McGraw-Hill Education

TOEFL
iBT

McGraw-Hill Education

TOEFL iBT

Tim Collins, PhD

Monica Sorrenson

New York Chicago San Francisco Athens London Madrid
Mexico City Milan New Delhi Singapore Sydney Toronto

Tim Collins, PhD, has taught test preparation since 1980 and has lived, worked, and taught in Europe, North Africa, Asia, and the United States. The author of more than twenty-five books and media publications for ESL/EFL and test preparation, he is a professor of ESL/EFL teacher education at National Louis University, Chicago, where he specializes in teaching courses in the assessment of ESL/EFL learners and test preparation. Dr. Collins's PhD is from the University of Texas at Austin.

Monica Sorrenson has taught English in the United Kingdom, New Zealand, Indonesia, Sudan, and Russia. She has tested students' English proficiency in China, Australia, Syria, Ukraine, and Oman. She has qualifications from the University of New South Wales, Sydney.

1 2 3 4 5 6 7 8 9 10   QVS/QVS   1 0 9 8 7 6 5 4 3

ISBN   978-0-07-179622-4 (book and disk set)
MHID   0-07-179622-3 (book and disk set)

ISBN   978-0-07-179619-4 (book for set)
MHID   0-07-179619-3 (book for set)

e-ISBN 978-0-07-179620-0
e-MHID   0-07-179620-7

Library of Congress Control Number 2013934652

Interior design by THINK Book Works
Interior photos by Michael Goss Photography
Interior artwork by Cenveo

TOEFL® and TOEFL iBT® are registered trademarks of Educational Testing Service (ETS), which was not involved in the production of, and does not endorse, this product.

McGraw-Hill Education products are available at special quantity discounts to use as premiums and sales promotions or for use in corporate training programs. To contact a representative, please visit the Contact Us pages at www.mhprofessional.com.

This book is printed on acid-free paper.

CONTENTS

CHAPTER 1

Introducing the TOEFL iBT®

Chapter at a Glance

In this chapter, you will learn:

About the TOEFL iBT. . . . . An overview of all four sections of the TOEFL and the kinds of questions you will encounter in each one.

About This Book and Disk . . . . An overview of all the chapters and features in this book and disk.

How to Use This Book and Disk . . . . Complete instructions on various ways to work through this book and disk.

Practical Information . . . . Suggestions for the day of the test and the night before to have a smooth test-taking experience.

Test-Wise Suggestions. . . . . Test-taking hints and tips you can use during the test to score your best.

Congratulations on your determination to take the TOEFL iBT! Whether your goal is to study abroad, gain admission to a university in your country, study online, get a visa, obtain employment in an English-speaking company, or simply gauge your level of English on a highly respected and internationally recognized measure of English ability, *McGraw-Hill Education: TOEFL iBT* contains everything you need to prepare for the test and accomplish your goal. It will teach you the knowledge required for this difficult exam, help you build your skills, and give you ample opportunities to test yourself with exercises and full-length practice TOEFL exams.

About the TOEFL iBT

The TOEFL iBT is a comprehensive test of your knowledge of English as it is used in higher education settings. It contains separate sections for Reading, Listening, Speaking, and Writing.

- **Reading** and **Listening** sections test your understanding of written passages you read on your computer screen and spoken passages you listen to using a special headset. Reading and Listening passages are all on topics typically encountered in North American university settings. These sections of the TOEFL iBT use multiple-choice items to check your understanding.
- The **Speaking** section tests your ability to speak on common personal and academic topics. Some of the items test only your speaking skills, while others ask you to integrate into your responses information you read on your computer screen, listen to using a special headset, or both.
- The **Writing** section tests your ability to write on common topics. One item asks you to write on an academic topic, integrating information from spoken and written sources. A second item simply asks you to write about a topic of general interest.

The sections of the TOEFL iBT, item types, and time limits are summarized in the following TOEFL iBT At a Glance chart. For more information on each section of the test, refer to the appropriate chapter.

AT A GLANCE

TOEFL iBT

SECTION	DESCRIPTION	TIME	FOR MORE INFORMATION
Reading	Read 3 passages of about 700 words each on academic topics.* Answer 42 multiple-choice items about the passages you read.	60 minutes	Chapter 3
Listening	Listen to 4 academic lectures and 2 conversations on campus-related topics.** Answer 34 multiple-choice items about the selections you listened to.	60 minutes	Chapter 4
Break		10 minutes	

SECTION	DESCRIPTION	TIME	FOR MORE INFORMATION
Speaking	Respond to 6 items in 45 to 60 seconds each. **Independent Speaking** • **Item 1.** State an opinion about a general-interest topic. • **Item 2.** State a choice of two possible actions or opinions on a campus-related or general-interest topic. **Integrated Reading, Listening, and Speaking** • **Item 3.** Read and listen to students talking about a short document on a campus-related topic. Respond to a question. • **Item 4.** Read a short passage and listen to part of a lecture on an academic topic. Respond to a question. **Integrated Listening and Speaking** • **Item 5.** Listen to two people talk about a campus-related topic. Respond to a question. • **Item 6.** Listen to part of a lecture on an academic topic. Respond to a question.	20 minutes	Chapter 5
Writing	Write 2 essays in 20 to 30 minutes each. **Integrated Reading, Listening, and Writing** • Read a 230- to 300-word passage (3 minutes) on an academic topic. • Listen to a 200- to 300-word lecture (2 minutes). • Write a 150- to 225-word essay (20 minutes). **Independent Writing** • Write a 300-word essay (30 minutes) on a general-interest topic.	60 minutes	Chapter 6

* In some administrations of the TOEFL, the Reading section will include 4 or 5 passages, have 56 to 70 items, and last from 80 to 100 minutes. These extra passages and questions are used to assess items before they are used in actual tests and do not count toward your score.

** In some administrations of the TOEFL, the Listening section will include as many as 5 lectures and/or 3 conversations, have up to 54 items, and last as long as 90 minutes. As in the Reading section, these extra selections and questions are used to assess items before they are used in actual tests and do not count toward your score.

Academic topics include readings, lectures, and discussions on academic subjects drawn from the arts and humanities (history, language, and literature), the social sciences (sociology, anthropology), and the natural sciences (earth science, physical sciences, and life science). On each section of the test, academic topics are drawn from a variety of subjects to avoid favoring certain majors or fields of study over others. You do not need any specialized knowledge to read these passages or answer the questions, and all the information you need to answer the questions is in the reading passage or listening selection. **General-interest topics** ask about your personal likes, dislikes, or preferences. **Campus-related topics** include subjects relating to life on a North American college or university campus, including student life, residence halls, transportation services, food services, university offices, university rules and regulations, and so on.

After you take the TOEFL iBT, your answers to the Reading and Listening sections are machine scored. Your responses to Speaking and Writing are sent to trained, professional human raters who evaluate your work using special scoring guides called rubrics. Then the raw scores for all four sections of the test are converted to standard scores. These standard scores are reported via Internet and postal mail to you and the institutions you designate.

About This Book and Disk

In *McGraw-Hill Education: TOEFL iBT* these features will help you score your best:

- In **this chapter**, you will find a complete overview of the TOEFL iBT, suggestions on how to use this book, ideas to help you on the day of the test, and test-wiseness tips that can help you score your best the day of the test.
- In **Chapter 2**, a complete practice TOEFL pretest lets you experience taking a full-length TOEFL test and helps you identify your areas of personal strength and the skills you need to improve.
- In **Chapters 3 through 6**, you will find complete intensive preparation for each TOEFL section: Reading, Listening, Speaking, and Writing. Each chapter has easy-to-follow instruction from an expert TOEFL coach, along with carefully crafted exercises to build your skills. A complete practice TOEFL iBT test section concludes each chapter and helps you identify your strengths and the skills you need to review before you go on to the next chapter.
- In **Chapters 7 and 8**, you will find two complete TOEFL iBT final practice tests. Use Final Practice Test 1 to check your progress and find remaining areas needing improvement. Then use Final Practice Test 2 as a last check of your skills before you take the actual TOEFL iBT.

- The **Appendixes** provide additional tools and learning aids, such as a list of academic vocabulary, lists of common topics that regularly appear on the TOEFL iBT, and reproducible rubrics you can use to evaluate your speaking and writing.

Throughout every chapter, you will find these features to help you:

- Abundant **exercises** in every chapter give you in-depth practice on every skill on the test, as well as regular cumulative review and end-of-chapter complete practice test sections.
- **Tips** give practical advice on areas of special difficulty, suggestions on how to answer items quickly and efficiently, and ways to avoid common errors.
- **Language boxes** give examples of common wording used on TOEFL items, which build familiarity with the way TOEFL items are written, as well as sample language you can use in Speaking and Writing responses to score high.
- Complete **Answers and Explanations** in each chapter provide explanations for correct and incorrect answers for every multiple-choice item in every exercise and practice test, plus sample answers, evaluation instructions, or both for every Speaking and Writing item.
- Easy-to-use **Personalized Study Planners** after each complete TOEFL iBT practice test help you pinpoint your strengths and areas for improvement, and tell you which page numbers to review to improve your score.
- User-friendly **rubrics** for evaluating Speaking and Writing responses that are based on the actual rubrics used to score the test. These learner-friendly rubrics help you evaluate your speaking and writing just as they are evaluated by real scorers.
- **Audio transcripts** provide complete scripts for all parts of the audio program. You can use these to check and build listening skills, practice taking notes, and help you understand English as it is actually spoken in North American colleges and universities.

The disk contains the following:

- Complete **audio recordings** for all the Listening passages in the book
- **Computer versions** of all the TOEFL iBT practice tests in this book so you can get experience taking a test online

How to Use This Book and Disk Program

To get the most out of this book and disk, follow this five-step program.

1. Gather Everything You Will Need

Along with this book, you will also need a disk player to play the accompanying audio recordings or a computer to take the practice tests on the disk. (You may also need a headset, earbuds, or a microphone.) For test items that ask you to speak, you will need to use the *record* function on your computer or mobile device to record and play back your responses. If your device does not have this function, ask a friend with strong English skills to listen to your responses. For test items that ask you to write, you will need a desktop computer or laptop to gain experience keyboarding your responses within the time limit.

2. Learn Important Facts About the TOEFL iBT

Read the "About the TOEFL iBT" section in this chapter to learn all about the test. You'll learn about the different question types, how the test is scored, and what you will see and hear when you take the TOEFL iBT.

3. Take the Practice Pretest

The complete practice pretest in Chapter 2 of this book is a simulated full-length TOEFL iBT test. Take it to launch your test-preparation program. You can take the test in either of two ways: (1) in the book, using the disk for the listening portions, or (2) entirely on computer, using the disk. After you take the pretest, use the Answers and Explanations to review your answers. The Answers and Explanations contain complete explanations for each correct and incorrect answer on the Reading and Listening sections, and evaluation instructions for Speaking and Writing. Use your results to pinpoint areas of strength and weakness in your knowledge base and your skill set. At the end of the test, you will find a TOEFL iBT Personalized Study Planner. For each test section, it will show you which kinds of questions are giving you the most difficulty and where to look in this book for learning material that will help you.

4. Prepare in Depth for Each TOEFL Test Section

After you take the pretest, use the results and the TOEFL iBT Personalized Study Planner to help you prepare your personal action plan. Chapters 3 through 6 provide intensive preparation for each TOEFL section: Reading, Listening, Speaking, and Writing. You can use the results of the pretest to work through the rest of this book in a variety of ways:

- You can work through all four chapters in order, completing all of the exercises and activities, and checking the Answers and Explanations for each one.
- You can use the pretest results to determine which skills—Reading, Listening, Speaking, or Writing—you need to improve the most. Then study those chapters first. If you have time, study the remaining chapters or use the TOEFL iBT Personalized Study Planner to identify the page numbers of the specific item types and skills you need to review.
- You can use the TOEFL iBT Personalized Study Planner to identify the page numbers of the specific item types and skills you need to study in each chapter.

No matter how you work through this book, use the Answers and Explanations for each practice test and exercise to check your correct and incorrect answers to multiple-choice items and to evaluate your speaking and writing responses. Then at the end of each chapter, use the complete TOEFL practice test section to check yourself. Review your answers and then use the TOEFL iBT Personalized Study Planner to identify the page numbers of the skills you need to practice before you continue to your next study task or take the actual test.

5. Take Final Practice Tests 1 and 2

Chapters 7 and 8 of this book each contain one full-length, simulated practice TOEFL iBT test with complete answers and explanations. Use these tests to check your progress and to gain added experience with the TOEFL format. Again, you may take both tests either in the book, using the disk for the listening portions, or entirely on computer using the disk. Use the Answers and Explanations after each practice test to check your correct and incorrect answers to multiple-choice items and to evaluate your speaking and writing responses. Then at the end of each final practice test, use the TOEFL iBT Personalized Study Planner to identify the page numbers of the skills you need to practice before taking the actual TOEFL iBT.

Practical Information for Taking the TOEFL iBT

Keep the following tips in mind before you take the TOEFL iBT:

- **Preparing for the test.** The best way to prepare for the TOEFL iBT is regular study. To do your best, don't cram by trying to study everything at the last minute. Use a special notebook to plan your studies and keep track of your progress. Take the practice tests on the disk to get used to keyboarding your essay and answering speaking items in short amounts of time. Become familiar with the directions commonly used on each section of the TOEFL iBT so you don't have to spend time and energy reading them the day of the test. Raise your level of general English by watching movies and TV, reading, listening to radio shows, and using the Internet and social media. Practice a relaxation technique to use if you become nervous during the test. For example, if you find you cannot concentrate because you are too nervous, close your eyes, breathe in, count to ten, exhale, and open your eyes.

- **The night before.** Make sure you know the location of the test center and find out information you need about public transportation, driving directions, parking, and so on. Organize the things you will need the day of the test (your identification card, driver's license, or other required identification and documents specified when you signed up to take the test), purse or wallet, glasses or contact lenses, car keys, tissue, and so on. Depending on the time of day you take the test, you may want to prepare a snack to eat just before you start the test. Try to relax and remember that your careful preparation will help you score your best. Eat a good meal the night before the test, and try to get a good night's sleep. Don't stay up late studying; that way you can feel rested and refreshed the day of the test. If you feel you must study, take a few minutes to review the tips throughout this book, as well as the test-wise suggestions that follow this section.

- **The day of the test.** Try to arrive a few minutes early. Turn in all materials prohibited in the exam room, in particular your mobile phone and any other electronic devices. The ETS has strict policies about not using or possessing these devices during the TOEFL iBT. Find out the rules for using the restroom during the test, as well as any other relevant rules. Make sure you understand the rules before the test begins. Set up your work areas with the mouse, keyboard, screen, and note paper positioned so you can use them with comfort and ease. Check the audio volume and microphone when the test prompts you to do so, and make sure you know how to use the controls if you have to adjust the audio volume or other settings during the test. Use your relaxation technique throughout the test if you feel nervous or overwhelmed.

- **After the test.** After you finish the test, reward yourself for your hard work. Enjoy a meal with friends or family, watch a movie, or do something else you enjoy. If you feel that you did not perform well on the test, you can cancel the scores for this administration before you leave the testing center. Use this option only if you are convinced that a serious problem prevented you from doing a good job on the test.

Test-Wise Suggestions

People who are test-wise use knowledge about standardized tests to improve their chances of selecting correct answers and raising their scores.

GENERAL

- Set up your work area for each section of the test. Position the mouse, keyboard, screen, and note paper so you can use them easily.
- Remember that you can take and use notes on all sections of the TOEFL iBT. Keep in mind that you can refer back to the reading passages, so you do not need to take notes during the Reading section.
- Use the relaxation technique you practiced if you find you cannot concentrate during the test.

READING AND LISTENING ITEMS

- On the TOEFL iBT, you have to answer many items in a short amount of time. Keep moving through the multiple-choice items. If you find yourself spending a lot of time on a Reading item, take a guess or skip the item and return to it later. In the Listening section, you cannot return to items later, so make sure you answer each item before moving to the next one.
- Don't change an answer unless you are certain your first answer is wrong.
- Read the question and then try to figure out the answer. Then read all the options. If the option you thought of is the best one, choose it. If not, try to find the best answer.
- If you still do not know the answer, use the process of elimination to improve your chances of answering correctly. If you can eliminate one option as definitely wrong, you have improved your odds of guessing correctly. If you can eliminate two options as wrong, you have improved your odds of guessing correctly to fifty-fifty.
- If you still cannot answer, guess. Do not leave items unanswered, because there is no penalty for guessing on the TOEFL iBT.

- Be careful with negative items. These items can be very confusing. To answer these items, consider each answer option individually, looking for the one option that is incorrect, contradicts the passage, or is not supported by the passage.
- If two options are similar, both are likely to be wrong, so choose neither of them.
- If two options are opposite, one is likely right. Choose the one that makes the most sense, or simply guess.
- The most general option is usually right; options with words like *all*, *always*, *never*, and so on are most likely wrong.
- Frequently, the longest answer option is correct. If you have no idea about how to answer an item, choosing the longest option may be a better idea than guessing, unless you are certain that the longest option is incorrect.

SPEAKING

- Take notes as you listen and read, and write your notes in the form of an outline that you can use when you give your response.
- Practice speaking many times with the program on disk (or with a timer) to get used to speaking with a short time limit.
- Content and fluency are the most important criteria in evaluating your responses, and accuracy is less important, as long as your response is comprehensible. Therefore, spend most of your preparation time on content and fluency, and worry less about correct pronunciation and grammar.

WRITING

- Take notes as you listen and read. Organize your notes in the form of an outline that you can use when you write your response.
- Content, organization, and use of signaling words and expressions (words that show the relationship among ideas) are the most important criteria used to evaluate essays, so focus on those and not on mechanics as you answer. If you have time remaining to review your essay when you take the test, check your grammar, spelling, and so on last.
- Learn to write a multiparagraph essay using a simple, consistent organizational pattern of an introductory paragraph to state the main idea of the essay, body paragraph(s) that support the main idea with detail and development, and a concluding paragraph that restates the main idea and sums up the essay. (Chapter 6 gives complete instruction on writing a multiparagraph essay.)
- Practice keyboarding. If you don't have a lot of experience keyboarding, develop this skill by using your computer to write essays, joining a social network, starting a blog, or doing something else to get a lot of experience keyboarding. Use the disk and a laptop or desktop computer to practice keyboarding an essay within the time limits of the test.

CHAPTER

2 TOEFL iBT Practice Pretest

Chapter at a Glance

In this chapter, you will learn:

TOEFL iBT Practice Pretest.................Your strengths and weaknesses on each section of the TOEFL iBT

TOEFL iBT Personalized Study Planner ....Your personalized plan for preparing for the TOEFL iBT

This TOEFL iBT Practice Pretest is designed to help you assess the skills you will need to score your best on the TOEFL iBT.

Completing the entire pretest takes about 3 hours and 30 minutes, the same amount of time as the actual TOEFL iBT. If possible, complete the test in one sitting to simulate the actual test experience. If you cannot complete the test in a single sitting, use the pretest At a Glance to help you plan how much time to allow for each part. The table also contains the materials you will need for each section of the pretest.

AT A GLANCE

TOEFL iBT Practice Pretest

SECTION	TIME	YOU NEED
Reading	60 minutes	Watch or timer on your computer or mobile phone
Listening	60 minutes	Watch or timer, disk, and player
Break	10 minutes	The actual TOEFL iBT includes a break between Listening and Speaking.
Speaking	20 minutes	Watch or timer, disk and player, audio recorder on your mobile phone or computer
Writing	60 minutes	Watch or timer, disk and player, computer to keyboard your response
All sections		Paper and pencil or pen for taking notes are needed for all sections of the TOEFL iBT. (Note-taking is allowed on all sections of the TOEFL iBT.)

After you take the TOEFL iBT Practice Pretest, use the Answers, Explanations, Audio Scripts, and Sample Responses on pages 82–102 to check your work. Then use the TOEFL iBT Personalized Study Planner on pages 74–81 to analyze your results and find the skills you need to focus on as you work through the rest of this book.

Reading

Directions: The Reading section of the TOEFL iBT assesses your ability to understand academic reading passages in English. To simulate actual TOEFL iBT conditions, follow these instructions:

- Use your watch or the timer on your mobile phone or computer to keep track of the time.
- Give yourself 20 minutes to read each passage and respond to the items that are about it.
- Allow 60 minutes to read all the passages and answer all the items.
- As on the actual TOEFL iBT, you may look back at the passage when answering items. You can skip items and return to them.
- If you do not finish all the items when the test ends, mark your place. Then continue working as quickly as you can. When you finish, take note of the total time. This will give you an idea of how quickly you need to work on the actual TOEFL iBT to answer all the items in 60 minutes.

Now begin the Reading section of the TOEFL iBT Practice Pretest.

Directions: Give yourself 20 minutes to read the passage and answer Items 1–14.

People's perception of the flavor of the food they consume is related not just to the sense of taste, but rather to all five senses. Human taste buds, which are located primarily on the top and sides of the tongue, can distinguish only five sensations: sweetness, sourness, saltiness, bitterness, and umami (which means "savory"). The sense of smell, detected by receptor cells in the nose, is responsible for perceiving many other aspects of flavor, including flavors imparted by herbs, spices, and aromas (such as the smell of coffee or tea). In fact, most of what we perceive as the flavor of food is supplied by the sense of smell, not the sense of taste. But other senses contribute to our perceptions of food as well. For example, the sense of hearing lets people perceive the crunch of a fresh carrot. The sense of sight lets people appreciate the golden yellow skin of an apple or colorful pink frosting on a cupcake. Even the sense of touch has a role. The way a food feels in our mouths and hands—crispy, tough, or tender—contributes to our perception of food.

One of the most common food flavors, hotness or spiciness, is determined primarily by the sense of touch. The chemical capsaicin, which occurs naturally in many plants, primarily various kinds of peppers, is responsible for the pungency, or hot spiciness, of many kinds of food they are used in. In fact, spicy peppers are one of the most common food ingredients, and they are used in cuisines the world over. Capsaicin is detected not by taste buds on the tongue, but rather by chemoreceptor nerve endings in the skin and mucous membranes. In general, contact with capsaicin produces a hot, burning, and sometimes painful sensation. Thus foods with high amounts of capsaicin will cause any part of the body they come into contact with to feel a warm, hot, or even burning sensation, according to the amount of the substance in the food and the sensitivity of the skin. Capsaicin that comes into contact with the mucous membrane in the mouth will cause greater pain than it would if it came into contact with a thick callous on a foot, for example. Even though capsaicin can produce a painful sensation, many people still like the pungent flavor of food containing hot peppers or other sources of capsaicin.

To measure the spiciness of food, a scale—the Scoville scale—was devised. The scale was created by pharmacist Wilbur Scoville in 1912. Scoville's method relied on human tasters, often working in a panel of five. First, Scoville dried the peppers and then used alcohol to extract the capsaicin. Then he diluted the solution with a mixture of sugar and water until the hotness of the chemical was no longer detectable by the tasters. The amount of dilution indicated the heat of the pepper. For example, green peppers, which contain no capsaicin, had a Scoville score of zero. A relatively mild pepper, such as a banana pepper, had a score of 900, indicating that the capsaicin had to be diluted 900 percent to be undetectable. A hotter pepper, the serrano pepper, had to be diluted 10,000 times to be undetectable, resulting in a Scoville score of 10,000. The hottest of peppers commonly found in North American supermarkets, the habanero, measures over 200,000 on the Scoville scale.

Scoville's method was good at determining the relative hotness of peppers, but it still had a considerable amount of error in detecting the exact hotness of a sample, because human tasters' subjective judgments were involved. Many scientists believe that the error in Scoville's method could be as high as 50 percent. As a result, scientists began analyzing the spiciness of peppers using other, more accurate chemical methods that can be used to determine the exact amount of capsaicin in parts per million. One part per million of capsaicin is called an ASTA pungency unit. Further study with both scales revealed that only an average estimate of the pungency of a variety of pepper could be determined, because the amount of capsaicin in individual peppers of the same species could vary widely based on factors such as soil composition, humidity, amount of exposure to sunlight, and other growing conditions.

Food producers, consumers, and scientists use these different measures in different ways. Food producers can accurately measure the spiciness of raw ingredients and finished products in order to ensure that their products appeal to customers. Some consumers, especially lovers of spicy food, use the ratings to find the hottest peppers they can, or to avoid overly spicy varieties. However, even a pepper that is normally mild may be hotter than expected because of growing conditions.

Directions: Now answer the questions.

People's perception of the flavor of the food they consume is related not just to the sense of taste, but rather to all five senses. Human taste buds, which are located primarily on the top and sides of the tongue, can distinguish only five sensations: sweetness, sourness, saltiness, bitterness, and umami (which means "savory"). The sense of smell, detected by receptor cells in the nose, is responsible for perceiving many other aspects of flavor, including flavors imparted by herbs, spices, and aromas (such as the smell of coffee or tea). In fact, most of what we perceive as the flavor of food is supplied by the sense of smell, not the sense of taste. But other senses contribute to our perceptions of food as well. For example, the sense of hearing lets people perceive the crunch of a fresh carrot. The sense of sight lets people appreciate the golden yellow skin of an apple or colorful pink frosting on a cupcake. Even the sense of touch has a role. The way a food feels in our mouths and hands—crispy, tough, or tender—contributes to our perception of food.

PARAGRAPH 1

1. According to paragraph 1, which of the following is true about people's perception of flavor?

   Ⓐ People can experience only five sensations: sweetness, sourness, saltiness, bitterness, and umami.

   Ⓑ Touch, taste, sight, smell, and hearing all contribute to how people experience the flavor of food.

   Ⓒ The sense of touch is the primary sense involved in how people experience food.

   Ⓓ The way food feels in our mouths is determined by the sense of smell.

2. Which of the following is NOT a way the sense of taste contributes to the way people experience food?

   Ⓐ A steaming bowl of soup makes us feel warm and cozy

   Ⓑ Salty popcorn makes us eat more and more

   Ⓒ A piece of white chocolate is sweet to eat

   Ⓓ A slice of lemon makes our tongues curl

One of the most common food flavors, hotness or spiciness, is determined primarily by the sense of touch. The chemical capsaicin, which occurs naturally in many plants, primarily various kinds of peppers, is responsible for the pungency, or hot spiciness, of many kinds of food they are used in. In fact, spicy peppers are one of the most common food ingredients, and they are used in cuisines the world over. Capsaicin is detected not by taste buds on the tongue, but rather by chemoreceptor nerve endings in the skin and mucous membranes. In general, contact with capsaicin produces a hot, burning, and sometimes painful sensation. Thus foods with high amounts of capsaicin will cause any part of the body they come into contact with to feel a warm, hot, or even burning sensation, according to the amount of the substance in the food and the sensitivity of the skin. Capsaicin that comes into contact with the mucous membrane in the mouth will cause greater pain than it would if it came into contact with a thick callous on a foot, for example. Even though capsaicin can produce a painful sensation, many people still like the pungent flavor of food containing hot peppers or other sources of capsaicin.

3. According to paragraph 2, which sense is primarily involved in sensing the spiciness of food?

Ⓐ taste

Ⓑ smell

Ⓒ touch

Ⓓ hearing

4. The word "pungency" in the passage is closest in meaning to

Ⓐ a strong, aromatic, smoky flavor

Ⓑ a strong, sharp, burning flavor

Ⓒ a strong, painful, cooling flavor

Ⓓ a strong, rich savory flavor

5. According to the passage, how is pungency detected?

Ⓐ Nerve endings in the nose sense a spicy aroma.

Ⓑ Taste buds on the top of the tongue sense a spicy food.

Ⓒ Special nerve cells in the mouth detect a pungent chemical.

Ⓓ Taste buds on the roof of the mouth detect capsaicin.

6. The word "substance" in the passage refers to

Ⓐ A pungency

Ⓑ mucous membrane

Ⓒ capsaicin

Ⓓ callous

P
A
R
A
G
R
A
P
H

2

One of the most common food flavors, hotness or spiciness, is determined primarily by the sense of touch. The chemical capsaicin, which occurs naturally in many plants, primarily various kinds of peppers, is responsible for the pungency, or hot spiciness, of many kinds of food they are used in. **A** In fact, spicy peppers are one of the most common food ingredients and are used in cuisines the world over. Capsaicin is detected not by taste buds on the tongue, but rather by chemoreceptor nerve endings in the skin and mucous membranes. In general, contact with capsaicin produces a hot, burning, and sometimes painful sensation. **B** Thus foods with high amounts of capsaicin will cause any part of the body they come into contact with to feel a warm, hot, or even burning sensation, according to the amount of the substance in the food and the sensitivity of the skin. **C** Capsaicin that comes into contact with the mucous membrane in the mouth will cause greater pain than it would if it came into contact with a thick callous on a foot, for example. Even though capsaicin can produce a painful sensation, many people still like the pungent flavor of food containing hot peppers or other sources of capsaicin. **D**

7. Look at the four squares (■) that indicate where the following sentence could be inserted into the passage.

> **In fact, many people add capsaicin to foods that normally would not be pungent, such as ice cream, chocolate, or hard candy, because they enjoy spicy food so much.**

Where would the sentence best fit?

P
A
R
A
G
R
A
P
H

3

To measure the spiciness of food, a scale—the Scoville scale—was devised. The scale was created by pharmacist Wilbur Scoville in 1912. Scoville's method relied on human tasters, often working in a panel of five. First, Scoville dried the peppers and then used alcohol to extract the capsaicin. Then he diluted the solution with a mixture of sugar and water until the hotness of the chemical was no longer detectable by the tasters. The amount of dilution indicated the heat of the pepper. For example, green peppers, which contain no capsaicin, had a Scoville score of zero. A relatively mild pepper, such as a banana pepper, had a score of 900, indicating that the capsaicin had to be diluted 900 percent to be undetectable. A hotter pepper, the serrano pepper, had to be diluted 10,000 times to be undetectable, resulting in a Scoville score of 10,000. The hottest of peppers commonly found in North American supermarkets, the habanero, measures over 200,000 on the Scoville scale.

8. Which of the following can be inferred about peppers sold in supermarkets?

Ⓐ Spicier peppers are more expensive than less spicy varieties.

Ⓑ Peppers with Scoville scores higher than 200,000 units are not safe to eat.

Ⓒ Peppers with Scoville scores higher than 200,000 are available less frequently than habanero peppers.

Ⓓ Peppers hotter than habanero peppers are never sold in supermarkets.

9. The word "dilute" in the passage is closest in meaning to

Ⓐ make a liquid weaker by adding a solution to it

Ⓑ make a liquid sweeter by adding sugar to it

Ⓒ make a liquid hotter by adding capsaicin to it

Ⓓ make a liquid clearer by adding water to it

Scoville's method was good at determining the relative hotness of peppers, but it still had a considerable amount of error in detecting the exact hotness of a sample, because human tasters' subjective judgments were involved. Many scientists believe that the error in Scoville's method could be as high as 50 percent. As a result, scientists began analyzing the spiciness of peppers using other, more accurate chemical methods that can be used to determine the exact amount of capsaicin in parts per million. One part per million of capsaicin is called an ASTA pungency unit. Further study with both scales revealed that only an average estimate of the pungency of a variety of pepper could be determined because the amount of capsaicin in individual peppers of the same species could vary widely based on factors such as soil composition, humidity, amount of exposure to sunlight, and other growing conditions.

10. Why does the author mention that Scoville scores are inaccurate because "human tasters' subjective judgments were involved"?

(A) To show that a more accurate test of pungency was required

(B) To prove that for scientific tests to be accurate, human judgments cannot be involved

(C) To show that Scoville was not a very good scientist

(D) To prove that Scoville scores cannot show the relative pungency of different kinds of peppers

11. Which of the following best expresses the essential information in the highlighted sentence? Incorrect choices change the meaning in important ways or leave out essential information.

(A) Further study of factors such as soil composition, humidity, amount of exposure to sunlight, and other growing conditions revealed that the amount of capsaicin in a species of pepper could vary widely.

(B) Further study showed that varied growing conditions cause individual peppers of the same species to have an average amount of capsaicin, so the pungency of individual peppers cannot be determined.

(C) Further study of individual species of pepper showed that only an average estimate of the pungency of any individual pepper could be determined.

(D) Further study showed that because individual peppers of one species may have different levels of capsaicin as a consequence of growing conditions, only an average estimate of the pungency of a pepper variety could be calculated.

P
A
R
A
G
R
A
P
H

5
Food producers, consumers, and scientists use these different measures in different ways. Food producers can accurately measure the spiciness of raw ingredients and finished products to ensure that their products appeal to customers. Some consumers, especially lovers of spicy food, use the ratings to find the hottest peppers they can or to avoid overly spicy varieties. However, even a pepper that is normally mild may be hotter than expected because of growing conditions.

12. The word "their" in the passage refers to

   (A) consumers'

   (B) peppers'

   (C) scientists'

   (D) food producers'

13. At the end of paragraph 5, why does the author mention that "even a pepper that is normally mild may be hotter than expected because of growing conditions"?

   (A) To remind readers not to rely on the variety of pepper to know how spicy an individual pepper may be

   (B) To remind readers that Scoville scores are less accurate than ASTA scores

   (C) To remind readers that eating extremely pungent varieties of peppers can be dangerous

   (D) To remind readers that certain varieties of peppers are considerably more pungent than others

14. Select from the seven phrases below the three phrases that correctly characterize Scoville units and the two phrases that correctly characterize ASTA pungency units. Two of the phrases will NOT be used.

Complete the table below to summarize information about the Scoville unit and the ASTA pungency unit. Match the appropriate statements to the unit with which they are associated.

ASTA PUNGENCY UNIT Select 2	SCOVILLE UNIT Select 3
•	•
•	•
	•

Answer Choices

A Showed that green peppers have a very high pungency level

B Uses alcohol to extract capsaicin from dried peppers

C Measures pungency in parts per million

D Measures pungency by having human raters make subjective judgments

E Has an inaccuracy rate as high as 50 percent

F Uses a chemical process to measure the units

G Has inaccurate measurements because the pungency of individual peppers varies widely

Directions: Give yourself 20 minutes to read the passage and answer Items 15–28.

One of the characteristics of a great work of art, whether a work of fiction, a musical composition, a film, or a piece of fine art, is that the work has stood the test of time and can continue to speak to us over the ages. One work that has remained fresh and vibrant over several centuries is the beloved Chinese opera *The Peony Pavilion,* which has remained popular since its first performance in 1598. This work, both an opera and a play, focuses on the story of two young lovers who struggle to find one another and then stay together. In *The Peony Pavilion*, a young woman, Mengmei, is kept isolated from friends and outsiders by her strict, traditional father, a high imperial official. She is not even allowed to leave home to go to school. Instead, a teacher comes to tutor her, but for only a few hours a day. Lonely for friends her own age and eager to find a suitable husband, she chafes at her father's harsh rules. One afternoon, she dozes off, and in her dream she sees a handsome young man and falls in love with him. On awakening, she tells everyone of the dream, but no one takes her seriously. Shortly thereafter, however, she believes she sees the young man passing by the house, but by the time she can run out to the street to find him, he has disappeared. Her father scolds her for leaving the house without permission. The young man she saw, Liniang, is a young scholar from a poor peasant family traveling to the capital city to take the imperial exam. If he passes the test, he can get a good job with the government.

Months go by, and Mengmei longs for the man she saw in the dream and then out of her window. Her father, not believing her, tries to get her to cheer up, but she becomes more and more depressed, stops eating, and finally falls into a deep sleep. In the meantime, the young man, returning from the exam, passes through town again. His horse slips in the snow, and he is thrown from the horse and almost dies of cold and exposure, but he is found by servants from Mengmei's home. He is brought in, revived, and treated by a doctor who recommends bed rest for a period of time. The father orders the head butler to take care of him. While recuperating, he learns of Mengmei and seeing her portrait, falls in love with her. He finds her almost lifeless body and kisses her. She awakes and they fall deeply in love. Eventually, they marry, and he is appointed to a high post in the government. The young lovers are separated again when war breaks out, but finally, after many hardships of war, they are happily reunited.

The original play and opera had almost immediate appeal when first produced, and both were extremely popular among women. The theme of freedom of love, which was denied to women at that time, appealed greatly to women, and the work became very popular among them. Reportedly, female audience members were so touched by the story that they wept and even fainted. This opera offers a compelling story, beautiful music, and a theme of enduring appeal, which explains why it has interested audiences until this day.

The opera itself is approximately 24 hours long, so adjustments are needed to make this work accessible to modern audiences. Modern versions focus on the love story and omit the entire second half of the opera, which is about the war, to reduce the opera to a manageable length. However, as recently as 1999, a 20-hour version was performed in New York. Of course, this is not the first time that this seminal work has been adapted or changed. In fact, soon after the opera's debut in 1598, much of the original music and lyrics were revised to make them easier to perform. Since then, there have been many different versions of this work, as directors have worked to make it relevant to new audiences. *The Peony Pavilion* has been produced many times and has been made into movies, plays, and novels. It is so popular that it even has been the basis of a video game focusing on Liniang's adventures at war.

While these efforts have brought this opera to new audiences, many of the changes have upset fans of traditional Chinese opera. Some productions of this opera have tried to remove some extra trappings added to the opera during the nineteenth century and return the work to its origins in the 1600s, but even these efforts have met with resistance from opera traditionalists, showing the enduring power and cultural importance of this work.

Directions: Now answer the questions.

> One of the characteristics of a great work of art, whether a work of fiction, a musical composition, a film, or a piece of fine art, is that the work has stood the test of time and can continue to speak to us over the ages. One work that has remained fresh and vibrant over several centuries is the beloved Chinese opera *The Peony Pavilion*, which has remained popular since its first performance in 1598. This work, both an opera and a play, focuses on the story of two young lovers who struggle to find one another and then stay together. In *The Peony Pavilion*, a young woman, Mengmei, is kept isolated from friends and outsiders by her strict, traditional father, a high imperial official. She is not even allowed to leave home to go to school. Instead, a teacher comes to tutor her, but for only a few hours a day. Lonely for friends her own age and eager to find a suitable husband, she chafes at her father's harsh rules. One afternoon, she dozes off, and in her dream she sees a handsome young man and falls in love with him. On awakening, she tells everyone of the dream, but no one takes her seriously. Shortly thereafter, however, she believes she sees the young man passing by the house, but by the time she can run out to the street to find him, he has disappeared. Her father scolds her for leaving the house without permission. The young man she saw, Liniang, is a young scholar from a poor peasant family traveling to the capital city to take the imperial exam. If he passes the test, he can get a good job with the government.

15. According to paragraph 1, *The Peony Pavilion* is a great work of art because

   Ⓐ audiences have continued to identify with it over the years

   Ⓑ it is a tale about the experiences of two young lovers

   Ⓒ it was composed over 400 years ago in Imperial China

   Ⓓ it is both an opera and a play

16. All of the following are true of the father EXCEPT:

   Ⓐ He has many old-fashioned ideas.

   Ⓑ He gives his daughter many rules to follow.

   Ⓒ He thinks that girls and young women should usually stay at home.

   Ⓓ He believes that every young woman should get a good education.

17. The phrase "chafes at" in the passage is closest in meaning to

Ⓐ submits to

Ⓑ struggles with

Ⓒ feels indifferent about

Ⓓ rebels against

P
A
R
A
G
R
A
P
H

2
Months go by, and Mengmei longs for the man she saw in the dream and then out of her window. Her father, not believing her, tries to get her to cheer up, but she becomes more and more depressed, stops eating, and finally falls into a deep sleep. In the meantime, the young man, returning from the exam, passes through town again. His horse slips in the snow, and he is thrown from the horse and almost dies of cold and exposure, but he is found by servants from Mengmei's home. He is brought in, revived, and treated by a doctor who recommends bed rest for a period of time. The father orders the head butler to take care of him. While recuperating, he learns of Mengmei and seeing her portrait, falls in love with her. He finds her almost lifeless body and kisses her. She awakes and they fall deeply in love. Eventually, they marry, and he is appointed to a high post in the government. The young lovers are separated again when war breaks out, but finally, after many hardships of war, they are happily reunited.

18. Which of these things do Liniang and Mengmei have in common?

Ⓐ They have similar levels of education.

Ⓑ They are both from wealthy, important families.

Ⓒ They both become very ill during the opera.

Ⓓ They are not free to travel or visit friends.

19. The word "he" in the passage refers to

Ⓐ the father

Ⓑ the doctor

Ⓒ the head butler

Ⓓ the young man

PARAGRAPH 2

Months go by, and Mengmei longs for the man she saw in the dream and then out of her window. **A** Her father, not believing her, tries to get her to cheer up, but she becomes more and more depressed, stops eating, and finally falls into a deep sleep. In the meantime, the young man, returning from the exam, passes through town again. His horse slips in the snow, and he is thrown from the horse and almost dies of cold and exposure, but he is found by servants from Mengmei's home. **B** He is brought in, revived, and treated by a doctor who recommends bed rest for a period of time. The father orders the head butler to take care of him. While recuperating, he learns of Mengmei, and seeing her portrait, falls in love with her. He finds her almost lifeless body and kisses her. She awakes and they fall deeply in love. **C** Eventually, they marry, and he is appointed to a high post in the government. The young lovers are separated again when war breaks out, but finally, after many hardships of war, they are happily reunited. **D**

20. Look at the four squares (■) that indicate where the following sentence could be inserted into the passage.

At first, Mengmei's father is opposed, but then a letter from the Emperor arrives telling Liniang that he scored first on the imperial exam and will soon be appointed to a high government post, which causes the father to accept Liniang as a future son-in-law.

Where would the sentence best fit?

PARAGRAPH 3

The original play and opera had almost immediate appeal when first produced, and both were extremely popular among women. The theme of freedom of love, which was denied to women at that time, appealed greatly to women, and the work became very popular among them. Reportedly, female audience members were so touched by the story that they wept and even fainted. This opera offers a compelling story, beautiful music, and a theme of enduring appeal, which explains why it has interested audiences until this day.

21. According to paragraph 3, why did this opera become popular among women?

Ⓐ Women loved the beautiful music.

Ⓑ Women identified with Mengmei's struggle to find love.

Ⓒ Women felt it was unfair that they could not receive a good education.

Ⓓ Women agreed with the father's strict, traditional values.

22. The phrase "touched by" in the passage is closest in meaning to

(A) interested in

(B) depressed by

(C) affected by

(D) worried about

23. The word "it" in the passage refers to

(A) the opera

(B) the story

(C) the music

(D) the theme

PARAGRAPH 4

The opera itself is approximately 24 hours long, so adjustments are needed to make this work accessible to modern audiences. Modern versions focus on the love story and omit the entire second half of the opera, which is about the war, to reduce the opera to a manageable length. However, as recently as 1999, a 20-hour version was performed in New York. Of course, this is not the first time that this seminal work has been adapted or changed. In fact, soon after the opera's debut in 1598, much of the original music and lyrics were revised to make them easier to perform. Since then, there have been many different versions of this work, as directors have worked to make it relevant to new audiences. *The Peony Pavilion* has been produced many times and has been made into movies, plays, and novels. It is so popular that it even has been the basis of a video game focusing on Liniang's adventures at war.

24. In which of these ways was the opera changed shortly after its debut in 1598?

(A) The opera was shortened by 4 hours.

(B) The lyrics and music were revised to make the opera easier to perform.

(C) The opera was reduced in length by half.

(D) A second part about a war was added to the opera.

25. Why does the author mention that a 20-hour version of *The Peony Pavilion* was performed in New York in 1999?

Ⓐ To show that the New York performance altered the opera improperly

Ⓑ To provide a contrasting example of a time when the opera was not shortened considerably

Ⓒ To show how modern productions cut up to half the original opera to meet the needs of today's audiences

Ⓓ To give an example of a recent, complete performance of the opera

26. Why does the author state that this opera has been used as the basis of a video game?

Ⓐ To show the wide appeal of this opera and its applicability to many kinds of media

Ⓑ To criticize video game makers for devaluing an important work of art

Ⓒ To show that this opera is not relevant to today's opera audiences

Ⓓ To criticize excessive video game playing by young people

While these efforts have brought this opera to new audiences, many of the changes have upset fans of traditional Chinese opera. Some productions of this opera have tried to remove some extra trappings added to the opera during the nineteenth century and return the work to its origins in the 1600s, but even these efforts have met with resistance from opera traditionalists, showing the enduring power and cultural importance of this work.

27. Which of the following best expresses the essential information in the highlighted sentence? Incorrect choices change the meaning in important ways or leave out essential information.

(A) Efforts to remove nineteenth-century trappings from the opera to return it to its origins in the 1600s have met with resistance, showing the work's enduring power and cultural relevance.

(B) Resistance to the work's enduring power and cultural importance led to efforts to return the opera to its origins in the 1600s.

(C) Efforts to restore trappings added to the opera in the nineteenth century and return it to its origins in the 1600s have met with resistance, showing the work's enduring power and cultural relevance.

(D) Efforts to return the opera to its origins in the 1600s have met with resistance, showing the work's nineteenth-century trappings.

28. An introductory sentence for a brief summary of the passage is provided. Complete the summary by selecting the THREE answer choices that express important ideas in the passage. Some sentences do not belong in the summary, because they express ideas that are not presented in the passage or are minor details in the passage. *This item is worth 2 points.*

Write the letters of your answer choices in the spaces where they belong.

> **The passage discusses a famous Chinese opera, *The Peony Pavilion*.**
>
> •
>
> •
>
> •

Answer Choices

A First performed in 1598, this opera, a love story about a young woman who falls in love with a young man she sees in a dream, has stood the test of time.

B The young woman's father, a high imperial official, did not allow her to have friends her own age or meet outsiders.

C This opera had strong appeal to women because it focuses on the theme of freedom of love, which was denied to women at the time.

D The young woman sees the young man riding by her house on horseback and tries to meet him.

E The second part of the opera, about the young man's adventures at war, is often omitted from modern productions of the opera.

F To remain relevant to audiences, the opera has been changed in many ways over the years, and novels, films, plays, stories, and even video games have been made from it.

Directions: Give yourself 20 minutes to read the passage and answer Items 29–42.

Color psychology is the study of color as a factor in determining human behavior. Proponents of color psychology believe that color has an observable and measurable effect on human behavior, and that color can be used to affect and manage human behavior. The color of the paint on a room's walls, the color of a product package, the color of a pill, and even the color of lighting can all affect us, according to color psychology. For example, a city in England recently changed the color of the light from its city streetlights to blue in some areas. The city found that crime went down in areas that had the blue street lighting. Medical researchers who studied people's perception of medicine showed that the color of pills affected people's judgments about their effectiveness. For example, when people were told that certain pills were a stimulant, they thought that the pills in the warm color range (red, orange, and yellow) would be stronger than pills in the cool color range (blue, green, and purple). However, when they thought that the pills were depressants, they thought that the pills in the cooler color range were stronger. The colors of furniture can have an effect, too. Dark and cool-colored furniture tends to encourage people to sit for longer periods of time than light and warm-colored furniture, which tends to encourage people to sit for shorter periods before they want to get up and move around again. For this reason, fast-food restaurants often choose warm, bright colors for their seating areas.

Color psychology has several main principles. The first principle of color psychology is that color can carry specific meaning. In the example about pills, color conveyed information about the strength and effectiveness of the medicine. In the example about light, blue light conveyed the meaning that the location was not a good place to commit a crime, perhaps because the odds of getting caught were higher. Second, the meaning of color may be learned or biologically innate. For example, for North Americans, the color red is associated with love, a positive emotion, but also with danger, such as a red emergency exit sign. However, in most other parts of the world, emergency exit signs are green, not red. For many Asians, red has none of these associations, but rather is associated with celebration. In the past, scientists have tried to find a biological link between color and behavior. They point to studies that show, for example, that many people prefer rooms that are painted blue or green. According to the researchers, these colors are associated with places where human beings have had evolutionary success—places where humans have lived and thrived for thousands of years. Scientists believe that people like blue rooms because blue is the color of large bodies of water. And in fact, humans have had evolutionary success in areas near large bodies of water because in those areas humans can access the water needed for drinking, washing, and bathing. Third, color scientists believe that humans evaluate color automatically. That is, people automatically and unconsciously make associations with colors as soon as they perceive them. Fourth, these associations force color-motivated behavior. That is, people exposed to blue street lighting automatically adjusted their behavior in ways that reduced crime. Finally, color meaning and effect are influenced by context. For example, scientists believe that the color of food has an effect on whether people will choose or like a certain kind of food. However, the color of the food is not the only color that matters to people. The other colors in the environment will also have an effect on them.

While psychologists continue to have doubts about the claims of color psychology, major companies use its insights to encourage people to buy their products or perceive their companies positively. Some studies show that consumers tend to make an initial decision about whether to consider buying a product within 60 to 90 seconds of becoming aware of the product in a store. These same studies show that at least 60 percent of the time, the color of the product is a factor in the consumer's decision about whether to buy the product. Some studies say that color is a determining factor as much as 90 percent of the time.

Color psychology is not used only by companies. Some psychologists believe in color therapy—using knowledge of color to improve people's behavior, mental health, and physical health. Practitioners of color therapy believe that they can use color to positively influence people. For example, some studies show that the color red tends to raise blood pressure and emotional levels. Thus hospitals tend to avoid the color red in order to avoid exciting heart patients excessively. Studies show that cool colors such as blue tend to be calming. Using this insight, many prisons have painted their walls blue to reduce prison violence.

Critics of color psychology point to a number of problems. They believe that the research methods may be shoddy and that the relationship between color and human behavior is not automatic or biological. They point out that associations with color are highly culturally bound and not very reliable. However, companies continue to follow the precepts of color psychology and say that they can see the benefits of color psychology in increased sales and customer loyalty when color psychology is used effectively.

Directions: Now answer the questions.

Color psychology is the study of color as a factor in determining human behavior. Proponents of color psychology believe that color has an observable and measurable effect on human behavior, and that color can be used to affect and manage human behavior. The color of the paint on a room's walls, the color of a product package, the color of a pill, and even the color of lighting can all affect us, according to color psychology. For example, a city in England recently changed the color of the light from its city streetlights to blue in some areas. The city found that crime went down in areas that had the blue street lighting. Medical researchers who studied people's perception of medicine showed that the color of pills affected people's judgments about their effectiveness. For example, when people were told that certain pills were a stimulant, they thought that the pills in the warm color range (red, orange, and yellow) would be stronger than pills in the cool color range (blue, green, and purple). However, when they thought that the pills were depressants, they thought that the pills in the cooler color range were stronger. The colors of furniture can have an effect, too. Dark and cool-colored furniture tends to encourage people to sit for longer periods of time than light and warm-colored furniture, which tends to encourage people to sit for shorter periods before they want to get up and move around again. For this reason, fast-food restaurants often choose warm, bright colors for their seating areas.

29. Why do fast-food restaurants choose bright, warm colors for their seating areas?

Ⓐ To encourage customers to finish their food quickly and leave

Ⓑ To provide background colors that make the food appealing

Ⓒ To make the seating areas inviting to customers

Ⓓ To encourage people to buy more food

30. According to the information in paragraph 1, which of the following is true about the color of pills and people's perceptions of their strength?

Ⓐ Color is the principal factor that determined people's perception of the pills' strength.

Ⓑ People generally associate yellow, orange, and red with strength and effectiveness.

Ⓒ People think that stimulants are stronger than depressants.

Ⓓ People's decisions are based on a combination of factors, including color.

31. The word "their" in the passage refers to

Ⓐ the pills'

Ⓑ the people's

Ⓒ the colors'

Ⓓ the medical researchers'

P
A
R
A
G
R
A
P
H

2

Color psychology has several main principles. The first principle of color psychology is that color can carry specific meaning. In the example about pills, color conveyed information about the strength and effectiveness of the medicine. In the example about light, blue light conveyed the meaning that the location was not a good place to commit a crime, perhaps because the odds of getting caught were higher. Second, the meaning of color may be learned or biologically innate. For example, for North Americans, the color red is associated with love, a positive emotion, but also with danger, such as a red emergency exit sign. However, in most other parts of the world, emergency exit signs are green, not red. For many Asians, red has none of these associations, but rather is associated with celebration. In the past, scientists have tried to find a biological link between color and behavior. They point to studies that show, for example, that many people prefer rooms that are painted blue or green. According to the researchers, these colors are associated with places where human beings have had evolutionary success— places where humans have lived and thrived for thousands of years. Scientists believe that people like blue rooms because blue is the color of large bodies of water. And in fact, humans have had evolutionary success in areas near large bodies of water because in those areas humans can access the water needed for drinking, washing, and bathing. Third, color scientists believe that humans evaluate color automatically. That is, people automatically and unconsciously make associations with colors as soon as they perceive them. Fourth, these associations force color-motivated behavior. That is, people exposed to blue street lighting automatically adjusted their behavior in ways that reduced crime. Finally, color meaning and effect are influenced by context. For example, scientists believe that the color of food has an effect on whether people will choose or like a certain kind of food. However, the color of the food is not the only color that matters to people. The other colors in the environment will also have an effect on them.

32. Which of the following is evidence that the meanings colors carry can be biologically innate?

(A) Emergency exit signs are green in many countries.

(B) People find rooms with blue walls pleasant and attractive.

(C) Many people associate the color red with celebration.

(D) Furniture in cool colors tends to encourage people to relax.

33. Which of the following is NOT one of the principles of color psychology?

(A) People's favorite colors provide insight into their personalities.

(B) The meanings of colors are both learned and biological.

(C) People make associations with colors as soon as they see them.

(D) Colors carry special meanings.

34. The word "odds" in the passage is closest in meaning to

(A) differences

(B) chances

(C) dangers

(D) reasons

35. The word "them" in the passage refers to

(A) scientists

(B) colors

(C) people

(D) food

While psychologists continue to have doubts about the claims of color psychology, major companies use its insights to encourage people to buy their products or perceive their companies positively. Some studies show that consumers tend to make an initial decision about whether to consider buying a product within 60 to 90 seconds of becoming aware of the product in a store. These same studies show that the color of the product is a factor in the consumer's decision about whether to buy the product at least 60 percent of the time. Some studies say that color is a determining factor as much as 90 percent of the time.

36. Which of the following can be inferred about color and consumers' decision to buy a product?

   Ⓐ Color has an immediate effect on purchasing decisions.

   Ⓑ Color has an influence only if the consumer has a positive perception of the color of a product.

   Ⓒ Color is not the most important factor in purchasing decisions.

   Ⓓ Certain colors will force consumers to buy a product.

37. Why does the author mention that some studies indicate that color is a factor in up to 90 percent of purchases?

   Ⓐ To show that color is an important part of purchasing decisions

   Ⓑ To show that the author does not believe those studies

   Ⓒ To show that color may be even more influential than authors of other studies believe

   Ⓓ To show that consumers will reject products if they do not like the color

P
A
R
A
G
R
A
P
H

3

A While psychologists continue to have doubts about the claims of color psychology, major companies use its insights to encourage people to buy their products or perceive their companies positively. Some studies show that consumers tend to make an initial decision about whether to consider buying a product within 60 to 90 seconds of becoming aware of the product in a store. **B** These same studies show that the color of the product is a factor in the consumer's decision about whether to buy the product at least 60 percent of the time. **C** Some studies say that color is a determining factor as much as 90 percent of the time. **D**

38. Look at the four squares (■) that indicate where the following sentence could be inserted into the passage.

> **For these reasons, companies pay careful attention to the colors of products and product packaging.**

Where would the sentence best fit?

P
A
R
A
G
R
A
P
H

4

Color psychology is not used only by companies. Some psychologists believe in color therapy—using knowledge of color to improve people's behavior, mental health, and physical health. Practitioners of color therapy believe that they can use color to positively influence people. For example, some studies show that the color red tends to raise blood pressure and emotional levels. Thus hospitals tend to avoid the color red in order to avoid exciting heart patients excessively. Studies show that cool colors such as blue tend to be calming. Using this insight, many prisons have painted their walls blue to reduce prison violence.

39. Why does the author indicate that prisons have painted their walls blue?

(A) To show that color therapy can solve many problems

(B) To provide an example of a failure of color therapy

(C) To show that both blue light and blue walls reduce violence

(D) To provide an example of the use of color therapy

40. The phrase "color therapy" in the passage is closest in meaning to

    Ⓐ using color to understand and affect behavior

    Ⓑ using color to reduce crime

    Ⓒ using color to reduce heart attacks

    Ⓓ using color to improve mental and physical health

PARAGRAPH 5

        Critics of color psychology point to a number of problems. They believe that the research methods may be shoddy and that the relationship between color and human behavior is not automatic or biological. They point out that associations with color are highly culturally bound and not very reliable. However, companies continue to follow the precepts of color psychology and say that they can see the benefits of color psychology in increased sales and customer loyalty when color psychology is used effectively.

41. Which of the following best expresses the essential information in the highlighted sentence? Incorrect choices change the meaning in important ways or leave out essential information.

    Ⓐ However, companies say that when color psychology is used effectively they can see its benefits, so they continue to follow its precepts.

    Ⓑ However, companies continue to use color psychology and say when it is used effectively, they can see its benefits in increased sales and customer loyalty.

    Ⓒ However, companies say they will continue to use color psychology to increase sales and customer loyalty.

    Ⓓ However, companies say that they can see the precepts of increased sales and customer loyalty when the benefits of color psychology are used.

42. An introductory sentence for a brief summary of the passage is provided below. Complete the summary by selecting the THREE answer choices that express important ideas in the passage. Some sentences do not belong in the summary, because they express ideas that are not presented in the passage or are minor details in the passage. *This item is worth 2 points.*

Write the letters of your answer choices in the spaces where they belong.

> **The passage discusses the definition and uses of color psychology.**
>
> •
>
> •
>
> •

Answer Choices

A Color psychology asserts that colors have learned and biological meanings.

B Color psychology studies the effects of color on people.

C The color red has different meanings for Asians than for people of other cultures.

D Color therapy can prevent heart attacks.

E Companies use color psychology to improve sales.

F The color blue tends to cause violence.

Answers and Explanations for the Reading section of the TOEFL iBT Practice Pretest begin on page 82.

Listening

Directions: The Listening section of the TOEFL iBT assesses your ability to understand conversations and lectures in English. To simulate actual TOEFL iBT conditions, follow these instructions:

- Listen to each conversation or lecture only once. You may take notes while listening and use your notes as you answer the items.
- After each selection, answer the items that follow in the order in which they appear. After you answer an item, do not return to it. Continue with each listening selection and its items until you complete the test or time has ended.
- Use your watch or the timer on your mobile phone or computer to keep track of the time. Allow 60 minutes to listen to all the selections and answer the questions.
- If you do not finish all the items when the test ends, mark your place. Then continue working as quickly as you can. When you finish, take note of the total time. This will give you an idea of how quickly you need to work on the actual TOEFL iBT to answer all the items in 60 minutes.

The Audio icon appears each time you need to listen to an audio track. For some items, you need to listen to another audio track besides the conversation or lecture in order to answer.

Now begin the Listening section of the TOEFL iBT Practice Pretest.

Directions: Listen to a conversation between a student and a professor.

Directions: Now answer the questions. Choose the letter of the answer.

1. Why does the student go to see the professor?

   (A) To apply for a scholarship

   (B) To discuss a field trip

   (C) To talk about painting

   (D) To ask for a reference

2. What is the student hoping to do?

   (A) Work on an archaeological site in Jordan

   (B) Work in the office of a research association in London

   (C) Work on restoring ancient art in Greece

   (D) Work on finding ancient paintings in Rome

3. What kind of work is the student hoping to do?

   (A) Discover caves of geological interest

   (B) Restore ancient Greek and Roman paintings

   (C) Explore caves with ancient paintings inside

   (D) Make a geological survey in the desert

4. Why is the professor happy to write a reference for her?

   (A) She completes her projects quickly.

   (B) She is well prepared academically.

   (C) She knows some languages other than English.

   (D) She gets along with people of different nationalities.

5. How does the professor feel about working on an archaeological site?

   (A) It is tedious but thrilling.

   (B) It is pure boredom.

   (C) It is glamorous but dangerous.

   (D) It is well paid and exciting.

Directions: Listen to part of a lecture in a class on botany. The professor is talking about tropism.

Aristotle

Giambattista della Porta

Thomas Browne

Albert Bernard Franck

Charles Darwin

Auxin

Directions: Now answer the questions. Choose the letter of the answer.

6. What is the professor mainly talking about?

   Ⓐ Understanding the growth patterns of plants

   Ⓑ Increasing food production by using auxin in fertilizer

   Ⓒ Mimicking the effects of auxin on plant growth

   Ⓓ Understanding how plants respond to light, gravity, and objects

7. What is the best definition of plant tropism?

   Ⓐ A view of plants as passive insensate organisms

   Ⓑ A plant's tendency to seek light, water, and minerals

   Ⓒ A plant's mechanism of hormonal control

   Ⓓ A plant's ability to turn in response to stimuli

8. Which is true of the following types of tropism?

   Place a check (✔) in the correct boxes. This item is worth 2 points.

	GEOTROPISM	PHOTOTROPISM	THIGMOTROPISM
A plant grows in a different direction due to contact with a solid object.			
A plant grows toward a light source.			
The roots of a plant go toward a gravitational source.			
It was described by della Porta in 1569.			

9. According to the professor, for what was the Aristotelian scientific model responsible?

   Ⓐ Misunderstanding of plants

   Ⓑ Lack of interest in plants

   Ⓒ Overexploitation of plants

   Ⓓ Too much experimentation with plants

10. What is the role of auxin in tropism?

    Ⓐ A weed killer that kills unwanted plants

    Ⓑ A plant hormone that controls geotropism and phototropism

    Ⓒ A fertilizer that makes plants grow more quickly

    Ⓓ A genome sequence that controls how plants grow

11. How is understanding tropism useful in modern food production?
    Choose 2 answers.

    Ⓐ It decreases the importance of fertilizer.

    Ⓑ It benefits the environment.

    Ⓒ It helps maximize plant yield.

    Ⓓ It provides suitable specimens for cloning.

Directions: Listen to part of a lecture in a psychology class. The professor is talking about crowdsourcing.

Western

Educated

Industrialized

Rich

Democratic

Crowdsourcing

Turker

Trolleyology

Benedikt Herrmann

public good games

Directions: Now answer the questions. Choose the letter of the answer.

12. What is the professor's overall view of crowdsourcing?

(A) Previous research methods were more reliable.

(B) It deserves to be a popular research method.

(C) It is not economically viable as a research method.

(D) It is hard to tell at present how useful it will be.

13. Which of the following is a reason why using many American graduate students in psychology research is problematic?

  Ⓐ American students are poorer than most people.

  Ⓑ American students are not representative of most people.

  Ⓒ American students will not accept low pay for their work.

  Ⓓ American students who participate in research studies are strange.

14. What kind of work did the two student Turkers do?

  Ⓐ Mainly linguistic

  Ⓑ Mainly psychology testing

  Ⓒ Scientific and marketing

  Ⓓ All kinds of work

15. What is significant about the Harvard University repeat of the trolleyology experiment?

  Ⓐ It found that religious Turkers are generally more moral.

  Ⓑ It suggests that academic research should pay more attention to moral issues.

  Ⓒ It somewhat modified previous findings.

  Ⓓ It completely overturned previous findings.

16. **AUDIO TRACK 4** Listen again to part of the lecture. Then answer the question.

  Ⓐ She thinks Herrmann is probably right.

  Ⓑ She is more interested in Herrmann's opinion than in the student's.

  Ⓒ She thinks punishment evolved as a form of self-interest.

  Ⓓ She believes some people punish as often as they collaborate.

17. What does the professor think about Turkers' pay?

  Ⓐ American Turkers do not receive adequate pay.

  Ⓑ Low pay could affect the quality of Turkers' work.

  Ⓒ Turkers are volunteers; they should not expect more pay.

  Ⓓ Turkers who come from developing countries are paid reasonably.

Directions: Listen to a conversation between a student and a university employee.

Directions: Now answer the questions. Choose the letter of the answer.

18. Why does the student want to speak to Mr. Wall?

  Ⓐ To move to another dorm

  Ⓑ To complain about students in his dorm

  Ⓒ To find out about a workshop

  Ⓓ To hand in an application

19. Why is Mr. Wall unable to help the student at present?

  Ⓐ Mr. Wall does not have the authority.

  Ⓑ Mr. Wall is out of the office.

  Ⓒ The student has not made an appointment.

  Ⓓ The student has not made up his mind.

20. Why does the student dislike the freshmen in his dorm?

  Ⓐ They watch loud hockey games on TV all night.

  Ⓑ They are unsociable.

  Ⓒ They have frequent loud parties.

  Ⓓ They make a lot of noise in the parking lot.

21. What is the disadvantage of McKinley Dorm?

(A) Its rooms face north.

(B) It has only single rooms.

(C) There is traffic noise from Lexington Road.

(D) It costs more than Johnson Dorm.

22. Listen again to part of the conversation. Then answer the question.

(A) He wants to prove he is a capable student

(B) He wants to provide the employee with more detail

(C) He wants to tell a joke about his situation

(D) He wants to present his case more strongly

Directions: Listen to part of a lecture in a class on public health. The professor is talking about malaria.

Public Health

4 billion

216 million

1.2 million

plasmodium parasites

Plasmodium falciparum

Education

Environment

Immunization

Insecticide-
treated nets

Directions: Now answer the questions. Choose the letter of the answer.

23. What is the professor mainly talking about?

Ⓐ Ways malaria can be prevented

Ⓑ Ways malaria can be cured

Ⓒ Ways malaria is spread to people and animals

Ⓓ Ways malaria kills people and animals

24. Why does the professor mention that scientists estimate that malaria has killed one out of every two people who ever lived?

    Ⓐ To show that death rates from malaria are increasing

    Ⓑ To show that malaria is a major public health problem today

    Ⓒ To show that malaria has afflicted humans for millennia

    Ⓓ To show that all people are at risk of getting malaria

25. Why is *Plasmodium falciparum* so dangerous?

    Ⓐ It can penetrate insecticide-treated nets.

    Ⓑ It attacks people who live in rural areas far from medical treatment.

    Ⓒ It is the most common kind of malaria parasite.

    Ⓓ It avoids detection by the human immune system.

26. According to the professor, which of the following will help eradicate malaria?

    Ⓐ Preventive education and environmental control

    Ⓑ A preventive vaccine

    Ⓒ Mutations of the malaria parasite

    Ⓓ Flooding areas where mosquitoes breed

27. Why does the professor mention the country Mauritius?

    Ⓐ To demonstrate that international aid is effective

    Ⓑ To show that malaria control is impossible

    Ⓒ To prove that malaria control need not be difficult or costly

    Ⓓ To illustrate the ease of malaria control on an island

28. The class discusses some important events related to malaria. Put the events in order from earliest to latest.

Write your answer choices in the spaces where they belong. You can either write the letter of your answer choice or you can copy the statement. The first one is done for you. *This item is worth 2 points.*

1.	Historically, malaria probably causes 50 percent of all deaths.
2.	
3.	
4.	
5.	

Answer Choices

A The World Health Organization begins using ITNs.

B Doubts arise about maintaining the decline in malaria mortality rates.

C A decade-long 25 percent reduction in mortality rates is achieved.

D A study finds that malaria-affected countries have greatly reduced per capita earnings.

Directions: Listen to part of a lecture in an art history class.

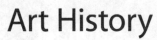

Directions: Now answer the questions. Choose the letter of the answer.

29. What does the professor mainly discuss?

(A) Differences between medieval and Renaissance art

(B) Differences between Humanism and religion

(C) Differences between art in northern and southern Europe

(D) Differences among four different artists' styles

30. Why does the professor discuss the four particular works of art?

(A) They are extremely valuable.

(B) They surpass medieval art.

(C) They represent the new ideals of the Renaissance.

(D) They are misunderstood by modern art historians.

31. Which were true of Italian city-states in the early fifteenth century? *Choose 2 answers.*

[A] Religious control was significant.

[B] New laws caused their wealth to increase.

[C] Knowledge of the sciences spread from them to other areas.

[D] There were few immigrants.

32. Which philosophy became influential in the Renaissance?

(A) Realism

(B) Classicism

(C) Humanism

(D) Republicanism

33. According to the professor, why are a mirror, fruit, shoes, a candle, and a dog highly significant in the Arnolfini portrait?

(A) They provide information on fifteenth-century wedding customs.

(B) They are religious symbols from the fifteenth century.

(C) They show van Eyck's great technical skill.

(D) They attest to the painted couple's wealth and social position.

34. Why does the professor end the lecture with Raphael's painting "The School of Athens"?

(A) To assert that it is the greatest of all Renaissance paintings

(B) To show the confidence of Renaissance-era people in their own achievements

(C) To prove the debt the Renaissance owed to the classical world

(D) To praise the painting's sophistication because it contains so many realistic figures

Answers and Explanations for the Listening section of the TOEFL iBT Practice Pretest begin on page 88.

Speaking

Directions: The Speaking section of the TOEFL iBT assesses your ability to speak in English on a variety of academic and general-interest topics. Some of the items assess only your speaking skills, while others assess your ability to integrate information from reading and/or listening passages into your speaking. To simulate actual TOEFL iBT conditions, follow these instructions:

- For items that integrate listening, listen to each conversation or lecture only once.
- For items that integrate reading, use your watch or timer to keep track of the time. After reading time is up, do not refer back to the reading as you answer.
- As you read, listen, and plan your response, you may take notes to use when giving your response.
- Use your computer's or mobile device's *record* function to record and play back your responses. If your device does not have this function, ask a friend with strong English skills to listen to your responses. You or your friend can evaluate your responses using the simplified scoring rubrics in this book.

 This icon appears each time you need to listen to an audio track.

When this icon appears, record your response on your computer or mobile device. If your device does not have a *record* function, ask a friend with strong English skills to listen to your response.

Now begin the Speaking section of the TOEFL iBT Practice Pretest.

1. You will now speak about a familiar topic. Prepare your response in 15 seconds. Then allow 45 seconds to record your response.

> Choose a place you used to visit as a child. Describe how it has changed since then. Include specific examples and details in your description.
>
> | Preparation Time: 15 seconds |
> | --- |
> | Response Time: 45 seconds |

2. You will now give your opinion about a familiar topic. Prepare your response in 15 seconds. Then allow 45 seconds to record your response.

> Some people spend their free time on activities such as walking or playing sports. Other people prefer to relax in their free time by watching movies or TV programs. Which do you think is better and why?
>
> | Preparation Time: 15 seconds |
> | --- |
> | Response Time: 45 seconds |

3. You will now read a short passage on a campus-related topic and listen to a conversation on the same subject. Then you will hear a question. Prepare your response in 30 seconds. Then allow 60 seconds to record your response.

Reading Time: 45 seconds

Announcement from the Head Librarian

The university has decided to change some of its library services next semester. Complete details for all campus libraries may be found online. The principal changes will be:

1. A reduction in opening hours for the Main Library. (Monday–Friday: 10 A.M.–8 P.M. Saturday: 10 A.M.–4 P.M. Sunday: closed.)
2. The permanent closure of the Ford Fine Arts Library. (From now on, its collection will be housed on Level 6 of the Main Library.)

 Now listen to two students discussing the announcement.

The woman expresses her opinion of the announcement by the Head Librarian. State her opinion and explain the reasons she gives for holding that opinion.

> Preparation Time: 30 seconds
> Response Time: 60 seconds

4. You will now read a short passage on an academic topic and listen to a talk on the same subject. Then you will hear a question. Prepare your response in 30 seconds. Then allow 60 seconds to record your response.

Reading Time: 45 seconds

Soil Composition and Pollution

Soil is the top layer of the Earth's surface, mostly created from weathered rock. It is made up of varying amounts of minerals; humus, or decayed organic matter; air; water; and useful living creatures like worms. The finest rock particles within soil form sticky clay; medium particles become silt; and the coarsest constitute sand. While there is sufficient moisture, soil supports vegetation, providing a habitat for a variety of animals.

Soil pollution from toxic compounds, salts, or disease-causing agents has a detrimental effect on all that lives and grows in the soil, and on humans consuming those products.

 Now listen to a talk on this topic in a geography class.

Describe how climate, relief, and pollution influence the health of soil. Use information from the reading and the talk.

Preparation Time: 30 seconds
Response Time: 60 seconds

5. You will now listen to part of a conversation about a campus-related situation. Then you will hear a question. Prepare your response in 20 seconds. Then allow 60 seconds to record your response.

The speakers discuss two possible solutions to the woman's problem. Describe the problem and the two solutions. Then explain what you think the woman should do and why.

Preparation Time: 20 seconds
Response Time: 60 seconds

6.  You will now listen to part of a lecture on an academic topic. Then you will hear a question. Prepare your response in 20 seconds. Then allow 60 seconds to record your response.

> Using points from the talk, explain why Pluto in the Kuiper Belt was made a dwarf planet in 2006.
>
> | Preparation Time: 20 seconds |
> | --- |
> | Response Time: 60 seconds |

Explanations and Sample Responses for the Speaking section of the TOEFL iBT Practice Pretest begin on page 99.

Writing

Directions: The Writing section of the TOEFL iBT assesses your ability to communicate in writing in academic settings.

This section has two items. To simulate actual TOEFL iBT conditions, follow these instructions.

ITEM 1: INTEGRATED WRITING

- Read the passage in 3 minutes. Use your watch or the timer on your mobile phone or computer to keep track of time. You may take notes as you read and listen, and use your notes when you answer the question.
- Start the audio program and listen to the passage one time as you take notes.
- Read the question, plan your response, and write it in 20 minutes. You may use your notes and refer back to the reading passage as you write.

ITEM 2: INDEPENDENT WRITING

- Set your timer for 30 minutes and start working. You may take notes to plan your essay and to use as you write.

 The Audio icon appears when you need to listen to an audio track.

If you do not finish your essays when the time ends, mark your place. Then continue working as quickly as you can. When you finish, take note of the total time. This will give you an idea of how quickly you need to work on the actual TOEFL iBT to write both essays in 60 minutes.

Now begin the Writing section of the TOEFL iBT Practice Pretest.

1. Integrated Writing

A. Read the passage in 3 minutes. Use your watch or the timer on your mobile phone or computer to keep track of the time. You may take notes in the space provided.

Reading Time: 3 Minutes

The concept of the digital native is one that became relevant as technology proliferated, and more new technology devices—computers, game devices, audio systems, and so on—became available. As devices were introduced and became more complex, it seemed to many observers that those who were born after the advent of the personal computer and other devices had experience with them as children and were adept with them, learned to use them easily, and seemed to integrate technology into their lives in natural ways. This contrasted sharply with older generations who continued to struggle with new technology and by some accounts, resisted it. We hear anecdotal evidence, for example, of young people effortlessly connecting printers, computers, audio systems, and other devices. While older generations pored over manuals and instructions, or went through struggles to do the same task, they marveled at the expertise of these younger generations.

The term *digital native* was coined to characterize the difference between older and younger technology users, whose differing levels of skill and expertise seem to correlate very highly to when they were born and to their degree of access to technology. Under this model, learning to use technology may be somewhat akin to learning a new language—the earlier you start, the easier it is, and to really be a native, you need to start as a young child.

B. Now listen to part of a lecture on the topic you just read about. You may take notes in the space provided.

_____

_____

_____

_____

_____

_____

_____

_____

_____

_____

_____

_____

_____

_____

C. Take 20 minutes to plan, write, and revise an essay of about 150 to 225 words. Use a watch or timer to keep track of time. You may refer to the reading and your notes as you plan and write your essay. Pay attention to the quality of your writing and on how well you present the points in the lecture and their relationship to the reading passage.

 Summarize the points made in the lecture you just heard, explaining how they cast doubt on the points made in the reading passage.

Response Time: 20 minutes

_____

_____

_____

_____

_____

_____

_____

_____

_____

_____

_____

_____

_____

2. Independent Writing

Take 30 minutes to plan, write, and revise an essay on the topic below. Use your mobile phone or computer to keep track of the time. As on the actual TOEFL iBT, use notepaper to gather and organize your ideas. Then keyboard your essay on a computer, if possible. An effective essay will be about 300 words.

Do you agree or disagree with the following statement?

> **The most important factor that influences students' success in school is a good teacher.**

Use specific reasons and examples to support your answer.

Response Time: 30 minutes

_____

_____

_____

_____

_____

_____

_____

_____

_____

_____

_____

_____

_____

_____

_____

_____

_____

_____

_____

_____

_____

_____

_____

_____

_____

_____

_____

Explanations and Sample Responses for the Writing section of the
TOEFL iBT Practice Pretest begin on page 101.

TOEFL iBT Personalized Study Planner

Reading

Use your answers to the Reading section of the TOEFL iBT Practice Pretest and this chart to focus your preparation for the actual TOEFL iBT. Follow these steps.

1. Review all your correct and incorrect answers in the Answers and Explanations, which begin on page 82.
2. In the chart, circle the number of each item you answered incorrectly.
3. Review again the Answers and Explanations for each item you answered incorrectly, this time in the order they are grouped in the chart.
4. For each item type and item format where you want to improve your performance, study the pages listed in the third column.

ITEM NUMBERS	ITEM TYPE	STUDY PAGES
1, 3, 5, 15, 21, 24, 29, 30, 32	Factual information	109–116
2, 16, 33	Negative factual information	116–121
4, 9, 17, 22, 34, 40	Vocabulary	122–131
6, 12, 19, 23, 31, 35	Reference	132–139
11, 27, 41	Sentence simplification	139–148
8, 18, 36	Inference	154–158
10, 13, 25, 26, 37, 39	Rhetorical purpose	159–162
7, 20, 38	Insert text	163–167
28, 42	Prose summary	170–176
14	Fill in a table	176–182

Listening

Use your answers to the Listening section of the TOEFL iBT Practice Pretest and these charts to focus your preparation for the actual TOEFL iBT. Follow these steps.

1. Review all your correct and incorrect answers in the Answers and Explanations, which begin on page 88.
2. In each chart, circle the number of each item you answered incorrectly.
3. Review again the Answers and Explanations for each item you answered incorrectly, this time in the order in which they are grouped in these charts.
4. For each item type and item format where you want to improve your performance, study the pages listed in the third column.

ITEM NUMBERS	ITEM TYPE	STUDY PAGES
6, 12, 23, 29	Gist-content	260–269
1, 18	Gist-purpose	270–274
2, 3, 8, 9, 11, 13, 19, 20, 21, 25, 26, 27, 32, 33	Supporting detail	275–281
16, 24	Understanding the function of what is said	284–286
5, 17, 22	Understanding the speaker's attitude	287–291
28	Understanding organization	294–300
7, 10, 15, 30, 31	Connecting content	300–304
4, 14, 34	Making inferences	304–307

ITEM NUMBERS	ITEM FORMAT	STUDY PAGES
11, 31	Special multiple choice	254
16, 22	Replay items	254–256
8	Check box items	256
28	Drag-and-drop items	257–258

Speaking

Use your responses to the Speaking section of the TOEFL iBT Practice Pretest and this chart to focus your preparation for the actual TOEFL iBT. Follow these steps.

1. Review your responses by comparing them to the sample responses that begin on page 99.

2. Evaluate your responses with the rubrics. If possible, ask a teacher or an English-speaking friend to help you. Or wait a day or two and evaluate yourself. Use the TOEFL iBT Simplified Independent Speaking Rubric on pages 370–371 to score your responses to Items 1 and 2. Use the TOEFL iBT Simplified Integrated Speaking Rubric on pages 398–399 to score your responses to Items 3–6. Write your scores on the lines.

   1. _____   3. _____   5. _____

   2. _____   4. _____   6. _____

3. Which skills do you do well? Which skills do you want to improve? Review your rubrics for Items 1 and 2 together, and check the boxes of the skills you do well. Then review the pages listed for the skills you want to improve.

ITEMS 1 AND 2: INDEPENDENT SPEAKING

SKILL	STUDY PAGES
☐ Answers the question	376–377
☐ Has a main idea	377
☐ Has supporting details	377–378
☐ Follows a logical order	378–379
☐ Uses signaling words and phrases to show relationships among ideas	380–382

4. Now review your completed rubrics for Items 3–6 together, and check the boxes of the skills you do well. Then review the pages listed for the skills you want to improve.

ITEMS 3 TO 6: INTEGRATED SPEAKING

SKILL	STUDY PAGES
☐ Answers the question	411, 420–421
☐ Has a main idea and supporting details	404–408, 422–423
☐ Integrates information from reading and/or listening passages	412–416
☐ Follows a logical order	434–435
☐ Uses order and signaling words and phrases to show relationships among ideas	413–416, 424

Writing

Use your responses to the Writing section of the TOEFL iBT Practice Pretest and these charts to focus your preparation for the actual TOEFL iBT.

ITEM 1: INTEGRATED WRITING

1. Review your responses by comparing them to the sample responses that begin on page 101. Evaluate your essay using the instructions on page 497.

   Write your score on the line. _____

2. Enter your rating in each row of the Integrated Writing Rubric that begins on this page.

3. Review your ratings in each row. Which areas do you want to improve? Study the pages listed for those areas in the column on the right.

SCORE	DESCRIPTION	STUDY PAGES
5	A **Level 5** response:	
	☐ Selects relevant and important information from the lecture and presents it in relation to similar information in the reading. Includes supporting detail and examples.	483–487
	☐ Is well organized and makes sense. Uses signaling words and phrases to connect information and show the relationships among ideas.	490–494
	☐ Includes occasional errors in vocabulary and grammar that do not result in inaccurate or confusing presentation of information or connections among ideas.	495–497
4	A **Level 4** response:	
	☐ Generally selects relevant and important information from the lecture and presents it in relation to relevant and important information in the reading, but may have minor inaccuracies, vagueness, or omissions that cause minor confusion to readers.	483–487
	☐ Includes errors in vocabulary and grammar that are more frequent than in a Level 5 response, but cause only minor problems with clarity or connection of ideas.	495–497

SCORE	DESCRIPTION	STUDY PAGES
3	A **Level 3** response: ☐ Contains some information from the listening and makes some connections to the reading	483–487
	A response at this level has one or more of these problems: ☐ The response addresses the task, but some information may be inaccurate or incomplete. Makes only general, vague, or unclear connections between points in the reading and the lecture.	483–487
	☐ The response omits one major point made in the lecture.	483–487
	☐ Some key points in the lecture or reading, or the connections between them, are unclear, incomplete, inaccurate, or general.	490–494
	☐ Vocabulary and grammar errors may be more frequent than in a Level 4 response and may cause confusion to readers.	495–497
2	A **Level 2** response: ☐ Has some relevant information from the lecture, but has inaccuracies or omissions of important ideas from the lecture.	483–487
	☐ Makes inaccurate or incomplete connections with information from the reading.	483–487
	A response at this level shows one or more of the following: ☐ Omits or inaccurately presents the relationship between the lecture and the reading.	483–487
	☐ Omits or inaccurately presents important points in the lecture.	483–487
	☐ Contains language errors or expressions that obscure meaning.	495–497
1	A **Level 1** response: ☐ Provides little or no meaningful or relevant information from the lecture.	483–487
	☐ Has problems with vocabulary and grammar that make the essay difficult to understand.	495–497
0	A response at this level contains only ideas copied from the reading passage, does not address the topic, is not written in English, or is blank.	

ITEM 2: INDEPENDENT WRITING

1. Evaluate your essay using the instructions on page 525.

   Write your score on the line. _____

2. Enter your rating in each row of the Independent Writing Rubric on this page.

3. Review your ratings in each row. Which areas do you want to improve?
   Study the pages listed for those areas in the column on the right.

SCORE	DESCRIPTION	STUDY PAGES
5	A **Level 5** response largely:	
	☐ Addresses the topic and the task.	515–517
	☐ Is organized and well developed; uses appropriate detail, examples, and explanations.	517–518
	☐ Stays on topic, flows, and makes sense.	519–520
	☐ Uses language well. Has variety in sentence patterns, vocabulary, and idioms, and only minor errors of vocabulary and grammar.	524–525
4	A **Level 4** response largely:	
	☐ Addresses the topic and the task, though some points are not well developed.	515–517
	☐ Is generally well organized and developed; uses appropriate detail, examples, and explanations.	517–518
	☐ Stays on topic, flows, and makes sense, but may have some problems with repetition, staying on topic, or unclear connection of ideas.	519–520
	☐ Uses language fairly well. Has variety in sentence patterns, vocabulary, and idioms, and only minor errors of vocabulary and grammar, but may have some errors in grammar, word form, or natural language that do not cause unclarity.	524–525
3	A **Level 3** response is characterized by one or more of the following:	
	☐ Addresses the topic and the task, but with somewhat developed detail, examples, and explanations.	515–517
	☐ Stays on topic, flows, and makes sense, but connection of ideas might be unclear at times.	517–518
	☐ May show inconsistent ability in grammar and vocabulary that may cause occasional unclarity.	524–525
	☐ Accurate but limited range of sentence structures and vocabulary.	524–525

SCORE	DESCRIPTION	STUDY PAGES
2	A **Level 2** response will show one or more of the following weaknesses:	
	☐ Development of topic and task is limited.	515–517
	☐ Poor organization or connection of ideas.	517–518
	☐ Not enough or inappropriate detail, examples, and explanations.	515–517
	☐ Poor choice of words or word forms.	524–525
	☐ Many errors of sentence structure or vocabulary.	524–525
1	A **Level 1** response is seriously harmed by one or more of these weaknesses:	
	☐ Disorganized or lacks development.	517–518
	☐ Little or no detail, examples, and explanations, or does not respond to the task.	515–517
	☐ Serious errors in sentence structure or vocabulary.	524–525
0	A response at this level contains only ideas copied from the topic, does not address the topic, is not written in English, or is blank.	

Answers, Explanations, Audio Scripts, and Sample Responses

Reading (Page 13)

1. **B** **Touch, taste, sight, smell, and hearing all contribute to how people experience the flavor of food. (Factual information)** Option B is correct because the paragraph mentions all of these senses as involved in how people experience the flavor of food. Option A is incorrect because these five sensations are all detected by the sense of taste, and the paragraph makes clear that other senses are involved, too. Option C is incorrect, therefore. Option D is contradicted by the passage. The sense of touch lets us experience how food feels in our mouths.

2. **A** **A steaming bowl of soup makes us feel warm and cozy. (Negative factual information)** Option A is correct because this is the only option that does not involve the sense of taste. Option A is about the sense of touch. Options B, C, and D are all about the sense of taste and are therefore incorrect.

3. **C** **touch (Factual information)** Option C is correct because this answer is stated directly in the passage: "One of the most common food flavors, hotness or spiciness, is determined primarily by the sense of touch." Therefore, the remaining options are incorrect.

4. **B** **a strong, sharp, burning flavor (Vocabulary)** Option B is correct because this answer is closest to the definition provided in the passage. The passage states that pungency is a strong, hot sensation, and *burning* is close to the meaning of *hot*.

5. **C** **Special nerve cells in the mouth detect a pungent chemical. (Factual information)** Option C is correct because the passage states that "chemoreceptor nerve endings in the skin and mucous membranes" detect pungency. Option A is about the sense of smell and is therefore incorrect. Option B is about the sense of taste and is therefore incorrect. Taste buds are on the tongue, not the roof of the mouth, so Option D is incorrect.

6. **C** **capsaicin (Reference)** Option C is correct because the substance that is being detected is capsaicin. Option A is incorrect because pungency is a sensation, the effect of capsaicin, not a substance. Options B and D are incorrect

because these are places where capsaicin might be detected by chemoreceptor cells, not a substance to be detected.

7. **D** **(Insert text)** Option D is correct because the sentence gives additional detail about people who like the pungent taste of foods with capsaicin. The only place where this sentence makes sense is after another sentence about people who like pungent food. Only Option D follows such a sentence. The sentence does not make sense in the locations in Options A, B, and C.

8. **C** **Peppers with Scoville scores higher than 200,000 are available less frequently than habanero peppers. (Inference)** Option C is correct because the passage states that habanero peppers have the highest Scoville score of peppers "commonly sold" in supermarkets. This implies that other, hotter varieties are less commonly available. Option A cannot be inferred from the passage, because the passage gives no information about the prices of peppers. Option B cannot be inferred from the passage, because the passage gives no information about the safety of eating foods with high Scoville scores. Option D is incorrect because peppers hotter than habaneros are not commonly available. It is not logical to infer from this information that such peppers are not available at all; rather, it can only be inferred that they are available less frequently.

9. **A** **make a liquid weaker by adding a solution to it (Vocabulary)** Option A is correct because according to the passage, a solution of water was added to the alcohol and capsaicin mixture until the "hotness of the chemical was no longer detectable." This implies that the alcohol mixture was made weaker. Options B, C, and D are contradicted by the information in the passage. The capsaicin was made weaker by adding the solution of water and sugar.

10. **A** **To show that a more accurate test of pungency was required (Rhetorical purpose)** Option A is correct because the paragraph goes on to discuss how a more accurate chemical test was developed. While Option B may be a true statement, this is not the reason the author included this piece of information. Rather, the

author includes this statement as a reason why a new test was needed. Option C is incorrect because the passage is not concerned with whether Scoville was a good scientist and never evaluates him in this way. The passage simply states that the test was not sufficiently accurate, which meant that another test was necessary. Option D is contradicted by the passage. Scoville scores can show the relative pungency of varieties of peppers, but these scores are only estimates or averages because of the effect of different growing conditions.

11. **D Further study showed that because individual peppers of one species may have different levels of capsaicin as a consequence of growing conditions, only an average estimate of the pungency of a pepper variety could be calculated. (Sentence simplification)** Option D is correct because only this option restates the essential ideas of the sentence without omitting information, introducing information that is incorrect or not in the passage, or changing the meaning. Option A is incorrect because it omits an important piece of information: because capsaicin levels vary among different individuals of the same variety of pepper, scientists can estimate only the average pungency of a pepper variety. Option B is incorrect because it misstates key information in the sentence. The sentence does not say that peppers have an average, or moderate, amount of capsaicin, but that only an average amount can be calculated for a variety of pepper because of differences among individual peppers of a single variety owing to different growing conditions.

Option C is incorrect because the pungency of individual peppers can be determined using the two methods; as a consequence, the pungency of a variety of pepper cannot be determined accurately, but only estimated.

12. **D food producers' (Reference)** Option D is correct because the passage makes it clear that food companies want to ensure that their products will be accepted by consumers. Option A does not make sense because *consumers'* and *customers'* refer to the same people. Option B is incorrect because peppers do not produce food products. Option C is incorrect because food companies produce these products, not scientists.

13. **A To remind readers not to rely on the variety of pepper to know how spicy an individual pepper may be (Rhetorical purpose)** The author includes this statement directly after a statement on how consumers can use Scoville or ASTA units to avoid overly spicy peppers; this reminder will help consumers remember to taste each pepper before using it to ensure that it is not excessively pungent. Therefore, Option A is correct. Option B is incorrect because while it is true that Scoville scores are less accurate than ASTA scores, this is not the reason why the author mentions the information. The author is concerned about individual differences among peppers due to growing conditions. Option C is not supported by information in the passage. Option D does not make sense. Consumers are already using the pungency scores to identify excessively pungent varieties of pepper.

14. **(Fill in a table)** The correctly completed table should look like this. Answers can be in any order. Answers are correct if only the letter is written.

ASTA PUNGENCY UNIT	SCOVILLE UNIT
Select 2	**Select 3**
• C Measures pungency in parts per million	• B Uses alcohol to extract capsaicin from dried peppers
• F Uses a chemical process to measure the units	• D Measures pungency by having human raters make subjective judgments
	• E Has an inaccuracy rate as high as 50 percent

These answers are correct for these reasons.

ASTA Pungency Unit

- **C Measures pungency in parts per million** The passage directly states that one ASTA pungency unit is one part per million of capsaicin.
- **F Uses a chemical process to measure the units** The passage indicates that the ASTA pungency unit is measured using a chemical process.

Scoville Unit

- **B Uses alcohol to extract capsaicin from dried peppers** The passage indicates that Scoville's process extracted capsaicin with alcohol, which then could be diluted using a solution of water and sugar.
- **D Measures pungency by having human raters make subjective judgments** The passage indicates that Scoville's method used a panel of five raters to make judgments about the spiciness of the solution of alcohol, capsaicin, water, and sugar.
- **E Has an inaccuracy rate as high as 50 percent** The passage directly states that the accuracy rate of Scoville's test was this low.

Incorrect options do not belong in the completed table for these reasons:

- **A Showed that green peppers have a very high pungency level** This option is contradicted by the passage. Green peppers have a Scoville score of 0, which means that they contain no capsaicin.
- **G Measurements are inaccurate because the pungency of individual peppers varies widely.** This statement is about differences among peppers of the same variety, primarily because of growing conditions, and not because of the inaccuracy of the tests. Different peppers of the same variety will have different levels of pungency not because of inaccuracy of the tests, but because of different growing conditions.

15. **A audiences have continued to identify with it over the years (Factual information)** Option A is correct because the passage says that one of the marks of a great work is that it "has stood the test of time and can continue to speak to us over the ages." Only Option A captures this meaning. Option B is incorrect because this is only a summary of the plot; it does not explain why the work is great. Option C only indicates the age of the work. The true test of greatness, according to the passage, is that the work "can continue to speak to us" over time, so Option C is therefore incorrect. Option D only says that this work existed in more than one genre, opera and drama. Option D does not meet the test of greatness as identified in the passage.

16. **D He believes that every young woman should get a good education. (Negative factual information)** Option D is correct because the passage says that "a teacher comes to tutor her, but only for a few hours a day." This shows that the father does not take his daughter's education very seriously. All the remaining options are incorrect because these options are supported by information in the passage. Option A is incorrect because the passage says that the father was traditional. Option B is incorrect because the passage says that the father is strict and didn't let his daughter leave their home frequently. This implies that the father had many rules for his daughter. Option C is directly stated in the passage and is therefore incorrect.

17. **B struggles with (Vocabulary)** Option B is correct because the passage indicates that despite the father's strict rules, Mengmei wants to have friends and find a husband. This indicates that she is caught in a struggle between her wishes and her father's wishes. Option A is incorrect because she does not submit to her father's rules. She runs out of the house to meet Liniang and then longs for him. Because she has strong feelings about Liniang and her father's rules, Option C is therefore incorrect. Option D is not supported by information in the passage. While Mengmei runs out of the house to try to meet Liniang, this is an impulsive act and not an act of rebellion.

18. **C They both become very ill during the opera. (Inference)** Option C is correct because Mengmei falls into a deep sleep caused by depression and lack of food. Mengmei falls from his horse in winter and nearly freezes to death. The doctor prescribes bed rest for him to recover. Option A is contradicted by information in the passage. While Liniang is a scholar, Mengmei is only allowed to meet with a tutor for a few hours a day. Option B is contradicted by the passage, too. Only Mengmei is from an important family. Liniang is from a poor peasant family. Option D is also contradicted by the passage. Only Liniang is free to travel and visit friends. Mengmei usually has to stay at home.

19. **D the young man (Reference)** Option D is correct because this sentence is clearly about Liniang, the young man, learning about and falling in love with the young woman while he is recovering from the fall from his horse. Options A, B, and C do not make sense because those persons already know about Mengmei and do not fall in love with her.

20. **C (Insert text)** Option C is correct because the new sentence is about the father agreeing to the marriage of the young lovers, and the only place where this sentence makes sense is after they fall in love and before they get married. Therefore, the other options are incorrect.

21. **B Women identified with Mengmei's struggle to find love. (Factual information)** Option B is correct because the passage states that the opera's theme, "freedom of love, which was denied to women at that time, appealed greatly to women." Option A is not supported by information in the passage. While the passage says that the music is good, it does not say that women in particular identified with it. Option C is not supported by information in the passage. While Mengmei does not receive a good education, this is not given as a reason why women identified with her or the opera. Option D is contradicted by the passage. Women identified with the opera's strong, unconventional view of the freedom to love, which contradicts the father's traditional values.

22. **C affected by (Vocabulary)** Option C is correct because female audience members related to Mengmei's struggle for freedom of love so strongly that they wept or fainted. Option A is incorrect because interest is not a strong enough feeling to provoke tears or fainting. Option B is incorrect because Mengmei's struggle for freedom to love did not depress the women but made them identify compassionately with her. Option D is incorrect because the women felt a strong sense of identification with Mengmei, not worry.

23. **A the opera (Reference)** Option A is correct because this pronoun clearly refers to the work as a whole, not to individual parts of the work (story, music, or theme). Options B, C, and D all refer to parts or aspects of the opera, so they are incorrect.

24. **B The lyrics and music were revised to make the opera easier to perform. (Factual information)** Option B is correct because this information is stated directly in paragraph 4.

Option A is incorrect because the opera was shortened by 4 hours in 1999. Option C is incorrect because this cut is one of the modern adaptations of this opera. Option D is contradicted by information in the passage. The second part was not added to the original opera. The second part of the original opera was cut to shorten the opera.

25. **B To provide a contrasting example of a time when the opera was not shortened considerably (Rhetorical purpose)** Option B is correct because the previous sentence discusses cutting the opera's length to meet the needs of modern audiences. The word *however* indicates that the sentence provides a contrasting example, in this case a relatively lengthy production in 1999. Option A is not supported by information in the passage. Option C is incorrect because this production maintains most of the opera. Other productions have cut more than half the opera by omitting the second half, which is about the war, not the love story. Option D is incorrect because even though this New York production is lengthy, it still is not the full 24-hour production.

26. **A To show the wide appeal of this opera and its applicability to many kinds of media (Rhetorical purpose)** Option A is correct because this information appears in a paragraph about ways that this work has been updated and brought to new genres (such as film and novel) to enhance its appeal to new audiences. Stating that it has been the basis of a video game provides one more example. This contradicts Option C, which is therefore incorrect. Option B is not supported by the passage. The author is not critical of the video game makers but rather seems to believe that making the video game is a good idea. Option D is not supported by information in the passage. Nowhere does the author mention or imply that people play video games excessively.

27. **A Efforts to remove nineteenth-century trappings from the opera to return it to its origins in the 1600s have met with resistance, showing the work's enduring power and cultural relevance. (Sentence simplification)** Option A is correct because only this option restates the essential ideas of the sentence without omitting information, introducing information that is incorrect or not in the passage, or changing the meaning. Option B is incorrect because it changes the meaning of the original sentence in an important way: the

original sentence says that there was resistance to removing the nineteenth-century trappings, not to the work's power and importance. Option B also omits the reference to nineteenth-century trappings, and consequently misstates the cause-effect relationship: efforts to remove the trappings and restore the opera to its origins caused the resistance, which show the opera's power and importance. Option C is incorrect because the efforts were to remove the nineteenth-century trappings, not to restore them. Option D is incorrect because resistance to the restorations shows the work's importance, not its nineteenth-century trappings.

28. **(Prose summary)** If you completed the summary correctly, it should look like this:

The passage discusses a famous Chinese opera, *The Peony Pavilion*.
- **A** First performed in 1598, this opera, a love story about a young woman who falls in love with a young man she sees in a dream, has stood the test of time.
- **C** This opera had strong appeal to women because it focuses on the theme of freedom of love, which was denied to women at the time.
- **F** To remain relevant to audiences, the opera has been changed in many ways over the years, and novels, films, plays, stories, and even video games have been made from it.

These answers are correct for these reasons.
- **A** **First performed in 1598, this opera, a love story about a young woman who falls in love with a young man she sees in a dream, has stood the test of time.** This option sums up several important ideas from the beginning of the passage, so it belongs in the summary.
- **C** **This opera had strong appeal to women because it focuses on the theme of freedom of love, which was denied to women at the time.** This option restates one of the main ideas of the passage, the theme and appeal of the opera, so it belongs in the summary.
- **F** **To remain relevant to audiences, the opera has been changed in many ways over the years, and novels, films, plays, stories, and even video games have been made from it.** This sentence sums up the different ways the opera has been changed to remain relevant, one of the main topics of the passage, so it belongs in the summary.

Incorrect options do not belong in the completed table for these reasons:
- **B** **The young woman's father, a high imperial official, did not allow her to have friends her own age or meet outsiders.** This option is a relatively minor plot detail, so it does not belong in the summary.
- **D** **The young woman sees the young man riding by her house on horseback and tries to meet him.** Like Option B, this option is a relatively minor plot detail, so it does not belong in the summary.
- **E** **The second part of the opera, about the young man's adventures at war, is often omitted from modern productions of the opera.** This information is one supporting detail about one of the main ideas of the passage, the changes made to keep the opera relevant to modern audiences, so it does not belong in the summary.

29. **A** **To encourage customers to finish their food quickly and leave (Factual information)** Option A is correct because fast-food restaurants encourage people to eat quickly and leave, and the passage says that warm-colored furniture encourages people to get up and move. The remaining options are not supported by information in the passage.

30. **D** **People's decisions are based on a combination of factors, including color. (Factual information)** Option D is correct because people combined their understanding of the kind of medicine (stimulant or depressant) with beliefs about color to make judgments about the strength of the medicine. For this reason, Option A is incorrect. Option B is contradicted by information in the passage. The perception of color is tied to other perceptions, such as the type of medicine. Option C is not supported by information in the passage.

31. **A** **the pills' (Reference)** Option A is correct because the study examined how color affected people's assessment of the strength of the medication. The other options do not make sense.

32. **B** **People find rooms with blue walls pleasant and attractive. (Factual information)** Option B is correct because the passage states that people prefer the color blue for evolutionary reasons—humans experienced evolutionary success in areas with water, so they have a biological preference for the color blue, which they associate with water. Options A and C

are examples of culturally bound meanings conveyed by color. While exit signs are green in many countries, they are red in others. The color red is associated with celebration in Asian cultures, according to the passage. Option D is not possible, because the passage does not state whether this meaning is learned or biologically innate.

33. **A** **People's favorite colors provide insight into their personalities. (Negative factual information)** Option A is not stated in the passage, so therefore it is correct. Options B, C, and D are all mentioned in the passage as principles of color psychology, so they are incorrect.

34. **B** **chances (Vocabulary)** *Odds* refers to the likelihood that something will happen. Option B is the only answer choice with this meaning. Therefore, the other options are incorrect.

35. **C** **people (Reference)** The paragraph is mainly about the effect of color on people, so Option C is correct. The remaining options do not make sense.

36. **A** **Color has an immediate effect on purchasing decisions. (Inference)** Option A is inferred correctly from information in the passage because the passage states that people make initial decisions about whether to purchase a product within 60 to 90 seconds of seeing the product, and because color is a factor in purchasing decisions at least 60 percent of the time. Therefore, it is correct to infer that color has an immediate effect on purchasing decisions. Option B is not supported by information in the passage and does not make sense. A negative perception of a color may influence a customer not to consider a product. Options C and D are not supported by information in the passage. The passage states only that color is an important factor in making purchasing decisions. The passage never states or implies that color will force consumers to purchase a product.

37. **C** **To show that color may be even more influential than authors of other studies believe (Rhetorical purpose)** This information comes after another sentence in which the author says 60 percent or more of purchasing decisions involve color. This sentence indicates that additional studies indicate that color may be even more influential, so Option C is correct. Option A is incorrect because this point has already been supported with other data earlier in the paragraph. There is no indication that the

author is suspicious of these studies, so Option B is incorrect. While people may reject a product because of the color, this is not the author's main idea at this point in the article, and this conclusion cannot be drawn from this supporting detail. The author never indicates that she believes that people reject products because of color, and the information in paragraph 3 does not support such a conclusion. Therefore, Option D is incorrect.

38. **D** **(Insert text)** Option D is correct because this sentence gives a consequence of the impact of color on consumer decisions. The logical place for this sentence to go is after all of the information that supports the belief that color has an effect on consumer decisions. Therefore, Options B and C are incorrect because in both of these positions, the inserted sentence interrupts the data that supports the belief. Option A is incorrect because the sentence needs to come after the information on the impact of color on consumer decisions.

39. **D** **To provide an example of the use of color therapy (Rhetorical purpose)** Option D is correct because this sentence is in a paragraph about color therapy. Reducing prison violence by painting walls blue is an example of using the calming effect of this color for color therapy. Option A is incorrect because this is only one use of color therapy. Option B is incorrect because the author is not criticizing color therapy in the part of the article where this example occurs. Option C is incorrect because the author does not bring up this example in reference to the effect of blue light, which is mentioned in another part of the article.

40. **D** **Using color to improve mental and physical health (Vocabulary)** Option D is the definition given for this term in the passage, so it is therefore correct. Option A is a definition of color psychology, not color therapy, so it is incorrect. Options B and C are examples of the use of color therapy, not definitions, so they are incorrect.

41. **B** **However, companies continue to use color psychology and say when it is used effectively, they can see its benefits in increased sales and customer loyalty. (Sentence simplification)** Option B is correct because only this option restates the essential ideas of the sentence without omitting information, introducing information that is incorrect or not in the passage, or changing the meaning. Option A is incorrect because it omits key information in increased sales and customer loyalty. Option C is incorrect because it omits key information on using color

psychology correctly. Option D is incorrect because it misstates key information in the original sentence. Increased sales and customer loyalty are benefits, not precepts, of color psychology.

42. (Prose summary) If you completed the summary correctly, it should look like this:

The passage discusses the definition and uses of color psychology.

- **A** Color psychology asserts that colors have learned and biological meanings.
- **B** Color psychology studies the effects of color on people.
- **E** Companies use color psychology to improve sales.

These answers are correct for these reasons.

- **A** **Color psychology asserts that colors have learned and biological meanings.** This option restates a main tenet of color psychology, so it belongs in the summary.
- **B** **Color psychology studies the effects of color on people.** This option restates one of the

main ideas of the passage, the definition of color psychology, so it belongs in the summary.
- **E** **Companies use color psychology to improve sales.** This sentence sums up another of the main topics of the passage, so it belongs in the summary.

Incorrect options do not belong in the completed table for these reasons:

- **C** **The color red has different meanings for Asians than for people of other cultures.** This option is a relatively minor supporting detail, so it does not belong in the summary.
- **D** **Color therapy can prevent heart attacks.** This option misstates information in the passage. While color therapy can improve health, this option is an overstatement of the benefits of color therapy.
- **F** **The color blue tends to cause violence.** This option contradicts information in the passage, so it does not belong in the summary. According to the passage, the color blue tends to calm people.

Listening (Page 41)

Questions 1–5

TRACK 1 AUDIO SCRIPT

Narrator: Listen to a conversation between a student and a professor.

Professor: Hello, Sofia. Take a seat.

Student: Thanks, Professor Green. As I said in my email, I'm looking for a letter of recommendation for a scholarship I'm applying for.

Professor: Yes. You're planning to spend time in London, right?

Student: Jordan, actually. The program's organized by a research institute in London, but the fieldwork takes place in Jordan.

Professor: Sounds exciting. Fill me in on the details.

Student: Well, I found out that if I do some fieldwork in Petra—that's the name of the site in Jordan—and submit a report to the institute in London, I can get credit towards my program here.

Professor: OK. So what's happening in Petra?

Student: A couple of years back, archaeologists working in a cave complex found some amazing paintings they think are more than two thousand years old and inspired by Greek and Roman art.

Anyway, the team from the institute is surveying more caves. The whole package—tuition, flights, and accommodation—is pretty expensive. I can't afford to go unless I get a scholarship.

Professor: I see. You do have an excellent academic record, and your final project for me showed real maturity. I'd be happy to write a reference. What do I need to do?

Student: Support my application with a one-page letter saying which courses I took and how I did.

Professor: I remember you took a couple of tough required courses with me and Advanced Dating Methods as an elective course, and got all As.

Student: That's right.

Professor: You know, it's going to be hot and boring scraping away the soot, dirt, and graffiti in a cave in Jordan on the off-chance you find anything.

Student: Do you think so?

Professor: In my experience, working on an archaeological site is ninety-nine parts boredom to one part incredible excitement.

Student: Hmm.

Professor: But, of course, that one part makes it all worthwhile, so best of luck.

ANSWERS AND EXPLANATIONS

1. **D To ask for a reference (Gist-purpose)**
Option D is correct because it is the only option about asking for a reference. The student says, "I'm looking for a letter of recommendation for a scholarship I'm applying for." She adds that she needs support for her application with a one-page letter saying which courses she took and how she performed in them. For this reason, Option A is incorrect. The student is applying to the research association in London for a scholarship. Option B is incorrect because the student is talking about fieldwork, not a field trip. Option C is incorrect because although the student mentions paintings, the purpose of the conversation is to ask for the letter.

2. **A Work on an archaeological site in Jordan (Detail)** Option A is directly stated by the student. When the professor says the student is "planning to spend time in London, right?" the student corrects him by saying, "Jordan, actually." Option B is incorrect because the sponsoring research organization is in London, but the site where the student wants to work is in Jordan. Options C and D are incorrect because the Greek and Roman paintings discussed in the conversation are located in Jordan, not Greece or Rome.

3. **C Explore caves with ancient paintings inside (Detail)** Option C is correct because the student says, "Archaeologists working in a cave complex found some amazing paintings they think are more than 2,000 years old." She adds, "The team from the institute is surveying more caves." Options A, B, and D are not supported by information in the conversation.

4. **B She is well prepared academically. (Inference)** Option B is correct because the professor says the student "took a couple of tough required courses with me and Advanced Dating Methods as an elective, and got all As." Options A, C, and D are not supported by information in the conversation.

5. **A It is tedious but thrilling. (Attitude)** Option A is correct because the professor says, "In my experience, working on an archaeological site is 99 parts boredom to one part incredible excitement." He adds, "Of course, that one part makes it all worthwhile." Therefore, Option B is only partially correct. Options C and D are contradicted by information in the conversation.

Questions 6–11

TRACK 2 AUDIO SCRIPT

Narrator: Listen to part of a lecture in a class on botany. The professor is talking about tropism.

Professor: In ancient Greek, the word *trope* means "a turning." There are many types of tropism; I shall touch on three: thigmotropism, phototropism, and geotropism.

Thigmotropism means a plant's changing the direction of its growth due to physical contact with a solid object. It's estimated that plants are roughly ten times more sensitive to touch than humans. The phenomenon is best illustrated by plant tendrils—you know, those long, thin shoots with coils at the end. In climbing beans or peas, tendrils feel their way towards support. In roots, if there is a rock or some other obstacle, a plant navigates around it.

The most well-known kind of tropism is phototropism—the turning of a plant towards a light source. I'm sure you've all seen indoor plants bending towards a window. This is positive phototropism. Negative phototropism is plant shoots that grow away from light, as some vines do, seeking dark solid objects ideal for climbing.

Geotropism is growth in response to the direction of gravity. Positive geotropism means primary roots burrow down towards the center of the Earth, where gravity is strongest. Negative geotropism means primary stems above ground grow perpendicular to the Earth while secondary stems and roots grow diagonally. If you picture trees clinging to a cliff, both phototropism and geotropism are in evidence: the trees don't grow out at right angles to the cliff, but curve up skyward; their roots don't burrow into the cliff, but trail down it.

In all cases, plants seek light, water, and mineral nutrients in the most efficient way possible. However, the hormonal mechanism that controls plant movement is so sophisticated it has only recently been unravelled.

Until the eighteenth century, the scientific paradigm of Aristotle placed logic above experimental evidence. In a religious universe, humans and other animals took precedence over plants and minerals; indeed, a major distinction between animals and plants was that the former could feel. As a result, plants were considered passive, insensate, and exploitable organisms.

While there are many early descriptions of tropism, they ascribe the phenomenon to other agents than plants themselves. This changed in 1569 when Giambattista della Porta observed that cucumber seedlings tend towards the light. He described this as "sympathy" in the same way that iron was sympathetic to a magnet, or a hen to an egg. We may chuckle at his notion of sympathy, but it opens up debate on the role of the plant, which is no longer completely passive as in the Aristotelian worldview.

More than one hundred years later, Thomas Browne experimented with mustard seedlings to prove that if plants growing in pots are rotated, the seedlings that first lean toward the light later turn back to it when they face the dark. Browne wrongly deduced that plants do this to avoid "bad air" from neighboring plants. Other investigators believed that plants turned toward a light source, like the sun, for heat. Only in 1878 did Albert Bernard Franck demonstrate that plants search for light itself. He did this by cultivating plants that continued to bend toward a lamp even after it had been extinguished. This suggested that plants maintain a degree of control over the direction of their own growth. In 1880, Charles Darwin proposed that a transmissible substance produced in the tip of a plant's stem induces curvature below. Technology at the time wasn't able to discover the minute amounts of plant hormone which make up that substance, but Darwin rightly anticipated that it controls both phototropism and geotropism.

In 1931, Fritz Kögl and Arie Jan Haagen-Smit finally isolated and named the hormone auxin. However, its transport and signaling remained largely unknown until after 2000. To outline the theory of transport and signaling, I'd need to introduce complex genetic terminology. But it's enough just to say that a number of plants have had their entire genome sequenced. As a result, we know much more today about auxin than we did five years ago.

What are the implications of tropism? In an era of massive food production, it's important to optimize crops by investing cleverly in the physical setup. Botanists now know which plants are best to clone; agricultural producers can predict which ones suit certain environments. Furthermore, fertilizers and weed killers that mimic auxins have proven effective.

ANSWERS AND EXPLANATIONS

6. **D** **Understanding how plants respond to light, gravity, and objects (Gist-content)** Option D is correct because the professor mainly discusses theories of how plants respond to certain stimuli. Option A is too general to be correct. Options B and C are only details mentioned in the lecture.

7. **D** **A plant's ability to turn in response to stimuli (Connecting content)** Option D is correct because it integrates information from the definitions of the three kinds of tropism provided by the professor. The professor says, "Thigmotropism means a plant's changing the direction of its growth due to physical contact with a solid object." She adds, "Phototropism [is] the turning of a plant towards a light source." She further adds, "Geotropism is growth in response to the direction of gravity." Option A is contradicted by information in the lecture. Option B, while true, is not a definition of tropism. Option C is not supported by information in the lecture and is too general to be correct.

8. (Detail/Check box)

	GEOTROPISM	PHOTOTROPISM	THIGMOTROPISM
A plant grows In a different direction due to contact with a solid object.			✔ The professor says, "Thigmotropism means a plant's changing the direction of its growth due to physical contact with a solid object."
A plant grows toward a light source.		✔ The professor says, "Phototropism—the turning of a plant towards a light source."	
The roots of a plant go toward a gravitational source.	✔ The professor says, "Geotropism is growth in response to the direction of gravity."		
It was described by della Porta in 1569.		✔ The professor says, "In 1569 . . . Giambattista della Porta observed that cucumber seedlings tend towards the light."	

9. **A Misunderstanding of plants (Detail)**
Option A is correct because the professor says that within the paradigm of Aristotle, "plants were considered passive, insensate, exploitable organisms." Options B and C are not supported by information in the lecture. Option D is incorrect because the professor mentions some early scientists who experimented with plants, but she does not suggest that they experimented too much.

10. **B A plant hormone that controls geotropism and phototropism. (Connecting content)**
Option B is correct because the professor says, "Charles Darwin proposed that a transmissible

substance produced in the tip of a plant's stem induces curvature below. Technology at the time wasn't able to discover the minute amounts of plant hormone which make up that substance, but Darwin rightly anticipated that it controls both phototropism and geotropism. In 1931, Fritz Kögl and Arie Jan Haagen-Smit finally isolated and named the hormone auxin." Options A, C, and D are incorrect. Although the professor mentions weed killers, fertilizer, and genome sequences, none of them is auxin.

11. **C It helps maximize plant yield. D It provides suitable specimens for cloning. (Detail/Special multiple choice)** Options C and

D are correct because the professor says, "In an era of massive food production, it's important to optimize crops by investing cleverly in the physical setup. Botanists now know which plants are best to clone." Option A is incorrect because it is contradicted in the lecture. Effective fertilizers mimic auxin; therefore, the importance of fertilizer would be greater. Option B is incorrect. The benefit of tropism to the environment is too general. Note that you must choose both correct options to receive credit for this item.

Questions 12–17

TRACK 3 AUDIO SCRIPT

Narrator: Listen to part of a lecture in a psychology class. The professor is talking about crowdsourcing.

Professor: Now, you may've had your sister or your high school friend call you "weird" because you're taking a psychology course.

Students: Yeah. Uh-huh. Sure.

Professor: Canadian researchers coined the term WEIRD to describe undergraduates who, until recently, comprised most of the test subjects of academic studies. They're human lab rats, if you like. Analysis of research published in leading psychological journals showed that American undergrads were four thousand times more likely to have participated in studies than anyone else!

The Canadians called these students WEIRD because they were nearly all Western, Educated, Industrialized, Rich, and Democratic. However, since they don't represent a cross-section of humanity, the research outcomes from studies in which they were involved may not be so valid.

Therefore, researchers are now rerunning psychological tests and conducting original research using Web-based subjects. Web contributors are a more diverse crowd: around sixty percent are university graduates, and thirty percent are American, but Indians constitute close to thirty percent, Indonesians and Bangladeshis make up more than fifteen percent each, and the remainder hail from 190 other countries. These people are called Turkers, and the concept is crowdsourcing. Has anyone here been a Turker?

Male Student: Yes. I ranked Spanish-language websites for the education department in my state. Then I had a night job as a security guard. About half the time I was online working for a crowdsourcing company. I voted on logos other Turkers had designed for sporting goods. I also

uploaded a video to YouTube for a documentary, but none of my footage was used.

Professor: Anyone else?

Female Student: I interpreted satellite images for an archaeological survey. The photos were taken over isolated places in the desert. I identified land formations that looked like ancient forts, city walls, or tombs. Later, an Italian team started digging at two of those sites. However, I quit because I made about a dollar an hour.

Professor: Low pay is certainly an issue with crowdsourcing. Did anyone do any psych tests?

Male Student: I took part in a Harvard University replication of the classic trolleyology experiment.

Professor: Really, Josh? Tell us more.

Male Student: In this dilemma, there's an out-of-control train car, or trolley, which is going to kill the passengers inside unless a bystander is pushed in front to slow it down. The subject of the experiment has to actively kill a single individual—the bystander—or passively let the passengers die.

Professor: What was interesting about the findings of the study done with Turkers?

Male Student: Turkers responded the same way as the WEIRD undergrad students *only* if they didn't hold strong religious beliefs.

Professor: Punishment is the other area of moral interest. Did you read the piece by Benedikt Herrmann from the UK? He's the guy who replicated a public good game in sixteen countries. In public good games, players share stuff with other players to get more points or to go up a level. These games reward cooperation as much as competition. D'you remember what Herrmann found?

Female Student: In four countries punishment was almost as common as collaboration.

Professor: What does Herrmann think this proves?

Female Student: Such behavior is rather disturbing. I thought people were beyond that.

Professor: But what does *Herrmann* think?

Female Student: Punishment didn't evolve to encourage cooperation. It's a form of self-interest—which could explain why my sister calls me "weird"!

Professor: So, some research is being repeated using more diverse participants. It's being done at roughly a tenth of the cost of using undergrads. And most interestingly, Turkers are now able to collaborate in real time. Whether Turkers continue to do all these tasks so cheaply remains to be seen.

Male Student: What's the problem? Crowdsourcing's voluntary. It's more like a hobby. You're learning something; you get a buzz from being part of new research.

Female Student: In my view, if the Canadians thought WEIRD undergrads were skewing results, when so many Turkers come from developing countries, that affects things too. I quit because I was paid so little, but in some places, a dollar an hour could seem decent money.

Professor: Uh-huh. Other criticisms include poor work done by Turkers who are often paid per item and the long time it takes to complete mundane research due to the high dropout rate of Turkers. Despite the glitches, I'm sure, as a research method, uh, crowdsourcing's here to stay. It's fast, cheap, diverse, and mostly reliable.

TRACK 4 AUDIO SCRIPT

Narrator: Listen again to part of the lecture. Then answer the question.

Female Student: In four countries punishment was almost as common as collaboration.

Professor: What does Herrmann think this proves?

Female Student: Such behavior is rather disturbing. I thought people were beyond that.

Professor: But what does *Herrmann* think?

Narrator: What does the professor mean when she says this?

Professor: But what does *Herrmann* think?

ANSWERS AND EXPLANATIONS

12. B **It deserves to be a popular research method. (Gist-content)** Option B is correct because the professor says, "As a research method, crowdsourcing's here to stay. It's fast, cheap, diverse, and mostly reliable." Option A is not supported by anything the professor says. Option C is contradicted when the professor says that some crowdsourcing research "is being done at roughly a tenth of the cost of using undergrads."

13. B **American students are not representative of most people. (Detail)** Option B is correct because the professor says American students are Westerners who are highly educated and from rich, industrialized, democratic countries. Option A is contradicted by information in the lecture. Options C and D are not supported by information in the lecture.

14. D **All kinds of work (Inference)** Option D is correct. The two student Turkers did all kinds

of work. The male student says he, "ranked Spanish-language websites." He "voted on logos." He "took part in . . . the classic trolleyology experiment." The female student says she "interpreted satellite images." Option A is incorrect because only one piece of work was linguistic. Option B is incorrect because only one piece of work involved psychology testing. Option C is incorrect because while some work was scientific or related to marketing, one student also did linguistic work.

15. C **It somewhat modified previous findings. (Connecting content)** Option C is correct because in the Harvard University repeat of the trolleyology experiment, previous findings were modified. The male student says that he took part in the experiment. He adds, "Turkers responded the same way [in the repeat] as the WEIRD undergrad students only if they didn't hold strong religious beliefs." Options A and B are not supported by information in the lecture. Option D is incorrect. It is too extreme to say, "It completely overturned previous findings." The word *overturned* suggests that the new findings would have been totally different from the old ones, but that was not true.

16. B **She is more interested in Herrmann's opinion than in the student's. (Function/Replay)** Option B is correct because when the professor says, "But what does *Herrmann* think?" she emphasizes her interest in Herrmann's opinion by the strong stress she places on the name "Hermann." Options A, C, and D are not supported by information in the audio replay.

17. B **Low pay could affect the quality of Turkers' work. (Attitude)** Option B is correct because the professor says, "Low pay is certainly an issue with crowdsourcing." She adds, "Other criticisms include poor work done by Turkers who are often paid per item." Option A is not supported by anything said in the lecture. Option C is incorrect. That volunteer Turkers should not expect more pay is the male student's opinion, not the professor's opinion. Option D is incorrect. That Turkers who come from developing countries are paid reasonably is the female student's opinion, not the professor's opinion.

Questions 18–22

TRACK 5 AUDIO SCRIPT

Narrator: Listen to a conversation between a student and a university employee.

Employee: Good morning. May I help you?

Student: I was speaking on the phone to Mr. Wall, the housing manager. Is he available?

Employee: I'm afraid he's in a workshop till Thursday. Didn't he mention that?

Student: No, he didn't. My appointment's on Friday, but I'm not sure the matter can wait.

Employee: Oh? What were you going to speak to him about?

Student: Well, I've been living in Johnson Dorm for the past year. Mostly it's OK. My roommate's fine, and we're on the south side of the building, so it's sunny, but unfortunately, it's really noisy.

Employee: Are you above Lexington Road? That can be busy with the buses and the parking lot right outside the window.

Student: No, we're on Lincoln. The problem isn't the noise from the parking lot. The problem is this group of freshmen who live across the hall. Seems they've been partying since the day they arrived. We can hear everything going on in their room—music, shouting, jumping around. One of the guys plays hockey, and he must invite the whole team back after practice. It's out of control.

Employee: I see. May I ask if you've followed the standard complaints procedure?

Student: You mean, talking to the guys, and putting something in writing?

Employee: Yes.

Student: Sure. But honestly, it won't make any difference. I'd rather move out of Johnson and into McKinley Dorm. Mr. Wall said there was space in McKinley. I know it's more expensive because most of the rooms are singles, but I've got to have some peace and quiet.

Employee: You will have to wait until Mr. Wall returns for his decision on this one; I'm not authorized to make transfers.

Student: Look, I'm on a scholarship, and if I don't get good grades, I may lose it. Right now, I'm bombing out in two subjects. To say I'm concerned is an understatement.

Employee: I do understand. However, it is beyond my jurisdiction to let students change dorms. I'll tell Mr. Wall you came by, and I'm sure he'll call you as soon as possible.

TRACK 6 AUDIO SCRIPT

Narrator: Listen again to part of the conversation. Then answer the question.

Employee: You will have to wait until Mr. Wall returns for his decision on this one; I'm not authorized to make transfers.

Student: Look, I'm on a scholarship, and if I don't get good grades, I may lose it. Right now, I'm bombing out in two subjects. To say I'm concerned is an understatement.

Narrator: What does the student mean when he says this?

Student: Right now, I'm bombing out in two subjects. To say I'm concerned is an understatement.

ANSWERS AND EXPLANATIONS

18. **A** **To move to another dorm** (Gist-purpose) Option A is correct. The student wants to speak to Mr. Wall about transferring to another dorm because he says, "I'd rather move out of Johnson and into McKinley Dorm." Option B is incorrect because the student has already complained about students in his dorm. This conversation has another purpose. Options C and D are not supported by information in the conversation.

19. **B** **Mr. Wall is out of the office. (Detail)** Option C is correct. Mr. Wall is unable to help the student at present because he is out of the office. The employee says, "I'm afraid [Mr. Wall is] in a workshop till Thursday." Option A is incorrect. It is the employee who is speaking, not Mr. Wall, who lacks the authority to help the student. Option C is incorrect. It is contradicted by information in the conversation. In fact, the student has made an appointment, but it is for a later date. Option D is not supported by information in the conversation.

20. **C** **They have frequent loud parties. (Detail)** Option C is correct because the student says, "Seems they've been partying since the day they arrived. We can hear everything going on in their room—music, shouting, jumping around." Option A is incorrect. While the freshmen do play hockey, the student does not say they watch it on TV. Option B is contradicted by information in the passage: the students are very sociable. Option D is not supported by information in the conversation.

21. **D** **It costs more than Johnson Dorm. (Detail)** Option D is correct because McKinley Dorm costs more than Johnson Dorm, which is a disadvantage. The student says, "Mr. Wall said there was space in McKinley. I know it's more

expensive because most of the rooms are singles." Option A is incorrect. The student does not mention which way rooms in McKinley Dorm face. Option B is incorrect. The student mentions that McKinley Dorm mainly has singles, but he does not say this is a disadvantage. Option C is incorrect. The employee mentions traffic noise from Lexington Road in connection to Johnson, not McKinley, Dorm.

22. **D He wants to present his case more strongly (Attitude/Replay)** Option D is correct. When the student says, "I'm bombing out in two subjects. To say I'm concerned is an understatement," he wants to present his case for changing dorms more strongly. The tone of his voice is assertive. Options A, B, and C are not supported by the audio replay.

Questions 23–28

TRACK 7 AUDIO SCRIPT

Narrator: Listen to part of a lecture in a class on public health. The professor is talking about malaria.

Professor: Last week, we looked at smoking and mortality, and public health measures to reduce these rates. Today, I'd like to review malaria. While this is a distressing topic, it's not all gloom and doom.

Before I begin, I'll be quoting a few statistics, so take notes. The first one is four billion. Any idea what that number refers to?

Female Student: People at risk of contracting malaria annually?

Professor: Well done. And what about 216 million?

Male Student: Umm . . . The number of malaria cases worldwide?

Professor: Yes. In 2010, of the 216 million cases reported, one point two million proved fatal. One point two million! That's like an entire city being wiped out each year. Sixty percent of those deaths occurred among children under the age of five, with pregnant women as the next-affected group. Many places in a broad band around the equator have the perfect conditions for malaria, but Africa experiences the most fatalities by far.

Not only are individual deaths heartrending, malaria is a burden on entire communities. A 1995 study compared average per capita earnings between countries with and without malaria. There was a five hundred percent difference. It was estimated, in 2012, that one percent of the gross domestic product is still being lost annually

in malaria-affected countries, and a staggering forty percent of public health expenditure there is devoted to the disease.

Now, malaria has been with us for millennia—as long as humans have been settled near fresh water. Scientists estimate it has killed one out of every two people who've ever lived!

Increased prevention and control measures reduced mortality rates by more than twenty-five percent globally between 2003 and 2013, but maintaining those rates may be difficult. Why so?

Female Student: Maybe because of the global economic recession. International aid decreases when rich countries have their own problems.

Professor: You're absolutely right. Any other reason?

Male Student: Are the mosquitoes getting cleverer? Has the malaria parasite mutated?

Professor: Indeed. Plasmodium parasites have become drug resistant, especially in Southeast Asia. While there *are* vaccines available, they're not very good.

Malaria is borne by female mosquitoes that carry plasmodium parasites they've picked up from an infected vertebrate source. These parasites multiply rapidly within a human or animal's liver and red blood cells, causing headache, fever, coma, liver failure, or death. A large number of malaria survivors suffer brain damage.

There are five species of parasite; *Plasmodium falciparum* is by far the most insidious, since it dodges human immune system surveillance by transforming into numerous proteins. That's why a decent vaccine is proving hard to create.

Now, let's look at four factors in the control of malaria. I'm going to write "E. I. E. and I." on the board. What does "E" stand for?

Female Student: Education? Preventive education?

Professor: Right. Making people more aware of the symptoms and encouraging them to seek medical treatment swiftly. Drugs like artemisinin can cure most malaria cases.

Male Student: Does "E" also stand for environment? Something like controlling the environment where mosquitoes breed?

Professor: Yes, it does. Spraying mosquitoes with moderate amounts of pesticide and encouraging water flow in stagnant pools or tanks are hugely significant. Larvae-eating fish have also been introduced into swamps and rivers to good effect. Recently, Mauritius, a country in the western Indian Ocean, spent about one US dollar per head of population on doing these things. It reduced infection and mortality rates dramatically, proving malaria control isn't rocket science and doesn't need big bucks.

What about "I"?

"I" stands for immunization—although, as I mentioned, it's not very effective. "I" is also for the use of ITNs—insecticide-treated nets—which are. They were first used by the World Health Organization in 1998.

Impregnated with pesticide, the bed nets last for three to five years, and if people have them, almost all of them use them. The problem seems to be with their distribution: fewer than two percent of children in urban areas of sub-Saharan Africa sleep under ITNs; in rural areas, the percentage is much lower.

So malaria remains a major killer, but some simple public health measures can reduce its impact. However, on a sobering note, it seems that from 2013, the decline in mortality rates was being questioned, and malarial infection may be rising again.

ANSWERS AND EXPLANATIONS

23. **A Ways malaria can be prevented (Gist-content)** Option A is correct because most of the lecture is about prevention of malaria. Option B is not supported by information in the lecture. Options C and D are details in the lecture, so they are incorrect.

24. **C To show that malaria has afflicted humans for millennia (Understand function)** Option C is correct because the professor says, "Malaria has been with us for millennia—as long as people have settled near fresh water." Option A is contradicted by information in the lecture; death rates have been falling. Option B is mentioned in the lecture, but it is not the reason the professor

brings up this statistic, which is related to history and not current events. Option D is contradicted by information in the passage. Malaria is prevalent in only certain countries around the world.

25. **D It avoids detection by the human immune system. (Detail)** Option D is correct because the professor says, "*Plasmodium falciparum* is by far the most insidious [parasite], since it dodges human immune system surveillance by transforming into numerous proteins." Options A, B, and C are not supported by information in the lecture.

26. **A Preventive education and environmental control (Detail)** Option A is correct because the female student says, "Preventive education." The male student adds, "Controlling the environment where mosquitoes breed." Option B is incorrect because the professor says that vaccines are ineffective against malaria. Options B and C are contradicted by information in the lecture. Mutations of the malaria parasite make it harder to control. Malaria-carrying mosquitoes breed in flooded areas, so this would have the opposite effect and increase malaria rates.

27. **C To prove malaria control need not be difficult or costly (Detail)** Option C is correct because the professor says, "Mauritius, a country in the western Indian Ocean, spent about one US dollar per head of population on [spraying pesticide, encouraging water flow, and introducing larvae-eating fish]. It reduced infection and mortality rates dramatically, proving malaria control isn't rocket science, and it doesn't need big bucks." Therefore, Option B is incorrect. Options A and D are not supported by information in the lecture.

28. (Organization/Drag-and-drop)

1.		Historically, malaria probably causes 50 percent of all deaths.
2.	**D**	A study finds malaria-affected countries have greatly reduced per capita earnings. The professor says, "A 1995 study compared average per capita earnings between countries with and without malaria. There was a five hundred percent difference."
3.	**A**	The World Health Organization begins using ITNs. The professor says, "[ITNs] . . . were first used by the World Health Organization in 1998."
4.	**C**	A decade-long twenty-five percent reduction in mortality rates is achieved. The professor says, "Increased prevention and control measures reduced mortality rates by more than twenty-five percent globally between 2003 and 2013, but maintaining those rates may be difficult."
5.	**B**	Doubts arise about maintaining the decline in malaria mortality rates. *See number 4.*

Questions 29–34

TRACK 8 AUDIO SCRIPT

Narrator: Listen to part of a lecture in an art history class.

Professor: Today, I'd like to discuss the works of four artists that illustrate the differences between Renaissance and medieval art.

But first, some background. In the early fifteenth century, the Italian city-states had cast off the burden of feudalism. Agricultural workers had gained a degree of freedom and were moving into cities. A rise in trade led to universal improvements in the standard of living. Collective and corporate liberty were enshrined in law. Guilds—premodern unions—and companies with shareholders became legal entities, bringing enormous wealth and influence.

Along with a growth in trade, particularly with the East, paper came into common use. Printing began. Scientific and cultural knowledge spread from Italian city-states across Europe. Artistic skills improved dramatically, especially with the invention of perspective. Painting and sculpture no longer carried explicit religious messages. Classical studies, landscape painting, and portraiture all rose in popularity.

Europe was still a continent of believers, but the power of the established church was waning; a philosophy known as Humanism gained ground. This was influenced by classical Rome and Greece, where texts and artworks espoused the emancipation of the individual and the value of reason. Humanism stressed living a successful life on earth rather than focusing on death with the assurance of salvation.

So let's look at some works of art. Take the Arnolfini portrait, painted by Jan van Eyck in 1434 for an Italian merchant. Even though you and I may find the clothing and the gestures of this man and wife odd, we're nevertheless struck by the clever play of light and the high degree of realism. The technical skill of the painter is consummate. But who is he honoring? For more than five hundred years, this painting was thought to be a wedding portrait, alluding to the sanctity of marriage. The objects around the couple—mirror, fruit, shoes, candle, dog—were considered religious symbols. But in my view, it's more likely this portrait is proof of the handsome couple's social status. I mean, they're rich enough to engage the services of van Eyck, and those accessories—mirror, fruit, shoes, candle, and dog—are just that: expensive accessories. So there's a sudden leap in the number of portraits painted in the Renaissance, and they celebrate the luxurious life of successful individuals, not their relationship to the church or the hereafter.

Here's a second difference between the medieval era and the Renaissance: formerly, there were virtually no works of art where a high degree of *emotion* was achieved. However, Albrecht

Dürer, who painted his final self-portrait in 1500, demonstrates his technical virtuosity *and* his emotional depth. The fur of his collar; his facial features; his skin, hair, and ringlets are rendered in photographic detail. When I saw this painting in Germany, during spring break, even I responded with a jolt. His frown and a tinge of sadness betray his humanity. I was suddenly aware that the painter, who died aged twenty-eight, not long after completing this work, was all too human.

Michelangelo also created numerous secular works like the sculpture *David*. This huge carved stone is three times the size of a normal man, and it symbolized the independence of the Florentine Republic. Now, however, it is the power and beauty of the figure and Michelangelo's technical achievement that awe viewers.

Lastly, Raphael's masterpiece, the *The School of Athens*. This was painted onto the wall of a private chamber of the reigning pope, proving how far Humanism had infiltrated the seat of religious power. It shows the Greek founding fathers of arithmetic, geometry, music, astronomy, grammar, logic, and philosophy. Its grand scale, lofty architecture, and dozens of realistic figures pay homage to classical scholarship and greatness, but also suggest that the Renaissance world would surpass it. And it certainly did.

ANSWERS AND EXPLANATIONS

29. **A** **Differences between medieval and Renaissance art (Gist-content)** Option A is correct because the professor states that this is the main idea of the talk at the beginning of the lecture. Options B and C are not supported by the lecture. Option D is incorrect because the professor uses the artists' styles to contrast the two kinds of art.

30. **C** **They represent the new ideals of the Renaissance. (Connecting content)** Option C is correct because the professor says these works "illustrate the differences between Renaissance and medieval art." In the lecture, the professor lists a number of new ideals, including "enormous wealth," "scientific and cultural knowledge," "a philosophy known as Humanism," an interest in classical Rome and Greece, and "a high degree of emotion" expressed in art. Options A and B may be true, but they are not the reasons the professor discusses the works of art. The professor does not mention the value of the paintings, and she is discussing them to show how people's view of the world changed during the Renaissance, not

whether the technical skills of artists increased. Option D is not supported by information in the lecture.

31. **B** **New laws caused their wealth to increase.** **C** **Knowledge of the sciences spread from them to other areas. (Connecting content/Special multiple choice)** Options B and C are correct. Option B is correct because the professor says, "Collective and corporate liberty were enshrined in law. Guilds—premodern unions—and companies with shareholders became legal entities." Option C is correct because the professor says, "Scientific and cultural knowledge spread from Italian city-states across Europe." Option A is incorrect because religious control was weaker, as suggested by "the power of the established church was waning." Option D is incorrect because "agricultural workers . . . were moving into cities," so there was high immigration. Note that you must choose both correct options to receive credit for this item.

32. **C** **Humanism (Detail)** Option C is correct. The professor says, "A philosophy known as Humanism gained ground." Options A, B, and D are not supported by information in the lecture.

33. **D** **They attest to the painted couple's wealth and social position. (Detail)** Option D is correct because the objects demonstrate the painted couple's wealth and social standing. The professor says, "Those accessories are just that: expensive accessories" and "This portrait is proof of the handsome couple's social status." Option A is incorrect because this painting is no longer thought to be a wedding portrait. Option B is contradicted by information in the lecture. Option C is incorrect. While the accessories do show van Eyck's great technical skill, this is not why they are "highly significant."

34. **B** **To show the confidence of Renaissance-era people in their own achievements (Inference)** Option B is correct because the professor says, "Its [the painting's] grand scale, lofty architecture, and dozens of realistic figures pay homage to classical scholarship and greatness, but also suggest that the Renaissance world will surpass it. And it certainly did." Options A and D are not supported by information in the lecture. Option C is incorrect. While the Renaissance did owe a debt to the classical world, this is not why she mentions the painting.

Speaking (Page 60)

Item 1

TRACK 9 AUDIO SCRIPT

Narrator: You will now speak about a familiar topic. Prepare your response in fifteen seconds. Then allow forty-five seconds to record your response.

Choose a place you used to visit as a child. Describe how it has changed since then. Include specific examples and details in your description.

Item 2

TRACK 10 AUDIO SCRIPT

Narrator: You will now give your opinion about a familiar topic. Prepare your response in fifteen seconds. Then allow forty-five seconds to record your response.

Some people spend their free time on activities such as walking or playing sports. Other people prefer to relax in their free time by watching movies or TV programs. Which do you think is better and why?

Item 3

TRACK 11 AUDIO SCRIPT

Narrator: You will now read a short passage on a campus-related topic and listen to a conversation on the same subject. Then you will hear a question. Prepare your response in thirty seconds. Then allow sixty seconds to record your response.

The University of Springfield is changing some of its library services. Read the announcement from the Head Librarian about the plan. You will have 50 seconds to read the announcement. Begin reading now.

TRACK 12 AUDIO SCRIPT

Narrator: Now listen to two students discussing the announcement.

Man: With everyone using the Internet and e-readers at home, there's hardly anyone in the library.

Woman: Hmm. It was pretty busy before final exams. Also, I work three days in town on a school art program while taking classes here at night. It'll be impossible for me to get out materials the professor recommends after class, whereas I can when the library's open till nine P.M. Sundays are also a great time for me to have a whole day of study in the library. Seems like I can kiss that one good-bye!

Man: It just means you'll have to organize your time differently.

Woman: It's all very well to cut costs—that's what relocating the art collection's about—but my concern is that we students don't see where the money goes that's being saved.

Man: I'm with you on that one.

Woman: Yeah, I bet we Fine Arts majors don't get a badly needed ceramics studio or a state-of-the-art video editing lab in the space where the Ford collection was. Probably the Dean will just enlarge her office.

Narrator: The woman expresses her opinion of the announcement by the Head Librarian. State her opinion and explain the reasons she gives for holding that opinion.

Item 4

TRACK 13 AUDIO SCRIPT

Narrator: You will now read a short passage on an academic topic and then listen to a talk on the same subject. Then you will hear a question. Prepare your response in thirty seconds. Then allow sixty seconds to record your response.

Now read the passage about soil composition and pollution. You have 45 seconds to read the passage. Begin reading now.

TRACK 14 AUDIO SCRIPT

Narrator: Now listen to a talk on this topic in a geography class.

Professor: There are many factors that contribute to healthy soil. Two major ones are climate and relief—that is, the height and shape of the land.

Temperature and precipitation—how much rain there is—are particularly important. Cold climates, like that of Siberian Russia or the high mountain ranges of the Andes, produce soils of little benefit to agriculture. Frozen for much of the year, humus does not form fast enough to improve the soil. Likewise, deserts abound in very hot places where soil is too dry or sandy to support much life. A moderate amount of rain in a temperate region falling on humus-rich worm-filled silt is a wonderful thing. In reality, many places have uneven precipitation. Soil itself may even become hazardous in a landslide.

Both the slope and the angle of the land affect the rate of water runoff and erosion. Steep slopes produce poor, thin soils. Low-lying flat land has deeper, more fertile soils, especially with the addition of rich material from rivers. However, rivers also flood, and flat land may not drain. Pollution is easily washed along a waterway, and most factories are built in cities on the plains.

Narrator: Describe how climate, relief, and pollution influence the health of soil. Use information from the reading and the talk.

Item 5

Narrator: You will now listen to part of a conversation about a campus-related situation. Then you will hear a question. Prepare your response in twenty seconds. Then allow sixty seconds to record your response.

Now listen to a conversation between two students talking about a problem one of them has in a class.

Man: Hi, Tara, how's it going?

Woman: Not so well, James.

Man: I'm sorry about that. Can I help?

Woman: Maybe. Well . . . as you know . . . , I've always been a pretty good student. Yesterday, for the first time, I failed a mechanical engineering project that's worth fifteen percent of our final grade, but I, I . . . don't think I deserved to fail.

Man: I see. Have you discussed it with your professor?

Woman: No, I'm too ashamed.

Man: There's got to be a reason for your poor performance.

Woman: There is. My father's ill, and the last week I was working on my project, I spent four days in the emergency room with him.

Man: Oh, dear.

Woman: But also, it was a group project. I did my part fine, even with all of my other problems. It was the others in my group who were, well . . . careless. One guy made some calculations that were faulty. One girl compared our model with some others, but copied off a student in another group. Naturally, the professor spotted that.

Man: I think you've got two options, Tara. You could get a note from the hospital so your professor knows the background. You could ask to be assessed only on your contribution.

Or you could let it go. After all, what's fifteen percent? If you complain, the students in your group are going to hate you. In a department like engineering, you've got to deal with those people for the next four years.

Woman: Thanks, James. I'll think about what you've said.

Narrator: The speakers discuss two possible solutions to the woman's problem. Describe the problem and the two solutions. Then explain what you think the woman should do and why.

Item 6

Narrator: You will now listen to part of a talk on an academic topic. Then you will hear a question. Prepare your response in twenty seconds. Then allow sixty seconds to record your response.

Now listen to part of a lecture in an astronomy class.

Professor: Astronomers have always been eager to find more planets. Over time, numerous bodies were proposed which were later downgraded to asteroids or dwarf planets. In 2005, Eris seemed a promising candidate. Although Eris is larger than Pluto, with a large moon, astronomers declared Eris a dwarf planet. Following this, Pluto's status was questioned. In 2006, it was reclassified as a dwarf.

But what is Pluto? Created about four point six thousand million years ago, it's a sphere made up of 98 percent nitrogen ice. Its mass is one-five-hundredth that of Earth's, which is significant to its status. It's roughly one-sixth the size of Earth, and at least 1,749 million miles beyond Neptune, in a region called the Kuiper Belt. So it's a light, small frozen ball way out there. However, Pluto does orbit the sun, and it does have five moons.

Why then did the International Astronomical Union downgrade Pluto? A planet must meet three criteria. It must orbit the sun. It must be massive enough to remain spherical. And it must clear the neighborhood around its orbit. Pluto fails to meet the third condition. Its mass cannot create enough gravity to draw in or scatter asteroids nearby, so it shares its orbit with many of them.

Narrator: Using information from the talk, explain why Pluto in the Kuiper Belt was made a dwarf planet in 2006.

EXPLANATIONS AND SAMPLE RESPONSES

There are many ways to answer these items. If you do not have a recording device, ask a friend to listen and evaluate your responses. If you have a recording device, ask a teacher or an English-speaking friend to listen to your responses and evaluate them. Or wait a day or two and evaluate them yourself. For Items 1 and 2, use a copy of the Independent Speaking Rubric in Appendix D. For Items 3 through 6, use a copy of the Integrated Speaking Rubric in Appendix D.

Compare your responses to these high-scoring responses.

 Item 1 Sample Response

 Item 2 Sample Response

 Item 3 Sample Response

 Item 4 Sample Response

 Item 5 Sample Response

 Item 6 Sample Response

After evaluating your responses, follow the instructions in the TOEFL iBT Personalized Study Planner on pages 76–77 to find ways to improve your performance.

Writing (Page 66)

Item 1

TRACK 17 AUDIO SCRIPT

Narrator: Now listen to part of a lecture on the topic you just read about.

Professor: This morning I decided to connect my new mobile phone to the audio system in my car. Well, needless to say, after fifteen minutes, I'd made no progress. Then my son reminded me that he needed me to drive him to school. On the way, he managed to connect the phone and the audio system almost immediately, while I'd struggled for fifteen minutes and almost made my son late for school. It seems like my son is a digital native, and I am not, but does this really explain my struggle?

Research says that being a digital native is not the main factor to consider in whether someone will be good at technology. In fact, the digital native model is overly simplistic. First, experts believe that people adopt technology in a very specific pattern. The first to accept a new technology are called pioneers. These are the people we see standing in line at a computer store when a new, desired device comes on the market. After that are the early adopters, those who adopt a new technology more quickly than others. These two groups have a number of factors in common. They tend to have more education than the general public and be older, too, and they tend to be

perceived as leaders by the community. The last to adopt a new technology are laggards—they tend to have less education and less social standing in the community. They are not perceived as leaders. Interestingly, the pioneers and early adopters tend to be somewhat older than the general population.

Actually, the reason that I struggle with technology may be the opposite of what is predicted by the digital native model. I am struggling because I am an early adopter or pioneer, not a resister. Of course, we are going to struggle more than others—we go into new ground and take risks to use technology.

TRACK 18 AUDIO SCRIPT

Narrator: Summarize the points made in the lecture you just heard, explaining how they cast doubt on the points made in the reading passage.

EXPLANATION

There are many ways to answer this item. Compare your answer to this high-scoring response. Then evaluate your essay. Follow the instructions on page 497. Use the Simplified Integrated Writing Rubric in Appendix E.

SAMPLE ESSAY RESPONSE

The reading and the lecture are on the topic of technology use and young people. The article says that young people are likely to be good at technology and use it, but not older people. The professor says that this view is simple and not true.

According to the reading, young people are digital natives. They were born after computer technology was invented, like to use it, and are good at it. They can connect a printer to a computer very easily, according to the reading. They also use technology a lot and it is part of their lives. Even the professor says that his son is good at connecting his mobile phone to car.

Even though the professor says that he uses technology and struggles, he not resisting technology. He wants to use it, but only struggles. The professor says that there is a specific pattern for people and new technology. According to professor, it's not necessary to be digital native to use new technology. The technology adaptation cycle shows that people who use technology first tend to be richer and older than others, but not friendly with them. They are working alone and looking for new ideas. They tend to be older than those who don't use technology or hate it.

In conclusion, the digital native idea doesn't work very well. It seems that young people may be good at connecting technology, but also seems that older people want technology, too, just like younger ones. Like the professor says, he struggles with technology because he wants it, not because he resists it.

Item 2

EXPLANATION

There are many ways to answer this item. Compare your answer to this high-scoring response. Then evaluate your essay. Follow the instructions on page 525. Use a copy of the Simplified Independent Writing Rubric in Appendix E.

SAMPLE ESSAY RESPONSE

I have been a student for many years, but not always a good one. So when this question is asked, I have many observations to offer from my experiences in school. I believe that a good teacher is only one factor for students to be successful in school. The other factors are parents and an interesting program.

To tell the truth, a good teacher helped me become a good student. When I was a young, I hated school. I thought it was a boring jail. I got better because of my high school teachers. My high school teachers were very good, and I begin to enjoy my studies more. My best teachers were my high school geometry teacher and my high school Spanish teacher. They were interesting teachers and made the classes fun. So I got interested in school and was a better student.

But a good program is also important. When I think about my elementary school and junior high school, I think that the teachers good but the program was not very interesting. In high school, we studied hard subjects, but was more interesting. Elementary school was not so interesting, and the classes were easy and boring. I got interested in school because of the teachers and the program.

The last factor is family. My mother and father are professors. They were always nagging me about school. So I was a bad boy and didn't study in elementary school. But my parents helped me find studies that interested me. When I entered high school, I had my choice of classes. My parents ask me to pick my classes, so I picked math and Spanish. Then they encouraged me and helped me. I studied more and more, and my grades get better. They stopped nagging me all the time. So my parents helped me a lot.

It is impossible to say that one factor is the most important for success in school. Good teachers, good program, and the help of the family are all factors that influence success in school.

After you evaluate your responses to Items 1 and 2, Use the TOEFL iBT Personalized Study Planner on pages 78–81 to find ways to improve your performance.

CHAPTER 3

TOEFL iBT Reading

Chapter at a Glance

In this chapter, you will learn:

Reading Passages . . . Common topics

Reading Items . . . . 3 item formats and 10 item types

Skills . . . . Techniques to help you answer each kind of item

Tips . . . . Hints to help you find the correct answers and avoid common mistakes

The TOEFL iBT Reading section assesses your ability to read and understand the kinds of academic texts frequently encountered in North American higher education settings. In general, the reading section:

- includes 3 reading passages of about 700 words each, with 12 to 14 items per passage
- has 42 items total
- lasts 60 minutes

You may encounter a test with four reading passages and a larger number of items. That test will have a different time limit, too.

Reading item types include:

- **Traditional multiple-choice items** with four options (answer choices) and one answer. These items can test **factual information**, **negative factual information**, **inferencing**, **rhetorical purpose**, **vocabulary**, **sentence simplification** (restating a sentence or sentences in simpler language), or **reference** (finding the word or phrase that another word or phrase refers to).

- **Insert text items**, which offer a sentence or sentences to be inserted into the passage in four possible places. To answer this type of item, you need to identify the organization of the passage and find the place where the sentence fits best.
- **Prose summary items**, which ask you to select from a number of statements those that best summarize the passage or a portion of the passage. These are sometimes called "drag-and-drop" items because on the actual TOEFL iBT, you use the cursor and mouse on your computer to drag and drop the text into the appropriate box of a table or chart on your computer screen.
- **Fill in a table items**, which require you to organize or structure information from the passage in a table. These are also drag-and-drop items.

Here is a sample drag-and-drop, fill in a table item.

KIND OF ASTRONOMICAL BODY	STATEMENTS
Planet	**Select 2**
	•
	•
Minor Planet	**Select 3**
	•
	•
	•

Use your cursor to drag the statements here.

Decide which statement belongs in which box; then drag each statement to the box.

Answer Choices

- A This group has eight recognized members.
- B Pluto should be reclassified as a member of this group.
- C They are round and their orbits around the sun are clear of other space debris.
- D This category was created in 2006.
- E This group has five recognized members.
- F Small space objects may share characteristics of this category and asteroids.
- G Pluto is a member.

Most items on the TOEFL iBT Reading section are worth 1 point, but some of the drag-and-drop items are worth 2 points. After you take the TOEFL, your total score will be calculated. This raw score will be converted to a scaled score of 0 to 30 and will be reported to you on a score report together with results on other sections of the test.

AT A GLANCE

TOEFL iBT Reading Section

Time Limit	60 minutes
Content	3 reading passages of about 700 words each, on academic subjects*
Items	12–14 per passage; 42 total

ITEM TYPES

Basic information
- Factual information
- Negative factual information
- Vocabulary
- Reference
- Sentence simplification

Inference
- Inference
- Rhetorical purpose
- Insert text

Reading to Learn
- Prose summary
- Fill in a table

ITEM FORMATS
- Standard multiple choice (4 options and 1 answer)
- Drag-and-drop items

* In some administrations of the TOEFL, the Reading section will include 4 or 5 passages, have 56 to 70 items, and last from 80 to 100 minutes. These extra passages and questions are used to assess items before they are used in actual tests and do not count toward your score.

TOEFL iBT Reading Passages

Reading passages on the TOEFL iBT are generally about 700 words long, though some may be shorter and some may be longer. The passages are similar to readings typically encountered in North American university classes. The reading selections will cover many topics, from natural sciences, social sciences, humanities, engineering, computer science, and so on. Passages may be expository, argumentative, or historical. No special knowledge is needed to read the passages or answer the questions. In order not to favor some test takers over others, the readings on each test will reflect a mixture of humanities, sciences, and business-related topics. Here are the subject areas that topics are drawn from.

TOEFL iBT Reading Subject Areas

Topics of reading passages on the TOEFL iBT are drawn from these academic subject areas:

- **Arts and humanities:** literature, art and art history, music and music history
- **Sciences:** life science, physical science, earth and space science, computer science, engineering
- **Social sciences:** geography, history, sociology, anthropology, psychology, economics
- **Business and management:** case studies

For a complete list of academic subject areas and sample topics, see Appendix B.

The following is a sample passage on the topic of climate change (earth science). On TOEFL iBT reading passages, definitions of key, difficult words are provided to you to aid comprehension. On the actual test, you can see these definitions by holding your computer's mouse over the words. In this book, these words will be indicated by footnotes.

Climate data released recently reveal that the arctic ice cap melted at an alarming rate during the summer of 2012, shattering the previous record for summer melting set in 2007. Rutgers University climatologist David Robinson said, "We thought that might be the record for quite a while. And here we are, just five years later, and we've shattered that record. We're seeing losses of sea ice I never thought I'd see in my career." Satellite photos of the ice cap show that the ice cap is the smallest it has ever been since scientists began taking satellite photos of the ice cap in 1980. The data also show that the ice that remains is thinner than before. Only a few years ago, scientists thought that the ice cap might disappear by 2050. Now some scientists think that day may be only a few years away.

Scientists believe that the cause of the melting is global warming. Global warming is the gradual increase in average temperatures observed in recent years. In fact, Earth's mean temperature has increased by 0.8° C since early in the twentieth century. Scientists believe that human activities, such as burning of fossil fuel and deforestation, are the cause. Even though temperatures are rising overall, the climate changes will be different in different places and may include extreme highs as well as extreme lows. Some locations may see a larger increase in mean temperatures, while in others temperatures may stay the same or fall. Locations may experience cooler than average summers, but winters may be warmer than previously. And precipitation rates may be altered. Scientists believe that global warming will cause an increase in all kinds of extreme weather, from droughts to floods. Areas of the United States are already experiencing reduced rainfall and even drought conditions, though other areas are seeing unusual heavy rains and flooding.

Other conditions are believed to be related to global warming. The break in the ozone layer over Antarctica, for example, is believed to be related to the release of certain gases, primarily from aerosol cans, but also from other sources. Increased temperatures have caused the hole to become larger, which allows even more sunlight to enter Earth's atmosphere, which then adds to the problem of rising temperatures. Recent extreme flooding in Thailand, a drought in much of the United States, and extreme summer heat in parts of Europe have all been attributed to global warming. Events such as these have begun to result in serious disruptions to agriculture. In 2012, many US farmers experienced crop failures. Corn crops were devastated in the Midwest, and rice crops failed in parts of the South. Reservoirs[1] in Texas that supply water to cities and to farmers have cut off water to farmers to conserve remaining water for city dwellers.

Even though scientific opinion is almost unanimous and most governments and international organizations agree, some governments continue to say that they do not believe in global warming or they do not accept the proposed solutions. Some of the countries believe that they are being asked to make great changes, while other, larger polluters are asked to do much less. While countries continue to oppose change, global

---

[1] A reservoir is a large artificial lake or building used to store water before it is used.

temperatures continue to rise, the ice cap continues to melt, and disruptions to usual weather patterns continue to grow in intensity. The record shrinkage of the ice cap in 2012 is only one example of how conditions continue to worsen. It is unclear what evidence it will take to convince all governments that action is needed.

In the Reading section of the TOEFL iBT, you are allowed to look back at the passage as you answer the questions. Therefore, you do not need to take notes as you read. However, you may want to use your note paper for other purposes, such as keeping track of items you skipped.

> **TIP** **Arrange the work area before you begin the actual TOEFL iBT Reading section!**
>
> Rearrange your work area so you can work efficiently on the Reading section. Since you only use your computer's mouse on this section, you might move the keyboard out of your way. Place your computer's mouse where it is easy for you to use. Keep your notepaper and pen or pencil handy.

TOEFL iBT Reading Items

In this section, we will examine all the item types and formats on the TOEFL iBT Reading section. TOEFL iBT Reading items fall into three main types: basic information items, inference items, and reading to learn items.

Answering Basic Information Items

Basic information items assess literal and negative literal comprehension, as well as vocabulary, reference, and sentence simplification. Some items involve understanding only a specific fact drawn directly from the text, while others assess your overall understanding of the passage or a part of the passage (such as a paragraph). TOEFL iBT basic information items are standard multiple-choice items with a question and four answer options, one of which is correct.

READING BASIC INFORMATION ITEMS AT A GLANCE

ITEM TYPES	ITEM FORMAT
• Factual information	• Standard multiple choice
• Negative factual information	• Standard multiple choice
• Vocabulary	• Standard multiple choice
• Reference	• Standard multiple choice
• Sentence simplification	• Standard multiple choice

Factual Information Items

These items require you to identify specific facts and information that are directly stated in the passage. Usually, the answer to a factual information item will be in one or two specific sentences in the passage. Factual information items may ask you to recognize relationships among information such as:

- Cause and effect
- Supporting detail
- Chronological order
- Steps in a process

Factual information items always refer to specific details. These items never involve integration of information or understanding the main idea. Factual information items usually contain language such as *cause*, *how*, *what happened*, and *why*. Study the chart.

RECOGNIZING FACTUAL INFORMATION ITEMS
According to the information in paragraph 2, **the cause** of the melting is . . . *(cause and effect)*
According to the passage, **how much** did temperatures rise **at first**? *(chronological order)*
According to the information, **what happened in the early twentieth century?** *(chronological order)*
According to the information, one of the **causes** of global warming is . . . *(cause and effect)*
According to the passage, **why** is the polar ice cap melting? *(cause and effect)*
The author's discussion of causes of global warming includes which of these **details**? *(supporting detail, exemplification)*
Which of the following is an **example** that the author gives of ways to reduce greenhouse gas emissions? *(supporting detail, exemplification)*

Factual information items are always standard multiple-choice items.

EXAMPLE

Factual Information Item

Reread the first paragraph from the longer reading passage on global warming. Then answer the item.

PARAGRAPH 1

   Climate data released recently reveal that the arctic ice cap melted at an alarming rate during the summer of 2012, shattering the previous record for summer melting set in 2007. Rutgers University climatologist David Robinson said, "We thought that might be the record for quite a while. And here we are, just five years later, and we've shattered that record. We're seeing losses of sea ice I never thought I'd see in my career." Satellite photos of the ice cap show that the ice cap is the smallest it has ever been since scientists began taking satellite photos of the ice cap in 1980. The data also show that the ice that remains is thinner than before. Only a few years ago, scientists thought that the ice cap might disappear by 2050. Now some scientists think that day may be only a few years away.

According to paragraph 1, which of the following is true about the arctic ice cap?

Ⓐ It melted faster in 2007 than in 2012.

Ⓑ It will disappear by 2050.

Ⓒ It was the smallest it has ever been in 1980.

Ⓓ It will melt completely sooner than first predicted.

   You know that this is a factual information item focusing on chronological order because it asks for a specific piece of data from the passage—a detail about when the ice cap will melt. The correct answer is Option D: "It will melt completely sooner than first predicted." This option is correct because the passage says, "Only a few years ago, scientists thought that the ice cap might disappear by 2050. Now some scientists think that day may be only a few years away." Option A is not correct because 2012 broke the record set in 2007. Option B is contradicted by information in the passage. According to the information, the ice cap will melt much sooner than 2050. Option C is also contradicted by the passage: the ice cap is now smaller than it has ever been since scientists began taking satellite photos of it in 1980.

> **TIP** **Eliminate answer options that are contradicted by the passage!**
>
> An answer option that is contradicted by information in the passage will never be the answer to a factual information item. Eliminate all answer options that are contradicted by the passage. In this example, options B and C are contradicted by the passage, so they can be easily eliminated.

EXAMPLE

Factual Information Item

Reread paragraph 1 from the longer reading passage on the polar ice cap. Then answer the item.

> According to paragraph 1, what do satellite photos of the arctic ice cap in 2012 show?
>
> Ⓐ It has completely disappeared.
>
> Ⓑ It grew between 2008 and 2011.
>
> Ⓒ It is smaller and thinner than ever.
>
> Ⓓ It has been melting at an increasing rate and may soon disappear.

> **TIP** **Always answer a factual information item with a detail!**
>
> The answer to a factual information item will always be a detail, not a main idea. Eliminate all answer options that are not details. In this example, Option D is incorrect because it is the main idea and needs much more support than just data from 2012.

You know that this is a factual information question because the answer is a fact drawn from specific sentences in the passage. The answer is Option C, "It is smaller and thinner than ever." The passage says, "Satellite photos show that the ice cap is the smallest it has ever been since scientists began taking satellite photos in 1980. The data also show that the ice that remains is thinner than before." Option A is contradicted by the passage. The passage says that the ice cap will continue to melt until it completely disappears. Option B is neither supported nor contradicted in the passage, so it is not a possible answer. Option D is incorrect because this is a main idea, not a detail, and cannot be concluded from the satellite data alone.

TIP **Answer detail items as quickly as possible!**

When you answer detail questions, try to answer quickly so that you can have more time on harder item types. Follow these steps:

1. As soon as you read the question, try to think of the answer. Then look at the answer options. If you find your answer there, select it, and move to the next item.
2. If you cannot remember the answer, but recognize one of the options as the answer, select it and move on.
3. If you do not recognize any of the options, quickly glance at the passage to find the answer. Scanning can help you find the answer quickly.

Scanning

When you scan, you search a text for a specific piece of information. Learning to scan quickly can help you improve your performance on the TOEFL iBT Reading section. To scan, choose a specific word or number (such as a date, amount of money, or the name of a person or place) to look for. Examine the passage from start to finish quickly, not reading every word, but looking only for words or numbers similar to the ones you selected. For example, you could scan the passage on global warming for dates or specific facts such as effects of global warming.

EXERCISE 1

Scanning

Scan the passage on global warming on pages 106–108. Answer the questions.

1. When was the most recent record set for melting of the polar ice cap?

_____

2. When was the previous record for melting of the ice cap set?

_____

3. Who is David Robinson?

_____

4. When did scientists first think the ice cap could disappear?

_____

5. When did scientists begin taking satellite photos of the polar ice cap?

_____

6. Where is the ozone hole located?

_____

7. How much have average global temperatures increased since the beginning of the twentieth century?

_____

8. Name three places where global warming has caused changes to weather patterns.

_____

9. Which country experienced extreme flooding?

_____

10. Where was water cut off to farmers?

_____

Answers for Exercise 1 begin on page 213.

EXERCISE 2

Factual Information Items

Read the selection from a longer reading passage and answer the items.

An eclipse is an astronomical[1] event in which light from one astronomical body is blocked by another astronomical body, such as the moon or Earth. The sun, Earth, and Earth's moon are all involved in two kinds of eclipses. A solar eclipse occurs when light from the sun is blocked by the moon. For a solar eclipse to occur, the sun, moon, and Earth must be in alignment, with the moon in the middle to block the sun's light. Alignments of this sort are rare and last for only a few minutes, as Earth and the moon continue on their orbits. During an eclipse, people on Earth see the sun with a dark circle cut out of it (partial solar eclipse) or completely blocked by the moon (total solar eclipse) so that sunlight shines only from the edges of the sun; the rest of the light is blocked by the moon. The shadow cast by the moon during an eclipse will darken the sky, especially during a total or near-total eclipse. Animals may believe that night is falling. Birds may begin to roost for the night, for example.

A lunar eclipse occurs when sunlight shining on the moon is blocked by Earth's shadow. For a lunar eclipse to happen, the sun, Earth, and the moon must all be in a row, with Earth in the middle so it can block the sun's light and cast a shadow on the moon. The shadow cast by Earth contains two parts, the

_____
[1] Related to objects in space (stars, planets, moons, etc.)

umbra and the penumbra. The umbra is the shadow cast directly by Earth. The penumbra is a larger area around the umbra where direct light from the sun is blocked but some light is able to get through indirectly. A penumbral lunar eclipse happens when the penumbra cast by Earth slightly darkens the surface of the moon. An umbral lunar eclipse takes place when the umbra falls on the moon's surface. A lunar eclipse may be partial or total, depending on whether the shadow cast falls completely or partially on the surface of the moon. In a penumbral total eclipse, the moon may appear partially darkened, and areas of the penumbra may appear darker if they are near the umbra. In an umbral total lunar eclipse, it may appear that the moon has disappeared from the sky for a period.

Generally, a lunar eclipse is visible only at night and when the moon is full. A senelion, a kind of eclipse that occurs under only highly exceptional conditions, is a rare astronomical event. A senelion is an eclipse that occurs when the sun and moon are opposite one another on the horizon and are aligned so that Earth's shadow hits the moon. Thus the sun and the eclipsed moon can be seen simultaneously. This is the only time when the sun and a lunar eclipse will both be visible together. This is also the only time that an eclipse can take place with daylight visible at the same time. The most recent senelion was on December 10, 2010. The next one will not take place for another eighty-four years.

1. According to the passage, what is the cause of a solar eclipse?

   Ⓐ Light from the sun is blocked by Earth.

   Ⓑ Light from the moon is blocked by Earth.

   Ⓒ Light from Earth is blocked by the moon.

   Ⓓ Light from the sun is blocked by the moon.

2. Which of the following things happens during a partial solar eclipse?

   Ⓐ The sun looks like a dark circle was cut from it.

   Ⓑ Light shines only from the edges of the sun.

   Ⓒ Animals believe that night is falling.

   Ⓓ A shadow is partially cast on the moon.

3. What is one difference between an umbral and a penumbral lunar eclipse?

   Ⓐ The moon appears darker in an umbral eclipse than in a penumbral eclipse.

   Ⓑ The moon appears darker in a penumbral eclipse than in an umbral eclipse.

   Ⓒ An umbral eclipse is a total eclipse, and a penumbral eclipse is a partial eclipse.

   Ⓓ A penumbral eclipse is a total eclipse, and an umbral eclipse is a partial eclipse.

4. Which of these events is the most unusual?

   Ⓐ An umbral lunar eclipse

   Ⓑ A partial solar eclipse

   Ⓒ A total solar eclipse

   Ⓓ A senelion

5. Which of the following is a characteristic of a senelion?

   Ⓐ The moon will block the sun's light.

   Ⓑ The sky may darken for a few minutes.

   Ⓒ The sun and eclipsed moon can be seen at the same time.

   Ⓓ A senelion is a total lunar eclipse.

Answers and Explanations for Exercise 2 begin on page 213.

Negative Factual Information Items

These items require you to identify information that is untrue or that is not included in the passage. For example, a passage may provide three examples that support a theory or argument. A negative factual information item will ask you to identify, from among the four answer options, the option that is NOT in the passage. Usually the correct option will not be mentioned in the passage at all or will contradict information in the passage. Negative factual information items always contain the words *not* or *except*. Study the chart.

RECOGNIZING NEGATIVE FACTUAL INFORMATION ITEMS
The passage says that global warming happens for all the following reasons **EXCEPT**:
All of the following contribute to increased greenhouse gas emissions **EXCEPT**:
Which of the following is **NOT** a cause of the ozone hole in the Antarctic?
According to paragraph 2, all of the following are true of global warming **EXCEPT**:

TIP **Identify a negative factual information item from the words *NOT* or *EXCEPT*!**

A negative factual information question will always have the word *NOT* or *EXCEPT* in capital letters.

EXAMPLE

Negative Factual Information Item

Read the selection from a longer reading passage. Then answer the item.

An urban myth is a kind of folktale or legend of recent invention. Urban myths are untrue stories that are told and retold, and spread orally throughout the culture. For instance, a long-standing rumor that alligators live in the sewer system of New York City and kill people is an example of an urban myth. Another is a story of a woman who died from the bites of spiders that were living inside her large, elaborate wig. A third example is a story about a hitchhiker who was brutally murdered and reappeared as a ghost. These stories are not true, but they gain credence because they are repeated widely. Folklorists who study these tales call them urban myths to distinguish them from older myths, legends, and folktales from the Middle Ages and earlier.

According to experts in urban myths, these contemporary folktales have a number of common characteristics. Urban myths are spread through an oral tradition of people telling and retelling them over and over again. But these stories can be spread even more widely through the media or the Internet. Tellers of an urban myth often claim that the story is actually the firsthand experience of "a friend of a friend." That is, the teller claims that a friend or relative knows someone who knows an individual who saw an alligator in the sewers. The stories usually involve some sort of horrible or shocking element, and they often serve as warnings. Hearers are reminded that it's not a good idea for them to hitchhike, for example. Finally, even though the story is very specific and the teller claims secondhand knowledge, the stories usually lack specific details about the time, place, and location of the alleged event.

All of the following are characteristics of urban myths EXCEPT:

(A) They contain warnings or cautions about behavior to avoid.

(B) They supposedly happened to a friend of a friend of the teller.

(C) They originated in the Middle Ages or earlier.

(D) They lack specific details.

You can tell that this is a negative factual information item because it contains the word *EXCEPT.* The answer is Option C. The passage says that traditional folktales and legends, not urban myths, originated in the Middle Ages. Urban myths are much more recent than traditional folktales. Options A, B, and D are all mentioned in the passage in relationship to urban myths, so they are all incorrect.

TIP **Take extra care with negative factual information items!**

These items are difficult to answer because sometimes the information you need to answer them is scattered throughout the passage. Take special care with these items. Allow extra time for these items, or skip them and save them for later, when you have finished all the other items. Use the Review feature in the actual TOEFL iBT to return to these items.

EXAMPLE

Negative Factual Information Item

Reread the selection from the longer reading passage on urban myths.
Then answer the question.

> Which of the following is NOT an example of an urban myth mentioned in the passage?
>
> (A) A woman died from the bites of spiders living on her head.
>
> (B) The ghost of a hitchhiker appeared to some motorists, who later discovered the accident scene where the hitchhiker had died hours earlier.
>
> (C) A child's stomach exploded because she ate a certain kind of candy after drinking soda.
>
> (D) Dangerous reptiles in the sewers of large American cities have attacked people.

This is clearly a negative factual information item because it includes the word *NOT*. All of the urban myths in the answer options are included in the passage except the one in Option C. Therefore, the answer is Option C. Notice that the incorrect answer options are paraphrases of the information in the passage. For example, the hitchhiker story contains additional details. This makes it harder to eliminate incorrect options quickly.

TIP **For negative factual information items, look for the wrong option!**

Negative factual information questions are hard to answer because you are looking for something that is incorrect or missing from the passage. While searching for the answer, it's very easy to forget this and choose an answer that is true instead, especially when you are working quickly. When answering these items, always keep in mind that the answer will be contradicted by the passage or missing from the passage. Always read all the options to help you choose correctly. If you have to scan the passage and use the process of elimination, use your note paper to keep track of which options are not the answer. Write the letters of the answer options on your note paper. Then check them off as you find them in the passage.

A. ✔

B. ✔

C.

D. ✔

EXERCISE 3

Negative Factual Information Items

Read the selection from a longer reading passage and answer the items.

The modern steel and glass building represents more than a building technique. It is the aesthetic[1] creation of architects such as Frank Lloyd Wright, Le Corbusier, and Ludwig Mies Van der Rohe. Of these architects, one of the most influential in the development of the modern style is the architect most people simply call Mies. Born in Germany, Mies achieved considerable professional success in the United States. His style made extensive use of steel girders to support buildings, rather than stone or brick walls. This innovation, pioneered by architects who came before Mies, allowed architects to replace thick walls with expansive windows because the steel girders, rather than the walls, supported the buildings. Interior spaces were large and open, with few or minimal interior columns or walls needed because the building's steel frame made them unnecessary structurally. The stark, sleek buildings created a dramatic counterpoint to older, often elaborately decorated buildings with carved stonework, elaborate metalwork decorations, and dark, enclosed interior spaces.

Mies strove toward a rich yet simple, consistent, and aesthetically complete style. The typical Mies building employed top-quality materials such as marble, chrome-plated metal, and plate glass, always deployed in straight lines and cubical forms, to create rich but simplistic forms. Mies insisted on designing interior furnishing and details, too. His buildings might include custom furniture. To give a uniform look to building exteriors, he even designed special window blinds. One of Mies's most famous sayings to describe his minimalistic approach was, "Less is more."

---

[1] Artistic

1. Which of the following is NOT a feature of Mies's architecture?

    Ⓐ many interior walls and columns

    Ⓑ expensive, high-quality materials

    Ⓒ cubical spaces

    Ⓓ open, sweeping floor plans

2. Mies used all of these materials in his buildings EXCEPT:

    Ⓐ marble

    Ⓑ plate glass

    Ⓒ chrome-plated metal

    Ⓓ elaborate carved stonework

3. Which of the following is NOT an example of how Mies designed rich, consistent, aesthetically complete buildings?

    Ⓐ curving lines

    Ⓑ custom furniture

    Ⓒ special window blinds

    Ⓓ high-quality material

4. All of the following provided support for older buildings EXCEPT:

    Ⓐ steel girders

    Ⓑ interior columns

    Ⓒ thick, heavy walls

    Ⓓ brick and stone materials

5. All of these were features of older building styles EXCEPT:

    Ⓐ dark interior spaces

    Ⓑ metal decorations

    Ⓒ brick or stone walls

    Ⓓ straight lines and cubical spaces

Answers and Explanations for Exercise 3 begin on page 213.

Vocabulary Items

TOEFL iBT vocabulary items test both your vocabulary knowledge and your ability to figure out the meanings of unknown words and phrases from the context and other clues. In general, words that are rarely encountered, are highly technical, or have specific or unusual meanings in the passage will have definitions provided for you as you read. You can recognize these words because they are indicated for you. The words in vocabulary items are generally more usual than these glossed words.

Figuring Out Unfamiliar Vocabulary

Because TOEFL iBT readings are drawn from a wide variety of subject areas, and no official word list is used to develop the test, it's not possible to study all the words that might be on the test. Rather, you should develop vocabulary skills to help you figure out the meanings of unfamiliar words. Here are some ways to do so:

- **Use the context.** The context is the overall content and meaning of a passage. The subject of the passage, the details, and the relationship among the ideas can help you figure out the meaning of an unfamiliar word. For example, read this sentence and try to figure out a word that completes it: "The stark, sleek buildings created a dramatic _____ to older, often elaborately decorated buildings with carved stonework, elaborate metalwork decorations, and dark, enclosed interior spaces." If you answered with a word such as *contrast,* you answered correctly.
- **Use word parts.** Prefixes, suffixes, and word parts can help you figure out the meaning of an unfamiliar word. For example, in the word *counterpoint,* you know that the word *point* means "idea" and that *counter* can mean "against." From these word parts, you can figure out that *counterpoint* means "something that goes against an idea" or "contrast."
- **Use embedded examples or illustrations.** Often the sentence or other sentences in the passage will include an example or definition that can help you figure out the meaning of the unknown word. Read the example: "An urban myth is a kind of folktale or legend of recent invention. Urban myths are untrue stories that are told and retold, and spread orally throughout the culture.'" You can figure out that *folktale* means "a popular story that is told and retold orally," since this definition is given in the next sentence.
- **Look for a word with a similar meaning elsewhere in the sentence or nearby sentences.** Often, a synonym of the target word will appear nearby in the passage. In the example about urban myths, the author uses the words *folktale* and *legend*. If you know the meaning of the word *legend* ("an old story about heroic adventures"), that definition can help you figure out the meaning of the word *folktale*.

A vocabulary item will always follow an excerpt from the passage with the tested word or phrase highlighted.

> The stark, sleek buildings created a dramatic counterpoint to older, often elaborately decorated buildings with carved stonework, elaborate metalwork decorations, and dark, enclosed interior spaces.

Vocabulary items always include the target word or phrase in quotation marks and use words such as *means* or *closest in meaning to*. Study the chart.

RECOGNIZING VOCABULARY ITEMS
The word "counterpoint" in the passage **is closest in meaning to** . . .
The phrase "dramatic counterpoint" in the passage **is closest in meaning to** . . .
In stating that "The stark, sleek buildings created a dramatic counterpoint to older, often elaborately decorated buildings," the author **means** that . . .

EXAMPLE

Vocabulary Item

Interior spaces were large and open, with few or minimal interior columns or walls needed because the building's steel frame made them unnecessary structurally.

The word "minimal" in the passage is closest in meaning to

(A) the smallest height necessary

(B) the smallest width necessary

(C) the thinnest necessary

(D) the smallest number necessary

If you chose Option D, you are correct! This answer can most easily be determined by the context. The passage states that "spaces were large and open, with few or minimal interior columns." *Minimal* is closest in meaning to "few in number," so only Option D is correct. The other options do not make sense.

EXAMPLE

Vocabulary Item

The typical Mies building employed top-quality materials such as marble, chrome-plated metal, and plate glass, always deployed in straight lines and cubical forms, to create rich but simplistic forms.

In stating that Mies created "rich but simplistic forms," the author means that

(A) Mies's buildings only appeared expensive

(B) Mies used high-quality materials in simple ways to create beautiful effects

(C) Mies wasted money because he used expensive materials in simple ways

(D) Mies's style was ironic because he used top-quality materials in simple ways

In this example, understanding the meaning of *rich* is important. While *rich* can refer to money or wealth, in this example, it refers to the attractiveness of Mies's architecture. Option B is correct because the combination of top-quality materials to create simple structures was visually attractive. Option A is incorrect because the passage does not indicate that that the buildings appeared expensive. Option C is incorrect because the passage does not imply that Mies's style wasted money. Option D is incorrect because the passage does not suggest that Mies's style was ironic.

TIP **Be careful of words with multiple meanings!**

Words with multiple meanings are often tested on the TOEFL iBT. For example, the word *rich* can refer to wealth. Or it can refer to the "complexity and depth" of something, such as "a rich visual effect." Generally, all the possible meanings of multimeaning words are included in the answer options. Therefore, always look for the answer option that is closest to the meaning of the target word as it is used in the passage.

EXERCISE 4

Vocabulary Items

Reread the paragraphs from a longer reading passage. Then answer the items.

An eclipse is an astronomical[1] event in which light from one astronomical body is blocked by another astronomical body, such as the moon or Earth. The sun, Earth, and Earth's moon are all involved in two kinds of eclipses. A solar eclipse occurs when light from the sun is blocked by the moon. For a solar eclipse to occur, the sun, moon, and Earth must be in alignment, with the moon in the middle to block the sun's light. Alignments of this sort are rare and last for only a few minutes, as Earth and the moon continue on their orbits. During an eclipse, people on Earth see the sun with a dark circle cut out of it (partial solar eclipse) or completely blocked by the moon (total solar eclipse) so that sunlight shines only from the edges of the sun; the rest of the light is blocked by the moon. The shadow cast by the moon during an eclipse will darken the sky, especially during a total or near-total eclipse. Animals may believe that night is falling. Birds may begin to roost for the night, for example.

---

[1] Related to objects in space (stars, planets, moons, etc.)

1. The word "solar" in the passage is closest in meaning to

Ⓐ having to do with the sun

Ⓑ having to do with the moon

Ⓒ having to do with Earth

Ⓓ having to do with orbits

2. In stating that Earth, the moon, and the sun must be "in alignment," the author means that the bodies must be

Ⓐ in a row

Ⓑ in the same place

Ⓒ touching one another

Ⓓ near one another

TIP **If you can't answer a vocabulary item, insert each answer into the original sentence!**

If you cannot figure out the answer, substitute each of the options into the original sentence. The option that makes the most sense is most likely the answer. In Item 2, only one option makes sense in the passage.

PARAGRAPH 2

A lunar eclipse occurs when sunlight shining on the moon is blocked by Earth's shadow. For a lunar eclipse to happen, the sun, Earth, and the moon must all be in a row, with Earth in the middle so it can block the sun's light and cast a shadow on the moon. The shadow cast by Earth contains two parts, the umbra and the penumbra. The umbra is the shadow cast directly by Earth. The penumbra is a larger area around the umbra where direct light from the sun is blocked but some light is able to get through indirectly. A penumbral lunar eclipse happens when the penumbra cast by Earth slightly darkens the surface of the moon. An umbral lunar eclipse takes place when the umbra falls on the moon's surface. A lunar eclipse may be partial or total, depending on whether the shadow cast falls completely or partially on the surface of the moon. In a penumbral total eclipse, the moon may appear partially darkened, and areas of the penumbra may appear darker if they are near the umbra. In an umbral total lunar eclipse, it may appear that the moon has disappeared from the sky for a period.

3. The phrase "umbral total lunar eclipse" in the passage is closest in meaning to

Ⓐ a lunar eclipse in which sunlight is totally blocked by Earth's penumbra

Ⓑ a lunar eclipse in which parts of the moon are darker than others

Ⓒ a lunar eclipse in which the moon is between Earth and the sun

Ⓓ a lunar eclipse in which sunlight is totally blocked by Earth's shadow

Generally, a lunar eclipse is visible only at night and when the moon is full. A senelion, a kind of eclipse that occurs under only highly exceptional conditions, is a rare astronomical event. A senelion is an eclipse that occurs when the sun and moon are opposite one another on the horizon and are aligned so that Earth's shadow hits the moon. Thus the sun and the eclipsed moon can be seen simultaneously. This is the only time when the sun and a lunar eclipse will both be visible together. This is also the only time that an eclipse can take place with daylight visible at the same time. The most recent senelion was on December 10, 2010. The next one will not take place for another eighty-four years.

PARAGRAPH 3

4. In stating that a senelion is a kind of eclipse that occurs "under only highly exceptional conditions," the author means that

   Ⓐ the conditions for such an eclipse seldom or rarely occur

   Ⓑ the cause of the eclipse is different from that of a normal eclipse

   Ⓒ the eclipse will be harder to see than a normal eclipse

   Ⓓ the weather conditions are good for observing the eclipse

---

TIP **On vocabulary items, read all the options before you answer!**

As you know, the TOEFL iBT assesses multimeaning words. Always look for an answer that expresses the meaning of the word as it is used in the passage. To do so, read all the answer options to make sure you are choosing the option with the correct meaning. Test your choice by substituting it into the original sentence.

Exceptional, in Item 4, can have two meanings, "highly unusual" and "extremely good." One of the options is related to the meaning "extremely good," which is incorrect. The passage is discussing why a certain type of eclipse is very unusual. Working too quickly, you might choose the incorrect option because you are familiar with that meaning of the word. Or, without looking at the passage, you choose the wrong meaning because you don't know which meaning is used.

5. The word "simultaneously" in the passage is closest in meaning to

Ⓐ at the only time

Ⓑ at the same time

Ⓒ separately

Ⓓ side by side

Answers and Explanations for Exercise 4 begin on page 214.

Academic Vocabulary

As you know, TOEFL iBT readings contain vocabulary specific to the topic. For example, a reading on astronomy would contain words such as *planet, moon, umbral, penumbral, senelion*, and other terms related directly to the topic.

It is impossible to learn all of the possible content vocabulary related directly to the topics on the TOEFL, and there is no official word list. However, many vocabulary words are common to academic speech in all subject areas. This vocabulary is called **academic vocabulary** because these words are common to all academic subjects. One such word is *classify*. This word can be used in many academic contexts. You can classify kinds of eclipes. You can also classify buildings or architects according to their styles. Increasing your academic vocabulary will help you with every listening selection on the TOEFL. Here is some common academic vocabulary:

analyze

average

classify

compare

contain

contrast

decrease

discuss

increase

mean

A complete list of academic vocabulary is in Appendix A.

Academic Vocabulary

A. Review the passage. Look at the highlighted words. Which are academic vocabulary? Which are content vocabulary? Complete the chart.

Climate data released recently reveal that the arctic ice cap melted at an alarming rate during the summer of 2012, shattering the previous record for summer melting set in 2007. Rutgers University climatologist David Robinson said, "We thought that might be the record for quite a while. And here we are, just five years later, and we've shattered that record. We're seeing losses of sea ice I never thought I'd see in my career." Satellite photos show that the ice cap is the smallest it has ever been since scientists began taking satellite photos in 1980. The data also show that the remaining ice is thinner than before. Only a few years ago, scientists thought that the ice cap might disappear by 2050. Now some scientists think that day may be only a few years away.

Scientists believe that the cause of the melting is global warming. Global warming is the gradual increase in average temperatures observed in recent years. In fact, Earth's mean temperature has increased by 0.8° C since early in the twentieth century. Scientists believe that human activities, such as burning of fossil fuel and deforestation, are the cause. Even though temperatures are rising overall, the climate changes will be different in different places and may include extreme highs as well as extreme lows. Some locations may see a larger increase in mean temperatures, while in others temperatures may stay the same or fall. Locations may experience cooler than average summers, but winters may be warmer than previously. And precipitation rates may be altered. Scientists believe that global warming will cause an increase in all kinds of extreme weather, from droughts to floods. Areas of the United States are already experiencing reduced rainfall and even drought conditions, though other areas are seeing unusual heavy rains and flooding.

Other conditions are believed to be related to global warming. The break in the ozone layer over Antarctica, for example, is believed to be related to the release of certain gases, primarily from aerosol cans, but also from other sources. Increased temperatures have caused the hole to become larger, which allows even more sunlight to enter Earth's atmosphere, which then adds to the problem of rising temperatures. Recent extreme flooding in

Thailand, a drought in much of the United States, and extreme summer heat in parts of Europe have all been attributed to global warming. Events such as these have begun to result in serious disruptions to agriculture. In 2012, many US farmers experienced crop failures. Corn crops were devastated in the Midwest, and rice crops failed in parts of the South. Reservoirs[1] in Texas that supply water to cities and to farmers have cut off water to farmers to conserve remaining water for city dwellers.

Even though scientific opinion is almost unanimous and most governments and international organizations agree, some governments continue to say that they do not believe in global warming or they do not accept the proposed solutions. Some of the countries believe that they are being asked to make great changes, while other, larger polluters are asked to do much less. While countries continue to oppose change, global temperatures continue to rise, the ice cap continues to melt, and disruptions to usual weather patterns continue to grow in intensity. The record shrinkage of the ice cap in 2012 is only one example of how conditions continue to worsen. It is unclear what evidence it will take to convince all governments that action is needed.

_____

[1] A reservoir is a large artificial lake or building used to store water before it is used.

Academic Vocabulary

1. reveal
2.
3.
4.
5.
6.
7.
8.
9.
10.

Content Vocabulary

1.
2.
3.
4.
5.
6.
7.
8.
9.
10.

B. Provide definitions for the academic vocabulary as the vocabulary is used in the passage.

1. _show_ _____

2. _____

3. _____

4. _____

5. _____

6. _____

7. _____

8. _____

9. _____

10. _____

Answers for Exercise 5 begin on page 214.

Reference Items

Reference items ask you to figure out which word or phrase in the passage a pronoun or other reference word refers to. A pronoun is a word such as *he, her, their,* and *ours*. A pronoun takes the place of another noun in the passage. Understanding the word or words a pronoun refers to is an important part of understanding a text.

Pronouns

Pronouns are words such as *it, she, them, which,* or *yourself* that refer to a noun in another place in the passage. Other words, such as *some, none, few,* and *many* can also be used to refer to nouns that are stated elsewhere in the passage. The word that a pronoun refers to is called its antecedent, because this word generally (but not always) comes before the pronoun in the sentence or passage. (*Ante* means "before.") Here are some common types of pronouns and other reference words:

Subject pronouns	I, you, he, she, it, they	Watson and Crick are seminal figures in the area of genetics. **They** discovered DNA.
Object pronouns	me, you, him, her, it, us, them	The scientific community owes a huge debt of gratitude to **them**.
Possessive adjectives	my, your, his, her, its, our, their	**Their** discovery is one of the most important scientific discoveries of all time.
Possessive pronouns	mine, yours, his, hers, its, ours, theirs	But the credit is not just **theirs**.
Relative pronouns	who, whose, that, which, where	A scientist **whose** prior studies anticipated Watson and Crick's discovery was Barbara McClintock.
Reference words	some, few, another, many, others	**Others** contributed important insights as well. Even though **many** contributed insights, only a **few** got credit.

Pronouns

What word or words do the numbered items refer to? Write your answers on the lines.

An urban myth is a kind of folktale or legend of recent invention. Urban myths are untrue stories that are told and retold, and spread orally throughout the culture. For instance, a long-standing rumor that alligators live in the sewer system of New York City and kill people is an example of an urban myth. **(1)** Another is a story of a woman who died from the bites of spiders that were living inside her large, elaborate wig. A third example is a story about a hitchhiker who was brutally murdered and reappeared as a ghost. These stories are not true, but **(2)** they gain credence because they are repeated widely. Folklorists who study these tales call them urban myths to distinguish them from older myths, legends, and folktales from the Middle Ages and earlier.

According to experts in urban myths, these contemporary folktales have a number of common characteristics. Urban myths are spread through an oral tradition of people telling and retelling **(3)** them over and over again. But these stories can be spread even more widely through the media or the Internet. Tellers of an urban myth often claim that the story is actually the firsthand experience of "a friend of a friend." That is, the teller claims that a friend or relative knows **(4)** someone who knows an individual who saw an alligator in the sewers. The stories usually involve some sort of horrible or shocking element, and they often serve as warnings. Hearers are reminded that it's not a good idea for **(5)** them to hitchhike, for example. Finally, even though the story is very specific and the teller claims secondhand knowledge, the stories usually lack specific details about the time, place, and location of the alleged event.

1. _____   4. _____

2. _____   5. _____

3. _____

Answers for Exercise 6 begin on page 215.

To answer a reference item, follow these steps:

1. Try to figure out the word that the pronoun refers to without reading the options. Then read all the options. If the word you think of is among the options, try it in the sentence. If it makes sense and does not change the meaning of the sentence, then select it and go on.

2. If you still cannot figure out the answer then look at the nouns in the passage that are before and after the pronoun. The antecedent will probably (but not always) come before the pronoun. The noun closest to the pronoun may not be the antecedent, so do not choose it automatically. If the pronoun is singular, look for only singular antecedents. If the pronoun is plural, look for only plural antecedents. When you find an answer, read all of the answer options. If the answer you thought of is among the options, check that answer by substituting it in the passage. If it makes sense, select it.

3. If you still cannot find the answer, review all the options, find the one that makes the most sense, try it in the sentence, and if it makes sense, select it.

A reference item always follows an excerpt of the text with the target word or phrase highlighted. The question will always include the phrase *refers to.*

RECOGNIZING REFERENCE ITEMS
The word "their" in the passage **refers** to . . .

> **EXAMPLE**

Reference Item

Reread the second paragraph of the passage on eclipses. Answer the item.

PARAGRAPH 2

A lunar eclipse occurs when sunlight shining on the moon is blocked by Earth's shadow. For a lunar eclipse to happen, the sun, Earth, and the moon must all be in a row, with Earth in the middle so it can block the sun's light and cast a shadow on the moon. The shadow cast by Earth contains two parts, the umbra and the penumbra. The umbra is the shadow cast directly by Earth. The penumbra is a larger area around the umbra where direct light from the sun is blocked but some light is able to get through indirectly. A penumbral lunar eclipse happens when the penumbra cast by Earth slightly darkens the surface of the moon. An umbral lunar eclipse takes place when the umbra falls on the moon's surface. A lunar eclipse may be partial or total, depending on whether the shadow cast falls completely or partially on the surface of the moon. In a penumbral total eclipse, the moon may appear partially darkened, and areas of the penumbra may appear darker if they are near the umbra. In an umbral total lunar eclipse, it may appear that the moon has disappeared from the sky for a period.

The word "it" in the passage refers to

(A) sun

(B) Earth

(C) moon

(D) eclipse

The phrases "the word 'it'" and "refers to," and the highlight on the target word indicate that this is a reference item. The correct answer is Option B, "Earth." That option is correct because according to the sentence, for a lunar eclipse to take place, Earth must be between the sun and the moon in order to cast a shadow. For these reasons, Options A and C are not correct. The sun cannot be in the middle, or there would be no shadow cast, and the moon cannot cast a shadow onto itself. Option D is not correct because an eclipse is the result of the position of the bodies. An eclipse does not cause a blockage of light. An eclipse is the result of a blockage of light.

> **TIP** **To answer a reference item, insert each option in the original sentence!**
>
> If you cannot figure out the answer, substitute each of the options into the original sentence. The option that makes the most sense is most likely the answer. For instance, in this example item, only "Earth" makes sense when substituted into the sentence.

EXAMPLE

Reference Item

Reread the selection from a longer reading passage on eclipses on page 135. Answer the item.

The word "they" in the passage refers to

Ⓐ areas

Ⓑ penumbra

Ⓒ eclipses

Ⓓ moon

The wording of the item, with the phrases "the word 'they'" and "refers to," and the highlight indicate that this is a reference item. Option A, "areas," is correct because it is the only answer that makes sense. The part of the penumbra nearest the umbra will be darker. Only Option A suggests that some parts of the penumbra will be darker than others. Option B, "penumbra," is incorrect for this reason. Option C is not correct because not all eclipses are penumbral. Option D is incorrect because the pronoun *they* refers to areas of the shadow that are darker than others, not to the moon, the body that the shadow is cast upon. In addition, *moon* cannot be the antecedent for *they*, because *moon* is singular and *they* is plural.

> **TIP** **On reference items, choose a singular answer if the pronoun is singular, plural if it is plural!**
>
> If a pronoun is singular, look for a singular answer option. If the pronoun is plural, look for a plural answer option. In this example, you can easily eliminate options B and D because the words in those answer options are singular and *they* is plural.

EXERCISE 7

Reference Items

Read the selection from a longer reading passage. Then answer the items.

P
A
R
A
G
R
A
P
H

1

Companies are examining new ways of organizing work teams to better meet the demands of the global economy. Effective organizations realize that structuring employees' work in traditional rigid departments and divisions does not meet their needs. Companies these days want to organize workers into cross-functional teams with expertise drawn from many departments of the company, not just one or two. Companies want teams that are flexible and can be easily changed as project needs change or as new projects come along. They also want teams whose leaders are strong and dynamic.

1. The word "their" in the passage refers to

    Ⓐ departments'

    Ⓑ teams'

    Ⓒ organizations'

    Ⓓ employees'

2. The word "one" in the passage refers to

    Ⓐ one employee

    Ⓑ one department

    Ⓒ one team

    Ⓓ one member

P
A
R
A
G
R
A
P
H

2

Research shows that one of the most effective ways to organize such a team is the heavyweight, cross-functional team. These teams involve cross-functional membership drawn from various parts of the company, according to the skills needed to accomplish the project. Each member of the team will have a functional leader (the individual's department manager) and a project team leader (the leader of the specific project team). Employees may be on teams for more than one project, and they may join or leave teams at different times. An individual employee may be a member or leader of one or more teams and may be the leader of one team and a member of another, depending on the needs of the company, the skills of the workers, and the time and skills required for each project. The team leader is called a "heavyweight" because her role is to listen to all of the team members, ensuring that all perspectives are considered, and then make decisions on behalf of the group, based on their recommendations. A good heavyweight team leader will always look to the team members for ideas and consensus and try to build consensus when necessary, but will always be ready to make important decisions—especially when there is disagreement—in order to ensure responsive, decisive project management.

3. The word "they" in the passage refers to

Ⓐ projects

Ⓑ teams

Ⓒ team leaders

Ⓓ employees

4. The word "another" in the passage refers to

Ⓐ an additional member

Ⓑ an additional leader

Ⓒ an additional company

Ⓓ an additional team

5. The word "her" in the passage refers to

Ⓐ team leader's

Ⓑ employee's

Ⓒ functional leader's

Ⓓ team member's

Answers and Explanations for Exercise 7 begin on page 215.

Sentence Simplification Items

These items require you to identify a sentence from four options that has the same meaning as a sentence from the reading passage. To be correct, an answer option must:

- include all of the ideas in the original sentence
- not contain any incorrect information
- not contradict the original sentence
- not add information not in the original sentence

Each TOEFL iBT will contain one or more of these items. A single set (passage and corresponding items) will never contain more than one of these items.

Paraphrasing

When you paraphrase, you rewrite a sentence in simpler language. A good paraphrase restates the original idea of the sentence without changing the meaning, adding additional information, or deleting information. Look at the example:

- **Original.** These teams involve cross-functional membership drawn from various parts of the company, according to the skills needed to accomplish the project well.
- **Paraphrase.** Cross-functional team members come from around the company, according to the skills needed for the project.

Paraphrasing

Provide a paraphrase of each sentence on the line.

1. Companies these days want to organize workers into cross-functional teams with expertise drawn from many departments of the company, not just one or two.

   _____

   _____

   _____

2. Companies want teams that are flexible and can be easily changed as project needs change or as new projects come along.

   _____

   _____

   _____

3. An individual employee may be a member or leader of one or more teams and may be the leader of one team and a member of another, depending on the needs of the company, the skills of the workers, and the time and skills required for each project.

   _____

   _____

   _____

4. Each member of the team will have a functional leader (the individual's department manager) and a project team leader (the leader of the specific project team).

_____

_____

_____

5. The team leader is called a "heavyweight" because her role is to listen to all of the team members, ensuring that all perspectives are considered, and then make decisions on behalf of the group, based on their recommendations.

_____

_____

_____

Answers for Exercise 8 begin on page 215.

On a sentence simplification item, you will first see a paragraph from the passage with the target sentence highlighted. Then you will be asked to identify which answer option best restates the sentence. Study the chart.

> **RECOGNIZING SENTENCE SIMPLIFICATION ITEMS**
>
> Which of the following best expresses the essential information in the highlighted sentence? Incorrect answer choices change the meaning in important ways or leave out essential information.

EXAMPLE

Sentence Simplification Item

Reread the selection from a longer reading passage. Then answer the item.

P
A
R
A
G
R
A
P
H

2

Research shows that one of the most effective ways to organize such a team is the heavyweight, cross-functional team. These teams involve cross-functional membership drawn from various parts of the company, according to the skills needed to accomplish the project. Each member of the team will have a functional leader (the individual's department manager) and a project team leader (the leader of the specific project team). Employees may be on teams for more than one project, and they may join or leave teams at different times. An individual employee may be a member or leader of one or more teams and may be the leader of one team and a member of another, depending on the needs of the company, the skills of the workers, and the time and skills required for each project. The team leader is called a "heavyweight" because her role is to listen to all of the team members, ensuring that all perspectives are considered, and then make decisions on behalf of the group, based on their recommendations. A good heavyweight team leader will always look to the team members for ideas and consensus and try to build consensus, but will always be ready to make important decisions, especially when there is disagreement, in order to ensure responsive, decisive project management.

Note: Unlike the actual TOEFL iBT, this passage has two simplification items to provide extra practice.

Which of the following best expresses the essential information in the first highlighted sentence? Incorrect answer choices change the meaning in important ways or leave out essential information.

(A) Company needs and employee skills and expertise determine whether an individual employee will be assigned to membership on one team or multiple teams.

(B) Individuals may be both leaders and members of different teams and may serve on different numbers of teams at different times, depending on company and project needs.

(C) Company needs, worker skills, and the time and expertise each project needs determine employee assignments, and individuals may have leadership roles on some teams and membership roles on others.

(D) Employees determine whether they serve as members or leaders on one or more teams, depending on company needs, employee skill sets, and the skills and time required for each project.

Option C is correct because only this option restates the essential ideas of the sentence without omitting information, introducing information that is incorrect or not in the passage, or changing the meaning. Option A is incorrect because it omits key information from the original sentence, "the time and skills required for each project." Option B is incorrect because it both adds an idea (may serve on different numbers of teams at different times) and omits a key idea (time and employee skill sets). Option D changes the meaning of the original sentence in a key way: it says that employees determine their assignments, while the original says that the company determines the assignments.

EXAMPLE

Sentence Simplification Item

Reread the selection from the longer reading passage on teams on page 142. Then answer the item.

Which of the following best expresses the essential information in the second highlighted sentence? Incorrect answer choices change the meaning in important ways or leave out essential information.

Ⓐ To have responsive, decisive project management and build consensus, a heavyweight team leader will always be ready to make important decisions, even when there is disagreement.

Ⓑ To build consensus, a good heavyweight team leader will be ready to make important decisions so that the team does not waste time giving ideas and suggestions.

Ⓒ Heavyweight team leaders ensure responsive, decisive project management by encouraging team members to offer ideas and build consensus and by being ready to make important decisions when there is disagreement.

Ⓓ Offering ideas and suggestions, building consensus, and making decisions when there is disagreement are all ways heavyweight team leaders can ensure responsive, decisive project management.

Option C is correct because only this option restates the essential ideas of the sentence without omitting information, introducing information that is incorrect or not in the passage, or changing the meaning. Option A is incorrect because the meaning changes. The original says that the purpose of making decisions is to have responsive, decisive management, not to build consensus. Option B is incorrect because it changes the original meaning. The original sentence does not say that presenting ideas and suggestions wastes time. Good leaders allow for those, and make decisions when there is disagreement. Option D is incorrect because it changes the original meaning. The original sentence indicates that the team leader encourages others to offer suggestions, while this sentence says that team leaders offer suggestions.

EXERCISE 9

Sentence Simplification Items

Read the paragraphs. (Each paragraph is drawn from a previous reading passage in this chapter.) Then answer the question after each paragraph.

PARAGRAPH 3

Other conditions are believed to be related to global warming. The break in the ozone layer over Antarctica, for example, is believed to be related to the release of certain gases, primarily from aerosol cans, but also from other sources. Increased temperatures have caused the hole to become larger, which allows even more sunlight to enter Earth's atmosphere, which then adds to the problem of rising temperatures. Recent extreme flooding in Thailand, a drought in much of the United States, and extreme summer heat in parts of Europe have all been attributed to global warming. Events such as these have begun to result in serious disruptions to agriculture. In 2012, many US farmers experienced crop failures. Corn crops were devastated in the Midwest, and rice crops failed in parts of the South. Reservoirs[1] in Texas that supply water to cities and to farmers have cut off water to farmers to conserve remaining water for city dwellers.

----

[1] A reservoir is a large artificial lake or building used to store water before it is used.

1. Which of the following sentences best expresses the essential information in the highlighted sentence in paragraph 3? Incorrect choices change the meaning in important ways or leave out essential information.

   (A) For example, scientists believe that the hole in the ozone layer over Antarctica is a consequence of the release into the atmosphere of gases from aerosol cans and other sources.

   (B) For example, scientists believe that the release of certain gases into the atmosphere caused the break in the ozone layer over Antarctica.

   (C) It is believed that break in the atmosphere over Antarctica is related to the release of certain gases, such as gases from aerosol cans, for example.

   (D) The release of certain gases into the atmosphere from aerosol cans and other sources is believed to be a consequence of the break in the ozone layer over Antarctica.

P
A
R
A
G
R
A
P
H

1

The modern steel and glass building represents more than a building technique. It is the aesthetic creation of architects such as Frank Lloyd Wright, Le Corbusier, and Ludwig Mies Van der Rohe. Of these architects, one of the most influential in the development of the modern style is the architect most people simply call Mies. Born in Germany, Mies achieved considerable professional success in the United States. His style made extensive use of steel girders to support buildings, rather than stone or brick walls. This innovation, pioneered by architects who came before Mies, allowed architects to replace thick walls with expansive windows because the steel girders, rather than the walls, supported the buildings. Interior spaces were large and open, with few or minimal interior columns or walls needed because the building's steel frame made them unnecessary structurally. The stark, sleek buildings created a dramatic counterpoint to older, often elaborately decorated buildings with carved stonework, elaborate metalwork decorations, and dark, enclosed interior spaces.

2. Which of the following sentences best expresses the essential information in the highlighted sentence in paragraph 1? Incorrect choices change the meaning in important ways or leave out essential information.

  Ⓐ An innovation pioneered by architects who came before Mies, steel girders allowed architects to replace expansive windows with thick walls.

  Ⓑ An innovation pioneered by architects who came before Mies, steel girders, instead of thick walls, supported buildings, which allowed architects to replace thick walls with expansive windows.

  Ⓒ Pioneered by Mies, this innovation allowed architects to replace thick walls with large windows because the steel girders, not the walls, supported the building.

  Ⓓ Thick walls instead of steel girders supported the buildings, which allowed architects to replace thick walls with expansive windows.

PARAGRAPH 3

A lunar eclipse occurs when sunlight shining on the moon is blocked by Earth's shadow. For a lunar eclipse to happen, the sun, Earth, and the moon must all be in a row, with Earth in the middle so it can block the sun's light and cast a shadow on the moon. The shadow cast by Earth contains two parts, the umbra and the penumbra. The umbra is the shadow cast directly by Earth. The penumbra is a larger area around the umbra where direct light from the sun is blocked but some light is able to get through indirectly. A penumbral lunar eclipse happens when the penumbra cast by Earth slightly darkens the surface of the moon. An umbral lunar eclipse takes place when the umbra falls on the moon's surface. A lunar eclipse may be partial or total, depending on whether the shadow cast falls completely or partially on the surface of the moon. In a penumbral total eclipse, the moon may appear partially darkened, and areas of the penumbra may appear darker if they are near the umbra. In an umbral total lunar eclipse, it may appear that the moon has disappeared from the sky for a period.

3. Which of the following sentences best expresses the essential information in the highlighted sentence in paragraph 3? Incorrect choices change the meaning in important ways or leave out essential information.

   Ⓐ A lunar eclipse can happen when the moon is in the middle between Earth and the sun so that Earth can cast a shadow on the moon.

   Ⓑ For a lunar eclipse to happen, the sun, Earth, and the moon must all be in a row with Earth in the middle so the moon can block the sun's light and cast a shadow on Earth.

   Ⓒ The sun, moon, and Earth must all be in a row for a lunar eclipse to happen, so that Earth can cast a shadow on the moon.

   Ⓓ Earth, the moon, and the sun must all be in a row with Earth in the middle to cast a shadow on the moon for a lunar eclipse to happen.

P
A
R
A
G
R
A
P
H

1

An urban myth is a kind of folktale or legend of recent invention. Urban myths are untrue stories that are told and retold and spread orally throughout the culture. For instance, a long-standing rumor that alligators live in the sewer system of New York City and kill people is an example of an urban myth. Another is a story of a woman who died from the bites of spiders that were living inside her large, elaborate wig. A third example is a story about a hitchhiker who was brutally murdered and reappeared as a ghost. These stories are not true, but they gain credence because they are repeated widely. Folklorists[1] who study these tales call them urban myths to distinguish them from older myths, legends, and folktales from the Middle Ages and earlier.

---

[1] Folklorists study folklore (popular beliefs, customs, and stories).

4. Which of the following sentences best expresses the essential information in the highlighted sentence in paragraph 1? Incorrect choices change the meaning in important ways or leave out essential information.

Ⓐ These tales are called urban myths by the folklorists who study them, to distinguish these tales from older myths, legends, and folktales from the Middle Ages and earlier.

Ⓑ To distinguish these tales from the folklorists who study older myths, legends, and folktales from the Middle Ages and earlier, they are called urban myths.

Ⓒ Folklorists distinguish myths, legends, and folktales as different from one another.

Ⓓ Older myths, legends, and folktales from the Middle Ages and earlier are called urban myths to distinguish them from folklorists.

Answers and Explanations for Exercise 9 begin on page 215.

EXERCISE 10

Answering TOEFL iBT Basic Information Items

Read the excerpt from a longer reading passage and answer the items about it.

Water moves around Earth in all three states—as vapor, a gas in the atmosphere; as a liquid in rain, rivers, and lakes; and as a solid as snow and ice. The process by which water moves about and changes state is called the hydrological cycle. The hydrological cycle has four stages: evaporation, condensation, precipitation, and runoff.

In the evaporation stage, liquid water becomes a gas and enters the atmosphere. Evaporation takes place in two main ways. Water in lakes, rivers, streams, and oceans—and virtually all water in liquid form on Earth's surface—is warmed by the sun and becomes a gas. In addition, water vapor is released by plants as part of the transpiration stage of photosynthesis. In transpiration, water produced as waste by the process of photosynthesis is released by the stomata in plants into the atmosphere. (Stomata are small openings in the underside of leaves that take in and release various gases.) Together, these two processes are called evapotranspiration.

Water vapor in the atmosphere rises, and water molecules come together to form small droplets suspended in the atmosphere. When there are enough of these droplets, they become visible as clouds or fog. The name of this phase is condensation.

Atmospheric conditions cause these droplets to come together to form larger and larger droplets, which when too heavy to remain suspended in the atmosphere, fall to Earth's surface in liquid or solid form as rain, sleet, snow, or hail. This third stage in the cycle is called precipitation.

Finally, water fallen to Earth's surface is called runoff. Runoff can evaporate directly back into the atmosphere soon after hitting the ground, especially if temperatures are warm. Runoff also can enter bodies of water, such as rivers, streams, lakes, and oceans. When water enters these bodies, it will continue to move on Earth's surface, often because of gravity, which causes rivers and streams to run downhill, where they will empty into larger rivers, lakes, or oceans. In lakes and oceans, water will continue to move. Two ways water moves are waves and currents. Some runoff will also be absorbed into the ground in a process called infiltration. This water provides moisture in the soil or is absorbed into underground aquifers. An aquifer is an underground area of loose material such as rock or sand where groundwater collects. Groundwater can move through the ground in underground rivers or streams or return to the surface through natural springs or wells dug by humans.

Some precipitation will not become runoff right away. Snow and ice may remain in solid form for some time before they melt and become a special form of runoff, snowmelt. Some precipitation never hits the ground or becomes runoff. Canopy interception—water caught on leaves on tree branches high in the forest—allows it to evaporate back into the atmosphere without touching the ground.

As water moves through the various stages, important things happen. Runoff adds moisture to the soil, which provides sustenance for plants to take in through their roots. Evaporation purifies water because as water evaporates, impurities are removed from the water. In addition, as underground water moves through aquifers, the crushed gravel or sand filters the water of impurities. Finally, water moves nutrients—such as dissolved minerals—all around Earth's surface. Plants and animals use these minerals as they take in water.

1. In saying that "water moves around Earth in all three states," the author means that

   (A) water moves around Earth in solid, liquid, and gas forms

   (B) water can move across only three of the fifty US states at a time

   (C) the water cycle has three stages

   (D) water has to change form to move around Earth's surface

2. The word "hydrological" in the passage is closest in meaning to

   (A) related to vapor

   (B) related to water

   (C) related to state

   (D) related to motion

3. Which part of a plant allows for water vapor to be released back into the atmosphere?

   Ⓐ Stomata

   Ⓑ Leaves

   Ⓒ Roots

   Ⓓ Branches

4. Which of the following is NOT a way that water can fall to Earth's surface as precipitation?

   Ⓐ Rain

   Ⓑ Hail

   Ⓒ Sleet

   Ⓓ Fog

5. The word "evapotranspiration" in the passage is closest in meaning to

   Ⓐ the process by which energy from the sun converts liquid water to vapor

   Ⓑ the process by which plants release water vapor as waste

   Ⓒ the process by which water vapor enters the atmosphere

   Ⓓ the process by which water moves around Earth's surface

6. Which of the following best expresses the essential information in the highlighted sentence?

> Atmospheric conditions cause these droplets to come together to form larger and larger droplets, which when too heavy to remain suspended in the atmosphere, fall to Earth's surface in liquid or solid form as rain, sleet, snow, or hail.

Incorrect answer choices change the meaning in important ways or leave out essential information.

Ⓐ Droplets come together and become larger because of atmospheric conditions, until they are too heavy to remain in the atmosphere and fall to Earth's surface in solid or liquid forms.

Ⓑ Water falls to the ground when droplets in the atmosphere are too heavy to stay in the air in solid or liquid form because of atmospheric conditions.

Ⓒ Atmospheric conditions cause rain, sleet, snow, and hail to form from tiny droplets of water vapor in fog, which fall to the ground when the droplets are too heavy to stay suspended in the air.

Ⓓ Solid or liquid water vapor forms when tiny droplets in the atmosphere join together and become larger and larger until they are too heavy to remain in the atmosphere and fall to the ground in the form of rain, sleet, snow, and hail.

7. Runoff enters an aquifer through

Ⓐ canopy interception

Ⓑ evaporation

Ⓒ infiltration

Ⓓ snowmelt

8. The word "it" in the passage refers to

Ⓐ leaves

Ⓑ water

Ⓒ branches

Ⓓ canopy interception

9. The word "sustenance" in the passage is closest in meaning to

Ⓐ hail

Ⓑ food

Ⓒ support

Ⓓ minerals

10. Which of the following is a benefit of the hydrological cycle?

Ⓐ Water in lakes and ponds evaporates.

Ⓑ Water is purified in aquifers.

Ⓒ Trees release water vapor produced as waste.

Ⓓ Some precipitation stays frozen for long periods of time.

Answers and Explanations for Exercise 10 begin on page 216.

Answering Inference Items

These items test your ability to use information that you read to figure out new information—an inference. For instance, the passage might identify several long-term causes of climate change, all related to harm caused to the environment by human activity. One inference that might be made is that human activity is the cause of global warming.

Items on TOEFL iBT Reading that involve inferencing include inference items, rhetorical purpose items, and insert text items

TOEFL IBT INFERENCE ITEMS AT A GLANCE

ITEM TYPES	ITEM FORMATS
• Inference	• Standard multiple choice
• Rhetorical purpose	• Standard multiple choice
• Insert text	• Standard multiple choice

Inference Items

The simplest type of inference items ask you to select an inference that can be drawn directly from information in the reading passage. To answer these items, follow these steps:

1. Read the item and try to answer without reading the answer options.
2. Read all the answer options. If your answer is among the options, check it by ensuring that there is evidence in the passage that supports the inference. Make sure that the option does not contradict any information in the passage.
3. If the answer you thought of in Step 1 is not among the options or cannot be inferred from the information in the passage, read all of the answer options again, looking for an answer that can be inferred from the evidence in the passage and that is not contradicted by the information in the passage.

Usually, an inference item contains words such as *imply, suggest, infer, probably,* or *likely.* Study the chart.

RECOGNIZING INFERENCE ITEMS
Which of the following can be **inferred** from the passage?
From the information in paragraph 1, which of the following is the **most likely** outcome of global warming?
The information in the passage **suggests** that global warming is . . .
The author of the passage **implies** that governments that do not agree that global warming is a significant problem . . .
Which of the following is **probably** an outcome of the droughts experienced in parts of North America?

Inference Item

Reread the selection from a longer reading passage. Then answer the item.

P A R A G R A P H 1

Climate data released recently reveal that the arctic ice cap melted at an alarming rate during the summer of 2012, shattering the previous record for summer melting set in 2007. Rutgers University climatologist David Robinson said, "We thought that might be the record for quite a while. And here we are, just five years later, and we've shattered that record. We're seeing losses of sea ice I never thought I'd see in my career." Satellite photos of the ice cap show that the ice cap is the smallest it has ever been since scientists began taking satellite photos of the ice cap in 1980. The data also show that the ice that remains is thinner than before. Only a few years ago, scientists thought that the ice cap might disappear by 2050. Now some scientists think that day may be only a few years away.

From the information in the paragraph, which of the following is the most likely reason the arctic ice cap might disappear completely earlier than originally predicted?

Ⓐ In 2007, the ice cap was the smallest it had been since 1980.

Ⓑ The ice cap is much thinner now than in previous years.

Ⓒ Prior to 1980, the ice cap was much smaller than it is today.

Ⓓ Scientists thought that the record set in 2007 would not be broken for many years.

You know this is an inference item because it asks you to speculate about a cause-and-effect relationship alluded to in the passage but never stated directly. The phrase "the most likely reason" also indicates that this is an inference item. Option B is correct because the ice cap was thinner in 2012 than in 2007. Option A is not correct because the ice cap was smaller in 2012. Option C is not supported by the information in the passage because 1980 is the first year that scientists began to take photographs of the ice cap and is merely a reference point. No inference about the size of the ice cap before 1980 can be drawn from this information since photographs are not available. Option D is incorrect because it is not a reason the ice cap will melt sooner than expected. Rather, it implies the opposite.

Inference Item

Reread the selection from a longer reading passage on the polar ice cap on page 155. Then answer the item.

Which of the following would probably be a result of the record-setting melting of the arctic ice cap in summer 2012?

(A) Global warming

(B) Higher ocean levels

(C) New records for ice melting

(D) Increased risk of earthquakes

You can tell that this is an inference item because it asks you to speculate about possible outcomes of melting of the arctic ice cap. The word *probably* also indicates that this is an inference item. The answer is Option B. Less ice means that more liquid water will be in the oceans, which will cause their levels to rise. Option A is incorrect because global warming is a possible cause of the loss of polar ice. Option C is incorrect because melting ice cannot be both the cause and the effect. Option D is incorrect because earthquakes are caused by stresses within Earth's crust, not by polar ice.

EXERCISE 11

Inference Items

Read the selection from a longer reading passage. Then answer the question.

When people think of sports medicine, they often think of professional or college team sports and the doctors and other health professionals who serve these highly trained athletes. But sports medicine is actually a much larger field that involves professional and nonprofessional sports and serves an increasing number of patients.

Sports medicine involves a number of medical and sports professionals, including athletic trainers, doctors, nurses, medical technicians, and physical therapists. To treat issues as diverse as broken bones, hurt or damaged muscles, heart and circulatory problems, and even injuries to the brain, many medical specialties are involved. Specialists in sports medicine are involved in emergency care, short-term recovery and rehabilitation, and treatment of long-term and chronic conditions that result from sports and exercise. Of course, sports medicine also focuses on preventing injuries.

When people think about sports medicine, they often think about a team doctor treating an injured player on the field, but sports medicine also includes prevention of injuries. This function is often exercised by the athletic trainer, whose training equips him or her to design effective workout and practice routines that build physical strength and help prevent injuries. If a player has a known problem, such as a baseball pitcher who is prone to arm injuries, the trainer can devise a practice schedule that works for the player, prescribe special exercises to relieve the arm, and even arrange for preventive medicine, if necessary. Sports medicine specialists can also ensure that athletes get appropriate nutrition, including proper levels of calories to meet the physical demands of the sport and adequate amounts of vitamins and protein to keep athletes' bodies strong. To do this work, sports medicine professionals need more than basic medical knowledge. They need to know about the physical demands and challenges posed by sports in general and by specific sports. But athletic trainers help more than just professionals. Individuals involved in many extreme or demanding sports also consult with athletic trainers or doctors specializing in sports medicine. Dedicated triathletes, amateur mountain climbers, and even avid skateboarders use the services of sports medicine professionals.

1. Which of the following can be inferred from the passage?

   Ⓐ Only professional athletes can benefit from sports medicine.

   Ⓑ Sports medicine's focus is on trauma care.

   Ⓒ Athletes have unique health concerns that require specialized attention.

   Ⓓ The knowledge required by a sports medicine physician is no different from the knowledge of a regular doctor

---

TIP **Options with words such as *always*, *never*, or *only* are almost always incorrect!**

Be careful with options that include limiting words such as *always*, *never*, or *only*. To be correct, these options have to have no exceptions. Therefore, options with these words are almost always incorrect. In Item 1, you can easily eliminate Option A because it has the word *only*.

2. From the information in the passage, which of the following is a case that a sports medicine specialist would most likely NOT take on?

(A) A high school football player keeps pulling the same muscle in his right leg.

(B) A snowboarder needs to develop stronger muscles to help steer the board.

(C) A repetitive stress injury prevents a worker from using the mouse on her computer.

(D) A backpacker is getting older and wants to know how to train for long hikes.

3. From the information in the passage, which of the following can be inferred about the emergence of sports medicine as a specialized field?

(A) The demand for sports medicine is rising because people increasingly participate in so many unsafe sports.

(B) Sports medicine has increased in demand because of the specialized knowledge required.

(C) Sports medicine will always remain a small field because it mainly serves professional athletes.

(D) Sports medicine does not greatly differ from other medical fields, because the problems it treats are no different from those experienced by the general public.

4. Which of the following can be inferred from the author's statement:

   Sports medicine specialists can also ensure that athletes get appropriate nutrition, including proper levels of calories to meet the physical demands of the sport and adequate amounts of vitamins and protein to keep athletes' bodies strong.

(A) Nutritionists work in the area of sports medicine.

(B) Many athletes have poor eating habits.

(C) Athletes can suffer from weight control problems.

(D) Players with adequate nutrition will not get injuries.

Answers and Explanations for Exercise 11 begin on page 217.

Rhetorical Purpose Items

Writers include information and ideas in their writing for specific purposes. A writer may include a specific fact to support the main idea. Or an author may cite a study that contradicts his or her point of view in order to refute the contradictory information. Or an author may include a quote from a noted expert to strengthen the argument. Rhetorical purpose items may focus on a certain fact, quotation, example, order or organizational pattern, or vocabulary word and ask you to infer the reason the author included it. Rhetorical purpose questions require an understanding of the main idea of the text and its organization. They also require you to infer the writer's overall stance toward the subject and purpose for writing, as well as the reason he or she included the specific information or ordered the text in a certain way.

A rhetorical purpose item will always identify a specific fact, example, quotation, vocabulary word, or organizational pattern. Frequently, rhetorical purpose items ask for a reason. Study the chart.

RECOGNIZING RHETORICAL PURPOSE ITEMS
Why does the author **introduce** climate data in paragraph 1?
The writer **mentions** the break in the ozone layer **in paragraph 3** because . . .
The author **refers to** the increase in Earth's mean temperature **in order to** . . .
Why does the author **discuss** the rise in Earth's mean temperature **before** she discusses the break in the ozone layer?
The **main purpose** of paragraph 3 is . . .

Rhetorical Purpose Item

Read the selection from a longer reading passage. Then answer the question.

Community psychology is a branch of psychology that emerged in the 1970s and 1980s. Psychology typically had focused mainly on individual mental health. Community psychology instead focuses on the structures and organization of communities, relationships among community members, and community members' actions, beliefs, and attitudes. Community psychology draws from many disciplines, including sociology, social work, political science, and public health. While counseling psychologists work directly with individuals, community psychologists work with groups, often engaging in projects involving community activism and social justice.

Why does the author include the statement "Psychology had typically focused mainly on individual mental health"?

(A) To show a similarity between community psychology and traditional psychology

(B) To indicate that psychology has many related subdisciplines and branches of study

(C) To clarify community psychology by showing how it is different from another kind of psychology that people are more familiar with

(D) To show that psychology studies more than communities

If you chose Option C, you are correct. Most people know that a major focus of psychology is the individual. Acknowledging this role is a good way to show the contrast with community psychology. Option A is incorrect because the information is a contrast, not a similarity. Option B is incorrect because while community psychology is a subdiscipline of psychology, the author's purpose is not to show the many subdisciplines of psychology. Option D is incorrect because psychology usually studies individuals.

> **TIP** **On rhetorical purpose items, choose an option that relates to the author's purpose!**
>
> Do not select an answer option to a rhetorical purpose item simply because it is true or a logical inference. Make sure that the answer is related directly to the author's purpose. For instance, it is true that psychology has many branches and subdisciplines, but this is not the reason the author includes detail about traditional psychology in the passage. The author wants to show a contrast between the two branches of psychology to help readers better understand community psychology.

EXAMPLE

Rhetorical Purpose Item

Reread the selection from a longer reading passage on the polar ice cap.
Then answer the item.

PARAGRAPH 1

Climate data released recently reveal that the arctic ice cap melted at an alarming rate during the summer of 2012, shattering the previous record for summer melting set in 2007. Rutgers University climatologist David Robinson said, "We thought that might be the record for quite a while. And here we are, just five years later, and we've shattered that record. We're seeing losses of sea ice I never thought I'd see in my career." Satellite photos of the ice cap show that the ice cap is the smallest it has ever been since scientists began taking satellite photos of the ice cap in 1980. The data also show that the ice that remains is thinner than before. Only a few years ago, scientists thought that the ice cap might disappear by 2050. Now some scientists think that day may be only a few years away.

Why does the author quote David Robinson in the article?

Ⓐ To provide an expert opinion that shows the large extent of the ice loss

Ⓑ To contradict evidence that ice loss is not a serious problem

Ⓒ To show that the cause of the melting is global warming

Ⓓ To show that ice loss is more of a personal concern than an environmental concern

The answer is Option A. The quote shows that an acknowledged academic expert believes that ice loss seems to be accelerating more quickly than scientists originally believed. Option B is incorrect because the passage does not offer evidence that ice loss is not a serious problem; therefore, there is nothing for the quote to contradict. Option C is incorrect because the quote does not mention that global warming is the cause of the ice loss. Option D is incorrect because the expert uses the time frame of his career to underline the speed of the loss, not to show that it is merely a personal concern.

EXERCISE 12

Rhetorical Purpose Items

Reread the passage on sports medicine on pages 156–157. Then answer the questions.

1. Why does the author introduce the example of a baseball pitcher who is prone to arm injuries?

   Ⓐ To illustrate the point that sports medicine has a preventive component

   Ⓑ To show the large number of medical specialties involved in sports medicine

   Ⓒ To illustrate the point that sports medicine treats both amateurs and professionals

   Ⓓ To show that all athletes need the services of sports medicine from time to time

2. Why does the author mention triathletes, mountain climbers, and skateboarders?

   Ⓐ To give examples of several kinds of professional athletes

   Ⓑ To show the many diverse sports people can participate in

   Ⓒ To show that many nonprofessional athletes benefit from sports medicine

   Ⓓ To give examples of athletes that each kind of specialist supports

Answers and Explanations for Exercise 12 begin on page 218.

Insert Text Items

Insert text items ask you to identify one of four possible locations in the text in which to insert an additional sentence. Insert text items assess your understanding of relevance and organization. To choose the location where the sentence belongs, you need to understand the organizational pattern of the reading selection and choose the place where the new sentence is the most relevant. You also need to understand the connection words in the passage and the new sentence to ensure that the new sentence is connected rhetorically to the rest of the passage. Connection words are words and phrases that are used to join sentences together and show the interrelationship of the ideas. Connection words include *first, second, third, last, in contrast, in addition, for instance, for example*, and *however*.

In an insert text item, you will see a selection from the reading passage with four black squares inserted into the text. Then you will see the directions:

> Look at the four squares (■) that indicate where the following sentence could be added to the passage. Where would the sentence best fit?

To answer this item on the TOEFL iBT, you use your cursor and mouse to click on the black square in the location where the sentence can best be inserted. In this book, each black box will have a letter in it (**A**) to identify each possible insertion point.

EXAMPLE

Insert Text Item

Reread the selection from a longer reading passage. Look at the four squares (■) that indicate where the following sentence could be added to the passage.

> **The earlier record was set after a record hot summer around the northern hemisphere with unusual weather around the globe.**

Where would the sentence best fit?

Climate data released recently reveal that the arctic ice cap melted at an alarming rate during the summer of 2012, shattering the previous record for summer melting set in 2007. **A** Rutgers University climatologist David Robinson said, "We thought that might be the record for quite a while. And here we are, just five years later, and we've shattered that record. We're seeing losses of sea ice I never thought I'd see in my career." Satellite photos of the ice cap show that the ice cap is the smallest it has ever been since scientists began taking satellite photos of the ice cap in 1980. **B** The data also show that the ice that remains is thinner than before. **C** Only a few years ago, scientists thought that the ice cap might disappear by 2050. **D** Now some scientists think that day may be only a few years away.

The answer is Option A. The sentence belongs at that point because it gives additional detail about the previous record that was set in 2007. Because the previous sentence discusses the 2007 record, location A is the most logical one for the new sentence. The remaining options do not make sense because the sentences that precede them are not about the 2007 record.

EXAMPLE

Insert Text Item

Reread the selection from a longer reading passage.

An eclipse is an astronomical event in which light from one astronomical body is blocked by another astronomical body, such as the moon or Earth. The sun, Earth, and Earth's moon are all involved in two kinds of eclipses. A solar eclipse occurs when light from the sun is blocked by the moon. For a solar eclipse to occur, the sun, moon, and Earth must be in alignment, with the moon in the middle to block the sun's light. Alignments of this sort are rare and last for only a few minutes, as Earth and the moon continue on their orbits. During an eclipse, people on Earth see the sun with a dark circle cut out of it (partial solar eclipse) or completely blocked by the moon (total solar eclipse), so that sunlight shines only from the edges of the sun; the rest of the light is blocked by the moon. **A** The shadow cast by the moon during an eclipse will darken the sky, especially during a total or near-total eclipse. Animals may believe that night is falling. Birds may begin to roost for the night, for example. **B**

A lunar eclipse occurs when sunlight shining on the moon is blocked by Earth's shadow. For a lunar eclipse to happen, the sun, Earth, and the moon must all be in a row, with Earth in the middle so it can block the sun's light and cast a shadow on the moon. The shadow cast by Earth contains two parts, the umbra and the penumbra. The umbra is the shadow cast directly by Earth. The penumbra is a larger area around the umbra where direct light from the sun is blocked but some light is able to get through indirectly. A penumbral lunar eclipse happens when the penumbra cast by Earth slightly darkens the surface of the moon. An umbral lunar eclipse takes place when the umbra falls on the moon's surface. A lunar eclipse may be partial or total, depending on whether the shadow cast falls completely or partially on the surface of the moon. In a penumbral total eclipse, the moon may appear partially darkened, and areas of the penumbra may appear darker if they are near the umbra. **C** In an umbral total lunar eclipse, it may appear that the moon has disappeared from the sky for a period.

Generally, a lunar eclipse is visible only at night and when the moon is full. A senelion, a kind of eclipse that occurs under only highly exceptional conditions, is a rare astronomical event. A senelion is an eclipse that occurs when the sun and moon are opposite one another on the horizon and are aligned so that Earth's shadow hits the moon. **D** Thus the sun and the eclipsed moon can be seen simultaneously. This is the only time when the sun and a lunar eclipse will both be visible together. This is also the only time that an eclipse can take place with daylight visible at the same time. The most recent senelion was on December 10, 2010. The next one will not take place for eighty-four years.

Look at the four squares (■) that indicate where the following sentence could be added to the passage.

In an umbral partial eclipse, part of the moon's surface is in partial shadow from the penumbra and another part of the moon is in a darker shadow from the umbra.

Where would the sentence best fit?

If you selected Option C, you are correct. The new sentence gives a detail about one kind of lunar eclipse—an umbral partial eclipse. The sentences around Option C give details about other kinds of umbral and penumbral lunar eclipses, so this is the best location for the new sentence. Options A and B are incorrect because this section of the passage is about solar eclipses, and the new sentence is about lunar eclipses. Option D is incorrect because this section of the passage is about a special kind of lunar eclipse, a senelion. The detail in the new sentence makes more sense when placed together with the detail about other lunar eclipses in the previous paragraph.

EXERCISE 13

Insert Text Items

Answer the questions.

PARAGRAPH 1

When people think of sports medicine, they often think of professional or college team sports, and the doctors and other health professionals who serve these highly trained athletes. But sports medicine is actually a much larger field that involves professional and nonprofessional sports and serves an increasing number of patients. **A**

PARAGRAPH 2

B Sports medicine involves a number of medical and sports professionals, including athletic trainers, doctors, nurses, medical technicians, and physical therapists. To treat issues as diverse as broken bones, hurt or damaged muscles, heart and circulatory problems, and even injuries to the brain, many medical specialties are involved. **C** Specialists in sports medicine are involved in emergency care, short-term recovery and rehabilitation, and treatment of long term and chronic conditions that result from sports and exercise. Of course, sports medicine also focuses on preventing injuries. **D**

1. Look at the four squares (■) that indicate where the following sentence could be added to the passage.

   Cardiologists, bone and muscle specialists, surgeons, and even dentists can be called upon for specific cases.

   Where would the sentence best fit?

PARAGRAPH 3

When people think about sports medicine, they often think about a team doctor treating an injured player on the field, but sports medicine also includes prevention of injuries. This function is often exercised by the athletic trainer, whose training equips him or her to design effective workout and practice routines that build physical strength and help prevent injuries. **A** If a player has a known problem, such as a baseball pitcher who is prone to arm injuries, the trainer can devise a practice schedule that works for the player, prescribe special exercises to relieve the arm, and even arrange for preventive medicine, if necessary. Sports medicine specialists can also ensure that athletes get appropriate nutrition, including proper levels of calories to meet the physical demands of the sport and adequate amounts of vitamins and protein to keep athletes' bodies strong. **B** To do this work, sports medicine professionals need more than basic medical knowledge. They need to know about the physical demands and challenges posed by sports in general and by specific sports. **C** But athletic trainers help more than just professionals. Individuals involved in many extreme or demanding sports also consult with athletic trainers or doctors specializing in sports medicine. **D** Dedicated triathletes, amateur mountain climbers, and even avid skateboarders use the services of sports medicine professionals.

P
A
R
A
G
R
A
P
H

3

2. Look at the four squares (■) that indicate where the following sentence could be added to the passage.

> **Specialists also need knowledge of the special demands posed by athletes' highly developed bodies.**

Where would the sentence best fit?

Answers and Explanations for Exercise 13 begin on page 218.

EXERCISE 14

Answering TOEFL iBT Inference Items

Read the excerpt from a longer reading passage and answer the items about it.

As we all know, water does not mix well with certain substances, such as oil. This is because the surface of water has a kind of tension that prevents certain kinds of substances from mixing with it. This is why oil and vinegar in salad dressing separate. This is also why cream rises to the top of milk.

Surfactants are chemicals that lower the surface tension of water. A low concentration of a surfactant will allow other substances to mix with the water. Surfactants have many uses. They are found in dishwashing liquid, shampoo, and skin cream. Detergents in dishwashing liquid allow grease and other oily substances to mix with water so they can be washed away. Surfactants in shampoo let sebum, an oily substance in the hair, mix with water so it can be washed away. Skin creams contain surfactants known as emollients to mix oily substances and water. Products such as sunblock and makeup contain emollients. Solubolizers are a kind of surfactant useful in perfumes and colognes. They are used to dissolve oily scent-bearing substances in water to create mixtures of different scents.

Surfactants are essential to many products people use every day, but there are some concerns. Some common surfactants have been associated with cancer and other health problems. Some experts believe that hazardous surfactants are used unnecessarily. For example, surfactants that are foaming agents are commonly used in shampoos and soap because people associate foam with cleansing, even though these materials are hazardous and foam is not needed to allow oil and water to mix. The most hazardous surfactants are derived from petroleum products.

1. Why does the author mention surfactants that are foaming agents?

   Ⓐ To give an example of an important use of surfactants

   Ⓑ To show that some surfactants are unnecessary

   Ⓒ To show how emollients work

   Ⓓ To show how surfactants can have more than one function

2. From the information in the passage, which kind of surfactant would be used to create a creamy salad dressing whose ingredients include a mixture of vinegar, water, and oil?

   Ⓐ Foaming agent

   Ⓑ Detergent

   Ⓒ Emollient

   Ⓓ Solubolizer

3. A foaming agent would be necessary for which of these purposes?

  Ⓐ To make bread that is light and fluffy

  Ⓑ To make strong hand soap that will wash away heavy grease

  Ⓒ To dissolve a flavorful oil in a liquid flavoring

  Ⓓ To make a kitchen cleanser to clean oily stove tops

P A R A G R A P H 3

  A Surfactants are essential to many products people use every day, but there are some concerns. Some common surfactants have been associated with cancer and other health problems. Some experts believe that hazardous surfactants are used unnecessarily. **B** For example, surfactants with foaming action are commonly used in shampoos and soap because people associate foam with cleansing, even though surfactants do not need to foam to allow oil and water to mix. **C** The most hazardous surfactants are derived from petroleum products. **D**

4. Look at the four squares (■) that indicate where the following sentence could be added to the third paragraph of the passage.

  For this reason, naturally derived surfactants are desirable whenever possible.

  Where would the sentence best fit?

Answers and Explanations for Exercise 14 begin on page 218.

Answering Reading-to-Learn Items

Each TOEFL iBT Reading test will have one reading-to-learn question, either a prose summary item or a fill in a table item. These items are both considered drag-and-drop items because on the TOEFL iBT, you use the cursor and mouse to select and drag text to the appropriate place in a table or chart. (This book uses letters and numbers to simulate the test-taking experience.)

TOEFL iBT READING-TO-LEARN ITEMS AT A GLANCE

ITEM TYPES	ITEM FORMATS
• Prose summary	• Drag-and-drop item
• Fill in a table	• Drag-and-drop item

Prose Summary Items

These items ask you to identify three sentences (from a selection of six) that best summarize the main ideas of the passage. You need to include sentences that summarize the main ideas, and eliminate sentences that include details or incorrect information. The result will be a brief summary of the passage restated in new language. You can select the options in any order. These items are worth two points, and the following scale is used:

CORRECT ANSWER OPTIONS	POINTS
0 to 1	0
2	1
3	2

The order of the sentences in the summary does not count.

Prose summary items will present you with directions, a box with an introductory sentence and places to insert the three sentences, and six answer options from which to choose. Here is an example:

> An introductory sentence for a brief summary of the passage is provided. Complete the summary by selecting the THREE answer choices that express important ideas in the passage. Some sentences do not belong in the summary, because they express ideas that are not presented in the passage or are minor details in the passage. *This question is worth 2 points.*
>
> Drag your answer choices to the spaces where they belong.

The passage discusses the causes and effects of global warming.

-
-
-

Prose Summary Item

Read the selection from a longer reading passage. Then answer the item.

Many organisms live in colonies, but not all of them are social organisms. A colony is defined as organisms of the same species living closely together with a shared purpose such as mutual defense or ability to attack bigger prey. Bacteria, ants, fish, and birds are all examples of organisms that live in colonies. A colony of bacteria is a group of the same bacteria living together on a medium. A small South American freshwater fish, the piranha, is another example. Alone, these small (14 to 26 cm), sharp-toothed fish are timid and have difficulty finding prey. But in large colonies, they can exhibit aggressive behavior and devour a very large organism in a few minutes. Living in schools also helps these small, timid fish fend off predatory birds. Certain bird species live in colonies. Bird colonies are of two types. Roosting colonies are flocks of birds that feed together and, when in need of rest, roost together in trees or other safe locations. Nesting colonies are birds that build their nests together for mutual protection from predators. Many seabirds live in nesting colonies during their reproductive cycle.

Even though all of these animals live in colonies, only a few of them are social organisms. Social organisms have a number of special characteristics that define them. First, social organisms practice communal brood care. That is, they care for their young collectively. The community's offspring are cared for by members of the colony, not just by the parents. Second, there are overlapping generations among the members of the colony. That is, at all times there are younger and older members living together at the same time. Overlapping generations give the colony the ability to continue over time, since the members will not die out at the same time. In addition, overlapping generations make cooperative brood care possible, since older generations can assist younger generations. The third characteristic of social animals is that there is reproductive division of labor. This means that only certain members of the colony produce offspring. Among some social insects, only one, the queen, will produce offspring, and the colony contains a small number of males and a large number of sexless workers whose jobs are to raise the young, gather food, and protect the colony.

Organisms that meet all the criteria of social organisms are called eusocial. Only a small number of organisms meet all the criteria of eusociality. Most of them are insects and include termites, ant, bees, and wasps. Two non-insect organisms are eusocial: naked mole rats, African rodents that live in underground tunnel colonies, and snapping shrimp, which live in colonies inside of sponges. Scientists do not uniformly agree on whether these non-insect species are truly eusocial. Some scientists say that a second species of mole rat is also eusocial, while others say that neither species meets the criteria fully. Many marine biologists believe that snapping shrimp are not truly eusocial, because although these colonies have a queen, a single organism responsible for producing offspring, other members of the colony can reproduce if the queen dies or if they are removed from the colony.

An introductory sentence for a brief summary of the passage is provided. Complete the summary by selecting the THREE answer choices that express important ideas in the passage. Some sentences do not belong in the summary, because they express ideas that are not presented in the passage or are minor details in the passage. *This question is worth 2 points.*

Write the letters of your answer choices on the lines where they belong.

> **The passage discusses the characteristics of social animals.**
>
> •
>
> •
>
> •

Answer Choices

A Eusociality is defined by meeting all three criteria of social animals.

B The naked mole rat is perhaps the only eusocial mammal.

C Eusocial animals are naturally friendly.

D Birds that reproduce in nesting colonies are an example of eusocial animals.

E Many animals live in colonies, but not all of them are social.

F Social animals are defined by three main characteristics.

If you completed the summary correctly, it should look like this:

The passage discusses the characteristics of social animals.

- **A** Eusociality is defined by meeting all three criteria of social animals.

- **E** Many animals live in colonies, but not all of them are social.

- **F** Social animals are defined by three main characteristics.

These answers are correct for these reasons.

- **A** **Eusociality is defined by meeting all three criteria of social animals.** This answer is correct because it summarizes a major point of the passage, the criteria for eusociality.
- **E** **Many animals live in colonies, but not all of them are social.** This answer is correct because it synthesizes information on colonies, social animals, and eusociality in the first paragraph.
- **F** **Social animals are defined by three main characteristics.** This sentence sums up important information in the passage: the characteristics of social animals.

Incorrect options do not belong in the completed table for these reasons:

- **B** **The naked mole rat is perhaps the only eusocial mammal.** This is a detail in the passage, so it does not belong in the summary.
- **C** **Eusocial animals are naturally friendly.** This idea is not mentioned in the passage and does not make sense. This option confuses the notion of social behavior with friendliness.
- **D** **Birds that reproduce in nesting colonies are an example of eusocial animals.** This statement is contradicted by the passage. The passage states that only a few animals that live in colonies exhibit eusocial behavior. Birds do not meet the criteria for eusocial animals, because they do not share responsibilities for raising their young.

TIP **When answering a prose summary item, quickly eliminate options that are details or incorrect!**

Focus on the statements that belong in the summary. Use your note paper to help you. Write letters from A to F. Then check or cross off the ones that are details, not in the passage, or incorrect. For example, on this item, you would first cross off B because it is a detail, C because it is not in the passage, and D because that statement is incorrect.

A   B✔   C✔   D✔   E   F

EXERCISE 15

Prose Summary Items

1. Reread the passage about sports medicine on pages 156–157. Then answer the question.

An introductory sentence for a brief summary of the passage is provided. Complete the summary by selecting the THREE answer choices that express important ideas in the passage. Some sentences do not belong in the summary, because they express ideas that are not presented in the passage or are minor details in the passage. *This item is worth 2 points.*

Write the letters of your answer choices in the spaces where they belong.

> **The passage discusses the work of sports medicine professionals and the athletes they serve.**
>
> •
>
> •
>
> •

Answer Choices

A Sports medicine is a growing field that serves professional and nonprofessional athletes.

B An athletic trainer can organize appropriate training routines and preventive care.

C Sports medicine professionals include many specialists.

D Preventive care includes monitoring nutrition.

E Sports medicine gives emergency care, treats long-term conditions, and provides preventive care.

F Health professionals who want to become sports medicine professionals require extensive training and professional certifications in sports medicine.

2. Reread the passage about eclipses on pages 164–165. Then answer the question.

An introductory sentence for a brief summary of the passage is provided. Complete the summary by selecting the THREE answer choices that express important ideas in the passage. Some sentences do not belong in the summary, because they express ideas that are not presented in the passage or are minor details in the passage. *This item is worth 2 points.*

Write the letters of your answer choices in the spaces where they belong.

The passage discusses different kinds of eclipses.

-
-
-

Answer Choices

A In a solar eclipse, the moon blocks light from the sun.

B Birds may roost during a total solar eclipse.

C A senelion is a very common kind of eclipse.

D In an umbral eclipse, the moon is completely dark.

E An eclipse happens when one astronomical body blocks light from another.

F In a lunar eclipse, Earth blocks light from the sun.

Answers and Explanations for Exercise 15 begin on page 219.

TIP **Do not worry about the order of your answer choices!**

Do not worry about the order of your choices in a summary item. The order of the options is not scored. So do not waste valuable time putting the statements in the same order as they occur in the passage. Just move the correct options to the summary box and move on.

Fill in a Table Items

Fill in a table items ask you to demonstrate your ability to structure and organize the information in the passage. In these items, you are presented with a number of statements and a table with two to three columns or rows. You use your cursor and mouse to drag the statements to their proper locations in the table. Usually, the table will be organized around a key critical thinking skill, such as analysis, classification, compare and contrast, steps in a process, chronological order, and so on.

Fill in a table items will present you with directions, a table with two to three columns or rows to insert five answers, and seven answer options from which to choose.

Select from the seven phrases below the two phrases that correctly characterize organisms that live in colonies and the three phrases that correctly characterize eusocial animals. Two of the phrases will NOT be used.

KIND OF ANIMAL	STATEMENTS
Organisms That Live in Colonies	**Select 2**
	•
	•
Eusocial Organisms	**Select 3**
	•
	•
	•

Correct fill in a table options:

- include accurate information from the passage
- are relevant to the categories in the table
- are main ideas of the passage, not minor details
- are correctly placed in the correct section of the table

Options may be incorrect because they are:

- factually incorrect
- unimportant details
- not mentioned in the passage
- incorrectly placed in the wrong section of the table

Fill in a table items are scored on whether you both selected the correct options and placed the options in the appropriate sections of the table. The order of the answers in the sections of the table is not scored. These items are worth three points, and the following scale is used:

CORRECT ANSWER OPTIONS	POINTS
0 to 2	0
3	1
4	2
5	3

EXAMPLE

Fill in a Table Item

Reread the passage on social animals on pages 171–172. Then answer the item.

Complete the following table to summarize information about the organisms discussed in the passage. Match the appropriate statements to the kind of animal with which they are associated.

Select from the seven phrases following the two phrases that correctly characterize organisms that live in colonies and the three phrases that correctly characterize eusocial organisms. Two of the phrases will NOT be used.

KIND OF ANIMAL	STATEMENTS
Organisms That Live in Colonies	**Select 2**
	•
	•
Eusocial Organisms	**Select 3**
	•
	•
	•

Answer Choices

A The organisms live together for a shared purpose, such as defense.

B The organisms raise their young together.

C Herons and swallows are two bird species that build nests together.

D Membership includes termites, ants, bees, and wasps.

E The organisms do not have differentiated functions, such as reproduction and food gathering.

F Overlapping generations ensure the organisms' long-term survival.

G Snapping shrimp fully practice reproductive division of labor.

If you completed the table correctly, it should look like this:

KIND OF ANIMAL	STATEMENTS
Organisms That Live in Colonies	**Select 2**
	• A The organisms live together for a shared purpose, such as defense.
	• E The organisms do not have differentiated functions, such as reproduction and food gathering.
Eusocial Organisms	**Select 3**
	• B The organisms raise their young together.
	• D Membership includes termites, ants, bees, and wasps.
	• F Overlapping generations ensure the organisms' long-term survival.

COLONIES

- **A The organisms live together for a shared purpose, such as defense.** This option is correctly placed in the colonies group because the passage clearly states that a main characteristic of these animals is that they "live closely together with a shared purpose such as mutual defense or ability to attack bigger prey."
- **E The organisms do not have differentiated functions, such as reproduction and food gathering.** This option is correctly placed in this group because the passage states that reproductive division of labor is a main characteristic of eusocial organisms. Therefore, this negative statement belongs with the information about colonies.

EUSOCIAL

- **B The organisms raise their young together.** Communal brood care is a main characteristic of eusocial animals, so this statement is correctly placed in this category.
- **D Membership includes termites, ants, bees, and wasps.** The passage indicates that all of these organisms are eusocial, so this option is correctly placed in this category.
- **F Overlapping generations ensure the organisms' long-term survival.** The passage identifies this as one of the principal identifying characteristics of eusocial organisms, so this option is correctly placed in this category.

> **TIP** **Do not worry about the order of the statements!**
>
> The order of the statements is not scored. Therefore, do not waste valuable time putting the statements in the same order as they occur in the passage. Just move the correct statements to the correct places in the table and move to the next item.

Incorrect options do not belong in the completed table for these reasons:

- **C Herons and swallows are two bird species that build nests together.** While it is correct that these two species of birds build nests together, this information is a relatively minor detail and the specific bird species are not mentioned in the passage. Therefore, other options belong in the table, not this one.

- **G Snapping shrimp fully practice reproductive division of labor.** This is a relatively minor detail and is stated incorrectly. The passage indicates that many marine biologists do not believe that snapping shrimp fully practice reproductive division of labor.

> **TIP** **Eliminate incorrect options before completing the table!**
>
> To avoid selecting an incorrect option, eliminate them before you begin to move options to the table. Use your note paper to help you. Write letters from A to G, then check or cross off the incorrect options. First eliminate answer options that are minor details. Then eliminate options that are incorrect. Then move the remaining options to their correct places in the table.

EXERCISE 16

Fill in a Table Items

1. Reread passage on sports medicine on pages 156–157. Then answer the item.

Select from the seven phrases following the two phrases that correctly characterize the popular view of sports medicine and the three phrases that correctly characterize the real view of sports medicine. Two of the phrases will NOT be used.

POPULAR VIEW OF SPORTS MEDICINE	REAL VIEW OF SPORTS MEDICINE
Select 2	Select 3
•	•
•	•
	•

Answer Choices

A It involves urgent and preventive care.

B It mainly treats college and professional athletes.

C Not a lot of specialized training is needed.

D It treats athletes in many kinds of professional and nonprofessional sports.

E It includes many kinds of health care professionals.

F Sports medicine specialists are mainly team doctors.

G Many nutritionists are involved in sports medicine.

2. Reread the passage on eclipses on pages 164–165. Then answer the item.

Select from the seven phrases following the two phrases that correctly characterize solar eclipses and the three phrases that correctly characterize lunar eclipses. Two of the phrases will NOT be used.

KIND OF ECLIPSE	STATEMENTS
Solar	**Select 2**
	•
	•
Lunar	**Select 3**
	•
	•
	•

Answer Choices

A The sun blocks the light of the moon.

B In a total eclipse, animals may think night has fallen.

C Earth blocks the light of the sun.

D A shadow is cast on the moon.

E The moon blocks the light of the sun.

F A shadow is cast on the sun.

G The darkest part of the shadow is the umbra.

Answers and Explanations for Exercise 16 begin on page 220.

TOEFL iBT Practice Reading Section

Directions: To simulate actual TOEFL iBT conditions, follow these instructions:

- Use your watch or the timer on your mobile phone or computer to keep track of the time.
- Give yourself 20 minutes to read each passage and respond to the items that are about it.
- Allow 60 minutes to read all the passages and answer all the items.
- As on the actual TOEFL iBT, you may look back at the passage when answering items. You can skip items and return to them.
- If you do not finish all the items when the test ends, mark your place. Then continue working as quickly as you can. When you finish, take note of the total time. This will give you an idea of how quickly you need to work on the actual TOEFL iBT to answer all the items in 60 minutes.

Now begin the TOEFL iBT Practice Reading section.

Give yourself 20 minutes to read the passage and answer Items 1–14.

Salsa is a rhythmic danceable Latin music style. While this term is often applied to music styles from locations such as Cuba, Puerto Rico, and the Dominican Republic, its origin and history are not clear. The word *salsa* means "sauce" in Spanish, and the term conjures up thoughts of rich, spicy Latin cooking. Many musicologists[1] believe that this energetic musical style emerged from the Latin jazz scene in New York City in the 1950s, 1960s, and 1970s. Others say that it emerged from Cuban and other music forms, such as *son*, a kind of Cuban music, or *merengue*, a music and dance style first popular in the Dominican Republic. Whatever the origin of the term, it seems that musicians distanced themselves from it, at least at first. Famed Latin musician Tito Puente, for example, was widely quoted as saying, "The only salsa I know is sold in a bottle called ketchup. I play Cuban music."

If the term didn't come from the musicians themselves, where did it come from? One of the first recorded uses of the term is the name of a Latin music program on local television in New York City, in the 1950s, hosted by a famous Latin music promoter. The music featured on that show included styles not now typically associated with salsa, such as certain Mexican traditional musical forms. Thus, the origin of this term may have been with music promoters involved in the presentation of the musicians' new stylings to the public, who struggled to find ways to package and present a new and emerging music in ways that non-Latin audiences could relate to. Adopting a term such as *salsa* to label the genre, even as the genre was being created and defined, would be helpful in encouraging the new genre's success because this word is easily pronounced by non-Spanish speakers and evokes such powerful associations. Later, the term was adopted by musicians, but for commercial reasons. They wanted their musical styles to be associated with the commercially accepted salsa. Even Tito Puente himself began to describe his music as salsa, but not for many years.

While it seems that the term *salsa* was invented in the 1950s or later, salsa grew out of a rich tradition of Cuban and Latin dance music in the New York City area that long predated the coining of the term now used to describe it. A number of Latin dance bands performed throughout the city beginning in the 1930s and 1940s. These bands had wide appeal. One of the most popular

---

[1] Musicologists study the history of music.

of these dance bands was led by Spanish-born and Cuban-raised Xavier Cugat. His band performed at the exclusive Waldorf-Astoria hotel in New York for more than sixteen years, drawing a diverse audience. Cugat, a classically trained musician, was criticized for the commercial appeal of his music, but he responded by saying that he would rather play his music and then sit by his swimming pool than play classical music and starve. In fact, many people, including Cugat, claim that Cugat was the inventor of the salsa music style. Many musicians who would go on to become famous salsa musicians got some of their most important experiences performing in Cugat's band. Tito Puente, for example, played for Cugat early in his career and, after Cugat's retirement, took over and led his band.

Salsa music included singers, both male and female. Of these, probably the most famous is Celia Cruz. Born in Cuba, Cruz developed an interest in music as a small child, but her parents encouraged her to become a teacher instead, so she focused on her studies. However, as a teenager she was told by one of her teachers that she could make more money in one day as an entertainer than a teacher makes in a month, so she became more serious about music as a career. She began performing in singing contests on a radio station and won several prizes. Her first prize was a cake! As she continued to perform and win prizes, she began to get the attention of other musicians. Eventually, she joined a band and performed all over Latin America. After the Cuban revolution, she refused to return to Cuba and settled in the United States, where her singing became more and more popular. Many people called her the Queen of Salsa.

Salsa is a rhythmic danceable Latin music style. While this term is often applied to music styles from locations such as Cuba, Puerto Rico, and the Dominican Republic, its origin and history are not clear. The word *salsa* means "sauce" in Spanish, and the term conjures up thoughts of rich, spicy Latin cooking. Many musicologists[1] believe that this energetic musical style emerged from the Latin jazz scene in New York City in the 1950, 1960s, and 1970s. Others say that it emerged from Cuban and other music forms, such as *son,* a kind of Cuban music, or *merengue,* a music and dance style first popular in the Dominican Republic. Whatever the origin of the term, it seems that musicians distanced themselves from it, at least at first. Famed Latin musician Tito Puente, for example, was widely quoted as saying, "The only salsa I know is sold in a bottle called ketchup. I play Cuban music."

---

[1] Musicologists study the history of music.

1. The word "salsa" as used in the passage is closest in meaning to

   (A) a kind of sauce used to enliven Latin food

   (B) a musical form derived directly from Dominican music

   (C) a style of popular Latin dance music

   (D) a name musicians used to describe an emerging Latin dance music

2. The word "its" in the passage refers to

   (A) music styles'

   (B) salsa music's

   (C) Cuba's

   (D) locations'

3. According to paragraph 1, which of the following is NOT a possible origin of salsa music?

   (A) *Merengue* music from the Dominican Republic

   (B) Latin jazz in the United States

   (C) *Son* music from Cuba

   (D) Spicy sauces from Puerto Rico

4. Why does the author include this quotation in paragraph 1: "The only salsa I know is sold in a bottle called ketchup. I play Cuban music"?

Ⓐ To show the importance of food in Latin culture

Ⓑ To show that salsa is not the real name of this music style

Ⓒ To show that salsa performers did not invent this term

Ⓓ To show that Tito Puente was not really a performer of Latin music

PARAGRAPH 2

If the term didn't come from the musicians themselves, where did it come from? One of the first recorded uses of the term is the name of a Latin music program on local television in New York City, in the 1950s, hosted by a famous Latin music promoter. The music featured on that show included styles not now typically associated with salsa, such as certain Mexican traditional musical forms. Thus, the origin of this term may have been with music promoters involved in the presentation of the musicians' new stylings to the public, who struggled to find ways to package and present a new and emerging music in ways that non-Latin audiences could relate to. Adopting a term such as *salsa* to label the genre, even as the genre was being created and defined, would be helpful in encouraging the new genre's success because this word is easily pronounced by non-Spanish speakers and evokes such powerful associations. Later, the term was adopted by musicians, but for commercial reasons. They wanted their musical styles to be associated with the commercially accepted salsa. Even Tito Puente himself began to describe his music as salsa, but not for many years.

5. Why did musicians eventually adopt the term *salsa* to describe their music?

Ⓐ The musicians wanted to make their music appealing to a broad audience.

Ⓑ Music promoters forced the musicians to accept the term.

Ⓒ They could incorporate other kinds of music, such as Mexican styles, in salsa.

Ⓓ They liked the association of their rich, rhythmic music with exotic food.

6. In stating that at one time music called salsa "included styles not now typically associated with salsa," the author means that

Ⓐ musicians didn't want their music labeled as salsa

Ⓑ the meaning of the term *salsa* included more than music

Ⓒ the meaning of the term *salsa* evolved over time

Ⓓ salsa is not a true variety of music

7. The word "who" in the passage refers to

Ⓐ musicians

Ⓑ music promoters

Ⓒ stylings

Ⓓ the public

8. Which of the following sentences best expresses the essential information in the highlighted sentence in paragraph 2? Incorrect choices change the meaning in important ways or leave out essential information.

Ⓐ The term *salsa*, which had powerful associations, was adopted because it would help define the genre, which was crucial for its success among non-Spanish speakers.

Ⓑ Adopting a label such as *salsa* for this new genre, even as it was being created, would help it succeed because it is a term with powerful associations that is easily pronounced by non-speakers of Spanish.

Ⓒ Even as it was being created and defined, the genre had powerful associations with non-Spanish speakers, and a name that was easy for them to pronounce was important to its future success.

Ⓓ Salsa music was created to have powerful associations, and adapting a label that was easy for non-Spanish speakers to pronounce would be critical to its success.

While it seems that the term *salsa* was invented in the 1950s or later, salsa grew out of a rich tradition of Cuban and Latin dance music in the New York City area that long predated the coining of the term now used to describe it. A number of Latin dance bands performed throughout the city beginning in the 1930s and 1940s. These bands had wide appeal. One of the most popular of these dance bands was led by Spanish-born and Cuban-raised Xavier Cugat. His band performed at the exclusive Waldorf-Astoria hotel in New York for more than sixteen years, drawing a diverse audience. Cugat, a classically trained musician, was criticized for the commercial appeal of his music, but he responded by saying that he would rather play his music and then sit by his swimming pool than play classical music and starve. In fact, many people, including Cugat, claim that Cugat was the inventor of the salsa music style. Many musicians who would go on to become famous salsa musicians got some of their most important experiences performing in Cugat's band. Tito Puente, for example, played for Cugat early in his career and, after Cugat's retirement, took over and led his band.

P A R A G R A P H 3

9. According to the passage, why did Xavier Cugat say that he would rather play his music and then sit by his swimming pool than play classical music and starve?

   (A) People wanted him to make classical music more popular.

   (B) Cugat's music was not popular or successful.

   (C) People criticized him for not using his training in classical music.

   (D) Cugat did not think that classical music was good.

10. The main purpose of paragraph 3 is to

   (A) explain the history of word *salsa* as a musical term

   (B) explain the development of salsa music in New York City

   (C) give reasons for salsa's popularity in New York City

   (D) explain the importance of Xavier Cugat in the history of salsa

P
A
R
A
G
R
A
P
H

4

Salsa music included singers, both male and female. Of these, probably the most famous is Celia Cruz. Born in Cuba, Cruz developed an interest in music as a small child, but her parents encouraged her to become a teacher instead, so she focused on her studies. However, as a teenager she was told by one of her teachers that she could make more money in one day as an entertainer than a teacher makes in a month, so she became more serious about music as a career. She began performing in singing contests on a radio station and won several prizes. Her first prize was a cake! As she continued to perform and win prizes, she began to get the attention of other musicians. Eventually, she joined a band and performed all over Latin America. After the Cuban revolution, she refused to return to Cuba and settled in the United States, where her singing became more and more popular. Many people called her the Queen of Salsa.

11. Why did Celia Cruz become more serious about popular music as a career?

Ⓐ She won a valuable prize in her first singing contest on the radio.

Ⓑ One of her teachers told her that careers in entertainment paid well.

Ⓒ She rebelled against her parents, who wanted her to be a teacher.

Ⓓ She loved listening to and singing popular Cuban music as a young child.

12. The information in the passage about Xavier Cugat and Celia Cruz suggests which of the following?

Ⓐ Musicians are not very interested in commercial success.

Ⓑ Musicians take financial considerations into account in their career decisions.

Ⓒ Careers that do not pay well can be rewarding in other ways.

Ⓓ Musicians did not like the term *salsa* and preferred to call their work Cuban music.

While it seems that the term *salsa* was invented in the 1950s or later, salsa grew out of a rich tradition of Cuban and Latin dance music in the New York City area that long predated the coining of the term now used to describe it. A number of Latin dance bands performed throughout the city beginning in the 1930s and 1940s. These bands had wide appeal. One of the most popular of these dance bands was led by Spanish-born and Cuban-raised Xavier Cugat. **A** His band performed at the exclusive Waldorf-Astoria hotel in New York for more than sixteen years, drawing a diverse audience. **B** Cugat, a classically trained musician, was criticized for the commercial appeal of his music, but he responded by saying that he would rather play his music and then sit by his swimming pool than play classical music and starve. **C** In fact, many people, including Cugat, claim that Cugat was the inventor of the salsa music style. Many musicians who would go on to become famous salsa musicians got some of their most important experiences performing in Cugat's band. Tito Puente, for example, played for Cugat early in his career and, after Cugat's retirement, took over and led his band. **D**

13. Look at the four squares (■) that indicate where the following sentence could be added to the third paragraph of the passage.

    Cugat further popularized this exciting, energetic music through live performances nationwide and starring roles in major Hollywood movies.

    Where would the sentence best fit?

14. An introductory sentence for a brief summary of the passage is provided. Complete the summary by selecting the THREE answer choices that express important ideas in the passage. Some sentences do not belong in the summary, because they express ideas that are not presented in the passage or are minor details in the passage. *This question is worth 2 points.*

Write the letters of your answer choices in the spaces where they belong.

> **The passage discusses the origins of salsa music.**
>
> •
>
> •
>
> •

Answer Choices

A Tito Puente did not like to call his music *salsa* at first.

B Salsa is a rhythmic and exciting Latin dance music.

C Xavier Cugat is one of the most famous of all salsa performers.

D The music has roots in Cuba, the Dominican Republic, and the United States.

E Salsa music was not very popular or successful commercially.

F The origin of the name *salsa* is not completely clear.

Give yourself 20 minutes to read the passage and answer Items 15–28.

As long as there have been farmers, farmers have saved seeds from the current year's crop to plant for the next year's crop. In fact, saving seeds is one of the oldest activities continuously performed by humans. Organized farming began during the Neolithic Revolution, the time about 12,000 years ago (8,000 to 10,000 BCE) when humans began to organize permanent settlements, cultivate crops, and raise animals for food. As long as farmers have been growing crops, they have been saving their seeds.

While farming has changed significantly over time, the need to save seeds is still a vital practice. However, this ancient practice has changed recently, for two reasons. First, some agricultural companies, which sell patented, often genetically modified seeds, often insist that farmers can no longer save seeds from one year's crop for the next, but need to buy new seeds from the manufacturer each year. Farmers and scientists praise the high yields and pest resistance of these seeds, but wonder about the wisdom of ending such an ancient practice as saving seeds. In fact, the companies' demand that farmers no longer save seeds has been highly controversial. This is not the principal concern about genetically modified plants, since critics believe that the modified plants may be inherently harmful or dangerous and may reduce biodiversity as the large number of biologically diverse varieties of important food crops such as rice, wheat, and corn are replaced with only a few hybrid varieties. Critics of genetically modified crops believe that the lack of diverse strains of these key foodstuffs makes us vulnerable to catastrophe. In fact, the small number of highly cultivated hybrid and genetically engineered varieties make the world's food supply highly susceptible to disease or pests. The lack of biodiversity, in fact, is a major risk factor of widespread use of hybrid and genetically modified seeds. In the case of wheat, there are hundreds of thousands of varieties of wild and cultivated wheat, but only a few are in active use in agriculture.

This situation has made another ancient agricultural practice, the seed repository, take on new importance. A seed repository is a safe place where a government, society, or culture can store a backup supply of seeds in case a natural or man-made catastrophe destroys crops and farmers' saved seeds, or if crops fail in successive years and farmers run out of saved seeds. Nowadays, the repositories store the seeds in dry conditions and subzero temperatures to preserve them. Some scientists believe that civilizations such as ancient Egypt, which had a highly developed agricultural economy, maintained seed repositories for just such purposes. Critics point out that the repositories, which typically maintain only small supplies of seeds, may not be able to replenish seed supplies in case of a catastrophe. However, they preserve important biodiversity that safeguards traditional plant varieties and may help scientists continue to develop new and improved hybrid seeds.

At present, there are about 1,400 seed repositories around the world. While this large number of repositories ensures that a wide variety of plant diversity will be maintained, there are still limitations. Seed repositories are very expensive to maintain, especially for third world countries, which have the largest portion of the world's biodiversity. In addition, only certain kinds of seeds can be stored in the cold, dry conditions of a repository for extended periods. Some seeds, such as cocoa and rubber tree seeds, cannot be stored in repositories. To preserve biodiversity among those species, scientists need to grow and regrow this kind of seed continually. However, even longer-lasting seeds deteriorate over time. Those seeds need to be sprouted and grown periodically, in carefully controlled environments to avoid cross-breeding with other varieties, and new seeds must be gathered and stored.

Redundancy of seed depositories is important, too. In case one depository is damaged or destroyed, similar seeds need to be available in another location. Recently, a seed repository in the Philippines was destroyed in a hurricane, and the contents of another one in Thailand were damaged by a flood. Yet another seed repository, in Iraq, was badly damaged during war. To ensure a backup supply of seeds, the Norwegian government recently opened a state-of-the-art seed repository north of the Arctic Circle. The repository serves to keep a supply of every kind of seed in the other first-line repositories around the world. To keep these valuable seeds safe, the repository is built into a mountain and seeds are stored at a constant low temperature. Though the seeds in these repositories represent only a fraction of the world's biodiversity, they are a valuable tool in preserving biodiversity for future generations.

PARAGRAPH 1

As long as there have been farmers, farmers have saved seeds from the current year's crop to plant for the next year's crop. In fact, saving seeds is one of the oldest activities continuously performed by humans. Organized farming began during the Neolithic Revolution, the time about 12,000 years ago (8,000 to 10,000 BCE) when humans began to organize permanent settlements, cultivate crops, and raise animals for food. As long as farmers have been growing crops, they have been saving their seeds.

15. Historically, why have farmers saved seeds?

Ⓐ To organize permanent settlements

Ⓑ To feed them to animals they grew for food

Ⓒ To save money

Ⓓ To use them in subsequent years' crops

16. The word "their" in the passage refers to

Ⓐ the crops'

Ⓑ the animals'

Ⓒ the settlements'

Ⓓ the companies'

P
A
R
A
G
R
A
P
H

2

While farming has changed significantly over time, the need to save seeds is still a vital practice. However, this ancient practice has changed recently, for two reasons. First, some agricultural companies, which sell patented, often genetically modified seeds, often insist that farmers can no longer save seeds from one year's crop for the next, but need to buy new seeds from the manufacturer each year. Farmers and scientists praise the high yields and pest resistance of these seeds, but wonder about the wisdom of ending such an ancient practice as saving seeds. In fact, the companies' demand that farmers no longer save seeds has been highly controversial. This is not the principal concern about genetically modified plants, since critics believe that the modified plants may be inherently harmful or dangerous and may reduce biodiversity as the large number of biologically diverse varieties of important food crops such as rice, wheat, and corn are replaced with only a few hybrid varieties. Critics of genetically modified crops believe that the lack of diverse strains of these key foodstuffs makes us vulnerable to catastrophe. In fact, the small number of highly cultivated hybrid and genetically engineered varieties make the world's food supply highly susceptible to disease or pests. The lack of biodiversity, in fact, is a major risk factor of widespread use of hybrid and genetically modified seeds. In the case of wheat, there are hundreds of thousands of varieties of wild and cultivated wheat, but only a few are in active use in agriculture.

17. Which of the following is NOT a reason people are concerned about company demands that farmers buy hybrid and genetically engineered seeds each year, rather than saving them?

(A) Buying new seeds each year is costly for farmers.

(B) Saving no seeds disrupts an ancient, time-tested practice.

(C) Farmers will not have saved seeds in case of a disaster.

(D) Farmers are impressed by the high yields of many hybrid seeds.

18. Which of the following best expresses the essential information in the highlighted sentence? Incorrect choices change the meaning in important ways or leave out essential information.

Ⓐ This is not the principal concern, because critics believe that the modified plants may be inherently dangerous, and as hybrid varieties of rice, wheat, and corn replace the large number of biologically diverse varieties, biodiversity will be reduced.

Ⓑ This is not the principal concern about genetically modified plants, because as the inherently harmful hybrid varieties of rice, wheat, and corn replace the large number of biologically diverse varieties, biodiversity will be reduced.

Ⓒ This is not the principal concern, since critics believe that genetically modified varieties may be inherently harmful and reduce biodiversity as biologically diverse varieties of important food crops such as rice, wheat, and corn replace the hybrid varieties.

Ⓓ This is not the principal concern, since the large number of hybrid and genetically modified varieties of important food crops such as rice, wheat, and corn replace biologically diverse varieties.

19. The word "strains" in the passage is closest in meaning to

Ⓐ separates

Ⓑ painful injuries

Ⓒ efforts

Ⓓ varieties

20. The word "susceptible" in the passage is closest in meaning to

Ⓐ likely to believe someone or something

Ⓑ likely to be criticized by someone

Ⓒ likely to be disagreed with

Ⓓ likely to be harmed by something

P
A
R
A
G
R
A
P
H

3

This situation has made another ancient agricultural practice, the seed repository, take on new importance. A seed repository is a safe place where a government, society, or culture can store a backup supply of seeds in case a natural or man-made catastrophe destroys crops and farmers' saved seeds, or if crops fail in successive years and farmers run out of saved seeds. The repositories store the seeds in dry conditions and subzero temperatures to preserve them. Some scientists believe that civilizations such as ancient Egypt, which had a highly developed agricultural economy, maintained seed repositories for just such purposes. Critics point out that the repositories, which typically maintain only small supplies of seeds, may not be able to replenish seed supplies in case of a catastrophe. However, they preserve important biodiversity that safeguards traditional plant varieties and may help scientists continue to develop new and improved hybrid seeds.

21. Why does the author mention seed repositories in ancient Egypt in paragraph 3?

Ⓐ To show that seed repositories did not prevent ancient Egypt from collapsing

Ⓑ To show that maintaining seed repositories is a long-standing practice

Ⓒ To show that ancient Egyptians grew genetically modified crops

Ⓓ To show that ancient Egyptians did not trust their farming skills

22. The word "they" in the passage refers to

Ⓐ critics

Ⓑ scientists

Ⓒ ancient Egyptians

Ⓓ repositories

At present, there are about 1,400 seed repositories around the world. While this large number of repositories ensures that a wide variety of plant diversity will be maintained, there are still limitations. Seed repositories are very expensive to maintain, especially for third world countries, which have the largest portion of the world's biodiversity. In addition, only certain kinds of seeds can be stored in the cold, dry conditions of a repository for extended periods. Some seeds, such as cocoa and rubber tree seeds, cannot be stored in repositories. To preserve biodiversity among those species, scientists need to grow and regrow this kind of seed continually. However, even longer-lasting seeds deteriorate over time. Those seeds need to be sprouted and grown periodically, in carefully controlled environments to avoid cross-breeding with other varieties, and new seeds must be gathered and stored.

23. Why do seeds in repositories need to be sprouted, grown, and replaced with new seeds periodically?

Ⓐ They are needed to replace seeds damaged in repositories in the Philippines, Thailand, and Iraq.

Ⓑ All seeds suffer damage after being stored for long periods, so they need to be replaced.

Ⓒ Seeds from plants such as the rubber tree cannot be stored successfully.

Ⓓ The repositories need to remove old seed varieties to make room for new hybrids.

24. Which of the following can be inferred from the passage?

Ⓐ Seed repositories will never be completely effective in preserving seed supplies and biodiversity.

Ⓑ Ancient practices are good models for us to follow today.

Ⓒ Seed repositories are too expensive to justify the limited benefits.

Ⓓ Critics are overly suspicious of hybrid and genetically modified seeds and do not understand their benefits.

P
A
R
A
G
R
A
P
H

4

At present, there are about 1,400 seed repositories around the world. While this large number of repositories ensures that a wide variety of plant diversity will be maintained, there are still limitations. ■ Seed repositories are very expensive to maintain, especially for third world countries, which have the largest portion of the world's biodiversity. ■ In addition, only certain kinds of seeds can be stored in the cold, dry conditions of a repository for extended periods. ■ Some seeds, such as cocoa and rubber tree seeds, cannot be stored in repositories. ■ To preserve biodiversity among those species, scientists need to grow and regrow this kind of seed continually. However, even longer-lasting seeds deteriorate over time. Those seeds need to be sprouted and grown periodically, in carefully controlled environments to avoid cross-breeding with other varieties, and new seeds must be gathered and stored.

25. Look at the four squares (■) that indicate where the following sentence could be added to paragraph 4.

These seeds, called recalcitrant seeds, are damaged by the cold, dry conditions of the repository.

Where would the sentence best fit?

P
A
R
A
G
R
A
P
H

5

Redundancy of seed depositories is important, too. In case one depository is damaged or destroyed, similar seeds need to be available in another location. Recently, a seed repository in the Philippines was destroyed in a hurricane, and the contents of another one in Thailand were damaged by a flood. Yet another seed repository, in Iraq, was badly damaged during war. To ensure a backup supply of seeds, the Norwegian government recently opened a state-of-the-art seed repository north of the Arctic Circle. The repository serves to keep a supply of every kind of seed in the other first-line repositories around the world. To keep these valuable seeds safe, the repository is built into a mountain and seeds are stored at a constant low temperature. Though the seeds in these repositories represent only a fraction of the world's biodiversity, they are a valuable tool in preserving biodiversity for future generations.

26. Why does the author of the passage mention damage to seed repositories in Thailand, Iraq, and the Philippines?

(A) To show that multiple repositories are needed to ensure that seed supplies are safe

(B) To criticize the lack of appropriate safeguards in the countries

(C) To prove that seed repositories will never safeguard the world's seed supply

(D) To prove that building a seed repository north of the Arctic Circle is a waste of time

27. Which of the following seeds would most likely NOT be stored in a seed repository?

(A) Corn

(B) Rice

(C) Wheat

(D) Cocoa

28. An introductory sentence for a brief summary of the passage is provided. Complete the summary by selecting the THREE answer choices that express important ideas in the passage. Some sentences do not belong in the summary, because they express ideas that are not presented in the passage or are minor details in the passage. *This item is worth 2 points.*

Write the letters of your answer choices in the spaces where they belong.

> **The passage discusses the importance of seed repositories.**
>
> •
>
> •
>
> •

Answer Choices

A Farmers and societies have long saved seeds.

B Seed repositories cannot safely store most kinds of seeds.

C Seed repositories, safe places for storing seeds, are important for preserving biodiversity.

D No one should eat food from genetically modified seeds.

E Seed repositories in Thailand, the Philippines, and Iraq were badly damaged recently.

F Seed repositories are important in case a catastrophe disrupts seed supplies.

Give yourself 20 minutes to read the passage and answer Items 29–42.

In July 1936, a military uprising in Spain led to the outbreak of a long and bloody civil war that lasted nearly three years and claimed the lives of hundreds of thousands, both military and civilian. The outbreak of this conflict had its roots in social and political divisions that emerged and deepened during the preceding years of the Second Spanish Republic.

The Second Spanish Republic was founded upon the overthrow of King Alfonse XIII in 1931. The first two years were dominated by a reformist agenda backed by a large majority of the people. During this time, the government made many important labor and social reforms. The government reformed land ownership, granted freedom of speech and association, gave women the right to vote, and reduced the enormous power and influence of the church. Some of the reforms, particularly those related to the military and the church, caused opposition to emerge. During this time, many extremist, ultraconservative organizations were founded, and violence increased. In the elections of 1933, conservatives gained power. During the following two years, the conservative leaders began to reverse many of the reforms. It was clear, however, that many Spaniards continued to support the reformist agenda of the first two years of the Republic. In fact, Spanish society was deeply divided over the reforms and their vision for Spain. In early 1936, new elections were held, and reformist groups gained control of the government again, but only by a narrow margin. The new government continued the reformist agenda, even as opposition, political instability, and violence became more and more prevalent.

In the meantime, four army generals began to organize plans for a military coup to end the republic and place a conservative government in power permanently. The four generals, Francisco Franco, Emilio Mola, José Sanjurjo, and Manuel Goded, had all been previously implicated in antigovernment activity and had been relieved of their prominent positions. However, the government did not consider the generals a risk, and instead of jailing them or removing them from the army, sent the four to less important posts away from the capital, Madrid. But from their distant assignments in places such as the Canary Islands, the city of Pamplona, and the Balearic Islands, these generals were able to plan and organize a military uprising secretively.

Their plan was to lead uprisings in their local posts, seize control of the Spanish army in colonial Morocco, and call for a general military uprising in the rest of Spain. They believed that popular support for the uprising would be strong because citizens, tired of the violence and controversial reforms of the church, would back the uprising. The generals accelerated their plans when in July 1936 the assassination of a prominent conservative leader provided a pretext for an uprising. The uprising began on July 17–18, 1936. The generals hoped to depict the uprising as a spontaneous patriotic uprising of the people at large. General Franco flew from the Canary Islands to Morocco and took control of the colonial army, as planned. The other generals seized control of key military installations. The generals believed that the rest of the army would follow their lead, but they underestimated support for the government in key locations throughout the country. In major cities such as Barcelona, Madrid, and Valencia, the army failed to rise or leaders loyal to the government defeated the uprising and retained control of the army. Rather than accepting defeat, the coup leaders began a long war of attrition using the forces that had rebelled. Madrid was surrounded by Franco's troops, making it difficult for food or supplies to enter. People starved in Barcelona, Madrid, and other government-controlled areas as the rebels tightened their grip. The relentless attacks wore down the people's resistance. General Franco became the leader of the military effort and consolidated political control as the other generals died in wartime casualties.

The uprising received major attention worldwide. The rebel generals received support from Nazi Germany and Fascist Italy. Both countries sent supplies to the rebel army. Direct military support included bombing raids conducted by the Italian Air Force, which stationed planes in the Balearic Islands, off the northeastern Spanish coast. The legitimate government in Madrid appealed to global powers for their support, but it was rebuffed. Nevertheless, thousands of volunteers from democratic countries traveled to Spain to fight on the side of the Republic.

P
A
R
A
G
R
A
P
H

2

The Second Spanish Republic was founded upon the overthrow of King Alfonse XIII in 1931. The first two years were dominated by a reformist agenda backed by a large majority of the people. During this time, the government made many important labor and social reforms. The government reformed land ownership, granted freedom of speech and association, gave women the right to vote, and reduced the enormous power and influence of the church. Some of the reforms, particularly those related to the military and the church, caused opposition to emerge. During this time, many extremist, ultraconservative organizations were founded, and violence increased. In the elections of 1933, conservatives gained power. During the following two years, the conservative leaders began to reverse many of the reforms. It was clear, however, that many Spaniards continued to support the reformist agenda of the first two years of the Republic. In fact, Spanish society was deeply divided over the reforms and their vision for Spain. In early 1936, new elections were held, and reformist groups gained control of the government again, but only by a narrow margin. The new government continued the reformist agenda, even as opposition, political instability, and violence became more and more prevalent.

29. In the first two years of the Second Spanish Republic, the government made all of these reforms EXCEPT:

   Ⓐ granting women the right to vote

   Ⓑ reducing the power of the church

   Ⓒ broadening land ownership

   Ⓓ strengthening the army

30. When the author says that the government "continued the reformist agenda, even as political instability and violence became more and more prevalent," the author means that the government continued to enact changes

   Ⓐ despite the growth of public unrest

   Ⓑ to quiet the increasing social disharmony

   Ⓒ to increase support among reform-minded citizens

   Ⓓ to avoid a military uprising

31. Which of the following can be inferred from the passage about popular support for the Second Spanish Republic?

(A) Most people supported the government at first, but opinion was divided by 1936.

(B) The government enjoyed the unwavering support of the military until the uprising of 1936.

(C) The church supported the government because its social reforms helped people.

(D) People supported the government until it lost the support of the military.

32. Why does the author mention in paragraph 2 that in 1936 reformers gained control of the government, but only by a narrow margin?

(A) To show that the government lacked public support and was ready to collapse

(B) To show that military force was needed to end the unpopular reforms

(C) To show that the government was ignoring the will of most people

(D) To show how divisions among the people caused the uprising to become a civil war

P A R A G R A P H 3

   In the meantime, four army generals began to organize plans for a military coup to end the republic and place a conservative government in power permanently. The four generals, Francisco Franco, Emilio Mola, José Sanjurjo, and Manuel Goded, had all been previously implicated in antigovernment activity and had been relieved of their prominent positions. However, the government did not consider the generals a risk, and instead of jailing them or removing them from the army, sent the four to less important posts away from the capital, Madrid. But from their distant assignments in places such as the Canary Islands, the city of Pamplona, and the Balearic Islands, these generals were able to plan and organize a military uprising secretively.

33. The phrase "relieved of" in the passage is closest in meaning to

(A) returned to

(B) removed from

(C) feeling relief from

(D) promoted to

34. At the outbreak of the Spanish Civil War, the leaders of the military uprising were posted to all of these locations EXCEPT:

(A) Madrid

(B) the Canary Islands

(C) the Balearic Islands

(D) Pamplona

P
A
R
A
G
R
A
P
H

4

Their plan was to lead uprisings in their local posts, seize control of the Spanish army in colonial Morocco, and call for a general military uprising in the rest of Spain. The generals believed that popular support for the uprising would be strong because citizens, tired of the violence and controversial reforms of the church, would back the uprising. They accelerated their plans when in July 1936 the assassination of a prominent conservative leader provided a pretext for an uprising. The uprising began on July 17–18, 1936. The generals hoped to depict the uprising as a spontaneous patriotic uprising of the people at large. General Franco flew from the Canary Islands to Morocco and took control of the colonial army, as planned. The other generals seized control of key military installations. The generals believed that the rest of the army would follow their lead, but they underestimated support for the government in key locations throughout the country. In major cities such as Barcelona, Madrid, and Valencia, the army failed to rise or leaders loyal to the government defeated the uprising and retained control of the army. Rather than accepting defeat, the coup leaders began a long war of attrition using the forces that had rebelled. Madrid was surrounded by Franco's troops, making it difficult for food or supplies to enter. People starved in Barcelona, Madrid, and other government-controlled areas as the rebels tightened their grip. The relentless attacks wore down the people's resistance. General Franco became the leader of the military effort and consolidated political control as the other generals died in wartime casualties.

35. The word "they" refers to

(A) the army

(B) uprisings

(C) leaders

(D) the generals

36. What was the goal of the generals' plot?

　Ⓐ Eliminate extremist conservative organizations

　Ⓑ Start a long, bloody civil war in Spain

　Ⓒ Avenge the death of a prominent conservative leader

　Ⓓ Replace the Republic with a conservative government

37. According to the passage, the generals accelerated their plan after the assassination of a conservative political leader because

　Ⓐ the generals wanted to retaliate against the government for the assassination

　Ⓑ the assassination provided a reason for the generals to move against the government

　Ⓒ the generals feared they would be sent to distant posts after the assassination

　Ⓓ the government wanted to continue its reforms of the church

38. The word "attrition" in the passage is closest in meaning to

　Ⓐ win by making many surprise attacks

　Ⓑ win by sending in overpowering force

　Ⓒ win by wearing down the enemy's resistance

　Ⓓ win by attacking by sea

39. Which of the following best expresses the essential information in the highlighted sentence? Incorrect answer choices change the meaning in important ways or leave out essential information.

(A) The generals underestimated support for the uprising and believed that the rest of the army would follow their example, but in key locations, the army failed to rise or loyal leaders defeated the uprising and retained control of the army.

(B) The generals believed that in key locations leaders loyal to the government would not follow the example of the generals and would fail to rise or defeat the uprising and retain control of the army.

(C) The generals underestimated support for the government and believed that the army would follow their example, but in key locations, the army failed to rise or the uprising was defeated and the government retained control of the army.

(D) The generals were confident about the army following their example, and in key locations local leaders rose up and gave control of the army to the rebels.

Their plan was to lead uprisings in their local posts, seize control of the Spanish army in colonial Morocco, and call for a general military uprising in the rest of Spain. They believed that popular support for the uprising would be strong because citizens, tired of the violence and controversial reforms of the church, would back the uprising. **A** The generals accelerated their plans when in July 1936 the assassination of a prominent conservative leader provided a pretext for an uprising. **B** The uprising began on July 17–18, 1936. The generals hoped to depict the uprising as a spontaneous patriotic uprising of the people at large. General Franco flew from the Canary Islands to Morocco and took control of the colonial army, as planned. The other generals seized control of key military installations. The generals believed that the rest of the army would follow their lead, but they underestimated support for the government in key locations throughout the country. In major cities such as Barcelona, Madrid, and Valencia, the army failed to rise or leaders loyal to the government defeated the uprising and retained control of the army. Rather than accepting defeat, the coup leaders began a long war of attrition using the forces that had rebelled. **C** Madrid was surrounded by Franco's troops, making it difficult for food or supplies to enter. People starved in Barcelona, Madrid, and other government-controlled areas as the rebels tightened their grip. The relentless attacks wore down the people's resistance. **D** General Franco became the leader of the military effort and consolidated political control as the other generals died in wartime casualties.

40. Look at the four squares (■) that indicate where the following sentence could be added to the fourth paragraph of the passage.

> **General Franco moved the colonial army from Morocco to Spain and used it to attack the government.**

Where would the sentence best fit?

The uprising received major attention worldwide. The rebel generals received support from Nazi Germany and Fascist Italy. Both countries sent supplies to the rebel army. Direct military support included bombing raids conducted by the Italian Air Force, which stationed planes in the Balearic Islands, off the northeastern Spanish coast. The legitimate government in Madrid appealed to global powers for their support, but it was rebuffed. Nevertheless, thousands of volunteers from democratic countries traveled to Spain to fight on the side of the Republic.

41. Which of the following is an example that the author gives of ways international support helped the Republic?

Ⓐ Fascist Italy bombed cities in Spain.

Ⓑ Volunteers went to Spain to fight.

Ⓒ Nazi Germany sent supplies.

Ⓓ Democratic governments sent troops.

42. Select from the seven phrases following the two phrases that correctly characterize supporters of the Republic and the three phrases that correctly characterize opponents of the Republic. Two of the phrases will NOT be used.

Complete the following table to summarize information about supporters and opponents of the Spanish government. Match the appropriate statements to the group with which they are associated.

SUPPORTERS OF THE REPUBLIC	OPPONENTS OF THE REPUBLIC
Select 2	Select 3
•	•
•	•
	•

Answer Choices

Ⓐ They were unhappy about changes to the church and the army.

Ⓑ They had broad support in 1936.

Ⓒ They wanted social and labor reforms.

Ⓓ They believed that the church was too powerful.

Ⓔ They won elections in 1933.

Ⓕ They wanted to start a civil war.

Ⓖ They included generals who had rebelled previously.

Answers and Explanations for the TOEFL iBT Practice Reading section begin on page 222.

TOEFL iBT Reading
Personalized Study Planner

Use your answers to the TOEFL iBT Practice Reading section and this chart to focus your preparation for the actual TOEFL iBT. Follow these steps:

1. Review all your correct and incorrect answers in the Answers and Explanations, which begin on page 222.
2. In the chart, circle the number of each item you answered incorrectly.
3. Review again the Answers and Explanations for each item you answered incorrectly, this time in the order they are grouped in the chart.
4. For each item type where you want to improve your performance, study the pages listed in the third column.

ITEM NUMBERS	ITEM TYPE	STUDY PAGES
5, 9, 11, 15, 23, 30, 36, 37, 41	Factual information	109–116
3, 17, 27, 29, 34	Negative factual information	116–121
1, 6, 19, 20, 33, 38	Vocabulary	122–131
2, 7, 16, 22, 35	Reference	132–139
8, 18, 39	Sentence simplification	139–148
12, 24, 31	Inference	154–158
4, 10, 21, 26, 32	Rhetorical purpose	159–162
13, 25, 40	Insert text	163–167
14, 28	Prose summary	170–176
42	Fill in a table	176–182

TOEFL iBT READING
Answers and Explanations

Exercise 1: Scanning (Page 113)

1. 2012
2. 2007
3. a climatologist (A scientist is also possible.)
4. 2050
5. 1980
6. over Antarctica

7. 0.8° C
8. Thailand, United States, and Europe (Texas, Midwest, and South are also possible.)
9. Thailand
10. Texas

Exercise 2: Factual Information Items (Page 114)

1. **D Light from the sun is blocked by the moon.** Option D is correct because in a solar eclipse the moon blocks light from the sun, casting a shadow on Earth. Therefore, the other options are incorrect.

2. **A The sun looks like a dark circle was cut from it.** Option A is stated directly in the passage and is therefore correct. Options B and C are incorrect because these are characteristics of a total solar eclipse. Option D is incorrect because it is a characteristic of a partial lunar eclipse.

3. **A The moon appears darker in an umbral eclipse than in a penumbral eclipse.** Option A is correct because in an umbral eclipse, Earth's shadow is cast directly on the moon. Option B is incorrect because in a penumbral eclipse, only the penumbra, a partial shadow, is cast on the moon. Options C and D are incorrect because both a penumbral and umbral eclipse can be partial or total, according to the information in the passage.

4. **D A senelion** Option D is correct because the passage states that a senelion occurs "under only highly exceptional conditions." Therefore, the other options are incorrect.

5. **C The sun and eclipsed moon can be seen at the same time.** According to the passage, "A senelion is an eclipse that occurs when the sun and moon are opposite one another on the horizon and are aligned so that Earth's shadow hits the moon." Therefore, Option C is correct. Option A is characteristic of a solar eclipse and a senelion is a lunar eclipse, so this option is incorrect. Option B is characteristic of a total solar eclipse and a senelion is a kind of lunar eclipse, so this option is incorrect. In addition, according to the passage, a senelion is the only time a lunar eclipse can take place with daylight visible. Option D is not supported by the passage. The passage gives no indication of whether a senelion can be partial or total.

Exercise 3: Negative Factual Information Items (Page 120)

1. **A many interior walls and columns** Option A is correct because interior walls and columns are features of older styles of buildings that predate Mies's buildings and that were made unnecessary by the steel girder frame he used. The remaining options are all mentioned in the passage as being features of Mies's architecture and are therefore incorrect.

2. **D elaborate carved stonework** Elaborate carved stonework was a feature of older styles; therefore, Option D is correct. The other options (marble, plate glass, and chrome-plated metal) are all mentioned in the passage as materials Mies used.

3. **A curving lines** Option A is correct because Mies used straight lines and cubic shapes. Curving lines were features of prior styles. The remaining options are all examples of features Mies used in his buildings.

4. **A** **steel girders** Option A is correct because the passage says, "His style made extensive use of steel girders to support buildings, rather than stone or brick walls." Options B and C are incorrect because the steel girders made interior columns and thick, heavy walls unnecessary. Option D is incorrect because the passage states that brick and stone were used in older building styles.

5. **D** **straight lines and cubical spaces** Option D is correct because the passage says that straight lines and cubical spaces were features of Mies's work. The passage mentions the other options in relation to older building styles.

Exercise 4: Vocabulary Items (Page 125)

1. **A** **having to do with the sun** Option A is correct because in a solar eclipse, the sun is partially or fully blocked. *Having to do with the sun* is the phrase that most closely expresses this meaning. Option B is incorrect because a lunar eclipse occurs when Earth's shadow is blocking sunlight from reaching the moon. For this reason, options C and D are also not possible.

2. **A** **in a row** Option A is correct because in several places, the passage uses the phrase "in a row" to describe the position of Earth, the moon, and the sun. Options B, C, and D are not possible because Earth and the moon are nearly 300,000 miles apart, both are millions of miles away from the sun, and the bodies do not become close together or touch.

3. **D** **a lunar eclipse in which sunlight is totally blocked by Earth's shadow** Option D is correct because the umbra is the shadow cast directly by Earth. Therefore, an umbral total eclipse happens when Earth's shadow totally blocks the sun's light from falling on the moon. Option A is incorrect because the penumbra is only a partial shadow. Some indirect light is able to get through. Option B is incorrect because a shadow of varying darkness is a characteristic of a penumbral eclipse, in which areas closer to the umbra appear darker than areas farther away. Option C describes conditions for a total solar eclipse, not a total lunar eclipse, so it is incorrect.

4. **A** **the conditions for such an eclipse seldom or rarely occur** Option A is correct because the passage makes it clear that this is the only time an eclipse will be visible during the day, and that the next similar eclipse will not be for eighty-four more years. Option B is incorrect because the cause of the eclipse has not changed—Earth and the moon are aligned, with Earth in the middle. Options C and D are incorrect because *the conditions* refers to the positions of the space objects, and not the viewing conditions.

5. **B** **at the same time** Option B is correct because the words *together* and *at the same time* in nearby sentences indicate that this option is nearest in meaning to the target word. Option A does not make sense. Options C and D are contradicted by the passage. The passage says that the eclipsed moon and the sun are visible together, which contradicts Option C. The passage says that the sun and moon are at opposite sides of the horizon, which contradicts Option D.

Exercise 5: Academic Vocabulary (Page 129)

A. The completed chart should look like this:

Academic Vocabulary	Content Vocabulary
1. reveal	1. climatologist
2. rate	2. deforestation
3. cause	3. drought
4. increase	4. ozone
5. mean	5. reservoirs
6. altered	6. polluters
7. related to	
8. attributed	
9. result in	

B. Many answers are possible. Compare your answers to these sample answers.
1. show
2. speed
3. reason something happens
4. gain
5. average
6. changed
7. caused by
8. blamed on
9. cause

Exercise 6: Pronouns (Page 133)

1. A different urban myth
2. the stories
3. urban myths

4. another person
5. hearers

Exercise 7: Reference Items (Page 137)

1. **C organizations'** Option C is correct because the companies are clearly worried about their own needs and want to organize workers in ways that accomplish the companies' goals. Option A is incorrect because the companies are trying to avoid rigid departments and divisions. Options B and D are incorrect because the teams are organized for the companies' benefit, not the teams' or the workers'.

2. **B one department** Option B is correct because the passage is talking about drawing members with different kinds of expertise from different departments of companies. Therefore, none of the other options makes sense.

3. **D employees** Option D is correct because the sentence is about team members, and this is the only option related to team members. Option

A is not correct because projects cannot join teams. Option B does not make sense. Option C is not correct because the sentence is about team members, not leaders.

4. **D an additional team** Option D is correct because the sentence is clearly talking about team membership. For this reason, Options A and B make no sense. Option C is incorrect because the employees are members of teams made up of small groups of company employees.

5. **A team leader's** Option A is correct because this sentence is about the role of the team leader. Therefore, Options B and D do not make sense. Option C is incorrect because a functional leader is the head of the employee's department, not the leader of the team.

Exercise 8: Paraphrasing (Page 140)

Many answers are possible. Compare your answers to these sample answers.

1. Now companies want workers in cross-functional teams with expertise from many parts of the company.
2. Companies want flexible teams that can be easily changed as projects change or new projects begin.

3. Individuals may lead teams and be members of others, depending on company needs, workers' skills, and project requirements.
4. Each team member has a functional leader (the department manager) and a project team leader.
5. The team leader is called a "heavyweight" because she should listen to all team members and make decisions based on the group's recommendations.

Exercise 9: Sentence Simplification Items (Page 145)

1. **A For example, scientists believe that the hole in the ozone layer over Antarctica is a consequence of the release into the atmosphere of gases from aerosol cans and other sources.** Option A is correct because only this option restates the essential ideas of the sentence without omitting information, introducing information that is incorrect or not in the passage, or changing the meaning. Option B

is incorrect because it omits an important detail, the source of the gases (aerosol cans and other sources). Option C is incorrect because it introduces an error to the sentence: there is a break in the ozone layer over Antarctica, not a break in the atmosphere. Option D is incorrect because it misstates the cause-and-effect relationship of the original sentence. The original sentence says that the gases are the cause of the break in the ozone layer. Option D says that the release of gases is a consequence of the break, which is contradicted by the passage and makes no sense.

2. **B An innovation pioneered by architects who came before Mies, steel girders, instead of thick walls, supported buildings, which allowed architects to replace thick walls with expansive windows.** Option B is correct because only this option restates the essential ideas of the sentence without omitting information, introducing information that is incorrect or not in the passage, or changing the meaning. Option A is incorrect because it changes the meaning of part of the sentence. Steel girders allowed architects to replace thick walls with expansive windows. For this reason, Option D is also incorrect. Option C is incorrect because the innovation was pioneered by architects who came before Mies.

3. **D Earth, the moon, and the sun must all be in a row with Earth in the middle to cast a shadow on the moon for a lunar eclipse to happen.** Option D is correct because only this option restates the essential ideas of the sentence without omitting information, introducing information that is incorrect or not in the passage, or changing the meaning. Option A is incorrect

because it misstates the order of the bodies. Earth needs to be between the moon and the sun for a lunar eclipse to occur. Option B is incorrect because Earth, not the moon, casts a shadow in a lunar eclipse. Option C is incorrect because it omits a key detail: Earth must be between the sun and the moon for a lunar eclipse to take place.

4. **A These tales are called urban myths by the folklorists who study them, to distinguish these tales from older myths, legends, and folktales from the Middle Ages and earlier.** Option A is correct because only this option restates the essential ideas of the sentence without omitting information, introducing information that is incorrect or not in the passage, or changing the meaning. Option B is incorrect because it says that the tales are called urban myths to distinguish them from the folklorists who study them, which does not make sense. The term is used to distinguish modern folktales from older ones. For this reason, Option D is incorrect, too. Option D is also incorrect because it incorrectly says that stories from the Middle Ages are called urban myths. Option C omits a key distinction: the modern stories are called urban myths to distinguish them from the older stories.

Exercise 10: Answering TOEFL iBT Basic Information Items (Page 149)

1. **A water moves around Earth in solid, liquid, and gas forms (Vocabulary)** Option A is correct because *state* refers to three states that matter can take: solid, liquid, and gas. Option B uses another meaning of *state*, which is related to government, not to science, and is therefore incorrect. Option C is incorrect because *state* refers to forms matter can take, not to the water cycle. In addition, the water cycle has four stages, not three. Option D is contradicted by the passage. In liquid form, for example, water moves through currents and waves.

2. **B related to water (Vocabulary)** Option B is correct because the passage is discussing the various physical states that water goes through. The word part *hydro-* refers to water. Therefore, the other options are incorrect.

3. **A Stomata (Factual information)** Option A is correct because the passage says "water . . . is released by the stomata in plants into the atmosphere." Option B is therefore incorrect

because stomata are only a part of leaves. Options C and D are mentioned in other parts of the passage, but not in relationship to stomata.

4. **D Fog (Negative factual information)** Option D is correct because only liquid or solid water can fall to the ground as precipitation. Fog is water vapor. The other options are all ways that water can fall to the ground, according to the passage, and are therefore incorrect.

5. **C the process by which water vapor enters the atmosphere (Vocabulary)** Option C is correct because according to the passage, *evapotranspiration* refers to the two main ways that water vapor enters the atmosphere: evaporation (water changing state from liquid to gas) and transpiration (water vapor released by plants as waste). Options A and B are incorrect because each one captures only part of the meaning of the word. Option D is related to the water cycle, of which evapotranspiration is only one part.

6.   **A   Droplets come together and become larger because of atmospheric conditions, until they are too heavy to remain in the atmosphere and fall to Earth's surface in solid or liquid forms. (Sentence simplification)** Option A is correct because only this option restates the essential ideas of the sentence without omitting information, introducing information that is incorrect or not in the passage, or changing the meaning. Option B omits important information, such as the types of precipitation and droplets joining together into bigger droplets. Option C is incorrect because it adds an additional, incorrect idea: that precipitation forms in fog. Fog is a cloud that is close to the ground. Rain, sleet, snow, and hail are formed in clouds high in the sky. In addition, Option C omits the idea that droplets come together to form larger droplets. Option D restates the information incorrectly. Water vapor cannot be solid or liquid. Water vapor is a gas.

7.   **C   infiltration (Factual information)** Option C is correct. The passage says, "runoff will also be absorbed into the ground in a process called infiltration." This water moves through the ground and is absorbed into aquifers. Option A, canopy interception, happens when precipitation does not reach the ground but is caught in tree leaves where it evaporates. Option B, evaporation, is the process by which liquid water becomes a gas and enters the atmosphere. Option D happens when frozen precipitation melts and becomes runoff.

8.   **B   water (Reference)** Option B is correct because the passage is about water and the water cycle. Options A and C are incorrect because the water that evaporates this way is caught in leaves in high tree branches. In addition, Option C is not possible because *it* is singular and *branches* is plural. Option D is incorrect because canopy interception is the name of the process by which precipitation evaporates without hitting the ground and becoming runoff.

9.   **C   support (Vocabulary)** Option C is correct. Sustenance is support such as food and water that keeps an organism alive. Option A is incorrect because hail is not a form of sustenance to living things. Though Option B also mentions a kind of sustenance, it is not the answer, because the passage is about water, which is not a kind of food. Option D is incorrect for the same reason. While certain minerals provide sustenance to plants, the passage is about water.

10.   **B   Water is purified in aquifers. (Factual information)** Option B is correct because it is the only option that presents a benefit of the hydrological cycle. The other options are part of the hydrological cycle but are not benefits.

Exercise 11: Inference Items (Page 156)

1.   **C   Athletes have unique health concerns that require specialized attention.** Option C is correct because the passage provides numerous examples of specialized attention required by various kinds of athletes. For this reason, Option D is incorrect. Option A is incorrect because the passage provides many examples of ways nonprofessionals can benefit from sports medicine. Option B is contradicted by the passage. Sports medicine provides treatment for recovery and rehabilitation, preventive care, and treatment of long-term and chronic conditions.

2.   **C   A repetitive stress injury prevents a worker from using the mouse on her computer.** Option C is correct because this injury is not sports related. The other options are all sports related, so they could be treated by a sports medicine specialist.

3.   **B   Sports medicine has increased in demand because of the specialized knowledge required.** Option B is an inference that is supported by information in the passage. The passage indicates that this is a growing field and gives many examples of the specialized knowledge required. Option A may be correct, but it is not supported by information in the passage. Options C and D are contradicted by information in the passage. The passage makes it clear that the field serves more than professionals and that athletes have specific needs and concerns that require specialized knowledge.

4.   **A   Nutritionists work in the area of sports medicine.** Option A can be correctly inferred from the information. Since sports medicine addresses nutrition, it is logical that nutritionists would be among the specialists involved. Option B may be true, but it is not supported by the information in the passage. To support this inference, the passage would need to give data on faulty nutrition among athletes. Options C and D are not supported by the passage.

Exercise 12: Rhetorical Purpose Items (Page 162)

1. **A** **To illustrate the point that sports medicine has a preventive component** Option A is correct because the details in the example are all preventive. The example also comes directly after a topic sentence about prevention. Option B is incorrect because this example focuses on only one sports medicine specialty. Option C, while discussed elsewhere in the passage, is not supported by this example. Option D cannot be inferred from this example.

2. **C** **To show that many nonprofessional athletes benefit from sports medicine** Option C is correct because the reference to triathletes, mountain climbers, and skateboarders follows a sentence about nonprofessionals. Option A is incorrect because the examples are clearly about nonprofessionals. Option B is incorrect because the passage is about sports medicine, not participation in sports. Option D is incorrect because the passage does not provide information relating specific sports to specific medical specialists.

Exercise 13: Insert Text Items (Page 166)

1. **C** The sentence belongs in this location because it gives a list of medical specialties and makes the most sense following the previous sentence, which is also about medical specialties. Option A is incorrect because the sentence does not make sense after the previous sentence, which is about patients, not medical specialists. Option B is incorrect because this sentence provides detail, so it should come after the topic sentence of the paragraph. Option D is incorrect because the sentence does not make sense after the previous sentence, which is about prevention, not medical specialties.

2. **C** Option C is correct because the sentence follows another sentence about specialized knowledge that sports medicine professionals need. Option A is incorrect because this part of the passage is not about special knowledge needed to practice sports medicine. Option B is incorrect because the sentence contains the word *also*, so it works better following this sentence. Option D is incorrect because this part of the passage is not about special knowledge needed for sports medicine.

Exercise 14: Answering TOEFL iBT Inference Items (Page 167)

1. **B** **To show that some surfactants are unnecessary (Rhetorical purpose)** Option B is correct because the passage says that foam is not necessary for surfactants to allow water and oil to mix. Option A is incorrect because even though one important use of surfactants is as foaming agents, the author is not concerned with whether they are commonly used, but rather with the idea that they are not necessary. Option C is incorrect because foaming agents are not emollients. Option D is incorrect because the author is not interested in describing surfactants that have more than one use (cleansing and foaming), but rather in showing that foaming agents are used unnecessarily.

2. **C** **Emollient (Inference)** An emollient is designed to mix oily substances with water to form products such as creams. A creamy salad dressing would be a similar use of an emollient, so Option C is correct. Option A is incorrect because a creamy salad dressing is not foamy. Option B is not correct because a salad dressing is not designed to clean products. Option D is incorrect because solubolizers are used to create perfumes, and a salad dressing is a food, not a perfume.

3. **A** **To make bread that is light and fluffy (Inference)** A foaming agent would add bubbles to make bread light and fluffy. Option B does not make sense because a detergent is needed to remove grease, and foaming agents are unnecessary for cleaning. Option C is not correct because a flavoring does not have bubbles or foam. Option D is incorrect because a detergent is used to clean oil.

4. **D** **(Insert text)** Option D is correct because logically, this sentence gives a contrasting

piece of information about different kinds of surfactants. Since petroleum-derived surfactants are dangerous, it follows that we should use naturally derived ones instead. Option A is incorrect because a reason does not precede the sentence that follows this position. Option B is

incorrect because it is not logical to use naturally derived surfactants because some surfactants are used unnecessarily. Option C is incorrect because unnecessary use of foaming agents has nothing to do with preferring naturally derived surfactants.

Exercise 15: Prose Summary Items (Page 174)

1. If you completed the summary correctly, it should look like this:

The passage discusses the work of sports medicine professionals and the athletes they serve.

- **A** Sports medicine is a growing field that serves professional and nonprofessional athletes.
- **C** Sports medicine professionals include many specialists.
- **E** Sports medicine gives emergency care, treats long-term conditions, and provides preventive care.

These answers are correct for these reasons.

- **A Sports medicine is a growing field that serves professional and nonprofessional athletes.** This option synthesizes the main idea of the passage, so it belongs in the summary.
- **C Sports medicine professionals include many specialists.** This option sums up information in the passage on the diverse medical specialties that serve the many health issues athletes face, so it belongs in the summary.
- **E Sports medicine gives emergency care, treats long-term conditions, and provides preventive care.** This sentence sums up the different kinds of care performed by sports medicine specialists, so it belongs in the summary.

Incorrect options do not belong in the completed table for these reasons:

- **B An athletic trainer can organize appropriate training routines and preventive care.** This option is a supporting detail, so it does not belong in the summary.
- **D Preventive care includes monitoring nutrition.** This option includes only one area addressed by sports medicine, so it does not belong in the summary.

- **F Health professionals who want to become sports medicine professionals require extensive training and professional certifications in sports medicine.** This information is not directly stated in the passage, so it does not belong in the summary.

2. If you completed the summary correctly, it should look like this:

The passage discusses different kinds of eclipses.

- **A** In a solar eclipse, the moon blocks light from the sun.
- **E** An eclipse happens when one astronomical body blocks light from another.
- **F** In a lunar eclipse, Earth blocks light from the sun.

These answers are correct for these reasons.

- **A In a solar eclipse, the moon blocks light from the sun.** This option is a main idea of the passage and thus belongs in the summary.
- **E An eclipse happens when one astronomical body blocks light from another.** This option summarizes the causes of both kinds of eclipses, so it also belongs in the passage.
- **F In a lunar eclipse, Earth blocks light from the sun.** This option is a main idea of the passage and belongs in the summary.

Incorrect options do not belong in the table for these reasons.

- **B Birds may roost during a total solar eclipse.** This is a minor detail in the passage and does not belong in the summary.
- **C A senelion is a very common kind of eclipse.** This information misstates a minor detail in the passage, so it therefore does not belong in the summary. A senelion is the least common type of eclipse.

- **D In an umbral eclipse, the moon is completely dark.** This option is only partially correct so it does not belong in the summary.

Only in a *total* umbral eclipse does the moon appear entirely dark, according to the passage.

Exercise 16: Fill in a Table Items (Page 181)

1. The following table is completed correctly. Answers can be in any order. Answers are correct if only the letter is written.

POPULAR VIEW OF SPORTS MEDICINE	REAL VIEW OF SPORTS MEDICINE
Select 2	Select 3
• B It mainly treats college and professional athletes.	• A It involves urgent and preventive care.
• F Sports medicine specialists are mainly team doctors.	• D It treats athletes in many kinds of professional and nonprofessional sports.
	• E It includes many kinds of health care professionals.

These answers are correct for these reasons.

Popular View of Sports Medicine

- **B It mainly treats college and professional athletes.** This information is presented as a popular view of sports medicine in the first sentence of the passage, so it is correctly placed in this section of the table.
- **F Sports medicine specialists are mainly team doctors.** The passage is clear that this statement is a popular misconception about sports medicine. Therefore, this option is correctly placed in this section of the table.

Real View of Sports Medicine

- **A It involves urgent and preventive care.** The passage states that sports medicine actually provides both of these kinds of care. This is one of the main ideas of the passage, so this option is correctly placed in this section of the table.
- **D It treats athletes in many kinds of professional and nonprofessional sports.** The passage mentions that sports medicine treats all kinds of athletes and mentions a variety of sports. Therefore, this option is correctly placed in this section of the table.

- **E It includes many kinds of health care professionals.** The passage indicates that sports medicine practitioners treat "broken bones, hurt or damaged muscles, heart and circulatory problems, and even injuries to the brain." These are all different medical specialties, so this option is correctly placed in this section of the table.

Incorrect options do not belong in the completed table for these reasons:

- **C Not a lot of specialized training is needed.** This idea is not mentioned in the passage and is inaccurate. Each of the medical professions referred to in the article requires specialized training.
- **G Many nutritionists are involved in sports medicine.** While the passage mentions that nutritionists may help athletes, the passage does not give an indication as to the number or proportion of nutritionists involved in sports medicine.

2. The following table is completed correctly. Answers can be in any order. Answers are correct if only the letter is written.

KIND OF ECLIPSE	STATEMENTS
Solar	**Select 2**
	• B In a total eclipse, animals may think night has fallen.
	• E The moon blocks the light of the sun.
Lunar	**Select 3**
	• C Earth blocks the light of the sun.
	• D A shadow is cast on the moon.
	• G The darkest part of the eclipse is the umbra.

These answers are correct for these reasons.

Solar Eclipse

- **B In a total eclipse, animals may think night has fallen.** This option is stated directly in the passage as happening during a total solar eclipse, and is therefore correct.
- **E The moon blocks the light of the sun.** This option is stated directly in the passage as the cause of a solar eclipse, and is also correct.

Lunar Eclipse

- **C Earth blocks the light of the sun.** This option is stated directly in the passage as the cause of a lunar eclipse, and is therefore correct.
- **D A shadow is cast on the moon.** This option is also stated directly in the passage as a characteristic of a lunar eclipse.

- **G The darkest part of the eclipse is the umbra.** This option is also stated directly in the passage as a characteristic of a lunar eclipse.

Incorrect options do not belong in the completed table for these reasons:

- **A The sun blocks the light of the moon.** This is not mentioned in the passage and does not make sense.
- **F A shadow is cast on the sun.** This is not mentioned in the passage and does not make sense. The sun is too bright for a shadow to be cast on it.

TOEFL iBT Practice Reading Section (Page 183)

1. **C a style of popular Latin dance music (Vocabulary)** Option C is closest to the definition given in the passage. Option A is related to the original, literal meaning of the term, not its meaning in music, as it is used in the passage. Option B is incorrect because salsa apparently borrows from many different types of Caribbean music. Option D is incorrect because musicians didn't use the term *salsa* at the time salsa music was being created. Musicians adopted the term later.

2. **B salsa music's (Reference)** The word *it* clearly refers to the phrase "this term" in the sentence, which refers to salsa music. Therefore, Option B is correct. Options A and D are not possible, because these answer options are plural and *it* is singular. Option C is not possible because the passage is not about Cuba's origin and history.

3. **D Spicy sauces from Puerto Rico (Negative factual information)** Option D is correct because the paragraph makes clear that the musical style grew out of other kinds of music (jazz, *son*, and merengue). *Salsa* is a food term later applied to the music; it was not an influence on its beginnings. Options A, B, and C are all mentioned in the passage as possible origins of salsa music and are therefore incorrect.

4. **C To show that salsa performers did not invent this term (Rhetorical purpose)** Option C is correct because the main idea of the paragraph is that salsa musicians did not invent this term. This quote is an example of how musicians rejected the term. Option A is not supported by the passage. Option B is contradicted by the passage. Salsa is the name of this musical style, even if it was not invented by musicians. Option D is contradicted by the passage. The passage makes clear that Tito Puente is a famous performer of Latin music.

5. **A The musicians wanted to make their music appealing to a broad audience. (Factual information)** Option A is correct because the passage says, "They wanted their musical styles to be associated with the commercially accepted salsa." Option B is not supported by information in the passage. Option C is contradicted by the passage. Mexican musical styles were not incorporated into salsa. Option D is incorrect because it is a reason that the term *salsa* appealed to audiences, not musicians.

6. **C the meaning of the term *salsa* evolved over time (Vocabulary)** Option C is correct

because the example that follows this sentence shows that the term *salsa* was not clearly defined originally, and the term became more specific as time passed. Evidence in the passage indicates that Option A may be a true statement, but this sentence is about the creation of the definition, not its acceptance. Therefore, Option A is incorrect. There is no evidence in the passage to support Option B or D.

7. **B music promoters (Reference)** Option B is correct because those who were struggling to present the new music to audiences were promoters. Option A is incorrect because musicians did not use or accept the term *salsa* right away. Option C is incorrect because stylings are a thing, and the antecedent of *who* is usually a person or an animal. Option D is incorrect because the promoters were trying to win approval of the public.

8. **B Adopting a label such as *salsa* for this new genre, even as it was being created, would help it succeed because it is a term with powerful associations that's easily pronounced by non-speakers of Spanish. (Sentence simplification)** Option B is correct because only this option restates the essential ideas of the sentence without omitting information, introducing information that is incorrect or not in the passage, or changing the meaning. Option A is incorrect because it omits a key detail: it helped define salsa as it was being created. Options C and D both change the meaning of the sentence and are therefore incorrect. Option C incorrectly says that the genre had powerful associations as it was being created. Option D says that salsa music was created to have powerful associations. Actually, the word *salsa* was selected because of its associations, according to the original sentence.

9. **C People criticized him for not using his training in classical music. (Factual information)** Option C is correct because the same sentence includes information on Cugat's classical training. Cugat's response was a defense of his reason for preferring popular music: playing popular music paid better. Option A is not supported by information in the passage. Option B is contradicted by the passage. Performing for sixteen years at an exclusive New York hotel is one indication that his music was popular. Option D is not supported by the information in the passage and most likely is not true: someone who

was classically trained probably would think that classical music is good.

10. **B** **explain the development of salsa music in New York City (Rhetorical purpose)** Option B is correct because the first sentence states that this is the intention of the paragraph. The remaining sentences give detail about the development of salsa in New York. Option A is not correct because this is the purpose of paragraph 2. Option C is not supported by the information in the paragraph. The paragraph does not give reasons for salsa's popularity. Option D is not correct because the information about Cugat is supporting detail about the development of salsa music in New York.

11. **B** **One of her teachers told her careers in entertainment paid well. (Factual information)** Option B is correct because the passage says one of her teachers told her she could make more money in one day as an entertainer than a teacher makes in a month. Option A is incorrect because the first prize she won was a cake. Option C is not supported by information in the passage. Though her parents wanted her to become a teacher, there is no evidence that she rebelled against them. Option D is contradicted by information in the passage. Though she was interested in music as a child, she focused on her schooling until her teacher spoke with her about entertainment.

12. **B** **Musicians take financial considerations into account in their career decisions. (Inference)** Option B is correct because both Xavier Cugat and Celia Cruz stated that they went into music to achieve financial success. Therefore, Option A is incorrect. Option C may be true but is not supported by information in the passage. Though Option D is discussed in the passage, it is incorrect because it is mentioned in reference to Tito Puente and not to Xavier Cugat or Celia Cruz.

13. **B** **(Insert text)** Option B is correct because this sentence adds an additional detail about Cugat's popularity and influence, so it best belongs following the first detail given about his music's success. For this reason, the other options are incorrect.

14. **(Prose summary)** If you completed the summary correctly, it should look like this:

The passage discusses the origins of salsa music.

- **B** Salsa is a rhythmic and exciting Latin dance music.
- **D** The music has roots in Cuba, the Dominican Republic, and the United States.
- **F** The origin of the name *salsa* is not completely clear.

These answers are correct for these reasons.

- **B** **Salsa is a rhythmic and exciting Latin dance music.** This answer is correct because it gives a definition of the topic of the passage.
- **D** **The music has roots in Cuba, the Dominican Republic, and the United States.** This answer is correct because it synthesizes data in the passage on the origins of salsa music.
- **F** **The origin of the name *salsa* is not completely clear.** This sentence sums up an important issue discussed in the passage: controversy about the name of this musical genre.

Incorrect options do not belong in the completed table for these reasons:

- **A** **Tito Puente did not like to call his music *salsa* at first.** While true, this information is a minor detail in the passage, so it does not belong in the summary.
- **C** **Xavier Cugat is one of the most famous of all salsa performers.** This information is a minor detail in the passage, so it does not belong in the summary.
- **E** **Salsa music was not very popular or successful commercially.** This information is not one of the main points of the reading, which is primarily focused on the origins of salsa, not its commercial success, and is contradicted by information in the passage.

15. **D** **To use them in subsequent years' crops (Factual information)** Option D is correct because the passage states, "Farmers have saved seeds from the current year's crop to plant for the next year's crop." Option B is not supported by the passage. While the passage mentions the raising of animals, it does not say that farmers used stored seeds to feed these animals. For this reason, Options A and C are also incorrect.

16. **A** **the crops' (Reference)** Option A is correct because logically the seeds to be saved for the following year need to come from the present year's crops. Therefore, the other options do not make sense.

17. **D** **Farmers are impressed by the high yields of many hybrid seeds. (Negative factual information)** Option D is correct because it is the only option that is not a concern about not saving hybrid seeds. Instead, it is an advantage of the seeds. All the other options are mentioned in the

passage as concerns about not saving seeds and therefore are incorrect.

18. **A** **This is not the principal concern, because critics believe that the modified plants may be inherently dangerous, and as hybrid varieties of rice, wheat, and corn replace the large number of biologically diverse varieties, biodiversity will be reduced. (Sentence simplification)** Option A is correct because only this option restates the essential ideas of the sentence without omitting information, introducing information that is incorrect or not in the passage, or changing the meaning. Option B is incorrect because it omits that the principal concerns are voiced by critics. In addition, it states as a fact, and not a belief, that genetically modified plants are inherently harmful. Option C incorrectly states that biologically diverse plants will replace hybrid and genetically modified varieties, so this option is incorrect. For this reason, Option D is also incorrect. In addition, Option D omits the critics' concern that the genetically modified plants are inherently harmful.

19. **D** **varieties (Vocabulary)** *Varieties* is used as a synonym for *strain* in paragraph 2, so Option D is correct. A strain is a variety of a species. The other options are all related to other meanings of the word *strain* that do not make sense in the passage and are therefore incorrect. Option A refers to the process of pouring a liquid through a filter to remove small solid pieces. In addition, *strain* is a noun, and *separates* is a verb. Option B refers to a kind of injury: a strain is a pulled or damaged muscle. Option C refers to the extra effort required to do a challenging task.

20. **D** **likely to be harmed by something (Vocabulary)** Option D is correct because the passage states that the plants are "susceptible to disease or pests." Since disease and pests cause harm, Option D is correct. Option A is related to another meaning of *susceptible:* someone who is susceptible is easily convinced to believe something. This meaning does not make sense in the passage, so Option A is incorrect. Options B and C do not make sense in the passage.

21. **B** **To show that maintaining seed repositories is a long-standing practice (Rhetorical purpose)** Option B is correct because the first sentence of the paragraph indicates that the seed repository is "another ancient agricultural practice." The information about ancient Egypt is a detail that supports this generalization. Option A is not supported by information in the passage,

and the overall thrust of the passage shows that the author believes that seed repositories are a good idea. Option C is not supported by information in the passage. Option D is not supported by the passage. The author gives no indication of the ancient Egyptians' opinions about their agriculture.

22. **D** **repositories (Reference)** Option D is correct because a main purpose of the repositories is to preserve biodiversity. Options A, B, and C do not make sense.

23. **B** **All seeds suffer damage after being stored for long periods, so they need to be replaced. (Factual information)** Option B is correct because the passage says that "Even longer-lasting seeds deteriorate over time." Option A may be true, but it is not supported by the passage. Option C is not relevant because seeds from this plant cannot be stored for long periods. The plants need to be grown and regrown to ensure a seed supply. Option D is contradicted by the passage. The repositories exist to ensure that the old varieties of plants are not replaced with new hybrids.

24. **A** **Seed repositories will never be completely effective in preserving seed supplies and biodiversity. (Inference)** Option A is correct because the passage points out the role and importance of seed repositories as well as their limitations. Option B is too general and is not supported by the information in the passage. Options C and D are not supported by information in the passage.

25. **D** **(Insert text)** Option D is correct because the sentence gives another detail about seeds that cannot be stored in cold, dry conditions. The only location that is a logical place for this detail is after a sentence that introduces this kind of seed. The sentence does not make sense in the other locations in the paragraph.

26. **A** **To show that multiple repositories are needed to ensure that seed supplies are safe (Rhetorical purpose)** Option A is correct because a key idea of this paragraph is that redundancy is needed so that seeds are available in one repository if another is damaged. For this reason, Option C is incorrect. Option B is not supported by information in the passage. The author makes no criticisms of the countries in the passage. Option D is contradicted by the passage. The new repository built by Norway is an example of the redundancy that the author believes is necessary for the seed repositories to work effectively.

27. D **cocoa (Negative factual information)**
Option D is correct because the passage identifies
the seed of the cocoa plant as one that cannot
be stored and needs to be regrown to obtain
seeds. The other options are all mentioned in the
passage as examples of plants whose seeds can
be stored for long periods of time, and they are
therefore incorrect.

28. **(Prose summary)** If you completed the summary
correctly, it should look like this:

The passage discusses the importance of seed
repositories.

- A Farmers and societies have long saved seeds.
- C Seed repositories, safe places for storing
  seeds, are important for preserving biodiversity.
- F Seed repositories are important in case a
  catastrophe disrupts seed supplies.

These answers are correct for these reasons.

- A **Farmers and societies have long saved
  seeds.** This sentence summarizes important
  background information about saving seeds.
- C **Seed repositories, safe places for
  storing seeds, are important for preserving
  biodiversity.** This option restates a key reason
  seed repositories are important, so it belongs in
  the summary.
- F **Seed repositories are important in case
  a catastrophe disrupts seed supplies.** This
  option summarizes a second reason for the
  importance of seed repositories, so it belongs in
  the summary.

Incorrect options do not belong in the completed
table for these reasons:

- B **Seed repositories cannot safely store
  most kinds of seeds.** This option includes
  incorrect information that is contradicted in the
  passage, so it does not belong in the summary.
  Only a few kinds of seeds cannot be stored in
  repositories.
- D **No one should eat food from genetically
  modified seeds.** This option misstates an idea
  in the passage. The passage says that critics
  believe the foods are not safe, but it does not
  say that no one should eat them. Therefore, this
  sentence does not belong in the passage.
- E **Seed repositories in Thailand, the
  Philippines, and Iraq were badly damaged
  recently.** This option contains unimportant
  supporting detail, so it does not belong in the
  summary.

29. D **strengthening the army (Negative factual
information)** Option D is correct because it is
the only option not mentioned in the passage.
The remaining options are all mentioned in the
passage and are therefore incorrect.

30. A **despite the growth of public unrest
(Factual information)** Option A is correct
because the government continued on its
reformist course while opposition grew. Option
B is incorrect because the disharmony was over
opposition to certain reforms, particularly army
and church reforms. Option C is incorrect because
reform-minded citizens already supported the
government. Option D is not supported by the
passage. Continuing the reforms angered the
army leaders.

31. A **Most people supported the government
at first, but opinion was divided by 1936.
(Inference)** Option A is correct because it
accurately sums up how support for the
government grew and shrank. Option B is
incorrect because the generals had rebelled
previously. Option C is contradicted by the
passage. The church would have opposed the
reforms because they reduced the power of the
church. Option D is not supported by information
in the passage.

32. D **To show how divisions among the people
caused the uprising to become a civil war
(Rhetorical purpose)** Option D is correct
because the passage makes it clear that the army
didn't rise up everywhere, because support for
it was limited. To take over the government, the
army had to fight a civil war. Option A is incorrect
because the government apparently had strong
support from much of the population and the
part of the army that remained loyal. Option B is
incorrect because military force was not the only
way to end the reforms. Previously, a conservative
government had reversed many of the reforms
from the first two years of the Republic. Option
C is incorrect because the government was
supported by a small majority of people and was
following their will. A large minority opposed the
government and its reforms.

33. B **removed from (Vocabulary)** Option B is
correct because the generals lost their powerful
positions and were sent to less powerful posts
far from Madrid. Therefore, Options A and D are
contradicted by the passage. The generals were
not returned to their powerful posts (Option A) or
promoted to powerful posts (Option D). Option
C uses another meaning of *relieve* ("to reduce

anxiety"), which does not make sense in the passage and is therefore incorrect.

34. **A** **Madrid (Negative factual information)** Option A is the only option that is not one of the distant posts the generals were assigned to, so it is correct. Therefore, all the other options are incorrect.

35. **D** **the generals (Reference)** Option D is correct because it is the only answer that makes sense. The generals accelerated their plan because of the pretext provided by the assassination. Option A is not possible because *army* is singular and *they* is plural. In addition, only four generals, not the entire army, organized the uprising and underestimated the support for the Republic. Option B does not make sense because there was one uprising, not several. Option C is incorrect because the army generals, not the Republican leaders, underestimated support for the Republic. The Republican leaders probably overestimated support for the Republic.

36. **D** **Replace the Republic with a conservative government (Factual information)** Option D is stated directly in the passage and is therefore correct. The generals' goal was to overthrow the reformist government and stop the reforms. Option A is incorrect because the extremist conservative organizations would support a military uprising against the government. Option B is contradicted by the passage. The generals believed that the government would fall easily. Option C is only the pretext the generals used to justify their uprising. Their actual goal was to overthrow the government, not merely to avenge a single death.

37. **B** **the assassination provided a reason for the generals to move against the government (Factual information)** Option B is correct because the passage says that the assassination provided a pretext. A pretext is a reason that is given for something in order to cover up the real reason. The generals intended to rise against the Republic all along and only used the assassination to justify the uprising in the public mind. Option A is incorrect because the army was not worried about retaliation. Its goal was ending the Republic. Option C is incorrect because the generals were already posted to distant points after rebelling against the Republic. Option D

is contradicted by the passage. The generals wanted an uprising to stop the church reforms, but this was only one of the things they wanted to stop. Their real goal was to end all the reforms by installing a conservative government; the assassination was the pretext for overthrowing the Republic.

38. **C** **win by wearing down the enemy's resistance (Vocabulary)** Option C is correct because the passage indicates that the generals deprived the Republicans of food and supplies and wore them down with relentless attacks. The other options are not supported by information in the passage.

39. **C** **The generals underestimated support for the government and believed that the army would follow their example, but in key locations, the army failed to rise or the uprising was defeated and the government retained control of the army. (Sentence simplification)** Option C is correct because it restates the essential information in the sentence, does not change the meaning, and does not add information or omit key information. Option A is incorrect because it misstates a key fact: the original sentence suggests that the generals overestimated support for the uprising; the option sentence says the opposite. Option B is incorrect because it completely changes the meaning of the sentence. The generals believed that the army would follow their example and rise up. Option D is incorrect because it misstates what happened. The army failed to rise up, or the local leaders put down the rebellion and kept control of the army.

40. **C** **(Insert text)** Option C is correct because this is the most logical place to give more detail on the colonial army. Options A, B, and D are incorrect because a detail about the colonial army does not make sense in any of these positions.

41. **B** **Volunteers went to Spain to fight. (Factual information)** Option B is stated directly in the passage and is therefore correct. Options A and C are examples of ways the two governments supported the rebel generals, not the Republic. Option D is incorrect because the democratic governments rebuffed the Republic's appeals and did not send help.

42. **(Fill in a table)** The correctly completed chart should look like this. Answers can be in any order. Answers are correct if only the letter is written.

SUPPORTERS OF THE REPUBLIC	OPPONENTS OF THE REPUBLIC
Select 2	**Select 3**
• C They wanted social and labor reforms.	• A They were unhappy about changes to the church and the army.
• D They believed that the church was too powerful.	• E They won elections in 1933.
	• G They included generals who had rebelled previously.

These answers are correct for these reasons.

Supporters of the Republic

- C **They wanted social and labor reforms.** The passage indicates that social and labor reforms were part of the government's plan.
- D **They believed that the church was too powerful.** The passage indicates that the reforms reduced the power of the church.

Opponents of the Republic

- A **They were unhappy about changes to the church and the army.** The passage indicates that opponents were unhappy about the reforms.
- E **They won elections in 1933.** The passage indicates that conservative forces gained control of the government and reversed many of the previous government's reforms.
- G **They included generals who had rebelled previously.** The passage indicates that leaders of the uprising had previously been punished for their antigovernment activities by being sent to distant posts.

Incorrect options do not belong in the completed table for these reasons:

- B **They had broad support in 1936.** Initially, the Republic had strong support, but controversial reforms caused the people to become divided, and by 1936, only a small majority supported the Republican government. In addition, the conservatives had support from less than half the people by 1936. Therefore, this option is incorrect and does not belong in either section of the table.
- F **They wanted to start a civil war.** This option is incorrect and does not belong in the table. The generals' intention was not to start a civil war but to overthrow the government. When the uprising failed but the generals did not back down, civil war became inevitable.

TOEFL iBT Listening

Chapter at a Glance

In this chapter, you will learn:

Listening Items . . . . .5 item formats and 8 item types

Skills . . . . .Techniques to help you answer each kind of item

Tips . . . . .Hints to help you find the correct answers and avoid common mistakes

The TOEFL iBT Listening section assesses your ability to listen to and understand language commonly heard in North American colleges and universities—both inside and outside the classroom.

In general, most TOEFL iBT listening test administrations:

- have 4 academic **lectures** with 6 items per lecture
- have 2 campus-related **conversations** with 5 items per conversation
- contain 34 items total
- last 60 minutes

Academic **lectures** are on topics common to higher education classrooms in North America. In some lectures, only the professor will speak, while in others, both professor and students may ask and answer questions or exchange ideas and information.

Campus-related **conversations** take place in faculty or university offices or other indoor or outdoor settings on campus (including hallways, student unions, bus stops, and residence halls). Subjects range from school and classroom topics (such as getting clarification on an assignment) to student service and student life topics (such as housing, parking, and registration). In campus-related conversations, a student may be talking to a professor, a university staff member, or another student.

AT A GLANCE

TOEFL iBT Listening Section

Time Limit 60 minutes

Content 4 academic lecture listening selections*
2 campus-related conversation listening selections

Items 6 items per academic lecture
5 items per campus-related conversation
34 items total

ITEM TYPES **Basic information**
- Gist-content
- Gist-purpose
- Supporting detail

Pragmatic understanding
- Understanding the function of what is said
- Understanding the speaker's attitude

Connecting information
- Understanding the organization
- Connecting content
- Making inferences

ITEM FORMATS - Standard multiple choice (4 options and 1 answer)
- Special multiple choice (4 options and 2 or more answers)
- Drag-and-drop items
- Check box items
- Replay items

* In some administrations of the TOEFL, the Listening section will include as many as 5 lectures and/or 3 conversations, have up to 54 items, and last as long as 90 minutes. These extra selections and questions are used to assess items before they are used in actual tests and do not count toward your score.

At the beginning of the Listening section, you will see a photograph of a test taker wearing the special headset used during the test. Instructions will tell you to put on the headset. You will be able to make sure it works and to adjust the volume. Use the listening toolbar to control and adjust the volume before and during the test.

> **TIP** **Arrange your work area before you begin the actual TOEFL iBT!**
>
> After you check the playback volume at the test center, arrange your work area for the Listening section. You will not use your computer's keyboard during this section, so put it to one side to make room for note paper and your computer's mouse. Arrange the note paper and mouse so you can use them with comfort and ease. Keep in mind whether you are right-handed or left-handed.

TOEFL iBT Listening Selections

Listening passages on the TOEFL iBT are of two types: academic lectures and campus-related conversations.

Academic Lectures

The academic lectures on each TOEFL iBT Listening section assess your ability to understand language commonly heard in North American higher education classrooms. Lectures include different teaching styles and class sizes commonly found in colleges and universities. Academic lectures may include:

- Formal lectures by a professor in an auditorium or lecture hall
- Teacher-led classroom discussions in which professor and students interact

Academic Lectures: Subject Areas and Topics

In general, lecture topics are on common topics from the subject areas of the arts, earth and physical sciences, life sciences, and social sciences. The contents of the lectures are designed to be accessible to all test-takers regardless of their majors or educational experiences, and do not require any special knowledge. Each TOEFL iBT test will include topics from a variety of subjects (arts, sciences, etc.) to not favor some test takers over others. Here are categories that topics are drawn from.

Academic Lecture Subject Areas

Lecture topics are drawn from these academic subject areas:

- **Arts and humanities:** literature, art and art history, music and music history
- **Sciences:** life science, physical science, earth and space science, computer science, engineering
- **Social sciences:** geography, history, sociology, anthropology, psychology, economics
- **Business and management:** case studies

For a complete list of academic subject areas and sample topics, see Appendix B.

Academic Lectures: Listening Format

Academic lectures follow a simple basic format. You will see these screens as you listen to each academic lecture.

First, you will see a TOEFL iBT listening screen that identifies the class:

Earth Science

Next you will see a photograph of a professor lecturing to a class or a professor talking with a class.

 Then the lecture will begin. Listen to the following example as you read along silently. (On the actual TOEFL iBT, you will only listen to the selection.)

Narrator: Listen to part of a lecture in a geography class. The professor is talking about plate tectonics.

Professor: Hello, everyone. Umm . . . let's get started. . . . Okay, today we are going to talk about plate tectonics. Plate tectonics is a relatively new description of Earth's crust. The theory of plate tectonics asserts that once all of Earth's continents were a single landmass, which broke up as the underlying plates separated and began to move apart. Prior to the development of plate tectonics and related theories, scientists believed that Earth was solid and that its surface features were largely fixed. Under this view, changes in Earth's physical features were largely the result of upward or downward movement. For example, mountains formed because pressure from within Earth pushed up rock to form new mountains. This was called the geosynclinal theory. However, this theory could not explain all the evidence. Even as early as 1596, it had been noted that the landmasses on either side of the Atlantic had similar features and looked as if they had fit together at some point. However, the assumption that Earth, or at least its crust, was solid made it difficult to explain how these landmasses had once fit together.

The theory of plate tectonics grew out of the theory of continental drift, which as proposed in the early twentieth century, noted that many of the continents seemed to have fit together once. An important assumption in accepting the theory of continental drift was agreement among scientists that Earth's core was, in fact, molten, which would permit the movement of the solid landmasses above.

Throughout the twentieth century, many scientists contributed data and theories that helped support two new theories: the theory of continental drift and the subsequent emergence of the theory of plate tectonics. Two discoveries, in particular, were critical. First, seismographic data began to indicate that earthquakes tended to be centered in the same areas. In particular, scientists noted that earthquakes tended to be concentrated along ridges deep in the ocean. The discovery of a complex system of ridges, and the occurrence of earthquakes along them, was a strong indication that the ridges were boundaries between plates.

Second . . . , studies of the ocean floor indicated the possibility of sea floor spreading—that is, that the sea floor seemed to be expanding in certain places, particularly the Atlantic Ocean, and contracting in others, such as the Pacific Ocean. This discovery explained how Earth's surface could remain relatively the same size overall, while continuing to expand in certain places. Many scientists began to accept the notion that Earth's surface was composed of plates of different thicknesses, which were floating on Earth's molten mantle. Currents within the molten mantle could explain why Earth's surface tended to expand in certain places (as plates moved apart and molten rock pushed up) or contract in others (as plates pushing toward one another pushed deeper into the molten mantle and melted themselves). The hardest part of this theory for many to accept was the notion that massive plates could float on molten rock. This was eventually explained by the relative density of the materials, the plates being less dense than the molten rock below, which allowed them to be buoyant and float on the molten rock.

Scientists realized that areas of geological activity, such as earthquakes and volcanoes, were likely the locations of plate boundaries, where movement of the plates would cause violent disruptions as rock pushed against rock or plate boundaries opened, allowing molten rock to rise to the surface. Scientists soon discovered that there were several kinds of plate boundaries, each associated with different kinds of activity. In the United States, an area of intense geologic activity is along the West Coast. This map shows the many fault lines just in the state of California.

Throughout each lecture, you may see one or more "board" screens with key words or phrases. In general, these are the kinds of words that professors might write on the board. These screens may appear at any time during the listening selection. In this book, the screens will appear together after the class screen.

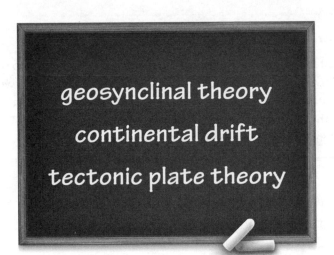

geosynclinal theory
continental drift
tectonic plate theory

TIP **Use the board art to help you understand the lecture!**

Use the words in the board art to help you understand key words as you listen to the lecture. Sometimes you may already know the meanings of words in the lecture but do not recognize the words when you hear them. Use the words in the board art to help you listen for and understand these key words. However, these words are not usually tested in items, so don't expect to use them when you answer the items.

Sometimes, you will see a screen with a photo, drawing, map, or table related to the lecture. These screens may appear at any time during the lecture. This map of fault lines in California might appear with the lecture on tectonic plates, for example.

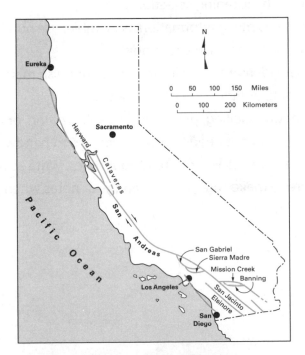

Main fault lines in California

TIP **Use the illustrations to help you as you listen!**

When you see an illustration during a listening selection, pay close attention to the drawing and to the professor. If the illustration has a caption (a label near or under the image), write it in your notes. For this illustration, you would write, Map: Main fault lines of California. If the professor or the students say something about the illustration, write that information in your notes, too. For this illustration, you might write, "US—intense geo. activ along w coast, many fault lines."

When the lecture is finished, the test will advance to the first item. You cannot view the items until the lecture has ended.

Taking Notes

As you listen to TOEFL listening selections, take detailed notes, just as you would in any college or university class. Since you cannot see the items until you finish listening, take as detailed notes as you can. The notes you take during the TOEFL iBT are for your use during the test. Your notes will be collected at the end of the test, but they will not be read or evaluated. Follow these instructions:

1. In lectures, write the name of the class or subject at the top of your notes.
2. Pay attention to the words on the board screens, and write them down, too, so you can refer to them as you listen and answer the items that follow. The words on the board screens may also help you understand difficult words in the listening selection.
3. To help you write as much information as possible, use numbers, abbreviations, and symbols in your notes.
4. Write down main ideas and details. To help distinguish main idea and detail, use a simple outline form in your notes.
5. Do not worry about spelling, punctuation, capitalization, or other details in your notes. You do not need to worry about good handwriting or printing either, as long as you can read your notes. Write as quickly as you can, taking care to make sure you can read your notes when it is time to answer the questions.

Listen again to the first part of the lecture on plate tectonics. As you listen, look at the notes a student wrote as she listened to this part of the lecture. What abbreviations and symbols did she use?

> **Earth Science**
> **Plate Tectonics**
> **New theory**
> **—all conts 1 landmass**
> **—conts broke up as plates under them moved**
> **Old theories**
> **—earth solid, fixed features, changes frm movmnt up + down**
>   **(geosynclinal th. Prob: conts looked like fit tog. But th.**
>   **can't expl this.**

What numbers and abbreviations did you find in the notes? (The notes use "1" for *one*, "+" for *plus*, and "conts" for *continents*, for example.)

Now you try it. Listen to the next part of the lecture. Write your notes in the space provided. When you finish taking notes, compare your notes to the sample notes that follow.

_____

_____

_____

_____

_____

_____

_____

Now compare your notes to these sample notes.

> **2 new theories cont drift, plate tectonics. Proof:**
> **—earthquakes in the same areas, espic nr ridges deep in ocean**
> **—shows the ridges were boundaries between plates**

Review your notes and make sure they are as complete and detailed as possible. Find other places to use numbers, abbreviations, and symbols in your notes.

EXERCISE 1

Taking Notes

 Listen to the lectures and conversations and take notes.

1.

_____
_____
_____
_____
_____
_____
_____
_____

2.

3.

Contemporary
Literature

_____

_____

_____

_____

_____

_____

_____

Answers for Exercise 1 begin on page 326.

Academic Lectures: Vocabulary

TOEFL iBT academic lectures contain vocabulary specific to the topic. For example, a lecture on plate tectonics would include words such as *continental drift, earthquake, sea floor spreading*, and other words related to geography. A lecture on photosynthesis would contain words such as *plant, water, oxygen, carbon dioxide*, and other terms related directly to the topic. A lecture on the history of salsa music would contain words related to music, such as *melody, rhythm, beat*, and so on. Particularly difficult content words might appear in the board art you see as you listen.

It is impossible to learn all of the important content vocabulary directly related to the topics on the TOEFL. However, many vocabulary words are common to academic speech in all subject matters. This vocabulary is called **academic vocabulary** because these words are common to all academic subjects. One such word is *classify*.

Academic Vocabulary

Academic vocabulary includes words that are used across one or more academic subject. Some common academic vocabulary includes:

classify
predict
analyze
graph
table

These words can be used in many academic contexts. You can classify kinds of music, such as jazz, classical, pop, and so on. You can also classify plants that use or do not use photosynthesis. Increasing your academic vocabulary will help you on every section of the TOEFL iBT. See Appendix A for a list of 150 top academic vocabulary words.

EXERCISE 2

Academic Vocabulary

 Listen to the lecture as you read along silently. Write the missing words you hear on the lines.

Life Science

Good afternoon, everyone. Today we are continuing with the topic of gases in the atmosphere. As we saw in our last class, scientists did not know until the late 1700s or early 1800s that the air we breathe is composed of different (1) _____. We also know that the identity of the actual (2) _____ of oxygen, Priestley or Lavoisier, is highly disputed. Though the actual discoverer is still the subject of controversy, we do know that their (3) _____ showed that the atmosphere is (4) _____ of different gases, and that oxygen is consumed by fire. All of this was discovered through a simple (5) _____ that nearly all of us have seen. Priestly noticed that when a candle was placed in a closed jar or bottle, the flame would eventually go out. That led him to believe that air (6) _____ of various gases and that the gas he discovered, (7) _____, was consumed by fire. Later, it would be discovered that fire also produced another gas, carbon dioxide. Later discoveries showed the (8) _____ of numerous other gases, including nitrogen, (9) _____, and hydrogen.

We now know that the atmosphere is composed (10) _____ of nitrogen and oxygen, with smaller amounts of other gases, including carbon dioxide, helium, hydrogen, and others, some of which exist only in very small quantities. These latter gases are called "trace gases." We also know that the amount of carbon dioxide in the atmosphere is rising because of the large amount of fossil fuel we now burn to provide energy.

Answers for Exercise 2 begin on page 327.

EXERCISE 3

Content Vocabulary or Academic Vocabulary?

Review your answers to Exercise 2. Are the missing words academic vocabulary or content vocabulary? Write the words in the correct columns.

ACADEMIC VOCABULARY	CONTENT VOCABULARY
	atmosphere

Answers for Exercise 3 begin on page 328.

Campus-Related Conversations

The two to three campus-related conversations on each TOEFL iBT Listening section assess your ability to understand the kinds of conversations that take place outside of class on North American college and university campuses:

- Individual student conversations with a professor, frequently in his or her office. The student may have a question about a test or an assignment. Or the student may want further information about a topic presented in class.
- Formal or informal conversation about school or student services with university staff members. The student may have a problem registering, parking, or using a service such as housing, financial aid, and so on.
- Casual conversations between students on school-related, nonacademic topics. Two students may be talking about campus news, student services, a class, class requirements, or another topic of campus interest.

> **TIP** **Use photos to identify campus-related conversations!**
>
> A campus-related conversation always begins with a photograph of the speakers. These photographs are set in a variety of campus locations, including hallways, offices, bus stops, and so on. They will not take place during class sessions. If the first image you see is a photo, you know that you are going to hear a campus conversation. If the first image you see is the name of a class, you know you are going to hear an academic lecture.

Campus-Related Conversations: Listening Topics

On each TOEFL iBT, one of the conversations will be in a professor's office on a class-related topic and another will be on a student service or school-related topic. Class-related topics might include asking a question about a grade, on a class requirement, or for clarification on an assignment or a topic raised in class. Student-service-related topics include asking about school services (registrar, parking, libraries), campus-related news and announcements, and student activities (entertainment, student clubs, and so on). A complete list of campus-related topics is in Appendix C.

School Services Language

Because many of the conversations on the TOEFL iBT involve school services, you need vocabulary and background knowledge about these services. Here are some common university offices and services that students may interact with.

- **Admissions and records.** This office handles student admission applications and records. If you need a transcript (an official list of courses and grades), you get it from this office or the registrar's office. Your transcript will show your grade point average or GPA, which is an average score based on your grades. If all your grades are A, your GPA will be 4.0. If your average grade is B, your GPA will be 3.0.
- **International student affairs.** This office helps international students and their families with admissions, visas, and support for life away from home.
- **Parking management.** This office handles campus parking, including issuing parking permits and parking tickets.
- **Recreational sports.** This service provides gyms, pools, and other facilities for students to get exercise and participate in intramural sports. (Intramural sports are team sports for students at the university. Intercollegiate sports are sports played by teams from different universities.) Large universities often offer extensive sports facilities to all students, often at very low prices or included in tuition.
- **Registrar.** This office handles student course registrations and academic records, such as grades.
- **Student accounts.** This office handles student bills for tuition, fees, and student housing; it sends bills and accepts payments.
- **Student housing.** This office is in charge of student residence halls and university apartments for students.
- **Student union.** This campus institution provides services that improve students' lives. The student union is frequently located in a special building with offices for student clubs and organizations, meeting rooms for guest speakers, and rooms for special events such as dances. Student unions may organize celebrations and special events for students, provide restaurants and food services, offer hotel rooms for university visitors, and provide study areas for students.

EXERCISE 4

Student Services

🎧 **AUDIO TRACK 30** Some students are talking about life on campus. Listen to the students. Give the letter of the student service that can help them. You can use each item more than once.

a. Admissions and records

b. International student affairs

c. Parking management

d. Recreational sports

e. Registrar

f. Student accounts

g. Student housing

h. Student union

1. _____

2. _____

3. _____

4. _____

5. _____

6. _____

7. _____

8. _____

9. _____

10. _____

Answers and Explanations for Exercise 4 begin on page 328.

Campus-Related Conversations: Listening Format

For each campus-related conversation, you will first see a picture of the speakers.

Next, the narrator will give a brief introduction to the listening selection. Then the listening selection will begin.

 Listen to the following example. Read along silently as you listen.

Narrator: Listen to a part of a conversation between a student and a university employee.

Student: Excuse me, can you help me? I need to replace my student ID card.

Employee: OK, you need to fill out this form and show me some other form of identification, such as your driver's license or passport. Then you pay a $25 fee. Then I can give a new ID card right away.

Student: OK. I brought my passport with me from home. Do you need to take my photo again?

Employee: No, we just use the photo that we took when you got your first ID card. It's right here in our computer system.

Student: That's good. My hair is a mess today. How can I pay the fee? I also lost my credit card, checkbook, and ATM card. And I am out of cash because I can't use the ATM.

Employee: Actually, we don't take cash or checks. We charge it to your student account. You'll get a bill at the end of the month.

Student: Really? Ummm . . . I didn't know I had a student account.

Employee: Yes, it's used for things like small fees, library fines, and other small payments to the university. You can also use it in the bookstore to buy your books each semester.

Student: I wish I'd known that last year when I didn't have money to buy my books. I had to borrow money from my roommate.

Employee: That's why the university gives all students a student account. You can use it for just about any small bill at the university, but you can't use it in the shops or restaurants in the student union food court. Just remember, if you don't pay it, your access to the library and other student services will be cut off.

The photograph will remain on the screen as you listen to the conversation. When the conversation is over, the test will advance to the first item. You cannot see the items until after you listen to the conversation.

Taking Notes

As on academic lectures, take detailed notes as you listen to the conversations. Since you cannot see the items until you finish listening, write down as much detail as you can. As on all parts of the TOEFL iBT, notes will be collected at the end of the test, but they will not be read or evaluated. Follow these instructions:

1. To help you write as much information as possible, use numbers, abbreviations, and symbols in your notes.
2. Write down main ideas and details. To help distinguish main idea and detail, use a simple outline form in your notes.
3. The first item after a conversation is almost always a gist-purpose item, so listen carefully for statements that indicate the reason the people are talking and include them in your notes. You will learn more about gist-purpose items on pages 270–274.
4. Do not worry about spelling, punctuation, capitalization, or other details in your notes. You do not need to worry about good handwriting or printing either, as long as you can read your notes. Write as quickly as you can, taking care to make sure you can read your notes when it is time to answer the questions.

Taking Notes

 Listen to the conversations and take notes.

1.

_____

_____

_____

_____

_____

_____

_____

_____

_____

2.

Answers for Exercise 5 begin on page 329.

Natural Language

TOEFL iBT listening selections present natural language used in North American higher educational settings. The features of everyday natural language include pauses, digressions, repetition, mispronunciations, and other errors typical of natural language. Speakers may be native speakers of English or learners of English with accents and errors typical of language learners.

Natural Language

Here are some common features of everyday natural speech you will likely encounter on the TOEFL iBT.

- **Getting listeners' attention.** To get listeners' attention before they speak, English speakers use expressions such as "Excuse me" before they begin their main point.
- **Pauses and fillers.** Though English speech may often seem fast, natural speech often has pauses and fillers such as "Umm" or "Uhh."
- **Reduced speech.** Speakers may use contractions, omit words, or run words together. For example, "What did you do?" might become, "Whatdidja do?"
- **Digressions.** Speakers may not always stick to the topic. Instead, they begin to talk about an unrelated point and then return to the main topic. One of the skills the TOEFL iBT tests is the ability to distinguish main ideas and relevant details from irrelevant digressions.
- **Asides.** Speakers may briefly state their own opinion about the main topic during a conversation. These asides may be useful in answering items about speakers' purposes and opinions. Asides are sometimes tested in playback items.
- **Interruptions.** In natural speech, listeners may interrupt with a question or comment, and these interruptions may be off topic.
- **Self-correction.** Sometimes, speakers will realize that they made a mistake and will correct themselves.

Get used to listening to natural English through English movies, TV, or the Internet. As you listen, pay attention to pauses, fillers, digressions, interruptions, and other features of natural, spoken English.

TOEFL iBT Listening Item Formats

TOEFL iBT Listening items include standard multiple-choice items as well as several kinds of special items.

TOEFL iBT LISTENING ITEM FORMATS

ITEM TYPE	DESCRIPTION
Standard multiple choice	Choose 1 answer from four options.
Special multiple choice	Choose 2 or more answers from four or more options.
Replay items	Listen to part of the selection again. Answer a multiple-choice item.
Check box items	Classify or evaluate information by checking boxes.
Drag-and-drop items	Organize information by placing sentences in a table.

Standard Multiple-Choice Items

Most items on the TOEFL iBT Listening section are standard multiple-choice items. These items have a question and four answer options. Here is an example, based on the conversation between a student and a university employee that you read previously.

According to the university employee, how can the student pay for her new student ID?

(A) Write a check.

(B) Use a credit card.

(C) Use her student account.

(D) Pay cash.

TIP **Answer multiple-choice items wisely!**

Several strategies can help you answer traditional multiple-choice items effectively. See the test-wiseness section on pages 9–10.

Special Multiple-Choice Items

These multiple-choice items have more than one answer. Usually, these items will have four options, two of which are correct. Here is an example, based on the lecture about plate tectonics that you read previously.

Which of the following discoveries were critical in the development of the theory of plate tectonics? *Choose 2 answers.*

A Earthquakes are concentrated around crevices in the ocean floor.

B Earth is solid.

C The sea floor is spreading.

D Earth's features are largely fixed.

TIP **Use small boxes to identify special multiple-choice items!**

When answer options have square boxes instead of circles, you know that the item is a special multiple-choice item with two or more answers. Check the directions carefully, and choose the correct number of options.

Replay Items

Some TOEFL iBT items ask you to listen again to part of the listening selection and then answer a question about that particular part. These items are called replay items or playback items. Here is an example of a replay item based on the lecture about plate tectonics that you read previously.

First, a screen appears that tells you that this kind of item is coming. You will see:

> Listen again to
> part of the lecture.
> Then answer the
> question.

Then you will hear again part of the listening selection that you just heard, followed by the question.

 Listen to the audio and read along silently as you listen.

Narrator: Listen again to part of the lecture. Then answer the question.

Professor: The hardest part of this theory for many to accept was the notion that massive plates could float on molten rock. This was eventually explained by the relative density of the materials, the plates being less dense than the molten rock below, which allowed them to be buoyant and float on the molten rock.

Narrator: Why does the professor say this?

Professor: The hardest part of this theory for many to accept was the notion that massive plates could float on molten rock.

Then you will see the item and answer options:

Ⓐ The professor wants to indicate that she disagrees with the theory of tectonic plates.

Ⓑ The professor wants to point out that most scientists continue to reject the theory for this reason.

Ⓒ The professor wants to indicate that this was an important objection the theory needed to overcome.

Ⓓ The professor wants to indicate that scientists believed that rock could float.

In this book, the audio icon next to a listening item will indicate that it is a replay item. In addition, you will see and hear the same directions as on the TOEFL iBT.

> **TIP**   **Use tone and intonation on playback items!**
>
> The speaker's tone and intonation are very important in answering replay items, since these can indicate the speaker's attitude. Listen for attitudes such as belief, skepticism, and confusion in speakers' tone and intonation. In this item, it's clear that the professor believes in the theory and is merely commenting on a part of the theory that was hard for other scientists to accept.

Check Box Items

These items ask you to evaluate information in a chart or table by checking (✔) boxes. You will see a table with a number of phrases or sentences and instructions asking you to examine and evaluate the information in some way. You might check boxes to indicate which of the items was mentioned or included in the listening selection. Or you might have to decide whether each of the items is related to or supports a certain idea or concept. For example, look at the following item. It is meant to accompany a conversation about ways to pay for things at the university. Based on the information you hear, you need to decide whether you can or cannot pay for an ID card, textbooks, or coffee in the ways described. On the actual TOEFL iBT you will use your cursor and mouse to check the appropriate boxes. In this book, you will write check marks (✔) in the boxes.

Indicate whether students can pay for things in these ways.

Put a check (✔) in the column for "Can" or "Cannot."

	CAN	CANNOT
Use a student account to pay for a new ID card.		
Use a student account to buy textbooks in the university bookstore.		
Use cash to pay for a new ID card.		
Use a student account to buy coffee in the student union.		

Drag-and-Drop Items

These items involve filling in a table with information from a list. On the actual TOEFL iBT, you will use your computer's mouse to click on and drag words, phrases, or sentences into the correct position in the table. In this book, you will provide the letters of the answer choices.

Ordering Items

One drag-and-drop format asks you to order past events or steps in a process by placing answer options in the correct order in a table. Look at the example:

> What are the steps the student can follow to get and pay for a replacement student ID card? Place the steps in order from first to last. The first one is done for you.

1.	Go to the ID Center and fill out a form.
2.	
3.	
4.	
5.	

(A) Pay the student account at the end of the month.

(B) Get a new ID card.

(C) Pay $25 using her student account.

(D) Show another form of ID, such as a passport.

TIP **Prepare for ordering items as you listen!**

You may need to order answer options by date in an ordering item. If a listening selection contains dates, make sure you include them in your notes.

You may also need to order answer options according to the steps in a process. If you hear steps in a process, write the steps in order in your notes, and number them. For example, in this conversation, your notes might read:

1. Fill out form ID center

2. Pay $25 w/ std acct

3. Show diff ID

Matching Items

This common drag-and-drop format asks you to sort answer options by matching them with headings in a table. Look at the example:

Match each of the following statements with the theory about Earth's structure to which it refers. Use your cursor to drag and drop the statements to the spaces where they belong.

GEOSYNCLINICAL THEORY	CONTINENTAL DRIFT	PLATE TECTONICS

Ⓐ Landmasses were joined together and slowly moved apart.

Ⓑ Landmasses ride on large structures that slowly move together or apart.

Ⓒ Pressure from within Earth pushes rock up to the surface.

TOEFL iBT Listening Item Types

TOEFL iBT listening item types cover a range of understandings, from basic comprehension (understanding the main idea or "gist," or distinguishing main idea and detail) to increasingly higher levels of understanding (understanding organization, classifying information, inferring speakers' purposes and attitudes, and making other kinds of inferences). The following section examines all the item types on the TOEFL iBT Listening section.

TOEFL IBT LISTENING ITEM TYPES

	ITEM TYPE	DESCRIPTION
Basic Comprehension	Gist-content	Understand the main idea.
	Gist-purpose	Understand the speaker's reason for speaking.
	Supporting detail	Identifying details that support the main idea.
Pragmatic Understanding	Understanding the function of what is said	Understand the speaker's reasons for saying something.
	Understanding the speaker's attitude	Understand the speakers' opinion or feelings about something.
Connecting Information	Understanding organization	Understand the overall organization of the listening selection. Understand the reason information is in the selection (example, reason, contrast, etc.).
	Connecting content	Organize information in the listening selection in new ways.
	Making inferences	Figure out information based on facts in the listening selection.

Answering Basic Comprehension Items

Basic comprehension items include gist-content, gist-purpose, and detail items. Frequently, the first item that follows the listening selection is a gist-content item or a gist-purpose item.

BASIC COMPREHENSION ITEMS

ITEM TYPE	ITEM FORMATS USED
Gist-content	Standard multiple choice
	Always follows a lecture
	May follow a conversation
Gist-purpose	Standard multiple choice
	Always follows a conversation
	May follow a lecture
Supporting detail	Standard multiple choice
	Special multiple choice

Gist-Content Items

The gist is the main idea. In general, gist-content items appear with academic lecture listening selections, but they can also occur with campus-related conversations.

Listening for the Main Idea

The main idea of the listening selection may be stated directly or indirectly in the lecture or conversation. In many listening selections, the speaker may state the main idea in the first few sentences or exchanges. In other listening selections, you may need to figure out, or infer, the main idea by listening to the entire selection and using the details of the lecture or conversation to determine the main idea.

Here are examples of two listening selections with the main idea stated directly or indirectly.

Listen to the excerpts. Then answer the questions.

 **EXCERPT 1**

What is the main idea?

How is the main idea stated, **directly** or **indirectly**? (Choose one)

 **EXCERPT 2**

What is the main idea?

How is the main idea stated, **directly** or **indirectly**? (Choose one)

For Excerpt 1, if you said that the main idea is stated directly, you are right. The selection states the main idea directly: "Plate tectonics is a relatively new description of Earth's crust. The theory of plate tectonics asserts that once all of Earth's continents were a single landmass, which broke up as the underlying plates separated and began to move apart."

For Excerpt 2, if you said that the main idea is stated indirectly, you are right. The main idea seems to be that even though consumers complain about inflation, inflation can be beneficial to consumers, particularly those who own certain kinds of assets.

Gist-content items frequently include language such as *main idea*, *main topic*, or *main point*. Study the chart.

RECOGNIZING GIST-CONTENT ITEMS
What is the (**main/primary**) **topic** of this (conversation/lecture)?
What is the (student) asking about?
What is the **main point** of this (conversation/lecture)?
What is the professor discussing with the students?

Gist-Content Item

 Listen to the selection from a longer lecture. Then answer the question.

Physics

Properties of light

Visible and invisible light

Colors of the spectrum

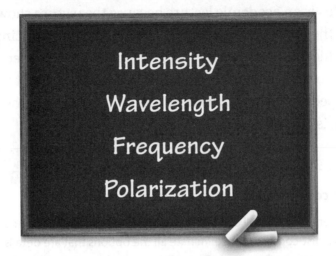

Intensity

Wavelength

Frequency

Polarization

What is the main idea of the lecture?

(A) Scientific terms have special meanings that are different from their ordinary meanings.

(B) The class will examine many properties of light in this unit of study.

(C) The class will study both invisible and visible light.

(D) Intensity refers to the rate of transfer of energy of a wave, such as a light wave.

TIP **Listen for the main idea at the beginning of each lecture!**

In lectures, the professor will often state the main idea of the lecture early in the lecture. Since the first item is almost always a gist item, listen for the main idea at the beginning of each lecture and write it in your notes. For example, in this lecture, the professor says, "Today we will turn our attention to the next topic in the syllabus, optics, or the study of light. When we think of light, we most often think of visible light and the colors in the spectrum, but we will touch upon many more topics in our study of light, including visible and invisible light, intensity of light, wavelength, frequency, and polarization." This sentence lets you know both the main idea of the lecture (properties of light) and key details (visible and invisible light, intensity of light, wavelength, frequency, and polarization). When you hear a clear statement of the main idea, write it in your notes. When you hear details, write them under the main idea using a simple outline format. Study the example:

Main idea: properties of light
—visible, invisible, intensity, wavelength, freq, polariz.

You know that this is an academic lecture because the picture shows a professor speaking to a class. The answer is Option B. The professor is introducing the topic of the next unit of study, which is the properties of light. Option A is incorrect because that is only one of the ideas in the selection. Option C is incorrect because it is too specific—it refers to only one aspect of light that the class will study. Option D, the scientific meaning of the term *intensity*, is also too specific.

TIP **Answer gist-content items with a generalization!**

The answer to a gist-content item will almost always be a generalization, not a detail. If you are not sure of the answer to a gist-content item, eliminate all the options that are details. For instance, in this example, you can eliminate Options A, C, and D because they are too specific. Only Option B is a generalization.

EXAMPLE

Gist-Content Item

 Listen to the selection from a longer conversation. Then answer the question. Circle the letter of the answer.

What is the main topic of this conversation?

Ⓐ The borders of the campus zone

Ⓑ The bus transportation system on campus

Ⓒ Buying a bus pass

Ⓓ Ways for student to get to campus

You can identify this item as a gist-content item because it asks for the main topic of the conversation. The answer is Option C, buying a bus pass. The student wants to buy a bus pass, so he is in the office finding out about the various plans and prices. Option A is incorrect because it is just one detail about the various plans and prices. Options B and D are incorrect because they are too broad. Option B would include other details, such as routes and schedules, which are not in the selection. Option D is about all means of transportation, not just bus passes, so it is incorrect.

> **TIP** **Choose the correct generalization!**
>
> Sometimes, the answer options to a gist-content item will contain more than one generalization. In most cases, one of the generalizations will be too broad. It will cover more than the topic of the selection. In this example, Options B and D are both too broad. The main idea of the selection is about bus passes. Option B is about the whole system, not just passes. It would include more information on routes, schedules, and fares. Option D is even broader, because it covers kinds of transportation not mentioned in the selection (such as driving and walking).

EXERCISE 6

Gist-Content Items

 Listen to selections from longer TOEFL iBT listening selections again. Then answer the item after each selection. Circle the letter of the answer.

1.

Microeconomics

What is the main topic of this lecture?

(A) A consumer boycott is a morally based consumer decision.

(B) Purchasing Fair Trade goods is one way consumers can feel that they are making good purchasing decisions.

(C) Fair Trade goods are of higher quality than similar goods that are not Fair Trade.

(D) Consumers base decisions on moral or ethical considerations.

2.

What is the main point of this conversation?

(A) Closed reserve items can be checked out for two hours or overnight.

(B) Closed reserve items can be photocopied or scanned.

(C) Closed reserve items have many special rules.

(D) Professors put library items on closed reserve when they are required reading for their students.

3.

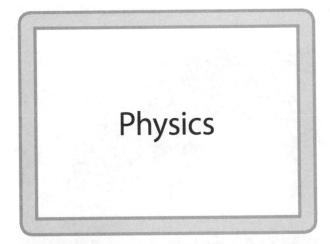

Physics

What is the primary topic of this lecture?

Ⓐ The first observations of the Doppler effect when trains became able to travel at high speeds

Ⓑ The relationship between the Doppler effect and sonic booms

Ⓒ How sound waves work

Ⓓ Changes in how we perceive sound because of the Doppler effect

4.

What is the main point of this conversation?

Ⓐ Midterms and quizzes in the student's class

Ⓑ Requirements for getting an A in the student's class

Ⓒ Dropping one quiz grade in the student's class

Ⓓ Possible term paper topics for the student's class

5.

Contemporary Literature

What is the main idea of this lecture?

(A) Most contemporary writing on the immigrant experience is by Asian or Hispanic authors.

(B) Hemon is not a true immigrant, because he did not choose to come to the United States.

(C) Stories of the immigrant experience are not an important part of contemporary American literature.

(D) Hemon's writing is an unusual example of literature of the immigrant experience.

Answers and Explanations for Exercise 6 begin on page 331.

Gist-Purpose Items

This second sort of gist item asks you to identify speakers' main purpose in communicating. One of these items will almost always follow campus-related conversations, but they may appear with academic lectures as well. Often, the purpose of the conversation is not stated directly. For example, in an office conversation with a professor, a student in marketing class might ask a number of questions about course content, but the student's purpose is finding out about the topics that will be covered on an upcoming midterm exam. Gist-purpose items frequently include language such as *why* or *main purpose*. Study the chart.

RECOGNIZING GIST-PURPOSE ITEMS
Why is (the student) talking to (the professor)?
Why is (the student) in (the registrar's office)?
What is the **main purpose** of this (conversation)?
Why does (the student) need (the employee's) assistance?

EXAMPLE

Gist-Purpose Item

 Listen again to the conversation between a student and a university services manager. Then answer the question.

Why does the services manager ask the student questions?

Ⓐ The student doesn't understand the manager.

Ⓑ The manager wants the student to know that the plans are not available to faculty and staff.

Ⓒ The manager wants to help the student find a plan that works for him.

Ⓓ The manager wants to tell the student that the Gold Plan is available at night.

This item begins with, "Why does the services manager ask . . . ," so it is a gist-purpose item. Option C is correct because the manager asks questions so that the student can compare his travel needs to the two plans. Option A is incorrect because the student clearly understands the manager. Option B is incorrect because the plans have different prices for students and faculty/staff. Option D is incorrect because this is only one detail from the conversation.

EXAMPLE

Gist-Purpose Item

 Listen to a part of a conversation between a student and a professor. Then answer the question.

Why is the student talking to the professor?

Ⓐ To find out why she got a low grade on a paper

Ⓑ To talk about the effect of market factors on food prices

Ⓒ To find out why her paper needs a concluding paragraph

Ⓓ To discuss the relationship between lettuce prices and consumer demand

This example is clearly a gist-purpose item because it uses the wording of one the most typical gist-purpose items. If you chose Option A, your answer is correct. Option A is the reason the student gives for speaking to the professor. Option B is not correct because it is the topic of the paper, not the conversation with the professor. Option C is not correct because it is a detail in the conversation. Option D is not correct because it is an example she could have added to her paper.

EXERCISE 7

Gist-Purpose Items

 Listen to the following listening selections from longer conversations. Then answer the item after each selection. Circle the letter of the answer.

1. Why does the student go to see the professor?

   (A) She has a family emergency.

   (B) She needs to make sure she can take a makeup exam.

   (C) She doesn't want to take the midterm exam.

   (D) She wants to tell her about the volleyball team's winning record.

2. Why is the man talking to the woman?

Ⓐ He has questions about extremist politics in Europe.

Ⓑ He doesn't want to write about military history.

Ⓒ He needs advice about whether to talk to the professor.

Ⓓ He needs advice about a term paper topic.

3. What is the main purpose of this talk?

Ⓐ To discuss why the progressive income tax is controversial

Ⓑ To tell students that the progressive income tax is the main topic of the midterm

Ⓒ To talk about topics covered on the exam next week

Ⓓ To talk about recent efforts to change tax rates on the rich

4. Why is the man talking to the woman?

    Ⓐ He wants her to know that single rooms are available in Roberts Hall.

    Ⓑ He wants her to know that he is tired from moving to another dorm room.

    Ⓒ He wants to tell her that he is moving to another room.

    Ⓓ He wants to complain about his roommate.

5. Why does the student go to see the professor?

    Ⓐ He is worried about an online class next week.

    Ⓑ He doesn't understand the instructions the professor sent.

    Ⓒ He lives 30 miles from campus and cannot come to class.

    Ⓓ He cannot participate in the online class because the keyboard on his phone is too small.

Answers and Explanations for Exercise 7 begin on page 334.

Supporting Detail Items

These items ask you to identify key details that support the main idea of the listening selection. A detail is a specific fact or piece of information that backs up, or supports, the main idea. For example, if the main idea of a lecture is exploring reasons children seem to learn language more easily than adults, supporting details might include that while adults struggle with a new language even when taking classes, children seem to learn a new language from exposure and without formal classes or instruction.

Main Idea and Detail

As you know, the gist is the main idea. The main idea is what the passage is mainly about. You will also need to know details—specific pieces of information that support, or back up, the main idea. For example, the main idea of the reading on plate tectonics is stated directly in the passage: "Plate tectonics is a relatively new description of Earth's crust. The theory of plate tectonics asserts that once all of Earth's continents were a single landmass, which broke up as the underlying plates separated and began to move apart." Details that support this main idea include the three theories used to describe Earth's crust: geosynclinal, continental drift, and plate tectonics.

EXERCISE 8

Main Idea or Detail?

Read each pair of sentences. Write *M* if the sentence is a main idea. Write *D* if the sentence is a detail. Follow the example.

1. __M__ **a.** People are becoming increasingly concerned about global warming.
   __D__ **b.** Average summer and winter temperatures have risen.

2. _____ **a.** The Center for Service Learning provides opportunities for students to engage in community-based learning experiences.
   _____ **b.** This holiday break, students can travel to New York City or New Orleans to participate in a volunteer project rebuilding public schools damaged by recent flooding.

3. _____ **a.** Diabetes and heart disease are becoming increasingly common.
   _____ **b.** Increasing rates of obesity are raising concerns about long-term health consequences.

4. _____ **a.** The technology adaptation cycle explains how new innovations are accepted by the public.
   _____ **b.** Individuals with high levels of education are more likely to adopt new technological innovations than individuals with less education.

5. _____ **a.** All campus parking lots are free to the public after 5 P.M., but overnight parking is not permitted except in the Green Street lot.
   _____ **b.** The Office of Parking Management is in charge of all off-street parking on campus.

Answers for Exercise 8 begin on page 336.

> **TIP** **Indicate main idea and detail in your notes!**
>
> As you listen and take notes, use a simple outline format to show the relationship between main idea and detail. Write the main points to the right. Indent the details under the main points.
>
> ### Why low grade?
> ### —no concl
> ### —problems w/ mechs, sp, commas
>
> Often, outlines use letters and numbers to show the relationship of ideas. Because you have to work quickly when taking the TOEFL iBT, you probably shouldn't spend time lettering and numbering.

Detail items may be standard multiple choice, special multiple choice, or negative factual information. Detail items frequently contain language such as *cause*, *result*, or *support*. Study the chart.

RECOGNIZING DETAIL ITEMS
What does the (professor) say about the **cause** of (global warming)?
According to the professor, **what** is **one important** (**cause/result**) of global warming?
According to the professor, **what does the theory** of (plate tectonics) **demonstrate**?
Which detail supports the professor's comment that average temperatures are rising?

EXAMPLE

Detail Item

 Listen again to part of a conversation between a student and a professor. Then answer the question. Circle the letters of the answers.

According to the professor, what does the student need to do to improve her paper? *Choose 2 answers.*

A Correct errors about supply and demand

B Correct the spelling errors

C Add a concluding paragraph

D Add an introductory paragraph

This is an example of a special multiple-choice item. If you chose Options B and C, you are correct. The professor tells the student that her paper is missing a concluding paragraph and has many spelling errors. Option A is not correct because the professor says that the student's paper shows a good understanding of supply and demand. Option D is not correct because the professor says the student's paper has a good introductory paragraph.

TIP **Answer special multiple-choice items as if they are true-or-false items!**

Special multiple-choice items are challenging because you need to select more than one answer. A good way to answer one of these items is to consider each of the answer options as a true-or-false item. Read the options one by one and decide whether each one answers the question (is true) or not. If it is true, select it. For example, Option A is not true. The professor never says that the paper contains errors about the theory of supply and demand. Option B is true because the student admits she needs to improve her spelling. Option C is true because the professor says that the student needs to add a concluding paragraph. Even though you have found two correct answer options, evaluate the final option, Option D, to ensure that you did not make a mistake with your other answers. Option D is, in fact, not true because the professor says that the student's paper already has a good introduction.

EXAMPLE

Detail Item

Answer this question based on the conversation you just heard in Audio Track 42. Circle the letter of the answer.

What is one of the student's problems with mechanics?

Ⓐ She needs to add another example.

Ⓑ She needs to indent all her paragraphs.

Ⓒ She needs to end all sentences with periods.

Ⓓ She needs to be more careful about commas.

If you selected Option D, you are correct. Option D is correct because the professor says that the student needs to correct problems with commas. Option A is not correct because examples are related to content, not mechanics. Option B is incorrect because though indenting paragraphs is a mechanics problem, the professor does not identify indentation as a problem. Option C is incorrect because periods are not mentioned in the conversation.

Negative Factual Information Items

Some factual information items use a negative word such as *not* in the question. These are called negative factual information items. Look at the example. Circle the letter of the answer.

Which of the following is NOT a problem the student needs to correct in her paper?

Ⓐ Spelling errors

Ⓑ Comma errors

Ⓒ Capitalization errors

Ⓓ Indentation errors

If you selected Option D, you are correct. Option D is the only problem the student does not need to fix. The professor says, "It looks like you indented all of your paragraphs." All of the other errors are things the professor says she needs to correct.

Negative items are hard to answer because we are used to choosing options that are correct. Negative items ask us to find the one option that is not in the selection or that is contradicted by it. Because negative items work differently from regular multiple-choice items and are difficult, the TOEFL iBT test writers always write the negative word in all capital letters in the question.

When you see a word such as *NOT* or *EXCEPT* in a question, remember to look for an answer option that is not supported, or is contradicted, by the selection. Read all the options carefully, and eliminate the ones that are true or supported by the lecture or conversation, and look for the one option that is untrue or not supported.

EXERCISE 9

Supporting Detail Items

 Listen to the selections from Exercise 6 again and answer the questions. Circle the letter of the answer.

1. What does the professor say about the cause of the Free Trade movement?

   Ⓐ Consumer decisions can have a big impact on economic activity.

   Ⓑ The Free Trade movement frequently focuses on agricultural products from developing nations.

   Ⓒ Consumers want to pay lower prices for everything.

   Ⓓ Consumers want products sourced in ways that they believe are moral or ethical.

2. Which of the following are ways a student can access closed reserve items? *Choose 2 answers.*

   A Use them in the library for two hours

   B Check them out for the weekend

   C Scan or photocopy them

   D Check them out for a month

3. In which of these situations would the people NOT observe the Doppler effect?

   Ⓐ Two passengers in a speeding train that is blowing its horn

   Ⓑ Two runners running on the side of the highway as a car speeds away blowing its horn

   Ⓒ Two police officers driving police cars toward one another rapidly and sounding their sirens

   Ⓓ Two pedestrians waiting to cross the highway as a truck drives toward them at high speed blowing its horn

4. Why does the student need to write a term paper?

   Ⓐ He got a C on three quizzes.

   Ⓑ He might have a B average for exams.

   Ⓒ He will probably get an A on the final exam.

   Ⓓ He wants to get an A for the course.

5. Why did Aleksander Hemon stay in the United States?

   Ⓐ He wanted to learn English and become an American writer.

   Ⓑ He wanted to write about the immigrant experience.

   Ⓒ He was on a short-term exchange program.

   Ⓓ His hometown was under air attack.

Answers and Explanations for Exercise 9 begin on page 337.

EXERCISE 10

Answering Basic Comprehension Items

 Listen to the selection. Answer the questions.

Psychology

1. What is the main topic of this talk?

   Ⓐ The goals of positive psychology

   Ⓑ The weaknesses of positive psychology

   Ⓒ Differences between traditional psychology and positive psychology

   Ⓓ An overview of positive psychology

2. What is the main purpose of this talk?

   Ⓐ To give students ways to find happiness in life

   Ⓑ To provide an introduction to a unit of study in the course

   Ⓒ To criticize the weaknesses and shortcomings of positive psychology

   Ⓓ To study positive psychology deeply and critically

3. Which of the following is NOT an area studied by positive psychology?

   Ⓐ Ways that people derive happiness from hobbies and entertainment

   Ⓑ Ways that people learn to think of their lives as meaningful and important

   Ⓒ Ways that people are made unhappy by abnormalities

   Ⓓ Ways that people's jobs and daily occupations make them feel good

4. According to the professor, what is one problem of mainstream psychology?

   Ⓐ It is unscientific.

   Ⓑ It is used to diagnose and treat mental illness.

   Ⓒ It gives a partial or incomplete view of people.

   Ⓓ It ignores abnormality.

5. Positive psychology studies "the meaningful life" by examining which of these things?

   Ⓐ The satisfaction people feel when they play a sport

   Ⓑ The satisfaction people get from their jobs

   Ⓒ The satisfaction people feel when they take a vacation

   Ⓓ The satisfaction people get from involvement in the community

Answers and Explanations for Exercise 10 begin on page 339.

> **TIP** **Look for answer options that stand out from others!**
>
> Sometimes, you can figure out the answer by finding an answer option that stands out as different from the others. For example, in Item 3, all of the options focus on happiness except one of them. Which one? Option C focuses on the unhappiness caused by abnormalities. All of the others are identified in positive terms. Option C is different from the other options, and it is, in fact, something that is studied by traditional psychology, not positive psychology, and, therefore, it is the answer.

Answering Pragmatic Understanding Items

While basic comprehension items involve literal and inferential comprehension, pragmatic understanding items involve higher-order thinking skills. Pragmatic understanding items test your understanding of speakers' attitude, degree of certainty, and motivation for speaking. Pragmatic understanding items are of two types: function items and attitude (stance) items. To answer these items, you need to go beyond literal meanings. Pragmatic understanding items often require test takers to use clues from speakers' stress and intonation to make inferences about the speakers' reasons for speaking.

Some pragmatic understanding items are replay items. For replay items, you will hear a part of the selection a second time and then answer a question about just that part. Other pragmatic understanding items may quote directly from the selection without playing the recording back.

PRAGMATIC UNDERSTANDING ITEMS

ITEM TYPE	ITEM FORMATS USED
Understanding the function of what is said	Standard multiple choice
	Special multiple choice
	Replay items
Understanding the speaker's attitude	Standard multiple choice
	Special multiple choice
	Replay items

Understanding the Function Items

Understanding the function items ask you to figure out why a speaker says something. For example, the question, "Do you know what time it is?" is not a literal question—the answer is not yes or no. The listener knows to respond by saying the time of day. Understanding the function items assess speakers' often unstated reasons for speaking. A speaker may say something to express agreement, disagreement, or skepticism. Or a speaker may want to give an example, apologize, provide clarification, or change the subject. Usually, the speaker's reasons are not stated directly but need to be figured out. Understanding the function items often include words such as *mean*, *imply*, or *purpose*. Study the chart.

RECOGNIZING UNDERSTANDING THE FUNCTION ITEMS
What does (the administrator) **imply/mean** when (she) says this? (replay)
What can you **infer** from (the professor's) response to (the student)? (replay)
Why does the professor say this? (replay)
What does the student **mean** when he says, . . . ?
Why does the professor **mention** . . . ?
What is the professor's **purpose** in saying . . . ?

> **EXAMPLE**

Understanding the Function Item

 Listen to a replay item from a conversation you have heard previously. Circle the letter of the answer.

Ⓐ She wants to hear an example or clarification.

Ⓑ She disagrees with the professor about her low grade.

Ⓒ She disagrees with the professor about mechanics.

Ⓓ She wants to change the subject.

If you selected Option A, you are correct. Option A is correct because the student's intonation indicates interest and curiosity. Options B and C are incorrect because her intonation does not indicate disagreement. Option D is incorrect because she is not changing the subject, but asking for more detail about it.

EXERCISE 11

Understanding the Function Items

 Listen again to parts of conversations that you heard previously. Then answer the questions. Circle the letter of the answer.

1. Ⓐ The professor is unwilling to change the rule.

   Ⓑ The student will have to do extra work if she is absent for the test.

   Ⓒ If a student has an unusual problem, the professor will make an exception to the rule.

   Ⓓ The professor is not really serious about enforcing the rule.

2. Ⓐ He really didn't like the topic of political extremism.

   Ⓑ He doesn't want to write about military history.

   Ⓒ He needs more information on the assignment.

   Ⓓ He really hates political history.

3. (A) She already understands the definition, and she has a question on another aspect of progressive income tax.

   (B) She wants to change the subject to a completely different topic.

   (C) She is a conservative and does not think that the progressive income tax is a good idea.

   (D) She has a few more questions about the details of a progressive income tax.

4. (A) She is not interested in his problem.

   (B) The man likes to play old music.

   (C) A lot of people have had that problem before the man.

   (D) She has already heard about that.

5. (A) The professor thinks that the small keyboard is not a serious problem.

   (B) The professor doesn't have time to help John.

   (C) The professor thinks that he can't solve John's problem with the small keyboard.

   (D) The professor thinks that John is not a very responsible student.

Answers and Explanations for Exercise 11 begin on page 341.

TIP **Do not choose the literal meaning for an understanding the function item!**

Understanding the function items assess your ability to listen and figure out the speaker's intention, which is expressed indirectly. Therefore, eliminate any answer options that include the literal meaning. For example, in Item 5, the professor says that she cannot solve all of the student's problems, but she is not speaking literally. Therefore, Options B and C are not possible. Rather, she means that having a small keyboard is not a big problem.

Understanding the Attitude (Stance) Items

Attitude (stance) items require test takers to figure out a speaker's attitude, opinion, likes, dislikes, feelings, or emotions. You might have to determine whether a speaker is amused, anxious, distrustful, disbelieving, or uncertain. Frequently, understanding the attitude items are replay items. These items often begin with language such as *attitude*, *opinion*, or *feel*. Study the chart.

RECOGNIZING UNDERSTANDING THE ATTITUDE (STANCE) ITEMS
What is the (man's) **attitude toward** . . . ?
What opinion does the (professor) express about . . . ?
How does (the man) seem to **feel** about . . . ?
Which sentence best expresses (the man's) **feelings**?

EXAMPLE

Understanding the Attitude Item

Listen to part of a talk in a life science class. Then answer the question. Circle the letter of the answer.

Life Science

What is the professor's attitude toward the scientists' hypothesis that symbiotic relationships are not truly mutual?

Ⓐ He is certain that symbiotic relationships are not truly mutual.

Ⓑ He wants the students to find ways to prove that symbiotic relationships are not truly mutual.

Ⓒ He is certain that scientists can prove their hypothesis about symbiotic relationships.

Ⓓ He believes that the hypothesis is not supported by current research.

If you chose Option D, you are correct. Right now, the professor believes that the hypothesis lacks proof. Words such as *although*, *however*, *so far*, and *supposition* indicate that he is doubtful. Option A is not correct because his attitude seems doubtful. Option B is incorrect because his comments are not directed toward the students. Option C is incorrect because he does not express an opinion about whether the scientists will be able to prove the hypothesis.

EXAMPLE

Understanding the Attitude Item

 Listen again to part of the lecture. Then answer the question.

Ⓐ He is certain that proof will never be found.

Ⓑ He thinks that proof has already been found.

Ⓒ He is open-minded about whether such proof will be found.

Ⓓ He is certain that other kinds of mutual relations exist.

TIP **Listen to tone and intonation on attitude (stance) items!**

On understanding the attitude items, pay attention to the speaker's tone and intonation, since these can change the meaning of a word or phrase completely. The word *may*, for example, in this sample item, can express possibility, doubt, or even disbelief, depending on the tone and intonation.

If you chose Option C, you are correct. Option C is correct because the professor's use of the word *may* indicates that he believes that finding such proof is possible. Therefore, Options A and B are incorrect. Option D is not discussed by the professor.

> **TIP** **Listen for tone and intonation on replay items!**
>
> Replay items are frequently understanding the function or understanding the attitude items. Tone and intonation are very important in answering these kinds of questions. When you encounter a replay item, prepare yourself to answer one of these two item types. To help you answer, as you listen to the audio excerpt, ask yourself questions such as, "What are the speakers' attitudes toward the topic?" or "Why did the speaker say this?"

EXERCISE 12

Understanding Tone and Intonation

 Listen to each conversation. What do the people mean? Circle the letter of the answer.

1. When the man says, "Yeah, right," what does he mean?

    Ⓐ He believes that John will be on time tomorrow.

    Ⓑ He believes that John will be late tomorrow.

2. When the woman says, "That sounds awfully easy," what does she mean?

    Ⓐ She believes it's a good deal.

    Ⓑ She believes it's a bad deal.

3. When the woman says, "Congratulations," what does she mean?

    Ⓐ She thinks the man got a better grade than usual.

    Ⓑ She thinks the man got a lower grade than usual.

4. When the man says, "Congratulations," what does he mean?

   Ⓐ He is happy for the woman.

   Ⓑ He is not happy for the woman.

5. When the woman says, "Great!" what does she mean?

   Ⓐ She is happy that class is canceled.

   Ⓑ She is not happy that class is canceled.

6. When the man says, "Of course," what does he mean?

   Ⓐ He is surprised that the concert is sold out.

   Ⓑ He is not surprised that the concert is sold out.

7. When the woman says, "Of course," what does she mean?

   Ⓐ She doesn't feel surprised about the quiz.

   Ⓑ She feels surprised about the quiz.

8. When the man says, "My goodness!" what does he mean?

   Ⓐ He thinks the news is bad.

   Ⓑ He thinks the news is good.

9. When the woman says, "My goodness!" what does she mean?

   Ⓐ She is impressed by his grades.

   Ⓑ She is not impressed by his grades.

10. When the man asks, "How did that work out for you?" what does he mean?

    Ⓐ He thinks the woman did well on the final.

    Ⓑ He thinks the woman did poorly on the final.

Answers for Exercise 12 begin on page 343.

EXERCISE 13

Understanding the Attitude (Stance) Items

 Listen again to the conversation. Then answer the replay items. Circle the letter of the answer.

1. Listen again to part of the conversation. Then answer the question.

   Ⓐ She feels bad because her job interferes with her studies.

   Ⓑ She thinks the professor is not sincere about his compliment.

   Ⓒ She is trying to be modest.

   Ⓓ She wants to brag about herself.

2. Listen again to part of the conversation. Then answer the question.

   Ⓐ She is forgetful and trying to remember if she applied for that fellowship already.

   Ⓑ She is excited and interested in hearing more about the scholarship.

   Ⓒ She is insecure and feels she may not be qualified for the scholarship.

   Ⓓ She is very busy and thinks that this conversation is a waste of time.

3. Listen again to part of the conversation. Then answer the question.

   Ⓐ He feels happy.

   Ⓑ He feels worried.

   Ⓒ He is indifferent.

   Ⓓ He is bored.

4. Listen again to part of the conversation. Then answer the question.

   Ⓐ He is uninterested.

   Ⓑ He is suspicious.

   Ⓒ He is skeptical.

   Ⓓ He is encouraging.

Answers and Explanations for Exercise 13 begin on page 343.

EXERCISE 14

Answering Pragmatic Understanding Items

 Listen to the conversation. Then answer questions 1 and 2.

1. What does the professor mean when he says, "The short answer is yes"?

   (A) The professor does not have much to say on this topic.

   (B) The professor is annoyed with the student.

   (C) The student can add the question but has to listen to a long explanation.

   (D) The professor thinks that the student's question is not serious.

2. Why does the professor say, "Yes, this kind of thing happens all the time in research"?

   (A) He wants to criticize researchers who make unnecessary mistakes.

   (B) He wants to reassure the student that adding a research question is not a problem.

   (C) He thinks that investigators add research questions to their work too frequently.

   (D) He thinks that adding research questions is a bad practice.

 Listen again to parts of the conversation. Then answer questions 3, 4, and 5.

3. (A) He feels angry because he thinks the professor is unreasonable.

   (B) He feels happy because he can add the research question to the project.

   (C) He feels anxious because he thinks a lot of extra work is required.

   (D) He feels annoyed because the professor didn't answer the question.

4. (A) This kind of problem is common in research.

   (B) Sometimes researchers make mistakes.

   (C) The student thinks he made a big mistake.

   (D) He is agreeing with the professor.

5. (A) He wants to add a second new research question.

   (B) He wants to ask another question about his project.

   (C) He wants to stop talking about the research project and talk about another subject.

   (D) He wants to give another reason why researchers change their research designs.

Answers and Explanations for Exercise 14 begin on page 344.

Answering Connecting Information Items

Connecting information items focus on the interrelationship of information in the listening selection. A connecting information item may focus on:

- Understanding how ideas are organized by the speakers (understanding organization)
- Finding relationships among the information and ideas presented (connecting content)
- Using details in the listening selection to make generalizations (making inferences)

In all of these items, you need to go beyond specific facts and details in the listening selection and use them to find a bigger picture.

CONNECTING INFORMATION ITEMS

ITEM TYPE	ITEM FORMATS USED
Understanding organization	Standard multiple choice
	Special multiple choice
	Drag-and-drop (ordering)
Connecting content	Standard multiple choice
	Special multiple choice
	Drag-and-drop (classifying)
	Check box
Making inferences	Standard multiple choice
	Special multiple choice

Understanding Organization Items

These items ask you to demonstrate understanding of how speakers organize and present information. Usually, these items accompany academic lectures, but sometimes they appear with campus-related conversations. These items might ask about the overall organization of the listening selection. Or they might ask about the interrelationship of specific facts or ideas in the selection. There are two types: overall organization items and relationship organizational items.

These items frequently include language such as *organized*, *purpose*, and *why*. Study the chart.

RECOGNIZING UNDERSTANDING ORGANIZATION ITEMS

OVERALL ORGANIZATION	RELATIONSHIP OF IDEAS
How are the (events/ideas) **organized** . . . ?	**Why** does the professor **include information about** . . . ?
Why does the professor talk about *X* first?	**What** is the **purpose of mentioning** *X* . . . ?
	Why does the (professor) **mention** . . . ?

Overall Organization Items

Items of this type require you to recognize major organizational patterns commonly used in academic speech, and apply them to ideas from the listening selection. Common organizational patterns include chronological order, cause and effect, and compare and contrast. Each of these patterns uses signaling words and phrases to show the interrelationship of the ideas. Many overall organization items are drag-and-drop.

COMMON ORGANIZATIONAL PATTERNS AND SIGNALING WORDS

PATTERN	SIGNALING WORDS AND PHRASES
Importance	more importantly
Chronological order	first, second, third, last, then, next, later
Process	first, second, third, last, then, next
Compare and contrast	however, but
Cause and effect	so, then, as a result, because

EXAMPLE

Overall Organization Item

 Listen to the excerpt from a longer lecture in a life science class. Then answer the questions.

What are the steps of the life cycle of a butterfly? Place the steps in order from first to last. The first one is done for you.

1.	B Egg
2.	
3.	
4.	

Ⓐ Adult

Ⓑ Egg

Ⓒ Chrysalis

Ⓓ Larva

Here is how the completed table should look:

1.	B Egg
2.	D Larva
3.	C Chrysalis
4.	A Adult

EXAMPLE

Overall Organization Item

How does the professor organize the information he presents to the class?

(A) In the order in which the stages occur

(B) In the order in which butterflies travel from place to place

(C) By the length of time each step takes

(D) By the kind of food consumed during each stage

If you selected Option A, you are correct. The ideas in the lecture are in the order in which the stages in the life cycle of a butterfly occur. The other options are not supported by the lecture.

Relationship Organizational Items

Other organizational items ask you about the relationship of ideas in the listening selection. Relationships include:

- The reason the speaker included a piece of information
- The relationship between two pieces of information in the selection
- The function of a specific statement in the selection (introduce a topic, gain listeners' attention, signal a change in topic, connect detail to the main idea, introduce an example, and so on)

EXAMPLE

Relationship Organizational Item

 Listen again to the excerpt from a longer lecture in a life science class. Then answer the question. Circle the letter of the answer. Then decide whether the item is about overall organization or relationship of ideas, and circle the correct category.

Why does the professor mention milkweed plants?

(A) Because all butterflies lay their eggs on these plants

(B) Because butterfly larvae eat only the leaf of this plant

(C) To give some additional detail about one of the stages

(D) To show that not all butterflies follow these stages

Overall Organization   Relationship of Ideas   (circle one)

If you selected Option C, you are correct. This organizational item is about the interrelationship of ideas in the lecture. This example gives additional detail explaining what happens during this stage in the life of a butterfly. Options A and B are not supported by the selection. Only monarch butterflies lay their eggs exclusively on this plant (Option A) because monarch caterpillars eat only the leaf of this plant (Option B). Option D is contradicted by the lecture, which states that all butterflies follow this pattern.

EXAMPLE

Relationship Organizational Item

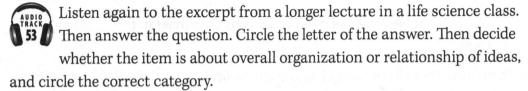 Listen again to the excerpt from a longer lecture in a life science class. Then answer the question. Circle the letter of the answer. Then decide whether the item is about overall organization or relationship of ideas, and circle the correct category.

Why does the professor include information about adult butterflies mating at the beginning and end of the information?

Ⓐ To show that the egg is really not the first stage in the cycle

Ⓑ To show that the stages can happen in any order

Ⓒ To show the relationship between the adult stage and the egg stage

Ⓓ To show that there is an additional stage in the life cycle

Overall Organization   Relationship of Ideas   *(circle one)*

If you selected Option C, you are correct. This organizational item is about the relationship of ideas in the selection. In order for eggs to be produced, adult butterflies have to mate first. Option A is incorrect because the egg is the first stage in the cycle. Options B and D are contradicted by the lecture. The stages happen in the order described by the professor, so Option B is incorrect. There are only four stages in the lifecycle, so Option D is incorrect.

EXAMPLE

Relationship Organizational Item

AUDIO TRACK 53

Listen again to the excerpt from a longer lecture in a life science class. Then answer the question. Circle the letter of the answer. Then decide whether the item is about overall organization or relationship of ideas, and circle the correct category.

Why does the professor begin the lecture by stating that cycles occur constantly in nature?

(A) To indicate that life cycles of other organisms are similar to the butterfly's life cycle

(B) To indicate that all patterns in nature are cyclical

(C) To indicate that the butterfly life cycle is consistent with a larger scientific principle

(D) To indicate that butterflies model their behavior on that of other organisms

Overall Organization   Relationship of Ideas   (*circle one*)

If you selected Option C, you are correct. This item is about the overall organization of the lecture. The professor says that so the students understand that the butterfly life cycle is not unusual, but merely an example of a general principle of how nature operates. Option A is not supported by the lecture. That many cycles occur in nature does not imply that all cycles follow the same or similar patterns. Option B is not a logical conclusion. From the information given in the lecture, it is not logical to conclude that all patterns in nature are cyclical. The professor merely states that cycles occur constantly. Option D is not supported by the lecture. The lecture gives no reason to conclude that butterflies are copying the behavior of other organisms.

EXERCISE 15

Understanding Organization Items

 Listen to part of a lecture in a marketing class. Then answer the questions. Circle the letter of the answer.

Marketing

1. Why is the professor talking about hotel prices?

Ⓐ Hotel prices follow the law of supply and demand in an unexpected way.

Ⓑ Hospitality is an important and fast-growing sector of the economy.

Ⓒ He is comparing them to the prices of vegetables.

Ⓓ Good marketing can help hotels increase sales by lowering prices.

2. How is the information ordered in this lecture?

   (A) According to cause-effect relationships

   (B) By comparing and contrasting

   (C) In the order in which the events happened

   (D) From most important to least important

3. What are the steps the hotel company followed? Place the steps in order from first to last.

1.	**B** The company lowered the prices of rooms at 11:00 every night.
2.	
3.	
4.	

   (A) The company raised the prices of rooms at 11:00 every night.

   (B) The company lowered the prices of rooms at 11:00 every night.

   (C) Company marketers studied check-in times at hundreds of hotels.

   (D) Demand stayed up, and profits went up.

4. Why did the professor include the example about hotel rooms?

   (A) To show an example of when lower prices increase demand

   (B) To show that the law of supply and demand applies to vegetables, but not to hotel rooms

   (C) To show an example of when higher prices affect demand

   (D) To show that consumer demand operates differently for different products

Answers and Explanations for Exercise 15 begin on page 346.

Connecting Content Items

Connecting content items ask you to identify relationships among ideas in the listening selection. Some connecting content items ask you to organize information in a different way than as it is presented in the selection. Other items may ask you to make inferences or draw conclusions using information in the selection. You might have to make a prediction based on the information, infer a possible cause or effect related to the information, or figure out the sequence of events based on clues in the information. In contrast to understanding information items, connecting content items ask you to figure out relationships among ideas, but not to assess the organization of the information. Often, connecting content items include drag-and-drop or matching item formats as well as check box formats. Connecting content items often begin with language such as *consequence*, *outcome*, and *imply*. Study the chart.

RECOGNIZING CONNECTING CONTENT ITEMS
What is a **possible consequence** of . . . ?
What is a **likely outcome** of . . . ?
What does the (man) **imply** about . . . ?

EXAMPLE

Connecting Content Item

 Listen again to part of a lecture in a life science class. Then answer the question.

Match each of the stages in the life of a butterfly with where the stage takes place. Write the letters under the correct heading.

EGG	LARVA	PUPA

Ⓐ In a hard case

Ⓑ On milkweed plants

Ⓒ On the underside of a milkweed leaf

The completed table should look like this:

EGG	LARVA	PUPA
C On the underside of a milkweed leaf	B On milkweed plants	A In a hard case

> **EXAMPLE**
>
> ## Connecting Content Item
> Answer the question. Circle the letter of the answer.
>
> What is a likely outcome if all the milkweed plants in an area die out?
>
> (A) Caterpillars in the area will not be able to find food.
>
> (B) Butterflies will move to different areas to lay their eggs.
>
> (C) Monarch butterflies will not lay their eggs in the area.
>
> (D) Monarch caterpillars in the area will not find food.

Option C is correct because monarch butterflies lay their eggs only on this kind of plant. Adult monarch butterflies therefore will not lay eggs in the area. Options A and B are incorrect because they are too general. Only monarch caterpillars eat milkweed leaves exclusively, so other species of caterpillars (Option A) or butterflies (Option B) will not be affected. Option D is incorrect because monarch butterflies lay their eggs only in areas that have milkweed plants. Therefore, no monarch caterpillars will be in the area either.

> **EXAMPLE**
>
> ## Connecting Content Item
> Answer the question.
>
> In which stage do the actions happen?
>
> *Place a check (✔) in the correct box.*
>
> | | EGG | LARVA | PUPA | ADULT |
> |------------------------------|-----|-------|------|-------|
> | Lays eggs | | | | |
> | Is on the underside of a leaf | | | | |
> | Is inside a hard case | | | | |

The completed table should look like this.

	EGG	LARVA	PUPA	ADULT
Lays eggs				✔
Is on the underside of a leaf	✔			
Is inside a hard case			✔	

EXERCISE 16

Connecting Content Items

 Listen again to the lecture in a marketing class. Then answer the questions.

1. What is the most likely consequence of increasing the price of unsold, ripe vegetables?

    Ⓐ The vegetables will go bad sooner.

    Ⓑ Demand will stay the same.

    Ⓒ No one will buy the vegetables.

    Ⓓ Demand will go down.

2. How do the pricing decisions affect demand?

    Place a check (✔) in the correct box.

	DEMAND GOES UP	DEMAND STAYS THE SAME	DEMAND GOES DOWN
The price of unsold, ripe vegetables is reduced.			
The price of hotel rooms is reduced after 11:00 P.M.			
The price of hotel rooms is raised after 11:00 P.M.			

3. According to the professor, what does hotel pricing demonstrate?

    Ⓐ Consumer demand is influenced by more than price.

    Ⓑ Lower prices increase demand.

    Ⓒ Higher prices reduce demand.

    Ⓓ Consumer demand is impossible to predict.

4. A coffee chain notices that demand for coffee is lower in the afternoon than in the morning. How can the coffee chain increase sales and income in the afternoon without reducing income from morning sales, according to the professor's theory?

(A) Reduce prices in the morning

(B) Reduce prices in the afternoon

(C) Reduce prices all day

(D) Raise prices all day

Answers and Explanations for Exercise 16 begin on page 348.

Making Inferences Items

Making inferences items ask you to use information in the selection to figure out new information. For example, imagine that you apply for admission to a university. Then you open your email and see that there is an email from the admissions office. You can infer that the university has made a decision about your application and that the news is in that email. On the TOEFL iBT, some inference items may be replay items. Making inferences items often contain language such as *infer*, *imply*, and *most likely*. Study the chart.

RECOGNIZING MAKING INFERENCES ITEMS
Which of the following can be **inferred** about . . . ?
What does the professor **imply** when he says this? (replay)
What will (the woman) **most likely** do next?

EXAMPLE

Making Inferences Item

 Listen to part of a longer conversation between a student and a university records administrator. Then answer the questions. Circle the letters of the answers.

What do you think the student will most likely do next?

(A) Complain to the administrator's boss in order to get a transcript

(B) Pay the late tuition with her own money so she can get a transcript

(C) Send a copy of her report card to the agency

(D) Ask the registrar's office to contact the agency

If you said that the answer is Option C, you are correct. This is the easiest way for the student to send the agency the information about her grades last term. Options A and B are incorrect because sending a copy of the report card is an easier way for the student to accomplish her goal than the courses of action in those options. Option D is contradicted by the information. The agency needs to contact the university.

> **EXAMPLE**
>
> ## Making Inferences Item
>
> Answer the question about the conversation between the student and the university records administrator. Circle the letter of the answer.
>
> What can be inferred about the administrator?
>
> Ⓐ She wants the student to pay nearly $8,000.
>
> Ⓑ She doesn't have much experience with scholarship agencies.
>
> Ⓒ She is trying her best to help the student.
>
> Ⓓ She doesn't want the student to get her scholarship money this term.

If you said that Option C is correct, you are right. Option C is correct because it is clear that the administrator understands the student's problem and helps her find a solution. Option A is contradicted by the conversation. The administrator wants the student to get her scholarship money. Option B is contradicted by the conversation, too. When the administrator says, "That happens all the time," she shows that she is experienced. Option D is incorrect because the administrator mentions several ways the student can solve the problem and get the scholarship money.

> **TIP** **The answer to an inference item is never stated directly in the listening selection!**
>
> Because an inference is new information and is a conclusion drawn from other information in the selection, the answer to an inference item will seldom be stated directly in the selection. You need to use information in the selection to figure out the answer.

EXERCISE 17

Making Inferences Items

Listen to part of a lecture in a life sciences class. Then answer the questions. Circle the letters of the answers.

Life Science

Migration

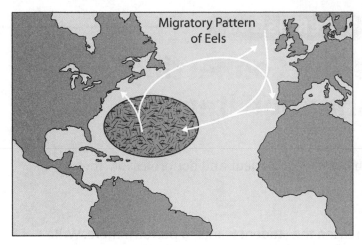

1. According to the professor, what is the main difference between the migration patterns of birds and European eels?

   Ⓐ A new generation of eels makes a return migratory trip, but bird migration includes older birds.

   Ⓑ The life span of birds is generally longer than the life span of eels.

   Ⓒ When eel larvae swim to Europe, they learn the route back to North America.

   Ⓓ Only birds migrate in groups.

2. A scientist interested in making a new discovery about European eels would most likely study which of these?

   Ⓐ The eels' habitats in Europe

   Ⓑ The eels' route from Europe to the Azores Islands

   Ⓒ The eels' route from the Azores Islands to North America

   Ⓓ The eels' route from North America to Europe

3. Why does the professor discuss eels and not monarch butterflies in class?

   Ⓐ They are the only animal in which a new generation migrates to a place they have never been to before.

   Ⓑ The students can see and learn about eels at the City Aquarium next week.

   Ⓒ The eels' migration pattern is better understood than the migration pattern of monarch butterflies.

   Ⓓ People do not like eels because they remind them of snakes.

Answers and Explanations for Exercise 17 begin on page 349.

EXERCISE 18

Answering Connecting Information Items

 Listen to a conversation between a student and her professor. Then answer the questions.

1. Match the concert with the reason the student wants to perform there. Write the letters under the correct headings.

JANUARY	MARCH	APRIL
Chicago	New York	Disneyland

Ⓐ She has a solo.

Ⓑ She has an audition for a summer job.

Ⓒ The concert is at her old high school.

2. The professor and the student discuss various solutions to the student's problem. Which suggestions work? Which ones do not work?

Place a check (✔) in the correct box.

	WORKS	DOES NOT WORK
Record the class and do an extra project		
Not perform in the concert		
Attend the class by telephone		

3. Why does the professor's attitude toward the student's request change?

Ⓐ He understands the reasons her request is valid.

Ⓑ He decides that the student is telling the truth.

Ⓒ He thinks the class on March 5 is very important.

Ⓓ He thinks that it's not a good idea to change the rules.

4. Another student missed one class session because he was sick. Now the same student wants to be absent a second time to have an extra-long spring break at the beach. What will the professor most likely tell the student?

Ⓐ "You will lose 50 points from your final grade."

Ⓑ "You can do a makeup project for the second absence."

Ⓒ "You can phone in from the beach."

Ⓓ "You can talk to the department head to see if she will approve the request."

5. What is another way that the student in the conversation could get the professor's permission to be absent two times?

Ⓐ Attend the professor's other section of the same course, which meets before she leaves for New York and Chicago

Ⓑ Attend an online session of the same course taught by a different professor

Ⓒ Offer to bring the professor a recording of the concert in New York

Ⓓ Offer to write an extra paper on the theories of another psychologist who is interested in child development

Answers and Explanations for Exercise 18 begin on page 350.

TOEFL iBT Practice Listening Section

Directions: To simulate actual TOEFL iBT conditions, follow these instructions:

- Listen to each conversation or lecture only once. You may take notes while listening and use your notes as you answer the items.
- After each selection, answer the items that follow in the order in which they appear. After you answer an item, do not return to it. Continue with each listening selection and its items until you complete the test or time has ended.
- Use your watch or the timer on your mobile phone or computer to keep track of the time. Allow 60 minutes to listen to all the selections and answer the questions.
- If you do not finish all the items when the test ends, mark your place. Then continue working as quickly as you can. When you finish, take note of the total time. This will give you an idea of how quickly you need to work on the actual TOEFL iBT to answer all the items in 60 minutes.

The Audio icon appears each time you need to listen to an audio track. For some items, you need to listen to another audio track besides the conversation or lecture in order to answer.

Now begin the TOEFL iBT Practice Listening section.

Listen to a conversation between a student and a university professor.

Now answer the questions. Circle the letter of the answer.

1. Why does the professor want to talk to the student?

    Ⓐ To ask about his health

    Ⓑ To check where he is going on a field trip

    Ⓒ To find out if he has completed his project

    Ⓓ To discuss his upcoming exam .

2. What prevents the student from joining the class on April 30?

    Ⓐ Surgery on that day

    Ⓑ Recovery from surgery

    Ⓒ A major basketball game

    Ⓓ An exam in another class

3. What must the student do to complete the assignment?

    Ⓐ Time his journey across the George Washington Bridge

    Ⓑ Visit restricted areas of the George Washington Bridge

    Ⓒ Photograph and measure one of Othmar Amman's bridges

    Ⓓ Survey the Verrazano Narrows Bridge by climbing a tall pylon

4. Why does the student think few of his classmates may be interested in the George Washington Bridge?

   Ⓐ It was built relatively recently, in 1981.

   Ⓑ It cost only a million dollars to build.

   Ⓒ They think it will be too hard to survey.

   Ⓓ They are overly familiar with it.

5. Listen again to part of the conversation. Then answer the question.

   Ⓐ She hopes to prevent students from copying one another's work.

   Ⓑ She hopes to encourage students to cooperate with each other.

   Ⓒ She is offering to work individually with each student.

   Ⓓ Her learning tasks are very difficult for most students.

Listen to part of a lecture in a math class. The professor is talking about graphs.

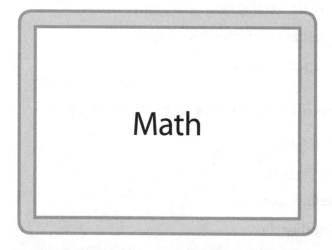

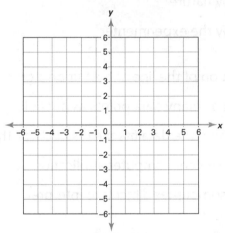

Coordinate Plane

Now answer the questions. Circle the letter of the answer.

6. Which aspects of graphs does the professor mainly talk about? *Choose 2 answers.*

    A Their recent history

    B Their drawbacks

    C Their usefulness

    D Their design rules

7. What did the political economist Playfair understand about graphs?

    Ⓐ They present complex information at a glance.

    Ⓑ They improve the accuracy of the data.

    Ⓒ They would become popular with social scientists.

    Ⓓ Scottish government and business would rely on them.

8. What purpose do graphs serve?

   Ⓐ They show the existence and form of mathematical relationships.

   Ⓑ They improve the accuracy of the data.

   Ⓒ They make high school mathematics more accurate and engaging.

   Ⓓ They improve our understanding of numerical constants.

9. What usually goes on the *y*-axis?

   Ⓐ Units of time

   Ⓑ A descriptive title

   Ⓒ Values determined by nature

   Ⓓ Values determined by the experimenter

10. What is the best description of the line of best fit on a graph?

    Ⓐ A line going through as many data points as possible

    Ⓑ A line used to show how the data fits the researchers' theory

    Ⓒ A line generated by a recent computer application

    Ⓓ A curved line that is sometimes difficult to interpret

11. How does the professor feel at the end of the lecture?

    Ⓐ Amused about errors his students make with graphs

    Ⓑ Irritated because students have not used graphs correctly in the past

    Ⓒ Excited because graphs can show information very clearly

    Ⓓ Disappointed because students will not have opportunities to make graphs in the future

Listen to part of a lecture in a class on contemporary theater.

Contemporary Theater

Augusto Boal

a "spect-actor"

Now answer the questions. Circle the letter of the answer.

12. What is the main topic of this lecture?

   Ⓐ A kind of theater in which audience members become actors

   Ⓑ A kind of theater that is used to spread propaganda

   Ⓒ A kind of theater that tries to give audiences skills to overcome oppression

   Ⓓ A kind of theater that encourages audiences to examine media critically

13. What did Boal think about the conclusions viewers should draw from Forum Theater plays?

   Ⓐ They must be simple enough for spect-actors to remember.

   Ⓑ They must present a clear discourse.

   Ⓒ They should be lifelike and dramatically appealing.

   Ⓓ They should not always favor the oppressed.

14. What was the purpose of the performance the professor filmed in India?

   Ⓐ To help managers in diversity training

   Ⓑ To help disadvantaged patients assume more control

   Ⓒ To show the complex relationships between doctors and patients

   Ⓓ To help school staff deal with rude or violent students

15. 🎧 **AUDIO TRACK 64** Listen again to part of the conversation. Then answer the question.

   Ⓐ He doubts that Forum Theater is useful.

   Ⓑ He approves of Forum Theater.

   Ⓒ He thinks Forum Theater is a government agency.

   Ⓓ He is very excited about Forum Theater.

16. The professor describes how Forum Theater functions. Put the events in order. Write your answer choices in the spaces where they belong. You can either write the letter of your answer choice or you can copy the statement. The first one is done for you. *This item is worth 2 points.*

1.	A spect-actor substitutes for an oppressed character.
2.	
3.	
4.	
5.	

Answer Choices

[A] The actors and spect-actor resolve the conflict.

[B] Audience members successfully apply conflict-resolution lessons they learned in the theater to the real world.

[C] The actors stop following the script. They use new ideas to go on with the play.

[D] Since the spect-actor cannot resolve the conflict in a realistic manner, another spect-actor takes over the role.

17. What do some of Augusto Boal's other types of theater try to do?

   (A) Encourage audience participation in traditional theater

   (B) Entertain audiences in more than 70 countries

   (C) Promote audience scrutiny of biased media

   (D) Expose the personal dramas of psychologists

Listen to a conversation between a student and a university employee.

Now answer the questions. Circle the letter of the answer.

18. Why does the student go to see the employee?

Ⓐ To complain about parking

Ⓑ To inquire about parking costs

Ⓒ To apply for a parking permit

Ⓓ To renew a parking permit

19. How are college parking fees calculated?

Ⓐ By day or by week

Ⓑ By week or by month

Ⓒ By day or by semester

Ⓓ By day, week, month, or semester

20. Why were some college parking rates discontinued?

Ⓐ They were too difficult for security to monitor.

Ⓑ They were too time-consuming for clerks to administer.

Ⓒ They could not compete with municipal parking rates.

Ⓓ They were too expensive for students.

21. What does the student need to know about the parking building on Maple Drive?

    Ⓐ It is a new facility.

    Ⓑ It is open 24 hours a day.

    Ⓒ Students can use it only during summer.

    Ⓓ Students cannot use it at all.

22. What will the woman most likely do next?

    Ⓐ Return to the office later to buy a permit

    Ⓑ Find out information about bus passes

    Ⓒ Load money onto her credit or debit card

    Ⓓ Park her car at home and walk to campus

 Listen to part of a lecture in an education class. The professor is talking about the value of homework.

Education

correlational analysis

Harris Cooper

Now answer the questions. Circle the letter of the answer.

23. What is the main point of this lecture?

Ⓐ Homework should be abolished because it does not help children learn.

Ⓑ The benefits and drawbacks of homework are not completely understood.

Ⓒ Homework is not beneficial because there is too much cheating.

Ⓓ High school students should get four hours of homework every night.

24. What does the professor think about the homework debate?

Ⓐ It shows that assigning a lot of homework results in academic success.

Ⓑ It has not produced many concrete results.

Ⓒ It solves an age-old riddle.

Ⓓ It is a fashionable topic.

25. What does the professor think is a myth?

Ⓐ Parents and policy makers believe in the utility of homework.

Ⓑ Asian students generally do better on tests because they do more homework.

Ⓒ Good students do more homework than weaker students.

Ⓓ A country's international competitiveness is improved by more homework.

26. Which kind of academic study does the professor think is the most valid?

    Ⓐ A causal study

    Ⓑ A correlational study

    Ⓒ A graded study

    Ⓓ An interview study

27. According to the professor or the students, how should parents involve themselves in their children's homework?

    Ⓐ By cowriting their history assignments

    Ⓑ By correcting their math homework

    Ⓒ By helping their children with art projects

    Ⓓ By participating in interactive science homework

28. What does the professor or the students say about the following?

Place a check (✔) in the correct box. This item is worth 2 points.

	ADVANTAGEOUS TO STUDENTS	DISADVANTAGEOUS TO STUDENTS	ITS VALUE IS NOT KNOWN
Noninstructional homework			
A lot of homework in grades one to five			
A student's low socioeconomic status			
Math homework			

Listen to part of a lecture in a class on chemical engineering. The professor is talking about rare earth elements, or REEs.

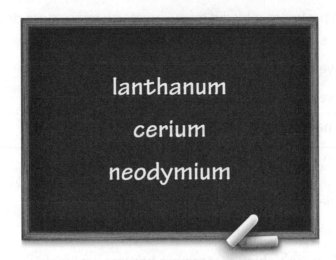

Now answer the questions. Circle the letter of the answer.

29. What is the main point of the lecture?

Ⓐ Rare earth elements are an amazing discovery.

Ⓑ There are ways to increase production of rare earth elements.

Ⓒ Rare earth elements have benefits and drawbacks.

Ⓓ Rare earth elements are more trouble than they are worth.

30. What does "rare" mean in the name "rare earth element"?

Ⓐ The element is located at the bottom of the periodic table.

Ⓑ The element does not exist abundantly in nature.

Ⓒ The element was discovered only relatively recently.

Ⓓ A large amount of raw material is needed to extract the element.

31. Which products does the professor say contain REEs? *Choose 2 answers.*

A Airplanes

B Air conditioners

C Computer screens

D Dishwashers

32. According to the professor, why did many rare-earth mines close down in the 1990s?

Ⓐ Labor costs were too high.

Ⓑ Known reserves of REEs were running out.

Ⓒ REEs did not have many industrial uses at the time.

Ⓓ Pollution from the mining process was too great.

33. Why did companies resume rare-earth mining recently?

Ⓐ Engineers developed better extraction techniques for REEs.

Ⓑ Prices for REEs were so high that mining became profitable.

Ⓒ Geologists discovered large undersea deposits of REEs.

Ⓓ Price spikes caused panic; mines reopened suddenly.

34. How does the professor feel about the future of the rare-earth industry?

Ⓐ She hopes that its excesses can be curbed.

Ⓑ She feels uncertain about it.

Ⓒ She believes scientists will not find better alternatives.

Ⓓ She does not show how she feels.

Answers and Explanations for the TOEFL iBT Practice Listening section begin on page 351.

TOEFL iBT Listening
Personalized Study Planner

Use your answers to the TOEFL iBT Practice Listening section and these charts to focus your preparation for the actual TOEFL iBT. Follow these steps:

1. Review all your correct and incorrect answers in the Answers and Explanations, which begin on page 351.
2. In each chart, circle the number of each item you answered incorrectly.
3. Review again the Answers and Explanations for each item you answered incorrectly, this time in the order in which they are grouped in these charts.
4. For each item type and item format where you want to improve your performance, study the pages listed in the third column.

ITEM NUMBERS	ITEM TYPE	STUDY PAGES
6, 12, 23, 29	Gist-content	260–269
1, 18	Gist-purpose	270–274
3, 7, 9, 10, 13, 17, 19, 20, 21, 24, 26, 28, 31, 32, 33	Supporting detail	275–281
5, 14	Understanding the function of what is said	284–286
11, 15, 34	Understanding the speaker's attitude	287–291
16	Understanding organization	294–300
8, 25, 27, 30	Connecting content	300–304
2, 4, 22	Making inferences	304–307

ITEM NUMBERS	ITEM FORMAT	STUDY PAGES
6, 31	Special multiple choice	254
5, 15	Replay items	254–256
28	Check box items	256
16	Drag-and-drop items	257–258

TOEFL IBT LISTENING
Answers, Explanations, and Audio Scripts

Exercise 1: Taking Notes (Page 238)

TRACK 28 AUDIO SCRIPT

Narrator: Number 1. Listen to part of a lecture in an economics class.

Professor: We can observe that consumer decisions can have a big impact on economic activity. At many different times, consumers' ethical and moral considerations can play a big part in individual or collective decisions they make. Consumers, for example, can make a decision to boycott, or avoid shopping at, certain national or global chains because they don't like the practices of that chain. At times, to meet consumer demand or expectation, organizations or movements are formed. One such organization, err, movement is the Fair Trade movement. Fair Trade responds to consumer desire for products, particularly agricultural products, that are sourced in ways the consumers consider ethical or moral. Fair Trade has several objectives, first and foremost that producers receive more of the proceeds from the sale of their products, which are typically things such as coffee, chocolate, or other agricultural products. But the concern is more than just fair prices for producers. Consumers also want to support sustainable, eco-friendly farming methods. A number of global organizations have responded by creating Fair Trade associations that set standards and certify producers as Fair Trade. Ethical and moral considerations are powerful—so powerful, in fact, that they may trump other considerations, such as lower consumer prices. Consumers may be willing to pay higher prices.

Narrator: Number 2. Listen to part of a lecture in a physics class.

Professor: The Doppler effect is a well-documented phenomenon about the perception of sound. The Doppler effect is observed when either the object making the sound or the individual perceiving the sound, or both, are in motion relative to each other. Basically, car and train horns, as well as sirens, produce sound at a constant frequency. But if the horn, for example, is in motion, as is the case when a car honks its horn at another vehicle, the sound will be perceived as changing pitch even though the sound actually never changes pitch. This phenomenon was first observed in the nineteenth century, when trains were able to operate fast enough to produce the effect. Basically, to an observer standing still, an approaching horn will sound as if it's at a higher pitch, and a receding horn will sound as if it's a lower pitch. But the frequency of the sound waves stays the same. How is that possible?

Student: Is it because of the movement?

Professor: Exactly. As the vehicle moves toward the listener, each sound wave is emitted slightly closer to the listener. Thus, to the listener, the waves seem to arrive in greater frequency, which makes the pitch go up. The opposite happens when the sound is moving away from the listener. The space between each sound wave is progressively larger, which makes it seem like the pitch is dropping.

Student: So what happens with supersonic aircraft? They move faster than the speed of sound. So can they sneak up silently?

Professor: Actually, it's the opposite. The noise from an aircraft is produced in waves, too. But in this case, the waves are produced by something moving faster than the speed of sound. So those sound waves tend to bunch up and produce what listeners below perceive as a sonic boom—a loud explosive sound produced by hearing all of the waves bunched up together. A supersonic aircraft will produce considerable noise. Plus, the aircraft would have trouble sneaking up because it could be spotted by most radar.

Narrator: Number 3. Listen to part of a lecture in a contemporary literature class.

Professor: Stories of the immigrant experience are an important part of the American literary tradition. As long as there have been immigrants to the United States, there have been chronicles of their journeys and experiences. It is sometimes troubling whether these authors are really American, since they may hold foreign nationality. However, since these writings are so closely linked to the American experience, and are often in English, we are including them in our class. Many of these writings are by Latino authors or Chinese authors, since speakers of these languages are the largest immigrant groups at present. Probably all of us have heard of Amy Tan and her writings about her family and life in the United States. But the author I want to talk about today is Aleksander Hemon. Hemon is a particularly interesting example because he did not choose to immigrate. Rather, immigration seemed to choose Hemon. Hemon was in Chicago on a short-term exchange program from his native country, then Yugoslavia. He was about to board a flight back to his native country when word was received that the capital city, Belgrade, was under air attack. He was prevented from traveling and became a refugee from war. He worked a variety of odd jobs as he learned English. A writer in his first language, he decided to learn enough English to write stories and novels in his new language. He published novels and short stories to high praise and later won an award of a million dollars.

ANSWERS

Many answers are possible. Compare your notes to these sample notes.

1.

Consumer decisions—big econ impact
—ethical
—moral
Boycott—not use bad businesses
Fair trade
—ex: coffee, choc.
—ethic. sourced
—pay fair price
—eco-friendly
Consumers pay more fair trade

2.

Doppler effect—sound perception
Motion—sound seems to change
—approaching—higher
—receding—lower
Sound waves seem to arrive more freq. bec motion
Sonic boom ≠ Doppler effect

3.

Immig. exp in lit
—not Am, but live in US
—many Asian, Latino
Hemon—didn't want immig, "imig chose him"
—in Chicago for visit
—war started in his country
—refugee
—learned Engl, wrote novels, stories
—won big prize for writing

Exercise 2: Academic Vocabulary (Page 243)

ANSWERS

1. gases
2. discoverer
3. research
4. composed
5. experiment
6. consisted
7. oxygen
8. existence
9. helium
10. primarily

Exercise 3: Content Vocabulary or Academic Vocabulary? (Page 244)

The completed chart should look like this:

ACADEMIC VOCABULARY	CONTENT VOCABULARY
discoverer	atmosphere
research	gases
composed	oxygen
experiment	helium
consisted	
existence	
primarily	

Exercise 4: Student Services (Page 247)

TRACK 30 AUDIO SCRIPT

Narrator: Number 1.

Male Student: A group of my friends in the engineering college started a student club for engineering students from our country. We plan to meet once a week for events and networking. Next week, an executive from a big company is coming to talk to us. He is from our country and a graduate of the university. We're going to have more events like this one. We just finished becoming a registered student organization. Now we want to use university meeting rooms for our activities.

Narrator: Number 2.

Female Student: I just got a letter from the education department of my country. To renew my scholarship for next year, I need to send a record of all my grades so far this year to the education office.

Narrator: Number 3.

Male Student: Oh, no. This letter says that I am still registered for a class that I dropped on the first day of the semester. I haven't been attending, but I need to drop it right away.

Narrator: Number 4.

Female Student: My parents are visiting next week. They are coming all the way from my country and then renting a car to drive the rest of the way here. Their hotel is a couple of miles away. What will they do with the car when they come to campus?

Narrator: Number 5.

Male Student: I just got a tuition bill for fall term. Right now, they are still waiting for my country to make the tuition payment for fall, but they always make it late. The letter says that if I don't pay by Friday, I won't be able to use the library or rec center. This happens every year. How do I stop getting cut off from using the library? I have a big paper due in two weeks!

Narrator: Number 6.

Female Student: I have a room in Roberts Hall, but it's too far from the computer science building. Most computer science students live in Asbury Hall, which is a lot closer. I want to move there next fall.

Narrator: Number 7.

Male Student: Since I got here in August, I have gained weight from so much studying. It seems that I never get out of the house, and now that there is snow on the ground, I can't ride my bike to campus, so I am not getting any exercise at all. I'd like to start swimming again, like I did in my country.

Narrator: Number 8.

Female Student: I just got a letter about my visa status. There is some sort of problem, but I can't figure out what is wrong. What if my visa is canceled?

Narrator: Number 9.

Male Student: I tried to register for my classes last night, but the online system says that my registration is blocked until I pay some library fines from last semester. I need to register for my classes right away, but the woman I spoke to in the registrar's office says that there is nothing she can do until I pay the fines.

Narrator: Number 10.

Female Student: Oh, no. I just got another ticket for an expired parking meter. I can't believe it! The maximum time on meters near the foreign languages building is two hours, but all my classes are two and a half hours, so I keep getting tickets. Where do I get a pass for the lot on Green Street?

ANSWERS AND EXPLANATIONS

1. **h   student union** This answer is correct because student clubs' and organizations' activities are organized through the student union.
2. **a   admissions and records** This answer is correct because the student needs to send a transcript to the education department. Admissions and records handles requests for transcripts.
3. **e   registrar** This answer is correct because the registrar's office handles issues related to current registrations and grades.
4. **c   parking management** The parents need information about parking on campus. Parking management is responsible for this function.
5. **f   student accounts** The student needs to talk to student accounts to find out how to pay the bill.
6. **g   student housing** This student is having a problem with living arrangements in university housing, so the student needs to talk to the student housing office.
7. **d   recreational sports** The student is concerned about lack of exercise. Recreational sports offers facilities and activities for students to participate in sports and exercise.
8. **b   international student affairs** This office handles issues related to visas and residency for international students.
9. **f   student accounts** The student can't register because of unpaid bills and must therefore talk to student accounts, which handles student payments to the university.
10. **c   parking management** The student is having trouble with parking tickets and permits and must therefore talk to parking management.

Exercise 5: Taking Notes (Page 250)

TRACK 32 AUDIO SCRIPT

Narrator: Exercise 5. Taking Notes. Number 1. Listen to part of a conversation in a library.

Librarian: OK, here you go. You need to have this item back in two hours.

Student: Two hours! I thought library loans were for a month.

Librarian: Usually, they are. But items placed on closed reserve are only available for two hours. They are also available overnight, but you have to return the item by 9 A.M. tomorrow when the library opens.

Student: Oh, so that's what closed reserve means. I don't think I can read this entire article in two hours, and I am busy tonight, so I can't read it even if I check it out overnight. Can I check it out over the weekend?

Librarian: No, you can only check it out for one night, not Friday and Saturday. But if you check it out on Saturday, you don't have to return it until Monday. That's because the library is closed on Sunday.

Student: Well, I am not sure I can get here by 5:00 on Saturday to check it out. I have to work at that time. And I can't read it in two hours.

Librarian: Well, you can make a photocopy for five cents a page, or you can scan it for free and save it to a USB drive.

Student: I didn't bring my USB drive with me today. And I don't want to make a copy. Can I check it out overnight?

Librarian: Yes, but you'll have to come back an hour before closing to check it out overnight. You can start reading now and then come back later to check it out overnight, unless another student asks for it.

Student: I see. I think I will check it out and go home and scan it, and make it back in two hours.

Librarian: OK, that's up to you. But if you're late, the fine is two dollars an hour.

Student: Well, for today, that's not a problem. From now on, I will keep my USB drive with me in case I need to scan here in the library.

Librarian: That's a good idea. We have eight scanners and they are completely free.

Narrator: Number 2. Listen to a part of a conversation between a student and a professor.

Student: Excuse me, professor. Do you have a minute?

Professor: Sure, how can I help you, David?

Student: Well, I had a question about the grading system for the class. I got an A on the midterm. So do I have to write a term paper?

Professor: Well, that depends. If you want to get an A for the course, you need to write a term paper and get an A on it. If you only want a B or C, then you don't have to do a term paper.

Student: I see. What if I get a B on the final exam?

Professor: Then it gets a little tricky. To get an A, you have to have an A average on the tests and quizzes, and you have to write an A term paper, too. You say you got an A on the midterm. How are your quiz grades?

Student: Well, I have an A-minus right now, I think. I scored well on all the quizzes except the first one. I got a high C on that one.

Professor: Well, that's a bit complicated, too. You are allowed to "throw out" your lowest quiz grade. That way, one of your quiz grades doesn't count toward your final grade.

Student: What do you mean?

Professor: We take eleven quizzes during the course, and only ten of them count. So your average is based on not counting one quiz. That's always the lowest grade. Everyone can have a bad day, so I always do that with one of the quizzes. With most students, it's the first quiz. Then they study harder.

Student: OK, without that low quiz, I am pretty sure I have an A average on the quizzes.

Professor: In that case, if you want an A, I would advise you to write a term paper. Have you considered any subjects . . . ?

ANSWERS

Many answers are possible. Compare your notes to these sample notes.

1.

> Wants check out closed res bk
> Closed res
> —2 hours
> —overnight, check out @ 5:00
> —return morning
> —copy, 5 cents
> —scan free
> —late = $2/hr
> He can't read in 2 hrs, no USB drive, wants scan @ home, return in 2 hrs

2.

> Student wants info on grading, whether should write term paper
> —for A, yes
> —must have A on tests and quizzes
> —one quiz doesn't count (10/11)
> —most students drop 1st quiz
> As on tests, quizzes, so write TP

Listening for the Main Idea (Page 261)

TRACK 34 AUDIO SCRIPT

Professor: Hello, everyone. Umm . . . let's get started. . . . Today we are going to talk about plate tectonics. Plate tectonics is a relatively new description of Earth's crust. The theory of plate tectonics asserts that once all of Earth's continents were a single landmass, which broke up as the underlying plates separated and began to move apart. Prior to the development of plate tectonics and related theories, scientists believed that Earth was solid and that its surface features were largely fixed. Under this view, changes in Earth's physical features were largely the result of upward or downward movement. For example, mountains formed because pressure from within Earth pushed up rock to form new mountains. This was called the geosynclinal theory. However, this theory could not explain all the evidence. Even as early as 1596, it had been noted that the landmasses on either side of the Atlantic had similar features and looked as if they had fit together at some point. However, the assumption that Earth, or at least its crust, was solid made it difficult to explain how these landmasses had once fit together.

TRACK 35 AUDIO SCRIPT

Professor: Good morning, class. Inflation, or the gradual, or not so gradual rise in prices, is of constant concern to consumers. Even in countries with low inflation rates, consumers complain that the constant rise of prices, without a corresponding increase in income, gradually erodes the value of their income. But is this view accurate? Consumers who own valuable assets, such as homes, may find that the value of that asset rises over time because of the impact of inflation. This, of course, does not apply to assets that depreciate, such as cars, but it certainly could apply to others in addition to real estate, such as artwork, precious metals, or even fine jewelry. Those assets tend to increase in value over time because of the effect of inflation. Of course, market factors can also influence the value of those assets. The value of precious metal, for example, has increased at a rate much higher than inflation. The historic and esthetic value of jewelry can also raise its value beyond the value of the metal and gemstones, too.

Example: Gist-Content Item (Page 262)

TRACK 36 AUDIO SCRIPT

Narrator: Listen to part of a lecture in a physics class.

Professor: Hello, class. Today we will turn our attention to the next topic in the syllabus, optics, or the study of light. When we think of light, we most often think of visible light and the colors in the spectrum, but we will touch upon many more topics in our study of light, including visible and invisible light, intensity of light, wavelength, frequency, and polarization. Some of these terms have special meaning in physics. When people talk about the intensity of light in nonscientific terms, they are referring to the strength of the light. When physicists talk about intensity of light, however, they are referring to rate of transfer of the energy.

Example: Gist-Content Item (Page 264)

TRACK 37 AUDIO SCRIPT

Male Student: Hello, I want to find out about getting a transit pass.

Male Manager: Sure. Staff or student?

Student: Student.

Manager: OK, that's good. A transit pass is much cheaper for students than staff. Basically, there are two plans. With the Economy Plan, you pay twenty dollars a month and you can ride between campus and town twice a day. Plus, you can ride for free on all bus lines within the campus zone. Are most of your classes in the campus zone?

Student: I don't know. What's the campus zone?

Manager: It's the area nearby campus. The boundaries are Green Street, Kennedy Avenue, Collins Boulevard, and Maple Street.

Student: Does that include the Performing Arts Center? A lot of my classes are in that building because I am a theater major.

Manager: Well, the Performing Arts Center is a block north of Green Street. You just need to walk a block south, and then you can ride for free to any other part of the campus.

Student: OK, that's good to know.

Manager: That's the Economy Plan. Do you plan to take the bus to and from home? Or do you plan to take the bus at night?

Student: Yes, sometimes, I have to be at the Performing Arts Center late at night. Plus, sometimes I go home for lunch or dinner, so I'll ride more than one round-trip per day.

Manager: In that case, you probably want to consider the Gold Plan. It's fifty dollars a month, but that's less than two dollars per day. It gives you unlimited rides on all buses, including late at night.

Student: How do I buy a pass?

Manager: Just fill out the form on this computer. Your student account will be charged fifty dollars each month, and your pass will automatically renew each month. And you don't need a special card. Just use your student ID when you board the bus.

Student: Great!

Exercise 6: Gist-Content Items (Page 266)

TRACK 38 AUDIO SCRIPT

Narrator: Number 1. Listen to part of a lecture in an economics class.

Professor: We can observe that consumer decisions can have a big impact on economic activity. At many different times, consumers' ethical and moral considerations can play a big part in individual or collective decisions they make. Consumers, for example, can make a decision to boycott, or avoid shopping at, certain national or global chains because they do not like the practices of that chain. At times, to meet consumer demand or expectation, organizations or movements are formed. One such organization, err, movement is the Fair Trade movement. Fair Trade responds to consumer desire for products, particularly agricultural products, that are sourced in ways the consumers consider ethical or moral. Fair Trade has several objectives, first and foremost that producers receive more of the proceeds from the sale of their products, which are typically things such as coffee, chocolate, or other agricultural products. But the concern is more than just fair prices for producers. Consumers also want to support sustainable, eco-friendly farming methods. A number of global organizations have responded by creating Fair Trade associations that set standards and certify producers as Fair Trade. Ethical and moral considerations are powerful—so powerful, in fact, that they may trump other considerations, such as lower consumer prices. Consumers may be willing to pay higher prices.

Narrator: Now answer the question.

Narrator: Number 2. Listen to part of a conversation in a library.

Librarian: OK, here you go. You need to have this item back in two hours.

Student: Two hours! I thought library loans were for a month.

Librarian: Usually, they are. But items placed on closed reserve are only available for two hours. They are also available overnight, but you have to return the item by nine A.M. tomorrow when the library opens.

Student: Oh, so that's what closed reserve means. I don't think I can read this entire article in two hours, and I am busy tonight, so I can't read it even if I check it out overnight. Can I check it out over the weekend?

Librarian: No, you can only check it out for one night, not Friday and Saturday. But if you check it out on Saturday, you don't have to return it until Monday. That's because the library is closed on Sunday.

Student: Well, I am not sure I can get here by 5:00 on Saturday to check it out. I have to work at that time. And I can't read it in two hours.

Librarian: Well, you can make a photocopy for five cents a page, or you can scan it for free and save it to a USB drive.

Student: I didn't bring my USB drive with me today. And I don't want to make a copy. Can I check it out overnight?

Librarian: Yes, but you'll have to come back an hour before closing to check it out overnight. You can start reading now and then come back later to check it out overnight, unless another student asks for it.

Student: I see. I think I will check it out and go home and scan it, and make it back in two hours.

Librarian: OK, that's up to you. But if you're late, the fine is two dollars an hour.

Student: Well, for today, that's not a problem. From now on, I will keep my USB drive with me in case I need to scan here in the library.

Librarian: That's a good idea. We have eight scanners and they are completely free.

Narrator: Now answer the question.

Narrator: Number 3. Listen to part of a lecture in a physics class.

Professor: The Doppler effect is a well-documented phenomenon about the perception of sound. The Doppler effect is observed when either the object making the sound or the individual perceiving the sound, or both, are in motion relative to each other. Basically, car and train horns, as well as sirens, produce sound at a constant frequency. But if the horn, for example, is in motion, as is the case when a car honks its horn at another vehicle, the sound will be perceived as changing pitch even though the sound actually never changes pitch. This phenomenon was first observed in the nineteenth century, when trains were able to operate fast enough to produce the effect. Basically, to an observer standing still, an approaching horn will sound as if it's at a higher pitch, and a receding horn will sound as if it's a lower pitch. But the frequency of the sound waves stays the same. How is that possible?

Student: Is it because of the movement?

Professor: Exactly. As the vehicle moves toward the listener, each sound wave is emitted slightly closer to the listener. Thus, to the listener, the waves seem to arrive in greater frequency, which makes the pitch go up. The opposite happens when the sound is moving away from the listener. The space between each sound wave is progressively larger, which makes it seem like the pitch is dropping.

Student: So what happens with supersonic aircraft? They move faster than the speed of sound. So can they sneak up silently?

Professor: Actually, it's the opposite. The noise from an aircraft is produced in waves, too. But in this case, the waves are produced by something moving faster than the speed of sound. So those sound waves tend to bunch up and produce what listeners below perceive as a sonic boom—a loud explosive sound produced by hearing all of the waves bunched up together. A supersonic aircraft will produce considerable noise. Plus, the aircraft would have trouble sneaking up because it could be spotted by most radar.

Narrator: Now answer the question.

Narrator: Number 4. Listen to a part of a conversation between a student and a professor.

Student: Excuse me, professor. Do you have a minute?

Professor: Sure, how can I help you, David?

Student: Well, I had a question about the grading system for the class. I got an A on the midterm. So do I have to write a term paper?

Professor: Well, that depends. If you want to get an A for the course, you need to write a term paper and get an A on it. If you only want a B or C, then you don't have to do a term paper.

Student: I see. What if I get a B on the final exam?

Professor: Then it gets a little tricky. To get an A, you have to have an A average on the tests and quizzes, and you have to write an A term paper, too. You say you got an A on the midterm. How are your quiz grades?

Student: Well, I have an A-minus right now, I think. I scored well on all the quizzes except the first one. I got a high C on that one.

Professor: Well, that's a bit complicated, too. You are allowed to "throw out" your lowest quiz grade. That way, one of your quiz grades doesn't count toward your final grade.

Student: What do you mean?

Professor: We take 11 quizzes during the course, and only 10 of them count. So your average is based on not counting one quiz. That's always the lowest grade. Everyone can have a bad day, so I always do that with one of the quizzes. With most students, it's the first quiz. Then they study harder.

Student: OK, without that low quiz, I am pretty sure I have an A average on the quizzes.

Professor: In that case, if you want an A, I would advise you to write a term paper. Have you considered any subjects . . . ?

Narrator: Now answer the question.

Narrator: Number 5. Listen to part of a lecture in a contemporary literature class.

Professor: Stories of the immigrant experience are an important part of the American literary tradition. As long as there have been immigrants to the United States, there have been chronicles of their journeys and experiences. It is sometimes troubling whether these authors are really American, since they may hold foreign nationality. However, since these writings are so closely linked to the American experience and are often in English, we are including them in our class. Many of these writings are by Latino authors or Chinese authors,

since speakers of these languages are the largest immigrant groups at present. Probably all of us have heard of Amy Tan and her writings about her family and life in the United States. But the author I want to talk about today is Aleksander Hemon. Hemon is a particularly interesting example because he did not choose to immigrate. Rather, immigration seemed to choose Hemon. Hemon was in Chicago on a short-term exchange program from his native country, then Yugoslavia. He was about to board a flight back to his native country when word was received that the capital city, Belgrade, was under air attack. He was prevented from traveling and became a refugee from war. He worked a variety of odd jobs as he learned English. A writer in his first language, he decided to learn enough English to write stories and novels in his new language. He published novels and short stories to high praise and later won an award of a million dollars.

Narrator: Now answer the question.

ANSWERS AND EXPLANATIONS

1. **B Purchasing Fair Trade goods is one way consumers can feel that they are making good purchasing decisions.** In the lecture, the professor directly states that purchasing Fair Trade goods is one way consumers feel they make good purchasing decisions, so Option B is correct. Option A is incorrect because it is too specific—it focuses on one minor detail, boycotts. The main part of the lecture is about Fair Trade as an example of a kind of consumer decision making. Option C is not mentioned in the lecture, so it is incorrect. Option D is incorrect because only some consumers base decisions on moral or ethical concerns.

2. **C Closed reserve items have many special rules.** Option C is correct because the employee and student spend considerable time discussing the special rules for closed reserve items. Options A and B are two ways to access closed reserve items. Option D is incorrect because this is a detail in the conversation.

3. **D Changes in how we perceive sound because of the Doppler effect** Option D is correct because the lecture is about how motion affects the perception of sound. Options A and B are incorrect because they are details. Option C is too general to be the main idea of this lecture. The lecture is about only the Doppler effect, not sound waves in general.

4. **B** **Requirements for getting an A in the student's class** The student asks several questions about what he has to do to get an A. Therefore, this is the main idea of the conversation. Options A and C are details about the grading system, so they are incorrect. Option D is not correct because term paper topics are only mentioned briefly.

5. **D** **Hemon's writing is an unusual example of literature of the immigrant experience.** Option D is correct because the professor made Hemon the topic of the lecture because he is an unusual example of a common kind of writing. Options A and B are details about immigrant writing and Hemon's background, so they are incorrect. Option C is contradicted by the information in the selection.

Example: Gist-Purpose Item (Page 270)

TRACK 39 AUDIO SCRIPT
See Track 37 audio script, page 331.

Example: Gist-Purpose Item (Page 271)

TRACK 40 AUDIO SCRIPT
Narrator: Listen to a part of a conversation between a student and a professor.

Student: Professor, I'd like some help with my paper. I'm not sure why I got a low grade. I thought I did a good job of explaining the research on how food prices are influenced by consumer demand and market supply.

Professor: Let's see. . . . Yes, the information on supply and demand is pretty good. You could have used another example or two, but that's not the problem.

Student: Yes, I wanted to add an example about lettuce prices. It seems that, for lettuce, consumer demand stays the same no matter how high the price goes. That's a big exception to the law of supply and demand.

Professor: That's very interesting, but to get a higher grade, you need to pay attention to what I taught you about writing a good paper. Your essay should have an introductory paragraph, at least three body paragraphs, and a concluding paragraph. You had a good introduction and good body paragraphs. But you didn't have a concluding paragraph. And you have some problems with mechanics. Good mechanics is a requirement, too.

Student: What do you mean by mechanics?

Professor: Mechanics includes things like spelling, punctuation, and indenting paragraphs. It looks like you indented all of your paragraphs. But your spelling needs some work. And you make a lot of mistakes with commas.

Student: Well, spell-check will help with spelling, and I will be more careful about commas.

Professor: Please pay attention to capitalization, too. Make sure you capitalize all proper nouns. Proper nouns are the names of people and places, for example.

Student: I will do that. I will hand in a revised paper on Friday. Thank you for your help, Professor.

Exercise 7: Gist-Purpose Items (Page 272)

TRACK 41 AUDIO SCRIPT
Narrator: Number 1.

Student: Excuse me, Professor Kean. Do you have a minute?

Professor: Sure, Sandra. How can I help you?

Student: Well, I play on the women's volleyball team and . . .

Professor: I know. I go to all the games. You guys are having a great season this year.

Student: Yes, we've won our last few games. And that's why I need to talk to you.

Professor: Oh. What's up?

Student: Well, we have a midterm next week, and if we win our game tonight, we will go to the state championship in Springfield. That's next week too. And you said that the only valid excuses for missing the midterm are being sick or a family emergency.

So I am worried that I won't be able to make up the exam.

Professor: Yes, I always tell students that the only valid excuses are sickness and family emergencies, but if you have a special situation, we can work it out.

Student: That's great, Professor Kean.

Narrator: Now answer the question.

Narrator: Number 2.

Male Student: Hey, Rhonda. Have you picked out a topic for your history term paper? I am really having a hard time. And it's due in only a couple of weeks.

Female Student: I know what you mean. Since the paper has to cover military and political history between World War I and II, I decided to study the Spanish Civil War. But I just made up my mind yesterday, and the professor approved the topic when I emailed him this morning.

Male Student: That's a great idea. But I didn't know that it had to cover military and political history only.

Female Student: Oh, yes. The professor said it in class the very first day.

Male Student: In that case, I really don't know what to write about. I am not interested in military history at all.

Female Student: It can cover politics, too. What about political extremism in Europe at this time? You really liked that topic when we discussed it in class.

Male Student: I don't know. I think I need to talk to the professor and find out what he has in mind.

Narrator: Now answer the question.

Narrator: Number 3.

Professor: Let's get started, class. Last time we said that we would answer questions about next Friday's midterms. Does anyone have any questions?

Female Student: Will income tax be one of the topics? I am still a little unclear about that.

Professor: Yes, it will be on the test. Who can help Stephanie? What is a progressive income tax?

Female Student: Actually, I am pretty clear on what a progressive income tax is. That's not what my question is about. A progressive income tax is one that has higher rates for the rich than for the poor. But why are they so controversial?

Professor: Good question, Stephanie. That will be on the test for sure. Progressive income taxes are a feature of tax codes worldwide, including this country's. Progressive income taxes have been around for well over a century, yet they continue to be controversial. Can anyone help Stephanie? Chuck?

Male Student: Well, lately, haven't there been big controversies over tax rates for the rich? Conservatives seem to want lower taxes for the rich, while liberals would rather raise their rates, to keep taxes low for the middle class and working class.

Professor: Yes, that's certain. But let's keep in mind that this controversy has been part of the discourse about the progressive income tax from its very inception. In fact, early opponents disagreed so strongly with the notion of a progressive income tax that they had it declared unconstitutional. It took a constitutional amendment to finally institute a progressive income tax, and even then the rates themselves remain controversial.

Narrator: Now answer the question.

Narrator: Number 4.

Man: Hi, Madge. Can you talk a minute?

Woman: Sure, Victor. What's wrong? You look a little tired.

Man: Yes, I'm changing rooms. Now I am in 109 Roberts Hall.

Woman: How come?

Man: It was my roommate. He was making me crazy.

Woman: Oh, yeah. You've been having trouble with him for a while, haven't you? So why did you decide to move?

Man: Well, he kept complaining about my music. You know that I can't study unless I have music playing. He kept telling me to turn down my music.

Woman: Well, that's nothing new.

Man: Well, then he decided to go to bed every night at 9:00, so that he can get up at five A.M. to study. I wanted to read at night, but he said that the light kept him up. So I couldn't play my music or stay up past ten.

Woman: You were lucky to get another dorm room so fast.

Man: I agree. I was lucky because I got a single room, too. But it's in Roberts Hall. It's so far from the academic quad that no one wants to live there. So I can have my music as loud as I want!

Narrator: Now answer the question.

Narrator: Number 5.

Student: Professor, I'm a little worried about next week's assignment.

Professor: What's the matter, John?

Student: Well, we have an online class next week, right?

Professor: Yes, we're having that class online because I have to be in Beijing to speak at a conference. I emailed instructions for the online discussion yesterday. Didn't you get them?

Student: Yes, but that's not the problem. I got the instructions and they are clear to me. The problem is my computer. It's out of order right now. And I live about thirty miles from campus, so I can't come to campus to use the computer center. I don't want to miss the class or the online discussion.

Professor: I see. What happened to your computer?

Student: I think that the hard drive crashed. I took it in to be repaired, but it won't be back in time for the online class.

Professor: Do you have a mobile phone?

Student: Yes, I do.

Professor: You can access our course discussion from your phone. There is a special app for that.

Student: That's great. But isn't the keyboard on the phone a little small?

Professor: John, I can't solve all your problems!

Narrator: Now answer the question.

ANSWERS AND EXPLANATIONS

1. **B** **She needs to make sure she can take a makeup exam.** Option B is correct because the student tells the professor that she wants to take a makeup exam because she has to be in a volleyball game the same day as the midterm. Option A is one of the reasons students can take a makeup exam, but it is not the reason the student is going to be absent from class. Option C is contradicted by the information in the conversation. The student clearly wants to take a makeup exam. She talks about the team's record with the professor, but this is not the reason she wanted to speak with the professor, so Option D is incorrect.

2. **D** **He needs advice about a term paper topic.** Option D is correct because the student says that he wants advice about how to pick a topic for a term paper. Option A is not supported by the information in the conversation. The student liked this subject when it was discussed in class and has

no questions about it at all. Option B is true, but it is not the reason the student is talking to the woman. Option C is incorrect because although the student wonders whether he needs to talk to the professor, that takes place after he talks to the woman.

3. **C** **To talk about topics covered on the exam next week** Option C is supported by the professor's opening question. He wanted to know if the class has questions about the topics on the upcoming test. Option A is incorrect because it is one of the topics on the test. Option B is incorrect because the professor is clear that this topic will be on the test, but it is not the only topic. Option D is incorrect because this is one way that the progressive income tax is controversial, but that is not the reason that the people are talking.

4. **C** **He wants to tell her that he is moving to another room.** At the beginning of the conversation, the man tells the woman that he is changing dorm rooms, so Option C is correct. Option A is not supported by the conversation. Option B is incorrect because the woman is the one who says that the man looks tired. Option D is incorrect. Details about the former roommate support the man's reason for moving, but news of the move, and not reasons for it, is the focus of this conversation.

5. **A** **He is worried about an online class next week.** Option A is correct because the student goes to the professor to talk about his concern that he will not be able to participate in an online class because his computer is not working. Option B is contradicted by the conversation. The student says that he understands the instructions. Option C is incorrect because distance from campus is not a problem for attending class since the class session is online. Option D is incorrect because the student was not planning on using his phone until after he spoke with the professor.

Exercise 8: Main Idea or Detail? (Page 276)

ANSWERS

1. a. M; b. D
2. a. M; b. D
3. a. D; b. M
4. a. M; b. D
5. a. D; b. M

Example: Detail Item (Page 277)

TRACK 42 AUDIO SCRIPT
See Track 40 audio script, page 334.

Exercise 9: Supporting Detail Items (Page 280)

TRACK 43 AUDIO SCRIPT

Narrator: Number 1. Listen to part of a lecture in an economics class.

Professor: We can observe that consumer decisions can have a big impact on economic activity. At many different times, consumers' ethical and moral considerations can play a big part in individual or collective decisions they make. Consumers, for example, can make a decision to boycott, or avoid shopping at, certain national or global chains because they don't like the practices of that chain. At times, to meet consumer demand or expectation, organizations or movements are formed. One such organization, err, movement is the Fair Trade movement. Fair Trade responds to consumer desire for products, particularly agricultural products, that are sourced in ways the consumers consider ethical or moral. Fair Trade has several objectives, first and foremost that producers receive more of the proceeds from the sale of their products, which are typically things such as coffee, chocolate, or other agricultural products. But the concern is more than just fair prices for producers. Consumers also want to support sustainable, eco-friendly farming methods. A number of global organizations have responded by creating Fair Trade associations that set standards and certify producers as Fair Trade. Ethical and moral considerations are powerful—so powerful, in fact, that they may trump other considerations, such as lower consumer prices. Consumers may be willing to pay higher prices.

Narrator: Now answer the question.

Narrator: Number 2. Listen to part of a conversation in a library.

Librarian: OK, here you go. You need to have this item back in two hours.

Student: Two hours! I thought library loans were for a month.

Librarian: Usually, they are. But items placed on closed reserve are only available for two hours. They are also available overnight, but you have to return the item by nine A.M. tomorrow when the library opens.

Student: Oh, so that's what closed reserve means. I don't think I can read this entire article in two hours, and I am busy tonight, so I can't read it even if I check it out overnight. Can I check it out over the weekend?

Librarian: No, you can only check it out for one night, not Friday and Saturday. But if you check it out on Saturday, you don't have to return it until Monday. That's because the library is closed on Sunday.

Student: Well, I am not sure I can get here by 5:00 on Saturday to check it out. I have to work at that time. And I can't read it in two hours.

Librarian: Well, you can make a photocopy for five cents a page, or you can scan it for free and save it to a USB drive.

Student: I didn't bring my USB drive with me today. And I don't want to make a copy. Can I check it out overnight?

Librarian: Yes, but you'll have to come back an hour before closing to check it out overnight. You can start reading now and then come back later to check it out overnight, unless another student asks for it.

Student: I see. I think I will check it out and go home and scan it, and make it back in two hours.

Librarian: OK, that's up to you. But if you're late, the fine is two dollars an hour.

Student: Well, for today, that's not a problem. From now on, I will keep my USB drive with me in case I need to scan here in the library.

Librarian: That's a good idea. We have eight scanners and they are completely free.

Narrator: Now answer the question.

Narrator: Number 3. Listen to part of a lecture in a physics class.

Professor: The Doppler effect is a well-documented phenomenon about the perception of sound. The Doppler effect is observed when either the object making the sound or the individual perceiving the sound, or both, are in motion relative to each other. Basically, car and train horns, as well as sirens, produce sound at a constant frequency. But if the horn, for example, is in motion, as is the case when a car honks its horn at another vehicle, the sound will be perceived as changing pitch even though the sound actually never changes pitch. This phenomenon was first observed in the nineteenth century, when trains were able to operate fast enough to produce the effect. Basically, to an observer standing still, an approaching horn will sound as if it's at a higher pitch, and a receding horn will sound as if it's a lower pitch. But the frequency of the sound waves stays the same. How is that possible?

Student: Is it because of the movement?

Professor: Exactly. As the vehicle moves toward the listener, each sound wave is emitted slightly closer to the listener. Thus, to the listener, the waves seem to arrive in greater frequency, which makes the pitch go up. The opposite happens when the sound is moving away from the listener. The space between each sound wave is progressively larger, which makes it seem like the pitch is dropping.

Student: So what happens with supersonic aircraft? They move faster than the speed of sound. So can they sneak up silently?

Professor: Actually, it's the opposite. The noise from an aircraft is produced in waves, too. But in this case, the waves are produced by something moving faster than the speed of sound. So those sound waves tend to bunch up and produce what listeners below perceive as a sonic boom—a loud explosive sound produced by hearing all of the waves bunched up together. A supersonic aircraft will produce considerable noise. Plus, the aircraft would have trouble sneaking up because it could be spotted by most radar.

Narrator: Now answer the question.

Narrator: Number 4. Listen to a part of a conversation between a student and a professor.

Student: Excuse me, professor. Do you have a minute?

Professor: Sure, how can I help you, David?

Student: Well, I had a question about the grading system for the class. I got an A on the midterm. So do I have to write a term paper?

Professor: Well, that depends. If you want to get an A for the course, you need to write a term paper and get an A on it. If you only want a B or C, then you don't have to do a term paper.

Student: I see. What if I get a B on the final exam?

Professor: Then it gets a little tricky. To get an A, you have to have an A average on the tests and quizzes, and you have to write an A term paper, too. You say you got an A on the midterm. How are your quiz grades?

Student: Well, I have an A-minus right now, I think. I scored well on all the quizzes except the first one. I got a high C on that one.

Professor: Well, that's a bit complicated, too. You are allowed to "throw out" your lowest quiz grade. That way, one of your quiz grades doesn't count toward your final grade.

Student: What do you mean?

Professor: We take eleven quizzes during the course, and only ten of them count. So your average is based on not counting one quiz. That's always the lowest grade. Everyone can have a bad day, so I always do that with one of the quizzes. With most students, it's the first quiz. Then they study harder.

Student: OK, without that low quiz, I am pretty sure I have an A average on the quizzes.

Professor: In that case, if you want an A, I would advise you to write a term paper. Have you considered any subjects . . . ?

Narrator: Now answer the question.

Narrator: Number 5. Listen to part of a lecture in a contemporary literature class.

Male Professor: Stories of the immigrant experience are an important part of the American literary tradition. As long as there have been immigrants to the United States, there have been chronicles of their journeys and experiences. It is sometimes troubling whether these authors are really American, since they may hold foreign nationality. However, since these writings are so closely linked to the American experience and are often in English, we are including them in our class. Many of these writings are by Latino authors or Chinese authors, since speakers of these languages are the largest immigrant groups at present. Probably all of us have heard of Amy Tan and her writings about her family and life in the United States. But the author I want to talk about today is Aleksander Hemon. Hemon is a particularly interesting example because he did not choose to immigrate. Rather, immigration seemed to choose Hemon. Hemon was in Chicago on a short-term exchange program from his native country, then Yugoslavia. He was about to board a flight back to his native country when word was received that the capital city, Belgrade, was under air attack. He was prevented from traveling and became a refugee from war. He worked a variety of odd jobs as he learned English. A writer in his first language, he decided to learn enough English to write stories and novels in his new language. He published novels and short stories to high praise and later won an award of a million dollars.

Narrator: Now answer the question.

ANSWERS AND EXPLANATIONS

1. **D Consumers want products sourced in ways that they believe are moral or ethical.** Option D is directly stated in the lecture. Option A is not a cause of the Fair Trade movement. It is a general statement of the impact of collective consumer decisions. Option B is not a cause of the Fair Trade movement, but simply a detail about one aspect of it. Option C is contradicted by the lecture. The professor says that consumers are willing to pay more because of their ethical considerations.

2. **A Use them in the library for two hours**
   C Scan or photocopy them. (Special multiple choice) This special multiple-choice item asks for two answers. Options A and C are both mentioned by the librarian, so they are correct. Option B is incorrect because items cannot be checked out for the whole weekend. But items checked out on Saturday night are not due back in the library until Monday morning. Option D is incorrect because this is the way to check out regular library items, not closed reserve items.

3. **A Two passengers in a speeding train that is blowing its horn (Negative factual information)** A negative factual information item such as this one is answered by information that is not in the listening selection or is contradicted by it. The Doppler effect is observed when a listener, a producer of a sound, or both are in motion relative to one another. Option A is the only option in which the people and sound are

not in motion relative to each other because the passengers are moving at the same speed and direction as the train. Therefore, the passengers would not observe the Doppler effect. Options B, C, and D are all situations in which the people would observe the Doppler effect because either the people, the source of the sound, or both are in motion relative to one another.

4. **D He wants to get an A for the course.** Option D is correct because the requirements for an A are an A average on tests and quizzes and an A grade on a term paper. The student's questions indicate that he wants to get that grade. Option A is contradicted by the conversation. The student got a C on one of the quizzes but As on the rest. Option B would not be a reason to write a term paper. Students need to write a term paper only if they want to get an A and have an A average on tests. Option C is not a reason to want to write a term paper. It's just one of the conditions for getting an A.

5. **D His hometown was under air attack.** Option D is correct because the professor says that the air attack started the day Hemon was supposed to return to his country. Option A is incorrect because Hemon started to do these things after he became stranded outside his country. Option B is incorrect because Hemon didn't want to immigrate. He chose to write about immigration after he became an involuntary immigrant. Option C is not a reason to stay in the United States.

Exercise 10: Answering Basic Comprehension Items (Page 281)

TRACK 44 AUDIO SCRIPT

Narrator: Listen to this talk by a professor. Answer the questions.

Professor: From time to time, new perspectives and insights will act to change an academic discipline entirely. That's the case with positive psychology, which has reshaped the way many people see psychology. From the very beginning, modern psychology has looked at abnormality, neurosis, and psychosis. The major thrust, in a certain sense, of mainstream psychology is a focus on diagnosis and treatment of various sorts of problems, or abnormalities.

Positive psychology takes a very different approach. Some people have even called it the study of happiness. The founders of positive psychology summed up their intent by saying,

"We believe that a psychology of positive human functioning will arise, which achieves a scientific understanding and effective interventions to build thriving individuals, families, and communities." The founders of positive psychology believe that studying only disorders gives a partial view of people. Goals and outcomes of positive psychology include encouraging and developing individuals' talents and making life more happy and fulfilling for people.

Positive psychologists study three overlapping areas. First, they study "the pleasant life," or ways that people derive happiness from hobbies, activities, entertainment, and relationships. Second, they study "the good life," ways that people gain satisfaction from activities such as work. Finally, they study "the meaningful life," the ways people gain satisfaction from involvement with activities they believe are meaningful or related to values, goals, and ideas, such as communities, organizations, and religion.

Of course, positive psychology is not without its critics. Many say that the methods used in positive psychology are unscientific, for example. In the next few weeks, we will deeply and critically examine positive psychology, with an eye toward understanding it, evaluating its validity, and even applying some of its findings in our own lives. I guess you might say that this unit of instruction is one place where your studies might help you find true happiness.

ANSWERS AND EXPLANATIONS

1. **D   An overview of positive psychology (Gist-content)** Option D is correct because the lecture defines positive psychology, compares it to traditional psychology, and summarizes major features—all characteristics of an overview of a topic. Options A, B, and C are incorrect because they are details or parts of the overview.

2. **B   To provide an introduction to a unit of study in the course (Gist-purpose)** Option B is correct because the professor states that she is giving an overview of the class's next topic of study. Option A is incorrect because this is a possible benefit of studying positive psychology, but it is not the purpose of this lecture. Option C is not correct because the professor does not actually criticize positive psychology in this lecture, but rather says that the class will study

criticism during the unit. Option D describes what the class will do in coming class sessions.

3. **C   Ways that people are made unhappy by abnormalities (Detail/Negative factual information)** Option C is correct because this is one of the purposes of traditional psychology. Options A, B, and D are all mentioned in the listening selection as examples of areas of study in positive psychology.

4. **C   It gives a partial or incomplete view of people. (Detail)** Option C is correct because this detail is stated directly in the selection. Option A is a criticism of positive psychology, not mainstream psychology. Option B is not a problem of mainstream psychology itself. The focus on abnormal psychology to the exclusion of other aspects is the problem. Option D is contradicted by the information because mainstream psychology focuses on abnormalities to the exclusion of other important considerations.

5. **D   The satisfaction people get from involvement in the community (Detail)** According to the professor, study of the meaningful life includes consideration of the happiness people feel from involvement in communities and organizations. Therefore, Option D is correct. Options A and C are examples of the area of positive psychology called "the pleasant life," so they are incorrect. Option B is incorrect because it is an example of an area studied as part of "the good life"—work and daily occupations.

Example: Understanding the Function Item (Page 285)

TRACK 45 AUDIO SCRIPT

Narrator: Listen again to part of a conversation that you heard previously. Then answer the question.

Professor: That's very interesting, but to get a higher grade, you need to pay attention to what I taught you about writing a good paper. Your essay should have an introductory paragraph, at least three body paragraphs, and a concluding paragraph.

You had a good introduction and good body paragraphs. But you didn't have a concluding paragraph. And you have some problems with mechanics. Good mechanics is a requirement, too.

Student: What do you mean by mechanics?

Narrator: What does the student mean when she says this?

Student: What do you mean by mechanics?

Exercise 11: Understanding the Function Items (Page 285)

Narrator: Listen again to parts of conversations that you heard previously. Then answer the questions. Number 1.

Student: Well, we have a midterm next week, and if we win our game tonight, we will go to the state championship in Springfield. That's next week, too. And you said that the only valid excuses for missing the midterm are being sick or a family emergency. So I am worried that I won't be able to make up the exam.

Professor: Yes, I always tell students that the only valid excuses are sickness and family emergencies, but if you have a special situation, we can work it out.

Student: That's great, Professor Kean.

Narrator: What does the professor imply when she says this?

Professor: Yes, I always tell students that the only valid excuses are sickness and family emergencies, but if you have a special situation, we can work it out.

Narrator: Number 2.

Female Student: It can cover politics, too. What about political extremism in Europe at this time? You really liked that topic when we discussed it in class.

Male Student: I don't know. I think I need to talk to the professor and find out what he has in mind.

Narrator: What does the man mean when he says this?

Male Student: I don't know. I think I need to talk to the professor and find out what he has in mind.

Narrator: Number 3.

Professor: Yes, it will be on the test. Who can help Stephanie? What is a progressive income tax?

Student: Actually, I am pretty clear on what a progressive income tax is. That's not what my question is about. A progressive income tax is one that has higher rates for the rich than for the poor. But why are they so controversial?

Narrator: Why does the woman say this?

Student: Actually, I'm pretty clear on what a progressive income tax is. That's not what my question is about.

Narrator: Number 4.

Man: Well, he kept complaining about my music. You know that I can't study unless I have music playing. He kept telling me to turn down my music.

Woman: Well, that's nothing new.

Narrator: What does the woman mean when she says this?

Woman: Well, that's nothing new.

Narrator: Number 5.

Professor: You can access our course discussion from your phone. There is a special app for that.

Student: That's great. But isn't the keyboard on the phone a little small?

Professor: John, I can't solve all your problems!

Narrator: What does the professor mean when she says this?

Professor: John, I can't solve all your problems!

ANSWERS AND EXPLANATIONS

1. **C If a student has an unusual problem, the professor will make an exception to the rule.** Option C is correct because *work it out* means "find a solution together." The student thanks the professor, which also shows that the professor is willing to make an exception to the rule. For this same reason, Option A is incorrect. Option B shows misunderstanding of the expression *work it out,* so this option is incorrect. Option D is incorrect because the professor's remark shows that she is willing to make exceptions in special circumstances, but she is still serious about the rule.

2. **C He needs more information on the assignment.** Option C is correct because the student feels confused about the term paper requirements, so he wants to get clarification directly from the professor. Option A is contradicted by the information in the conversation. Option B is a true statement, but it is not why the student said he needs more information. Option D is not supported by the conversation. The student does not express a feeling about political history.

3. **A She already understands the definition and has a question on another aspect of progressive income tax.** The student has a question about this kind of tax, but the question is not about the definition of a progressive income tax. Therefore, Option A is correct. Option B is incorrect because the student is not interested in changing the subject completely, but in shifting to another aspect of the tax. Option C is not supported by the information in the lecture. Since the student does not have questions about the definition of a progressive income tax, Option D is not possible.

4. **D She has already heard about that.** Option D is correct because the context shows that the female student is already aware of the man's problem with his roommate over noise and that

other problems occurred that caused the man to want to change rooms. Option A is contradicted by the conversation. The woman student shows a lot of interest in the man's problem and the solution he has found. Option B does not make sense since the conversation gives no information on the kind of music the student liked. Option C does not make sense because the conversation is not about comparing the man's experiences with others'.

5. A   The professor thinks that the small keyboard is not a serious problem. The professor's ironic tone and laughter show that she thinks that the small keyboard is not a big problem. Therefore, Option A is correct. Option B is contradicted by the conversation. The professor spends a lot of time problem solving with the student. Option C is not supported by the selection. This is the literal meaning of the sentence, but the ironic tone and laughter indicate that the professor has another meaning in mind rather than the literal one. Option D is not supported by the conversation.

Example: Understanding the Attitude Item (Page 287)

TRACK 47 AUDIO SCRIPT

Narrator: Listen to part of a talk in a life science class.

Professor: Today, we will continue our study of various relationships among organisms that live together. As we said yesterday, parasitism describes a relationship between two organisms in which one of the organisms benefits and the other, the host, is harmed. Often, when we think of parasitism, we think of organisms such as worms that live in the gut, or digestive systems, of various animals, including humans. But there are other types of parasites as well, such as the plasmodium parasite, which lives in the bloodstreams of humans and other vertebrates and causes malaria. The amount of harm that a parasite can cause to its host can vary. Many digestive parasites, for example, do not endanger the host's survival, but merely make the host's life more difficult. The host may suffer from loss of nutrition, stomachaches, and other discomforts, but the host is usually not harmed. But malaria can cause great harm to its host.

Many scientists believe that there are mutually beneficial relationships among other kinds of organisms that live together. These relationships are called symbiotic. For example, many scientists believe that certain birds, called plovers, are in a symbiotic relationship with crocodiles. These birds will go directly into the crocodile's mouths in order to eat pieces of food caught in the teeth as well as harmful parasites that might be there. The crocodile gets a free teeth cleaning, and the plover gets a meal.

Although relationships such as these seem mutually beneficial, some scientists disagree that they are truly mutual. They believe that there may be some harmful effects to one of the partners, even though the harm may be slight or unobservable. They point out, for example, that even though bacteria that live in cows' digestive systems help the animals digest the plants they eat, the bacteria may be harming the hosts in some undetected way. In order to prove this hypothesis, however, scientists need to find ways to detect the harm caused. So far, their position is only supported by supposition. Of course, such proof may be found someday.

Example: Understanding the Attitude Item (Page 288)

TRACK 48 AUDIO SCRIPT

Narrator: Listen again to part of the lecture. Then answer the question.

Professor: In order to prove this hypothesis, however, scientists need to find ways to detect the harm caused. So far, their position is only supported by supposition. Of course, such proof *may* be found someday.

Narrator: What does the professor mean when he says this?

Professor: Of course, such proof *may* be found someday.

Exercise 12: Understanding Tone and Intonation (Page 289)

TRACK 49 AUDIO SCRIPT

Narrator: Listen to each conversation. What do the people mean? Circle the letter of the answer. Number 1.

Woman: John says that he will be on time to work tomorrow.

Man: Yeah, right. He was late today, yesterday, and the day before.

Narrator: Number 2.

Man: I just read that you can earn a hundred dollars a day working from your home. That sounds like a good deal. I need some extra money.

Woman: That sounds awfully easy.

Narrator: Number 3.

Man: I got a B in Professor Bloom's class. That's the first time I ever got a B in college.

Woman: Congratulations. Now you know how a regular student feels, Mr. A-plus average!

Narrator: Number 4.

Woman: I just found out I was accepted to Harvard.

Man: Congratulations! Now you just have to find a way to pay for it!

Narrator: Number 5.

Man: Dr. Smith just sent everyone in class an email. Class is canceled tomorrow.

Woman: Great! Now how can we ask him questions about the test on Friday?

Narrator: Number 6.

Woman: The concert at the student union is sold out.

Man: Of course! That's why I bought my ticket last week.

Narrator: Number 7.

Man: I think that Dr. Quinn is going to give a quiz today.

Woman: Of course. It's Monday. She wants to see if we did our homework over the weekend.

Narrator: Number 8.

Woman: Look, you got a parking ticket while we were in the restaurant.

Man: My goodness! That's my first parking ticket since 2010!

Narrator: Number 9.

Man: I just checked my grades online. I got all As.

Woman: My goodness! That's quite a record.

Narrator: Number 10.

Woman: I stayed up all night three nights in a row studying for the chemistry final.

Man: How did that work out for you?

ANSWERS

1. b
2. b
3. b
4. a
5. b
6. b
7. a
8. a
9. a
10. b

Exercise 13: Understanding the Attitude (Stance) Items (Page 291)

TRACK 50 AUDIO SCRIPT

Narrator: Listen to the conversation. Then answer the questions.

Professor: Hi, Christina. Thanks for coming by my office. I wanted to talk to you because of your outstanding work the past few semesters. All the professors are really impressed with your work here at the university.

Student: Well, thank you, Professor. I just try to work hard.

Professor: Well, we are very impressed, so we have decided to ask if you want to apply for the Hall Fellowship.

Student: Oh, my! I'm not sure I've heard of that fellowship.

Professor: The fellowship is named for the wife of the first dean of this college, Mildred Hall, who died over one hundred years ago. Apparently, she was from a wealthy family and donated a lot of money for fellowships for women scholars. If you get it, it will pay all of your tuition next year, and you can renew it for two more years. That's long enough for you to finish your degree and graduate. If you're interested, we will fill out a nomination form, and the financial aid office will contact you. Then you need to fill out an application and do a few more things.

Student: Well, I feel really honored. Thank you, Professor.

Professor: There is just one issue. Do you have any other financial aid?

Student: Well, I am a lab assistant for an undergrad course.

Professor: OK. We want to make sure that we nominate students who don't have scholarships, so that every student has support.

Student: Oh, well, I don't have a scholarship. I just help the professors in the lab. Do you think that I will be able to keep that job if I get the fellowship?

Professor: Good luck with that! The fellowship requires you to take a full load, and you cannot take a full load and work in a lab, according to the university's financial aid rules.

Narrator: Listen again to parts of the conversation. Then answer the questions. Number 1.

Professor: Hi, Christina. Thanks for coming by my office. I wanted to talk to you because of your outstanding work the past few semesters. All the professors are really impressed with your work here at the university.

Student: Well, thank you, Professor. I just try to work hard.

Narrator: What does the woman mean when she says this?

Student: Well, thank you, Professor. I just try to work hard.

Narrator: Number 2.

Professor: Well, we are very impressed, so we have decided to ask if you want to apply for the Hall Fellowship.

Student: Oh, my! I'm not sure I've heard of that fellowship.

Narrator: What does the woman mean when she says this?

Student: Oh, my! I'm not sure I've heard of that fellowship.

Narrator: Number 3.

Student: Well, I feel really honored. Thank you, Professor.

Professor: There is just one issue. Do you have any other financial aid?

Narrator: Which sentence expresses how the professor feels?

Narrator: Number 4.

Student: Oh, well, I don't have a scholarship. I just help the professors in the lab. Do you think that I will be able to keep that job if I get the fellowship?

Professor: Good luck with that!

Narrator: How does the professor seem to feel about the woman working in the lab if she gets the fellowship?

ANSWERS AND EXPLANATIONS

1. **C** **She is trying to be modest.** The student's tone and intonation show that she is trying to accept the professor's compliment without sounding proud or ungrateful. Therefore, Option C is the best answer. Options A and B are not supported by the information in the conversation. Option D is the opposite of what the student is trying to do. She is trying to be modest about her accomplishments.

2. **B** **She is excited and interested in hearing more about the scholarship.** The woman's tone and intonation communicate interest and excitement, so Option B is correct. None of the other options make sense.

3. **B** **He feels worried.** The professor's tone and intonation, as well as his words, indicate that he is worried about a potential problem if the student already has a scholarship. Therefore, Option B is correct. The other options do not make sense.

4. **C** **He is skeptical.** Option C is correct because the professor's tone shows that he is not convinced that the student will be able to work in the lab if she gets the scholarship. The other options do not make sense.

Exercise 14: Answering Pragmatic Understanding Items (Page 292)

TRACK 51 AUDIO SCRIPT

Narrator: Listen to the conversation. Then answer questions 1 and 2.

Student: Professor, do you have time for a question?

Professor: Sure, Mitch. How can I help you?

Student: Well, I am getting ready to analyze the data for my statistics project and I have a few questions.

Professor: Let's see. . . . You were going to survey student opinions about fast-food restaurants and then analyze the results, right?

Student: Yes. The problem I am having is with the data analysis. When I looked at the raw data, I noticed that there is a big difference between male and female students. I hadn't planned on analyzing my data in this way, so I want to know if that's OK.

Professor: Well . . . The short answer is yes. But you're going to have to make some adjustments to your write-up.

Student: Adjustments . . . ?

Professor: Yes, this kind of thing happens all the time in research. Sometimes you don't know all the research questions until you begin the research. Then, suddenly, a new pattern in the data jumps out at you. Or a new question that you forgot to ask emerges.

Student: Well, in this case, both.

Professor: There are a few things you need to do. In the introduction to your paper, make sure that you state that you added a research question. Then, in the results section, give the data analysis. Finally, in the discussion part of the paper, analyze and interpret the data just as you would for your original research questions. What were those?

Student: I had two research questions originally. First, I wanted to see who eats more fast food, freshmen and sophomores, or juniors and seniors. Second, I wanted to see if the two groups preferred the same kinds of fast food.

Professor: Fascinating. I hope I don't get hungry reading your paper.

Student: That wasn't as bad as I thought. But there is something else. I am having trouble finding software to analyze the data I gathered. My new research question makes the analysis a lot more complicated.

Professor: I can see that. But there's an easy answer this time. Here. Check out the statistics program on this CD. It's called Statpack. I am pretty sure that the software you need is on this CD.

TRACK 52 AUDIO SCRIPT

Narrator: Listen again to parts of the conversation. Then answer questions 3, 4, and 5. Question 3.

Professor: Well . . . The short answer is yes. But you're going to have to make some adjustments to your write-up.

Student: Adjustments . . . ?

Narrator: Which sentence best expresses how the student feels?

Narrator: Question 4.

Professor: Sometimes you don't know all the research questions until you begin the research. Then, suddenly, a new pattern in the data jumps out at you. Or a new question that you forgot to ask emerges.

Student: Well, in this case, both.

Narrator: What does the student mean when he says this?

Student: Well, in this case, both.

Narrator: Question 5.

Student: That wasn't as bad as I thought. But there is something else. I am having trouble finding software to analyze the data I gathered. My new

research question makes the analysis a lot more complicated.

Narrator: How does the student feel when he says this?

Student: But there is something else.

ANSWERS AND EXPLANATIONS

1. **C** **The student can add the question but has to listen to a long explanation. (Understanding the function)** The professor says that this happens frequently, but gives a long explanation, so Option C is correct. Option A is contradicted by the information in the conversation. The professor gives a long explanation. Option B is contradicted by the conversation. The professor seems happy with the student, in fact. Option D is contradicted by the conversation. The professor seems pleased with the student's research project and takes the student's question seriously.

2. **B** **He wants to reassure the student that adding a research question is not a problem. (Understanding the function)** The professor's positive tone and supportive attitude show that he wants to make sure the student doesn't feel bad about adding a research question. Option A is not supported by the information in the conversation. Option C is contradicted by the professor's supportive tone. Option D is contradicted by the conversation. The professor clearly believes that researchers add research questions for good reasons.

3. **C** **He feels anxious because he thinks a lot of extra work is required. (Understanding the attitude)** The student's tone and intonation show that he feels anxious or afraid, so Option C is correct. The other options are contradicted by the tone and intonation used by the student and the information in the conversation.

4. **D** **He is agreeing with the professor. (Understanding the function)** Option D is correct because the student saw a new pattern in the data and added a new research question, so he is agreeing with the professor. Option A is incorrect because the student is not talking about whether these things are common, but rather simply stating that the things happened during his project. Options B and C are not supported by the information in the conversation. The people are not talking about mistakes in research (Option B). The student may have thought that he made a mistake, but here he is not admitting he made

a mistake. Rather, he is saying that changes are common during research (Option C).

5. **B** **He wants to ask another question about his project. (Understanding the attitude)**
The student clearly wants to change the subject to another question related to his study, data analysis, so Option B is correct. The remaining options are contradicted by the information in the conversation. The student wants to ask a different question about the project, not add a second new research question, so Option A is incorrect. He doesn't change the topic to a completely different subject, but asks another question about the research project, so Option C is incorrect. The student doesn't give another reason, but goes on to a question about data analysis, so Option D is incorrect.

Example: Overall Organization Item (Page 295)

TRACK 53 AUDIO SCRIPT

Narrator: Listen to the following excerpt from a longer lecture in a life science class. Then answer the questions.

Professor: As we have been discussing, cycles occur constantly in nature. The lives of organisms are no different. Different organisms present different life cycles. Take butterflies as an example. The life cycle of a butterfly begins when two adult butterflies mate. The female lays eggs, generally on the leaves of a plant. Some butterflies prefer certain plants that they use exclusively. The monarch butterfly is one example. That butterfly always lays its eggs on milkweed plants. When the eggs hatch, larvae emerge. Larvae, or caterpillars, look like long worms with many legs. The caterpillars use the leaves of the plant for food. Caterpillars eat a lot! In a single day, a caterpillar may eat several times its weight in leaves, which can cause great damage to the plant. After a while, the caterpillar hangs upside down from a branch or twig, sheds its skin, and grows a hard covering, or case. Inside the case, the organism, now called a pupa, undergoes an amazing transformation, and after a few weeks, an adult butterfly emerges from the case. After the butterfly emerges, it needs to let its wings dry and harden in the fresh air and sun. As soon as that is over, the butterfly is ready to fly off to look for nourishment—nectar from flowers—and to find mates and start the cycle again.

Exercise 15: Understanding Organization Items (Page 299)

TRACK 54 AUDIO SCRIPT

Narrator: Listen to the following lecture in a marketing class. Then answer the questions. Circle the letter of the answer.

Professor: A good knowledge of the law of supply and demand can help marketers price products appropriately, often in unusual or unexpected ways. A particularly interesting example is drawn from hospitality, one of the fastest-growing sectors of the economy. A certain budget hotel chain was wondering if their rooms were priced appropriately. This company owned a lot of inexpensive hotels alongside interstate highways. They advertised the price of the rooms on large neon signs along the road. The prices were written in neon lights and could be changed according to consumer demand. The hotel marketers wondered when consumer demand would be the highest. So they studied check-in times gathered from hundreds of the company's hotels across the country. Then they made an interesting discovery. Hotel check-ins increased dramatically at about eleven P.M. This made them think that they needed to adjust their pricing strategy. So they did a test. What do you think they did? Karla?

Female student: They probably lowered the price at eleven P.M. so they could rent the room that night. Even a few dollars is better than a room going unrented for a night.

Professor: Interesting response, Karla. But actually, that was their old strategy. The strategy worked similarly to the pricing strategy of supermarkets. If some vegetables are about to go bad, supermarkets lower the price to get at least a little money before the vegetables had to be thrown away. With vegetables, that usually works. Supermarkets are able to get rid of unsold products before they go bad. But hotel rooms are not the same as vegetables, even if both can go unsold. The hotel chain found that lower prices late at night had no effect on the number of rooms they rented, even if they rented the rooms at or below cost. Any other ideas?

Male Student: Maybe they raised prices.

Professor: Good thought, Max. Why could they raise prices?

Male Student: Supply and demand, I think . . .

Professor: That's right. They noticed that demand went up at 11:00. People were tired and didn't want to drive any further. So they paid less attention to the price and checked into the first hotel they saw. Because demand after eleven was so high, the chain could still charge more and not see demand decrease. This insight earned the company millions of dollars in profits just from a relatively small price increase. So you can see, a knowledge of economic theory can help you be a better marketer.

ANSWERS AND EXPLANATIONS

1. **A** **Hotel prices follow the law of supply and demand in an unexpected way.** Option A is correct because higher prices do not lower demand at certain times of day when demand is strongest. Option B is only a detail about the hotel industry and not the reason the professor is talking about prices. Option C is incorrect because the professor adds the example of vegetable prices to clarify why the woman's answer was incorrect. Option D is contradicted by the information in the lecture. Lower prices after 11:00 did not increase demand. That is why the company undertook the study.

2. **C** **In the order in which the events happened** Option C is correct because the events are in the order in which they happened. Therefore, the other options are not possible.

3. The completed chart should look like this:

1. **B**	The company lowered the prices of rooms at 11:00 every night.
2. **C**	Company marketers studied check-in times at hundreds of hotels.
3. **A**	The company raised the prices of rooms at 11:00 every night.
4. **D**	Demand stayed up, and profits went up.

4. **D** **To show that consumer demand operates differently for different products** Option D is correct because the professor says that the example is about an unusual pattern of supply and demand. Time of day has a big effect on demand for hotel rooms, but not on the price of vegetables. Option A is incorrect because lower prices do not increase consumer demand for hotel rooms late at night. Option B is incorrect because the law of supply and demand applies to both, but it works in different ways because demand for vegetables is different from demand for hotel rooms, especially at certain times of day. Option C is contradicted by the information. Demand for hotel rooms was not affected when prices were raised after 11 P.M. because price is not the only factor that affects demand.

Example: Connecting Content Item (Page 301)

TRACK 55 AUDIO SCRIPT
See Track 53 audio script, page 346.

Exercise 16: Connecting Content Items (Page 303)

TRACK 56 AUDIO SCRIPT
See Track 54 audio script, page 346.

ANSWERS AND EXPLANATIONS

1. **D** **Demand will go down.** Option D is correct because the law of supply and demand predicts that as prices decrease, demand increases. Therefore, Options B and C are incorrect. Option A does not make sense because raising the price will affect sales, which is unrelated to increasing the speed in which the vegetables go bad.

2. The completed table should look like this.

	DEMAND GOES UP	DEMAND STAYS THE SAME	DEMAND GOES DOWN
The price of unsold, ripe vegetables is reduced.	✔		
The price of hotel rooms is reduced after 11:00 P.M.		✔	
The price of hotel rooms is raised after 11:00 P.M.		✔	

3. **A** **Consumer demand is influenced by more than price.** Option A is correct because consumer demand is affected by people's need for sleep after a certain time of day. Options B and C are contradicted by the information in the lecture. Option D is incorrect because data from hotel check-in times show that demand increases predictably at a certain time of day.

4. **B** **Reduce prices in the afternoon** Option B is most likely to increase sales and income. Since sales are low in the afternoon, reducing afternoon prices is the most likely way to increase sales and income overall. Option A is incorrect because demand is high in the morning, so customers will pay higher prices. For this reason, Option C is incorrect. Option C will increase sales and income in the afternoon but will reduce income in the morning when demand is high. Option D is incorrect because while income will increase in the morning, when demand is high, sales will decrease in the afternoon, when demand is low.

Example: Making Inferences Item (Page 304)

TRACK 57 AUDIO SCRIPT

Narrator: Listen to part of a longer conversation between a student and a university records administrator. Then answer the questions.

Administrator: Hello, can I help you?

Student: Yes, I have a scholarship from my country to study at the university. I need to send a transcript to my country's scholarship agency, but the registrar's website says that my account is on hold, so I can't order a transcript. And I really need that transcript in order to get my tuition paid.

Administrator: Let me see your student ID, and I can check . . . Hmmmm. Yes, it looks like your tuition for this term is late. Right now, you owe nearly eight thousand dollars in tuition and fees for this term.

Student: Eight thousand dollars! I don't have that much money. The scholarship agency needs my transcript from last term in order to renew my scholarship for this term and pay the eight thousand dollars.

Administrator: I see. Yes, that happens all the time. Your country's scholarship office needs to contact us directly. Or maybe they will accept another document, such as your report card.

Student: Let's see . . . Here is the email they sent me.

Administrator: Yes, look here. They will accept a copy of your report card, too. You're in luck. A transcript costs twenty-five dollars and a report card is free. And it looks like they will accept a photocopy or electronic file, too.

Exercise 17: Making Inferences Items (Page 306)

Narrator: Listen to part of a lecture in a life sciences class.

Professor: Class, as you know, we have been studying migration of birds for the past few sessions. When people think of animal migration, they most likely think of birds, many, but not all species of which fly between northern and southern locations in order to live in warm locations year-round. Many species of butterfly migrate seasonally, including the Cloudless Sulpher and the Gulf Fritillary, yellow and bright orange North American species, and the Purple Crow butterfly, a beautifully colored species found only in Taiwan. Of all insect migratory patterns, that of the monarch butterfly is probably the most studied. These hardy travelers fly between North America and Mexico annually.

We do not have time to talk about butterfly migration in this course, but today we are going to talk in detail about migration of yet another animal form, the European eel. These eels, long, bony, snake-like fish, live in freshwater rivers, streams, and creeks in Europe. Though these animals are frightening to some of us, they are an important source of food in many countries, including Spain.

For centuries people wondered how these creatures reproduce, because no one had ever seen their eggs. In fact, not until recently did scientists realize that these amazing creatures make a six-thousand-kilometer journey to reproduce in North America. However, eel migration is unlike bird migration, in which the same generations will migrate in both directions, often multiple times over the course of the birds' lives. Presumably, new offspring follow older generations to learn the migration routes. However, in the case of eel migration, the parents all die off in North America. A new generation, tiny larvae, makes the migratory return trip each time alone, unguided by older generations. This is an amazing capacity, for each year the eel larvae swim to a place they have never been to before and that is known only to their ancestors.

Until recently, scientists didn't know that the eels reproduced in North America, and scientists are still trying to figure out the exact route the eels follow. Using tracking devices, scientists have determined that eels first swim to the Azores, a chain of islands west of Africa. From there, their route across the Atlantic to North America is still being traced. We do know, however, that the tiny eel larvae are aided by the Gulf Stream, a strong Atlantic water current that they ride back to Europe.

Eels are not the only species in which a new generation migrates unaided by older generations. Monarch butterflies also reproduce several times before they make their return trip. The butterflies that made the trip die out by the time of the return journey. Unlike eels' migratory pattern, the monarch's route is now well documented.

Some of you may want to write your term papers about European eels. We will learn more about European eels when we visit the City Aquarium on our field trip next week. In addition, those of you who go on our annual study trip to the Bahamas may actually be able to see eels in the wild and meet the scientists who study them.

ANSWERS AND EXPLANATIONS

1. **A A new generation of eels makes a return migratory trip, but bird migration includes older birds.** Option A includes correct information about both birds and eels. Options B and D are not supported by information in the lecture. Option C is not a difference between eels and birds and is contradicted by the lecture. The eels follow different routes to and from Europe.

2. **C The eels' route from Europe to the Azores Islands** Option C is correct because this is the only part of the route that is still not yet understood, according to the professor. Therefore, the other options are incorrect.

3. **B The students can see and learn about eels at the City Aquarium next week.** Option B is the only option that makes sense. The students can see eels and learn about them during the trip to the Aquarium. Option A is contradicted by information in the selection. Some butterflies migrate to places they have never been before. Option C is contradicted by the lecture. Parts of the eels' route are still unknown, while the butterflies' route is better documented. Option D may be true, but it is not a reason to study or not study an organism.

Exercise 18: Answering Connecting Information Items (Page 308)

Narrator: Listen to the following conversation between a student and her professor.

Student: Excuse me, Professor Martin. Do you have a couple of minutes to talk to me?

Professor: Sure, Martha. What's up?

Student: Well, I have concern about the attendance requirement for our class.

Professor: OK, sure.

Student: Well, according to the syllabus, we are allowed one free absence. After that, we lose half a letter grade for each absence unless we have your permission or a valid excuse.

Professor: That's right. The points on all assignments total to one thousand points. The cutoffs for an A, B, and C are nine hundred points, eight hundred points, and seven hundred points. So a letter grade is one hundred points. If you are absent more than one time, I will deduct fifty points. I do that because our class only meets once a week for four hours. If you miss a class, that's a week's work.

Student: OK, thanks. Actually, I already understood that. But I have a special problem. I am in the University Concert Orchestra this semester. We have three performances this semester that are out of town. We are performing at a high school in Chicago next week, and in March, we are performing in a college orchestra competition in New York. Then in April, we are going to perform at Disneyland.

Professor: Well, it's not fair to the other students to let you be absent three times, when everyone else has only one free absence. Rules are rules, you know. Can't you skip one of the concerts?

Student: Well, as it turns out, the concert in Chicago is in my old high school. I attended that high school three years ago when I was an exchange student. The principal wants me to meet some of the students at the school, and I really want to see my old orchestra teacher. So I really want to go back there with the orchestra. And in the concert in New York, I am going to have a solo. The conductor just told me that. And all my friends told me that Disneyland hires a lot of musicians in summer, so I have an audition for one of those jobs when I am there.

Professor: Well, it sounds like you really need to go to all three concerts. Hmmm. Let's see. Can you call in to class those days? I can bring a phone conference unit to class, and you can listen on your mobile phone and participate.

Student: I already thought of that. Our performances in New York and Chicago are at the same time as our class, so that won't work. But I can do that for the April class. Our performance is in the afternoon that day.

Professor: OK, so the April class is not a problem. Show me the dates of the other concerts on the syllabus.

Student: Look, here . . . The concerts are January 24 and March 7.

Professor: I see. Well, it's OK to miss one class, but the March 7 class is very important. It's the week before the midterm. Can you ask another student to record the class for you? If you record the class and do a short make-up project, I am willing to let you miss both classes.

Student: Actually, I already thought of that. My friend Carter says he can record both classes for me, and he promised to give me his notes, too. But what kind of project should I do?

Professor: Well, on March 5, we are talking about Piaget's ideas about child development. How about if you read a research article about Piaget? I can refer you to a couple of articles, and you can choose one and write a report about it. That will help you prepare for the midterm, too.

Student: That seems fair. Thank you, Professor. How can I find the article?

Professor: Well, just give me a minute. I have a couple of ideas about articles that you might use.

ANSWERS AND EXPLANATIONS

1. **(Connecting content/Drag-and-drop)** The completed table should look like this:

JANUARY	MARCH	APRIL
Chicago	New York	Disneyland
C The concert is at her old high school.	A She has a solo.	B She has an audition for a summer job.

2. **(Connecting content/Check box)** The completed table should look like this:

	WORKS	DOES NOT WORK
Record the class and do an extra project	✓	
Not perform in the concert		✓
Attend the class by telephone		✓

3. A **He understands the reasons her request is valid. (Making inferences)** Option A is correct because the reasons the student gives convince the professor that her absences are justified. Option B Is Incorrect because the professor never questioned the student's truthfulness. Option C is true, but it is a reason for him to deny her request, so it is incorrect. Option D is incorrect because it is also a reason to deny her request.

4. A **"You will lose 50 points from your final grade." (Making inferences)** Option A is correct. It is highly probable that the professor will not approve the student's request for a long spring break because he was so unwilling at first to accept the woman's legitimate reasons to be absent. For this reason, Options B and C do not make sense. The professor would probably not refer the student to the department head (Option D), because he seems convinced that students need to follow the rules.

5. A **Attend the professor's other section of the same course, which meets before she leaves for New York and Chicago (Making inferences)** Option A is correct because the professor would likely accept this idea because the student will not miss any class sessions. Option B would not appeal to the professor because the other professor's class is different and the student would not get the information she needs for the midterm. Because the professor is so focused on students attending class, he would not accept Option C. Option D is incorrect because the professor believes that the student needs to study Piaget, who is an important topic of the class.

TOEFL iBT Practice Listening Section (Page 310)

Questions 1–5

TRACK 60 AUDIO SCRIPT

Narrator: Listen to a conversation between a student and a university professor.

Professor: Hi, Harry. Got a minute?

Student: Sure, Professor Brown.

Professor: I haven't seen you for a while. Is everything OK?

Student: Not really. I injured my left shoulder. In fact, I've been out of action since the big basketball game last week.

Professor: Oh dear. I hear you're pretty good.

Student: I *was* pretty good. I need surgery now, and who knows how long I'll be sitting on the bench after that.

Professor: I'm sorry to hear that. Umm . . . I don't suppose you've chosen your field trip location, have you?

Student: Err . . . I'm afraid not. I am just getting back on my feet, and . . . I hadn't thought about it much.

Professor: Well, . . . most of the class is visiting the Verrazano Narrows Bridge on April 30th.

Student: Hmm. That's the day after my surgery's scheduled. I'll be flat on my back while you're on the bridge or maybe even climbing the Staten Island pylons.

Professor: Unfortunately, this isn't "Extreme Engineering"! We're just doing a standard survey.

Student: Well, the date for my surgery is set, so I can't participate on that day.

Professor: Never mind. I'm sure Othmar Amman will forgive you.

Student: Othmar Amman?

Professor: The designer of the bridges. But you still have to do the fieldwork. . . . You'll have to visit either Amman's George Washington Bridge or his Verrazano Narrows on your own time. You'll need to document everything photographically and take all the measurements. Whichever structure you choose, I'll try to organize access to off-limits areas with a bridge employee.

Student: Thanks.

Professor: Although it's not necessary for you to complete your assignment.

Now that I think of it, I'd prefer you survey the George Washington Bridge; 'cause not so many students are doing that. Maybe they think that just because it opened in 1931 it's not an engineering feat.

Student: Or perhaps familiarity breeds contempt. Most of us live in New Jersey, and we've crossed that bridge a million times. I barely even notice it.

Professor: True. By the way, I've devised individualized learning tasks, so no one can—shall we say—collaborate? I'll send you yours closer to the date.

TRACK 61 AUDIO SCRIPT

Narrator: Listen again to part of the conversation. Then answer the question.

Student: Or perhaps familiarity breeds contempt. Most of us live in New Jersey, and we've crossed that bridge a million times. I barely even notice it.

Professor: True.

By the way, I've devised individualized learning tasks, so no one can—shall we say—collaborate?

Narrator: What does the professor mean when she says this?

Professor: By the way, I've devised individualized learning tasks, so no one can—shall we say—collaborate?

ANSWERS AND EXPLANATIONS

1. **B To check where he is going on a field trip (Gist-purpose)** Option B is correct because the professor says, "I don't suppose you've chosen your field trip location, have you?" While the professor and the student discuss Option A, the student's health, this subject comes up only in relationship to the field trip. Options C and D are not supported by information in the selection.

2. **B Recovery from surgery (Inference)** Option B is correct because the student says, "That's the day after my surgery's scheduled. I'll be flat on my back." Option A is incorrect because surgery is not on the day of the field trip but the day before. Options C and D are not supported by information in the selection.

3. **C Photograph and measure one of Othmar Amman's bridges (Detail)** Option C is correct because the professor says, "You still have to do the fieldwork. You'll have to visit either Amman's George Washington Bridge or his Verrazano-Narrows on your own time. You'll need to document everything photographically and take all the measurements." Option A is not supported by information in the selection. Option B is incorrect. While visiting restricted areas of a bridge is mentioned, this activity is not required, and the name of the bridge is not given. Option D is incorrect because the professor says, "This isn't 'Extreme Engineering'! We're just doing a standard survey."

4. **D They are overly familiar with it. (Inference)** Option D is correct because the student says, "Familiarity breeds contempt. Most of us live in New Jersey, and we've crossed that bridge [the George Washington Bridge] a million times." Option A is incorrect because the bridge was built in 1931, not 1981. Options B and C are not supported by information in the selection.

5. **A She hopes to prevent students from copying one another's work. (Understanding the function/Replay)** Option A is correct because the professor indicates that she hopes to prevent copying when she says, "I've devised individualized learning tasks, so no one can—shall we say—collaborate?" If a task is individualized, it can only be done by one person. Her tone of voice is light but firm. Options B, C, and D are not supported by the replay.

Questions 6–11

TRACK 62 AUDIO SCRIPT

Narrator: Listen to part of a lecture in a math class. The professor is talking about graphs.

Professor: Umm . . . I'm sure you're all familiar with graphs, but today I'd like to discuss their origins, effectiveness, and design conventions.

In the modern world, graphs are everywhere. Businesses, organizations, and governments rely on them to follow trends and make decisions. Scientists, including social scientists, use them for analysis and reporting.

So, when did graphs first appear? Well, way back in the fourteenth century, a Frenchman, Nicole Oresme, created the bar chart to plot velocity against time. It seems Oresme was interested in this 300 years before Isaac Newton. Then . . . in the early nineteenth century, the Scottish political economist, William Playfair, popularized line graphs and later pie charts. He realized that the visual representation of data allows readers to grasp complex information instantly.

OK. Let's consider why we need graphs. There are four basic reasons. The first is to identify gross errors in experimental data. You know, you're checking the current through a lightbulb, and, in one experiment, the current seems really low for the amount of voltage put through it. All the other points on your graph ascend and then plateau out, but one point hangs down below the plateau. Alert to this deviation, you conduct that experiment again.

The second reason we need graphs is to discover the *existence* of a mathematical relationship between two measured quantities. Let's say your high school math teacher asked you to survey classmates about their average earnings per year and the distance they could throw a ball. Well, this graph will have a whole lot of random data points. However, if you note the average distance from the sun and a planet's period of orbit, you'll end up with a neat data set and a graph showing a connection between the two measured quantities.

Which leads me to . . . three. The third reason for using a graph is to determine the *form* of the relationship between two measured quantities. The final reason for using graphs is to evaluate numerical constraints.

Now, let's look at the two axes of a graph. Remember . . . , the plural of *axis* is *axes*—A. X. E. S; it's like *analysis* and *analyses* or *crisis* and *crises*. So, how do you decide what goes on which axis? Well,

the *x*-quantity—the one on the horizontal axis—is usually an *independent* variable. That means that *you* choose the values for it. It's also conventional to put time on the *x*-axis. On the vertical axis, or *y*-axis, a *dependent* variable is found. The *y*-quantity is a value for which *nature*—something like the laws of, umm, physics—determines the values. On both axes, make sure your choice of scales is sensible and that they're divided into regular intervals. Also, you often need zero on your graph to make interpretation of information easier, although this would be silly if something like the distance from the sun were being measured. Next, label the axes with the names of the quantities and their units, which follow in parentheses. You'd be amazed how many students forget to do this. Lastly, put a title above your graph.

These days, all kinds of graphs can be made with computer applications, but make sure you learn your software. I mean, can you generate a line of best fit? This line goes through as many data points as possible, averaging out the small errors or uncertainties in those individual points. For mathematical analysis, it's best to use the line and ignore the points. The most easily interpretable line of best fit is a straight line. Curves are problematic due to their deceptive appearance. For example, if you plot height against time for a stone dropped from a tall building, it seems as though the data points fit a parabola. However, if you square time, you find the points actually fit a straight line. The reason for needing that straight line is to assess constants.

As I said earlier, graphs are ubiquitous. I hope, now, you'll take considerably more care in transmitting your academic discoveries to your readers, so I won't have to give this lecture again!

ANSWERS AND EXPLANATIONS

6. **C Their usefulness D Their design rules (Gist-content/Special multiple choice)** Options C and D are correct because the professor says, "I'd like to discuss [graphs'] origins, effectiveness, and design conventions." Options A and B are not supported by information in the selection.

7. **A They present complex information at a glance. (Detail)** Option A is correct because the professor says, "[Playfair] realized that the visual representation of data allows readers to grasp complex information instantly." Option B is incorrect because the accuracy of the data will remain the same, no matter how it is presented. Visual representation affects the presentation

of the data, not its quality. Options C and D are incorrect because even though graphs became popular with social scientists, governments, and businesspeople, the professor does not say that Playfair made this prediction.

8. **A** **They show the existence and form of mathematical relationships. (Connecting content)** Option A is correct because the professor says, "We need graphs . . . to discover the existence of a mathematical relationship between two measured quantities." He adds, we need graphs "to determine the form of the relationship between two measured quantities." Options B and C are not supported by information in the listening selection. Option D is contradicted by information in the listening selection.

9. **C** **Values determined by nature (Detail)** Option C is correct because the professor says, "It's also conventional to put time on the *x*-axis. On the vertical axis, a dependent variable is found. The *y*-quantity is a value for which *nature*—something like the laws of physics—determines the values." Options A and D are incorrect because time and values determined by the experimenter go on the *x*-axis. Option B is incorrect because the title goes above the graph.

10. **A** **A line going through as many data points as possible (Detail)** Option A is correct because the professor says, "This line goes through as many data points as possible, averaging out the small errors or uncertainties in those individual points." Option B is contradicted by the information. The line of best fit is used to interpret the data, not to show how it supports a certain theory. In addition, Option B is not a definition of a line of best fit, which is what the question is asking for. Option C is not supported by information in the selection. Option D is incorrect. The line of best fit may sometimes be curved and difficult to interpret, but this does not define the line.

11. **B** **Irritated because students have not used graphs correctly in the past (Understanding the attitude)** Option B is correct because the professor says, "I hope, now, you'll take considerably more care in transmitting your academic discoveries to your readers, so I won't have to give this lecture again!" His tone of voice shows irritation, and his words imply that students had not used graphs correctly in the past. Options A, C, and D are not supported by the information in the selection.

Questions 12–17

TRACK 63 AUDIO SCRIPT

Narrator: Listen to part of a lecture in a class on contemporary theater.

Professor: The Brazilian writer and director Augusto Boal, who died in 2009, created a unique kind of theater known as Forum Theater. Initially influential in South America, Forum Theater has spread around the world.

Boal's early attempts to break down the barriers between actors, action, and the audience took place in the 1950s. He called these "simultaneous dramaturgy." Over time, he developed them into Forum Theater and other kinds of theater that try to empower audiences through their examination of oppression.

In Forum Theater, a member of the audience called a "spect-actor" is allowed to stop a performance and suggest alternative actions. Usually, this happens in scenes where one character is being oppressed. I mean, he or she is the victim of some kind of abuse—violence, fraud, theft, exploitation, etc. The spect-actor's intervention assists the oppressed character, while the other actors improvise to continue the play.

Student: What if the spect-actor's suggestion is unrealistic?

Professor: Hmm. Members of the audience judge this. If they think it is unrealistic, they shout out: "Magic!" Then, the spect-actor has to revise the suggestion, or the play goes on until another spect-actor calls out "Stop!" and makes a better suggestion. The play continues until the actors and spectators resolve the problem.

In order to prevent chaos or an overly simplistic case against oppression, the actors may cleverly argue for the oppressors. So the conclusion, according to Boal, still favors the oppressed, but it is more realistic and more dramatically appealing. This is a play, remember, not merely a discourse.

In another variant, spect-actors are invited on stage to replace first the oppressed, then the oppressors. By the oppressed assuming the role of the oppressors, more creative solutions to the conflict may be found.

Boal was careful to note that Forum Theater should not show one correct path, but examine several possible paths.

Student: Professor, are there any theater companies that use Forum Theater now?

Professor: Well . . . , yes, there are, in more than seventy countries. . . . Its form has remained pure with the Cardboard Citizens Company in the UK, but undergone metamorphosis elsewhere. In many theater companies, much of a play is written and stops only at designated points.

Forum Theater is also used in management or diversity training and in public health education. When I was in France a few years ago, I saw it used in a workshop on dealing with abusive high-school students. Teachers and administrative staff were the audience, and the actors played the students. I became a spect-actor myself in one scenario. In Canada, last semester, I watched immigrants who had experienced oppression from landlords and neighbors learn to take control. In India, I filmed a performance in which patient care in hospital and community settings was dealt with. Many poor, uneducated patients are fearful of doctors and of the medical hierarchy. They seldom voice their concerns about their treatment; Forum Theater empowers them to do so. I interviewed both doctors and patients afterwards. The doctors said they'd been largely unaware of the detrimental effect they had on patients until they saw the Forum Theater play.

Student: Umm . . . Are there any real gains from this? It sounds like propaganda to me.

Professor: It's promotion rather than propaganda. But participants gain additional skills beyond just conflict resolution. Audiences develop language skills and enjoy the special vocabulary and atmosphere of theater. Spect-actors improve their gestures, body awareness, and overall confidence. To paraphrase the novelist Charles Dickens, on stage they become the heroes of their own lives. Furthermore, when a similar oppressive situation occurs in real life, the audience and spect-actors have rehearsed effective actions, so they're more likely to succeed with their demands.

Student: Was Boal involved in any other types of theater?

Professor: Yes, in many others. Next week, we'll look at Newspaper Theater, Invisible Theater, and Rainbow Theater. Some of these are about encouraging audiences to scrutinize media more carefully in light of class- or state-sanctioned oppression; others are more personal and are popular with psychologists who use drama therapy.

TRACK 64 AUDIO SCRIPT

Narrator: Listen again to part of the lecture. Then answer the question.

Professor: Many poor, uneducated patients are fearful of doctors and of the medical hierarchy. They seldom voice their concerns about their treatment; Forum Theater empowers them to do so. I interviewed both doctors and patients afterwards. The doctors said they'd been largely unaware of the detrimental effect they had on patients until they saw the Forum Theater play.

Student: Are there any real gains from this? It sounds like propaganda to me.

Narrator: What does the student mean when he says this?

Student: Are there any real gains from this? It sounds like propaganda to me.

ANSWERS AND EXPLANATIONS

12. **C   A kind of theater that tries to give audiences skills to overcome oppression (Gist-content)** Option C is correct because the professor says that the goal of Forum Theater is "to empower audiences through their examination of oppression." Option A is incorrect because the use of spect-actors is only one detail about Forum Theater. Option B is incorrect because it is only the opinion of one of the students in the class. Option D is a characteristic of other kinds of theater mentioned in the lecture, such as Newspaper Theater.

13. **C   They should be lifelike and dramatically appealing. (Detail)** Option C is correct because the professor says, "In order to prevent chaos or an overly simplistic case against oppression, the actors may cleverly argue for the oppressors. So the conclusion, according to Boal, still favors the oppressed, but it is more realistic and more dramatically appealing. This is a play, remember, not merely a discourse." Options A and B are not supported by information in the selection. Option D is contradicted in the selection: conclusions should always favor the oppressed.

14. **B   To help disadvantaged patients assume more control (Understanding the function)** Option B is correct because the professor says, "Many poor, uneducated patients are fearful of doctors and of the medical hierarchy. They seldom voice their concerns about their treatment; Forum Theater empowers them to do so." Option A is incorrect because the professor refers to diversity training but does not say it takes place in India. Option C is incorrect because the performance the professor filmed showed the complex relationships between doctors and patients, but this was not the purpose of

the performance. Option D is incorrect because Forum Theater is used to help school staff deal with abusive students in France, not India.

15. A He doubts that Forum Theater is useful. (Understanding the attitude/Replay) Option

A is correct. The male student doubts Forum Theater is useful when he says, "It sounds like propaganda to me." This is shown by his slightly aggressive tone of voice. Options B, C, and D are not supported by the replay.

16. (Organization/Drag-and-drop)

1. A spect-actor substitutes for an oppressed character.	
2. C The actors stop following the script. They use new ideas to go on with the play.	The professor says, "The spect-actor's intervention assists the oppressed character while the other actors improvise to continue the play."
3. D Since the spect-actor cannot resolve the conflict in a realistic manner, another spect-actor takes over the role.	"The play goes on until another spect-actor calls out "Stop!" and makes a better suggestion."
4. A The actors and spect-actor resolve the conflict.	"The play continues until the actors and spectators resolve the problem."
5. B Audience members successfully apply conflict-resolution lessons they learned in the theater to the real world.	"When a similar oppressive situation occurs in real life, the audience and spect-actors have rehearsed effective actions, so they're more likely to succeed with their demands."

17. C Promote audience scrutiny of biased media (Detail) Option C is correct because the professor says, "Some of these are about encouraging audiences to scrutinize media more carefully in light of class or state-sanctioned oppression." Options A and D are not supported by information in the selection. Option B is incorrect because Forum Theater, not the other types of theater that Boal created, is used in more than seventy countries.

Questions 18–22

TRACK 65 AUDIO SCRIPT

Narrator: Listen to a conversation between a student and a university employee.

Employee: Good afternoon. Can I help you?

Student: Uhh . . . I wonder if I'm in the right place. Do you issue parking permits here?

Employee: Yeah, we do. Is that what you want—a parking permit?

Student: Well, I'm not quite sure . . .

Employee: If you don't mind my saying, it's a bit late in the year to apply with two weeks of classes left. We charge a flat fee per semester; your permit will only be valid until August thirty-first.

Student: I see . . . I just bought my car on Saturday, but I will be here over the summer doing some research. Do you have weekly or monthly parking rates?

Employee: Only daily or semester. All others were discontinued last year; enforcement took up too much of security's time.

Student: I see.

Employee: Have you parked long-term on campus before?

Student: No, this is the first time.

Employee: I'll need to see a valid driver's license and your student ID.

Student: Uh-huh. But I'm not certain I want a permit.

Employee: Oh? If you park on campus every day from now until August 31st, you'd spend seven hundred forty-two dollars if you pay daily. Of course, it's unlikely you'd do that. But even if you were here one day in two, that'd amount to three hundred seventy dollars. A semester permit is just three hundred fifty dollars.

Student: Hmm. I imagine I'll drive to college one day in three, so I'll try the daily rate. How do I pay to park that way?

Employee: Uhh . . . We use Pay Wave here. Load up your credit or debit card, and wave it across the sensor at the entrance to the parking lot you use. When the machine issues your ticket, don't forget to place it on your dashboard. Security's pretty fussy about the validity and visibility of the ticket.

Student: OK, sure.

Employee: One more thing. Even over summer, students aren't allowed to use the Maple Drive lot; it's strictly for faculty members and other staff. Your car'll be towed away if you park there.

Student: I understand.

ANSWERS AND EXPLANATIONS

18. **B** **To inquire about parking costs (Gist-purpose)** Option B is correct. The student is inquiring about parking costs. Options A and D are not supported by information in the selection. Option C is incorrect. Initially, the university employee asks if the student wants to apply for a parking permit, but the student says she isn't sure. As the conversation continues, it is clear the student is only inquiring about parking costs. Ultimately, she does not purchase any kind of permit, choosing to pay for parking on a daily basis, which does not require a permit.

19. **C** **By day or by semester (Detail)** Option C is correct because the employee says the college has "only daily or semester" rates. Therefore, the other options are incorrect.

20. **A** **They were too difficult for security to monitor. (Detail)** Option A is correct because the employee says, "All others [parking rates] were discontinued last year; enforcement took up too much of security's time." Options B, C, and D are not supported by information in the selection.

21. **D** **Students cannot use it at all. (Detail)** Option D is correct because the employee says, "Students aren't allowed to use the Maple Drive lot; it's strictly for faculty members and other staff. Your car'll be towed away if you park there." Options A and B are not supported by information in the selection. Option C is incorrect because students

are forbidden from using the Maple Drive facility even over summer.

22. **C** **Load money onto her credit or debit card (Inference)** Option C is correct because the student has decided to pay the daily rate, and the university uses Pay Wave for that. The employee tells her that in order to use Pay Wave, she needs to add money to her card. Option A is incorrect because the student says she is not interested in buying a parking permit. Options B and D are not supported by information in the conversation. The student clearly wants to drive to campus, not take the bus or walk.

Questions 23–28

TRACK 66 AUDIO SCRIPT

Narrator: Listen to part of a lecture in an education class. The professor is talking about the value of homework.

Professor: OK, class, let's get started. The homework debate has fierce proponents and opponents. Or should I say, there are fashions in homework: pile it on, one year; pare it back, the next. In many cases, people cling to myths rather than research findings. Furthermore, some research remains flawed by poor methodology. The long debate has probably raised more questions than it has answered conclusively.

So, umm, let's define homework. Basically, it's tasks assigned by schoolteachers for students to be completed outside class hours. It's divided into instructional and noninstructional tasks. The former include practice, preparation, extension, and integration homework. The latter include work assigned for personal development or for improving parent-child relationships. Almost no research has been done into the effects of noninstructional homework.

An additional difficulty in this debate is that much research is skewed in favor of the *purpose* of homework rather than in comparing the *effects* of homework on academic success. The relationship between homework and academic achievement is hard to establish due to conflicting research, poor correlational analysis, and few longitudinal studies.

But what are the benefits of homework according to the research you read for homework?

Female Student: Well . . . older students, in grades six and above, get more out of it. A very small amount is fine for younger students.

Professor: Yes, that holds up.

Male Student: Around four hours a night in senior high school is probably the optimal amount.

Professor: Four sounds right.

Female Student: Its nonacademic functions contribute to life skills like time management and taking responsibility. If students go on to college, they need a routine of concentrated independent study from high school.

Male Student: Umm, parents and policy makers also like homework.

Professor: I think that's a *consequence* rather than a benefit.

Male Student: Another advantage is that without significant amounts of homework, countries lose their competitive edge in, in . . . the global knowledge economy.

Professor: Be careful! That's a myth. Remember the results from Japan and Finland? High-school students there get less homework than in the US, but outperform Americans in an array of tests. The economies of Japan and Finland both enjoy a significant amount of technological product innovation.

Male Student: Uh-huh. But what about math? Doesn't Harris Cooper conclude that more math homework improves math scores on international aptitude tests?

Professor: Yeah, he does. And so do many other experts. But for arts subjects there's no correlation unless the homework is preparatory—getting ready for the next topic.

What about the drawbacks of homework?

Female Student: A loss of interest in school. Plus a lack of leisure time. Things like sports, hobbies, and spending time with friends are good for kids.

Male Student: At my school, cheating was an issue. Rich moms and dads did their kids' homework for them. Those children almost invariably got higher grades in long history or art projects. There were also kids whose parents worked around the clock at poorly paid jobs or who weren't working at all who seldom seemed to do their homework. Yet I read somewhere that if *science* homework is interactive—and done with a family member or classmate—that *can* be fruitful.

Female Student: It also matters whether a teacher grades the homework. In very large classes, teachers often write "Good" or "Very good" at the bottom without making any corrections or suggestions. As a result, students feel ripped off; homework is one more meaningless chore.

Male Student: Hmm. That's not so bad. As adults, we all have to do things we don't like. It may be disappointing getting homework back unmarked, but that's life.

Professor: Returning to Cooper, what did he think was deficient in many studies into homework's positive effects?

Male Student: Well, the studies are correlational—they show that one or more factors are *associated* with others, not that they *cause* them. Causal relationships are much more conclusive.

Professor: Good. Or should that be "Very good"? Now, what are the five variables in homework?

Female Student: Subject matter, amount, nature of the assignment, and, umm, classroom factors like decent materials and follow-up discussions.

Male Student: *And* parental involvement.

Professor: For sure. As you said earlier, parental involvement is beneficial if it's interactive or supportive rather than directive.

Female Student: Is that why Asian Americans whose parents have high expectations of their children benefit from homework more than other ethnic groups?

Professor: Apparently so. In all this, there remains a riddle: does homework create better students, or do better students do more homework?

I'll leave you to consider that for . . . homework.

ANSWERS AND EXPLANATIONS

23. **B** **The benefits and drawbacks of homework are not completely understood. (Gist-content)** Option B is correct because the professor points out some advantages of homework, but he also indicates that much is not known about the benefits of homework. Option A is contradicted by information in the selection. The passage points out a number of benefits of homework. Options C and D are details in the selection, not main ideas, so they are incorrect.

24. **C** **It has not produced many concrete results. (Detail)** Option C is correct because the professor says, "The long debate has probably raised more questions than it has answered conclusively." Option A is incorrect because the selection indicates that large amounts of homework do not result in academic success for younger children. Options B and D are not supported by information in the passage.

25. **D** **A country's international competitiveness is improved by more homework. (Connecting content)** Option D is correct because when the male student says, "Without significant amounts of homework, countries lose their competitive edge in the global knowledge economy," the

professor responds, "Be careful! That's a myth." The professor gives examples of Japan and Finland—countries with less homework than the US—that "enjoy a significant amount of technological product innovation." Options A, B, and C are not supported by information in the selection.

26. **A A causal study (Detail)** Option A is correct because the professor says, "Causal relationships are much more conclusive [than correlational ones]." Option B is contradicted by the selection. Options C and D are not supported by information in the selection.

27. **D By participating in interactive science homework (Connecting content)** Option D is correct because the male student says, "If science homework is interactive—and done with a family member or classmate—that can be fruitful." Options A and C are mentioned in the selection, but these kinds of parental participation are considered disadvantageous. Option B is not supported by information in the selection.

28. **(Detail/Check box)**

	ADVANTAGEOUS TO STUDENTS	DISADVANTAGEOUS TO STUDENTS	ITS VALUE IS NOT KNOWN
Noninstructional homework			✔ The professor says, "Almost no research has been done into the effects of noninstructional homework."
A lot of homework in grades one to five		✔ The female student says, "Older students, in grades six and above, get more out of [homework]. A very small amount is fine for younger students."	
A student's low socioeconomic status		✔ The male student says, "There were also kids whose parents worked around the clock at poorly paid jobs or who weren't working at all who seldom seemed to do their homework."	
Math homework	✔ The professor agrees that Harris Cooper, a homework expert, concluded that math homework improves math scores on international aptitude tests.		

Questions 29–34

Narrator: Listen to part of a lecture in a class on chemical engineering. The professor is talking about rare earth elements, or REEs.

Professor: By the end of this year, the worldwide demand for rare earth elements, or REEs, will outstrip supply. In the future, chemists and engineers—like you—will have to use fewer, recycle more, or find alternatives. Or mines will need to step up production.

In fewer than thirty years, REEs have become essential. I mean, would you, err, forgo your sunglasses just because they're coated with erbium, or forfeit your computer with its europium screen? Should we dispense with lanthanum batteries, which . . . lanthanum batteries are less toxic than cadmium or lead-based ones? Should the textile industry do without red cerium dyes? Even green technologies, like wind turbines, fluorescent lamps, and refrigeration systems, contain neodymium and seventeen other REEs.

On the periodic table, REEs form two rows at the bottom, constituting elements 57 through 71, and 89 through 102. Only six were known before 1850, and most are late twentieth-century discoveries. There's a theory that the super-actinide elements, 122 through 153, are yet to be found.

REEs are called "earth" elements because their commonest form is neither liquid nor gas. In one sense, they're not rare: cerium, for instance, is almost as plentiful as copper—the twenty-fifth most abundant element on earth. REEs are rare because they never exist alone in the same way that gold or tin does. This makes their refinement complex due to their wide dispersion, low concentration, or complex combinations with other minerals. Only since the 1960s have there been cost-effective extraction processes.

But there are downsides to this industry—enormous pollution for one. Some REEs exist in combination with radioactive elements like uranium or thorium. Their waste disposal may be less than . . . ideal. Others require powerful acids for refinement. As a result, mines in almost all countries closed down in the 1990s.

To counter this, mining processes have improved. In 2009, the UN launched a project to track discarded electronic waste, aiming to boost the recycling of REEs. Japanese companies led the way. One firm researched the cost of reusing neodymium and dysprosium from its washing machines and air conditioners. Another claims recycling will soon fill ten percent of its needs.

The Japanese are also considering ocean mining. Typically, this is expensive and dirty, but its damage could be controlled. A 2011 study of Pacific Ocean seabed mud showed high concentrations of REEs. Over millions of years, minerals have been thrown up through hydrothermal vents and deposited on the seafloor. One patch of mud only two point three kilometers wide might contain enough REEs to meet global demand for a year.

In 2010, when the price per kilogram of REEs reached a peak, mining companies worldwide resumed production. One US firm that had closed a large Californian mine, reopened it. Australian, Brazilian, Japanese, and Malaysian consortia operate small mines with more substantial projects on the drawing board.

The volatility of rare-earth prices has been extreme—lanthanum and cerium, historically around ten dollars a kilogram, rose to one hundred in 2011. Dysprosium, always more expensive, hit three thousand dollars a kilo. As we know from the oil crisis of the 1970s, commodity spikes seriously affect the global economy, but as long as we drive cars with catalytic converters, enjoy highly polished diamond rings, or wear little earbuds to listen to phones or music, we're part of an economic cycle prey to market forces.

Mining is a dirty business—and the extraction, refinement, and disposal of rare earth elements is no exception. The best we can do is limit contamination and political fallout over market control. Hmm . . . Maybe one day one of you guys might win a Nobel Prize for finding reliable substitutes!

ANSWERS AND EXPLANATIONS

29. **C** **Rare earth elements have benefits and drawbacks. (Gist-content)** Option C is correct because the professor says, "REEs have become essential," which means they are beneficial. Later she adds, "There are downsides to this industry—enormous pollution for one." Option A is incorrect because while rare earth elements are extremely useful, the lecture is not mainly about their discovery. Option B is not supported by information in the selection. Option D focuses on only the disadvantages of rare earth elements, while the selection is also about the benefits of rare earth elements, so it is incorrect.

30. **D** **A large amount of raw material is needed to extract the element. (Connecting content)** Option D is correct because the professor says, "REEs are rare because they never exist alone in the same way that gold or tin does. This makes their refinement complex due to their wide dispersion, low concentration, or complex combinations with other minerals." Option A is incorrect because position on the periodic table does not relate to the rarity of an element. Option B is incorrect because some rare earth elements, like cerium, exist abundantly in nature. Option C is incorrect because the recent discovery of these elements is not connected to their name.

31. **B** **Air conditioners** **C** **Computer screens (Detail/Special multiple choice)** Option B is correct because the professor says, "One firm researched the cost of reusing neodymium and dysprosium from its washing machines and air conditioners." Therefore, REEs are found in air conditioners. Option C is correct because the professor indicates that computers have europium in their screens. Option A is not supported by information in the selection. Option D is incorrect because washing machines, not dishwashers, contain REEs.

32. **D** **Pollution from the mining process was too great. (Detail)** Option D is correct because the professor says, "There are downsides to this industry—enormous pollution for one. As a result, mines in almost all countries closed down in the 1990s." Options A, B, and C are not supported by information in the selection.

33. **B** **Prices for REEs were so high that mining became profitable. (Detail)** Option B is correct because the professor says, "In 2010, when the price per kilogram of REEs reached a peak, mining companies worldwide resumed production." Option A is incorrect because while mining processes have improved, the professor talks only about recycling, not extraction techniques. Option C is incorrect because while Japanese geologists have discovered large undersea deposits of REEs, the professor does not mention that these deposits are now being mined. Option D is incorrect because the professor does not say that mines reopened suddenly.

34. **A** **She hopes that its excesses can be curbed. (Understanding the attitude)** Option A is correct because the professor says, "The best we can do is limit contamination and political fallout over market control." Options B and D are not supported by information in the selection. Option C is incorrect because the professor indicates that she believes scientists will find better alternatives when she says, "one of you [students] might win a Nobel Prize for finding reliable substitutes."

CHAPTER 5

TOEFL iBT Speaking

Chapter at a Glance

In this chapter, you will learn:

Speaking Topics . . . . Common general-interest, campus-related, and academic topics

Speaking Items . . . . . 6 item types

Skills . . . . Techniques to help you answer each kind of item

Tips . . . . Hints to help you find the correct answers and avoid common mistakes

The TOEFL iBT Speaking section assesses your ability to speak in common situations on North American college and university campuses—both in and out of the classroom.

As in the Listening section, you will use a special headset during the Speaking section. You will hear short conversations or academic lectures on the headset, and you will see short written materials on your computer screen. You will then see and hear questions about these items, and you will be asked to speak briefly in response to the questions. The microphone on your headset will record your responses.

The Speaking section lasts for about 20 minutes and consists of six items:

- **Two independent speaking items**, in which you respond to two questions on general-interest or campus-related topics. You will both see these items on your screen and listen to them on your headset. For each item, you will have 15 seconds to prepare your response and 45 seconds to give your response. Item 1 will ask you to state an opinion about a general-interest topic such as a familiar person, place, event, or object. Item 2 will ask you to state a choice among two possible situations, actions, or opinions on a general-interest or campus-related topic.

- **Two integrated listening, reading, and speaking items**, in which you read a short passage, listen to a short lecture or conversation on the same subject, and then respond to a question about the material. For each item, you will have 30 seconds to prepare your response and 60 seconds to give your response. Item 3 will ask you to integrate information from a reading and a conversation on a campus-related topic. Item 4 will ask you to synthesize general written information and specific spoken information on an academic topic.

- **Two integrated listening and speaking items**, in which you listen to a conversation or lecture and then respond to a question about the material. For each item, you will have 20 seconds to prepare your response and 60 seconds to give your response. Item 5 will ask you to listen to a conversation about a campus-related problem or dilemma and give a solution. Item 6 will ask you to listen to a talk on an academic subject and summarize key information.

TOEFL iBT Speaking Topics

The Speaking selections of the TOEFL iBT are on general-interest, campus-related, and academic topics. Items on **general-interest topics** ask about your personal likes, dislikes, or preferences:

- A place you like to visit
- A place you like to study, read, have fun, etc.
- An important event in your life
- A person, event, class, or experience that influenced you.

Items on **campus-related topics** are on subjects relating to life on a North American college or university campus, including student life, residence halls, university offices, and university services.

TOEFL iBT Speaking Campus-Related Topics

- Campus events, including performances, guest speakers, etc.
- Campus transportation
- Class announcements
- Food service
- Library and computer services
- Parking regulations
- University policies on academic honesty, class attendance, mobile phones, etc.

For a complete list of campus-related topics, see Appendix C. For information on the various offices that handle key campus functions, see page 246.

Items on **academic topics** focus on topics students might encounter in classes in the arts, humanities, social sciences, and natural sciences.

TOEFL iBT Speaking Academic Subject Areas

- **Arts and humanities:** literature, art and art history, music and music history
- **Sciences:** life science, physical science, earth and space science, computer science
- **Social sciences:** geography, history, sociology, anthropology, psychology, economics
- **Business and management:** case studies

For a list of sample academic topics, see Appendix B.

After you take the TOEFL iBT, your responses will be sent to trained raters who will score your work using special scoring guides, called rubrics. The rubrics, which are different for independent and integrated tasks, focus on:

- **Delivery:** fluency and clarity, including pronunciation and intonation
- **Language use:** appropriate and effective use of grammar and vocabulary
- **Topic development:** the completeness and accuracy of your response, organization and flow of your ideas, and integration of information from readings and listening selections (on integrated items)

Listening to Selections. Throughout this book, this icon appears to tell you when you need to listen to a listening selection.

 Recording Your Practice Responses. In this chapter and throughout this book, you will be asked to record your responses to Speaking practice questions. When this icon appears, record your response on your computer or mobile device. If your device does not have a *record* function, ask a friend with strong English skills to listen to your response. You may want to record and play back each of your responses several times to make sure that you can give complete responses within the time limits.

AT A GLANCE

TOEFL iBT Speaking Section

Time Limit   20 minutes

Content   General-interest, campus-related, and academic topics

Items   6 items total

ITEM TYPES   **Independent Speaking**
- **Item 1:** State an opinion about a general-interest topic.
- **Item 2:** State a choice of two possible actions or opinions on a campus-related or general-interest topic.

Integrated Reading, Listening, and Speaking
- **Item 3:** Read and listen to students talking about a short document on a campus-related topic. Respond to a question.
- **Item 4:** Read a short passage and listen to part of a lecture on an academic topic. Respond to a question.

Integrated Listening and Speaking
- **Item 5:** Listen to two people talk about a campus-related problem. Respond to a question.
- **Item 6:** Listen to part of an academic lecture. Respond to a question.

At the beginning of the Speaking section, you will see a photograph of a test taker wearing the special headset used during the test. Instructions will tell you to put on your headset. You will be able to make sure it works and to check and adjust the playback and recording volume. Use the speaking toolbar to control and adjust the volume before and during the test.

> **TIP** **Arrange your work area before you begin the actual TOEFL iBT!**
>
> After you check your headset's playback and recording volume at the test center, you should arrange your work area for the Speaking section. You will not use your computer's keyboard during this section, so put it to one side to make room for notepaper and your computer's mouse. Arrange the notepaper and mouse so you can use them with comfort and ease. Keep in mind whether you are right-handed or left-handed. You can take and use notes during any part of the Speaking section, so arrange your note paper to make it easy to use.

Independent Speaking: Items 1 and 2

The two independent speaking items ask you to give your opinion or choice about two general-interest or campus-related topics.

Item Format

When you take the TOEFL iBT, Items 1 and 2 will appear on the screen and you will hear them read aloud.

You will see:

> 🎤 You will now speak about a familiar topic. Prepare your response in 15 seconds. Then allow 45 seconds to record your response. Some students sign up for their classes weeks or months before classes begin. Other students wait until the term begins and visit several classes before choosing the ones they will take. Which method of choosing classes do you think is better for students and why?
>
> **Preparation Time: 15 seconds**
> **Response Time: 45 seconds**

You will hear:

Narrator: You will now speak about a familiar topic. Prepare your response in 15 seconds. Then allow 45 seconds to record your response. Some students sign up for their classes weeks or months before classes begin. Other students wait until the term begins and visit several classes before choosing the ones they will take. Which method of choosing classes do you think is better for students and why? Begin speaking after the beep.

The item will stay on the screen, and the timer will count down 15 seconds of preparation time. You can use this time to organize your thoughts. You are allowed to take notes.

After 15 seconds have passed, you will hear a beep. The question will stay on the screen and a new timer will appear. You will have 45 seconds to record your answer. After 45 seconds have passed, the recorder will turn off, and the test will advance to the next item.

> 🎤 You will now speak about a familiar topic. Prepare your response in 15 seconds. Then allow 45 seconds to record your response. Some students sign up for their classes weeks or months before classes begin. Other students wait until the term begins and visit several classes before choosing the ones they will take. Which method of choosing classes do you think is better for students and why?
>
> **Response Time: 45 seconds**

Item 1: Express an Opinion

The first independent speaking item asks you to express your opinion about a topic of general interest. No special knowledge is assumed or needed. The topics include describing favorite or important places, pastimes, people, and activities; expressing likes, dislikes, and values; and retelling important past events.

> **EXAMPLE**
>
> ### Item 1: Express an Opinion
>
> Read this sample TOEFL iBT Speaking opinion item. On the real test, you will hear the item at the same time as you read it on the screen.
>
> > Think of a class that influenced your life and why it had such a big influence on you. Include details and examples to support your opinion.
>
> | Preparation Time: 15 seconds |
> | --- |
> | Response Time: 45 seconds |

This item asks for your opinion on a common topic any student could answer, a class that had an influence on you. Like all TOEFL iBT independent speaking items, it asks you to give an answer and support it with details and examples.

Evaluating Independent Speaking Responses

All TOEFL iBT Speaking responses are evaluated by trained raters using a special scoring rubric. Understanding the rubric can help you prepare for the test. The following pages show a simplified version of the TOEFL iBT Independent Speaking Scoring Rubric that you can use as a checklist to prepare for the test and to evaluate your speaking yourself.

TOEFL IBT SIMPLIFIED INDEPENDENT SPEAKING SCORING RUBRIC

SCORE	GENERAL DESCRIPTION	DELIVERY	LANGUAGE USE	TOPIC DEVELOPMENT
4	**The response:** • Answers the question • Is complete • Is understandable • Makes sense • Stays on topic • Has few pauses, hesitations, or interruptions • Includes ALL of the items listed in the columns to the right	**The speech:** • Is well paced • Is fluent • Is clear • May include minor problems with pronunciation or intonation • Is understandable overall	**The language:** • Shows effective use of correct grammar and vocabulary • Shows good control of basic and advanced structures • Has minor errors that do not affect understanding	**The content:** • Answers the question • Is sustained (has no pauses or interruptions) • Stays on topic • Has a main idea • Includes supporting details • Has ideas and details in a logical order • Uses signaling words and phrases to show the relationships among ideas
3	**The response:** • Answers the question, but is not complete • Is generally understandable • Has fluid expression, but there may be some pauses or gaps in expression • Includes TWO of the items listed in the columns to the right	**The speech:** • Is generally clear • May have minor pronunciation or intonation problems that require the listener to pay attention to understand • Is understandable overall	**The language:** • Shows fairly effective use of correct grammar and vocabulary • May have some improper or limited use of grammar and vocabulary that reduces fluency but not clarity	**The content:** • Generally makes sense most of the time • Is mostly sustained • Has limited development of ideas • Lacks detail • At times, the relationship among ideas is not clear

SCORE	GENERAL DESCRIPTION	DELIVERY	LANGUAGE USE	TOPIC DEVELOPMENT
2	**The response:** • Answers the question • Has limited detail and development • Has problems with delivery or completeness and meaning is unclear at times; but is understandable overall • Includes TWO of the items listed in the columns to the right	**The speech:** • Is basically understandable, though listeners need to pay attention to understand • Has pronunciation, intonation, or rhythm problems that make meaning unclear in places	**The language:** • Shows limited range and use of grammar and vocabulary that prevents full expression of ideas • Uses only simple sentence structures correctly • Consists mainly of short sentences with simple or unclear connections among ideas • Lists ideas or joins them with simple linking words and expressions such as *and*	**The content:** • Answers the question, but number of ideas or their development is limited • Uses mostly basic ideas • Has limited development or detail • Is vague or repeats at times • Has unclear connections among ideas • Has poor or limited use of linking words and phrases
1	**The response:** • Is very limited in content, is only minimally connected to the question, or is mainly not understandable • Includes TWO of the items listed in the columns to the right	**The speech:** • Has consistent problems with pronunciation, stress, and intonation that make comprehension difficult • Is choppy or fragmented • Has frequent unnatural pauses and hesitations	**The language:** • Shows limited grammar and vocabulary that prevent expression of ideas • Has limited use of linking words and expressions • May make heavy use of practiced or memorized vocabulary and expressions	**The content:** • Lacks relevant ideas except for the most basic • Does not use the time available or answer the question • May repeat the question to fill time
0	No response, response is off topic, or response is not understandable.			

Here is a sample response to the example TOEFL iBT Speaking opinion item. Read it and listen to it. Then use the scoring rubric to figure out the score it received.

 Sample Response 1

> The most important class, umm, that I ever took was a class in geometry . . . in high school. I had a really good teacher that year. In this class, I liked to solving the problems with logic. This class was important for me because I like math for the first time. Before this class, I hated math. After this class, I decided to take another math class. Then I began to like math more and more. So I decided to major in math in college.

If you said that this response scored a 4, you are correct. This response earned this score because it:

- ✔ Is on topic, answers the question, and is complete
- ✔ Has some pauses and hesitations but flows fluently and is understandable overall
- ✔ Has some minor grammar problems, but these small errors do not interfere with understanding. For example, *like* is used in place of *liked,* but the response is understandable, and the past tense is used correctly in other places throughout the response.
- ✔ Includes details that make sense and are relevant
- ✔ Is in a logical order
- ✔ Uses a number of signaling words and expressions (*before, after, then, so*) to show the relationships among the ideas

Here are some more sample answers to this example item. Read and listen to each one, and then give it a score. Then note the score that each one received and why it received that score.

 Sample Response 2

> Of all my classes, the most important was piano performance. I took this class my second year at university. In this class, we studied with a very famous pianist. She was very experienced. This teacher taught us many ways to perform better. She know a lot about how to play for a audiences. How to focus. How to listen, too. She help us feel more comfortable on stage. Now, when I am prepare for a concert, I think of this class. She gave us a lot of good advice.

If you said that this response scored a 3, you are correct. This response earned this score because it:

- ✔ Models clear speech, though it has a number of pronunciation problems that slightly interfere with understanding
- ✔ Has fairly good grammar and vocabulary but has a number of errors. Sentence fragments (such as *How to focus*) made the response choppy but still clear.
- ✔ Is sustained, despite the choppiness
- ✔ Has relevant ideas but does not follow an effective order
- ✔ At times, has unclear relationship among ideas. Better use of signaling words would make the relationship among ideas clearer. For example, it is not clear how listening better will help her perform better.

 ## Sample Response 3

The most important class I took was physical chemistry. Call this class p-chem. This class is very hard; students are always afraid. I study very hard in this class, get good grade. Learned many things. I feel good because I work hard in difficult class, get good grade. After that, feel can do good in hard class. Know that I am good at chemistry.

If you said that this response scored a 2, you are correct. This response

- ✔ Is understandable overall but requires listeners to pay attention carefully to understand
- ✔ Has choppy delivery and the pronunciation is hard to understand in places
- ✔ Has limited control of grammar and vocabulary and has several basic errors, such as sentences with missing subjects
- ✔ Addresses the question but has limited ideas. It focuses on just one idea and restates it several ways.
- ✔ Has only limited use of signaling words, which makes understanding the relationships among ideas difficult

Sample Response 4

TOEFL prep course very important class for me. Learn a lot about very hard test important for life. TOEFL test is very, very . . . difficult. Listening, speaking, reading, write. Study all these things to get ready. TOEFL test very important . . . to future. Want to go to Canada if passing TOEFL. TOEFL very hard test . . . study a lot. Get good grade, go to Canada for to studying, get married after graduate, have good life.

If you said that this response scored a 1, you are correct. This response

- ✔ Has very limited content
- ✔ Has unclear pronunciation, choppy delivery, and several unnatural pauses
- ✔ Includes only basic ideas
- ✔ Does not use the time available

EXERCISE 1

Understanding the Independent Speaking Scoring Rubric

Here is another sample TOEFL iBT Speaking opinion item. Read it, remembering that on the real test, you will hear the question at the same time as you read it on the screen.

> Choose a place that you like very much and explain why you like it so much. Include details and examples to support your opinion.

| Preparation Time: 15 seconds |
| Response Time: 45 seconds |

Now listen to the responses. Score them from 1 to 5 using the Simplified Independent Speaking Scoring Rubric on pages 370–371. Write the score on the line.

1. Response 1: _____

2. Response 2: _____

3. Response 3: _____

4. Response 4: _____

Answers and Explanations for Exercise 1 begin on page 451.

Responding to an Opinion Item

An effective response to an opinion item includes this information:

- Your opinion on the topic—the person, place, object, or idea that the item asks your opinion about—and a bit of detail about this answer
- One to two reasons to support your opinion

> **TIP** **Have enough reasons!**
>
> Examining the rubric shows that while giving one reason is enough to score a 2 or possibly a 3, most responses that score a 3 or 4 generally include two or more reasons. So make sure that you always have at least two reasons to back up your opinion. In the example response in which the student said that geometry class was an important influence, the reasons are (1) starting to like math, (2) taking more math courses, and (3) deciding to major in math.

In your response, you need to present strong ideas. You also need to use a logical order, such as more important to less important, time (the order events happened), or cause and effect. Listen to and read again this high-scoring response.

The most important class, umm, that I ever took was a class in geometry . . . in high school. I had a really good teacher that year. In this class, I liked to solve the problems with logic. This class was important for me because I liked math for the first time. Before this class, I hated math. After this class, I decided to take another math class. Then I began to like math more and more. So I decided to major in math in college.

> Your opinion and some detail about it
>
> Reason 1
>
> Reason 2

This response includes all the parts of an effective response.

✔ The first sentence clearly states the candidate's opinion in response to the question.

✔ The following two sentences give detail about the answer. Detail includes relevant information such as having a good teacher and solving problems with logic.

 The candidate gives two good reasons for why this class was important to her. First, in this class, she started to like math. Second, she took more math classes and decided to major in math.

✔ The information is in a logical order. The reasons are in order of time and also show a cause-and-effect relationship. Because the candidate liked math and took more courses, she eventually decided to major in math.

Preparing Your Response to an Opinion Item

When you prepare your response, first make sure you understand the question and what it is asking for. Each question asks for a specific answer. Look again at the question from Exercise 1. The answer to this question is a specific place.

> **TIP** **Choose an answer that is easy to talk about!**
>
> When responding to an opinion item, think about an answer that is easy to talk about. For example, for this TOEFL Speaking item, there are many places that you could use in your answer. Choose the place that is easiest for you to talk about in English.

Now look again at the first example question. What kind of answer does it ask for?

> Think of a class that influenced your life and why it had such a big influence on you. Include details and examples to support your opinion.

If you said that the answer to this question is a specific class, you are correct. Once you know your answer, write it on your note paper. While this seems obvious, having the answer written in front of you will help you gather ideas. It will also help you stay on topic when you give your response.

During the 15 seconds you have to prepare your response, you should gather and organize your ideas. You can plan mentally or write brief notes. You will not have enough time to write your complete response.

Gather Ideas and Take Notes

In general, your notes should state your opinion and give reasons for your opinions. In this section, we will look at steps for preparing good notes and then using them to deliver an effective response.

An effective response needs to give detail about your opinion and your reasons for holding that opinion. One good way to think of detail and reasons is a process called brainstorming. When you brainstorm, you think of ideas and write them down quickly in a few words in your notes. Because you have only a few seconds to prepare on the TOEFL iBT Speaking section, stop brainstorming when you have two or three details and two or three reasons. Write your details and reasons in your notes. Because you have limited time, use only brief words, abbreviations, numbers, and symbols. For example, the candidate wrote *gd* instead of *good*. What other abbreviations, numbers, and symbols do you see in the notes? What words do they stand for?

Geometry
—gd teacher
—like solving probs
Reasons
—took more, majored in math
—liked math for 1st time

If you said that the abbreviations were *probs* and *1st*, you are correct. The abbreviation *probs* stands for *problems* and *1st* for *first*.

> **TIP** **Focus on ideas in your notes!**
>
> To give a strong response, you need good ideas. So focus on ideas, not spelling, capitalization, or punctuation, in your notes. Use abbreviations and symbols in notes to write quickly. Periods, capital letters, and correct spelling are not necessary in notes, so don't worry about them.

In a good response, your ideas are in a logical order. So your notes should indicate the order. Look at your notes. If the ideas are not in the correct order, then number them in order. Use the most effective order you can think of. Here are some possible ways to order the information:

- Importance (more important to less important, or less important to more important)
- Time (the order in which events happened)
- General to specific
- Cause and effect

Here are the notes written by the candidate speaking about her geometry class. How did she order the information?

> **Geometry**
> —gd teacher 1
> —like solving probs 2
> **Reasons**
> —took more, majored in math 2
> —liked math for 1st time 1

For the details about the geometry class, the order goes from general to specific. First the candidate talks about having a good teacher. Then she gives a very specific detail about why she liked geometry, using logic to solve the problems. The reasons for her opinion are in cause-and-effect order: she began to like math, which caused her to take more courses. Taking more courses led her to major in math.

EXERCISE 2

Preparing Notes

Listen to and read the following TOEFL iBT independent speaking opinion items. For each one, you will have 15 seconds to write brief notes to prepare your response. Write your notes on a sheet of paper. After 15 seconds, a beep will sound and the next item will begin. Save your notes for Exercise 3, when you will use your notes to give responses to the questions. Make sure that your notes:

- Answer the question
- Give detail about your answer
- Give reasons to support your answer
- Order the ideas

1. Who is the person, besides your relatives, who had the most positive influence on you, and why? Use details and examples to support your explanation.
2. Describe your favorite food and explain why this food is your favorite. Use details and examples to support your explanation.
3. Describe your favorite hobby or pastime and explain why you enjoy it. Use details and examples to support your explanation.
4. Describe the city you enjoy the most and explain why you like it so much. Use details and examples to support your explanation.
5. Describe your dream home and explain why you want to live in this type of home. Use details and examples to support your explanation.

Sample Responses for Exercise 2 begin on page 451.

TIP **Use idea-gathering techniques to think of ideas quickly!**

Here are some simple ways to help you brainstorm ideas in a short amount of time.

- Ask yourself the questions *who, what, where, when,* and *why.*
- Ask yourself, "What happened first, second, third, etc.?"
- Ask yourself, "What are the causes? What are the effects?"

Giving Your Response

To give an effective response, expand each idea in your notes into one or two sentences.

> **TIP** **Do not repeat the question in your response!**
>
> Sometimes, test takers repeat part of the question in their responses to fill time or because they do not know what to say. The TOEFL iBT Speaking Scoring Rubric scores these responses as 1. So avoid repeating the question in your response. Instead, use brainstorming to gather ideas.

Always begin your response with a general statement of your opinion. Give an opening statement that gives some background, shows some thought, or gives an idea of how you determined your answer. Here are possible opening statements for two of the previous items:

- Of all the places I have visited, Barcelona is my favorite.
- Of course, many people have influenced me, but the biggest influence was my first-grade teacher, Miss Appleby.

If you are uncertain how to begin your response, start with an appropriate signaling expression, such as "In my opinion" or "I believe."

- **In my opinion,** Barcelona is the nicest city in the world.
- **I believe that** my first-grade teacher, Miss Appleby, was the biggest influence on me.

The chart shows some common signaling phrases for introducing your opinion.

SIGNALING WORDS AND PHRASES FOR EXPRESSING AN OPINION
In my opinion, ...
I believe ...
In my experience, ...
I think (that) ...

Items may ask you to express a like, dislike, preference, or ideal. Use appropriate language to express your preferences.

- **My favorite place is** Barcelona.
- Of all places, **I love** Barcelona **the most**.

The chart shows some common signaling phrases for stating a preference.

SIGNALING WORDS AND PHRASES FOR EXPRESSING A PREFERENCE
My **favorite** . . .
My **least favorite** . . .
I **prefer** . . .
I **really like** . . . (Barcelona) the most.
I **love** . . . (Barcelona) the most.

Your response should also use appropriate signaling words to link your ideas together and show relationships among them. For opinion items, you need to use appropriate signaling words to introduce your reasons. Look at the examples:

- This class was important for me **because** I liked math for the first time.
- **Before** this class, I hated math very much.
- **After** this class, I decided to take another math class.
- **Then** I began to like math more and more. **So** I decided to major in math in college.

Use the words and phrases in the chart to introduce reasons that support your opinion and show the relationships among the reasons.

SIGNALING WORDS AND PHRASES FOR INTRODUCING REASONS

SIGNALING WORDS AND PHRASES	PATTERN
Chronological order; order of importance	First, Second
Chronological order	Next, Then
Chronological order	Before, After
Order of importance	More importantly
Information	In addition, and
Example	For example, For instance
Contrast	However, but
Cause and effect	So, Then, As a result, because

If you have time when you prepare your response, write signaling words in your notes so you can use them when you respond. Look at the example:

Geometry
—gd teacher 1 *and*
—like solving probs 2
Reasons
—took more, so majored in math 2
— after class liked math for 1st time 1

EXERCISE 3

Responding to Opinion Items

A. Review your notes from Exercise 2 and use them to respond to the questions. Listen to and read the questions again. For each question, use 15 seconds to review your notes and prepare. Then use 45 seconds to record your response. Use the recorder on your computer or mobile phone to record your responses. If your device does not have a *record* function, ask a friend with strong English skills to listen to your response.

1. Who is the person, besides your relatives, who had the most positive influence on you, and why? Use details and examples to support your explanation.

    Record your response on your computer or mobile device.

2. Describe your favorite food and explain why this food is your favorite. Use details and examples to support your explanation.

   Record your response on your computer or mobile device.

3. Describe your favorite hobby or pastime and explain why you enjoy it. Use details and examples to support your explanation.

   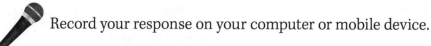 Record your response on your computer or mobile device.

4. Describe the city you enjoy the most and explain why you like it so much. Use details and examples to support your explanation.

 Record your response on your computer or mobile device.

5. Describe your ideal home and explain why you want to live in this type of home. Use details and examples to support your explanation.

 Record your response on your computer or mobile device.

B. Now listen to your responses and evaluate them. If possible, ask a teacher or an English-speaking friend to help you. Or wait a day or two and evaluate yourself. Use the Simplified Independent Speaking Rubric on pages 370–371. Then compare your responses to the high-scoring sample responses in the Answers and Explanations. Write your scores on the lines.

1. _____   2. _____   3. _____   4. _____   5. _____

Sample Responses for Exercise 3 begin on page 452.

TIP **Raise your score on opinion items!**

These suggestions can help you raise your score on the TOEFL iBT opinion items:

- Use brainstorming and notes to prepare a response with an opinion, detail, and one or two reasons.
- Put your ideas in a logical order.
- Combine short sentences into longer, more complex ones by using words such as *and, but, or, nor,* and *for* to link ideas together.
- Use signaling words and phrases to show how your ideas and reasons relate to each other.
- Practice speaking until you can speak for the full time without pausing or hesitating.

Item 2: Express a Choice

The second independent speaking item asks you to make a choice between two options and explain or defend your choice. As on Item 1, you will have 15 seconds to prepare your response and 45 seconds to say it. The topics are subjects of general interest, and no special knowledge is needed. On these items, you may have to take and defend a position or make and justify a recommendation.

SAMPLE TOPICS FOR ITEM 2: EXPRESS A CHOICE

Whether you prefer to study at home or at a library

Whether students should have cars on campus

Whether you prefer to watch movies on TV or at a theater

Whether you prefer to attend a university in a small town or large city

Whether you prefer online or face-to-face classes

> **EXAMPLE**

Item 2: Express a Choice

Read this sample TOEFL iBT Speaking choice item. Remember that on the real test, you will hear the question at the same time as you read it on screen.

> Some students prefer to attend a university in a small town, while others prefer to attend a university in a large city. Explain which view you prefer and why. Use details and examples to explain your answer.

Preparation Time: 15 seconds
Response Time: 45 seconds

Responding to a Choice Item

An effective response to a choice item includes this information:

- Your choice and a bit of detail about your choice
- A reason why the other choice is not such a good option
- Two reasons why your choice is a better option

As on opinion items, your response needs to present strong ideas. You also need to use a logical order, such as more important to less important, chronological order (the order in which events happened), or cause and effect. Listen to and read this high-scoring response.

I have attend universities in both a small town and large cities. Both are good options, but I prefer a small town. In a large city, there are many distractions. Life there is fun, but is hard to study. I like a small town because it's easier to focus on your studies. However, even though universities in small towns are quieter, they usually have many interesting activities for students. They have gyms, concerts, and guest speakers. There is always plenty to do.

> Your choice
>
> A reason why the other choice is not good
>
> Two more reasons your choice is better

Preparing Your Response to a Choice Item

As on the opinion item, you should make sure you understand the question. For a choice item, your response should always be one of the choices in the question. Look at the example. What are the choices?

Some students prefer to attend a university in a small town, while others prefer to attend a university in a large city. Explain which view you prefer and why. Use details and examples to explain your answer.

If you said that the choices are attending a university in a small town or a large city, you are correct.

> **TIP** **On choice items, always choose one of the options in the question!**
>
> When you answer a choice item, you need to stay on topic and answer the question exactly as stated. So always choose one of the options in the question. If the question asks whether you prefer to study in the library or at home, choose one of those options. Don't make your answer about studying at another place.

As on the opinion items, during the 15 seconds you have to prepare your response to the choice item, you can plan mentally or write brief notes.

Gathering Ideas and Taking Notes

In general, your notes should state and explain your choice and give reasons for it. In this section, we will look at steps for preparing good, brief notes in a short amount of time and then using them to give an effective response.

As on opinion items, begin your notes by writing your choice at the top and underlining it. For the example response, the answer is the preferred location, a small town. To save time, use abbreviations in your notes. What abbreviation did the candidate use for "small"?

> <u>Sm town</u>

If you said *sm*, you are correct.

An effective response needs to give detail about your choice and your reasons for making that choice. Use the same brainstorming and organizing techniques you used with opinion items to gather ideas for your response. Write notes as quickly as possible using words, phrases, and abbreviations. If you have time, number the ideas in order to reflect a logical organization pattern, such as order of importance, time, general to specific, or cause and effect. Look at the notes for the example topic:

> <u>Sm town</u>
> City—distracting
> Small town
> —many activs 2
> —easier to focus 1

Look at how the candidate ordered the reasons she prefers a small town. She put "easier to focus" first. This follows logically from the previous idea that going to school in the city is too distracting. Then she added the idea that even though a small town is less distracting, life there is still interesting.

EXERCISE 4

Preparing Notes

🎧 **AUDIO TRACK 77** Listen to and read the following TOEFL iBT independent speaking choice items. For each one, you will have 15 seconds to write brief notes to prepare your response. After 15 seconds, a beep will sound and the next item will begin. Write your notes on a sheet of paper. Keep your notes because you will use them again in Exercise 6 to give responses to the items. Make sure that in your notes you:

- Answer the question
- Give detail about your answer
- Give reasons to support your answer
- Order the ideas

Do you agree or disagree with the following statements? Why or why not? Use details and examples to support your response.

1. Spending time with your family is much more important than spending time at work.

2. Some people want to work for the same company for a long time. Others want to change jobs from time to time, or even frequently. Which do you think is better? Use details and examples to support your response.

3. Some people like to go to the movie theater to see a movie. Others prefer to watch movies at home on TV. Which do you prefer? Why? Use details and examples to support your response.

4. Because of computer technology, many books and magazines are available online and in print form. State which you prefer and tell why. Use details and examples to support your response.

5. Some people like to live in a big city. Others prefer to live in a small town. Which do you prefer? Why? Support your response with details and examples.

Sample Responses for Exercise 4 begin on page 452.

Giving Your Response

To give an effective response, you should expand each idea in your notes into one or two sentences.

Your response should always begin with a general statement of your choice. If you are uncertain how to begin your response, start with an appropriate signaling expression, such as "In my opinion" or "I believe." Then expand each idea in your outline into one or two sentences.

As you speak, use appropriate language. For example, to compare two options, use comparatives and superlatives. Look at the chart:

COMPARATIVES AND SUPERLATIVES
I like a small town because it's **easier** to focus on your studies.
However, even though universities in small towns are **quieter**, they usually have many interesting activities for students.
Of all the places on campus, the library is usually the **quietest**.

Comparative and superlative forms of adjectives are used to compare things. To form comparatives and superlatives, we use *-er than* and *the –est*, or *more . . . than* and *the most*. Follow these rules for forming comparatives and superlatives.

FORMING COMPARATIVES AND SUPERLATIVES

RULE	EXAMPLES		
Use *-er than* and *the -est* with one-syllable adjectives and two-syllable adjectives that end in *-y*.	big happy	bigg**er than** happi**er than**	**the** bigg**est** **the** happi**est**
Use *more . . . than* and *the most* with two-syllable adjectives that do not end in *-y* and three- and four-syllable adjectives.	careful important	**more** careful **than** **more** important **than**	**the most** careful **the most** important
Some adjectives have irregular forms.	good bad	**better than** **worse than**	**the best** **the worst**

EXERCISE 5

Comparatives and Superlatives

Complete the sentence. Write the comparative or superlative form of the adjective on the line. Follow the example.

1. I believe that spending time with your family is _more important than_ (**important**) spending time at work.

2. Reading online is _____ (**good**) reading a printed book.

3. Going to the movies is _____ (**expensive**) staying home and watching TV.

4. I prefer to live in Mexico City. It's _____ (**big**) city in North America.

5. Eating lunch with your family is _____ (**good**) way to spend a relaxing Sunday afternoon.

6. For many adults, taking classes at night is _____ (**convenient**) studying during the day.

7. The Cineplex 22 is _____ (**nice**) movie theater in town.

8. Stephan's old job was much _____ (**bad**) his new job.

9. Email is _____ (**fast**) sending a letter.

10. People who live in small towns feel _____ (**happy**) people who live in large cities.

Answers for Exercise 5 begin on page 453.

Since a choice is a kind of opinion, the language for expressing opinions you learned with opinion items is useful on choice items. Look at the examples.

- **In my opinion**, it's better to live in the city than in a small town.
- **I believe** (that) it's better to live in the city than in a small town.

English has a number of phrases that are useful for expressing choices. Study the chart:

SIGNALING WORDS AND PHRASES FOR STATING CHOICES
I like/love living in a city.
I like/love to live in a city.
I would rather (live in the city).
I would rather (live in the city) **than** (live in a small town).
I prefer (living/to live) in the city.
I prefer (living in the city) **to** (living in a small town).

Item 2 asks you to contrast two different choices. Look at the examples.

- Small towns are quieter than cities. **However,** small towns usually have many interesting activities for students.
- **While** cities are exciting, small towns are friendlier.
- Many people say that cities are fun places to live. **On the other hand,** there is also more crime and danger.

Common words for expressing contrast include *however*, *in contrast*, and *although*. Study the chart.

SIGNALING WORDS AND PHRASES FOR SHOWING CONTRAST
However,
In contrast,
On the other hand,
While (cities are exciting), (small towns are friendly).
Although (cities are exciting), (small towns are friendly).

EXERCISE 6

Responding to Choice Items

A. Review your notes from Exercise 4 and use them to give responses to the items. Listen to and read each TOEFL iBT Speaking choice item again. After 15 seconds, a beep will sound. Then take 45 seconds to record your response. Then another beep will sound, and the next item will begin. Use the recorder on your computer or mobile phone to record your responses. If your device does not have a *record* function, ask a friend with strong English skills to listen to your response.

> Do you agree or disagree with the following statements? Why or why not? Use details and examples to support your response.

1. Spending time with your family is much more important than spending time at work.

    Record your response on your computer or mobile device.

2. Some people want to work for the same company for a long time. Others want to change jobs from time to time, or even frequently. Which do you think is better? Use details and examples to support your answer.

    Record your response on your computer or mobile device.

3. Some people like to go to the movie theater to see a movie. Others prefer to watch movies at home on TV. Which do you prefer? Why? Use details and examples to support your answer.

    Record your response on your computer or mobile device.

4. Because of computer technology, many books and magazines are available online and in print form. State which you prefer and tell why. Use details and examples to support your answer.

   Record your response on your computer or mobile device.

5. Some people like to live in a big city. Others prefer to live in a small town. Which do you prefer? Why? Support your answer with details and examples.

Record your response on your computer or mobile device.

B. Now listen to your responses and evaluate them. If possible, ask a teacher or an English-speaking friend to help you. Or wait a day or two and evaluate your work yourself. Use the Simplified Independent Speaking Rubric on pages 370–371. Then compare your responses to the high-scoring sample responses in the Answers and Explanations. Write your scores on the lines.

1. _____ **2.** _____ **3.** _____ **4.** _____ **5.** _____

Sample Responses for Exercise 6 begin on page 453.

TIP   **Raise your score on choice items!**

These suggestions can help you raise your score on the TOEFL iBT Speaking section:

* Choose one of the options in the question as your answer.
* Provide detail and reasons for your choice in your response.
* Use signaling words and phrases to show relationships among your ideas.
* Avoid repeating the question in your response.

Integrated Reading, Listening, and Speaking: Items 3 and 4

Items 3 and 4 integrate reading and listening with speaking. First you read written material on your computer screen and use your headset to listen to a conversation or a lecture on the same topic. You may take notes as you read and listen. Then you answer a question that relates to both the reading and the listening and requires you to integrate information from both of them. You will have:

- 45 seconds to read
- 60 to 80 seconds to listen
- 30 seconds to prepare your response
- 60 seconds to respond

Item 3 focuses on a campus-related topic, and Item 4 focuses on an academic topic.

Item Format

Items 3 and 4 follow identical formats. You will first hear the narrator give a brief introduction to the topic of the reading and tell you how long you have to read it.

You will hear:

Narrator: The university sent an email to all students about the university's plan for a weather emergency. You will have 45 seconds to read the email. Begin reading now.

The reading will appear on the screen, along with a timer that counts down 45 seconds of reading time.

Reading Time: 45 seconds

Campus Closing at 3:00 Because of Weather

The National Weather Service has advised that a large snowstorm is affecting the east central area of the state, including the university campus. The snow had been expected to pass north of the metro area, but it began to affect the city and the campus at about noon. Snow is expected to continue to fall tonight and tomorrow. Altogether, 2 to 3 feet of snow is expected.

Because of the extreme weather, the university will close at 3:00 today. All campus offices will be closed, and all classes and scheduled activities will be canceled. The university will remain closed tomorrow and reopen on Wednesday, January 23.

When reading time is up, the reading text and timer will be replaced with a picture of people talking. The narrator will introduce the listening passage, and then the listening selection will begin.

AUDIO TRACK 79 You will hear a lecture or a conversation on the same topic. Listen to the following conversation. Read along as you listen. (On the actual TOEFL, you will only listen to the selection.)

Narrator: Now listen to two students discussing the plan.

Male Student: Wow! Look at how hard the snow is falling, Mary. It looks kind of dangerous out there. Do you think the university will close?

Female Student: Hmm. Check your email. I just got a notice that the campus is closing because of the snow.

Male Student: Really? Let me check my email. Oh, I see.

Female Student: Good thing too—I want to get home before the snow gets worse. Apparently at least 2 feet of snow is expected.

Male Student: Well, I wish they'd tell us these things earlier so we can plan ahead. I always get a ride home from a guy in my 4:00 class. Now I need to find a way to get home.

Female Student: I think that I can give you a ride.

Male Student: It's really important that the university plan ahead better. Look . . . Almost 6 inches of snow have already fallen. They need to make these decisions sooner. They should have closed the campus at noon when the snow started.

Female Student: Well, look at the announcement again. Snow wasn't in the forecast, so I don't think we can blame the university for not closing earlier. But at least we get a free day to prepare for the big test on Thursday. Are you ready to leave? I can drive you home now.

When the listening passage is completed, the photograph goes away and is replaced with the question screen.

You will hear the question at the same time as you read it on screen.

> The man expresses his opinion about the plan described in the announcement. Briefly summarize the plan. Then state his opinion and explain the reasons he gives for holding that opinion.
>
> **Preparation Time: 30 seconds**
> **Response Time: 60 seconds**

After 30 seconds have passed, you will hear a beep. The question will stay on the screen and a new timer will appear. You will have 60 seconds to record your response.

> The man expresses his opinion about the plan described in the announcement. Briefly summarize the plan. Then state his opinion and explain the reasons he gives for holding that opinion.
>
> **Response Time: 60 seconds**

After 60 seconds of response time have passed, the recorder will turn off, and the test will advance to the next item.

Natural Language

You will encounter common features of everyday natural speech in the listening portions of the TOEFL Listening, Speaking, and Writing sections. You may want to include them in your own spoken English. The features of everyday natural language include pauses, digressions, repetition, mispronunciations, and other errors typical of natural language. Here are some common features of everyday natural speech you will likely encounter on the TOEFL iBT.

- **Getting listeners' attention:** To get listeners' attention before they speak, English speakers use expressions such as "Excuse me" before they begin their main point.
- **Pauses and fillers:** Though English speech may often seem fast, natural speech often has pauses and fillers such as "Umm" or "Uhh."
- **Reduced speech:** Speakers may use contractions, omit words, or run words together. For example, "What did you do?" might become, "Whatdidja do?"
- **Digressions:** Speakers may not always stick to the topic. TOEFL iBT listening selections may include such digressions. One of the skills the TOEFL iBT tests is the ability to distinguish main ideas and relevant details from irrelevant digressions.
- **Interruptions:** In natural speech, listeners may interrupt with a question or comment, and these interruptions may be off topic.
- **Self-correction:** Sometimes, speakers will realize that they made a mistake and will correct themselves.

Get used to listening to natural English through English movies, TV, or the Internet. As you listen, pay attention to pauses, fillers, digressions, interruptions, and other features of natural, spoken English.

Item 3: Integrated Reading, Listening, and Speaking: Campus-Related Topics

For Item 3, the reading passage may be a simulated real-life campus document, such as a news article, an official letter, an announcement, or a notice from a campus office. The listening passage will be a conversation between two students, between a student and a professor, or between a student and a university staff member talking about the information in the document.

Item 3 assesses your ability to summarize, paraphrase, and integrate information from two different sources, one written and another spoken. To do so, you need to identify the main points and key details in each information source. You also have to identify and explain the speaker's attitude or opinion about the information in the campus document.

Evaluating Integrated Speaking Responses

All TOEFL iBT Speaking responses are evaluated by trained raters using a special scoring rubric. There are slightly different rubrics for independent and integrated speaking. Understanding the rubrics can help you prepare for the test. The following pages show a simplified version of the TOEFL iBT Integrated Speaking Scoring Rubric that you can use as a checklist to prepare for the test and to evaluate your own speaking.

TOEFL iBT SIMPLIFIED INTEGRATED SPEAKING SCORING RUBRIC

SCORE	GENERAL DESCRIPTION	DELIVERY	LANGUAGE USE	TOPIC DEVELOPMENT
4	**The response:** • Answers the question • Is complete • Is understandable • Makes sense • Stays on topic • Has few pauses, hesitations, or interruptions • Includes ALL of the items in the columns to the right	**The speech:** • Is generally fluent and sustained • May have small problems with pace as speakers try to remember information • Is generally clear • May have minor problems with pronunciation or intonation • Is highly understandable overall	**The language:** • Shows effective use of correct grammar and vocabulary that allows for automatic expression of ideas • Shows good control of basic and advanced structures • Has only minors errors that do not affect understanding or meaning	**The content:** • Includes information necessary to answer the question • Is in a logical order • Uses order and signaling devices to show relationships among ideas • Includes appropriate detail, though there may be small errors or omissions of detail
3	**The response:** • Answers the question, but is not complete • Is generally understandable • Has fluid expression, but there may be some pauses or gaps in expression • Includes TWO of the items in the columns to the right	**The speech:** • Is generally clear and somewhat fluent • May have minor pronunciation, intonation, or pacing problems that require the listener to pay attention to understand • Is understandable overall	**The language:** • Shows fairly effective use of correct grammar and vocabulary • May have some improper or limited use of grammar and vocabulary that reduces fluency but not clarity of the information	**The content:** • Is sustained • Gives relevant information to answer the question • Has some incompleteness or inaccuracy • Lacks some detail, or has unclear or choppy progression of ideas because of improper order or lack of signaling devices

SCORE	GENERAL DESCRIPTION	DELIVERY	LANGUAGE USE	TOPIC DEVELOPMENT
2	**The response:** • Answers the question but lacks some information or is inaccurate • Contains some understandable speech, but problems with understandability or relevance may make meaning unclear at times • Includes TWO of the items in the columns to the right	**The speech:** • Is clear at times, but has problems with pronunciation or intonation that may require significant listener effort • May not be sustained at a consistent level • Has problems with understandability that make meaning unclear at times	**The language:** • Has limited range and control of grammar and vocabulary • Contains errors in complex structures • Lacks automatic use of structures except in memorized phrases • Has limited or vague expression of relevant ideas or inaccurate use of signaling devices	**The content:** • Includes some relevant information, but is incomplete or inaccurate • Omits key ideas or refers to key ideas vaguely • Lacks understanding of key ideas from the stimulus • Presents unrelated or unordered ideas or lacks appropriate signaling devices to show relationships among ideas
1	**The response:** • Has very limited content, is only minimally connected to the question, or is mainly not understandable • Includes TWO of the items in the columns to the right	**The speech:** • Has consistent problems with pronunciation, stress, and intonation that make understanding difficult • Is choppy or fragmented • Has frequent unnatural pauses and hesitations	**The language:** • Shows limited grammar and vocabulary that prevent expression of ideas • Has limited use of signaling devices • May rely on only words or phrases to communicate ideas	**The content:** • Fails to give relevant information • Is often inaccurate, vague, or repetitive (including repeating the question)
0	No response, response is off topic, or response is not understandable.			

Here is a response to the example TOEFL iBT Integrated Reading, Listening, and Speaking item. Read it and listen to it. Then try to figure out the score it received.

 ### Sample Response 1

Umm . . . The university just announced that the campus will close at 3 o'clock because of bad weather. Snow is falling across the region and on the university campus, too. So all activities are canceled, and the university will not open for a day. The man is unhappy because he thinks that the news is too late. He thinks that the university should close at 12 o'clock because that's when the snow started to fall. He also thinks it's a problem because he can't get home since he will not see his classmate and get a ride.

If you said that this response was rated a 4, you are correct. The response:

✔ Summarizes the weather announcement briefly and restates the reasons the man is unhappy about the announcement
✔ Integrates information from the reading and the conversation
✔ Flows fluently and uses signaling words such as *so* and *because*
✔ Shows command of vocabulary and grammar, despite a few errors with difficult structures. For example, the candidate says he thinks the university "should close at 12:00," but "should have closed" is required.
✔ Has clear pronunciation. Despite a few mispronounced words, the response is highly understandable.

Here are some more sample responses to this example item. Read and listen to each one. Try to figure out the score each one received. Then read the score that each one received and the reason it received that score.

 ### Sample Response 2

The announcement says the university is close because snow. The weather is very bad, so the university will close tomorrow, too. The man does not liked this decision. He thinks the university should close sooner. Now he has problem getting home. Usually, he goes home with his classmate. But the class is canceled. So the announcement made it hard for him.

If you said that this response scored a 3, you are correct. The response:

✔ Answers the question with accurate information but lacks some relevant detail, especially about the reading

✔ Orders ideas in a way that makes sense and uses signaling words and phrases that show relationships among ideas

✔ Has generally clear pronunciation, and pronunciation errors do not impede understanding, but they do require listeners to pay attention to understand

✔ Has some grammar errors, but they do not affect understandability

 ## Sample Response 3

According announcement, university is closing at 3 o'clock because snow is bad. Nobody expected snow; it was surprising. The man felt surprising, too. He think that the university should be close earlier. Snow started at 12 o'clock, so the university should be close then. Now student have trouble return home. Usually, he meet a friend at 4. Now won't see friend. So he have problem.

If you said that this response scored a 2, you are correct. This response:

✔ Includes some relevant information, but the information is vague and incomplete

✔ Does not present ideas in a logical order and lacks signaling words and phrases in some places

✔ Models clear speech only at times

✔ Shows limited control of vocabulary and has many basic grammar errors

 ## Sample Response 4

Announcement say university take decision close . . . because snow bad. The man didn't like decision because snow already bad . . . early in day. The man complain a lot. I don't like this man. He complain . . . too many . . . Why not call friend . . . to get ride home? Where is friend? Plus, he have free day, can study or have fun with snow. He only complain . . . I don't understand why snow problem, look beautiful.

If you said that this response scored a 1, you are correct. This response:

✔ Lacks relevant detail

✔ Includes some repetitive or irrelevant information

✔ Does not order ideas logically and lacks signaling devices to show relationships among them

✔ Is hard to understand because of pronunciation and intonation problems

✔ Has limited vocabulary and shows a lack of control of basic grammar

---

EXERCISE 7

Understanding the Integrated Speaking Scoring Rubric

🎧 **AUDIO TRACK 84** In this exercise, you will use the rubric to evaluate four student responses to a TOEFL iBT item. You have 45 seconds to read a short news article from a campus newspaper. Then you will hear two students discussing the article. After that, you will hear four responses. Listen and evaluate the responses using the rubric.

Reading Time: 45 Seconds

Changes to Bus Service Announced

Yesterday campus services announced changes to the bus service between the main campus and the downtown campus starting today. A new route will be added from South Tower to downtown to supplement the existing route from the Student Union. Now students, faculty, and staff traveling between campuses will have their choice of two routes from two different parts of campus. Route 1 will continue to leave from the Student Union, but the frequency will be reduced from every 10 minutes to every 20 minutes. Route 2 will travel from South Tower to downtown every 15 minutes. The price per ride will increase by twenty-five cents to cover rising gas prices.

 🎧 **AUDIO TRACK 85** Now listen to two students talking about the same topic as the passage.

The woman expresses her opinion about the changes to campus bus service described in the article. Briefly summarize the changes. Then state her opinion and explain the reasons she gives for holding that opinion.

Now you will hear four sample responses. Rate the responses using the Simplified Integrated Speaking Scoring Rubric on pages 398–399. Write the score on the line.

1. Response 1: _____

2. Response 2: _____

3. Response 3: _____

4. Response 4: _____

Answers and Explanations for Exercise 7 begin on page 453.

Responding to Item 3

To respond to Item 3 successfully, you need to integrate information from the written document with the opinion expressed by one of the speakers. A good response will include:

- A summary of the gist of the document
- A summary of the speaker's opinion
- One or two reasons for the speaker's opinion

Listen to and read this high-scoring response again and see how the candidate addressed the parts of a good response.

Umm . . . The university just announced that the campus will close at 3 o'clock because of bad weather. Snow is falling across the region and on the university campus, too. So all activities are canceled, and the university will not open for a day.

Summary of the written information

The man is unhappy because he thinks that the news is too late. He thinks that the university should close at 12 o'clock because that's when the snow started to fall. He also thinks it's a problem because he can't get home since he will not see his classmate and get a ride.

Summary of the man's opinion

Reasons for his opinion

Preparing Your Response to Item 3

To prepare an effective response to Item 3, you need to gather information from the written information and listening selection. Taking brief notes as you listen and read is a good way to gather information for your response.

Reading and Taking Notes: Gist and Details

As you know, the gist is the main idea. When taking the TOEFL iBT Speaking section, you will need to read for the gist of the written information. You will also need one or two key details—specific pieces of information that support the main idea. Review the information in the reading. Then look at the sentences. Which is the main idea? Which are the details? Write **M** for main idea or **D** for detail on the line.

Campus Closing at 3:00 Because of Weather

The National Weather Service has advised that a large snowstorm is affecting the east central area of the state, including the university campus. The snow had been expected to pass north of the metro area, but it began to affect the city and the campus at about noon. Snow is expected to continue to fall tonight and tomorrow. Altogether, 2 to 3 feet of snow is expected.

Because of the extreme weather, the university will close at 3:00 today. All campus offices will be closed, and all classes and scheduled activities will be canceled. The university will remain closed tomorrow and reopen on Wednesday, January 23.

_____ **1.** About 2 to 3 feet of snow is expected.

_____ **2** The university will close today at 3:00 because of a bad snowstorm.

_____ **3.** All campus offices will close at 3:00.

_____ **4.** All classes and scheduled activities are canceled.

If you said that Sentence 2 is the main idea, you are right. This sentence sums up what is happening on campus and why. Sentence 1 is a specific detail about the amount of snow. Sentences 3 and 4 are specific details about the closings and cancellations.

Since the response time is brief, the notes you take in the TOEFL iBT Speaking section only need to summarize the main idea and a few details. To do so, as you read the document, try to sum up the main idea in a phrase or short sentence. Then write down a few of the key details. As with all notes, use abbreviations, symbols, and content words to write your ideas down quickly as you read. Look at the written information from the sample item again. Then look at the notes.

> Univ closing @ 3 bec snow
> —Up to 3'
> —Not expected, started @ 12
> —Offices closed 3:00
> —Classes, activs canceled today, tomm

Notice how the candidate wrote the main idea first, using abbreviations, such as _Univ_ ("university") and _bec_ ("because"). Notice, too, that the candidate used the symbol @ ("at") to save time. The candidate also left off small words such as _of_ and _is_. The complete main idea is: "The university is closing at 3:00 because of snow."

Under the main idea, the candidate included details and used dashes and a simple outline form to show the details that support the main idea. The candidate also used abbreviations and symbols in the details. Look at the notes again. Find the abbreviations or symbols for these words. Write the answer on the line.

1. feet _____

2. activities _____

3. tomorrow _____

If you said that the symbol for feet is ', you are correct. In the notes, the word _activities_ is abbreviated as _activs_ and _tomorrow_ as _tomm_.

EXERCISE 8

Reading and Taking Notes

Read and take notes on reading passages for the TOEFL iBT Speaking Item 3. Use the timer on your mobile phone or computer to count down 45 seconds for each one. As you read, write brief notes on the lines. Use symbols and abbreviations.

1.   **Historic Memorial Auditorium to Be Renovated**

Memorial Auditorium will be completely renovated beginning in January. Memorial Auditorium is one of the oldest and most historic spaces on campus. The renovation will include restoring historic features of the auditorium to their original state, while installing new, state-of-the-art sound and lighting systems. The seating is in poor condition and will be replaced with new, more comfortable seating that matches the original 1876 design with greater comfort. The auditorium will be closed in December to begin preparations for the renovation, which is expected to last one year. This week, workers will begin to remove the paintings in the auditorium so that they can be stored safely during the renovation.

Notes:

_____

_____

_____

_____

2.   **New Guest Speaker Series**

The university is pleased to announce a new guest speaker series for spring semester. Each Friday at 11:00 A.M. in Convocation Hall, a different speaker will address the campus community. Nationally and internationally recognized scholars and thinkers will be invited to share their thoughts with the community. We expect to invite scientists, business leaders, philosophers, novelists, poets, and many others. The kick-off event will take place on Friday,

September 10, when noted documentary filmmaker Charles White will talk about his new film *Living with Hope: My Struggle to Rebuild*. The film chronicles White's struggle to rebuild his home and business after they were destroyed by a hurricane.

Notes:

_____

_____

_____

_____

3. **New Fee Implemented**

For next year, tuition will remain at the same level as this year. But the university is adding a new technology fee. This fee is designed to cover the cost of installing a new, high-speed, campus-wide wireless network in all buildings. Work on the new network has already begun and will be completed in the next five months. Network speeds will be up to ten times faster for most users. After the new network is paid for, proceeds from the fee will be used to pay for upgrades to the network. The fee will be $15 per semester.

Notes:

_____

_____

_____

_____

4. **New Writing Requirement**

In order to improve graduates' writing skills, the university has decided to modify the graduation requirements to include a writing-intensive course in every major. The purpose of the course is to improve students' writing skills in the area related to their majors. Each program and department will be required to offer a writing-intensive class in the area of the major. Each course will focus on the kinds of writing expected in the student's field or major. The requirement is expected to improve students' employability after graduation.

Notes:

_____

_____

_____

_____

5.   **Announcement: New Director of Libraries**

      The university is pleased to announce that Dr. Kathleen Walsh is being promoted from head of digital collections to director of libraries. As head of digital collections, Dr. Walsh helped the university develop our outstanding online collections, which include thousands of online journals, books, and films. In addition, she has overseen the scanning and digitization of millions of pages from the university's archives. As director of libraries, Dr. Walsh will continue the work of developing expanded digital collections, as well as directing all library services. Please join in congratulating Dr. Walsh on her promotion.

Notes:

_____

_____

_____

_____

Sample Responses for Exercise 8 begin on page 454.

After you read and take notes, you will listen to a conversation about the document you just read. As you listen, you need to pay attention to the speakers' opinions, because you will be asked about them when you speak.

Listening and Taking Notes: Opinions

To respond to Item 3 successfully, you need to understand the opinion expressed by one of the speakers in the listening passage. Since you don't know which of the speakers the question will ask about, make sure you understand both speakers' opinions.

To focus your listening and gather ideas for your response, take notes as you listen. Write down the speakers' opinions and their reasons for having those opinions. As before, use abbreviations and symbols to write more quickly, and use a very simple outline form to show the relationship of the ideas.

AUDIO TRACK 87 Listen again to the two students discussing the university's announcement that it is closing because of snow. What do these abbreviations stand for: *U, in*? Which speaker is happy about the announcement? Which one is unhappy?

> Man: U tell us sooner
> —6 in snow already
> —Needs ride home
> Woman: Happy U closing
> —Wants get home
> —Can't blame U for snow
> —Free day to study—happy

If you said that *U* stands for *university* and *in* for *inches*, you are correct. The woman is happy about the announcement, while the man is upset about it. With these notes, the candidate is ready to respond whether the question asks about the woman's opinion or the man's.

EXERCISE 9

Listening and Taking Notes

Listen to the conversations and take notes. Focus on the speakers' opinions about the written information.

1. Notes:

_____

_____

_____

_____

2. Notes:

_____

_____

_____

_____

3. Notes:

_____

_____

_____

_____

4. Notes:

_____

_____

_____

5. Notes:

_____

_____

_____

Sample Responses for Exercise 9 begin on page 455.

Giving Your Response

After you finish listening, you will see the question and have 30 seconds to organize the ideas you gathered from the written information and the listening passage. Here again is the example question:

> The man expresses his opinion about the plan described in the announcement. Briefly summarize the plan. Then state his opinion and explain the reasons he gives for holding that opinion.

To give a good response, first make sure that you understand the item. In particular, you need to pay attention to which speaker's opinion you need to summarize in your response. This question asks about the man's opinion.

Next, you need to organize your notes and ideas so that they follow this pattern:

- Summarize the written material briefly.
- State the speaker's opinion.
- Give reasons for the speaker's opinion.

Because you have only 30 seconds to organize your information, you do not have time to write a new outline. Just use the information in the notes you already took. Look at the notes again.

> <u>Univ closing @ 3 bec snow</u>
> —Up to 3'
> —Not expected, started @ 12
> —Classes, activs canceled today, tomm
> <u>Man: U tell us sooner</u>
> —6 in snow already
> —Needs ride home
> <u>Woman: Happy U closing</u>
> —Wants get home
> —Can't blame U for snow
> —Free day to study—happy

When you give your response, you should first summarize the gist of the written information in a sentence and then give a bit more detail.

Summarizing

When you summarize, you restate information in fewer words. On Item 3, you need to give a very brief summary of the written material. Because you have only 60 seconds to respond, and because you need to include other information from the listening passage, your summary of the written information should be very short—no more than one or two sentences.

When you summarize the written information, use your notes to say a short summary of the main idea of the written information.

- The university just announced that the campus will close at 3 o'clock because of bad weather.

Signaling Words and Phrases for Starting a Summary

There are many ways to begin your summary. Here are a few:

- **According to the announcement,** the university will close at 3:00 because of bad weather.
- **The announcement is about** the university closing at 3:00 because of bad weather.
- **The announcement says** that the university is closing at 3:00 because of a bad snowstorm.

Use language that reflects the type of written material (announcement, notice, article, email, etc.).

After the introductory sentence, give one to two more sentences with relevant details. Use fewer words in your summary than in the original, and focus only on the most important information that is relevant to answering the question. Compare the original to the summary.

Original

The National Weather Service has advised that a large snowstorm is affecting the east central area of the state, including the university campus. The snow had been expected to pass north of the metro area, but it began to affect the city and the campus at about noon. Snow is expected to continue to fall tonight and tomorrow. All together, 2 to 3 feet of snow is expected.

Because of the extreme weather, the university will close at 3:00 today. All campus offices will be closed, and all classes and scheduled activities will be canceled. The university will remain closed tomorrow and reopen on Wednesday, January 23.

Summary

Heavy snow is falling across the region and on the university campus, too. So all activities are canceled, and the university will not open for a day.

Notice how the summary includes key detail, such as the extent of the snow (across the region and on the university campus) and the effects of the snowfall (the university will close and stay closed the following day; all activities are canceled). Notice, too, how the ideas are stated more simply and directly. For example, the sentence "All campus offices will be closed, and all classes and scheduled activities will be canceled" becomes "all activities are canceled."

EXERCISE 10

Summarizing

Use your notes from Exercise 8: Reading and Taking Notes to summarize the written information as you would for TOEFL iBT Speaking Item 3. Write your summaries on the lines.

1. _____

_____

_____

2. _____

_____

_____

3. _____

_____

_____

4. _____

_____

_____

5. _____

_____

_____

Sample Responses for Exercise 10 begin on page 456.

Paraphrasing. Next, you need to summarize the man's opinion about the information and give the reasons he holds that opinion. You can summarize the speaker's opinion in a sentence. Look at the example:

- The man is unhappy because he thinks that the news is too late.

This sentence is an effective summary of the man's opinion. He feels angry about the news because it snowed for some time before the university made its decision.

The following sentences paraphrase the reasons he gives. When you paraphrase, you restate someone's idea in different words. Look at the example:

- He thinks that the university should have closed at 12:00 because that's when the snow started to fall. He also thinks it's a problem because he can't get home since he will not see his classmate and get a ride.

The difference between a summary and a paraphrase is that a summary is always shorter than the original and sums up the main idea. A paraphrase uses different words and may be longer or shorter than the original.

Reported Speech. The sentences use reported speech to state the man's reasons. Reported speech is a way to quote another person's words indirectly. Reported speech is usually introduced by phrases such as *He says*, *He thinks*, and the like. Reported speech does not use quotation marks. Look at the examples:

- **He thinks that** the university should have closed at 12:00 because that's when the snow started to fall.
- **He also says** it's a problem because he can't get home since he will not see his classmate and get a ride.

English uses phrases such as *thinks (that)* and *says (that)* to introduce reported speech. The word *that* is optional. Study the chart.

SIGNALING DEVICES FOR REPORTED SPEECH
The man **says** (that) . . .
The man **thinks** (that) . . .
The man **told his friend** (that) . . .

Stating Reasons. To score high, you will also need to use in your response appropriate signaling words and phrases to give the speaker's reasons. Look again at the example:

> He thinks that the university should have closed at 12:00 **because** that's when the snow started to fall. He also thinks it's a problem **because** he can't get home **since** he will not see his classmate and get a ride.

In this example, the speaker uses *because* and *since* to state the man's reasons. There are many other ways to state reasons. Study the chart.

SIGNALING DEVICES FOR GIVING REASONS
since
because
so
The reason that . . .
One reason that . . .

TIP **Raise your score on Item 3!**

These suggestions can help you raise your score on the TOEFL iBT Speaking section Item 3:

- Take brief notes on the written information and listening selection as you listen.
- Read the question carefully. Make sure you know which speaker the question is about.
- Use signaling words and phrases to show relationships among your ideas.
- Avoid repeating the question in your response.

EXERCISE 11

Responding to Item 3

A. Review your answers to Exercise 8: Reading and Taking Notes (pages 406–408) and Exercise 9: Listening and Taking Notes (pages 410–411). Use your notes on the written information and the listening selections to respond to the TOEFL iBT questions. For each item, take 30 seconds to prepare your response. Then take 60 seconds to give your response. Use a watch or a timer to time yourself. Use the recorder on your computer or mobile phone to record your responses. If your device does not have a *record* function, ask a friend with strong English skills to listen to your response.

1. The woman expresses her opinion about the renovation of the auditorium. State her opinion and explain the reasons she gives for holding that opinion.

    Record your response on your computer or mobile device.

2. The man expresses his opinion about the new guest speaker series. State his opinion and explain the reasons he gives for holding that opinion.

    Record your response on your computer or mobile device.

3. The woman expresses her opinion about the new technology fee. State her opinion and explain the reasons she gives for holding that opinion.

    Record your response on your computer or mobile device.

4. The woman expresses her opinion about the new writing requirement. State her opinion and explain the reasons she gives for holding that opinion.

    Record your response on your computer or mobile device.

5. The woman expresses her opinion about the work of the new head of the library. State her opinion and explain the reasons she gives for holding that opinion.

    Record your response on your computer or mobile device.

B. Now listen to your responses and evaluate them. If possible, ask a teacher or an English-speaking friend to help you. Or wait a day or two and evaluate your responses yourself. Use the Simplified Integrated Speaking Rubric on pages 398–399. Then compare your responses to the high-scoring sample responses in the Answers and Explanations. Write your scores on the lines.

1. _____   **2.** _____   **3.** _____   **4.** _____   **5.** _____

Sample Responses for Exercise 11 begin on page 457.

Item 4: Integrated Reading, Listening, and Speaking: Academic-Related Topics

The format of Item 4 is identical to that of Item 3, but with academic, rather than campus-related content. For Item 4, the written information will be an excerpt from the reading for a course that will give general or theoretical information about an academic topic. The listening passage will be an excerpt from a lecture on the same topic. The lecture will include a specific example or illustration related to the topic of the reading. Your task is to integrate the general and specific information from the two sources and identify how they agree, disagree, or both.

EXAMPLE

Item 4: Integrated Reading, Listening, and Speaking Academic Topic

Listen to and read the sample TOEFL iBT Speaking section Item 4.

You will hear:

> **Narrator:** You will now read a short passage and listen to a lecture on the same topic. You will then be asked a question about them. After you hear and see the question, you will have 30 seconds to prepare your response and 60 seconds to record your response.

The reading will appear on the screen, along with a timer that counts down 45 seconds of reading time.

Reading Time: 45 seconds

Advertising Spokespersons

Ads often include a recurring spokesperson who touts the advantages of the product to potential consumers. A spokesperson may be a fictional character or a real person, famous or not. Regardless of the kind of spokesperson, a number of characteristics will influence the spokesperson's effectiveness. For example, the spokesperson should be someone whom consumers can identify with. The spokesperson should resemble the consumer in some way or be someone whom the customer wants to be like, look like, or respect. Of course, since consumers and their behavior change, sometimes a product will need to change or modify its spokesperson. Second, the spokesperson should be instantly recognizable. If he or she is supposed to be a worker, the spokesperson should wear appropriate clothing or a uniform.

When reading time is up, the reading text and timer are replaced with a picture of people talking. The narrator introduces the listening selection, and the selection begins.

 Listen to and read the example. (On the actual TOEFL iBT, you will only hear, and not see, the listening selection.)

Narrator: Now listen to part of a lecture on this topic in an advertising class.

Professor: As you know, one of the most effective advertising techniques is using a spokesperson. Even though there are some criteria that determine whether a spokesperson will be effective, the specific spokesperson will be different as consumer taste and behavior changes. Advertising for coffee is a good example. In the 1960s and 1970s, the two most popular spokespersons were older women. That's because at that time, there weren't large coffee chains such as Starbucks, and many middle-class women didn't work outside the home. A high percentage of coffee was made by women for at-home consumption. So it was logical that a warm, friendly, older woman would be the spokesperson, since a housewife might look to such a person for advice about making good coffee. Now, however, a much larger proportion of coffee is consumed away from the home. And the spokespeople are different too. Now, the spokesperson for coffee is more likely a young, energetic, working adult—just like the people who buy coffee at coffee stores.

When the listening passage is completed, the picture goes away and is replaced with the question screen. You will see:

The professor describes different kinds of advertising spokespersons for coffee. Explain how they are effective choices for promoting coffee.

| Preparation Time: 30 seconds |
| Response Time: 60 seconds |

You will hear:

Narrator: The professor describes different kinds of advertising spokespersons for coffee. Explain how they are effective choices for promoting coffee. Begin speaking after the beep. Use the 30 seconds before the beep to prepare your response. Use the timer to keep track of the time.

When 30 seconds have passed, you will hear a beep. The question will stay on the screen and a new timer will appear. You will have 60 seconds to record your response.

The professor describes different kinds of advertising spokespersons for coffee. Explain how they are effective choices for promoting coffee.

| Response Time: 60 seconds |

After 60 seconds of response time have passed, the recorder will turn off, and the test will advance to the next item.

Responding to Item 4

An effective response to Item 4 includes this information:

- A one-sentence statement about the topic of the reading
- A brief summary of the main point of the reading
- A one-sentence statement about the topic of the lecture
- A few sentences that explain how the information in the reading and lecture are related

Listen to and read this high-scoring response.

In general, the reading is about advertising spokespersons. | **Statement of the reading topic**

According to the reading, customers should like the spokesperson for the ad to be effective. The advertiser should choose people who are similar than their customers. | **Summary of the main point of the reading**

Statement of the lecture topic | The example the professor gives is about speakers for coffee. Because coffee buyers changed, the spokespeople changed, too. For example, many years ago, when housewifes made coffee a lot at home, the spokesperson was an older woman who housewifes respect. Now, the spokespersons are different. They are young and have a lot of energy, like people who buy coffee at a coffee chain store. So the criteria for choosing a spokesperson is the same, but the speakers are different because consumers have changed. | **How the general information in the reading and specific information in the lecture are related**

This response includes all of the parts of a high-scoring response. The response:

✔ Restates the main topic of the reading in the first sentence: an important criterion for choosing an advertising spokesperson is that customers will identify with the spokesperson

✔ Gives a bit more detail about the main idea in the second sentence

✔ Introduces the specific topic addressed in the lecture in the third sentence: spokespeople for coffee changed as coffee consumers changed, but they are still people customers can identify with

✔ Has fluid delivery, and the few pronunciation problems do not interfere with understanding

✔ Has good vocabulary and grammar, including some fairly advanced grammatical structures

✔ Has only a few errors, such as using *speakers* for *spokespersons*, or *housewifes* instead of *housewives*, which are minor and do not interfere with understanding

Preparing Your Response to Item 4

As on Item 3, you should do these things to prepare to respond to Item 4:

• Read the passage and take brief notes.
• Listen to the lecture and take brief notes.

As before, use abbreviations and symbols in your notes.

To respond to Item 4 successfully, you need to relate specific facts and examples in the lecture to the more general statements they support, or contradict, in the reading. Having an understanding of general and specific information will help you prepare a high-scoring response.

General and Specific

A general statement is one that is broad. A general statement, or generalization, applies to all members of a group, class, or category. Read the examples:

- Companies often use spokespersons in ads to represent a product or service.
- Spokespersons who resemble customers are effective.

A specific statement is one that is narrow and focused. It applies to only one or a few members of a group or category. Look at the examples:

- A few years ago, older housewives were the spokespersons for coffee sold in supermarkets.
- Today, coffee spokespersons are energetic working adults like those who buy coffee in coffee stores.

One of the specific details in the listening is that the spokesperson in a coffee ad is most likely an energetic working adult who buys coffee in coffee stores. What general statement in the reading is this specific example related to?

    (A) The spokesperson should be someone whom consumers can identify with.

    (B) Since consumers and their behavior change, sometimes a product will need to change or modify its spokesperson.

    (C) The spokesperson should be instantly recognizable.

If you picked Option A, you are correct. Advertisers choose spokespersons like this to attract the attention of the many young people who buy coffee at coffee stores. Option B is incorrect because the example is not about change, but about ads today. Option C is incorrect because the generalization is about relating to the spokesperson, not identifying him or her.

EXERCISE 12

General and Specific

Read each pair of sentences. One is general and one is specific. Write **G** for general or **S** for specific on the line.

1. _____ a. Scientists are worried that average temperatures are rising because of global warming.

   _____ b. Last year was the warmest year on record.

2. _____ a. Public health studies show that frequent hand-washing reduces disease.

   _____ b. Washing your hands five times a day reduces the risk of getting a cold by 45 percent.

3. _____ a. A contributing factor to the crash of flight 441 was that the pilot had been flying for 15 hours without a rest.

   _____ b. A common cause of airplane accidents is pilot fatigue.

4. _____ a. Prices tend to rise and fall based on supply and demand.

   _____ b. The world price of rice doubled in one year because crops failed in several countries.

5. _____ a. Studies show that water pollution can come from unexpected sources.

   _____ b. Runoff of rainfall from golf courses can cause dangerous chemicals to enter the water supply.

Answers for Exercise 12 begin on page 457.

Giving Your Response

When you give your response to Item 4, you need to use signaling words and phrases to summarize and to indicate general and specific ideas. We have already examined signaling words and phrases for summarizing on page 413, so you may want to review that information now.

A number of signaling phrases indicate whether information is general or specific. Study the chart.

SIGNALING WORDS AND PHRASES FOR GENERAL AND SPECIFIC INFORMATION

GENERAL	SPECIFIC
• The reading is **about** . . . • The reading **gives an overview of** . . . • **In general**, the reading **is about** . . . • The reading **gives a general explanation** of . . . • **Overall**, the reading discusses . . . • **In most cases** . . .	• The professor **provides two examples of** . . . • **Specifically**, the professor . . . • According to the professor, **an example** of . . . is . . . • **The example** the professor gives **is about** . . . • **For example** . . . • **For instance** . . .

EXERCISE 13

Responding to Item 4

A. (AUDIO TRACK 91) For each item, you will read a short passage and listen to a lecture on the same topic. You will then be asked a question about them. After you hear and see the question, you will have 30 seconds to prepare your response and 60 seconds to record your response. The audio program will guide you through the items. Take notes as you read and listen. Then record your response to each question on your computer or mobile phone.

1. Read the passage about scientific discoveries from a life science class. You have 45 seconds to read the passage. Begin reading now.

We often give credit to individual scientists for major discoveries. However, the work of scientists builds progressively, with contributions from many scientists coming together to lead to a major discovery. In fact, major discoveries are rarely the work of just one or two scientists, but are almost always the result of the work of many scientists. The discovery of

DNA is one example. Two scientists, Watson and Crick, are credited for this discovery. But their work built on scientific discoveries previously made by other scientists. The scientist who gets credit for the discovery is often the scientist who announces the discovery first. But the work of the other scientists who came before may be just as important as the work of the scientist who gets the credit.

Notes:

_____

_____

_____

Now listen to part of a lecture on this topic in life science class.

Notes:

_____

_____

_____

What was Barbara McClintock's discovery? How does her work show that scientists build on one another's work?

| Preparation Time: 30 seconds |
| Response Time: 60 seconds |

Record your response on your computer or mobile device.

2. Read the passage about television programs from a communications class. You have 45 seconds to read the passage. Begin reading now.

Scripted and Reality TV

Television programs can be grouped into many categories. One main distinction is between scripted programs and reality programs. Scripted programs are the comedies, crime shows, and medical dramas so common on television. Scripted programs show imaginary characters in humorous or dramatic situations. These programs, in general, are filmed using scripts created by writers, which is why they are called scripted programs. Reality television, in contrast, shows real people in real situations. Camera crews follow the people as they work through dramatic or humorous real-life situations. These programs do not have scripts. Though reality television is not new, it has gained popularity with audiences lately. Television networks seem to like reality shows because they are popular and cheaper to produce than scripted programs.

Notes:

_____

_____

_____

Now listen to part of a lecture on this topic from a communications class.

Notes:

_____

_____

_____

What are the main differences between scripted and reality TV programs?
How are cooking contests a good example of reality TV?

| Preparation Time: 30 seconds |
| Response Time: 60 seconds |

 Record your response on your computer or mobile device.

B. Now listen to your responses and evaluate them. If possible, ask a teacher or
an English-speaking friend to help you. Or wait a day or two and evaluate
your work yourself. Use the Simplified Integrated Speaking Rubric on
pages 398–399. Then compare your responses to the high-scoring sample
responses in the Answers and Explanations. Write your scores on the lines.

1. _____   **2.** _____

Sample Responses for Exercise 13 begin on page 457.

> **TIP** **Raise your score on Items 3 and 4!**
>
> Follow these suggestions to raise your score on Items 3 and 4.
>
> * Take brief notes while you read and listen.
> * Use the preparation time to organize your ideas.
> * Give both general information from the reading and specific detail from the lecture.
> * Use signaling words and phrases to show the relationship among ideas. Focus on signaling words for summarizing and general/specific.

Integrated Listening and Speaking: Items 5 and 6

Items 5 and 6 integrate listening with speaking. First you listen to a conversation or a lecture. As on Items 3 and 4, you may take notes as you listen. Then you give a response to a question that relates to the listening. Item 5 will focus on a campus-related topic. You will hear a conversation between two students, between a student and a professor, or between a student and a staff member about a campus-related problem and two possible solutions. You will summarize the information and give your opinion about which solution is preferable. Item 6 will focus on an academic topic. You will hear a short lecture on an academic topic and then summarize it briefly. You will have:

* 60 to 90 seconds to listen
* 20 seconds to prepare your response
* 60 seconds to respond

Item Format

Items 5 and 6 follow identical formats. You will first hear the narrator give a brief introduction and then the listening selection.

You will hear:

Narrator: Now listen to a conversation between two students.

A photo of the speakers will appear and you will hear the listening passage. Listen to and read the example. (On the actual TOEFL iBT, you will hear, but not see, the listening selection.)

Male Student: Oh, my goodness! Remember when I applied to the Summer Research Institute? Well, they just accepted my application.

Female Student: That's great, Jason. That lab is really well known. That means you can spend the whole summer in Canada studying cell reproduction.

Male Student: But here's the problem: I didn't think I would get accepted, so I took a job working in Professor Bell's lab. Now I have to turn down one. What should I do?

Female Student: Well, what do you think you should do?

Male Student: Well, I really like Professor Bell, and all the other students who work in his lab like working there. And he only takes a few undergraduate students each year, so it's a big honor. Maybe I should turn down the Summer Research Institute.

Female Student: Are you sure that you want to do that? I think you should go to the institute. Even fewer undergraduate students get accepted there. It's a really big honor for you and the university. I'm sure that the professor will want you to go. You should talk to him.

Male Student: I don't know. What if he can't find another student to take my place?

Female Student: I think that there are plenty of other students who can work in Professor Bell's lab. Why don't you ask his advice?

Male Student: But what if he gets upset with me?

When the listening passage is completed, the photograph goes away and is replaced with the question screen.

You will see:

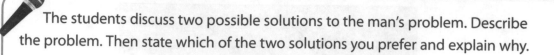

The students discuss two possible solutions to the man's problem. Describe the problem. Then state which of the two solutions you prefer and explain why.

> Preparation time: 20 seconds
> Response time: 60 seconds

You will hear:

Narrator: The students discuss two possible solutions to the man's problem. Describe the problem. Then state which of the two solutions you prefer and explain why. Begin speaking after the beep.

Use the 20 seconds before the beep to prepare your response. Use the timer to keep track of the time.

After 20 seconds have passed, you will hear a beep. The question will stay on the screen and a new timer will appear. You will have 60 seconds to record your response.

The students discuss two possible solutions to the man's problem. Describe the problem. Then state which of the two solutions you prefer and explain why.

> Response time: 60 seconds

After 60 seconds of response time have passed, the recorder will turn off, and the test will advance to the next item.

Item 5: Integrated Listening and Speaking: Campus-Related Topics

For Item 5, the listening passage will be a conversation between two students, between a student and a professor, or between a student and a university staff member. They will be talking about a problem one of them is experiencing and two possible solutions to the problem.

Item 5 assesses your ability to summarize the problem and the two possible solutions in the conversation, give your opinion about which solution is better and provide some justification for your opinion.

Evaluating Integrated-Speaking Responses

Items 5 and 6 are evaluated using the same rubric as Items 3 and 4. Use the Simplified Integrated Speaking Rubric on pages 398–399 as a checklist to prepare for the test and to evaluate your own speaking. Listen to and read the following response to the sample item. What score do you think it received? Use the rubric.

The . . . man got . . . uh . . . expected to a famous summer research institute in Canada and also took a job in Professor Bell's lab for summer. Now he is confused about what to do. He can go to institute or work in Bell's lab. In my opinion, it is better for him to go to the institute. First, working at the institute is a much bigger honor than working in the lab. If he talks to the professor, the professor will probably agree that going to the institute is an honor for the university too. In addition, Professor Bell can find another student from the university to work in his lab. He will meet new friends and teachers at the institute. And another student will have opportunity to work in Bell's lab. So everyone will benefit.

If you said that this response scored a 4, you are correct. The response received this score because it:

✔ Summarizes the problem and possible solutions. The candidate chose one of the solutions and provided two good reasons for that option.

✔ Has accurate pronunciation, and the few mispronunciations (such as *expected* instead of *accepted*) do not interfere with comprehension

✔ Uses grammar and vocabulary accurately. A number of different tenses are used automatically.

✔ Uses signaling words such as *and*, *now*, *in my opinion*, and *so* to show relationships among ideas

Responding to Item 5

To respond to Item 5 successfully, you need to summarize the problem and possible solutions, express your opinion about which solution is better, and justify it. A good response will include:

- A summary of the problem
- A summary of the possible solutions
- Your opinion about which possible solution is better
- Reasons you believe that solution is preferable

Listen to and read this high-scoring response again and see how the candidate included the parts of a good response.

	The . . . man got . . . uh . . . expected to a famous summer research institute in Canada and also took a job in Professor Bell's lab for summer. Now he is confused about what to do. → **Summary of the problem**
Summary of possible solutions	He can go to institute or work in Bell's lab. In my opinion, it is better for him to go to the institute. → **Your opinion about which possible solution is better**
	First, working at the institute is a much bigger honor than working in the lab. If he talks to the professor, the professor will probably agree that going to the institute is an honor for the university too. In addition, Professor Bell can find another student from the university to work in his lab. He will meet new friends and teachers at the institute. And another student will have opportunity to work in Bell's lab. So everyone will benefit. → **Reasons the solution is preferable**

Preparing Your Response to Item 5

To give an effective response to Item 5, you need to gather information from the listening selection. In your response, you will need to summarize the problem and possible solutions the speakers discuss. Then you need to add reasons (from the listening and of your own) to support your choice of possible solutions.

Use the note-taking skills you developed for Items 3 and 4 to take notes as you listen. At the top of your notes write the problem. Below that, write the two speakers and their ideas. As you listen, try to choose which possible solution you want to talk about in your response, and circle it. Then as you continue to listen, you can write in your notes the reasons that support that solution.

<u>Problem: Work in lab or go to summer institute</u>
Man—lab
—like prof Bell
—other students like lab
—big honor
—Bell upset if go institute
Woman—institute
—bigger honor
—Bell agree big honor
—talk to prof

> **TIP** **Choose the possible solution carefully!**
>
> Item 5 asks for an opinion, but the solution you choose does not need to reflect your own opinion. Choose the solution that you can best support with reasons drawn from the listening passage and your own experience. If you only hear or understand one of the solution options, you will have to use that one in your response. Do not go off topic by offering your own idea or solution, because that could result in a lower score. Choose one of the solutions in the conversation and defend it in your response.

After you finish listening and taking notes, you will see the question screen and have 20 seconds to organize the ideas you gathered from the listening passage. Here is the question again, for reference:

> The students discuss two possible solutions to the man's problem. Describe the problem. Then state which of the two solutions you prefer and explain why.

If you have not done so already, you should choose the possible solution and circle it now. Then make sure you have enough reasons to support your opinion. If necessary, add one or two ideas to your notes.

Problem: Work in lab or go to (summer institute)
Man—lab
—like prof Bell
—other students like lab
—big honor
—Bell upset if go institute
Woman—institute
—bigger honor
—Bell agree big honor
—talk to the prof
—another student work in lab

Last, organize your notes. Because you only have 20 seconds to organize your information, you do not have time to write a new outline. If your ideas are already in order, you do not need to do anything more. If any ideas need to be in a different order, number them as quickly as you can.

Problem: Work in lab or go to (summer institute) 1
Man—lab
—like prof Bell
—other students like lab
—big honor
—Bell upset if go institute
Woman—institute
—bigger honor 2
—Bell agree big honor 4
—talk to the prof 3
—another student work in lab 5

Giving Your Response

 Listen to and read the sample response again.

The . . . man got . . . uh . . . expected to a famous summer research institute in Canada and also took a job in Professor Bell's lab for summer. Now he is confused about what to do. He can go to institute or work in Bell's lab. In my opinion, it is better for him to go to the institute. First, working at the institute is a much bigger honor than working in the lab. If he talks to the professor, the professor will probably agree that going to the institute is an honor for the university too. In addition, Professor Bell can find another student from the university to work in his lab. He will meet new friends and teachers at the institute. And another student will have opportunity to work in Bell's lab. So everyone will benefit.

When you give your response, you first summarize the problem and the possible solutions. If necessary, review summarizing on pages 412–413. Then state your opinion. Use the language for stating opinions on page 380. The sample answer uses the phrase "In my opinion" to introduce the speaker's opinion.

After that, give reasons to back up your opinion. Use the language for stating reasons on page 381. The sample response uses signaling words and phrases such as *First*, *In addition*, and *And* to introduce reasons and show the relationships among them.

Follow your outline as you speak. If new ideas occur to you as you are speaking, add them. For example, as the candidate gave his response, he added this idea: He will meet new friends and teachers at the institute.

If time remains, add a brief concluding sentence. In the example, the candidate added, "So everyone will benefit." This final sentence shows that the candidate's opinion is the preferable option because it is the most beneficial to everyone. The candidate used the signaling word *so* to show a cause-and-effect relationship between the student going to the institute and everyone benefiting.

___

EXERCISE 14

Responding to Item 5

A. For each item, you will listen to a conversation. You will then be asked a question about it. After you hear and see the question, you will have 20 seconds to prepare your response and 60 seconds to record your response. The audio program will guide you through the items. Take notes as you listen. Then record your response on your computer or mobile phone. If your device does not have a *record* function, ask a friend with strong English skills to listen to your response.

1.  Listen to the conversation. Then answer the question.

Notes:

_____

_____

_____

The students discuss two possible solutions to the woman's problem. Describe the problem. Then state which of the solutions they think will work. Do you agree? Why?

 Record your response on your computer or mobile device.

2. Listen to the conversation. Then answer the question.

Notes:

_____

_____

_____

The student and the academic advisor discuss two solutions to the man's problem. Briefly summarize the problem. Then state which of the two solutions from the conversation you would recommend. Explain the reasons for your recommendation.

 Record your response on your computer or mobile device.

B. Now listen to your responses and evaluate them. If possible, ask a teacher or an English-speaking friend to help you. Or wait a day or two and evaluate yourself. Use the Simplified Integrated Speaking Rubric on pages 398–399. Write your scores on the lines.

1. _____   2. _____

Sample Responses for Exercise 14 begin on page 458.

Item 6: Integrated Listening and Speaking: Academic-Related Topics

The format of Item 6 is identical to that of Item 5, but with academic content, rather than a campus-related situation. For Item 6, the listening passage will be an excerpt from a lecture. Your task is to summarize key parts of the lecture.

Topics for Item 6 will be drawn from various academic subjects, but no special knowledge or background is required to respond successfully.

Item 6: Integrated Listening and Speaking Academic Topic

Listen to and read the sample TOEFL iBT Speaking section Item 6. You will hear:

Narrator: Now listen to part of a talk in a linguistics class.

A photo of the speaker will appear and you will hear the listening selection.

 Listen to and read the example. (On the actual TOEFL iBT, you will only hear the selection.)

Female Professor: Over the years, linguists have offered two basic theories to explain how people acquire language. One theory states that language is innate to human beings. Other linguists believe that languages are learned.

Scientists who believe that language is innate support their position with several kinds of evidence. First, all human beings seem to acquire language. Moreover, they tend to start producing language at about the same time and follow a similar pattern. First, children begin to utter sounds. All children, regardless of where they are from, tend to produce the "m" sound first. Then children produce one-word sentences and two-word sentences. Then, regardless of what language they speak, they jump to multiword sentences. In addition, children tend to make the same sorts of errors. And even when corrected by parents or teachers, the children tend to make the same error until they are ready to move to the correct grammar. Brain research also supports this position. Studies of the brain show, for example, that in most people, vocabulary is stored in the same general area of the brain. Other parts of the brain support other language functions in most people.

Linguists who believe that language is learned point to other evidence to support their position. They point to the great differences among languages. How can language be innate when languages are as different as Chinese, Spanish, and Arabic? The diversity among languages, to them, shows that languages are learned. In addition, if children are not exposed to a language, they will not learn it. The linguists say that this proves that language is not built in but learned from exposure.

When the listening passage is completed, the photograph will go away and be replaced with the question screen.

You will see:

> Using points and examples from the talk, explain the different ways scientists think humans acquire language.
>
> **Preparation Time: 20 seconds**
> **Response Time: 60 seconds**

You will hear:

Narrator: Using points and examples from the talk, explain the different ways scientists think humans acquire language. Begin speaking after the beep.

Use the 20 seconds before the beep to prepare your response. Use the timer to keep track of the time.

After 20 seconds have passed, you will hear a beep. The question will stay on the screen and a new timer will appear. You will have 60 seconds to record your response.

> Using points and examples from the talk, explain the different ways scientists think humans acquire language.
>
> **Response Time: 60 seconds**

After 60 seconds of response time have passed, the recorder will turn off, and the test will advance to the next section.

Responding to Item 6

An effective response to Item 6 includes this information:

- A one-sentence statement about the topic of the lecture
- A brief summary of each main point and the supporting detail

Listen to and read this high-scoring response.

The lecture is about two different theories about learning languages. According to one theory, language is innate. According to the lecture, language is innate because all people learn language following the same pattern. Also, the brain seems to be set up for learning language. Vocabulary and grammar are stored in the same part of everyone's brain. People who believe that language is learned point out that languages are very different. They feel that if language is innate, there would not be so many different languages. Also, children some are not taught a language. So they will not learn one. So language learning is not automatic.

Statement of the lecture topic

Main point 1

Supporting detail for main point 1

Main point 2

Supporting detail for main point 2

This response includes all of the parts of a high-scoring response. The first sentence restates the main topic of the reading: two theories of language learning. The second sentence states the first theory: language is innate. The following sentences provide supporting details. Then sentence 6 sums up the second theory: language is learned. Then two following sentences give supporting details. The response has fluid delivery, and the few pronunciation problems do not interfere with comprehension. The vocabulary and grammar are quite good. The candidate uses some fairly advanced grammar automatically. The few errors are minor and do not interfere with comprehension.

Preparing Your Response to Item 6

As on Item 5, you should take brief notes as you listen. Use the note-taking skills you developed for Items 3, 4, and 5. At the top of your notes write the topic of the lecture. Then use a simple outline style to write down brief notes on each main idea and the details that support them. As before, use symbols and abbreviations to help you take notes.

To respond to Item 6 successfully, you need to summarize main ideas and supporting details. Review these skills on pages 412–413, if necessary.

EXERCISE 15

Responding to Item 6

A. For each item, you will listen to a part of a lecture. You will then be asked a question about it. After you hear and see the question, you will have 20 seconds to prepare your response and 60 seconds to record your response. The audio program will guide you through the items. Take notes as you listen. Then record your response on your computer or mobile phone.

1. [AUDIO TRACK 99] Listen to the lecture. Then answer the question.

Notes:

_____

_____

_____

Using the example of employees in a refreshment stand, explain the operation of the law of diminishing returns.

 Record your response on your computer or mobile device.

2. Listen to the lecture. Then answer the question.

Notes:

_____

_____

_____

Using examples provided by the professor, explain the reasons fiction authors use secondary characters.

 Record your response on your computer or mobile device.

B. Now listen to your responses and evaluate them. If possible, ask a teacher or an English-speaking friend to help you. Or wait a day or two and evaluate yourself. Use the Simplified Integrated Speaking Rubric on pages 398–399. Then compare your responses to the high-scoring sample responses in the Answers and Explanations. Write your scores on the lines.

1. _____   **2.** _____

Sample Responses for Exercise 15 begin on page 459.

TOEFL iBT Practice Speaking Section

Directions: To simulate actual TOEFL iBT conditions, follow these instructions:

- For items that integrate listening, listen to each conversation or lecture only once.
- For items that integrate reading, use your watch or timer to keep track of the time. After reading time is up, do not refer back to the reading as you answer.
- As you read, listen, and plan your response, you may take notes to use when giving your response.
- Use your computer's or mobile device's *record* function to record and play back your responses. If your device does not have this function, ask a friend with strong English skills to listen to your responses. You or your friend can evaluate your responses using the simplified scoring rubrics in this book.

 This icon appears each time you need to listen to an audio track.

When this icon appears, record your response on your computer or mobile device. If your device does not have a *record* function, ask a friend with strong English skills to listen to your response.

Now begin the TOEFL iBT Practice Speaking section.

1. 🎧 AUDIO TRACK 100 You will now speak about a familiar topic. Prepare your response in 15 seconds. Then allow 45 seconds to record your response.

🎤 Describe an important event in your life and explain why it was important. Include specific examples and details in your description.

Preparation Time: 15 seconds
Response Time: 45 seconds

2. 🎧 AUDIO TRACK 101 You will now give your opinion about a familiar topic. Prepare your response in 15 seconds. Then allow 45 seconds to record your response.

🎤 Some people think it is necessary to earn an advanced degree. Other people are happy to have just a bachelor's degree. Which do you think is better and why?

Preparation Time: 15 seconds
Response Time: 45 seconds

3. 🎧 AUDIO TRACK 102 You will now read a short passage on a campus-related topic and listen to a conversation on the same subject. Then you will hear a question. Prepare your response in 30 seconds. Then allow 60 seconds to record your response.

Reading Time: 45 seconds

Announcement from the President

The university will become a smoke-free environment effective September 1. There will be no smoking in any building on campus or in the open air. There will be designated areas at four campus gates for smokers to extinguish their smoking materials before entering college grounds.

Residents of dormitories within the nonsmoking area will be permitted to smoke in their own rooms but not in public areas.

Fines for violations will be posted online. The University Health Service will offer all students, faculty, and staff free classes and support on quitting smoking.

Now listen to two students discussing the announcement.

The man expresses his opinion of the announcement by the president. State his opinion and explain the reasons he gives for holding that opinion.

Preparation Time: 30 seconds
Response Time: 60 seconds

4. You will now read a short passage on an academic topic and listen to a talk on the same subject. Then you will hear a question. Prepare your response in 30 seconds. Then allow 60 seconds to record your response.

Reading Time: 50 seconds

Public Services

Some services would probably not be provided if the state did not do so, for example, a police force. These are called public services. Everyone consumes them, and no one can be excluded from their consumption. They are nonrival because one person's use does not diminish the amount left for another. A public service is also not rejectable. For example, a child aged six to fifteen has to attend school in most countries. The child cannot reject the services of teacher training, funding, and facilities provided by the state whether the child attends a public or private school.

Now listen to a lecture on this topic in an economics class.

🎤 Explain how streetlights are examples of public services, but cars are examples of private goods. Use information from the reading and lecture.

Preparation Time: 30 seconds
Response Time: 60 seconds

5.  You will now listen to part of a conversation about a campus-related situation. Then you will hear a question. Prepare your response in 20 seconds. Then allow 60 seconds to record your answer.

The speakers discuss possible solutions to the man's problem. Describe the problem and the solutions. Then explain what you think the man should do and why.

Preparation time: 20 seconds
Response time: 60 seconds

6. You will now listen to part of a talk on an academic topic. Then you will hear a question. Prepare your response in 20 seconds. Then allow 60 seconds to record your answer.

Using information from the lecture, give reasons why people of the Incan Empire may have abandoned the city of Machu Picchu.

Preparation Time: 20 seconds
Response Time: 60 seconds

Sample Responses for the TOEFL iBT Practice Speaking section begin on page 461.

TOEFL iBT Speaking
Personalized Study Planner

Use your answers to the TOEFL iBT Practice Speaking section and this chart to focus your preparation for the actual TOEFL iBT. Follow these steps:

1. Review your responses by comparing them to the sample responses in the Answers and Explanations, which begin on page 461.

2. Evaluate your responses with the rubrics. If possible, ask a teacher or an English-speaking friend to help you. Or wait a day or two and evaluate yourself. Use the TOEFL iBT Simplified Independent Speaking Rubric on pages 370–371 to score your responses to Items 1 and 2. Use the TOEFL iBT Simplified Integrated Speaking Rubric on pages 398–399 to score your responses to Items 4 to 6. Write your scores on the lines.

   1. _____   3. _____   5. _____

   2. _____   4. _____   6. _____

3. What skills do you do well? Which skills do you want to improve? Review your rubrics for Items 1 and 2 together, and check the boxes of the skills you do well. Then, for the skills you want to improve, review the pages listed in the second column.

ITEMS 1 AND 2: INDEPENDENT SPEAKING

SKILL	STUDY PAGES
☐ Answers the question	376–377
☐ Has a main idea	377
☐ Has supporting details	377–378
☐ Follows a logical order	378–379
☐ Uses signaling words and phrases to show relationships among ideas	380–382

4. Now review your completed rubrics for Items 3 to 6 together, and check the boxes of the skills you do well. Then review the pages covering the skills you want to improve.

ITEMS 3 TO 6: INTEGRATED SPEAKING

SKILL	STUDY PAGES
☐ Answers the question	411, 420–421
☐ Has a main idea and supporting details	404–408, 422–423
☐ Integrates information from reading and/or listening passages	412–416
☐ Follows a logical order	434–435
☐ Uses order and signaling words and phrases to show relationships among ideas	413–416, 424

TOEFL IBT SPEAKING
Answers, Explanations, Audio Scripts, and Sample Responses

Exercise 1: Understanding the Independent Speaking Scoring Rubric (Page 374)

ANSWERS AND EXPLANATIONS

1. This response most likely scored a 4. The response:
   - ✔ Answers the question completely
   - ✔ Uses plenty of detail
   - ✔ Models fluid and understandable speech
   - ✔ Has only minor pronunciation errors
   - ✔ Has some grammar problems, but good vocabulary. Errors are minor and do not affect understanding.
   - ✔ Uses signaling words and phrases, such as *because*, *more importantly*, and *after*, to show relationships among ideas

2. This response most likely scored a 1. This response:
   - ✔ Does not use the time available
   - ✔ Has limited content and partially repeats the question to fill the time
   - ✔ Has unnatural and choppy pronunciation, stress, and intonation
   - ✔ Shows weak control of grammar
   - ✔ Has many incomplete sentences
   - ✔ Includes some detail, but detail is very limited

3. This response probably scored a 3. The response:
   - ✔ Answers the question, but not completely
   - ✔ Is clear, but has enough pronunciation problems that listeners may have to pay attention to understand
   - ✔ Has obvious grammar errors, but they do not interfere with understanding
   - ✔ Presents ideas one after another, without making the relationship among the ideas clear, because signaling words and phrases are not used consistently

4. This response probably scored a 1. This response
   - ✔ Answers the question, but with limited detail and development
   - ✔ Is understandable overall, but the meaning is not completely clear at all times
   - ✔ Has limited vocabulary and grammar
   - ✔ Uses very few signaling words
   - ✔ Answers the question, but with limited ideas

Exercise 2: Preparing Notes (Page 379)

SAMPLE RESPONSES

There are many ways to answer these questions. Compare your notes with these notes for high-scoring responses.

1.
   First college biology teach, Prof. Chen
   —gd teacher
   —took 5 classes
   Reasons
   —made sci interesting
   —helped students
   —fun, jokes

2.
   Pizza
   —cheese
   —vegetables
   Reasons
   —delicious
   —convenient
   —healthy

3.
   Skateboarding
   —board with wheels
   —street, sidewalk
   Reasons
   —exercise
   —transportation, go anywhere
   —skateboard park

4.
Venice
—beaut
—Italy
—canals
Reasons
—lots of hist
—beaut bldgs
—romantic

5.
apart in NYC
—small
—high floor, gd view
Reasons
—exciting
—culture

Exercise 3: Responding to Opinion Items (Page 382)

SAMPLE RESPONSES

A. There are many ways to respond to these questions. Listen to Track 108 to hear high-scoring responses. These responses scored high because they:

✓ Answer the questions completely
✓ Use plenty of detail
✓ Model fluid and understandable speech
✓ Have only minor pronunciation errors
✓ Have some grammar problems, but good vocabulary. Errors are minor and do not affect understanding.
✓ Use signaling words and phrases, such as *also*, *too*, and *for example*, to show relationships among ideas

B. Calculate your average score. Then look at the rubric again. What do you need to improve before you take the TOEFL iBT?

Exercise 4: Preparing Notes (Page 387)

SAMPLE RESPONSES

There are many ways to prepare notes for these speaking questions. Compare your notes to these sample notes.

1.
Family more impt
Family always there for us
Love of family impt
Need be resp for fam, take care kids, elders

2.
Better change jobs freq
Get raise
Get diff exp
Meet new coworkers
Get away bad boss

3.
Watch movies at home
Cheaper
More convenient
Snacks cheaper
Can talk
Others not disturb us

4.
Read online
Can order online, get faster
Doesn't waste paper
Online books cheaper, never get lost

5.
Big city
More fun, excitement
More jbs
Museums, theaters, parks
Hv many friends

Exercise 5: Comparatives and Superlatives (Page 389)

ANSWERS

1. more important than
2. better than
3. more expensive than
4. the biggest
5. the best

6. more convenient than
7. the nicest
8. worse than
9. faster than
10. happier than

Exercise 6: Responding to Choice Items (Page 391)

SAMPLE RESPONSES

A. There are many ways to respond to these questions. Listen to Track 109 to hear high-scoring responses. These responses scored high because they:
   - ✔ Answer the questions completely
   - ✔ Use plenty of detail
   - ✔ Model fluid and understandable speech

- ✔ Have only minor pronunciation errors
- ✔ Have some grammar problems, but good vocabulary. Errors are minor and do not affect understanding.
- ✔ Use signaling words and phrases, such as *also*, *too*, and *for example*, to show relationships among ideas

B. Calculate your average score. Then look at the rubric again for your score level. What do you need to improve before you take the TOEFL iBT?

Exercise 7: Understanding the Integrated Speaking Scoring Rubric (Page 402)

TRACK 84 AUDIO SCRIPT

Narrator: In this exercise, you will use the rubric to evaluate four student responses to a TOEFL iBT item. You have forty-five seconds to read a short news article from a campus newspaper. Then you will hear two students discussing the article. After that, you will hear four responses. Listen to and evaluate the responses using the rubric.

   The university is making some changes to campus bus services. You will have forty-five seconds to read an article in the campus newspaper about the change. Begin reading now.

TRACK 85 AUDIO SCRIPT

Narrator: Now listen to two students talking about the same topic as the article.

Woman: Where's the bus? I'm late for work. The bus should have been here ten minutes ago.

Man: Don't you know? The bus schedule just changed. Now this bus operates every twenty minutes, not every ten minutes like before.

Woman: Seriously?

Man: Yes, the article from today's paper is right here on my phone. Take a look. Now buses are every twenty minutes, not every ten minutes like before.

Woman: I can't believe that they made the schedule worse. So now I am going to be late for work. I work in a lab, so I need to be on time.

Man: Well, they added a new route to and from South Tower. I live near there, so when I go home, I can take the bus there. It's a lot shorter than walking home from the Student Union.

Woman: The new bus doesn't help me at all. I never go near South Tower. But now I'm going to be late for work every day because of the new schedule.

Man: Look, here comes the bus. Right on time.

Narrator: The woman expresses her opinion about the changes to campus bus service described in the article. Briefly summarize the changes. Then state her opinion and explain the reasons she gives for holding that opinion.

   Next, you will hear four sample responses. Rate the responses using the scoring rubric. Write the score on the line.

ANSWERS AND EXPLANATIONS

1. This response scored a 2. The response received this score because it:
   ✔ Includes some relevant information, but the information is incomplete and inaccurate
   ✔ Has unclear pronunciation at times
   ✔ Shows limited control of grammar and vocabulary

2. This response scored a 3. The response received this score because it:
   ✔ Includes relevant information, but some details are incorrect, such as the frequency of the bus from the Student Union
   ✔ Has generally fluid speech, but contains some errors, pauses, and hesitations that require attention to understand
   ✔ Has some grammar and vocabulary errors, but those errors do not affect meaning

3. This response scored a 4. This response received this score because it:
   ✔ Fully answers the question
   ✔ Provides a detailed summary of the changes and the woman's opinion about them

   ✔ Follows a logical order and makes good use of signaling words (*so, because, she says she,* etc.) to indicate the relationship among the ideas
   ✔ Has fluent and sustained speech with only minor pronunciation problems
   ✔ Uses a variety of complex sentence patterns automatically
   ✔ Has only minor grammar errors that do not interfere with understanding

4. This response scored a 1. The response received this score because it:
   ✔ Has very limited content and repeats part of the question
   ✔ Has incomplete, repetitive information and includes an irrelevant detail about bus fare going up. The detail about the bus being late is unclear and does not agree with what the student said.
   ✔ Is choppy and fragmented

Exercise 8: Reading and Taking Notes (Page 406)

SAMPLE RESPONSES

There are many ways to take notes on these readings. Compare your notes to these sample notes.

1.
   Renov Mem Auditorium—January
   —old, historic
   —restore
   —new sound, lighting, seats
   Close Dec for 1 year

2.
   Guest Speakers,
   —Friday, 11:00
   —scholars, thinkers
   Sept 10: Charles White, filmmaker

3.
   New tech fee
   —pay for wireless net
   —high speed, all buildings
   —$15/mo

4.
   Writing Req
   —writing course all majors
   —focus: writing in that subject
   —improve employability

5.
   New Library Dir
   —Kathleen Walsh
   —was head digital
   —dev excel online resources
   —now dir

Listening and Taking Notes: Opinions (Page 409)

TRACK 87 AUDIO SCRIPT
See Track 79, page 394.

Exercise 9: Listening and Taking Notes (Page 410)

Narrator: Conversation number 1.

Woman: I found out why our class was moved from Memorial Auditorium. It's closed for renovation.

Man: Yes, I just saw the notice. Isn't it great? That place might be historic, but right now it is kind of depressing. It's so old and dark. The renovation will make it a lot better.

Woman: Maybe. I am a little worried that they will damage it. It's such an old, important place. Did you know that seven US presidents have spoken there?

Man: Well, I'm glad that they're replacing the seating. It's tough to sit in those seats for a whole class. Last term I had a two-hour lecture class in that room, and it was awful.

Woman: What about the paintings in that room? I wonder what will happen to them . . .

Man: I don't know, but it sounds like they will put them back in the auditorium when it's finished.

Woman: If they don't damage the paintings or the auditorium.

Narrator: Conversation number 2.

Man: I am so bored with life on campus. Nothing interesting happens.

Woman: Are you sure, Mack? Look at this notice about the new lecture series. Every Friday, a different speaker will be here.

Man: Well, I bet the speakers are no good.

Woman: Well, the first speaker is a filmmaker. And you're in the film department. So that would interest you, wouldn't it?

Man: Who's the filmmaker?

Woman: Charles White.

Man: Really? I've seen all of his films. It's really exciting that he's coming here to campus.

Woman: I didn't know you were that interested in him.

Man: Yes, he's one of my favorite filmmakers.

Woman: According to the notice, writers, poets, and scientists will be coming too.

Man: I guess that this school isn't so boring after all . . .

Narrator: Conversation number 3.

Man: Hey, Ann. Look at this. The university is installing a new high-speed wireless network. It's about time. My downloads keep getting slower and slower. The new network will be a lot faster than the one we have now.

Woman: Yes, but now we have another new fee to pay for it. Costs here keep going up and up.

Man: Fifteen dollars a semester isn't much to pay. Some people pay a lot more than that for their personal data plans every month. Plus, tuition is staying the same next year.

Woman: Well, I already have a great data plan on my phone. I don't need a high-speed network.

Man: Well, you can probably connect your computer and your phone to the new network and save some money. Plus, you will be able to access all the university computing services for free.

Woman: Maybe it's not such a bad deal after all. I will check into whether I can get a cheaper plan on my phone.

Narrator: Conversation number 4.

Woman: Look. A new requirement has been added to all majors. Now we all will have to take a writing course to graduate.

Man: Yes, I saw the notice. I think it's great. A lot of employers complain that graduates lack writing skills. If our university has this requirement, maybe it will help us get jobs when we graduate.

Woman: I see what you mean. I just thought of it from the point of view of more work.

Man: Not only that, but it will help us in our other courses. We have some writing in all of our courses, but the only writing class we take is English 101. Taking another writing class will make all those term papers and essay tests easier.

Woman: I see what you mean. I wonder who will teach the writing course in our program. I hope it's Dr. Williams. He helped me a lot with my term paper last semester.

Man: Yes, he would be a good choice.

Narrator: Conversation number 5.

Woman: Hi, Carlos. What are you up to? You look busy . . .

Man: Yes, I am headed up to the library to pick up a couple of books. I am so tired of going over there to get books.

Woman: Well, you are in luck. I just read that the library has a new director. Before, she was the director of digital collections. So maybe soon you won't have to go to the library any more.

Man: Well, I'm not so sure. If she did such a good job in her old job, then why do I have to go to the library now?

Woman: Come on, Carlos. You can get a lot of materials online right now. And if the material is a book, you can have it sent to your dorm room or campus mailbox.

Man: Really? I didn't know that. You mean that I don't have to go to the library right now?

Woman: No. You can use the library's online catalog to look up items and read them right on your

computer or mobile phone. Look, here's a journal
article I downloaded a few minutes ago, right on
my phone screen.

Man: I didn't know that.

Woman: I think that research will get easier and easier
with this new head librarian.

Man: You're probably right. I am going back to my
computer and have the books I need sent to me
right away. Thanks for letting me know.

SAMPLE RESPONSES

Many responses are possible. Compare your responses
to the ones here.

1.
Man: Likes renov
—aud old + dark now
—seats not comfy
Woman: worried
—damage audit
—damage paintings

2.
Man: campus boring
—nothing happens
—speakers not good
—likes Charles White
Woman:
—speaker series coming
—many good speakers

3.
Man—happy
—wants fast network
—$15 cheap
Woman—not happy
—exp
— has internet on phone
—costs keep↑

4.
Man—likes
—help get jobs
—make other cl easier
Woman
—more work

5.
Man: not excited
—has to go to library now
—new dir didn't do good job bef
Woman—excited
—digital library excl
—new dir make more digital

Exercise 10: Summarizing (Page 414)

SAMPLE RESPONSES

Many answers are possible. Compare your summaries
to these summaries.

1. According to the information, Memorial
Auditorium will be closed for repairs in January.
Memorial Auditorium is old and historic, and it
will be restored. It will get new lights and seating.

2. The article says that the university is starting a
new guest speaker series each Friday at 11:00.
Each Friday, a famous speaker will speak. The
first speaker is a filmmaker. The series will be in
Convocation Hall.

3. The notice says that university tuition will not go
up next year, but the university will have a new

technology fee. The fee will pay for a new wireless
network in all campus buildings. The fee is $15
per semester.

4. The article says that the university is starting a
new writing requirement for all students. Each
student will take a writing course as part of his
or her major. The course will focus on writing
needed for that major. The requirement will help
students get jobs after graduating.

5. The library has a new director. The new director
was in charge of digital collections before. She
helped the library build an excellent digital
collection. The new director will continue this
work and be in charge of all library services.

Exercise 11: Responding to Item 3 (Page 416)

SAMPLE RESPONSES

A. There are many ways to respond to these questions. Listen to Track 110 to hear high-scoring responses. These responses scored high because they:

- ✔ Fully answer the question
- ✔ Provide a detailed summary of the reading passage and the people's opinions about them

- ✔ Follow a logical order and makes good use of signaling words to indicate the relationship among the ideas
- ✔ Use a variety of complex sentence patterns automatically
- ✔ Have only minor grammar errors that do not interfere with understanding

B. Calculate your average score. Then look at the rubric again. What do you need to improve before you take the TOEFL iBT?

Exercise 12: General and Specific (Page 423)

ANSWERS

1. a. G
    b. S
2. a. G
    b. S
3. a. S
    b. G

4. a. G
    b. S
5. a. G
    b. S

Exercise 13: Responding to Item 4 (Page 424)

TRACK 91 AUDIO SCRIPT

Narrator: For each item, you will read a short passage and listen to a lecture on the same topic. You will then be asked a question about them. After you hear and see the question, you will have thirty seconds to prepare your response and sixty seconds to record your response. The audio program will guide you through the items. Take notes as you read and listen. Then record your response to each question on your computer or mobile phone.

Number 1. Read the passage about scientific discoveries from a life science class. You have forty-five seconds to read the passage. Begin reading now.

Narrator: Now listen to a lecture on this topic in a life science class. The professor is discussing genetics.

Professor: The work of Barbara McClintock is a good example of ways that scientists build upon the work of one another. She noticed that corn from related corn plants suddenly changed color. So she carefully counted the colors in ears of a special South American corn. She was able to show that genes will suddenly change and cause corn to change color.

This work verified the work of an earlier scientist, Thomas Hunt Morgan. Morgan noticed that the eyes of related fruit flies were all the same, but suddenly one with a different eye color appeared unexpectedly. McClintock's work explained Morgan's observation.

McClintock's work, in turn, laid a foundation for later discoveries, including the discovery of DNA by Watson and Crick. Though Watson and Crick received credit for the discovery of DNA, the insights provided by McClintock and Morgan helped them reach their conclusions. That's why McClintock received the Nobel Prize for medicine. But Watson and Crick got all the credit for the discovery of DNA.

Narrator: What was Barbara McClintock's discovery? How does her work show that scientists build on one another's work?

Narrator: Number 2. Read the passage about television programs from a communications class. You have forty-five seconds to read the passage. Begin reading now.

Narrator: Now listen to part of a discussion on this topic from a communications class.

Professor: How many of you watched *Cook-Off!* on TV last night? Wasn't it exciting when Stephan won first prize and got one hundred thousand dollars to open his new restaurant? Though this might seem like a silly or irrelevant show, reality shows are more and more popular with audiences these days. So what makes *Cook-Off!* a reality show?

Female Student: Well, the reading says that reality shows are cheap to produce, but Stephan just won a fortune.

Professor: Good observation. But to a TV network, that is not much money compared to the cost of a scripted program. Scripted programs need stars, writers, and a script. A cooking show like *Cook-Off!* just needs a few volunteers who are willing to accept low pay in return for a small payoff. Plus the network does not have to pay writers to create a script. Audiences seem to like *Cook-Off!* too. It was the highest-rated program on television last week and probably this week, too. What other traits does it share with reality programs?

Male Student: Well, it's just like all other reality shows. The cameras follow the contestants as they prepare a different meal each week. The people are placed in a dramatic situation each week. They have to prepare an original meal in a short amount of time. Last week, they had to cook at the beach. They had to buy or bring everything they needed.

Professor: That's right. The producers create a dramatic situation each week, as we watch the people cook. And then we watch as we find out who wins and loses each week.

Narrator: What are the main differences between scripted and reality TV programs? How are cooking contests a good example of reality TV?

SAMPLE RESPONSES

A. There are many ways to respond to these questions. Listen to Track 111 to hear high-scoring responses. These responses scored high because they:

- ✓ Fully answer the question
- ✓ Integrate information from the reading passages and the listening selections
- ✓ Follow a logical order and make good use of signaling words to indicate the relationships among the ideas
- ✓ Have fluent and sustained speech, with only minor pronunciation problems
- ✓ Use a variety of complex sentence patterns automatically
- ✓ Have only minor grammar errors that do not interfere with understanding

B. Calculate your average score. Then look at the rubric again. What do you need to improve before you take the TOEFL iBT?

Exercise 14: Responding to Item 5 (Page 435)

TRACK 96 AUDIO SCRIPT

Narrator: Number 1. You will now listen to a conversation. You will then be asked a question about it. After you hear the question, you will have twenty seconds to prepare your response and sixty seconds to speak.

Narrator: Listen to a conversation between two students.

Man: Hi, Francesca, you look kind of upset.

Woman: I am, Mark. Look! I just got another parking ticket. I am so sick of getting parking tickets.

Man: Really? Why don't you just pay the meter?

Woman: I always pay the meter when I park, but you have to pay the meter every hour. I have a lot of two-hour classes, and all the parking meters are only for an hour. I can't run out and pay the meter, so I get a ticket.

Man: I see. So that won't work. Well, why don't you take the bus to school?

Woman: Well, I live on the other side of town. There isn't a bus to campus.

Man: That's too bad. Oh, wait. I have an idea. My bus stops at the parking lot just north of downtown. Why don't you park there? You can buy a monthly pass for the lot. Then you can take the bus from there. And with your student ID, the bus is free.

Woman: That's a good idea, but isn't a parking pass expensive?

Man: The sign by the lot says it's fifty dollars a month to park there.

Woman: Wow! That's a lot less money than what I pay the parking meters on campus.

Narrator: The students discuss two possible solutions to the woman's problem. Describe the problem. Then state which of the solutions they think will work. Do you agree? Why?

Narrator: Number 2. You will now listen to a conversation. You will then be asked a question about it. After you hear the question, you will have twenty seconds to prepare your response and sixty seconds to speak.

Narrator: Listen to a conversation between a student and an academic advisor.

Female Advisor: So how can I help you, Anson?

Male Student: Well, I hate to admit it, but I am having trouble with my classes. They all have such heavy reading loads. I have to stay up all night just to get all the reading done. I never have time for fun. And I had to stop going to the gym, too.

Advisor: Staying up all night and not exercising are a bad combination. This is a common problem and not just for international students. I struggled to keep up with the reading when I was in college.

Student: Really? That makes me feel a little better. What did you do?

Advisor: Well . . . a couple of things. I took a class in speed reading from the Academic Support Center. That probably helped the most.

Student: Really? I never heard of that.

Advisor: The Academic Support Center is an office that helps students improve their studies.

Student: Won't that take more time? I mean I hardly have time now, and now you want to add a speed reading class?

Advisor: In the class, each student reads the assignments from their own classes.

Student: OK, I'll think about it.

Advisor: If you don't like that idea, why don't you talk to the professor? I went to the professor and explained the problem. I asked him to show me which parts of the assignments were the most important. It turned out that he really wanted us to focus on the examples. So I spent most of my time

studying those. That way, I did a lot better on the tests.

Student: I'm not sure I should disturb the professor . . .

Narrator: The student and the academic advisor discuss two solutions to the student's problem. Briefly summarize the problem. Then state which of the two solutions from the conversation you would recommend. Explain the reasons for your recommendation.

SAMPLE RESPONSES

A. There are many ways to respond to these questions. Listen to Track 112 to hear high-scoring responses. These responses scored high because they:
- ✔ Fully answer the question
- ✔ Provide a detailed summary of the problem and defend one of the possible solutions as preferable
- ✔ Follow a logical order and makes good use of signaling words to indicate the relationship among the ideas
- ✔ Have fluent and sustained speech, with only minor pronunciation problems
- ✔ Use a variety of complex sentence patterns automatically
- ✔ Have only minor grammar errors that do not interfere with understanding

B. Calculate your average score. Then look at the rubric again. What do you need to improve before you take the TOEFL iBT?

Exercise 15: Responding to Item 6 (Page 441)

TRACK 99 AUDIO SCRIPT

Narrator: Number 1. You will now listen to part of a longer lecture from an economics class. You will then be asked a question about it. After you hear the question, you will have twenty seconds to prepare your response and sixty seconds to speak.

Professor: The law of diminishing returns is one of the most fundamental economic principles. It's used primarily in the area of production theory, the theory of how goods and services are created. Various factors contribute to production, including material and labor. Material and labor can each include individual factors, such as each type of material used and workers with different skills.

The law of diminishing returns says that increasing any single individual factor without increasing the others will eventually result in lower returns, or production. Let's take the example of a small refreshment stand in a theater. The stand is very busy, and the single employee cannot take care of all the customers during the short time the stand is open before performances and during intermissions. So the theater manager hires a second worker to take care of more customers. As a result, sales go up. So the manager could hire a third worker. Sales might go up or might stay the same, because consumer demand for refreshments is stable. Adding additional workers beyond two or three might even make the stand's profitability go down, since demand is stable while labor costs are increasing. In addition, because the stand is small, the workers' efficiency might decrease as the increasing number of workers get in one another's way in the small space of the stand.

Narrator: Using the example of employees at a refreshment stand, explain the operation of the law of diminishing returns.

Narrator: Number 2. You will now listen to part of a longer lecture from a world literature class. You will then be asked a question about it. After you hear the question, you will have twenty seconds to prepare your response and sixty seconds to speak.

Professor: Today we begin our study of *Don Quijote*, one of the greatest Western novels. This novel, which has two parts, is considered to be one of the first modern novels, if not the first, in the West. Of course, distinctions such as this are highly subjective and not very important when we consider the overall value of these works.

This comic Spanish novel is about a foolish man who, after reading numerous stories about knights, decides to become a knight himself and sets off on a series of ridiculous adventures. A knight was a heroic figure from the Middle Ages, a gentleman warrior with a horse, armor, and weapons.

Even though the novel is called *Don Quijote*, the name the man adopts when he becomes a knight, a secondary character, Sancho Panza, is quickly introduced. This character is Don Quijote's constant companion, and he has many adventures of his own in the novel. So why, we ask, is a secondary character needed in a novel that is supposedly about only one person? Yet we see similar secondary characters in novel after novel. There are several reasons. First, having a character like Sancho Panza permits the use of dialogue. Without dialogue, the novel would need a narrator. And in fact, throughout the novel Sancho Panza and Don Quijote have many rich and lively

conversations about philosophy and life. Second, a secondary character can provide commentary on the main character's actions. Don Quijote, for example, decides that some large windmills are giants and decides to attack them. Sancho Panza's role is to point out to readers how foolish Don Quijote is. Finally, a secondary character like Sancho Panza can be used to compare and contrast. Don Quijote and Sancho Panza are very different. For example, Don Quijote is tall and thin, if not gaunt, while his companion is short and fat. Putting the two side by side accentuates and clarifies Don Quijote's appearance and personality by comparison.

Narrator: Using examples provided by the professor, explain the reasons fiction authors use secondary characters.

SAMPLE RESPONSES

A. There are many ways to respond to these questions. Listen to Track 113 to hear high-scoring responses. These responses scored high because they:

- ✓ Fully answer the question
- ✓ Provide a detailed summary of relevant information in the lecture
- ✓ Follow a logical order and make good use of signaling words to indicate the relationships among the ideas
- ✓ Have fluent and sustained speech, with only minor pronunciation problems
- ✓ Use a variety of complex sentence patterns automatically
- ✓ Have only minor grammar errors that do not interfere with understanding

B. Calculate your average score. Then look at the rubric again. What do you need to improve before you take the TOEFL iBT?

TOEFL iBT Practice Speaking Section (Page 444)

There are many ways to respond to these questions. Compare your answers to the high-scoring responses in this section. Then read about why each answer received the score it did. Follow the instructions in the TOEFL iBT Personalized Study Planner on pages 449–450 to score your essays with the rubrics and find ways to improve your performance.

Item 1

TRACK 100 AUDIO SCRIPT

Narrator: Item 1. You will now speak about a familiar topic. Prepare your response in fifteen seconds. Then allow forty-five seconds to record your response.

Describe an important event in your life and explain why it was important. Include specific examples and details in your description.

SAMPLE RESPONSE

Listen to Track 114 to hear a sample response to Item 1. This response received a high score because it:

- ✔ Is on topic, answers the question, and is complete
- ✔ Has some pauses and hesitations, but flows fluently and is understandable overall
- ✔ Has some minor grammar problems, but these small errors do not interfere with understanding
- ✔ Includes details that make sense and are relevant
- ✔ Is in a logical order
- ✔ Uses a number of signaling words and expressions to show the relationships among the ideas

Item 2

TRACK 101 AUDIO SCRIPT

Narrator: Item 2. You will now give your opinion about a familiar topic. Prepare your response in fifteen seconds. Then allow forty-five seconds to record your response.

Some people think it is necessary to earn an advanced degree. Other people are happy to have just a bachelor's degree. Which do you think is better and why?

SAMPLE RESPONSE

Listen to Track 115 to hear a sample response to Speaking Item 2. This response received a high score because it:

- ✔ Is on topic, answers the question, and is complete
- ✔ Has some pauses and hesitations, but flows fluently and is understandable overall
- ✔ Has some minor grammar problems, but these small errors do not interfere with understanding
- ✔ Includes details that make sense and are relevant
- ✔ Is in a logical order
- ✔ Uses a number of signaling words and expressions to show the relationships among the ideas

Item 3

TRACK 102 AUDIO SCRIPT

Narrator: Item 3. You will now read a short passage on a campus-related topic and listen to a conversation on the same subject. Then you will hear a question. Prepare your response in thirty seconds. Then allow sixty seconds to record your response.

McKinley University is making its campus smoke-free. Read the announcement from the president about the plan. You will have forty-five seconds to read the announcement. Begin reading now.

TRACK 103 AUDIO SCRIPT

Narrator: Now listen to two students discussing the announcement.

Woman: You better enjoy that cigarette while you can, Mark.

Man: Yeah. If I hadn't paid my tuition fees for next year, I'd be looking for another school.

Woman: Really?

Man: Before we know it, the college'll be telling us to wear a uniform like schoolkids, or . . . or to stop chewing gum because it's too expensive to clean up.

Woman: Well . . .

Man: Isn't it my own choice to take five years off my own life by smoking?

Woman: But there are people around you who can't make that choice.

Man: You mean, passive smokers?

Woman: Uh-huh.

Man: I don't get what the big deal is. Smoking's already forbidden in classroom buildings and offices. And I really can't understand why we can't smoke outdoors. It's not like we're breaking any state or federal law.

Woman: I suppose the college is following the trend in other public places. In many cities, smoking is banned in cafés and restaurants. I've heard in some countries college campuses stopped it a few years ago.

Man: Personally, I think it's just another way for the college to raise revenue through fines. If they're anything like the parking fines, I'm gonna be broke as well as chewing a lot of gum.

Narrator: The man expresses his opinion of the announcement by the president. State his opinion and explain the reasons he gives for holding that opinion.

SAMPLE RESPONSE

Listen to Track 116 to hear a sample response to Speaking Item 3. This response received a high score because it:

- ✓ Fully answers the question
- ✓ Provides a detailed summary of the reading passage and the man's opinions about it
- ✓ Follows a logical order and makes good use of signaling words to indicate the relationships among the ideas
- ✓ Has fluent and sustained speech, with only minor pronunciation problems
- ✓ Uses a variety of complex sentence patterns automatically
- ✓ Has only minor grammar errors that do not interfere with understanding

Item 4

TRACK 104 AUDIO SCRIPT

Narrator: Item 4. You will now read a short passage on an academic topic and then listen to a talk on the same subject. Then you will hear a question. Prepare your response in thirty seconds. Then allow sixty seconds to record your response.

Now read the passage about public services and private goods. You have forty-five seconds to read the passage. Begin reading now.

TRACK 105 AUDIO SCRIPT

Narrator: Now listen to a lecture on this topic in an economics class.

Professor: So we've been talking about public services like police services, trash collection, or customs. Let's move on to their opposite, if you like: private goods.

Private goods are excludable, rival, and rejectable. I'll say that again. Private goods are excludable, rival, and rejectable.

Take the example of a chair. Maybe I go to a furniture store and buy a nice comfy armchair. Once I've bought it, I can pretty much do what I like with it. I can take it home and sit in it, or I can chop it up and use it for firewood. I can let other people sit in it, but if my house is burgled, and my chair's taken, this becomes theft. Therefore, private goods are *excludable*; I can exclude others from their use or possession.

They're also *rival* in the sense that once I've bought my chair, there's one fewer left for others. If my chair were on sale, and the only item, then there'd be none left. This doesn't matter so much in the case of an armchair, but it could if the item were a famous painting or a unique piece of jewelry. The amount of rivalry, or competition, there is for any object will affect its market value.

Private goods are also *rejectable*. If I don't like the color, or the material the armchair's covered in, I don't have to buy it.

Narrator: Explain how streetlights are examples of public services, but cars are examples of private goods. Use information from the reading and the lecture.

SAMPLE RESPONSE

Listen to Track 117 to hear a sample response to Speaking Item 4. This response received a high score because it:

- ✓ Fully answers the question
- ✓ Integrates information from the reading passage and the listening selection
- ✓ Follows a logical order and makes good use of signaling words to indicate the relationships among the ideas

- ✔ Has fluent and sustained speech, with only minor pronunciation problems
- ✔ Uses a variety of complex sentence patterns automatically
- ✔ Has only minor grammar errors that do not interfere with understanding

Item 5

TRACK 106 AUDIO SCRIPT

Narrator: Item 5. You will now listen to part of a conversation about a campus-related situation. Then you will hear a question. Prepare your response in twenty seconds. Then allow sixty seconds to record your answer.

Now listen to a conversation between two students.

Woman: Hello, Adam, how are you?

Man: A bit down, actually, Ella. D'you have some time to chat?

Woman: Sure. No problem.

Man: You know, I took a year's leave from college and went to work for my uncle. I needed to save up some money, and . . . and I guess I wasn't sure elementary education was the right major.

Woman: Uh-huh.

Man: I've been back six months now, and I'm one hundred percent sure it isn't. The only thing that interests me is the math part of our program. I'd probably make a decent high-school math teacher, but if I change to the high-school program, I'll have to go to school another year, which I can't afford. Frankly, I'm about to quit college altogether and go back to work for my uncle.

Woman: Oh dear. That might be an overreaction. There are several ways to view your situation. If you really believe high-school math is for you, then borrow some money and join the program. Or, complete your elementary education degree, even though you don't much like it, and do something completely different in grad school. You might not think so, but plenty of employers value education graduates. There's lots of training in the workplace these days that's done by people just like you. Whatever you decide, completing your degree is a must; otherwise, your prospects really are really limited.

Man: Thanks, Ella. I'll think about you've said.

Narrator: The speakers discuss possible solutions to the man's problem. Describe the problem and the solutions. Then explain what you think the man should do and why.

SAMPLE RESPONSE

Listen to Track 118 to hear a sample response to Speaking Item 5. This response received a high score because it:

- ✔ Fully answers the question
- ✔ Provides a detailed summary of the problem and defends one of the possible solutions as preferable
- ✔ Follows a logical order and makes good use of signaling words to indicate the relationships among the ideas
- ✔ Has fluent and sustained speech, with only minor pronunciation problems
- ✔ Uses a variety of complex sentence patterns automatically
- ✔ Has only minor grammar errors that do not interfere with understanding

Item 6

TRACK 107 AUDIO SCRIPT

Narrator: Item 6. You will now listen to part of a talk on an academic topic. Then you will hear a question. Prepare your response in twenty seconds. Then allow sixty seconds to record your answer.

Now listen to part of a lecture in an archaeology class.

Professor: High in the mountains of Peru, a ruined city bears testimony to the great civilization of the Incas.

Most archaeologists agree Machu Picchu was built around 1450 A.D. as a country retreat for an Incan emperor. It may also have been a religious center. One hundred and forty stone structures remain: temples, palaces, communal buildings, houses, and parks. Machu Picchu was well supplied with water, and its land could feed four times its population. Stone trails connected it to the outside world. Despite its grandeur, the city was abandoned around 1570. But why?

Perhaps the Spanish captured it. They'd invaded in 1532. But that's not the case. The Spanish were virtually unaware of the *existence* of Machu Picchu, resulting in its excellent preservation.

Perhaps disease ravaged the city. In 1520, Spanish settlers landed at Panama to the north. From this fleet came fatal new diseases like smallpox. Around two-thirds of the Incan population perished *before* the arrival of Spanish soldiers. But disease wasn't the only factor.

More likely, the Incan Empire was too weak to preserve Machu Picchu. By 1550, it had endured disease, invasion, and civil war. Besides, jungle grows fast. Within a year, Machu Picchu and its trails would've been reclaimed by jungle, concealing the city and its few remaining inhabitants until 1911.

Narrator: Using information from the lecture, give reasons why people of the Incan Empire may have abandoned the city of Machu Picchu.

SAMPLE RESPONSE

Listen to Track 119 to hear a sample response to Speaking Item 6. This response received a high score because it

- ✔ Fully answers the question
- ✔ Provides a detailed summary of relevant information in the lecture
- ✔ Follows a logical order and makes good use of signaling words to indicate the relationships among the ideas
- ✔ Has fluent and sustained speech, with only minor pronunciation problems
- ✔ Uses a variety of complex sentence patterns automatically
- ✔ Has only minor grammar errors that do not interfere with understanding

EVALUATION

There are many ways to answer these items. If you do not have a recording device, ask a friend to listen and evaluate your responses. If you have a recording device, ask a teacher or an English-speaking friend to listen to your responses and evaluate them. Or wait a day or two and evaluate them yourself. For Items 1 and 2, use the Independent Speaking Rubric on pages 370–371. For Items 3 to 6, use the Integrated Speaking Rubric on pages 398–399.

Chapter at a Glance

In this chapter, you will learn:

Writing Items . . . . 2 item types

Writing Topics . . . . . . Common general-interest and academic topics

Skills . . . . Techniques to help you write each kind of essay

Tips . . . . Hints to help you find the correct answers and avoid common mistakes

The TOEFL iBT Writing section assesses your ability to write the kinds of academic prose students in North American colleges and universities commonly have to write. The Writing section lasts for 60 minutes and consists of two items:

- **Integrated writing**, in which you write a 150- to 225-word essay in 20 minutes that integrates information from a written passage (about 230 to 300 words, 3 minutes) and a lecture (about 200 to 300 words, 2 minutes) on the same academic subject. Topics include subjects drawn from arts and humanities, sciences, social sciences, business, and management.
- **Independent writing**, in which you write an essay of about 300 words in 30 minutes on a general-interest topic in response to a question. Topics include entertainment, education, travel, friends and family, transportation, and technology.

AT A GLANCE

TOEFL iBT Writing Section

Time Limit   60 minutes total

Content   Integrated Reading, Listening, and Writing: Academic topic
Independent Writing: Your opinion on a general-interest topic

Items   2

ITEM TYPES   **Integrated Reading, Listening, and Writing**
• Read a 230- to 300-word passage (3 minutes)
• Listen to a 200- to 300-word lecture (2 minutes)
• Write a 150- to 225-word essay (20 minutes)

Independent Writing
• Write a 300-word essay (30 minutes)

For the integrated writing item, you will wear a special headset during the actual TOEFL iBT, just as in the Listening and Speaking sections of the test. You will read a short passage on an academic topic on your computer screen and hear a short academic lecture on the same topic on your headset. For both integrated and independent items, you will be able to take and use notes to prepare and write your essays. You will keyboard both essays on your computer. Your notes will be collected at the test center, but they will not be used or considered when your writing is evaluated.

At the beginning of the Writing section, you will see a photograph of a test taker wearing the special headset used during the test. Instructions will tell you to put on the headset. You will be able to make sure it works and to check and adjust the playback volume. Use the writing toolbar to control and adjust the volume before and during the test.

> **TIP** **Arrange your work area before you begin the actual TOEFL iBT!**
>
> After you check your headset's playback and recording volume at the test center, you should arrange your work area for the Writing section. You will use your computer's keyboard during this section; therefore, arrange the keyboard, mouse, and notepaper so you can use them with comfort and ease. Keep in mind whether you are right-handed or left-handed. You can take and use notes during any part of the Writing section, so arrange your notepaper to make it easy to use.

After you take the TOEFL iBT, your essays will be sent to trained raters who will score your work using special scoring guides called rubrics. The rubrics, which are different for the integrated and independent tasks, focus on these aspects of your writing ability:

- **Response to the task:** The essay addresses the topic and question.
- **Content:** Integrated item: the essay selects and integrates key important ideas and details from the reading and listening. Independent item: the essay supports a main idea with examples and detail.
- **Organization and development:** The essay uses appropriate examples, explanations, and details. The essay follows an appropriate organizational pattern, is unified, and flows.
- **Language use:** The essay uses vocabulary and grammar effectively and correctly, including variety in sentence patterns and appropriate vocabulary. The essay uses signaling words and phrases to show relationships among ideas.

Because the total time to prepare and write your essays is only 20 or 30 minutes, you will probably want to practice with the disk that accompanies this book. Practice writing until you can write complete essays within the time limits. This book will give you plenty of opportunities to build your writing skills and practice writing essays within the time limit.

Integrated Reading, Listening, and Writing: Item 1

Item 1 integrates reading and listening with writing. First, you read written material on your computer screen. Next, you use your headset to listen to a lecture on the same topic. You may take notes as you read and listen. Then you answer a question that relates to both the reading and the listening and requires you to integrate information from both. You can refer back to the reading passage as you write your essay. You will have:

- 3 minutes to read and take notes on a 230- to 300-word reading passage
- 2 minutes to listen to and take notes on a 200- to 300-word listening passage on the same topic
- 20 minutes to plan and write a 150- to 225-word essay in response to a question

Integrated Writing Item Format

Understanding TOEFL iBT item formats and directions before you take the actual test can help you work more quickly on the day of the test because you will not have to spend time or energy reading and understanding the directions. Item 1 follows this format.

You will first see the Item 1 directions on your computer screen:

> For Item 1, you will have 3 minutes to read a passage about an academic topic. Then the passage will disappear from your screen and you will hear a talk or lecture on the same topic. You may take notes while you read and listen.

Since you already are familiar with these directions from studying with this book, don't spend a lot of time reading them. Begin working right away. The reading passage will then appear on your screen, along with a timer that counts down 3 minutes of reading time.

Reading Time: 3 minutes

Milk chocolate, a solid, sweet confection made of cocoa extracts with added sugar, condensed or dry milk, and other ingredients, is a good illustration of the challenges of new product development. While milk chocolate may be a common, ordinary product today, its history is a story of technological innovation and competition on a multinational scale.

Candy makers had long desired to make a solid, sweet chocolate. Up until the nineteenth century, solid chocolate was only available in dark unsweetened or semisweet forms. The chief technological issue in making solid milk chocolate was removing the water from the milk. Chocolate has a high content of fat, and previous attempts to create milk chocolate were foiled by the water in milk, because water and fat will not mix. Therefore, chocolate makers began working to find ways to remove the water from milk. At this point, two major competitors emerged. In Switzerland, a candy maker named David Peter, later joined by business partner Henri Nestlé, began developing a process to remove water from milk. At about the same time, in the United States, Milton Hershey began to develop a different process. The challenge that they faced was that as water was extracted from milk, the milk tended to develop a bad taste from fermentation. Peter's solution was to extract the water in a vacuum, which prevented the milk from turning sour. However, Peter's process required a longer research and development process. To reach the market quickly, Hershey developed another process. That process, still a trade secret, used a special method to break down some of the fats in milk. The fats produced butyric acid, which tended to stop the fermentation but produced an odd sour taste. Hershey was thus able to beat Peter and Nestlé to market, ensuring the dominance of his company in the market.

When reading time is up, the reading text disappears and is replaced with a photograph of a professor speaking to a class. The narrator introduces the listening passage.

You will see:

You will hear:

Narrator: Now listen to part of a lecture on the topic you just read about.

Professor: Ummm . . . Good morning class. Today we are continuing our study of factors that result in a product's success. While speed to market is a key factor in capturing and retaining market share, there are other factors that can contribute to one competitor's dominance in the market. Let's take the example of milk chocolate. It's clear, first of all, that Peter's process resulted in a better-tasting bar of milk chocolate than Hershey's process. H-H-However, (*stammering*) customers accepted Hershey's competing product despite the inferior taste. I am sure that all of you have tasted both kinds and have noticed the difference. All factors being equal, it would seem logical that consumers would prefer the superior taste of Peter's chocolate after tasting it. After all, both products have been in the market nearly the same amount of time.

So what's the difference? Well, . . . there are at least two factors that we should consider. First, price. Hershey's process was much cheaper than Peter's. Peter's process took longer in the factory, consumed more energy, and milk had to be much fresher than in Hershey's process. As a result, Hershey could produce and sell his product at a lower price than Peter. Soooo (*short pause*) price became a factor.

Second, economic nationalism also played a role. You see, Hershey was unwilling to pay a foreign company a fee to use its process, and consumers wanted to buy a product made in their own country.

These two factors, then, contributed to the acceptance of Hershey's product even when both were side by side in the market. And consumers not only accepted the odd taste of Hershey's chocolate, they began to expect it. That's why today, some candy companies add butyric acid to their products just to duplicate the flavor customers are accustomed to. So we can conclude that consumer behavior is not always logical and that many factors will play into which product consumers will buy.

When the listening passage is completed, the photograph will disappear and the reading passage will reappear on your screen along with instructions and the question you will answer in your essay.

You have 20 minutes to plan and write your response. Your response will be judged on the quality of your writing and on how well you present the points in the lecture and their relationship to the reading passage. An effective response will typically be 150 to 225 words. | Instructions

Summarize the points made in the lecture you just heard, explaining how they cast doubt on the points made in the reading passage. | Question

Response Time: 20 minutes

The timer will start and count down 20 minutes for you to plan and write your essay. After 20 minutes, you will be told that time is up, and your essay will be saved. Then the test will advance to Item 2.

Natural Language

TOEFL iBT listening selections present natural language used in North American higher educational settings. The features of everyday natural language include pauses, digressions, repetition, mispronunciations, and other errors typical of natural language. For more information on natural language, see page 252.

Integrated Writing Item Topics

The academic topics in the integrated writing item are similar to those that appear in other sections of the TOEFL iBT. To answer a TOEFL iBT integrated writing item, no specialized knowledge is required. All the information you need is contained in the reading passage and listening selection. The task, integrating information from the two sources, is accessible to all test takers, and you will receive ample preparation in this book. Here is a list of academic subjects that topics are drawn from.

Academic Subjects for Integrated Writing

- **Arts and humanities:** literature, art and art history, music and music history
- **Sciences:** life science, physical science, earth and space science, computer science, engineering
- **Social sciences:** geography, history, sociology, anthropology, psychology, economics
- **Business and management:** case studies

For a complete list, see Appendix B.

Integrated Writing Item Types

TOEFL iBT integrated writing items require you to integrate information from the reading and listening passages. Usually, the question will ask you to say how the information in the lecture **challenges or contradicts** the information in the reading. Sometimes, the question may ask you to say how the information in the lecture **strengthens or supports** the information in the passage. Each item type follows a specific pattern. Study the examples. Key words are **in bold**.

INTEGRATED WRITING ITEM TYPES

THE LECTURE CONTRADICTS THE READING	THE LECTURE SUPPORTS THE READING
• Summarize the points made in the lecture, making sure to explain how they **cast doubt on/oppose/challenge** the **claims/ arguments/theories/specific points** made in the reading passage.	• Summarize the points made in the lecture, making sure to explain how they **support/ strengthen** the **explanations/points** in the reading. • Summarize the points made in the lecture, making sure to explain how they **answer the problem** raised in the reading passage.

> **TIP** **Passages that contradict are common on the TOEFL, so study for those!**
>
> Most writing tasks on the TOEFL iBT are based on readings and lectures that contradict each other in some way. Passages that support one another are much less common. Therefore, spend most of your time studying how to write an essay on contradicting passages.

Evaluating Integrated Writing Responses

All TOEFL iBT Writing responses are evaluated by trained raters using a special scoring rubric. There are slightly different rubrics for integrated and independent writing items. Understanding the rubrics can help you prepare for the test. The following pages show a simplified version of the TOEFL iBT Integrated Writing Scoring Rubric that you can use to guide you in preparing for the test, to evaluate your own writing, and to find ways to improve your writing.

TOEFL IBT SIMPLIFIED INTEGRATED WRITING SCORING RUBRIC

SCORE	DESCRIPTION
5	A **Level 5** response: • Selects relevant and important information from the lecture and presents it in relation to similar information in the reading. Includes supporting detail and examples. • Is well organized and makes sense. Uses signaling words and phrases to connect information and show the relationships among ideas. • Includes occasional errors in vocabulary and grammar that do not result in inaccurate or confusing presentation of information or connections among ideas.
4	A **Level 4** response: • Generally selects relevant and important information from the lecture and presents it in relation to relevant and important information in the reading, but may have minor inaccuracies, vagueness, or omissions that cause minor confusion to readers. • Includes errors in vocabulary and grammar that are more frequent than in a Level 5 response, but cause only minor problems with clarity or connection of ideas.
3	A **Level 3** response contains some information from the listening and makes some connections to the reading, but it has one or more of these problems: • The response addresses the task, but some information may be inaccurate or incomplete. • Makes only general, vague, or unclear connections between points in the reading and the lecture. • The response omits one major point made in the lecture. • Some key points in the lecture or reading, or the connections between them, are unclear, incomplete, inaccurate, or general. • Vocabulary and grammar errors may be more frequent than in a Level 4 response and may cause confusion to readers.
2	A **Level 2** response has some relevant information from the lecture but has inaccuracies or omissions of important ideas from the lecture or makes inaccurate or incomplete connections with information from the reading. A response at this level shows one or more of the following: • Omits or inaccurately presents the relationship between the lecture and the reading. • Omits or inaccurately presents important points in the lecture. • Contains language errors or expressions that obscure meaning.
1	A **Level 1** response: • Provides little or no meaningful or relevant information from the lecture. • Has problems with vocabulary and grammar that make the essay difficult to understand.
0	A response at this level contains only ideas copied from the reading passage, does not address the topic, is not written in English, or is blank.

Here is a response to the example TOEFL iBT integrated writing item. Read it, and then try to figure out the score it received. Write your score on the line.

Sample Response 1

Score: _____

The lecture and the reading are on competition and innovation in making milk chocolate. Milk chocolate was impossible to make for a long time because of water in the milk. The fat and water in the chocolate and milk didn't mix. Two different processes were developed to make milk chocolate. In Swizterland, a man named Peter removed water from milk with special process. But it took a long time to developing the process. Hershey developed another process, but the chocolate had bad taste. But it's not clear whether the reason Hershey won was because of speed to market or other factors discussed by professor.

According to the reading, customers accepted Hershey's product even though it tasted bad, because it was first to market. People wanted milk chocolate, so they accept the bad taste.

The professor gives some other factors. First, Hershey's chocolate was cheaper than Peter's Peter needed fresh milk and an expensive process to remove the milk. Hershey didn't need very fresh milk, and his process was faster and cheaper than Peter's. So that's one reason that people buyed Hershey's chocolate.

The second factor that the professor mention is economic nationalism. People in Europe prefer products from there. And people in U.S. wanted products from their country.

Apparently, people accepted the bad taste because of price and nationalism and not speed to market. They didn't buy Peter's chocolate after they tasted it. So there are many reasons why consumers make decisions, and the reasons are not always obvious.

If you said that this response was rated a 5, you are correct. This response received this score because it:

✔ Addresses the question (how the lecture casts doubt on the reading). The reading focuses on one aspect, speed to market. In the lecture, the professor says that speed to market is not the only factor, and that other factors (price and economic nationalism) are important.

✔ Integrates information from both sources, is organized logically, and contains accurate, relevant information

✔ Uses signaling words and phrases to show the relationship among the ideas

✔ Has only minor errors in vocabulary and grammar that do not interfere with understanding

Here are some more sample responses to this example item. Read each one. Try to figure out the score each one received. Then read the score that each one received and the reason it received that score.

Sample Response 2

Score: _____

Reading and lecture is about competition for inventing milk chocolate process. There were too processes for making milk chocolate. The reading and the professor disagree about the reason customers choose one process.

The reading says that there were too process for making milk chocolate. One process used very fresh milk. This chocolate tasted very good, but it took a long time to invent the process, and was expensive. Other process was cheaper because the milk didn't need to be fresh, and it was faster. It was faster to invent. But the chocolate didn't taste very good because the process used acid.

The reading says that Hershey's process was popular because it was first to market. The professor disagree with this idea. He says that customers don't prefer Hershey's chocolate because it was first to market. They prefer it because of price and pride. They bought the chocolate because it was cheap and because it was from their country. Professor called this economic nationalism.

So, the two sources disagree. Consumer decisions are not always logic. Consumers consider many factors, like price, country, and first to market. These will cause them to buy a product even if taste bad.

If you said that this response was rated a 4, you are correct. This response received this score because it:

- ✔ Integrates key information from both sources, but the information is more vague than in the Level 5 response
- ✔ Flows well, is organized, is clear, and contains only relevant details
- ✔ Has more frequent vocabulary and grammar errors than the Level 5 response, but the errors do not interfere with understanding

Sample Response 3

Score: _____

The reading say that inventing milk chocolate was difficult. Two people tryed to invent it, and one succeeded because was first to market. The professor disagree, and think that a different reason is more important.

The reading say that Switzerland process different from US process. Peter and Hershey wanted to make milk chocolate. Peter process was expensive but chocolate very delicious. However, Peter taking long time to make process. Hershey think of a different process, it is cheaper, but the chocolate not so good like Peter's. Hershey put acid in chocolate to make it quickly, but taste bad. But people by Hershey chocolate because it first to market. They hungry for chocolate, not worry about taste so much.

Professor disagree with reading. He think people buy Hershey chocolate because that chocolate cheaper. Those customers worry about price, not taste.

So professor think that customers not logical. For some consumer, logical to by cheaper candy. For another customer, logical to buy very delicious candy. Maybe different customers, both have own logic.

If you said that this response was rated a 3, you are correct. The response received this score because it:

- ✔ Contains many of the key points of the reading and lecture but omits an important key point, economic nationalism
- ✔ Integrates information from both sources, but the information is more vague than in the Level 4 response
- ✔ Contains the writer's own opinion, which is not relevant to answering the question
- ✔ Is well organized and flows
- ✔ Has more frequent vocabulary and grammar errors than in the Level 4 response, and at times meaning is unclear

Sample Response 4

Score: _____

> The reading say that two kinds of milk chocolate, one taste good another taste bad. Reading say people buy bad chocolate because first to market, but professor disagree.
>
> Professor think that people buy bad chocolate because not logical. They want bad product because cheap. Customers should buy product from their country, not because cheap. People hate foreign companies, not buy their product.
>
> I think professor tells right idea. People make bad decisions, want bad chocolate because not logical.

If you said that this response was rated a 2, you are correct. The response received this score because it:

✔ Attempts to present information from both sources but restates ideas from the reading and listening incorrectly, makes unclear or incorrect connections between ideas, and omits key ideas

✔ Is choppy and disorganized and does not flow fluently

> **TIP** **Avoid offering your opinion on Item 1!**
>
> Integrated writing assesses your ability to synthesize information from two different sources. Avoid focusing on your personal opinion in your essay. Focus instead on comparing and contrasting information from the two sources.

Sample Response 5

Score: _____

> Professor and reading about chocolate. Some chocolate taste bad because acid. Other chocolate taste good. People like chocolate, not me. Can't eat chocolate because get fat. I am dancer, dancer can't eat chocolate, get fat, can't dance. Professor and reading not tink about me in their idea. Need new chocolate not make fat, taste good. Then more customer buy chocolate.

If you said that this response was rated a 1, you are correct. The response received this score because it:

✔ Does not address the topic

✔ Does not draw on key ideas from the reading and lecture but instead offers the writer's personal opinion, which is not relevant to the essay topic

✔ Has vocabulary and grammar errors that make ideas unclear and the essay hard to follow

---

EXERCISE 1

The Integrated Writing Scoring Rubric

In this exercise, you will use the Integrated Writing Rubric to evaluate four responses to this TOEFL iBT integrated writing item.

A. Read the passage in 3 minutes. Use the timer on your phone or computer to keep track of the time.

Reading Time: 3 minutes

A recent study sheds new light on a common human behavior—telling a lie. The study examined how well people can lie. Specifically, the study considered whether practicing telling a lie made people better at convincing others that they are telling the truth. The design of the study used volunteers who agreed to tell lies to other volunteers who were listeners. Some of the liars were required to practice telling lies before telling them to other volunteers. Other liars didn't get any practice.

The listeners had to evaluate whether the liars were telling the truth. The listeners rated each liar on a scale of how truthful they believed the liars to be. Analysis of the data showed that the liars who had practice telling lies were more convincing than liars who had no practice.

Experts questioned the value and ethical foundations of a study that examines how people can lie effectively. However, this is not the purpose of the study, the researchers clarified. They believe that the results of the study will be useful in understanding how people lie. They say that understanding how people practice lies can help them figure out better ways to tell when someone has told a lie. They believe that the results will help develop ways to train police officers and other workers who have to distinguish lies from the truth. They believe that the results will be helpful when large numbers of people need to be screened, which takes place in airport security lines, border crossings, and other locations where many people are questioned on a daily basis and it is not practical to use lie detectors or other kinds of technology.

B. Now listen to part of a lecture on the topic you just read about.

C. Read the question and the four responses. Evaluate the responses using the rubric on page 473. Write the score on the line.

 Summarize the points made in the lecture you just heard, explaining how they challenge the points made in the reading passage.

1. Score: _____

Professor not a nice guy, think students big liars. Reading is about study about lying. Turns out liars get good from practice lying. Practice make perfect, so more liars practice, more lie good. Professor thinks he can catch liar students who tell lies. He think students maybe learn practice lies, but he can catch them because he expert in lying. Maybe he lying expert, but not nice. Mean to students, not trusting them.

2. Score: _____

The reading is about a study about lying. The study considers practicing lying. The reading says that this study is valuable and helps the police and others find liars. But the professor disagrees.

The study ask people to tell lies to other people. Some people who tell lies practice first, but others do not. The listeners decide who is lying. The results show that liars who practice are better liars. The reading says that this is a good way to research and it helps us catch liars.

The professor disagree with some of these ideas. The professor think that the research methods teaches people to lie. It is not good to teach people to lie. So there are problems with study.

Also, study does not help us tell when people are lying. Police and others need to know how to catch a liar. Other studies will show that. This study does not help police or other catch liars. It only helps people learn to lie.

The reading and lecture ask questions about the lying study. Apparently, the study does not help us catch liars and teaches us to lie. The class will read other studies that will give better ideas.

3. Score: _____

The reading is about a study some psychologists made about lying. The professor questions some of those ideas, and thinks that the study is not so good.

Reading say that the study of liars shows that by practicing telling lies, liars can become good liars. In the study, some volunteers told lies to some listeners. The lies were better when the liars practiced their lies first. The listeners think the liars as telling truth when they practice a lot. The reading says that this insight can help police and others catch liars.

The professor disagree with the reading. The professor think that the study have a problem with ethics. Teaching people to lie is not good. The study needs to have valuable results to prove that it's OK to teach people to lie. But this study does not have valuable results. It only shows that people who practice lies won't get caught.

The professor also thinks that the study doesn't tell us how to figure out if someone is lying. Other things, like eyes and detail in the lies, can help police and others decide if someone is lying.

The professor contradict the reading in several way. The professor's points show a lot of problems with the research study in the reading.

4. Score: _____

The reading and lecture are about psychology and lying. The reading is about a study of lying. The study shows that liars can't get caught if they practice their lies. The writer thinks that the study is good because it will help police.

The lecture says that lying is very bad, so study is no good. The psychologists should not teach people to tell the lies. That is a bad example for everyone. So the study has big problems, no one should pay attention to this study.

Answers and Explanations for Exercise 1 begin on page 544.

> **TIP** **Use the scoring rubric to evaluate yourself!**
>
> The scoring rubric is a good way to evaluate your own writing as you work through this book, especially if you are using this book for self-study. If possible, set each essay aside for a day or two before you evaluate it, so that you can look at your writing with increased objectivity. When you are ready, evaluate your writing with the rubric and figure out your score. Then compare your essay to the corresponding sample essay in the Answers, Explanations, Audio Scripts, and Sample Responses section.

Responding to Item 1

An effective response to an integrated writing item does these things:

- Summarizes the key points of the lecture accurately
- Makes accurate connections to key points in the reading
- States and develops ways that points in the reading support or contradict points in the lecture
- Is organized effectively, stays on topic, and flows
- Uses grammar and vocabulary effectively and correctly to convey ideas clearly and accurately

---

TIP **Focus on key points in the lecture and their connections to the reading!**

The Integrated Writing Scoring Rubric emphasizes accurate presentation of key points in the listening, accurate connections to key ideas in the reading, clarity, and organization. Therefore, spend most of your time working on those aspects of your writing.

The Five-Paragraph Essay

A good way to write a clear, well-organized essay is the five-paragraph essay. A five-paragraph essay follows this pattern:

- The first paragraph (or **introduction**) introduces the topic, summarizes the main idea of the listening and the reading, and gives a general statement of whether the reading and listening support or contradict one another (a thesis statement). The first paragraph is organized from general to specific.
- Three body (or **development**) paragraphs each give a different main point about a specific way that the listening and the reading support or contradict one other. If there are only two main points, then use only two body paragraphs.
- A final paragraph (or **conclusion**) summarizes and restates the main idea of the essay and gives a final, general concluding statement. The final paragraph is organized from specific to general.

Read this high-scoring response again. Look at how it follows the organization of a five-paragraph essay.

> The lecture and the reading are on competition and innovation in making milk chocolate. Milk chocolate was impossible to make for a long time because of water in the milk. The fat and water in the chocolate and milk didn't mix. Two different processes were developed to make milk chocolate. In Swizterland, a man named Peter removed water from milk with special process. But it took a long time to developing the process. Hershey developed another process, but the chocolate had bad taste. But it's not clear whether the reason Hershey won was because of speed to market or other factors discussed by professor.

Introduction

According to the reading, customers accepted Hershey's product even though it tasted bad, because it was first to market. People wanted milk chocolate, so they accept the bad taste.

The professor gives some other factors. First, Hershey's chocolate was cheaper than Peter's Peter needed fresh milk and an expensive process to remove the milk. Hershey didn't need very fresh milk, and his process was faster and cheaper than Peter's. So that's one reason that people buyed Hershey's chocolate.

The second factor that the professor mention is economic nationalism. People in Europe prefer products from there. And people in U.S. wanted products from their country.

Apparently, people accepted the bad taste because of price and nationalism and not speed to market. They didn't buy Peter's chocolate after they tasted it. So there are many reasons why consumers make decisions, and the reasons are not always obvious.

Body paragraphs

Conclusion

Preparing Your Response to Item 1

Because you have only a short time to plan and write your essay, having an organized approach will help you work effectively. In general, following these four steps will help you prepare a good essay in a short amount of time:

- **Gather ideas:** Take notes as you listen and read, analyze the question, and check your notes.
- **Organize ideas:** Put your ideas in a logical order.
- **Write your essay:** Use your organized ideas to write an essay in sentences and paragraphs.
- **Revise your essay:** Check your essay for content (clear, relevant ideas), order (logical order and flow), and correct language use (grammar, spelling, capitalization, and punctuation).

Gathering Ideas

Because of the short time limit, you should begin gathering ideas as you read and listen. One good way to gather ideas is to take notes. Before the Writing section begins, make sure paper and pencils or pens are ready so you can begin taking notes as soon as the reading and lecture begin. First take notes on the reading. You need to take detailed notes to have enough information when it is time to write your essay. As you read, follow these suggestions:

1. Write "Reading" at the beginning of the reading notes. Then write the reading topic.
2. Write down the main points and supporting ideas as you read. Use a simple outline format to show the relationships among the ideas.
3. To help you write as much information as possible, use numbers, abbreviations, and symbols in your notes.

Look at the sample notes. Then answer the questions that follow. If necessary, review the reading passage on pages 468–469.

<u>Reading</u>
Candy makers wanted make milk choc
—Main prob: remove H_2O frm milk bec water + fat don't mix
2 major competitors
—Switzerland, Petter & Nestlé
—US, Hershey, diff process.
Prob: milk got bad taste
<u>Solution</u>
—P-use vacuum, milk not sour, but slow research
—H-fast research, break down fats, but acid makes choc taste bad
H first to market, dominated

1. What is the first important idea? Circle it.
2. What is the first supporting point? Underline it.
3. What do *P* and *H* stand for? _____
4. What is one number, symbol, or abbreviation? Circle it.

The first main idea is, "Candy makers wanted make milk choc." The first detail is "Main prob: remove H_2O frm milk bec water + fat don't mix." *P* stands for *Peter* and *H* for *Hershey*. One symbol in the notes is H_2O, which stands for "water."

Repeat the same note-taking steps with the listening. As you know, most integrated writing items ask how the information in the lecture conflicts with, opposes, challenges, or casts doubt on the information in the reading, or answers a problem posed in the reading. Therefore, as you listen, try to find ways that the two sources of information disagree or present opposing viewpoints. Look at the sample notes. The student marked the first contradictory piece of information with a **C**. Mark another piece of contradictory information the same way. If necessary, review the listening transcript on page 470.

<u>Listening</u>
Getting market share—choc
—speed to market—H
—better taste—P
Peo didn't buy P's choc even tho tasted better than H's
<u>Other factors</u>
—price—H's process cheaper C
—econ nat—people buy prods frm their country
Peo made decisions on econ nat + price, not taste: not always logical

What contradictory information did you mark with a **C**? Another piece of contradictory information is economic nationalism.

EXERCISE 2

Taking Notes

A. Read the TOEFL iBT passage in 3 minutes. Use the timer on your phone or computer to keep track of the time. Take notes in the space provided.

Reading Time: 3 minutes

Matter on Earth's surface exists in three states: solid, liquid, and gas. Each of these states of matter has distinct properties and characteristics. Matter in a solid state has a fixed shape and volume. When matter is in a solid state, the molecules are packed tightly together. The closeness of the molecules is what gives a solid its fixed shape. Matter in a liquid state has a fixed volume, but not a fixed shape. A liquid will take the shape of its container. When matter is in a liquid state, the molecules are close together but able to move freely. Matter in a gaseous state has neither fixed volume nor fixed shape. The molecules are not tightly packed together, and they have enough freedom of motion to move about and take the shape of a closed container.

Transition of phase happens when a substance changes from one state of matter to another because of a change in its temperature. Every kind of matter has a temperature at which it will change state. If heated enough, any solid will transition phase and become a liquid, and then a gas. The melting point and freezing point of a substance is the temperature at which it will change from a solid to a liquid or a liquid to a solid. The vaporization point and condensation point of a substance is the temperature at which the substance will change from a liquid to a gas or a gas to a liquid. Some substances will exist in all three states on Earth's surface. Water, for example, has a freezing/melting point of 0° C and a vaporization/condensation point of 100° C. Other substances with much higher or lower melting points or vaporization points may exist on Earth's surface in only one or two states. Carbon dioxide has a melting point of −78° C and a vaporization point of −57° C. Since these temperatures are well below normal temperatures on Earth's surface, carbon dioxide will generally be in gaseous form, except when people purposefully create solid or liquid forms.

_____

_____

_____

_____

_____

_____

_____

_____

_____

_____

_____

_____

B. Now listen to part of a TOEFL iBT lecture on the topic you just read about. Take notes in the space provided. Write **C** next to contradictory information.

_____

_____

_____

_____

_____

_____

_____

_____

_____

_____

_____

Explanation and Sample Response for Exercise 2 begin on page 545.

Understanding the Question

When you finish listening, the photograph on the screen will disappear and the question will appear. Pay attention to the time, because the 20 minutes you have to plan, write, and revise your essay begin as soon as the question appears. When the question appears, analyze it and check your notes to make sure you have the right information to answer the question.

Each TOEFL iBT integrated writing question asks for a specific answer. Look at the question again:

> Summarize the points made in the lecture you just heard, explaining how they cast doubt on the points made in the reading passage.

The phrase *cast doubt* shows that this question asks you to find out how the lecture contradicts the information in the reading passage. The word *points* shows that your answer should focus on the main ideas of the passage.

TIP **Check your notes as soon as you see the question!**

The readings and listenings in a TOEFL iBT integrated writing item are deliberately created to include very specific ways that the listening and reading passages support or contradict one another. So as soon as you see the question, figure out how the materials support or contradict one another. Then make sure that your notes include enough information to write a 150- to 225-word essay. A high-scoring essay will probably have three, or at least two, ways the reading and listening support or contradict one another.

Since the question tells you the kind of information the question references, such as explanations, specific points, claims, arguments, theories, or problems posed in the reading passage, make sure that your notes include the correct type of information, and add information from the listening and reading, if necessary. Look at the idea added to the notes about chocolate:

<u>Reading</u>
Candy makers wanted make milk choc
—Main prob: remove H_2O frm milk bec water + fat don't mix
—Up to then, milk choc only avail as drink $\rbrack$ New idea added
2 major competitors
—Switzerland, Peter & Nestlé
—US, Hershey, diff process.
Prob: milk got bad taste
Solution
—P—use vacuum, milk not sour, but slow research
—H—fast research, break down fats, but acid produced
    makes chocolate taste bad
H first to market, dominated
<u>Listening</u>
Getting market share—choc
—speed to market—H
—better taste—P
Peo didn't buy P's choc even tho tasted better than H's
Other factors
—price—H's process cheaper C
—econ nat—people buy prods frm their country C
Peo made decisions on econ nat + price, not taste: not always
    logical C

EXERCISE 3

Understanding the Question

Look at the question. Then review your notes for Exercise 2: Taking Notes.
Add one or two ideas to your notes to ensure that they are complete. Since
you can see the reading during the TOEFL iBT, you can refer to it as you check
your notes.

Summarize the points made in the lecture you just heard, explaining how they
cast doubt on the points made in the reading passage.

Explanation and Sample Response for Exercise 3 begin on page 545.

Organizing Ideas

Before you write, you should take a few minutes to organize your notes so that you can write an organized essay. The TOEFL iBT scoring rubric gives great importance to organization, so paying attention to it before you write can help you raise your score.

You will probably not have time to write a complete outline and a 150- to 225-word essay in 20 minutes. To work faster, organize your notes by numbering ideas, drawing circles, and writing lines. You should organize your ideas into the structure of a five-paragraph essay. Study the example:

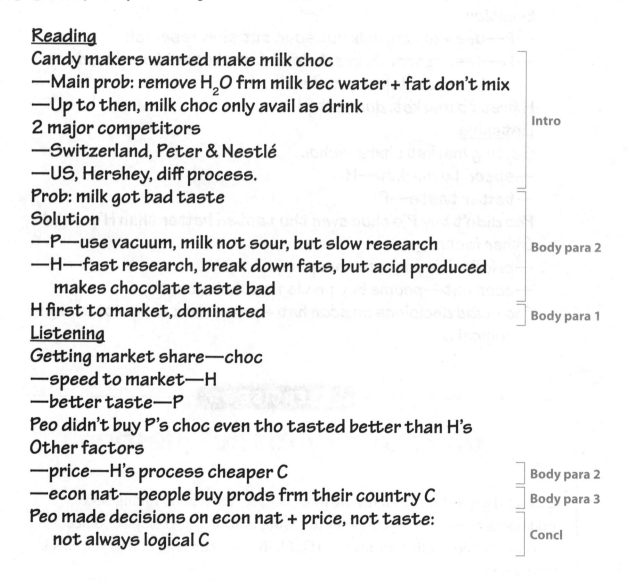

Reading

Candy makers wanted make milk choc

—Main prob: remove H_2O frm milk bec water + fat don't mix

—Up to then, milk choc only avail as drink

2 major competitors

—Switzerland, Peter & Nestlé

—US, Hershey, diff process.   Intro

Prob: milk got bad taste

Solution

—P—use vacuum, milk not sour, but slow research

—H—fast research, break down fats, but acid produced   Body para 2
  makes chocolate taste bad

H first to market, dominated   Body para 1

Listening

Getting market share—choc

—speed to market—H

—better taste—P

Peo didn't buy P's choc even tho tasted better than H's

Other factors

—price—H's process cheaper C   Body para 2

—econ nat—people buy prods frm their country C   Body para 3

Peo made decisions on econ nat + price, not taste: Concl
  not always logical C

Notice how the notes are organized into each part of the five-paragraph essay. The introduction begins with some general background on the goal, making solid milk chocolate, and on the two rival processes. Body paragraph 1 focuses on the idea developed in the reading: being first to market was critical to Hershey's success. Body paragraphs 2 and 3 introduce the contrasting information from the listening. Body paragraph 2 focuses on price as a factor. Body paragraph 3 focuses on economic nationalism. Finally, the conclusion draws on information from the listening to restate and sum up the writer's main idea: being first to market was not the key factor; price and economic nationalism played roles, too.

EXERCISE 4

Organizing Your Notes

Review the notes from Exercise 3: Understanding the Question. Organize them to write a five-paragraph essay using numbers, circles, and lines.

Sample Response for Exercise 4 begins on page 546.

Writing Your Essay

Once you have organized your ideas, you are ready to write. If you organized your ideas into the format of a five-paragraph essay, you can now take the information from your outline and use it to write sentences and paragraphs.

The **introductory paragraph** gives general background on the topic. This paragraph is organized from general to specific, and it ends with a thesis statement, which sums up the main idea of the essay. Look at the example. It begins with a general statement and provides some background on Peter's and Hershey's processes, and it ends with a thesis statement that sums up the disagreement between the reading and the lecture:

The lecture and the reading are on competition and innovation in making milk chocolate. Milk chocolate was impossible to make for a long time because of water in the milk. The fat and water in the chocolate and milk didn't mix. Two different processes were developed to make milk chocolate. In Swizterland, a man named Peter removed water from milk with special process. But it took a long time to developing the process. Hershey developed another process, but the chocolate had bad taste. But it's not clear whether the reason Hershey won was because of speed to market or other factors discussed by professor.

General introduction and background

Thesis statement

As you write your introduction, you will probably begin to summarize points in the reading and lecture. When you summarize, you restate an idea in new, simpler wording. For example, look at this statement in the reading:

- In Switzerland, a candy maker named David Peter, later joined by business partner Henri Nestlé, began developing a process to remove water from milk. Peter's solution was to extract the water in a vacuum, which prevented the milk from turning sour. However, Peter's process resulted in a longer research and development process.

The information is summarized in the essay in this way:

- In Swizterland, a man named Peter removed water from milk with special process. But it took a long time to developing the process.

Summaries are frequently introduced with signaling words to indicate a summary is coming. Look at the example:

- **The lecture and the reading are on** competition and innovation in making milk chocolate.

There are many ways to begin your summary. Study the chart.

SIGNALING WORDS AND PHRASES FOR STARTING A SUMMARY
The lecture and the reading **are on the topic of** . . .
The reading **covers** . . .
The lecture gives information on/about . . .
According to the professor/reading, . . .
The reading **addresses** . . .
The professor **states** . . .

The **first body paragraph** focuses on the reason identified by the professor: being first to market. The paragraph begins with a topic sentence, a sentence that sums up the main idea of the paragraph. Then there is one sentence of detail to support the topic sentence. The paragraph also uses another signaling phrase for summarizing another's words, "According to . . ." Look at the example:

> According to the reading, customers accepted Hershey's product even though it tasted bad, because it was first to market. — **Topic sentence**
> People wanted milk chocolate, so they accept the bad taste. — **Supporting sentence**

The **second body paragraph** focuses on price. Like the first body paragraph, it has a topic sentence that states the main idea of the paragraph. Then the following support sentences give detail to back up the topic sentence.

> The professor gives some other factors. First, Hershey's chocolate was cheaper than Peter's. Peter needed fresh milk and an expensive process to remove the milk. Hershey didn't need very fresh milk, and his process was faster and cheaper than Peter's. So that's one reason that people buyed Hershey's chocolate.

(Topic sentence / Supporting sentences)

The second body paragraph also introduces contrasting information. The sentence, "The professor gives some other factors," tells the reader that contrasting information is coming. The chart shows some other common ways to introduce contrasting information.

SIGNALING WORDS AND PHRASES FOR SHOWING CONTRAST
However, . . .
In contrast, . . .
On the other hand, . . .
While (Peter's process made delicious chocolate), (Hershey's process was less expensive).
Although (Peter's process required fresh milk), (Hershey's process didn't).

The **third body paragraph** focuses on economic nationalism. Like the other body paragraphs, it has a topic sentence that states the main idea of the paragraph. Then supporting sentences give additional detail.

> The second factor that the professor mention is economic
> nationalism. People in Europe prefer products from there.
> And people in U.S. wanted products from their country.

Topic sentence

Supporting sentences

In order to back up your ideas, you need to introduce reasons. In the third body paragraph, a second reason is introduced in this way.

- The second factor that the professor mention is economic nationalism.

The chart shows some common ways to introduce reasons and examples. Use these words and phrases to introduce reasons that support your opinion and show the relationships among the reasons.

SIGNALING WORDS AND PHRASES FOR INTRODUCING REASONS

PATTERN	SIGNALING WORDS AND PHRASES
Chronological order; order of importance	**First, Second**
Chronological order	**Next, Then**
Chronological order	**Before, After**
Order of importance	**More importantly**
Additional information	**In addition, and**
Example	**For example, For instance**
Contrast	**However, but**
Cause/effect	**So, Then, As a result, because**

The **concluding paragraph** sums up the ideas in the essay and restates them in a general way. This paragraph is always organized from specific to general, and it ends with a general restatement of the writer's conclusion. In this case, the writer sums up the three possible reasons proposed for Hershey's success and states which of them are true.

> Apparently, people accepted the bad taste because of
> price and nationalism and not speed to market. They didn't
> buy Peter's chocolate after they tasted it. So there are many
> reasons why consumers make decisions, and the reasons are
> not always obvious.

Summarizing statements

General concluding statement

EXERCISE 5

Writing Your Essay

Review the notes you organized in Exercise 4. Then take 10 minutes to write your response. Pay attention to the quality of your writing and on how well you present the points in the lecture and their relationship to the reading passage. An effective response will typically be 150 to 225 words.

Summarize the points made in the lecture you just heard, explaining how they cast doubt on the points made in the reading passage.

If possible, keyboard your essay on a computer. Use your watch or the timer on your phone to keep track of the time.

Sample Response for Exercise 5 begins on page 546.

Revising Your Essay

After you write, you should revise your writing. Look at how the TOEFL test taker revised the essay on chocolate. Corrections are in boldface so you can see them. (In the actual TOEFL iBT, you will correct your essay using the word processor, and your corrections will not display differently from the rest of the text.)

The lecture and the reading are on competition and innovation in making milk chocolate. Milk chocolate was impossible to make for a long time because of water in the milk. The fat and water in the chocolate and milk didn't mix. Two different processes were developed to make milk chocolate. In **Switzerland,** a man named Peter removed water from milk with special process. But it took a long time to developing the process. Hershey developed another process, but the chocolate **tasted bad**. But it's not clear whether the reason Hershey won was because of speed to market or other factors discussed by professor.

According to the reading, customers accepted Hershey's product even though it tasted bad, because it was first to market. People wanted milk chocolate, so they accept the bad taste. **Because Peter reached market later, people had already got used to the taste, and thought it was the way chocolate should taste.**

The professor gives some other factors. First, Hershey's chocolate was cheaper than Peter's. Peter needed fresh milk and an expensive process to remove the **water**. Hershey didn't need very fresh milk, and his process was faster and cheaper than Peter's. So that's one reason that people buyed Hershey's chocolate.

The second factor that the professor mention is economic nationalism. People in Europe prefer products from there. And people in U.S. wanted products from their country. **That's why Hershey's company became successful in the U.S., while Peter's products were more popular in Europe.**

Apparently, people accepted the bad taste because of price and nationalism and not speed to market. They didn't buy Peter's chocolate after they tasted it. So there are many reasons why consumers make decisions, and the reasons are not always obvious.

Content and organization are much more important in the TOEFL iBT Integrated Writing Scoring Rubric than grammar and vocabulary. Therefore, you should focus your revisions on content. So first you should revise for content. In particular, ensure that your answer clearly compares and contrasts the information in the reading and the information in the lecture, showing how they contradict or support one another. Then if there is time remaining, revise for things like grammar, vocabulary, and spelling.

In the example essay, the student added two sentences to ensure that support was complete and clear. After that, the student corrected a spelling error. (*Switzerland* was misspelled in the original.) And the student corrected a grammar error: "had bad taste" is an unnatural construction in English. The student rewrote it as "tasted bad." The student also added a missing period between sentences in body paragraph 2.

TIP **Focus your revision on content and organization!**

The most important criteria in the scoring rubric focus on content and organization, so focus on those when you revise:

1. Make sure you show how the lecture and reading contradict or support one another.
2. Make sure that your essay contains information from both the reading and the lecture.
3. Make sure all your ideas are relevant. Delete any irrelevant ideas.
4. Make sure your essay is in a logical order.
5. Make sure you use signaling words and phrases to show the interrelationship among ideas.

While vocabulary and grammar are important, they count less than content and organization. So check those last.

EXERCISE 6

Revising Your Essay

Take 5 minutes to review the essay you wrote for Exercise 5. First revise the content. Then revise the grammar and vocabulary.

Answers and Explanations for Exercise 6 begin on page 547.

> **TIP** **Plan your time!**
>
> To avoid running out of time, you should carefully plan your time for the remaining steps of the writing process. Here are some suggested times:
>
> - **Understanding the question:** 1–2 minutes
> - **Organizing your ideas:** 5 minutes
> - **Writing your essay:** 10 minutes
> - **Revising your essay:** 2–3 minutes

Evaluating Your Essay

After you write, you should evaluate your writing using the TOEFL iBT Simplified Integrated Writing Rubric on page 473. If possible, ask a teacher to evaluate your writing. If that is not possible, ask a friend with a high level of English to review your work. If no one can help you, then evaluate your writing yourself using the rubric. Put your writing aside for a day or two so that you can look at it freshly. Then use the rubric to determine your score.

After you figure out your score, use the sample high-scoring essay on page 474 and this special version of the rubric to help you figure out which areas to review before trying another practice essay.

1. Compare your essay to the sample high-scoring essay.
2. Check the box of each statement that describes your writing. The row with the most check marks will give you an indication of your score.
3. Look at the boxes you checked. How do you want to improve your writing? Study the page numbers in the second column.

Study the example for the sample essay on chocolate.

SCORE	DESCRIPTION	STUDY PAGES
5	A **Level 5** response:	
	☐ Selects relevant and important information from the lecture and presents it in relation to similar information in the reading. Includes supporting detail and examples.	483–487
	☐ Is well organized and makes sense. Uses signaling words and phrases to connect information and show the relationships among ideas.	490–494
	☐ Includes occasional errors in vocabulary and grammar that do not result in inaccurate or confusing presentation of information or connections among ideas.	495–497
4	A **Level 4** response:	
	☐ Generally selects relevant and important information from the lecture and presents it in relation to relevant and important information in the reading, but may have minor inaccuracies, vagueness, or omissions that cause minor confusion to readers.	483–487
	☐ Includes errors in vocabulary and grammar that are more frequent than in a Level 5 response, but cause only minor problems with clarity or connection of ideas.	495–497
3	A **Level 3** response	
	☐ Contains some information from the listening and makes some connections to the reading.	483–487
	A response at this level has one or more of these problems:	
	☐ The response addresses the task, but some information may be inaccurate or incomplete. Makes only general, vague, or unclear connections between points in the reading and the lecture.	483–487
	☐ The response omits one major point made in the lecture.	483–487
	☐ Some key points in the lecture or reading, or the connections between them, are unclear, incomplete, inaccurate, or general.	490–494
	☐ Vocabulary and grammar errors may be more frequent than in a Level 4 response and may cause confusion to readers.	495–497
2	A **Level 2** response:	
	☐ Has some relevant information from the lecture but has inaccuracies or omissions of important ideas from the lecture.	483–487
	☐ Makes inaccurate or incomplete connections with information from the reading.	483–487
	A response at this level shows one or more of the following:	
	☐ Omits or inaccurately presents the relationship between the lecture and the reading.	483–487
	☐ Omits or inaccurately presents important points in the lecture.	483–487
	☐ Contains language errors or expressions that obscure meaning.	495–497

SCORE	DESCRIPTION	STUDY PAGES
1	A **Level 1** response:	
	☐ Provides little or no meaningful or relevant information from the lecture.	483–487
	☐ Has problems with vocabulary and grammar that make the essay difficult to understand.	495–497
0	A response at this level contains only ideas copied from the reading passage, does not address the topic, is not written in English, or is blank.	

EXERCISE 7

Evaluating Your Essay

Have a teacher or an English-speaking friend review the essay you wrote on state of matter, or wait a day or two and review your essay yourself. Use the Integrated Writing Rubric on page 473 to evaluate your writing. Then use the sample high-scoring essay in the Answers and Explanations and a copy of the special Integrated Writing Rubric in Appendix F to figure out the areas you need to review before you tackle Exercise 8. Follow the instructions on page 497.

Evaluating Your Response for Exercise 7 begin on page 547.

EXERCISE 8

TOEFL iBT Integrated Writing Practice

A. Read the passage in 3 minutes. Use the timer on your phone or computer to keep track of the time. Take notes in the space provided.

Reading Time: 3 minutes

Manga and anime are two interrelated Japanese popular culture phenomena. Manga is a Japanese comic-book style, while anime is a uniquely Japanese style of animation. The word *manga* basically means "whimsical illustrations," and themes include love and romance, comedy, science fiction, fantasy, sports, and historical drama. Manga is a major presence in Japanese publishing and represents a multibillion-dollar industry. In recent years, industry sales have soared to nearly $4 billion (US). The word *anime* is a shortened form of the English word *animation*, and this genre also enjoys widespread popularity. Anime is a typically Japanese form of animation with themes similar to those of manga. Fans of anime can access it in theaters, on TV, on DVD, and online.

Manga originated in the eighteenth and nineteenth centuries as artists and writers began to use the medium of print to publish illustrated stories. Modern manga developed in the period following World War II. Critics believe that foreign comics brought to Japan after the war were a major influence on the genre and contributed to the boom in manga publishing in the 1940s and 1950s.

Anime, of course, is much younger than manga. The first anime appeared in about 1917 and was only a few minutes long. The first talking anime appeared in 1933, and the first full-length anime film appeared in 1945. As with manga, critics point out foreign influences, particularly in the employment of sophisticated, hand-drawn animation techniques pioneered by Walt Disney in the 1930s.

In the 1970s, manga boomed, and the two genres converged, as manga stories and characters were brought to life in anime. Interest also burgeoned as manga and anime drew fans throughout Asia and the rest of the world.

_____

_____

_____

_____

_____

B.  Now listen to part of a lecture on the topic you just read about. Take
notes in the space provided.

_____

_____

_____

_____

_____

_____

_____

_____

_____

_____

_____

_____

_____

_____

_____

C. Take 20 minutes to plan, write, and revise an essay of about 150 to 225 words. Use the timer on your phone to keep track of time. Pay attention to the quality of your writing and on how well you present the points in the lecture and their relationship to the reading passage.

Summarize the points made in the lecture you just heard, explaining how they contradict the points made in the reading passage.

_____

_____

_____

_____

_____

_____

_____

_____

_____

_____

_____

_____

_____

_____

_____

_____

Explanation and Sample Response for Exercise 8 begins on page 548.

Independent Writing: Item 2

The independent writing item asks you to write an essay about your opinion or personal preference on a topic of general interest. Typically, the independent-writing item provides a statement and asks whether you agree or disagree with it:

Do you agree or disagree with the following statement?

People today spend too much time working and studying and not enough time with their families.

Use specific reasons and examples to support your answer.

Independent Writing Item Format

When you begin Item 2, you will first see directions.

In this section, you will have 30 minutes to plan, write, and review your essay on the topic below. An effective essay will be about 300 words.

Then you will see the essay question, and the timer will start and count down 30 minutes for you to plan and write your essay. You will see:

Do you agree or disagree with the following statement?

People today spend too much time on computers, mobile phones, and other kinds of technology and not enough time with one another.

Use specific reasons and examples to support your answer.

Response Time: 30 minutes

After 30 minutes, you will be told that time is up, and your essay will be saved. At that point you will have completed all four sections of the TOEFL iBT.

Independent Writing Topics

Independent writing items ask you to give and support your opinion or personal preference on an important topic of general interest. The answer is based on your personal knowledge and experiences, and no special background or knowledge is required. Topics will never address controversial issues, such as politics. Here is a list of topics that questions might be drawn from.

General Interest Topics for Independent Writing

- **Career:** good jobs, career plans
- **Communication:** email, mobile phones
- **Culture and entertainment:** art, theater, museums, books, TV, films, music, concerts
- **Education:** schools, teachers, favorite subjects, difficult classes, study habits, class size
- **Famous people:** people you admire
- **Food:** favorite foods
- **Friends and friendship:** your best friend, the traits of a good friend
- **Future:** your future plans; what will the future be like?
- **Places:** favorite or preferred places to live, study, spend vacations, etc.
- **Sports:** favorites, exercise habits
- **Technology:** computers, mobile phones
- **Travel:** preferred means of transportation, favorite places to travel to

Evaluating Independent Writing Responses

As with responses to Item 1, responses to Item 2 are evaluated by trained raters using a special scoring rubric. The following pages show a simplified version of the TOEFL iBT Independent Writing Scoring Rubric that you can use as a checklist to prepare for the test and to evaluate your own writing.

TOEFL IBT SIMPLIFIED INDEPENDENT WRITING RUBRIC

SCORE	DESCRIPTION
5	A **Level 5** response largely: • Addresses the topic and the task. • Is organized and well developed; uses appropriate detail, examples, and explanations. • Stays on topic, flows, and makes sense. • Uses language well. Has variety in sentence patterns, vocabulary, and idioms and only minor errors of vocabulary and grammar.
4	A **Level 4** response largely: • Addresses the topic and the task, though some points are not well developed. • Is generally well organized and developed; uses appropriate detail, examples, and explanations. • Stays on topic, flows, and makes sense, but may have some problems with repetition, staying on topic, or unclear connection of ideas. • Uses language fairly well. Has variety in sentence patterns, vocabulary, and idioms and only minor errors of vocabulary and grammar, but may have some errors in grammar, word form, or natural language that do not cause unclarity.
3	A **Level 3** response is characterized by one or more of the following: • Addresses the topic and the task, but with somewhat developed detail, examples, and explanations. • Stays on topic, flows, and makes sense, but connection of ideas might be unclear at times. • May show inconsistent ability in grammar and vocabulary that may cause occasional unclarity. • Accurate but limited range of sentence structures and vocabulary.
2	A **Level 2** response will show one or more of the following weaknesses: • Limited development of topic and task. • Poor organization or connection of ideas. • Not enough or inappropriate detail, examples, and explanations. • Poor choice of words or word forms. • Many errors of sentence structure or vocabulary.
1	A **Level 1** response is seriously harmed by one or more of these weaknesses: • Disorganized or lacks development. • Has little or no detail, examples, and explanations, or does not respond to the task. • Serious errors in sentence structure or vocabulary.
0	A response at this level contains only ideas copied from the topic, does not address the topic, is not written in English, or is blank.

Here is a response to the example TOEFL iBT independent writing item. Read it and then try to figure out the score it received. Write your score on the line.

Sample Response 1

Score: _____

> These days, many people say that people spend too much time on computers and mobile phones, and not enough time with other people. But the people who complain don't really understand computers and phones, because these tools help us be with other people.
>
> I use my computer to stay in touch with my family and friends. All of the activities on my phone help me stay in contact with other people. I use email, chat, and social networking websites. I can communicate with friends, relatives, and others. I love to send email to my grandmother. She lives far from me in the country, and she loves to get my email, too. I like to buy things with my computer, too.
>
> I also use my phone to communicate with other people. I can talk on my phone, and use it to send email, too. I really like my phone because I can text. I can send texts to all my friends. When I am going to be late getting home, I always text my mom. Then she doesn't worry.
>
> Finally, I use technology to have fun with friends. I love to play video games online. My mom told me I need to go out and play with my friends, but we play together online from our own homes. So I am not alone, but always with friends.
>
> People say that we don't spend time with family and friends because of phones and computers. But the people do not understand technology very well. With technology you are never alone.

If you said that this response was rated a 5, you are correct. This essay

✔ Addresses the topic, and it gives plenty of detail and examples to back up its main idea
✔ Flows, makes sense, and stays on topic
✔ Has lots of variety in sentence patterns and effective use of vocabulary

Here are more sample responses to this example item. Read each one. Try to figure out the score each one received. Then for each one, read the score and the reason for that score.

Sample Response 2

Score: _____

Mobile phones and computers are everywhere today. They make our lives easier, but make us lonely, too. I think people should spend less time with computers and more time with people.

I am a student right now. Before, I study in a class at school. But now I take online class. I feel really lonely in online class. I like to see my classmates, and it's fun to be in school with friends. I don't like my online class.

When I go to coffee shop, see a lot of people with phones. They are always alone, and they are always texting their friends. I am sure that they feel lonely, too, because they always look for friends online.

On weekend, I like to have fun with friends, go places, and enjoy. But now all my friends are busy, never have time for me, always working on computer.

In conclusion, people are lonely because of computers and phones. People need to stop using these things, spend time with people.

If you said that this response was rated a 4, you are correct. This essay received this score because it:

✔ Responds to the task and is organized and well developed, yet less well developed than a Level 5 essay
✔ Has some repetition
✔ Has minor errors in vocabulary and grammar that do not interfere with understanding

Sample Response 3

Score: _____

Many people complain about phones, computers, say they don't spend time with friends. I donot agree, phones and computers help us contact friends.

I like email a lot. I send maybe 15 or more email every day to friend. And not all in my town. Now I have alot of friends in alot towns, and I send them email.

I like phone alot, too. Phone good to talk to friend, have fun chatting and talking. I send text message with phone, two. Phone makes friendly easy.

Phone and email help me communicate friends, talk and share ideas. Like to text photos, use website to get information about friends.

If you said that this response was rated a 3, you are correct. This essay received this score because it:

✔ Addresses the topic, but has limited detail and support

✔ Stays on topic and flows, but the connections among ideas are not clear

✔ Has errors of vocabulary and grammar that make meaning unclear at times

Sample Response 4

Score: _____

Question ask about phones and computers, say they cause problems. People dont spend time together, always with computer. I am agree with this idea. I hate my computer. Don't like to work on it all the time, want to be with my friends. And friends always busy on computer, no time for others friends. So think that phone is not so good, not help me be with friends, just alone allways.

If you said that this response was rated a 2, you are correct. This essay received this score because it:

✔ Has very limited information to support the main idea, and the information is not clear or well connected

✔ Has errors in grammar and vocabulary that make the essay hard to understand

Sample Response 5

Score: _____

People spend too much time with phones and computers, not with family and friends. Family and friends are very important, much more important than work or other things. All happiness in life comes from friends, now computers destroy friends.

I hate computer, always working on it, never with family. I stop working at 11 night, always on computer. Too busy, friends busy, too, always with computer.

Hope can stopped using computers all time, have time for friend, family, fun, entertainment.

If you said that this response was rated a 1, you are correct. This essay received this score because it:

✔ Does not address the topic directly
✔ Contains little or no detail
✔ Has many errors of vocabulary and grammar that make ideas unclear

---

EXERCISE 9

The Independent Writing Scoring Rubric

In this exercise, you will use the rubric to evaluate student responses to the TOEFL iBT independent writing item below. Read each student response and evaluate it using the rubric. Write the score on the line.

Do you agree or disagree with the following statement?

People should stop using cars and use public transportation instead.

Use specific reasons and examples to support your answer.

1. Score: _____

I having really good new car, like to drive it everywhere, except city. Lots of trafficjam in city, hard to find parking lot, too. My car is big, so not a lot of parking lots are big for my car. Prefer to take taxi when I go downtown, not take public transportation because too many people, not safe, dangerous. So I prefer to take car or taxi, not public transportation.

2. Score: _____

Many people believe taking public transporatation better than taking cars, but I not agree. Driving is alot better.

First reason is that driving is comfort. My car is very comfort and nice, so I like to drive it. Public transportation is not comfort, sometimes you can't get a seat. And trains and buses are slow and dirty in my town. I like clean, so car better for me.

Second reason is car make freedom. Public transportation doesn't run at night, so I can't go out late or visit friends. And public transportation not go all places. Only go busy places, downtown.

Third reason is car more safe. Many danger people on public transportation. I cant wear nice clothes or jewelry on public transportation because danger. Much safer in car.

Three reasons for not using public transportation. I hate public transportation and will always use car.

3. Score: _____

Many people ask about using public transportation or cars. My city bans half of all cars each day. That helps a lot, so I think even more people should take public transportation.

Public transportation is cleanest transportation. In my city, air contamination was very terrible. Then city decided that only half the cars can drive each day. Now air is clean.

Public transportation is the cheapest transportation. To travel by car, car needs gas, license, and other expenses. That's very expensive. Public transportation is very cheaper in my city. Public tranportation is only a few pennies a day.

Public transportation is the fast transportation, too. In my town, the subway is very fast. No traffic. And buses travel in special bus roads, so they can travel fast, too. People arrive to work very fast in my town with public transportation.

In conclusion, public transportation is a lot better than car. So think that city government needs to stop all cars driving downtown.

4. Score: _____

People should stop driving cars and use public transportation. In my opinion, taking a car is good. Public transportation not so good. I like taking a car because very convenient. With car, I can go anywhere. I go any time, too. My house far from town, so without car, not possible to go out at night when public transportation is off.

Public transportation good because not so expensive. Car is expensive. So maybe poor people consider public transportation, but rich people need cars.

Car is best transportation because comfortable, too. I like car because nice seats and air conditioning. I hate hot weather, so car is more nicer.

For these reasons, car is better than public transportation, but for others like poor man, public transportation good, too.

Answers and Explanations for Exercise 9 begin on page 549.

Responding to Item 2

An effective response to an independent writing item includes this information:

- A statement of the topic you are responding to
- A statement of your opinion or point of view
- Reasons to support your point of view

In your response, you need to present strong ideas. You also need to use a logical order, such as more important to less important, time (the order events happened), or cause and effect. A good way to write a clear, well-organized essay is the same five-paragraph essay format you used for Item 1. As you know, a five-paragraph essay follows this pattern:

- Introduction
- Three body paragraphs
- Conclusion

For more information on the parts of a five-paragraph essay, review pages 482–483.

Read this high-scoring response again. Look at how it follows the organization of a five-paragraph essay.

Introduction

> These days, many people say that people spend too much time on computers and mobile phones, and not enough time with other people. But the people who complain don't really understand computers and phones, because these tools help us be with other people.

— Topic

— Writer's opinion

— Writer's opinion

Body paragraphs

> I use my computer to stay in touch with my family and friends. All of the activities on my phone help me stay in contact with other people. I use email, chat, and social networking websites. I can communicate with friends, relatives, and others. For example, I love to send email to my grandmother. She lives far from me in the country, and she loves to get my email, too. I like to buy things with my computer, too.

> I also use my phone to communicate with other people. I can talk on my phone, and use it to send email, too. I really like my phone because I can text. I can send texts to all my friends. When I am going to be late getting home, I always text my mom. Then she doesn't worry.

> Finally, I use technology to have fun with friends. I love to play video games online. My mom told me I need to go out and play with my friends, but we play together online from our own homes. So I am not alone, but always with friends.

Conclusion

> In conclusion, people say that we don't spend time with family and friends because of phones and computers. But the people donot understand technology very well. With technology you are never alone.

This essay includes all the parts of an effective response. The first sentence clearly states the topic of the essay: whether people spend too much time with technology and not enough time with their families. The second sentence states the writer's opinion: "But the people who complain don't really understand computers and phones, because these tools help us be with other people." The following three paragraphs give three good reasons that support the opinion. The conclusion sums up the essay and restates the writer's opinion.

Preparing Your Response to Item 2

Because you have only a short time to plan and write your essay, the same four-step process of gathering ideas, organizing ideas, writing, and revising that you followed for Item 1 will help you prepare a good response to Item 2. In fact, following these steps is much easier for Item 2 because no reading or listening is involved. For more information on the steps, review pages 483–497.

> **TIP** **Pay attention to time!**
>
> To avoid running out of time, you should plan your time carefully. Suggested times for Item 2 are provided for each step.
>
> - **Gathering ideas:** 5 minutes
> - **Organizing ideas:** 5 minutes
> - **Writing your essay:** 15 minutes
> - **Revising your essay:** 5 minutes

Gathering Ideas

An effective response to Item 2 needs to give detail about your opinion and your reasons for holding that opinion. One good way to think of detail and reasons is the same process you used in Speaking: brainstorming. When you brainstorm, you think of ideas and write them down quickly in a few words in your notes. If necessary, review the information on brainstorming on page 377.

> **TIP** **Organize your notes into three groups!**
>
> Since a strong TOEFL iBT essay has three body paragraphs, save time by organizing your ideas into three groups as you take brainstorm and take notes. This way, you will have an organized list when you are ready to start writing.

As in other sections of the TOEFL iBT, use an outline form and use only brief words, abbreviations, numbers, and symbols when you take notes. Look at the notes that follow. Name one or two abbreviations, numbers, and symbols that you see in the notes. What words do they stand for? How did the writer put the ideas into three groups?

Fun w/ friends—play video gms online
—w/ friends
— mom thinks alone—not alone
Phone—communicate w/ peo
—talk
—email
—text friends +text mom if late
—read books on phone
Computer—stay in touch family + friends Body para 1
—email, chat, social networking
—friends, rels, + others
—email grandma—country
Concl—w/ tech never alone

Abbreviations in the notes include *w/ (with)*, *peo (people)*, and *+ (and)*. The writer put the ideas into groups according to type of technology: computer, phone, and online games. Having these three groups will help the writer save time in the next step, organization.

EXERCISE 10

Gathering Ideas

Read the TOEFL iBT independent writing item.

Do you agree or disagree with the following statement?

In order to get work experience, all university students should be required to hold part-time jobs.

Use specific reasons and examples to support your answer.

Now gather ideas. Allow about 5 minutes. Use the timer on your phone or computer to keep track of time.

_____

_____

_____

_____

_____

_____

_____

_____

_____

_____

_____

_____

_____

_____

Sample Response for Exercise 10 begins on page 549.

Organizing Ideas

Since organization is an important part of the scoring rubric, you should take a few minutes to organize your ideas. If you used an outline form, your ideas should already be organized into groups. Then check the following:

- Make sure you have enough information for three body paragraphs. Add ideas if necessary.
- Cross off any ideas that do not belong.
- Put the groups of ideas in order. Choose an organization pattern that makes sense, such as chronological order or order of importance (most important to least important, or least important to most important).
- Last, you should add information on the introduction and conclusion.

Intro: complainers don't understand tech, tech helps us be
    w/ others
Fun w/ friends—play video gms online
—w/ friends   **Body para 3**
—mom thinks alone—not alone, always w/ someone
Phone—communicate w/ peo
—talk
—email   **Body para 2**
—text friends +text 1mom if late
—~~read books on phone~~
Computer—stay in touch family + friends
—email, chat, social networking
—friends, rels, + others   **Body para 3**
—email grandma—country
Concl—w/ tech, never alone

Notice how the writer crossed off one idea that is not related: reading books on the phone. This is not a social activity, so it does not support the main idea. The writer also added an idea to show that when playing video games, people are not alone, but with another person. The writer numbered the groups in order and added information for the introduction and conclusion.

If your ideas are not already written in outline form, organize them using numbers, lines, and circles, as you did with Item 1. Then add information for the body and conclusion.

EXERCISE 11

Organizing Your Notes

Review your notes from Exercise 10: Gathering Ideas. Organize them to write a five-paragraph essay.

Sample Response for Exercise 11 begins on page 549.

Writing Your Essay

Once you have organized your ideas, you are ready to write. If you organized your ideas into the format of a five-paragraph essay, you can now take the information from your outline and use it to write sentences and paragraphs.

Look at the example of the **introductory paragraph**. It begins with a general statement of the topic and states the writer's point of view in the thesis statement.

> These days, many people say that people spend too much time on computers and mobile phones, and not enough time with other people. But the people who complain don't really understand computers and phones, because these tools help us be with other people.

Statement of the topic

Thesis statement

The **first body paragraph** focuses on the first reason identified by the writer, using a computer to send email. The paragraph has a topic sentence that gives the main idea of the paragraph and then more detail in the supporting sentences.

> I use my computer to stay in touch with my family and friends. All of the activities on my phone help me stay in contact with other people. I use email, chat, and social networking websites. I can communicate with friends, relatives, and others. For example, I love to send email to my grandmother. She lives far from me in the country, and she loves to get my email, too. I like to buy things with my computer, too.

Topic sentence

Supporting sentences

To back up your ideas, you need to introduce reasons. Study the example:

- **For example,** I love to send email to my grandmother.

Review the language for introducing reasons on page 494.

The **second body paragraph** focuses on communicating by phone. Like the first body paragraph, it has a topic sentence that states the main idea of the paragraph. Then the following support sentences give detail to back up the topic sentence.

> I also use my phone to communicate with other people. I can talk on my phone, and use it to send email, too. I really like my phone because I can text. I can send texts to all my friends. When I am going to be late getting home, I always text my mom. Then she doesn't worry.

Topic sentence

Supporting sentences

The **third body paragraph** focuses on fun with technology. Like the other body paragraphs, it has a topic sentence that states the main idea of the paragraph. Then supporting sentences give additional detail.

> Finally, I use technology to have fun with friends. I love to play video games online. My mom told me I need to go out and play with my friends, but we play together online from our own homes. So I am not alone, but always with friends.

Topic sentence

Supporting sentences

The **concluding paragraph** sums up the ideas in the essay and restates them in a general way. This paragraph is always organized from specific to general, and it ends with a general restatement of the writer's conclusion.

> In conclusion, people say that we don't spend time with family and friends because of phones and computers. But the people donot understand technology very well. With technology you are never alone.

Summarizing statements

General concluding statement

In this case, the writer restates the original opinion and ends with a strong closing statement: With technology you are never alone. The writer begins the paragraph with the phrase, *In conclusion.* This phrase is a very simple way to signal to the reader that the conclusion is beginning.

- **In conclusion,** people say that we don't spend time with family and friends because of phones and computers.

EXERCISE 12

Writing Your Essay

Take 15 minutes to write your response to the essay question. Use the notes you prepared and organized in Exercises 10 and 11.

Do you agree or disagree with the following statement?

In order to get work experience, all university students should be required to hold part-time jobs.

Use specific reasons and examples to support your answer.

If possible, keyboard your essay on a computer. Use your phone to keep track of the time. An effective response will typically be about 300 words.

_____

_____

_____

_____

_____

_____

_____

_____

_____

_____

_____

_____

_____

Sample Response for Exercise 12 begins on page 550.

Revising Your Essay

Look at how the TOEFL test taker revised the essay on computers and cell phones. Corrections are in boldface so you can see them. (In the actual TOEFL iBT, you will correct your essay using the word processor, and your corrections will not display differently from the rest of the text.)

These days, many people say that people spend too much time on computers and mobile phones, and not enough time with other people. But the people who complain don't really understand computers and phones, because these tools help us be with other people.

I use my computer to stay in touch with my family and friends. All of the activities on my phone help me stay in contact with other people. I use email, chat, and social networking websites. I can communicate with friends, relatives, and others. For example, I love to send email to my grandmother. She lives far from me in the country, and she loves to get my email, too. ~~I like to buy things with my computer, too.~~

I also use my phone to communicate with other people. I can talk on my phone, and use it to send email, too. I really like my phone because I can text. I can send texts to all my friends. When I am going to be late getting home, I always text my mom. Then she doesn't worry. **I also text my friends to say Hi or have fun chatting.**

Finally, I use technology to have fun with friends. I love to play video games online. My mom told me I need to go out and play with my friends, but we play together online from our own homes. So I am not alone, but always with friends.

In conclusion, people say that we don't spend time with family and friends because of phones and computers. But the people **don't** understand technology very well. With technology you are never alone.

In the example essay, the student deleted a sentence about shopping because it is irrelevant. In addition, the student added a sentence to paragraph 3 to strengthen the support. The student also changed the spelling of *donot* to *don't*.

> **TIP** **Pay attention to content and organization when you revise!**
>
> Content and organization are much more important in the TOEFL iBT Independent Writing Scoring Rubric than grammar and vocabulary. Therefore, you should focus your revisions on content. Then if there is time remaining, revise for grammar, vocabulary, and spelling.

EXERCISE 13

Revising Your Essay

Revise the essay you wrote in Exercise 12: Writing Your Essay. Take 5 minutes to make your revisions. First revise for content. Then revise for vocabulary and grammar.

Sample Response for Exercise 13 begins on page 550.

Evaluating Your Essay

After you write, you should evaluate your writing using the Simplified Independent Writing Rubric. If possible, ask a teacher to evaluate your writing. If that is not possible, ask a friend with a high level of English to review your work. If no one can help you, then evaluate your writing yourself using the rubric. Put your writing aside for a day or two so that you can look at it freshly.

After you figure out your score, use the sample high-scoring essay on page 550 and the following special version of the rubric to help you figure out which areas to review before trying another practice essay.

1. Compare your essay to the high-scoring essay on page 550.
2. Check the box of each statement that describes your writing. The row with the most check marks will give you an indication of your score.
3. Review the pages that are listed following each box you **did not** check in that row.
4. Look at the row above the row of your score. Study the pages that are listed following the boxes you **did not** check in that row, too. Study the example that a student prepared for the sample essay on computers and cell phones.

SCORE	DESCRIPTION	STUDY PAGES
5	A **Level 5** response largely:	
	☐ Addresses the topic and the task.	515–517
	☐ Is organized and well developed; uses appropriate detail, examples, and explanations.	517–518
	☐ Stays on topic, flows, and makes sense.	519–520
	☐ Uses language well. Has variety in sentence patterns, vocabulary, and idioms, and only minor errors of vocabulary and grammar.	524–525
4	A **Level 4** response largely:	
	☐ Addresses the topic and the task, though some points are not well developed.	515–517
	☐ Is generally well organized and developed; uses appropriate detail, examples, and explanations.	517–518
	☐ Stays on topic, flows, and makes sense, but may have some problems with repetition, staying on topic, or unclear connection of ideas	519–520
	☐ Uses language fairly well. Has variety in sentence patterns, vocabulary, and idioms, and only minor errors of vocabulary and grammar, but may have some errors in grammar, word form, or natural language that do not cause unclarity.	524–525
3	A **Level 3** response is characterized by one or more of the following:	
	☐ Addresses the topic and the task, but with somewhat developed detail, examples, and explanations.	515–517
	☐ Stays on topic, flows, and makes sense, but connection of ideas might be unclear at times.	517–518
	☐ May show inconsistent ability in grammar and vocabulary that may cause occasional unclarity.	524–525
	☐ Accurate but limited range of sentence structures and vocabulary.	524–525
2	A **Level 2** response will show one or more of the following weaknesses:	
	☐ Development of topic and task is limited.	515–517
	☐ Poor organization or connection of ideas.	517–518
	☐ Not enough or inappropriate detail, examples, and explanations.	515–517
	☐ Poor choice of words or word forms.	524–525
	☐ Many errors of sentence structure or vocabulary.	524–525
1	A **Level 1** response is seriously harmed by one or more of these weaknesses:	
	☐ Disorganized or lacks development.	517–518
	☐ Little or no detail, examples, and explanations, or does not respond to the task.	515–517
	☐ Serious errors in sentence structure or vocabulary.	524–525
0	A response at this level contains only ideas copied from the topic, does not address the topic, is not written in English, or is blank.	

EXERCISE 14

Evaluating Your Essay

Have a teacher or an English-speaking friend review the essay you wrote on working while in school or wait a day or two and review your essay yourself. Use the Simplified Independent Writing Rubric on page 507 to evaluate your writing. Then use the sample high-scoring answer in the Answers and Explanations and the special Independent Writing Rubric in Appendix F to figure out the areas you need to improve before you tackle Exercise 15. Follow the instructions on page 525.

Sample Response for Exercise 14 begins on page 550.

EXERCISE 15

TOEFL iBT Independent Writing Practice

Take 30 minutes to plan, write, and revise an essay on the topic below. Use your mobile phone or computer to keep track of the time. As on the actual TOEFL iBT, use notepaper to gather and organize your ideas. Then keyboard your essay on a computer, if possible. An effective essay will be about 300 words.

Do you agree or disagree with the following statement?

All children should be required to play at least one sport regularly during their years in school.

Use specific reasons and examples to support your answer.

Response Time: 30 minutes

Sample Response for Exercise 15 begins on page 551.

TOEFL iBT Practice Writing Section

Directions: The Writing section of the TOEFL iBT assesses your ability to communicate in writing in academic settings. This section has two items. To simulate actual TOEFL iBT conditions, follow these instructions.

ITEM 1: INTEGRATED WRITING

- Read the passage in 3 minutes. Use your watch or the timer on your phone or computer to keep track of time. You may take notes as you read and listen and use your notes when you answer the question.
- Start the audio program and listen to the passage one time as you take notes.
- Read the question, plan your response, and write it in 20 minutes. You may use your notes and refer back to the reading passage as you write.

ITEM 2: INDEPENDENT WRITING

- Set your timer for 30 minutes and start working. You may take notes to plan your essay and to use as you write.

 The Audio icon appears when you need to listen to an audio track.

If you do not finish your essays when the time ends, mark your place. Then continue working as quickly as you can. When you finish, take note of the total time. This will give you an idea of how quickly you need to work on the actual TOEFL iBT to write both essays in 60 minutes.

Now begin the TOEFL iBT Practice Writing section.

1. Integrated Writing

A. Read the passage in 3 minutes. Use the timer on your phone or computer to keep track of the time. Take notes in the space provided.

> **Reading Time: 3 minutes**

When we think of city planning, we often think of building new constructions and creating new spaces. However, some of a city planner's most interesting tasks involve preserving historic buildings for the future and finding new uses for buildings whose original purposes are no longer relevant. One city that has many examples of historical preservation is Chicago.

Chicago was a vibrant, rapidly growing city for many years. In the mid-nineteenth century, most of the city, which was largely made of wood, burned. This created the opportunity to build anew in large sections of the city. However, by the 1970s, many of those buildings, now close to 100 years old, were in disuse or in bad repair. One example is old movie theaters. Many large, ornate movie theaters were built in the 1930s and 1940s. After the invention of television, people stopped going to the movies frequently, and these buildings fell into disuse. City planners preserved two of these theaters in downtown, and with investment of public money, converted them into live theater spaces. Another theater was converted into an indoor shopping mall.

A second example is some of the many large factories and warehouses in Chicago. These buildings were no longer used as factories and were abandoned and in bad repair. Planners had the option of destroying them or finding new purposes. Many of these buildings were converted into dramatic, attractive apartments. The buildings were cheaper than new buildings and they preserved the historical exteriors while creating new uses inside.

_____

_____

_____

_____

_____

B.  Now listen to part of a lecture on the topic you just read about.
Take notes in the space provided.

_____

_____

_____

_____

_____

_____

_____

_____

_____

_____

_____

_____

_____

C. Take 20 minutes to plan, write, and revise an essay of about 150 to 225 words. Use the timer on your phone to keep track of time. Pay attention to the quality of your writing and on how well you present the points in the lecture and their relationship to the reading passage.

 Summarize the points made in the lecture you just heard, explaining how they cast doubt on the points made in the reading passage.

Response Time: 20 minutes

_____

_____

_____

_____

_____

_____

_____

_____

_____

_____

_____

_____

_____

_____

_____

_____

2. Independent Writing

Take 30 minutes to plan, write, and revise an essay on the following topic. Use your mobile phone or computer to keep track of the time. As on the actual TOEFL iBT, you may refer back to the reading, but do not replay the listening. Use notepaper to take notes to gather and organize your ideas. Then keyboard your essay on a computer, if possible. An effective essay will be about 300 words.

Do you agree or disagree with the following statement?

Soda and other high-sugar drinks are bad for people's health, so their sale should be banned.

Use specific reasons and examples to support your answer.

Response Time: 30 minutes

_____

_____

_____

_____

_____

_____

_____

_____

_____

_____

Explanations and Sample Responses for the TOEFL iBT Practice Writing section begin on page 551.

TOEFL iBT Writing Personalized Study Planner

Use your answers to the TOEFL iBT Practice Writing section and these special rubrics to focus your preparation for the actual TOEFL iBT.

ITEM 1: INTEGRATED WRITING

1. Evaluate your essay using the instructions on page 497.
2. Compare your essay with the sample high-scoring essay in the Answers and Explanations.
3. Enter your rating on each row of the Integrated Writing Rubric on this page.
4. Review your ratings in each row. Which areas do you want to improve? Study the pages that are listed for these areas in the column on the right.

SCORE	DESCRIPTION	STUDY PAGES
5	A **Level 5** response: ☐ Selects relevant and important information from the lecture and presents it in relation to similar information in the reading. Includes supporting detail and examples.	483–487
	☐ Is well organized and makes sense. Uses signaling words and phrases to connect information and show the relationships among ideas.	490–494
	☐ Includes occasional errors in vocabulary and grammar that do not result in inaccurate or confusing presentation of information or connections among ideas.	495–497
4	A **Level 4** response: ☐ Generally selects relevant and important information from the lecture and presents it in relation to relevant and important information in the reading, but may have minor inaccuracies, vagueness, or omissions that cause minor confusion to readers.	483–487
	☐ Includes errors in vocabulary and grammar that are more frequent than in a Level 5 response, but cause only minor problems with clarity or connection of ideas.	495–497

SCORE	DESCRIPTION	STUDY PAGES
3	A **Level 3** response:	
	☐ Contains some information from the listening and makes some connections to the reading.	483–487
	A response at this level has one or more of these problems:	
	☐ The response addresses the task, but some information may be inaccurate or incomplete. Makes only general, vague, or unclear connections between points in the reading and the lecture.	483–487
	☐ The response omits one major point made in the lecture.	483–487
	☐ Some key points in the lecture or reading, or the connections between them, are unclear, incomplete, inaccurate, or general.	490–494
	☐ Vocabulary and grammar errors may be more frequent than in a Level 4 response and may cause confusion to readers.	495–497
2	A **Level 2** response:	
	☐ Has some relevant information from the lecture but has inaccuracies or omissions of important ideas from the lecture.	483–487
	☐ Makes inaccurate or incomplete connections with information the reading.	483–487
	A response at this level shows one or more of the following:	
	☐ Omits or inaccurately presents the relationship between the lecture and the reading.	483–487
	☐ Omits or inaccurately presents important points in the lecture.	483–487
	☐ Contains language errors or expressions that obscure meaning.	495–497
1	A **Level 1** response:	
	☐ Provides little or no meaningful or relevant information from the lecture.	483–487
	☐ Has problems with vocabulary and grammar that make the essay difficult to understand.	495–497
0	A response at this level contains only ideas copied from the reading passage, does not address the topic, is not written in English, or is blank.	

ITEM 2: INDEPENDENT WRITING

1. Evaluate your essay using the instructions on page 525.
2. Compare your essay with the sample high-scoring essay in the Answers and Explanations.
3. Enter your rating on each row of the Independent Writing Rubric on this page.
4. Review your ratings in each row. Which areas do you want to improve? Study the pages that are listed for those areas in the column on the right.

SCORE	DESCRIPTION	STUDY PAGES
5	A **Level 5** response largely:	
	☐ Addresses the topic and the task.	515–517
	☐ Is organized and well developed; uses appropriate detail, examples, and explanations.	517–518
	☐ Stays on topic, flows, and makes sense.	519–520
	☐ Uses language well. Has variety in sentence patterns, vocabulary, and idioms, and only minor errors of vocabulary and grammar.	524–525
4	A **Level 4** response largely:	
	☐ Addresses the topic and the task, though some points are not well developed.	515–517
	☐ Is generally well organized and developed; uses appropriate detail, examples, and explanations.	517–518
	☐ Stays on topic, flows, and makes sense, but may have some problems with repetition, staying on topic, or unclear connection of ideas.	519–520
	☐ Uses language fairly well. Has variety in sentence patterns, vocabulary, and idioms, and only minor errors of vocabulary and grammar, but may have some errors in grammar, word form, or natural language that do not cause unclarity.	524–525
3	A **Level 3** response is characterized by one or more of the following:	
	☐ Addresses the topic and the task, but with somewhat developed detail, examples, and explanations.	515–517
	☐ Stays on topic, flows, and makes sense, but connection of ideas might be unclear at times.	517–518
	☐ May show inconsistent ability in grammar and vocabulary that may cause occasional unclarity.	524–525
	☐ Accurate but limited range of sentence structures and vocabulary.	524–525
2	A **Level 2** response will show one or more of the following weaknesses:	
	☐ Limited development of topic and task.	515–517
	☐ Poor organization or connection of ideas.	517–518
	☐ Not enough or inappropriate detail, examples, and explanations.	515–517
	☐ Poor choice of words or word forms.	524–525
	☐ Many errors of sentence structure or vocabulary.	524–525

SCORE	DESCRIPTION	STUDY PAGES
1	A **Level 1** response is seriously harmed by one or more of these weaknesses:	
	☐ Disorganized or lacks development.	517–518
	☐ Little or no detail, examples, and explanations, or does not respond to the task.	515–517
	☐ Serious errors in sentence structure or vocabulary.	524–525
0	A response at this level contains only ideas copied from the topic, does not address the topic, is not written in English, or is blank.	

TOEFL iBT WRITING
Answers, Explanations, Audio Scripts, and Sample Responses

Exercise 1: The Integrated Writing Scoring Rubric (Page 478)

TRACK 120 AUDIO SCRIPT

Narrator: Now listen to part of a lecture on the topic you just read about.

Professor: As you know, insights from psychology can inform fields as diverse as human resources, law enforcement, and even customer service. Let's take the example of the study on lying that you read about for homework. As you know, the study asked volunteers to prepare and tell lies to one another. Clearly, this type of research is disturbing, since it trained people to lie more effectively. W-w-we (*stammering*) do not want to encourage lying! So . . . in order to justify research of this type, the value of the research outcomes needs to outweigh the problems raised by the method.

In this case, the study raises little of value in distinguishing lies from the truth. Right now, the only thing that this study tells us is that in lying, practice makes perfect. That's probably something we could have figured out on our own. In addition, the study gives no insights on how to tell when someone is lying. Psychology does have insight to offer to answer this question, but this study does not provide those insights. A better study might compare different methods for distinguishing lies from the truth. Other studies have examined whether listeners can use physical and other cues to tell lies from the truth. For example, usually a lie will lack detail. Training listeners to listen for detail might be an effective way to help them find out if someone is lying. Liars often tend not to look directly at listeners when telling a lie. Sometimes their eyes will look up while they think of ways to lie.

So this study, while interesting, has ethical problems and really does not result in ways to help us distinguish lies from the truth. But remember, I know quite a bit about distinguishing lies from the truth. Keep that in mind if you have to explain why your paper is late or you are absent for class or a test.

TRACK 121 AUDIO SCRIPT

Narrator: Summarize the points made in the lecture you just heard, explaining how they challenge the points made in the reading passage.

ANSWERS AND EXPLANATIONS

1. This response probably scored a 1. The response received this score because it:
   - ✔ Shows that the writer completely misunderstands the information in the reading and lecture
   - ✔ Takes the professor's last comment out of context, when in fact this comment is irrelevant for responding to the prompt

2. This response probably scored a 4. The response received this score because it:
   - ✔ Responds to the prompt and sums up and compares key ideas from the reading and the lecture. However, the ideas are stated somewhat vaguely.
   - ✔ Has good vocabulary and grammar, but errors sometime make ideas unclear

3. This response probably scored a 5. The response received this score because it:
   - ✔ Is more detailed than the Level 4 response
   - ✔ Sums up the key ideas in the reading and lecture and compares them

4. This response probably scored a 2. The response received this score because it:
   - ✔ Omits key ideas from the lecture
   - ✔ Has frequent vocabulary and grammar errors that make meaning hard to understand
   - ✔ Is too short and lacks adequate detail and support

Exercise 2: Taking Notes (Page 485)

TRACK 122 AUDIO SCRIPT

Narrator: Now listen to part of a lecture on the topic you just read about. Take notes in the space provided.

Professor: Today, umm, we are continuing our study of matter. I am sure that all of you have heard of the three states of matter: solid, liquid, and gas. And all of us have heard that matter will transition from phase to phase in an orderly progression from solid to liquid to gas as the temperature changes. But this represents a highly simplistic view of state of matter. Depending on who you talk to, you may hear about other states of matter. In fact, most matter in the universe is in none of these states, but in a fourth state called plasma. Plasma is a state of matter in which, like a gas, molecules can move about freely and fill a closed container. But unlike a gas, matter in the plasma state can conduct electricity and produce magnetic fields. Plasma is common on Earth. It occurs in lightning, fluorescent lights, and neon lights.

Scientists also know that not all matter transitions from solid to liquid to gas. There are . . . two processes, . . . sublimation and deposition, that also occur. Sublimation happens when a solid changes directly to a gas. An example is solid carbon dioxide, or "dry ice." Because the melting point and vaporization points are so close together and so low, when dry ice is placed in an area at room temperature, it will change directly from solid to gaseous state. Another example is freezing fog. (*brief pause*) Fog, as you know, consists of water vapor suspended in the air. Fog may exist at temperatures below freezing, but the water droplets in fog have no place to condense. If the fog gets in contact with something colder than the freezing point of water, such as a metal bridge or railing, the water in fog may freeze directly, without passing through a liquid state. That's deposition.

EXPLANATION AND SAMPLE RESPONSE

There are many ways to take notes. Compare your notes to these sample notes.

<u>Reading</u>
3 states matter, solid, liq, gas
Solid
—fixed shape + vol
—mols packed tog
Liq
—fixed volume, not fixed shape
—take shape container
—mols close together, able move freely
Gas
—no fixed volume, shape
—mols not packed tog, can move + take shape container
Transition of phase— change from one state of matter bec temp
—melting, freezing point temp change solid to liq or liq solid
—vaporization and condensation point—temp changes liq to gas or gas to liq
Water—3 states on Earth: freezing 0° C and vap 100° C.
CO_2 melt point -78° C, vap -57° C. Usually gas.
<u>Listening</u>
3 states too simple C
Fourth state—plasma C
—like a gas, mols move about freely
—unlike gas, conducts electricity
—common on Earth
—in lightning, neon lights
sublimation and deposition—change directly gas to solid, or solid to gas C
—CO_2—change solid to gas
—freezing fog—gas to solid

Exercise 3: Understanding the Question (Page 489)

EXPLANATION AND SAMPLE RESPONSE

Many answers are possible. Ensure that your notes have enough information to write a 150- to 225-word essay. Add information that is missing or will help you answer the question. Look at the ideas this test taker added to the notes.

<u>Reading</u>
3 states matter, solid, liq, gas
Solid
—fixed shape + vol
—mols packed tog
Liq
—fixed volume, not fixed shape
—~~take shape container~~ fill closed container
—mols close together, able move freely

Gas
—no fixed volume, shape
—mols not packed tog, can move + take shape
    container
Transition of phase— change from one state of
    matter bec temp
—melting, freezing point temp change solid to
    liq or liq solid
—vaporization and condensation point—temp
    changes liq to gas or gas to liq
Water—3 states on Earth: freezing 0° C and
    vap 100° C.
CO_2 melt point -78° C, vap -57° C. Usually gas.

Listening
3 states too simple C
Fourth state—plasma C
—like a gas, mols move about freely
—unlike gas, conducts electricity + mag field
—common on Earth
—in lightning, neon lights
sublimation and deposition—change directly
    gas to solid, or solid to gas C
—CO_2—change solid to gas
—freezing fog—gas to solid

Exercise 4: Organizing Your Notes (Page 491)

SAMPLE RESPONSE

There are many ways to organize your notes for a five-paragraph essay. Look at this example.

Reading
3 states matter, solid, liq, gas—Intro
Solid
—fixed shape + vol
—mols packed tog
Liq
—fixed volume, not fixed shape
—~~take shape container~~ fill closed container
—mols close together, able move freely
Gas
—no fixed volume, shape
—mols not packed tog, can move + take
    shape container

Body
para
1

Transition of phase— change from one state of
    matter bec temp
—melting, freezing point temp change solid to
    liq or liq solid
—vaporization and condensation point—temp
    changes liq to gas or gas to liq
Water—3 states on Earth: freezing 0° C and
    vap 100° C.
CO_2 melt point -78° C, vap -57° C. Usually gas.
Listening
3 states too simple C
Fourth state—plasma C
—like a gas, mols move about freely
—unlike gas, conducts electricity + mag field
—common on Earth
—in lightning, neon lights

Body
para
2

sublimation and deposition—change directly
    gas to solid, or solid to gas C
—CO_2—change solid to gas
—freezing fog—gas to solid

Body
para
3

Concl—art too simple, state more compl

Exercise 5: Writing Your Essay (Page 495)

SAMPLE RESPONSE

There are many ways to write a five-paragraph essay. Look at this example of a high-scoring essay.

    According to the reading, exist three states of matter: solid, liquid, and gas. Exist matter in all states. And matter change state because of temperature. The professor say that this is not complete understanding of state of matter.
    The reading says that each state of matter is different. A solid has fixed shape and volume.

A liquid as fixed volume. And a gas doesn't have fixed shape or volume. A gas will fit any closed container. The difference is that molecules are packed different for each one. The reading also says that matter will change from solid to liquid to gas based on temperature.
    Professor say that this view too easy. First, there other states of matter. Fourth state of matter plasma. Plasma is like a gas, but is electric and magnetic.

Second, not all matter change from solid to liquid or gas to liquid. Some matter change from gas to solid directly, like freezing fog. Other matter change from solid gas. Example is dry ice. Dry ice melting point and evaporation point very low. If dry ice is in room temperature, changes directly to gas.

Therefore, the article gives a view of state of matter too simple. State is more complicated.

Exercise 6: Revising Your Essay (Page 497)

ANSWERS AND EXPLANATIONS

There are many ways to revise this essay to get a higher score. Look at how the test taker revised this high-scoring essay. The errors the student corrected are in boldface.

According to the reading, **there are** three states of matter: solid, liquid, and gas. Matter **exists** in all states. And matter change state because of temperature. The professor say that this is not complete understanding of state of matter.

The reading says that each state of matter is different. A solid has fixed shape and volume. A liquid as fixed volume. And a gas doesn't have fixed shape or volume. A gas will fit any closed container. The difference is that molecules are packed different for each one. The reading also says that matter will change from solid to liquid to gas based on temperature.

Professor say that this view too easy. First, there other states of matter. Fourth state of matter plasma. Plasma is like a gas, but is electric and magnetic.

Second, not all matter change from solid to liquid or gas to liquid. Some matter change from gas to solid directly, like freezing fog. Other matter change from solid gas. Example is dry ice. Dry ice melting point and evaporation point very low. If dry ice is in room temperature, changes directly to gas. **The names of these processes are sublimation and deposition.**

Therefore, the article gives a view of state of matter too simple. State is more complicated.

The test taker added a sentence to state the names of the two processes discussed in the previous sentences, sublimation and deposition. The test taker also corrected two problems with the word *exist*. The candidate had first used the expression "Exist three states of matter," which is not an English construction, but changed it to the more natural "There are three states of matter." The writer also wrote, "Exist matter," another unnatural expression, but then changed it to the more natural, "Matter exists . . ."

Exercise 7: Evaluating Your Essay (Page 499)

EVALUATING YOUR RESPONSE

Evaluate your essay with the rubric on page 473. Then follow the instructions:

1. Compare your essay with the high-scoring essay on page 474.
2. Use a copy of the special rubric in Appendix E. Check the boxes that apply to your writing. The row with the most boxes checked is most likely your score on the actual TOEFL.
3. To improve your performance, review the page numbers next to the boxes you **did not** check in that row and the row above.

Exercise 8: TOEFL iBT Integrated Writing Practice (Page 499)

TRACK 123 AUDIO SCRIPT

Narrator: Now listen to part of a lecture on the topic you just read about. Take notes in the space provided.

Professor: Ummm . . . While historians and critics of popular culture agree that manga and anime are vital parts of Japanese culture, they disagree, often fervently, about the relationship between the two genres. The history and cultural influences on each of the genres themselves are also highly disputed grounds.

While many critics state that there has been a convergence between anime and manga, there are still differences. First, err, manga is a much larger business than anime. Second, even though manga characters and stories have been brought to anime, manga continues to develop its own heroes and story lines that are independent of anime. In this sense, manga-influenced anime is only one part of the anime genre. So, a more accurate way to state the relationship between manga and anime is that manga has had an influence on anime, and some stories have crossed over, but that they are still separate genres.

Critics also dispute foreign influences on the two genres, though more about manga than anime. Anime . . . clearly was made possible by technological advances in film production in countries such as the United States and Russia, and the influence of advances in animation quality pioneered by Disney clearly had an effect. Nevertheless, Disney's animation techniques were adapted and simplified in Japan in order to speed production. The result was a uniquely Japanese style of animation only partially influenced by outside sources, while the content remained grounded in Japanese themes.

Many people believe that manga is influenced by comic book styles brought to Japan after World War II. While these comics may have had a limited influence, manga developed and maintained a unique drawing style, particularly in the way people are depicted. Also, while imported comic books were frequently in color, manga has often maintained its original black-and-white format. In addition, manga's themes grow directly out of concerns of Japanese society and people of the postwar era, a time of sweeping cultural change in Japan. In this sense, manga is just one part of a larger cultural flowering in Japan, as a new generation of Japanese began to express the concerns of the postwar society in art, film, writing, and popular culture.

Clearly, belief that manga and anime grow directly out of foreign influences is exaggerated at best, and in many ways misstates the genres' profound grounding in Japanese history, culture, artistic traditions, and values.

TRACK 124 AUDIO SCRIPT

Narrator: Summarize the points made in the lecture you just heard, explaining how they contradict the points made in the reading passage.

EXPLANATION AND SAMPLE RESPONSE

There are many ways to write a high-scoring response to this item. Compare your essay to this example of one way to write a high-scoring response.

Manga and anime are two related entertainment forms from Japan. Manga are special Japanese comic books, and anime is special Japanese animation. According to reading, manga and anime are very similar, but professor does not agree with this idea.

According to reading, manga is older than anime. According reading, after anime invented, manga stories brought to anime. Reading also say anime influenced by foreign animation, especially from Disneyland.

Professor disagree with this idea. First, professor say that only some manga stories are in anime. Manga still separate, and only a few manga stories cross over to anime.

Professor also agree that anime not completely influenced by Disneyland. Russian animation have influence, too. Also, anime has special Japan style of animation that is different from others.

So manga and anime are similar, but also different. And anime is now Japanese style, not foreign or from Disneyland.

Then have a teacher or an English-speaking friend review your essay, or wait a day or two and review your essay yourself. Use a copy of the Simplified Integrated Writing Rubric on page 473. Then use a copy of the special Integrated Writing Rubric in Appendix E to find the areas you need to improve before you complete the TOEFL iBT Practice Writing section later in this chapter. Review the boxes you checked in the special rubric. The row with the most boxes checked is most likely your score on the actual TOEFL iBT. To improve your performance, review the pages listed next to the boxes you **did not** check in that row, as well as in the row above.

Exercise 9: The Independent Writing Scoring Rubric (Page 511)

ANSWERS AND EXPLANATIONS

1. This essay probably scored a 2. This response deserves this score because it:
   - ✔ Does not address the prompt or provide much development
   - ✔ Does not present ideas in a logical order
   - ✔ Has many vocabulary and grammar errors that make the essay hard to understand

2. This essay probably scored a 4. This response deserves this score because it:
   - ✔ Addresses the topic and detail is somewhat developed
   - ✔ Stays on topic and flows
   - ✔ Has errors in vocabulary and grammar that interfere with clarity from time to time

3. This essay probably scored a 5. This response deserves this score because it:
   - ✔ Is organized and flows
   - ✔ Has plenty of support from a single example, the traffic control program
   - ✔ Has some minor errors of vocabulary and grammar, but they do not interfere with understanding

4. This essay probably scored a 3. This response deserves this score because it:
   - ✔ Has some development but lacks detail
   - ✔ Has frequent vocabulary and grammar errors and unconnected ideas that make the essay hard to follow

Exercise 10: Gathering Ideas (Page 516)

SAMPLE RESPONSE

There are many ways to gather ideas for this topic. Study these sample notes.

Hard find job now
—economy bad
—companies want expd workers
—easy get job aft. grad w/ exp.

University expensive
—get money for education
—even rich help family
Learn values
—value of money
—responsibility
—arrive on time

Exercise 11: Organizing Your Notes (Page 518)

SAMPLE RESPONSE

There are many ways to organize your notes for a five-paragraph essay. Look at the example. The writer added two ideas and ordered the ideas logically. The writer also crossed off an idea that is not relevant.

Intro: Agree—getting job help stds
Hard find job now
—economy bad
—companies want expd workers   Body
—easy get job aft. grad w/ exp.   para 2

University expensive
—get money for education   Body
—even rich help family—get pocket money   para 1
Learn values
—value of money   Body
—responsibility   para 3
—arrive on time
—respect coworkers + boss
Concl: job can help stds get money for school
    and exp for get job

Exercise 12: Writing Your Essay (Page 521)

SAMPLE RESPONSE

There are many ways to write a five-paragraph essay. Look at this example of a high-scoring essay.

Some people say that college students should be required to have part time jobs when they are in school. I agree with this idea because it can really help students.

First, going to university is expensive. If all students have a part time job, they will have money for their education. Even if they have scholarship or money from parents, they will help their family by getting pocket money.

Second, work experience will help student get job. Right now very hard to get a job these days. The economy is very bad, and companies hire experience workers only. These days, most college students have no experience, so hard to find a job. If they have experience, getting job after graduate easy.

Third, college students learn good values. Learn value of money from working. And learn responsibility, too. Going to work every day teaches them to arrive on time and respect boss and coworkers.

In conclusion, it's a great idea that college students find job during school. They will get money, help family, and learn responsible.

Exercise 13: Revising Your Essay (Page 525)

SAMPLE RESPONSE

There are many ways to revise your essay. First revise for content, and then for grammar and vocabulary. Look at how the student revised the essay on part-time jobs. The errors the student corrected are in boldface.

Some people say that college students should be required to have part time jobs when they are in school. I agree with this idea because it can really help students.

First, going to university is expensive. If all students have a part time job, they will have money for their education. Even if they have scholarship or money from parents, they will help their family by getting pocket money.

Second, work experience will help student**s** get job**s**. Right now **it is** very hard to get a job ~~these days~~. The economy is very bad, and companies hire experience workers only. These days, most college students have no experience, so **it is** hard to find a job. If they have experience, getting **a** job after **graduation** easy.

Third, college students learn good values. **They** learn **the** value of money from working. And **they** learn responsibility, too. Going to work every day teaches them to arrive on time and respect **their** boss and coworkers.

In conclusion, it's a great idea that college students find job during school. They will get money, help family, and learn **to be** responsible.

Exercise 14: Evaluating Your Essay (Page 527)

EVALUATING YOUR RESPONSE

Evaluate your essay with the rubric on page 507. Then use a copy of the special rubric in Appendix E. Check the boxes that apply to your writing. The row with the most boxes checked is most likely your score on the actual TOEFL. To improve your performance, review the pages listed next to the boxes you **did not** check in that row and the row above.

Exercise 15: TOEFL iBT Independent Writing Practice (Page 527)

SAMPLE RESPONSE

There are many ways to write a high-scoring response to this item. Compare your essay to this example of one way to write a high-scoring response.

Many people believe that sports are good for people, so all children should play one sport when children. I agree with this idea, because sport are good for us.

First, sport is healthy. From sport, we get exercise in the fresh air and sun. Exercise make children strong.

Sport teaches children important lessons. In sports we learn to cooperate. We learn teamwork. Team leaders get leadership skills. These skills make us good in school and life.

Last, sport develop good habits. If children learn to exercise, they will keep this habit all their life. I started to swim when child. Now I swim every day because of this good habit.

In conclusion, is good idea to require children to practice one sport to develop these good habits and values.

Then have a teacher or an English-speaking friend review your essay, or wait a day or two and review your essay yourself. Use a copy of the Simplified Independent Writing Rubric on page 507. Then use a copy of the special integrated rubric in Appendix E to find the areas you need to improve before you complete the TOEFL iBT Practice Writing section later in this chapter. Review the boxes you checked in the special rubric. The row with the most boxes checked is most likely your score on the actual TOEFL iBT. To improve your performance, review the pages listed next to the boxes you **did not** check in that row as well as in the row above.

TOEFL iBT Practice Writing Section (Page 531)

TRACK 125 AUDIO SCRIPT

Narrator: Now listen to part of a lecture on the topic you just read about. Take notes in the space provided.

Professor: Ummm, while historical preservation has its place, it has a number of disadvantages, too. Preservation, err, has its place, but it also has its price. In the case of Chicago, it's not completely clear whether all examples of historic preservation have been successful. For example, while one of the restored theaters is successful, the second one is largely unoccupied. The brightly lit exterior hides a dark interior that is used only a few times a year. And Chicago planners don't like to talk about what happened to Union Station, a large train station that was extensively renovated about twenty years ago. The building is in excellent condition, thanks to the renovation, but it's completely unused because train travel is not very popular. The building is beautiful but empty.

Many successful apartment buildings have been created from old warehouses and factories, too, but these buildings also pose challenges. Often, these buildings are very expensive to heat and cool because of the high ceilings. And it's often hard to install new technology in them. For example, wireless computer networks will not work in many of these buildings because the walls are so strong and thick. So I think that historical preservation has had mixed success at best.

TRACK 126 AUDIO SCRIPT

Narrator: Summarize the points made in the lecture you just heard, explaining how they cast doubt on the points made in the reading passage.

EXPLANATIONS AND SAMPLE RESPONSES

1. There are many ways to answer this question. Compare your essay to this example of one way to write a high-scoring response.

The reading and the lecture are about city planning and historical preservations. According to the reading, historical preservations created interesting uses for old buildings, but the professor says preservations not always succeed.

One example is old theaters. Chicago had many old theaters, and they fell into disuse after television was invent. So these beautiful old buildings were not useded. City planners made two of them live theaters, but that not completely succeed. Only one theater is succeed. The other is always empty without shows.

Another example is old warehouse and factory. These buildings not needed any more, so they were empty and dangerous. But the city planners changed them to apartment buildings. The buildings have nice exteriors, and the interiors all new. So modern house in old building. But the professor say that this not completely successful, too. The apartment buildings are expensive and technology doesn't work. The walls are thick and strong, so the people can't have wireless network.

The examples from professor and reading show that historical preservations seems like good idea, but is not always succeed. Planners need to plan carefully so that the buildings are good places for today.

EVALUATION

Have a teacher or an English-speaking friend review your essay, or wait a day or two and review your essay yourself. Use a copy of the Integrated Writing Rubric in Appendix E to evaluate your writing. Review the boxes you checked in the rubric. The row with the most boxes checked is most likely your score on the actual TOEFL iBT. Then use the TOEFL iBT Personalized Study Planner on pages 540–543 to find ways to improve your writing.

2. There are many ways to answer this question. Compare your essay to this example of one way to write a high-scoring response.

Recently, many people complain soft drinks. They say that sugar in drinks is bad for people, so sale should be stop. Soft drinks have many advantages, so I do not agree with this idea.

First, soft drinks taste good. Everyone likes the flavor of their favorite soda. They taste great and the bubbles are funny.

Second, soda does not contain alcohol. Many people drink alcohol, which causes social problems. So why are we worried so much about soda. Personally, I do not drink alcohol, so why ban my drink when other drinks that also can cause problems, are legal?

Third, not all soda contain sugar. They contain fake sugar. That fake sugar is very dangerous, maybe cause cancer. So why are we so worried about sugar? Other soda more dangerous. Sugar is natural product.

So for these reasons, I do not agree about banning soda with sugar. Other products are dangerous but we don't ban them. Soda is fun and not so dangerous, so we should drink it.

EVALUATION

Have a teacher or an English-speaking friend review your essay, or wait a day or two and review your essay yourself. Use a copy of the Independent Writing Rubric in Appendix E to evaluate your writing. Review the boxes you checked in the rubric. The row with the most boxes checked is most likely your score on the actual TOEFL iBT. Then use the TOEFL iBT Personalized Study Planner on pages 540–543 to find ways to improve your writing.

CHAPTER

7

TOEFL iBT Final Practice Test 1

Chapter at a Glance

In this chapter, you will learn:

TOEFL iBT Final Practice Test 1 . . . . Your strengths and weaknesses on each section of the TOEFL iBT

TOEFL iBT Personalized Study Planner . . . . Your personalized plan for preparing for the TOEFL iBT

This TOEFL iBT Final Practice Test 1 is designed to help you assess the skills you will need to score your best on the TOEFL iBT.

Completing the entire test takes about 3 hours and 30 minutes, the same amount of time as the actual TOEFL iBT. If possible, complete the test in one sitting to simulate the actual test experience. If you cannot complete the test in a single sitting, use the TOEFL iBT Test At a Glance to help you plan how much time to allow for each part. The table also indicates the materials you will need for each section of this test.

AT A GLANCE

TOEFL iBT Final Practice Test 1

SECTION	TIME	YOU NEED
Reading	60 minutes	Watch or timer on your computer or mobile phone
Listening	60 minutes	Watch or timer, disk, and player
Break	10 minutes	The actual TOEFL iBT includes a break between Listening and Speaking.
Speaking	20 minutes	Watch or timer, disk and player, audio recorder on your mobile phone or computer
Writing	60 minutes	Watch or timer, disk and player, computer to keyboard your response
All sections		Paper and pencil or pen for taking notes during all sections of the TOEFL iBT. (Note-taking is allowed on all sections of the TOEFL iBT.)

After you take this test, use the Answers, Explanations, Audio Scripts, and Sample Responses on pages 620–639 to check your work. Then use the TOEFL iBT Personalized Study Planner on pages 614–619 to analyze your results and find the skills you need to review before you take TOEFL iBT Final Practice Test 2 and the actual TOEFL iBT.

Reading

Directions: The Reading section of the TOEFL iBT asseses your ability to understand academic reading passages in English. To simulate actual TOEFL iBT conditions, follow these instructions:

- Use your watch or the timer on your mobile phone or computer to keep track of the time.
- Give yourself 20 minutes to read each passage and respond to the items that are about it.
- Allow 60 minutes to read all the passages and answer all the items.
- As on the actual TOEFL iBT, you may look back at the passage when answering items. You can skip items and return to them.
- If you do not finish all the items when the test ends, mark your place. Then continue working as quickly as you can. When you finish, take note of the total time. This will give you an idea of how quickly you need to work on the actual TOEFL iBT to answer all the items in 60 minutes.

Now begin the Reading section of TOEFL iBT Final Practice Test 1.

Directions: Give yourself 20 minutes to read the passage and answer Items 1–14.

In psychology and medicine, the term *stress* is a relatively new one, the first usage of the term being noted around 1930. Up until that time, the word *stress* was mostly used in physical sciences, architecture, and engineering to describe the strains that force and motion put on objects. A building might exhibit stress as a strong wind blows on it, for example. Psychology and medicine had not much addressed or discussed the strain that life and events of daily living can put on people, the physiological responses those strains can trigger in our bodies, and the effects of those responses on our health.

The concept of stress, as it is defined in medicine today, is closely related to the concept of homeostasis, or equilibrium. The concept of homeostasis refers to the way our bodies operate. Our bodies always try to reach a state of balance in their physical operations. Our rate of breathing, blood flow, digestion, and so on all operate in a constant state of flux around an idealized state of equilibrium. Our bodies try to achieve an appropriate and consistent rate of breathing, for example, to support our current level of activity. As our bodies experience change, such as a need to move, a change in air temperature, or the need to digest food, the operations of our bodies increase or decrease proportionately in order to maintain homeostasis. Stress is typically defined as an event that disrupts homeostasis excessively, with negative consequences. Our heart rates go up, blood pressure increases, digestion slows, and other reactions happen. These reactions themselves have negative consequences for our bodies.

When a difficult event happens, the typical response of the human body is the "fight-or-flight syndrome." This reaction is considered to be rooted in our distant past, when humans had to fight off predators to survive. The physical reactions of the fight-or-flight syndrome—increased heart rate, elevated blood pressure, and other changes—were designed to help our bodies marshal all their strength and resources to fight off the enemy. Today, other kinds of danger cause our bodies to react in the same way even though we no longer need to fight off opponents physically. When a threatening event happens, both the nervous system and the endocrine system increase their activity to respond to the threat or perceived threat. The central nervous system, especially the spinal cord and brain, become active to be able to handle the increased nerve and muscle activity demanded by responding to a threat. Another part of the nervous system, the sympathetic nervous system (which regulates basic functions of organs), becomes active to increase functions such as breathing, heart rate, and so on so that the body can be more physically responsive. Increased blood flows to the brain to support nervous system activity. Increased breathing rate, heart rate, and blood flow ensure that the body will have oxygen for extra activity required. Finally, the endocrine system (the system of glands that release chemicals that regulate many bodily functions) releases hormones to help the body respond to the threat. One in particular, cortisol, is thought to help the body redistribute energy evenly through the body so that all parts of the body will have energy to respond to the perceived threat. All of these reactions, however, are themselves stressful to the body. Blood pressure increases, digestion slows, and extra strain is placed on the heart, for example.

Stress is considered the negative impact of these physiological responses. Different scientists define stress differently. Some say that the body's response to any perceived threat is stressful, while others believe that only a bodily response that "exceeds the body's capacities to respond" is a stress event. In either case, excessive stress is considered to be a medical condition of its own that can have harmful consequences.

Stress has long been hypothesized to be a contributing factor to many medical conditions, such as decreased immunity to disease, high blood pressure, and excessive or unwanted weight gain. To measure stress and connect it to illness, Thomas Holmes and Richard Rahe developed a scale to measure stress and its association with illness. Using their Social Readjustment Rating Scale (SRRS), more commonly known as the Holmes and Rahe Stress Scale, they asked respondents to state whether they had recently experienced forty-three different events deemed to be stressful, such as losing one's job, experiencing a divorce or separation, becoming pregnant, and so on, in the previous six months. Then the respondents' health was tracked for the next six months. Results showed a strong correlation between scoring high on the stress scale in the previous six months and experiencing an illness in the next six months. Subsequent studies by other researchers have provided further validation, and investigators have developed specialized scales for teenagers and young adults, whose sources of stress are different from adults'.

Directions: Now answer the questions.

P A R A G R A P H 1

In psychology and medicine, the term *stress* is a relatively new one, the first usage of the term being noted around 1930. Up until that time, the word *stress* was mostly used in physical sciences, architecture, and engineering to describe the strains that force and motion put on objects. A building might exhibit stress as a strong wind blows on it, for example. Psychology and medicine had not much addressed or discussed the strain that life and events of daily living can put on people, the physiological responses those strains can trigger in our bodies, and the effects of those responses on our health.

1. According to the information in paragraph 1, which of the following is true of stress?

Ⓐ Stress begins because of a physiological problem.

Ⓑ Stress is not serious when it affects buildings and objects.

Ⓒ The concept of stress is relatively new to medicine and psychology.

Ⓓ Before 1930, people did not experience stress.

2. The word "trigger" in the passage is closest in meaning to

Ⓐ shoot

Ⓑ cause

Ⓒ increase

Ⓓ endanger

P A R A G R A P H 2

The concept of stress, as it is defined in medicine today, is closely related to the concept of homeostasis, or equilibrium. The concept of homeostasis refers to the way our bodies operate. Our bodies always try to reach a state of balance in their physical operations. Our rate of breathing, blood flow, digestion, and so on all operate in a constant state of flux around an idealized state of equilibrium. Our bodies try to achieve an appropriate and consistent rate of breathing, for example, to support our current level of activity. As our bodies experience change, such as a need to move, a change in air temperature, or the need to digest food, the operations of our bodies increase or decrease proportionately in order to maintain homeostasis. Stress is typically defined as an event that disrupts homeostasis excessively, with negative consequences. Our heart rates go up, blood pressure increases, digestion slows, and other reactions happen. These reactions themselves have negative consequences for our bodies.

3. According to paragraph 2, what does the strain of everyday life cause?

   (A) psychological problems

   (B) intense headaches

   (C) physical responses

   (D) a change in air temperature

4. Which of the following is NOT a way that stress has been defined in medicine and psychology?

   (A) The strains that force and motion put on objects

   (B) An event that causes the "fight-or-flight syndrome"

   (C) The effect of an event on homeostasis, or equilibrium

   (D) The long-term medical effects of the changes caused by a difficult event

5. The word "flux" in the passage is closest in meaning to

   (A) motion

   (B) tension

   (C) change

   (D) decrease

6. Which of the following best expresses the essential information in the highlighted sentence? Incorrect choices change the meaning in important ways or leave out essential information.

   (A) As our bodies maintain homeostasis, changes such as the need to move, changes in air temperature, or the need to digest food, cause the operations of our bodies to stay constant.

   (B) To maintain homeostasis, our bodies' operations adjust as we experience change, such as a need to move, a change in air temperature, or the need to digest food.

   (C) Our bodies' operations maintain homeostasis by increasing or decreasing change, such as the need to move, changes in air temperature, or the need to digest food.

   (D) To increase or decrease our bodies' operations to maintain homeostasis, our bodies experience change, such as a need to move, a change in air temperature, or the need to digest food.

When a difficult event happens, the typical response of the human body is the "fight-or-flight syndrome." This reaction is considered to be rooted in our distant past, when humans had to fight off predators to survive. The physical reactions of the fight-or-flight syndrome—increased heart rate, elevated blood pressure, and other changes—were designed to help our bodies marshal all their strength and resources to fight off the enemy. Today, other kinds of danger cause our bodies to react in the same way even though we no longer need to fight off opponents physically. When a threatening event happens, both the nervous system and the endocrine system increase their activity to respond to the threat or perceived threat. The central nervous system, especially the spinal cord and brain, become active to be able to handle the increased nerve and muscle activity demanded by responding to a threat. Another part of the nervous system, the sympathetic nervous system (which regulates basic functions of organs), becomes active to increase functions such as breathing, heart rate, and so on, so that the body can be more physically responsive. Increased blood flows to the brain to support nervous system activity. Increased breathing rate, heart rate, and blood flow ensure that the body will have oxygen for extra activity required. Finally, the endocrine system (the system of glands that release chemicals that regulate many bodily functions) releases hormones to help the body respond to the threat. One in particular, cortisol, is thought to help the body redistribute energy evenly through the body so that all parts of the body will have energy to respond to the perceived threat. All of these reactions, however, are themselves stressful to the body. Blood pressure increases, digestion slows, and extra strain is placed on the heart, for example.

7. According to the passage, which of these is true about the "fight-or-flight syndrome"?

Ⓐ It causes us to avoid facing our problems.

Ⓑ It is a remainder from our past.

Ⓒ It is an effective way to respond to the strains of life.

Ⓓ It only occurs when animals attack people.

8. Why does the author state that "Today, other kinds of danger cause our bodies to react in the same way even though we no longer need to fight off opponents physically"?

    (A) To show that physiological change in our bodies is no longer a logical reaction to a threat

    (B) To indicate that because stress is a natural reaction to a threat, we should not worry about its consequences

    (C) To show that our bodies are preprogrammed for violence

    (D) To indicate that the physical reactions to a threat are the result of a deeply rooted automatic defense mechanism

9. The word "one" in the passage refers to

    (A) a gland

    (B) a threat

    (C) a hormone

    (D) a body

PARAGRAPH 4

Stress is considered the negative impact of these physiological responses. Different scientists define stress differently. Some say that the body's response to any perceived threat is stressful, while others believe that only a bodily response that "exceeds the body's capacities to respond" is a stress event. In either case, excessive stress is considered to be a medical condition of its own that can have harmful consequences.

10. Which of the following can be inferred from the information in paragraph 4?

    (A) The word *stress* refers to the impact on our bodies of our body's responses to a threat.

    (B) All threats will have negative physiological effects on our bodies.

    (C) It is impossible to manage stress because it is the result of an automatic physiological process.

    (D) Scientists do not agree that stress has significant consequences on our health.

11. Why does the author state, "In either case, excessive stress is considered to be a medical condition of its own that can have harmful consequences"?

   (A) To indicate the author's disapproval of the controversy over the definition of stress

   (B) To indicate that stress is not a problem when it is not excessive

   (C) To indicate that the controversy disproves a possible link between stress and health

   (D) To indicate that even though scientists do not agree on whether all physiological changes cause stress, they do agree that excessive stress is harmful to our bodies

PARAGRAPH 5

Stress has long been hypothesized to be a contributing factor to many medical conditions, such as decreased immunity to disease, high blood pressure, and excessive or unwanted weight gain. To measure stress and connect it to illness, Thomas Holmes and Richard Rahe developed a scale to measure stress and its association with illness. Using their Social Readjustment Rating Scale (SRRS), more commonly known as the Holmes and Rahe Stress Scale, they asked respondents to state whether they had recently experienced forty-three different events deemed to be stressful, such as losing one's job, experiencing a divorce or separation, becoming pregnant, and so on, in the previous six months. Then the respondents' health was tracked for the next six months. Results showed a strong correlation between scoring high on the stress scale in the previous six months and experiencing an illness in the next six months. Subsequent studies by other researchers have provided further validation, and investigators have developed specialized scales for teenagers and young adults, whose sources of stress are different from adults'.

12. The word "whose" in the passage refers to

   (A) other researchers'

   (B) investigators'

   (C) teenagers' and young adults'

   (D) adults'

A Stress has long been hypothesized to be a contributing factor to many medical conditions, such as decreased immunity to disease, high blood pressure, and excessive or unwanted weight gain. **B** To measure stress and connect it to illness, Thomas Holmes and Richard Rahe developed a scale to measure stress and its association with illness. Using their Social Readjustment Rating Scale (SRRS), more commonly known as the Holmes and Rahe Stress Scale, they asked respondents to state whether they had recently experienced forty-three different events deemed to be stressful, such as losing one's job, experiencing a divorce or separation, becoming pregnant, and so on, in the previous six months. **C** Then the respondents' health was tracked for the next six months. Results showed a strong correlation between scoring high on the stress scale in the previous six months and experiencing an illness in the next six months. **D** Subsequent studies by other researchers have provided further validation, and investigators have developed specialized scales for teenagers and young adults, whose sources of stress are different from adults'.

13. Look at the four squares (■) that indicate where the following sentence could be inserted into the passage.

   The medical problems respondents experienced in the following months ranged from increased susceptibility to coughs and colds to higher rates of high blood pressure and heart attack.

   Where would the sentence best fit?

14. An introductory sentence for a brief summary of the passage is provided. Complete the summary by selecting the THREE answer choices that express important ideas in the passage. Some sentences do not belong in the summary because they express ideas that are not presented in the passage or are minor details in the passage. *This item is worth 2 points.*

   Write the letters of your answer choices in the spaces where they belong.

   The passage discusses the causes and effects of stress.

   -
   -
   -

Answer Choices

[A] Stress is the result of physiological changes that are a natural response to a threat in the environment.

[B] The purpose of the "fight-or-flight syndrome" is increased readiness to flee an attacker.

[C] Recent studies have shown that there is a relationship between high levels of stress and increased incidence of other health problems.

[D] High blood pressure is one of the principal effects of stress.

[E] Cortisol, a hormone produced during a stressful event, increases our ability to perceive risks in the environment.

[F] The concept of stress as a medical condition did not exist until relatively recently.

Directions: Give yourself 20 minutes to read the passage and answer Items 15–28.

The Arts and Crafts movement was an influential international design movement that lasted from about 1860 to 1910. Emphasizing handcrafting and decoration styles drawn from traditional and medieval motifs, the movement started in England and spread from there to industrialized parts of Europe as well as North America. Though considered mainly as a design movement, it was as much a social and political movement opposed to the excesses of industrialization as it was a design movement.

The Arts and Crafts movement had its origins in dissatisfaction with mass-produced goods made possible by the Industrial Revolution. The application of steam power to manufacturing led to mass production of household goods in large factories. Suddenly, common household objects that previously were produced by hand could be produced cheaply in mass quantities. However, the goods were often excessively ornate or unattractive, especially when compared to traditional, handmade products made by workers using old-fashioned methods. The poor quality and unattractive design of manufactured goods became apparent to many during the Great Exhibition of 1851 in London. This event, often called the Crystal Palace Exhibition, was in fact a celebration of the Industrial Revolution and England's leading role in it. England, the center of the Industrial Revolution, was the most industrialized nation in the world at the time. The Crystal Palace Exhibition was designed to be a showcase of England's industrial power and prestige. The exhibition, named for the large glass building in a London park where it took place, displayed the cloth, ceramics, furniture, and other goods whose mass production was made possible by the Industrial Revolution. Critics, however, noted that the new, mass-produced objects lacked the aesthetic appeal of handcrafted items. One influential critic, John Ruskin, wrote, "all machine work is bad; as work . . . it is dishonest." Almost immediately, many designers, including some of the organizers of the exhibition, began to call for design reform, though these first critics did not reject machine manufacture entirely.

The most influential exponent of the Arts and Crafts movement in England was William Morris, who wanted design reform but also backed social reform. Disturbed by the effects of the Industrial Revolution on the working classes, who labored for long hours in terrible conditions to produce shoddy merchandise of poor quality and unappealing design, Morris wanted to return to handcrafting and hoped to revitalize the role of the individual artisan, replace shoddy manufactured items with beautiful handmade ones, and return dignity to the common laborer. In an 1877 publication, Morris wrote, "I do not want art for a few any more than education for a few, or freedom for a few!" Morris and a few friends started a company to produce handcrafted objects. Among the objects the company first produced were furniture, stained glass, textiles such as cloth with hand-printed designs and embroidery, wallpaper, and hand-painted ceramic tiles. After a few years, the company was reorganized as William Morris and Company and began to create and sell tapestries and rugs in addition to the other items. Others encouraged the formation of small groups or cooperatives of artisans and designers.

The model for these organizations of workers and artists was the medieval craft guild. Medieval craft guilds were organizations of skilled experts in their crafts. There were guilds for candle makers, weavers, silversmiths, and every craft that existed. Guild members generally worked individually or in small groups and made everything by hand. Morris attempted to re-create this production process in his company, which operated as a kind of cooperative in which artists created designs for jewelers, furniture makers, weavers, ceramicists, and others to craft by hand.

Morris's company built interest in the movement, and in the 1880s its ideas were adapted and spread by a second generation of artists' cooperatives led by Arthur H. Mackmurdo, an English architect and designer who organized the Century Guild, an artists' cooperative similar to Morris's.

Mackmurdo also revitalized other crafts, such as preindustrial methods of book manufacturing. Printers, bookbinders, and artists produced beautifully bound and illustrated volumes. Other cooperatives began to spring up, and the ideals of the Arts and Crafts movement were adopted by artists and intellectuals. Their influence spread the movement's ideals even further afield, and the movement began to affect fine art and architecture. Many artists and intellectuals began to believe that there was no difference between fine and applied art, and design began to emerge as a profession of its own. At this time, the movement also spread to other centers of the Industrial Revolution, including North America, Germany, France, and Spain.

However, the movement was not without its critics. Many people believed that the Arts and Crafts movement was not practical in a modern, industrial society. In fact, only the very wealthy could afford the handcrafted items, and ironically, many of the biggest consumers of the objects were the captains of the Industrial Revolution themselves. In response to an 1893 exhibition, one critic stated that the movement was "the work of a few for a few." However, the ideas continued to spread and began to influence other styles such as Art Nouveau. Today, the jewelry, furniture, books, textiles, and other objects produced by the movement are coveted by collectors for their beauty and rarity.

Directions: Now answer the questions.

P
A
R
A
G
R
A
P
H

1

The Arts and Crafts movement was an influential international design movement that lasted from about 1860 to 1910. Emphasizing handcrafting and decoration styles drawn from traditional and medieval motifs, the movement started in England and spread from there to industrialized parts of Europe as well as North America. Though considered mainly as a design movement, it was as much a social and political movement opposed to the excesses of industrialization as it was a design movement.

15. According to the information in paragraph 1, which of the following is true of the Arts and Crafts movement?

Ⓐ It was a global design movement.

Ⓑ It was a reform movement focused on the future.

Ⓒ It encouraged using new technology to change society.

Ⓓ It supported social change as well as cultural change.

P
A
R
A
G
R
A
P
H

2
The Arts and Crafts movement had its origins in dissatisfaction with mass-produced goods made possible by the Industrial Revolution. The application of steam power to manufacturing led to mass production of household goods in large factories. Suddenly, common household objects that previously were produced by hand could be produced cheaply in mass quantities. However, this abundance of goods was not without its price. Moreover, the goods were often excessively ornate or unattractive, especially when compared to traditional, handmade products made by workers using old-fashioned methods. The poor quality and unattractive design of manufactured goods became apparent to many during the Great Exhibition of 1851 in London. This event, often called the Crystal Palace Exhibition, was in fact a celebration of the Industrial Revolution and England's leading role in it. England, the center of the Industrial Revolution, was the most industrialized nation in the world at the time. The Crystal Palace Exhibition was designed to be a showcase of England's industrial power and prestige. The exhibition, named for the large glass building in a London park where it took place, displayed the cloth, ceramics, furniture, and other goods whose mass production was made possible by the Industrial Revolution. Critics, however, noted that the new, mass-produced objects lacked the aesthetic appeal of handcrafted items. One influential critic, John Ruskin, wrote, "all machine work is bad; as work . . . it is dishonest." Almost immediately, many designers, including some of the organizers of the exhibition, began to call for design reform, though these first critics did not reject machine manufacture entirely.

16. According to paragraph 2, all of the following were problems caused by the Industrial Revolution EXCEPT:

(A) Mass production made inexpensive goods widely available.

(B) Mass-produced goods were unattractive.

(C) Mass production resulted in difficult working conditions.

(D) Mass-produced goods were often not well made.

17. Which of the following can be inferred from information in the passage?

(A) The Crystal Palace Exhibition was led by social reformers opposed to the Industrial Revolution.

(B) The Crystal Palace Exhibition unintentionally led to criticism of the Industrial Revolution.

(C) The Crystal Palace Exhibition encouraged cheap, shoddy manufacturing.

(D) The Crystal Palace Exhibition proved that high-quality goods could not be produced in mass quantities.

18. The word "it" in the passage refers to

(A) the Industrial Revolution

(B) the exhibition

(C) a London park

(D) a building made of glass

PARAGRAPH 3

The most influential exponent of the Arts and Crafts movement in England was William Morris, who wanted design reform but also backed social reform. Disturbed by the effects of the Industrial Revolution on the working classes, who labored for long hours in terrible conditions to produce shoddy merchandise of poor quality and unappealing design, Morris wanted to return to handcrafting and hoped to revitalize the role of the individual artisan, replace shoddy manufactured items with beautiful handmade ones, and return dignity to the common laborer. In an 1877 publication, Morris wrote, "I do not want art for a few any more than education for a few, or freedom for a few!" Morris and a few friends started a company to produce handcrafted objects. Among the objects the company first produced were furniture, stained glass, textiles such as cloth with hand-printed designs and embroidery, wallpaper, and hand-painted ceramic tiles. After a few years, the company was reorganized as William Morris and Company and began to create and sell tapestries and rugs in addition to the other items. Others encouraged the formation of small groups or cooperatives of artisans and designers.

19. According to paragraph 3, why did Morris back social reform?

Ⓐ Industrialization resulted in shoddy merchandise.

Ⓑ Workers had to endure dreadful conditions.

Ⓒ The Crystal Palace Exhibition revealed that workers were exploited.

Ⓓ He believed workers were incapable of producing good products.

20. Why does the author include this quotation from Morris's 1877 publication: "I do not want art for a few any more than education for a few, or freedom for a few!"?

Ⓐ To show that Morris was more interested in education and freedom than design

Ⓑ To show that the Arts and Crafts movement was a social movement as well as a design movement

Ⓒ To show that the Arts and Crafts movement valued art more than craft

Ⓓ To show that Morris was a radical who wanted to overthrow the government and start a revolution

21. The word "textiles" in the passage is closest in meaning to

Ⓐ designs

Ⓑ stained glass

Ⓒ wallpaper

Ⓓ cloth

P
A
R
A
G
R
A
P
H

4
The model for these organizations of workers and artists was the medieval craft guild. Medieval craft guilds were organizations of skilled experts in their crafts. There were guilds for candle makers, weavers, silversmiths, and every craft that existed. Guild members generally worked individually or in small groups and made everything by hand. Morris attempted to re-create this production process in his company, which operated as a kind of cooperative in which artists created designs for jewelers, furniture makers, weavers, ceramicists, and others to craft by hand.

22. According to paragraph 4, how were medieval guilds and Morris's company similar?

Ⓐ In both of them, artists and workers worked side by side.

Ⓑ In both of them, workers worked individually.

Ⓒ In both of them, workers crafted goods by hand.

Ⓓ In both of them, workers focused on only one craft.

23. Which of the following best expresses the essential information in the highlighted sentence? Incorrect choices change the meaning in important ways or leave out essential information.

Ⓐ Morris tried to re-create this process in his company, a kind of cooperative in which artists created designs for artisans to handcraft.

Ⓑ Morris's company, re-created this kind of cooperative, in which artists created designs for artisans to craft by hand.

Ⓒ In Morris's company, a kind of cooperative, Morris re-created the process of having artists create designs for artisans to craft by hand.

Ⓓ Morris's company, which operated as a kind of cooperative, created designs for artists, jewelers, furniture makers, weavers, and ceramicists to craft by hand.

P
A
R
A
G
R
A
P
H

5

Morris's company built interest in the movement, and in the 1880s, its ideas were adapted and spread by a second generation of artists' cooperatives led by Arthur H. Mackmurdo, an English architect and designer who organized the Century Guild, an artists' cooperative similar to Morris's. Mackmurdo also revitalized other crafts, such as preindustrial methods of book manufacturing. Printers, bookbinders, and artists produced beautifully bound and illustrated volumes. Other cooperatives began to spring up, and the ideals of the Arts and Crafts movement were adopted by artists and intellectuals. Their influence spread the movement's ideals even further afield, and the movement began to affect fine art and architecture. Many artists and intellectuals began to believe that there was no difference between fine and applied art, and design began to emerge as a profession of its own. At this time, the movement also spread to other centers of the Industrial Revolution, including North America, Germany, France, and Spain.

24. The word "revitalized" in the passage is closest in meaning to

(A) industrialized

(B) reformed

(C) modernized

(D) brought new life to

25. The word "their" in the passage refers to

(A) ideals'

(B) artists' and intellectuals'

(C) Mackmurdo's

(D) Arts and Crafts'

P
A
R
A
G
R
A
P
H

5

Morris's company built interest in the movement, and in the 1880s its ideas were adapted and spread by a second generation of artists' cooperatives led by Arthur H. Mackmurdo, an English architect and designer who organized the Century Guild, an artists' cooperative similar to Morris's. **A** Mackmurdo also revitalized other crafts, such as preindustrial methods of book manufacturing. Printers, bookbinders, and artists produced beautifully bound and illustrated volumes. **B** Other cooperatives began to spring up, and the ideals of the Arts and Crafts movement were adopted by artists and intellectuals. Their influence spread the movement's ideals even further afield, and the movement began to affect fine art and architecture. Many artists and intellectuals began to believe that there was no difference between fine and applied art, and design began to emerge as a profession of its own. **C** At this time, the movement also spread to other centers of the Industrial Revolution, including North America, Germany, France, and Spain. **D**

26. Look at the four squares (■) that indicate where the following sentence could be inserted into the passage.

> **The movement's influence spread as far as Japan, where the focus on traditional forms and skillful handcrafting by master artisans had great appeal.**

Where would the sentence best fit?

P
A
R
A
G
R
A
P
H

6

However, the movement was not without its critics. Many people believed that the Arts and Crafts movement was not practical in a modern, industrial society. In fact, only the very wealthy could afford the handcrafted items, and ironically, many of the biggest consumers of the objects were the captains of the Industrial Revolution themselves. In response to an 1893 exhibition, one critic stated that the movement was "the work of a few for a few." However, the ideas continued to spread and began to influence other styles such as Art Nouveau. Today, the jewelry, furniture, books, textiles, and other objects produced by the movement are coveted by collectors for their beauty and rarity.

27. Why does the author include in paragraph 6 a critic's comment that the products produced by the Arts and Crafts movement were "the work of a few for a few"?

  (A) To show that the movement affected only a few areas of art and design

  (B) To show that the movement did not have the impact on society that Morris envisioned

  (C) To show that the movement was undermined by the leaders of the Industrial Revolution

  (D) To show that the movement would not be important until it affected Art Nouveau

28. Select from the seven phrases following the two phrases that correctly characterize production during the Industrial Revolution and the three phrases that correctly characterize the Arts and Crafts movement. Two of the phrases will NOT be used.

Complete the following table to summarize information about the Industrial Revolution and the Arts and Crafts movement. Match the appropriate statements to the group with which they are associated.

INDUSTRIAL REVOLUTION	ARTS AND CRAFTS MOVEMENT
Select 2	Select 3
•	•
•	•
	•

Answer Choices

  [A] Only the wealthy could afford the products.

  [B] Steam power was used to produce goods.

  [C] It used cooperatives to make goods in mass quantities.

  [D] It used traditional and medieval decorations.

  [E] Its beautiful handcrafted products were displayed in the Crystal Palace Exhibition.

  [F] Goods were produced in large factories.

  [G] It tried to improve conditions for workers.

Directions: Give yourself 20 minutes to read the passage and answer Items 29–42.

In nature, any adaptation that provides an animal with a better chance of survival gives it a competitive advantage over others. One of the most common of these adaptations is camouflage, an animal's ability to hide itself. While a tiger's stripes or a bird's bright green color may appear unique and attractive to us, these kinds of coloration actually serve an important purpose. Camouflage gives organisms two advantages. First, the camouflage helps the organisms hide from predators and avoid becoming prey. Second, camouflage helps predators increase their likelihood of finding prey by hiding from prey until it is too late for the prey to escape. Probably the best known and one of the most sophisticated kinds of camouflage is that of the chameleon. This small lizard has the amazing ability to change color to match its surroundings. However, the chameleon is not the only animal with the ability to change color, nor does all camouflage involve blending into the environment. Camouflage can be divided into three types: crypsis (blending into the environment), mimesis (imitating another organism), or motion dazzle (confusing coloration that makes the organism easy to see but hard to locate). Camouflage can be accomplished through coloration, transparency, and illumination. Camouflage most commonly involves the sense of sight, but many scientists believe that the senses of smell and hearing can also be involved.

Crypsis is the most commonly found camouflage in nature, and coloration is the most common form of crypsis. Many animals use coloration to blend into the environment so they are harder for predators to spot. For example, deer and squirrels, which live among trees, have a brown or tawny coat to help them blend into the background. The peppered moth has a brown and spotted coloration that helps it blend into the bark of trees. Other moths have a brownish coloration that helps them blend into dried leaves lying on the ground. Certain birds that live high in trees, such as parakeets, are bright green to blend into the leaves of trees. However, these are among the simplest kinds of crypsis. As mentioned previously, the chameleon, as well as several other animals, such as certain frogs, octopi, and flatfish, can change color using special cells in their skin. These organisms can change color very quickly. Other animals, typically ones that live in environments with snowy winters, change color slowly by changing the color of their fur or feathers. The arctic hare (a kind of rabbit), the arctic fox, and the rock ptarmigan (a bird) all molt and grow new feathers or fur twice a year to change color to hide from predators or prey year-round. In winter they are white, and in spring they shed their winter fur and change back to colors that match the spring and summer environment. Molting also lets the animals grow warm winter coats to endure the cold, harsh arctic winter.

In addition to coloration, crypsis can involve movement, scent, and sound. For example, the leafy green seadragon, a relative of the seahorse, lives among seaweed. It uses both appearance and movement as camouflage. Its body has green and leafy-looking growths that make it resemble seaweed. In addition, it mimics the movement of the surrounding seaweed in the sea currents to blend in. Several organisms use scent as a form of crypsis. For instance, some spiders mimic the smell of ants to trick the ants. When the ants come near the spiders, the spiders eat them. Some scientists have thought that certain moths use sound to avoid being eaten by bats. Scientists thought that the moths made sounds that deliberately confused the bats or imitated the sounds of moths that were not edible, but subsequent research failed to replicate these findings. Scientists are continuing to study how insects use sound to avoid or confuse predators.

Mimesis involves adopting the appearance of another organism. For example, the shape and coloration of the flower mantis, an insect, resembles an orchid. This helps the mantis both avoid predators and catch prey. When an insect arrives to drink the orchid's nectar, the mantis can surprise and devour the unsuspecting insect.

Motion dazzle is a kind of camouflage often used by extremely fast-moving animals. In general, crypsis is effective only when the animal is not moving. This is why deer stand motionless in the forest when they sense that a predator is nearby. Many scientists believe that the stripes on animals such as tigers and zebras serve as a kind of camouflage. The scientists hypothesize that the stripes make it difficult to detect the speed and direction of the animals as they run.

Directions: Now answer the questions.

In nature, any adaptation that provides an animal with a better chance of survival gives it a competitive advantage over others. One of the most common of these adaptations is camouflage, an animal's ability to hide itself. While a tiger's stripes or a bird's bright green color may appear unique and attractive to us, these kinds of coloration actually serve an important purpose. Camouflage gives organisms two advantages. First, the camouflage helps the organisms hide from predators and avoid becoming prey. Second, camouflage helps predators increase their likelihood of finding prey by hiding from prey until it is too late for the prey to escape. Probably the best known and one of the most sophisticated kinds of camouflage is that of the chameleon. This small lizard has the amazing ability to change color to match its surroundings. However, the chameleon is not the only animal with the ability to change color, nor does all camouflage involve blending into the environment. Camouflage can be divided into three types: crypsis (blending into the environment), mimesis (imitating another organism), or motion dazzle (confusing coloration that makes the organism easy to see but hard to locate). Camouflage can be accomplished through coloration, transparency, and illumination. Camouflage most commonly involves the sense of sight, but many scientists believe that the senses of smell and hearing can also be involved.

29. According to the passage, why do animals use camouflage?

   Ⓐ To have the amazing ability of changing color

   Ⓑ To have beautiful and unique coloration

   Ⓒ To escape from prey

   Ⓓ To increase their chances of survival

30. Which of the following is NOT an example of a kind of camouflage?

   Ⓐ A snake hides in a cave during the day to avoid the hot desert sun.

   Ⓑ A deer's coloration blends into the forest environment.

   Ⓒ A fish has a silver coating that reflects light but makes it hard to locate.

   Ⓓ A bird resembles a predatory bird to scare away other birds.

31. The word "it" in the passage refers to

Ⓐ adaptation

Ⓑ animal

Ⓒ survival

Ⓓ advantage

P
A
R
A
G
R
A
P
H

2

Crypsis is the most commonly found camouflage in nature, and coloration is the most common form of crypsis. Many animals use coloration to blend into the environment so they are harder for predators to spot. For example, deer and squirrels, which live among trees, have a brown or tawny coat to help them blend into the background. The peppered moth has a brown and spotted coloration that helps it blend into the bark of trees. Other moths have a brownish coloration that helps them blend into dried leaves lying on the ground. Certain birds that live high in trees, such as parakeets, are bright green to blend into the leaves of trees. However, these are among the simplest kinds of crypsis. As mentioned previously, the chameleon, as well as several other animals, such as certain frogs, octopi, and flatfish, can change color using special cells in their skin. These organisms can change color very quickly. Other animals, typically ones that live in environments with snowy winters, change color slowly by changing the color of their fur or feathers. The arctic hare (a kind of rabbit), the arctic fox, and the rock ptarmigan (a bird) all molt and grow new feathers or fur twice a year to change color to hide from predators or prey year-round. In winter they are white, and in spring they shed their winter fur and change back to colors that match the spring and summer environment. Molting also lets the animals grow warm winter coats to endure the cold, harsh arctic winter.

32. Why does the arctic hare molt in spring?

Ⓐ To blend into the snow

Ⓑ To match the brown summer colors

Ⓒ To shed its cool summer coat

Ⓓ To change color very quickly

33. The word "endure" in the passage is closest in meaning to

(A) enjoy

(B) escape from

(C) last through

(D) avoid

PARAGRAPH 3

In addition to coloration, crypsis can involve movement, scent, and sound. For example, the leafy green seadragon, a relative of the seahorse, lives among seaweed. It uses both appearance and movement as camouflage. Its body has green and leafy-looking growths that make it resemble seaweed. In addition, it mimics the movement of the surrounding seaweed in the sea currents to blend in. Several organisms use scent as a form of crypsis. For instance, some spiders mimic the smell of ants to trick the ants. When the ants come near the spiders, the spiders eat them. Some scientists have thought that certain moths use sound to avoid being eaten by bats. Scientists thought that the moths made sounds that deliberately confused the bats or imitated the sounds of moths that were not edible, but subsequent research failed to replicate these findings. Scientists are continuing to study how insects use sound to avoid or confuse predators.

34. How does the leafy green seadragon use movement as camouflage?

(A) It lives among seaweed.

(B) It has green finlike growths.

(C) It mimics the effects of sea currents.

(D) It uses its fins to swim and find food.

35. The word "it" in the passage refers to

(A) seahorse

(B) seaweed

(C) sea currents

(D) seadragon

36. Which of the following best expresses the essential information in the highlighted sentence? Incorrect choices change the meaning in important ways or leave out essential information.

    (A) Later studies failed to replicate findings that moths made sounds that confused bats or imitated the sounds of inedible moths.

    (B) Subsequent research failed to replicate findings that moths made sounds that confused bats or imitated the sounds of inedible bats.

    (C) Scientists thought that subsequent research failed to disprove that moths made sound that confused bats or imitated the sounds of inedible moths.

    (D) Scientists disproved later studies that failed to replicate findings that moths made sounds that confused bats or imitated the sounds of inedible moths.

37. Why does the author mention in paragraph 3 that scientists are continuing to study how insects use sound to avoid or confuse predators?

    (A) To indicate that more research is necessary to clarify contradictory results about whether insects use sound camouflage

    (B) To indicate that scientists are convinced they will find insects that use sound camouflage if they keep investigating

    (C) To indicate that scientists believe that the subsequent studies are wrong

    (D) To indicate that scientists do not trust the results of previous studies of sound camouflage

P
A
R
A
G
R
A
P
H

3

In addition to coloration, crypsis can involve movement, scent, and sound. For example, the leafy green seadragon, a relative of the seahorse, lives among seaweed. It uses both appearance and movement as camouflage. **A** Its body has green and leafy-looking growths that make it resemble seaweed. In addition, it mimics the movement of the surrounding seaweed in the sea currents to blend in. **B** Several organisms use scent as a form of crypsis. For instance, some spiders mimic the smell of ants to trick the ants. When the ants come near the spiders, the spiders eat them. **C** Some scientists have thought that certain moths use sound to avoid being eaten by bats. Scientists thought that the moths made sounds that deliberately confused the bats, or imitated the sounds of moths that were not edible, but subsequent research failed to replicate these findings. Scientists are continuing to study how insects use sound to avoid or confuse predators. **D**

38. Look at the four squares (■) that indicate where the following sentence could be inserted into the passage.

> **A second example is the large blue Butterfly caterpillar, which secretes a sweet-smelling substance that tricks ants into bringing it into their nest where they feed from it, but later the caterpillar begins to eat the ants' eggs and larvae.**

Where would the sentence best fit?

P
A
R
A
G
R
A
P
H

4

Mimesis involves adopting the appearance of another organism. For example, the shape and coloration of the flower mantis, an insect, resembles an orchid. This helps the mantis both avoid predators and catch prey. When an insect arrives to drink the orchid's nectar, the mantis can surprise and devour the unsuspecting insect.

39. The word "mimesis" in the passage is closest in meaning to

(A) taking

(B) imitating

(C) making

(D) accepting

Motion dazzle is a kind of camouflage often used by extremely fast-moving animals. In general, crypsis is effective only when the animal is not moving. This is why deer stand motionless in the forest when they sense that a predator is nearby. Many scientists believe that the stripes on animals such as tigers and zebras serve as a kind of camouflage. The scientists hypothesize that the stripes make it difficult to detect the speed and direction of the animals as they run.

<small>PARAGRAPH 5</small>

40. Why is motion dazzle camouflage beneficial to animals that can move very quickly?

   Ⓐ It helps them avoid detection as they hide behind bushes waiting for prey.

   Ⓑ It helps the animals increase the advantage of their extreme speed.

   Ⓒ It alerts predators that the animals can run away very quickly.

   Ⓓ It alerts prey that a predator is rapidly approaching.

41. Why does the author mention that scientists "hypothesize" that stripes make it difficult to detect the speed and direction of the animals?

   Ⓐ To indicate that the scientists are not completely sure about this idea

   Ⓑ To indicate that the scientists reject this idea completely

   Ⓒ To indicate that the scientists are certain that this idea is correct

   Ⓓ To indicate that the scientists feel confused when they see these animals running

42. An introductory sentence for a brief summary of the passage is provided. Complete the summary by selecting the THREE answer choices that express important ideas in the passage. Some sentences do not belong in the summary because they express ideas that are not presented in the passage or are minor details in the passage. *This item is worth 2 points.*

Write the letters of your answer choices in the spaces where they belong.

> **The passage discusses the purposes and types of camouflage.**
>
> •
>
> •
>
> •

Answer Choices

A   Mimesis is the most common kind of camouflage.

B   Camouflage means "blending into the environment."

C   Camouflage gives animals a competitive advantage.

D   Camouflage can involve the senses of sight, smell, and hearing.

E   Three main types of camouflage are crypsis, mimesis, and motion dazzle.

F   All animals use one sort of camouflage or another.

Answers and Explanations for the Reading section of TOEFL iBT Final Practice Test 1 begin on page 620.

Listening

Directions: The Listening section of the TOEFL iBT assesses your ability to understand conversations and lectures in English. To simulate actual TOEFL iBT conditions, follow these instructions:

- Listen to each conversation or lecture only once. You may take notes while listening and use your notes as you answer the items.
- After each conversation or lecture, answer the items that follow in the order in which they appear. After you answer an item, do not go back. Continue with each passage and its items until you complete the test or time has ended.
- Use your watch or the timer on your mobile phone or computer to keep track of the time. Allow 60 minutes to listen to all the passages and answer the questions.
- If you do not finish all the items when the test ends, mark your place. Then continue working as quickly as you can. When you finish, take note of the total time. This will give you an idea of how quickly you need to work on the actual TOEFL iBT to answer all the items in 60 minutes.

The Audio icon appears each time you need to listen to an audio track. For some items, you need to listen to another audio track besides the conversation or lecture in order to answer.

Now begin the Listening section of TOEFL iBT Final Practice Test 1.

Directions: Listen to a conversation between a student and a professor.

Directions: Now answer the questions. Circle the letter of the answer.

1. Why is the student talking to the professor?

Ⓐ She is unsure about how to organize her term paper.

Ⓑ She does not have time to finish her term paper.

Ⓒ She has not read enough research for her term paper.

Ⓓ She would like to change the topic of her term paper.

2. According to the research, what usually happens when a coyote leaves the pack?

Ⓐ It is much more likely to die.

Ⓑ It is a little more likely to die.

Ⓒ It is much less likely to die.

Ⓓ It is a little less likely to die.

3. Listen again to part of the conversation. Then answer the question.

Ⓐ He wants to show that he agrees with the student.

Ⓑ He wants to make the student feel embarrassed.

Ⓒ He wants to persuade the student to give his own opinion.

Ⓓ He wants to encourage the student to think more deeply.

4. What did de Waal conclude about chimpanzees?

Ⓐ They greatly enjoy grooming each other.

Ⓑ They return favors in the same way humans do.

Ⓒ Gratitude is a mechanism for their social cohesion.

Ⓓ Chimp society is more cohesive than human society.

5. What is the most likely topic of the student's term paper?

Ⓐ Differences in human and animal values

Ⓑ Fundamental human and animal values

Ⓒ Selfish behavior in humans and animals

Ⓓ Recent discoveries in human and animal psychology

Directions: Listen to part of a lecture in a class on Japanese cinema. The professor is talking about the films of Yasujiro Ozu.

Japanese Cinema

Yasujiro Ozu

tatami mat

Directions: Now answer the questions. Circle the letter of the answer.

6. What is the lecture mainly about?

   Ⓐ How Yasujiro Ozu's films compare to other great films made in Japan

   Ⓑ What makes Yasujiro Ozu's films so magnificent

   Ⓒ Why critics think Yasujiro Ozu's films are overrated

   Ⓓ How Yasujiro Ozu's films are similar to Hollywood movies

7. According to the professor, which of these themes is characteristic of Ozu's films?

   Ⓐ The adventure and excitement of modern life

   Ⓑ The boredom of a simple, uneventful life

   Ⓒ The disintegration of the extended family

   Ⓓ The dangers of life in a large, dynamic city

8. How does Ozu feel about the characters in *Tokyo Story*?

   Ⓐ He finds them cruel and petty.

   Ⓑ He does not judge them.

   Ⓒ He considers them low-class.

   Ⓓ He does not think their lives are eventful.

9. How does the professor define "ellipsis"?

   Ⓐ Important events like weddings

   Ⓑ Events that should not be shown on screen

   Ⓒ A series of insignificant events

   Ⓓ Major events that happen off screen

10. In what ways do Ozu's films differ from standard Hollywood films?

   Ⓐ They are more static and less melodramatic.

   Ⓑ They won many awards, but cost less to make.

   Ⓒ Their soundtracks contain more music.

   Ⓓ Their characters do not rely so much on dialogue.

11. In the professor's opinion, what can modern viewers gain from Ozu's films?

Ⓐ A deeper understanding of Japanese cinema

Ⓑ Ways to improve the quality of their own lives

Ⓒ An appreciation of film restoration

Ⓓ An evening's light entertainment

Directions: Listen to part of a lecture in a class on the history of science. The professor is talking about the invention of zero.

History
of Science

zero as a number

zero as an empty
placeholder

the Babylonians

the Mayans

Directions: Now answer the questions. Circle the letter of the answer.

12. What is the main idea of this lecture?

   Ⓐ Zero is an ancient idea.

   Ⓑ Zero has caused much confusion.

   Ⓒ Zero is difficult to understand.

   Ⓓ Zero has a curious history.

13. How did the early Babylonians deal with zero as an empty placeholder?

   Ⓐ By context

   Ⓑ By adding symbols like stars

   Ⓒ By writing zero as a big O

   Ⓓ By writing zero as a little o

14. How was zero used as an empty placeholder in ancient Greece?

   Ⓐ By architects to construct buildings

   Ⓑ By astronomers to track the positions of stars

   Ⓒ By engineers to design roads

   Ⓓ By merchants to keep track of accounts

15. Why does the professor give the example of the ancient Greek farmer?

   Ⓐ To tell the students an amusing anecdote

   Ⓑ To suggest that ancient Greeks were mainly practical people

   Ⓒ To demonstrate why the number zero was not needed

   Ⓓ To refute arguments about a lack of intelligence in the ancient world

16. The professor mentions some important events related to zero. Put the events in order from earliest to latest.

   Write your answer choices in the spaces where they belong. You can either write the letter of your answer choice or you can copy the statement. The last one is done for you. *This item is worth 2 points.*

1.	
2.	
3.	
4.	
5.	Around 1600 AD, zero as a number becomes widely used in Europe.

   Answer Choices

   A The Mayans start to use zero as a number.

   B The Babylonians start to use zero as an empty placeholder.

   C The symbol for zero first appears in a Chinese document.

   D An Indian mathematician tries to give rules for zero as a number.

17. Why does the professor tell his story about New Year's Day 2000?

   Ⓐ To exhibit his deep understanding of this topic

   Ⓑ To suggest that our current calendar should be reformed

   Ⓒ To show that understanding zero as a number remains problematic

   Ⓓ To show that people understand zero correctly these days

Directions: Listen to a conversation between a student and a university employee.

Directions: Now answer the questions. Circle the letter of the answer.

18. What does the student want to do?

Ⓐ Get a gym membership

Ⓑ Register a sports club

Ⓒ Join a cultural club

Ⓓ Register a cultural club

19. Who does Reading Reach-Out want to help?

Ⓐ Students majoring in education

Ⓑ Adults in the wider community

Ⓒ Young children in town

Ⓓ High school students

20. What will be one activity of Reading Reach-Out?

Ⓐ Giving away children's books

Ⓑ Teaching children to read

Ⓒ Selling children's books

Ⓓ Writing children's books

21. How can the student apply for college funding for Reading Reach-Out?

Ⓐ Make a short speech to the Student Union

Ⓑ Fill out a form and prepare a budget

Ⓒ Write 500 words for a student magazine

Ⓓ Ask a student committee to recommend funding

22. 🎧 AUDIO TRACK 132 Listen again to part of the conversation. Then answer the question.

Ⓐ She wants to show her approval of the rule.

Ⓑ She wants to show her awareness of the rule.

Ⓒ She wants to show her uncertainty about the rule.

Ⓓ She wants to show her disregard for the rule.

Directions: Listen to part of a lecture in an engineering class. The professor is talking about geothermal energy.

Engineering

Geothermal energy

Solar energy

Directions: Now answer the questions. Circle the letter of the answer.

23. What aspect of geothermal energy does the professor mainly discuss?

Ⓐ The history of geothermal energy

Ⓑ Reasons to avoid using geothermal energy

Ⓒ Uses of geothermal energy in countries around the world

Ⓓ The advantages and disadvantages of geothermal energy

24. Overall, how does the professor feel about geothermal energy?

Ⓐ She thinks solar power is preferable.

Ⓑ She thinks it is worth developing.

Ⓒ She thinks it is not worth developing yet.

Ⓓ She thinks it is a fantasy.

25. According to the professor, when do geothermal wells become cost-effective?

Ⓐ When they produce water or steam at 120 degrees Celsius

Ⓑ When people can drill down to Earth's core

Ⓒ When energy rising to Earth's surface is equal to energy from the sun

Ⓓ At night or when the sun's light is blocked by weather

26. What kind of geothermal system does France prefer?

Ⓐ One that requires inexpensive pumping equipment

Ⓑ One that uses naturally occurring hot water or steam

Ⓒ One that can supply the United Kingdom via a deep-sea cable

Ⓓ One that uses water artificially circulated through hot rock

27. Which is true of the following energy sources?

    Place a check (✔) in the correct box. This item is worth 2 points.

	GEOTHERMAL	SOLAR	OIL AND GAS
Intermittent supply			
Endless supply			
Low maintenance costs			
Greenhouse gases produced			

28. What are the main disadvantages of geothermal energy at present?
    Choose 2 answers.

    A Hot rocks cool down within 10 years.

    B Occasional explosions make wells unsafe for workers.

    C Initial investment in a well is high.

    D Technology is not advanced enough to drill deep wells.

AUDIO TRACK 134

Directions: Listen to part of a lecture in a zoology class. The professor is talking about birds.

Zoology

Western scrub-jay

New Caledonian crow

palm cockatoo

theory of mind

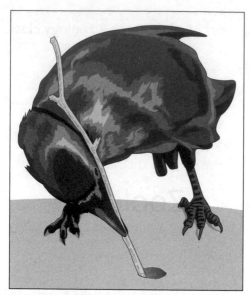

A New Caledonian crow using a twig

A palm cockatoo drumming

Directions: Now answer the questions. Circle the letter of the answer.

29. Why does the professor talk about these three birds?

Ⓐ They all live a very long time.

Ⓑ They are changing scientists' views on the intelligence of birds.

Ⓒ They make tools from branches and other plant material.

Ⓓ They are threatened with extinction.

30. According to the professor, which one of the following is true of New Caledonian crows?

Ⓐ Much of their behavior is instinctive.

Ⓑ They have a very unusual beak.

Ⓒ They make hooked tools.

Ⓓ They live in Australia.

31. Why does the professor mention bats' wings?

Ⓐ To prove that feathered birds are more intelligent than bats

Ⓑ To indicate that bats are mammals, not birds

Ⓒ To show that bats are inferior to birds

Ⓓ To make an interesting but irrelevant comment

32. What are two reasons that a male palm cockatoo might drum? *Choose 2 answers.*

Ⓐ To attract mates

Ⓑ To stake out territory

Ⓒ To demonstrate his musical skill

Ⓓ To assess the size of a potential nest cavity

33. What is a "theory of mind"?

Ⓐ The ability to understand another individual's experience

Ⓑ The ability to pay attention to detail

Ⓒ The ability to project one's own experience onto another individual's

Ⓓ The ability to learn complex new information

34. What evidence is there that Western scrub-jays have sophisticated thought processes?

Ⓐ They use memories of past experience to plan their future.

Ⓑ They conceal stolen food so carefully that only they can find it.

Ⓒ They produce a variety of complex calls.

Ⓓ They successfully avoid dangerous traffic.

Answers and Explanations for the Listening section of TOEFL iBT Final Practice Test 1 begin on page 626.

Speaking

Directions: The Speaking section of the TOEFL iBT assesses your ability to speak in English on a variety of academic and general-interest topics. Some of the items assess only your speaking skills, while others assess your ability to integrate information from reading and/or listening passages into your speaking. To simulate actual TOEFL iBT conditions, follow these instructions:

- For items that integrate listening, listen to each conversation or lecture only once.
- For items that integrate reading, use your watch or timer to keep track of the time. After reading time is up, do not refer back to the reading as you answer.
- As you read, listen, and plan your response, you may take notes to use when giving your response.
- Use your computer's or mobile device's *record* function to record and play back your responses. If your device does not have this function, ask a friend with strong English skills to listen to your responses. You or your friend can evaluate your responses using the simplified scoring rubrics in this book.

The Audio icon appears each time you need to listen to an audio track.

 When this icon appears, record your response on your computer or mobile device. If your device does not have a *record* function, ask a friend with strong English skills to listen to your response.

Now begin the Speaking section of TOEFL iBT Final Practice Test 1.

1. You will now speak about a familiar topic. Prepare your response in 15 seconds. Then allow 45 seconds to record your response.

Describe a local festival from your hometown that you enjoy. Include specific examples and details in your description.

Preparation Time: 15 seconds
Response Time: 45 seconds

2. 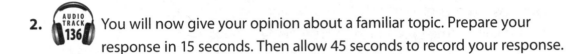 You will now give your opinion about a familiar topic. Prepare your response in 15 seconds. Then allow 45 seconds to record your response.

Some people take a year off between high school and college or university. Other people prefer to go directly from high school into college or university. Which do you think is better for students? Explain why.

Preparation Time: 15 seconds
Response Time: 45 seconds

3. You will now read a short passage on a campus-related topic and listen to a conversation on the same subject. Then you will hear a question. Prepare your response in 30 seconds. Then allow 60 seconds to record your response.

Announcement from Student Services

Beginning in fall semester, the university will pilot a new on-campus bus service operating between 7 P.M. and 11. P.M. The pilot will last one semester.

The service will be a figure eight, taking in campus Gates 2 and 8 at its extremities and passing by Memorial Student Union, the Academic Quadrangle, McKinley Library, and the Red Parking Building. All stops will be lighted and equipped with digital displays that provide the estimated time of arrival of the next bus. Buses will run approximately every 20 minutes.

The bus will be free to all university staff and students.

 Now listen to two students discussing the announcement.

The woman expresses her opinion of the announcement by Student Services. Briefly summarize the announcement. Then state her opinion about the announcement and explain the reasons she gives for holding that opinion.

| Preparation Time: 30 seconds |
| Response Time: 60 seconds |

4. You will now read a short passage on an academic topic and then listen to a talk on the same subject. Then you will hear a question. Prepare your response in 30 seconds. Then allow 60 seconds to record your response.

Reading Time: 50 seconds

Roman Temples

A temple in the Roman world performed a different role from a modern religious building. People did not gather inside. Most activities, including sacrifices, took place in the open air. Instead, a temple was a sanctuary, or sacred home, for gods. The dark, unlit room in which statues of the gods stood was called a *cella* in Latin—the language of the Romans.

The feeling of grandeur inspired by a temple bestowed pride upon the locals who had built it while reminding them of the great power of the Roman Empire.

Now listen to part of a lecture on this topic in an art history class.

The professor describes the Temple of Bacchus at Baalbek. Explain the temple's functions and how its design is typical of Roman temples. Use information from the reading and the talk.

Preparation Time: 30 seconds
Response Time: 60 seconds

5.  You will now listen to part of a conversation about a campus-related situation. Then you will hear a question. Prepare your response in 20 seconds. Then allow 60 seconds to record your response.

Summarize briefly the problem that the speakers are talking about. Then say which of the two solutions from the conversation you would recommend. Explain your reasons for your recommendation.

Preparation Time: 20 seconds
Response Time: 60 seconds

6.  You will now listen to part of a lecture on an academic topic. Then you will hear a question. Prepare your response in 20 seconds. Then allow 60 seconds to record your response.

Using points and examples from the talk, explain which factors influence taste and pleasure in food consumption.

| Preparation Time: 20 seconds |
| Response Time: 60 seconds |

Explanations and Sample Responses for the Speaking section of TOEFL iBT Final Practice Test 1 begin on page 635.

Writing

Directions: The Writing section of the TOEFL iBT assesses your ability to communicate in writing in academic settings. This section has two items. To simulate actual TOEFL iBT conditions, follow these instructions.

ITEM 1: INTEGRATED WRITING

- Read the passage in 3 minutes. Use your watch or the timer on your phone or computer to keep track of time. You may take notes as you read and listen and use your notes when you answer the question.
- Start the audio program and listen to the passage one time as you take notes.
- Read the question, plan your response, and write it in 20 minutes. You may use your notes and refer back to the reading passage as you write.

ITEM 2: INDEPENDENT WRITING

- Set your timer for 30 minutes and start working. You may take notes to plan your essay and to use as you write.

 The Audio icon appears when you need to listen to an audio track.

If you do not finish your essays when the time ends, mark your place. Then continue working as quickly as you can. When you finish, take note of the total time. This will give you an idea of how quickly you need to work on the actual TOEFL iBT to write both essays in 60 minutes.

Now begin the Writing section of the TOEFL iBT Final Practice Test 1.

1. Integrated Writing

A. Read the passage in 3 minutes. Use your watch or the timer on your phone or computer to keep track of the time. You may take notes in the space provided.

Reading Time: 3 minutes

In recent years, the question of who owns essential cultural artifacts has challenged museums, collectors, and governments. Many cultural artifacts were removed from countries during war, occupation, and colonization. Some of the most renowned objects that have been removed include the so-called Elgin marbles, beautiful stone carvings from the Parthenon in Athens, Greece; burial remains and other artifacts from ancient Egypt; and thousand-year-old paintings from churches in northeastern Spain. Sometimes the objects were removed with the permission of local authorities. The Elgin marbles, for example, were taken from Athens under a permit from the government in power at the time. However, the Rosetta Stone, a trilingual stone carving that was key in helping scholars understand ancient Egyptian writing, was found by a French soldier but then was captured by the British army and taken to London. Thousand-year-old paintings were taken from the walls of village churches in Spain by collectors, who sometimes paid for the works and other times removed them surreptitiously late at night when villagers were asleep. Many governments have reclaimed these objects on grounds that they were removed by force or without appropriate permission. The institutions that house these objects have been reluctant to return them because the objects are often their most renowned exhibits. The Rosetta Stone, for example, is the most visited exhibit in the British Museum in London. Museums often argue that they acquired the objects in good faith and that the objects are too valuable, too fragile, or too impractical to move. Returning the Elgin Marbles to Greece, for example, would involve packing, moving, and shipping tons of ancient stone carvings hundreds of miles. Returning the paintings to Spain would involve transporting fragile mural paintings thousands of miles. Nevertheless, museums have returned many objects acquired in dubious or unclear ways.

_____

_____

_____

_____

B. Now listen to part of a lecture on the topic you just read about. You may take notes in the space provided.

C. Take 20 minutes to plan, write, and revise an essay of about 150 to 225 words. Use a watch or timer to keep track of time. You may refer to the reading and your notes as you plan and write your essay. Pay attention to the quality of your writing and on how well you present the points in the lecture and their relationship to the reading passage.

 Summarize the points made in the lecture, being sure to explain how they oppose the points made in the reading passage.

Response Time: 20 minutes

2. Independent Writing

Take 30 minutes to plan, write, and revise an essay on the following topic. Use your mobile phone or computer to keep track of the time. As on the actual TOEFL iBT, use notepaper to gather and organize your ideas. Then keyboard your essay on a computer, if possible. An effective essay will be about 300 words.

Response Time: 30 minutes

Do you agree or disagree with the following statement?

Students should not get married until they complete their studies.

Use specific reasons and examples to support your answer.

_____

_____

_____

_____

_____

_____

_____

_____

_____

_____

_____

_____

*Explanations and Sample Responses for the Writing section of
TOEFL iBT Final Practice Test 1 begin on page 638.*

TOEFL iBT Personalized Study Planner

Reading

Use your answers to the Reading section of TOEFL iBT Final Practice Test 1 and this chart to focus your preparation for the actual TOEFL iBT. Follow these steps.

1. Review all your correct and incorrect answers in the Answers and Explanations, which begin on page 620.
2. In the chart, circle the number of each item you answered incorrectly.
3. Review again the Answers and Explanations for each item you answered incorrectly, this time in the order they are grouped in the chart.
4. For each item type and item format where you want to improve your performance, study the pages listed in the third column.

ITEM NUMBERS	ITEM TYPE	STUDY PAGES
1, 3, 7, 15, 19, 22, 29, 32, 34	Factual information	109–116
4, 16, 30	Negative factual information	116–121
2, 5, 21, 24, 25, 33, 39	Vocabulary	122–131
9, 12, 18, 31, 35	Reference	132–139
6, 23, 36	Sentence simplification	139–148
10, 17, 40	Inference	154–158
8, 11, 20, 27, 37, 41	Rhetorical purpose	159–162
13, 26, 38	Insert text	163–167
14, 42	Prose summary	170–176
28	Fill in a table	176–182

Listening

Use your answers to the Listening section of TOEFL iBT Final Practice Test 1 and these charts to focus your preparation for the actual TOEFL iBT. Follow these steps.

1. Review all your correct and incorrect answers in the Answers and Explanations, which begin on page 626.
2. In each chart, circle the number of each item you answered incorrectly.

3. Review again the Answers and Explanations for each item you answered incorrectly, this time in the order they are grouped in these charts.

4. For each item type and item format where you want to improve your performance, study the pages listed in the third column.

ITEM NUMBERS	ITEM TYPE	STUDY PAGES
6, 12, 23, 29	Gist-content	260–269
1, 18	Gist-purpose	270–274
2, 7, 8, 9, 10, 11, 14, 19, 20, 21, 25, 26, 27, 28, 30, 32, 33	Supporting detail	275–281
3, 22, 31	Understanding the function of what is said	284–286
24	Understanding the speaker's attitude	287–291
16	Understanding organization	294–300
4, 13, 34	Connecting content	300–304
5, 15, 17	Making inferences	304–307

ITEM NUMBERS	ITEM FORMAT	STUDY PAGES
28, 32	Special multiple choice	254
3, 22	Replay items	254–256
27	Check box items	256
16	Drag-and-drop items	257–258

Speaking

Use your answers to the Speaking section of TOEFL iBT Final Practice Test 1 and this chart to focus your preparation for the actual TOEFL iBT. Follow these steps.

1. Review your responses by comparing them to the sample responses that begin on page 635.

2. Evaluate your responses with the rubrics. If possible, ask a teacher or an English-speaking friend to help you. Or wait a day or two and evaluate yourself. Use the TOEFL iBT Simplified Independent Speaking Rubric on pages 370–371 to score your responses to Items 1 and 2. Use the TOEFL iBT Simplified Integrated Speaking

Rubric on pages 398–399 to score your responses to Items 3 to 6. Write your scores on the lines.

1. _____   3. _____   5. _____

2. _____   4. _____   6. _____

3. What skills do you do well? Which skills do you want to improve? Review your rubrics for Items 1 and 2 together and check the boxes of the skills you do well. Then review the pages that are listed for the skills you want to improve.

ITEMS 1 AND 2: INDEPENDENT SPEAKING

SKILL	STUDY PAGES
☐ Answers the question	376–377
☐ Has a main idea	377
☐ Has supporting details	377–378
☐ Follows a logical order	378–379
☐ Uses signaling words and phrases to show relationships among ideas	380–382

4. Now review your completed rubrics for Items 3 to 6 together and check the boxes of the skills you do well. Then review the pages that are listed for the skills you want to improve.

ITEMS 3 TO 6: INTEGRATED SPEAKING

SKILL	PAGES
☐ Answers the question	411, 420–421
☐ Has a main idea and supporting details	404–408, 422–423
☐ Integrates information from reading and/or listening passages	412–416
☐ Follows a logical order	434–435
☐ Uses order and signaling words and phrases to show relationships among ideas	413–416, 424

Writing

Use your responses to the Writing section of TOEFL iBT Final Practice Test 1 and these charts to focus your preparation for the actual TOEFL iBT.

ITEM 1: INTEGRATED WRITING

1. Review your responses by comparing them to the sample responses that begin on page 638. Evaluate your essay using the instructions on page 497.

   Write your score on the line. _____

2. Check the box of your rating in each row of the Integrated Writing Rubric that begins on this page.

3. Review your ratings. Which areas do you want to improve? Study the pages listed for those areas in the column on the right.

SCORE	DESCRIPTION	STUDY PAGES
5	A **Level 5** response: ☐ Selects relevant and important information from the lecture and presents it in relation to similar information in the reading. Includes supporting detail and examples.	483–487
	☐ Is well organized and makes sense. Uses signaling words and phrases to connect information and show the relationships among ideas.	490–494
	☐ Includes occasional errors in vocabulary and grammar that do not result in inaccurate or confusing presentation of information or connections among ideas.	495–497
4	A **Level 4** response: ☐ Generally selects relevant and important information from the lecture and presents it in relation to relevant and important information in the reading, but may have minor inaccuracies, vagueness, or omissions that cause minor confusion to readers.	483–487
	☐ Includes errors in vocabulary and grammar that are more frequent than in a Level 5 response but cause only minor problems with clarity or connection of ideas.	495–497

(continued)

SCORE	DESCRIPTION	STUDY PAGES
3	A **Level 3** response: ☐ Contains some information from the listening and makes some connections to the reading	483–487
	A response at this level has one or more of these problems: ☐ The response addresses the task, but some information may be inaccurate or incomplete. Makes only general, vague, or unclear connections between points in the reading and the lecture.	483–487
	☐ The response omits one major point made in the lecture.	483–487
	☐ Some key points in the lecture or reading, or the connections between them, are unclear, incomplete, inaccurate, or general.	490–494
	☐ Vocabulary and grammar errors may be more frequent than in a Level 4 response and may cause confusion to readers.	495–497
2	A **Level 2** response: ☐ Has some relevant information from the lecture, but has inaccuracies or omissions of important ideas from the lecture.	483–487
	☐ Makes inaccurate or incomplete connections with information from the reading.	483–487
	A response at this level shows one or more of the following: ☐ Omits or inaccurately presents the relationship between the lecture and the reading.	483–487
	☐ Omits or inaccurately presents important points in the lecture.	483–487
	☐ Contains language errors or expressions that obscure meaning.	495–497
1	A **Level 1** response: ☐ Provides little or no meaningful or relevant information from the lecture.	483–487
	☐ Has problems with vocabulary and grammar that make the essay difficult to understand.	495–497
0	A response at this level contains only ideas copied from the reading passage, does not address the topic, is not written in English, or is blank.	

ITEM 2: INDEPENDENT WRITING

1. Evaluate your essay using the instructions on page 525.

   Write your score on the line. _____

2. Check the box of your rating in each row of the Independent Writing Rubric on the next page.

3. Review your ratings in each row. Which areas do you want to improve? Study the pages listed for those areas in the column on the right.

SCORE	DESCRIPTION	STUDY PAGES
5	A **Level 5** response largely:	
	☐ Addresses the topic and the task.	515–517
	☐ Is organized and well developed; uses appropriate detail, examples, and explanations.	517–518
	☐ Stays on topic, flows, and makes sense.	519–520
	☐ Uses language well. Has variety in sentence patterns, vocabulary, and idioms, and only minor errors of vocabulary and grammar.	524–525
4	A **Level 4** response largely:	
	☐ Addresses the topic and the task, though some points are not well developed.	515–517
	☐ Is generally well organized and developed; uses appropriate detail, examples, and explanations.	517–518
	☐ Stays on topic, flows, and makes sense, but may have some problems with repetition, staying on topic, or unclear connection of ideas.	519–520
	☐ Uses language fairly well. Has variety in sentence patterns, vocabulary, and idioms, and only minor errors of vocabulary and grammar, but may have some errors in grammar, word form, or natural language that do not cause unclarity.	524–525
3	A **Level 3** response is characterized by one or more of the following:	
	☐ Addresses the topic and the task, but with somewhat developed detail, examples, and explanations.	515–517
	☐ Stays on topic, flows, and makes sense, but connection of ideas might be unclear at times.	517–518
	☐ May show inconsistent ability in grammar and vocabulary that may cause occasional unclarity.	524–525
	☐ Accurate but limited range of sentence structures and vocabulary.	524–525
2	A **Level 2** response will show one or more of the following weaknesses:	
	☐ Limited development of topic and task.	515–517
	☐ Poor organization or connection of ideas.	517–518
	☐ Not enough or inappropriate detail, examples, and explanations.	515–517
	☐ Poor choice of words or word forms.	524–525
	☐ Many errors of sentence structure or vocabulary.	524–525
1	A **Level 1** response is seriously harmed by one or more of these weaknesses:	
	☐ Disorganized or lacks development.	517–518
	☐ Little or no detail, examples, and explanations, or does not respond to the task.	515–517
	☐ Serious errors in sentence structure or vocabulary.	524–525
0	A response at this level contains only ideas copied from the topic, does not address the topic, is not written in English, or is blank.	

Answers, Explanations, Audio Scripts, and Sample Responses

Reading (Page 555)

1. **C** **The concept of stress is relatively new to medicine and psychology. (Factual information)** Option C is correct because the passage directly states that the term was not used before 1930, and up until then medicine and psychology did not give much attention to stress. Option A is incorrect because the passage states that stress is caused by the challenges of everyday life. Option B makes no sense because it is related to the use of this term in physical sciences, architecture, and engineering, not medicine and psychology. Option D is not supported by information in the passage. Just because the term *stress* was not used until 1930 does not mean that people did not experience strain from everyday life.

2. **B** **cause (Vocabulary)** Option B is correct because the paragraph discusses the cause-and-effect relationships among the strains caused by daily life, our bodies' responses to those strains, and the effects of those responses. Option A is related to the literal meaning of the word *trigger*, the part of the gun that causes it to fire, which does not make sense in this context. Option C is incorrect because the passage is discussing how stress begins, not how it increases. Option D does not make sense.

3. **C** **physical responses (Factual information)** According to the information in the passage, everyday strain causes physical responses in our bodies, so Option C is correct. Options A and B are not supported by information in the passage. Option D is incorrect because a change in temperature is an environmental change that affects homeostasis and is not related to stress.

4. **A** **The strains that force and motion put on objects (Negative factual information)** Option A is correct because this meaning of stress is related to physical science, not medicine or psychology. The meanings given in the remaining options are all related to medicine and psychology, so they are incorrect.

5. **C** **change (Vocabulary)** Option C is correct because the paragraph is discussing ways that the strains of life cause physiological changes in our bodies. Option A is incorrect because the passage is discussing changes within our bodies, not the movement of our bodies. Option B is incorrect because tension is related to emotions caused by stress, not the physiological changes caused by stress. Option D is incorrect because the passage makes clear that the effect of stress causes physiological processes to increase and decrease.

6. **B** **To maintain homeostasis, our bodies' operations adjust as we experience change, such as a need to move, a change in air temperature, or the need to digest food. (Sentence simplification)** Option B is correct because only this option restates the essential ideas of the sentence without omitting information, introducing information that is incorrect or not in the passage, or changing the meaning. Option A is incorrect because it misstates a key idea: our bodies do not keep functions constant when there is change, but rather adjust them so that functions stay in equilibrium. Option C also misstates key information: our bodies adjust bodily functions, not changes such as the need to move, in order to maintain homeostasis. Option D is incorrect because it also misstates key information: our bodies do not experience change in order to maintain homeostasis. Rather, our bodies adjust bodily functions in response to change.

7. **B** **It is a remainder from our past. (Factual information)** Option B is correct because this information is stated directly in the passage: "This reaction is considered to be rooted in our distant past, when humans had to fight off predators to survive." Option A does not make sense because only flight causes us to avoid facing our problems. Option C is contradicted by information in the passage. This type of response was effective in the distant past, not now. Option D is contradicted by information in the passage. The fight-or-flight syndrome happens in response to other threats, too.

8. **D** **To indicate that the physical reactions to a threat are the result of a deeply rooted automatic defense mechanism (Rhetorical purpose)** Option D is correct because the point of the paragraph is that an outmoded defense mechanism is the cause of stress. While Option A may be a true statement, the author introduces this information to show the cause-and-effect relationship between a threat and the fight-or-flight syndrome, not to say that the relationship is illogical. The point is made in another place in the passage. Option B is contradicted by information in the passage. Even though stress is a natural reaction to a threat, the passage makes clear that stress has important health consequences. Option C is not supported by information in the passage.

9. **C** **a hormone (Reference)** Option C is correct because this sentence is about the effect of chemicals produced by the endocrine system. The chemicals produced by the endocrine system are called hormones. Option A is incorrect because glands in the endocrine system release hormones, so this option does not make sense. Option B is incorrect because a threat causes release of hormones. Option D does not make sense.

10. **A** **The word *stress* refers to the impact on our bodies of our body's responses to a threat. (Inference)** Option A is correct because as used in the paragraph, *stress* refers to the harmful consequences of physiological changes that are caused by the fight-or-flight syndrome. Option B is contradicted by the passage: scientists disagree whether all physiological reactions are strong enough to have harmful effects on our bodies. Option C is not supported by information in the passage. Option D is contradicted by the passage. The scientists agree that stress is harmful. They disagree only on what constitutes a stress event.

11. **D** **To indicate that even though scientists do not agree on whether all physiological changes cause stress, they do agree that excessive stress is harmful to our bodies (Rhetorical purpose)** Option D is correct because the preceding sentences give two conflicting ideas on what constitutes stress, but they agree that stress has harmful consequences for our health. Option A is not supported by information in the passage. The author seems more interested in the consequences of stress than in controversy over its definition. Options B and C are not supported by information in the passage.

12. **C** **teenagers' and young adults' (Reference)** Option C is correct because the sentence is talking about the various kinds of threats that affect different kinds of people. Threats that affect adults have already been discussed, so Option D does not make sense. Options A and B do not make sense because researchers and investigators are mentioned because they are studying stress, not because they are experiencing it. Therefore, Option A is the only possible answer.

13. **D** **(Insert text)** Option D is correct because this sentence gives detail about the kinds of health problems research subjects with high stress experience, and this is the only location where this detail makes sense because It follows a sentence about a correlation between high stress and health problems. Option A does not make sense because a general topic sentence, not detail, belongs at the beginning of a paragraph. Option B does not make sense because the preceding sentence is about a hypothesized connection between stress and disease, and the inserted sentence contains detail about actual results of research subjects. Option C does not make sense because the inserted sentence gives detail about the kinds of problems caused by stress, and the preceding sentence is about the causes of stress, not the effects.

14. **(Prose summary)** If you completed the summary correctly, it should look like this:

    The passage discusses the causes and effects of stress.
    - **A** Stress is the result of physiological changes that are a natural response to a threat in the environment.
    - **C** Recent studies have shown that there is a relationship between high levels of stress and increased incidence of other health problems.
    - **F** The concept of stress as a medical condition did not exist until relatively recently.

    These answers are correct for these reasons.
    - **A** **Stress is the result of physiological changes that are a natural response to a threat in the environment.** This response sums up the cause of stress, which is one of the main ideas of the passage, so it belongs in the summary.
    - **C** **Recent studies have shown that there is a relationship between high levels of stress and increased incidence of other health problems.** This option summarizes one of the main ideas of the passage, proof of the

hypothesized relationship between stress and other health conditions, so it belongs in the summary.

- **F The concept of stress as a medical condition did not exist until relatively recently.** This sentence sums up a key idea in the passage—the notion of stress is a fairly new one—so it belongs in the summary.

Incorrect options do not belong in the completed table for these reasons:

- **B The purpose of the "fight-or-flight syndrome" is increased readiness to flee an attacker.** This option is a relatively minor detail and omits a key idea (the fight-or-flight syndrome also increases ability to fend off an attack), so it does not belong in the summary.
- **D High blood pressure is one of the principal effects of stress.** This option is a relatively minor detail in the passage, so it does not belong in the summary.
- **E Cortisol, a hormone produced during a stressful event, increases our ability to perceive risks in the environment.** This option misstates the function of cortisol, which increases our bodies' ability to respond to a threat, so it does not belong in the summary.

15. **D It supported social change as well as cultural change. (Factual information)** Option D is correct because this information is stated directly in paragraph 1: "it was as much a social and political movement opposed to the excesses of industrialization as it was a design movement." Option A is incorrect because according to the paragraph, the movement's international impact was in only a few countries in Europe and North America. More countries would have to be involved for the movement to be considered global. Option B is incorrect because the paragraph indicates that the movement was focused on old methods of manufacturing and traditional and medieval decoration. Option C is contradicted by information in the passage.

16. **A Mass production made inexpensive goods widely available. (Negative factual information)** Option A is the only option mentioned that is not a problem caused by the Industrial Revolution. In fact, the widespread availability of inexpensive goods is an advantage. Options B, C, and D are all mentioned in the passage as problems caused by the Industrial Revolution and are therefore incorrect.

17. **B The Crystal Palace Exhibition unintentionally led to criticism of the Industrial Revolution. (Inference)** Option B is correct because the exhibition was designed to show off England's industrial might, but it caused even some of its organizers to recognize that the goods were unattractive. This led to the formation of the Arts and Crafts movement. For this reason, Options A and C are incorrect. The organizers of the exhibition were proud of the Industrial Revolution, but the exhibition ironically led some of them to oppose aspects of the Industrial Revolution. Option D is not supported by the information in the passage. Though some of the organizers thought that the goods were cheap and shoddy, this does not mean that it was impossible to manufacture quality goods in mass quantities. In addition, even though some organizers of the exhibition became disillusioned because of the quality of the goods, they "did not reject mass manufacturing entirely," according to the passage.

18. **B the exhibition (Reference)** Option B is correct because the sentence is about the exhibition, so *exhibition* is the correct antecedent. Options A, C, and D are incorrect because they are details about where the exhibition took place and its name.

19. **B Workers had to endure dreadful conditions. (Factual information)** Option B is correct because the passage says that workers "labored for long hours in terrible conditions." Option A is incorrect because though it is true that the merchandise was shoddy, this was not the reason that Morris backed social reform. Option C is not supported by information in the passage. The exhibition revealed the low quality of some of the merchandise, but it did not show that workers were exploited. Option D is incorrect because the passage states that workers could produce good products when using old-fashioned methods. According to Morris, manufactured goods were shoddy because of industrial methods of production.

20. **B To show that the Arts and Crafts movement was a social movement as well as a design movement (Rhetorical purpose)** Option B is correct because it reflects Morris's desire to improve the lives of working people by returning to handcrafting. Option A is incorrect because Morris was interested in all of these things. Option C is incorrect because the movement gave equal importance to design and handcrafting, and the primary products were crafts, not fine art. Option D is not supported by information in the passage.

21. **D   cloth (Vocabulary)** Option D is correct because the phrase "such as" shows that it is an example or illustration of what a textile is. A textile is any material woven from thread, such as cloth, a rug or carpet, or a tapestry, all of which are mentioned in the passage. Therefore, the other options are incorrect.

22. **C   In both of them, workers crafted goods by hand. (Factual information)** Option C is correct because the passage states that guild workers and company workers created goods by hand. Option A is incorrect because artists and workers worked side by side only in Morris's company. Option B is incorrect because only guild workers worked individually or in small groups. Morris organized small groups of workers into a large company focused on many crafts, not one. For this same reason, Option D is also incorrect.

23. **A   Morris tried to re-create this process in his company, a kind of cooperative in which artists created designs for artisans to handcraft. (Sentence simplification)** Option A is correct because only this option restates the essential ideas of the sentence without omitting information, introducing information that is incorrect or not in the passage, or changing the meaning. Option B is incorrect because it misstates a key fact: Morris's company tried to re-create the medieval process in a new way, a kind of artist's cooperative. Option C is incorrect because medieval guilds did not include artists. Option D is incorrect because it misstates a key fact: artists, not the company, created designs for the jewelers, furniture makers, weavers, and ceramicists to craft by hand.

24. **D   brought new life to (Vocabulary)** Option D is correct because the movement focused on returning to, or restoring, older ways of manufacturing. Only Option D captures this meaning. For this reason, Option C is incorrect.

Option A does not make sense because Mackmurdo, like all members of the movement, was not interested in industrialization. Option B is incorrect because the movement was interested in reforming the Industrial Revolution, not the traditional ways of manufacturing, which it wanted to restore or revitalize.

25. **B   artists' and intellectuals' (Vocabulary)** Option B is correct because the artists' and intellectuals' influence spread the ideals. Option A does not make sense. Option C is not possible because *their* requires a plural antecedent and Mackmurdo is singular. In addition, the ideals were not just Mackmurdo's, but belonged to the whole movement. Option D does not make sense.

26. **D   (Insert text)** The sentence makes the most sense in position D because it gives an example of the most distant place the movement influenced. Therefore, it makes the most sense after the list of less distant places. For this reason, Option C is incorrect. The sentence does not make sense in positions A and B because in those locations, the article is not talking about places the movement spread to.

27. **B   To show that the movement did not have the impact on society that Morris envisioned (Rhetorical purpose)** Option B is correct because Morris had hoped that the movement would result in better lives and products for everyone. Instead, only a few people benefited—the few workers who produced the objects and the few wealthy people who could afford them. Option A is contradicted by information in the rest of the passage. The movement affected many areas of art and design. For this reason, Option D is also incorrect. Option C is contradicted by information in paragraph 6: that the leaders of the Industrial Revolution bought the products showed that they liked the beautiful Arts and Crafts designs.

28. **(Fill in a table)** The correctly completed table should look like this. Answers can be in any order. Answers are correct if only the letter is written.

INDUSTRIAL REVOLUTION	ARTS AND CRAFTS MOVEMENT
Select 2	**Select 3**
• **B** Steam power was used to produce goods.	• **A** Only the wealthy could afford the products.
• **F** Goods were produced in large factories.	• **D** It used traditional and medieval decorations.
	• **G** It tried to improve conditions for workers.

These answers are correct for these reasons.

Industrial Revolution
- **B Steam power was used to produce goods.** This option is correct because it is stated directly in the passage.
- **F Goods were produced in large factories.** This option is correct because it is stated directly in the passage.

Arts and Crafts Movement
- **A Only the wealthy could afford the products.** This option is correct because it is stated directly in the passage.
- **D It used traditional and medieval decorations.** This option is correct because it is stated directly in the passage.
- **G It tried to improve conditions for workers.** This option is correct because it is stated directly in the passage.

Incorrect options do not belong in the completed table for these reasons:
- **C It used cooperatives to make goods in mass quantities.** This option is incorrect because the cooperatives made high-quality, well-designed goods in small quantities.
- **E Its beautiful handcrafted products were displayed in the Crystal Palace.** This option is incorrect because machine-made products from factories were displayed in the Crystal Palace Exhibition.

29. **D To increase their chances of survival (Factual information)** Option D is correct because the passage directly states that camouflage helps animals avoid predators and catch prey. Option A is incorrect because the chameleon does not have this ability to amaze but to survive. Option C is incorrect because animals use camouflage to capture prey and escape from predators.

30. **A A snake hides in a cave during the day to avoid the hot desert sun. (Negative factual information)** Option A is correct because it is not an example of camouflage, which is designed to avoid detection by other animals. The snake is avoiding the sun, not other animals. Option B is incorrect because coloration that blends into the environment is a kind of camouflage. Option C is incorrect because the silver coloration makes the fish hard to locate, so it is a form of camouflage. Option D is incorrect because resembling another organism is a kind of camouflage.

31. **B animal (Reference)** Option B is correct because the passage is about how camouflage increases the ability of an animal to survive. The other options do not make sense.

32. **B To match the brown summer colors (Factual information)** Option B is correct because in spring, the snow melts and the environment returns to its natural tawny color. The hares shed their white fur and grow fur that matches the summer environment. For this reason, Option A is incorrect. Option C is incorrect because according to the passage, arctic animals grow warmer coats in fall and cooler coats in spring. Option D is a characteristic of how animals such as chameleons and squid change color. Molting and growing a new coat take much longer than the few seconds a chameleon or squid needs to change color.

33. **C last through (Vocabulary)** Option C is correct because *endure* means "patiently suffer through something difficult." This meaning can be derived from the context: arctic animals have to last through a very harsh winter, and a warm coat can help them live through the harsh winter. Only Option C captures this meaning. Therefore, the other options are incorrect.

34. **C It mimics the effects of sea currents. (Factual information)** Option C is correct because according to the passage, mimicking the sea currents helps the seadragon blend into the seaweed it lives among. Option A is incorrect because this option does not explain how the animal uses movement to blend into the surroundings. Option B is incorrect because it is an example of coloration, not movement. Option D is incorrect because it explains how the animal moves to find food, not how it moves to blend into the environment.

35. **D seadragon (Reference)** Option D is correct because the paragraph is focused on how this animal uses color and movement as camouflage. Option A is incorrect because the seahorse is a relative of the seadragon and is mentioned only to provide an additional, clarifying detail about the seadragon. Option B is incorrect because seaweed is part of the environment in which the seadragon lives. Option C is incorrect because the seadragon imitates the effect of sea currents on sea plants.

36. **A Later studies failed to replicate findings that moths made sounds that confused bats or imitated the sounds of inedible moths. (Sentence simplification)** Option A is correct because only this option restates the essential ideas of the sentence without omitting information, introducing information that is

incorrect or not in the passage, or changing the meaning. Option B is incorrect because it changes a key idea: the moths supposedly imitate the sounds of inedible moths, not inedible bats. Option C is incorrect because it changes the meaning of the sentence completely: the scientists did not believe that the subsequent research "failed to disprove" that the moths used sound camouflage. Rather, the scientists did not believe that the subsequent research replicated findings that moths used sound camouflage. Option D is incorrect because it changes the meaning of the sentence. The scientists did not disprove the subsequent research. They accepted the later studies' findings, which failed to replicate findings that moths used sound camouflage.

37. **A To indicate that more research is necessary to clarify contradictory results about whether insects use sound camouflage (Rhetorical purpose)** Option A is correct because so far results of later studies have failed to replicate the earlier studies. Therefore, more research is necessary. Options B, C, and D are not supported by information in the passage.

38 **C (Insert text)** Option C is correct because the sentence is a second example of scent camouflage. Location C follows the first example of scent camouflage in the passage, so the sentence belongs in this position. In the other locations, the preceding sentences are not examples of scent camouflage, so they are not logical places to insert the sentence.

39. **B imitating (Vocabulary)** Option B is correct because the passage indicates that mimesis involves adopting another's appearance. *Imitating* is the only answer option that is close in meaning to "adopting another's appearance." Therefore, Options A, C, and D are incorrect.

40. **B It helps the animals increase the advantage of their extreme speed. (Inference)** Option B is correct because motion dazzle helps the animals take greater advantage of their speed, since other animals will not be able to tell the exact speed or direction. Thus, the speeding animal will be harder to catch or avoid. For this reason, Option D is incorrect. Option A is incorrect because motion dazzle is only effective when an animal is moving. When one of these animals is standing still, it is easy to see. Option C is not supported by information in the passage.

41. **A To indicate that the scientists are not completely sure about this idea (Rhetorical purpose)** When scientists hypothesize, they develop a theory that they test scientifically to see if it is correct. Only Option A captures this meaning. Therefore, the other options are incorrect.

42. **(Prose summary)** If you completed the summary correctly, it should look like this:

The passage discusses the purposes and types of camouflage:
- **C** Camouflage gives animals a competitive advantage.
- **D** Camouflage can involve the senses of sight, smell, and hearing.
- **E** Three main types of camouflage are crypsis, mimesis, and motion dazzle.

These answers are correct for these reasons.
- **C Camouflage gives animals a competitive advantage.** This option sums up the reason camouflage is an important adaptation, so it belongs in the summary.
- **D Camouflage can involve the senses of sight, smell, and hearing.** This option gives important information on different kinds of camouflage discussed in the passage, so it belongs in the summary.
- **E Three main types of camouflage are crypsis, mimesis, and motion dazzle.** The passage is mostly about explaining each of these kinds of camouflage, so this sentence belongs in the summary.

Incorrect options do not belong in the completed table for these reasons:
- **A Mimesis is the most common kind of camouflage.** Crypsis, not mimesis, is the most common kind of camouflage according to the passage, so this sentence does not belong in the summary.
- **B Camouflage means "blending into the environment."** This option is contradicted by motion dazzle, which involves standing out from the environment in a confusing way. Therefore, this example does not belong in the summary.
- **F All animals use one sort of camouflage or another.** This option may be true but is not stated in the passage, so it does not belong in the summary.

Listening (Page 583)

Questions 1–5

TRACK 127 AUDIO SCRIPT

Narrator: Listen to a conversation between a student and a professor.

Professor: So, how's the psychology course going, Alex?

Student: I'm enjoying it, although it's time-consuming. For this term paper on values, I read at least twenty articles, and I'm still not sure I'm on track.

Professor: What do you mean?

Student: Well, I understand what one such value is: altruism or unselfishness. I even learned that an area of the human brain has recently been associated with it. But frankly, I find the animal studies confusing. I don't know how to incorporate them into my writing.

Professor: Hmm.

Student: I guess what I'm saying is, I don't know how to structure my paper.

Professor: OK. Let's start with the animal studies. Did you read the ones on coyotes and chimpanzees?

Student: Yes.

Professor: So what's Marc Bekoff trying to prove?

Student : If a coyote leaves the pack because it refuses to be part of the social group—not because it's ill—then its mortality rate is fifty-five percent as opposed to only twenty percent if it stays in the pack.

Professor: That's the data; what are the implications?

Student: That social relationships dramatically improve a coyote's chance of staying alive.

Professor: Right. And what about the work by Frans de Waal on chimpanzees and grooming?

Student: You mean, when one chimp picks out the bugs in another chimp's hair?

Professor: Uh-huh.

Student: He noted that each animal remembers who groomed him or her and how often.

Professor: What was his conclusion?

Student: Just like humans, chimps return favors by grooming the animals who groomed them or helping those chimps get some bananas. They're grateful.

Professor: How does that benefit chimp society?

Student: It remains cohesive.

Professor: Correct. Seems you understand the reading. What you've got to do now is tie the threads together into an argument.

Student: Something like: humans and animals both do things that demonstrate underlying altruistic values?

Professor: Absolutely.

Narrator: Now answer questions 1 to 5. Circle the letter of the answer.

TRACK 128 AUDIO SCRIPT

Narrator: Listen again to part of the conversation. Then answer the question.

Student: If a coyote leaves the pack because it refuses to be part of the social group—not because it's ill—then its mortality rate is fifty-five percent as opposed to only twenty percent if it stays in the pack.

Professor: That's the data; what are the implications?

Narrator: What does the professor mean when he says this?

Professor: That's the data; what are the implications?

ANSWERS AND EXPLANATIONS

1. **A** **She is unsure about how to organize her term paper. (Gist-purpose)** Option A is correct because the student says, "I don't know how to structure my paper." Options B and D are not supported by information in the conversation. Option C is incorrect because the student mentions she's read "at least twenty articles."

2. **A** **It is much more likely to die. (Detail)** Option A is correct because the student says, "If a coyote leaves the pack because it refuses to be part of the social group—not because it's ill—then its mortality rate is fifty-five percent as opposed to only twenty percent if it stays in the pack." Options B, C, and D are incorrect. They are about the likelihood of the coyote's death, but they do not describe the ratio of fifty-five percent to twenty percent.

3. **D** **He wants to encourage the student to think more deeply. (Function/Replay item)** Option D is correct because in the replay the professor speaks a little loudly, and he stresses the words *data* and *implications*. His tone of voice means he wants the student to think about the implications again. Options A, B, and C are not supported by the replay.

4. **C** **Gratitude is a mechanism for their social cohesion. (Connecting content)** Option C is correct because the student says that Frans de Waal "noted that each animal remembers who groomed him or her and how often. Just like

humans, chimps return favors by grooming the animals who groomed them, or helping those chimps get some bananas. They're grateful." When asked by the professor how these activities benefit chimp society, the student says, "It remains cohesive." Option A is incorrect because while it may be true that chimpanzees greatly enjoy grooming each other, this is not de Waal's conclusion. Option B is incorrect because while it may be true that chimpanzees return favors in the same way humans do, this is not de Waal's conclusion. Option D is not supported by information in the lecture.

5. **B Fundamental human and animal values** (Inference) Option B is correct because the student says, "Humans and animals both do things that demonstrate underlying altruistic values." Option A is incorrect because the term paper discusses similarities in human and animal values, not differences. Option C is contradicted by information in the conversation. Option D is incorrect because while the student is writing about recent discoveries in human and animal psychology, this is too general for the topic of a term paper.

Questions 6–11

TRACK 129 AUDIO SCRIPT

Narrator: Listen to part of a lecture in a class on Japanese cinema. The professor is talking about the films of Yasujiro Ozu.

Professor: Today's lecture is entitled, "We shouldn't want too much"—a line from a film by Yasujiro Ozu. It sums up the philosophy of the many ordinary, slightly disillusioned postwar Japanese who inhabit his films. For Ozu himself, it's far from true, for he was a perfectionist—doing up to twenty takes of the simplest of shots. And *he* had it all. He was a popular, prolific part of the Japanese studio tradition yet renowned for cinematic innovation. Several of his works are considered masterpieces. Many critics rate *Tokyo Story* from 1953 as the best film ever made, and I, for one, am in complete agreement.

Yasujiro Ozu lived from 1903 to 1963. The 1950s, when he reached his peak, are known as the Golden Age of Japanese cinema. Akira Kurosawa and Kenji Mizoguchi also produced their best work then.

Let's look first at Ozu's themes, which are deeply human. As a realist, he grapples with tradition versus modernization, in which he chronicles the disintegration of the extended family, selfishness versus altruism, and respect for elders versus independence. You certainly can't accuse Ozu of having nothing to say.

The plots of Ozu films are extremely simple and contain few external catalysts. Ozu portrays the seemingly uneventful lives of the Japanese middle and lower classes. *Tokyo Story*, for example, is a slice of the Hirayama family's life. It shows mother, father, children, in-laws, and grandchildren over a short period of time in Tokyo and provincial Onomichi. It focuses on their restrained gestures and mannerisms, on their daily rituals, and their simple acts of kindness. In their conversations, what is unsaid is more important than what is said. Viewers may find the Hirayamas dysfunctional; Ozu judges no one. *Tokyo Story* comes complete with cruelty and death, but these are balanced by a subtle beauty and by a profound awareness of the passage of time.

As for technique, Ozu was a minimalist. In narrative structure, he favored simple progression—there are no flashbacks. He also loved ellipsis. That is when significant events are left out. In the film *An Autumn Afternoon*, a wedding is mentioned in one scene, but in the next, a reference to the same wedding indicates that it's already taken place. The wedding itself is never shown on screen. To reject melodrama, Ozu skips over what Hollywood would feast on.

Ozu's deceptively simple camera work also violates Hollywood conventions. He avoids many standard shot types. In fact, he invented a very low-angle shot, called a *tatami* shot, where the camera is placed at the eye level of a person kneeling on a Japanese *tatami* mat. Such shots provide intimacy in scenes where people are conversing. Yet when they contain empty space, they suddenly disorient the viewer.

The static nature of Ozu's cinema is its most jarring feature for modern viewers used to helicopter, Steadicam, and tracking shots—all Hollywood staples. As his career progressed, Ozu moved his camera less and less, completely dispensing with tracking in his color films. *Tokyo Story* has a single tracking shot, which is emotionally charged because it happens right after the elderly couple has been evicted from their child's home. The modern world may demand perpetual motion, but for Ozu, harmony resides in stillness. A current Hollywood film, by contrast, has a vast majority of moving shots. Consequently, cinema now does little more than give us a roller-coaster ride.

Ozu did not transition between scenes conventionally either. He frequently edited in static objects or used direct cuts rather than fades or dissolves. During transitions, music played on the soundtrack. He rarely used music in any other way. This quasidocumentary technique lends authenticity to his work. The audience is not instructed to feel an emotion by a blaring soundtrack as in most films today.

Nevertheless, Ozu has his detractors. Japanese directors of the 1960s found his work too slow, too plotless.

Personally, I think we should expect *more* from movies. We should watch Ozu to appreciate the greatest cinematic craft and to learn that our own busy, distracted, destructive lives may be restored through tranquility, beauty, and devotion.

Narrator: Now answer questions 6 to 11. Circle the letter of the answer.

ANSWERS AND EXPLANATIONS

6. **B What makes Yasujiro Ozu's films so magnificent (Gist-content)** Option B is correct. The professor says, "Several of [Ozu's] works are considered masterpieces. Many critics rate *Tokyo Story* from 1953 as the best film ever made, and I, for one, am in complete agreement." She then goes on to explain how the themes, plots, and cinematic techniques of Ozu's films all contribute to their extraordinarily high quality. The other options are not supported by the information.

7. **C The disintegration of the extended family (Detail)** Option C is directly stated by the professor. The remaining options are not supported by the information.

8. **B He does not judge them. (Detail)** Option B is correct because the professor says, "Ozu judges no one." Option A is not supported by information in the lecture. Options C and D are incorrect because while the professor mentions that some of Ozu's characters are lower class and do not lead eventful lives, these factors do not relate to Ozu's feelings toward them.

9. **D Major events that happen off screen (Detail)** Option D is correct because the professor defines "ellipsis" as "when significant events are left out." Option A is incorrect because though the professor mentions an off-screen wedding as an example of ellipsis, the wedding itself is not a definition. Option B is incorrect because Hollywood directors often show events on screen

that Ozu might choose not to. Option C is not supported by information in the lecture.

10. **A They are more static and less melodramatic. (Detail)** Option A is correct because the professor says, "The static nature of Ozu's cinema is its most jarring feature for modern viewers used to helicopter, Steadicam, and tracking shots—all Hollywood staples." She says, "To reject melodrama, Ozu skips over what Hollywood would feast on." Options B and D are not supported by information in the lecture. Option C is contradicted by the information. Ozu mainly uses music as transition between scenes, unlike in Hollywood films.

11. **B Ways to improve the quality of their own lives (Detail)** Option B is correct because the professor thinks modern viewers can find ways to improve the quality of their own lives by watching Ozu's films. She says, "We should watch Ozu . . . to learn that our own frantic, distracted, destructive lives may be restored through tranquility, beauty, and devotion." Option A is incorrect because the professor infers viewers may gain a deeper understanding of themselves, not of Japanese cinema, by watching Ozu's films. Options C and D are not supported by information in the lecture.

Questions 12–17

TRACK 130 AUDIO SCRIPT

Narrator: Listen to part of a lecture in a class on the history of science. The professor is talking about the invention of zero.

Professor: I'm going to start today with some numbers: 1970 and 104. How do these relate to me?

Student: One hundred four's your office number. I guess nineteen seventy's your date of birth.

Professor: Right. And what do they have in common?

Student: Um . . . There's zero in both of them.

Professor: And these days, we couldn't survive without zero—either zero the empty placeholder or zero the number—because zero . . . well, zero expresses two different concepts.

Let's consider the year 1970. This shows zero the empty placeholder since the date 197 is pretty different from 1970. However, in many ancient cultures with sophisticated mathematical systems, like the Babylonians in the Middle East, zero the empty placeholder didn't exist for a long time. And I mean a really long time—around a thousand years. No one seemed too concerned about its absence; context indicated which number was being discussed. Zero as an empty placeholder came into existence for the Babylonians around 700 BC. Little hooks were used to denote the empty place. However, zero still didn't occur at the end of a number, so 1907 would exist, but not 1970. Again, context signaled which number was intended. The other thing to note about the Babylonians was that they used a place-value number system—theirs was base-sixty whereas ours is base-ten—while the ancient Greeks did not.

Student: Then how did the Greeks make all those mathematical advances and build such amazing architecture?

Professor: They used geometry—the description of lines—rather than math. They left math to the merchants, who didn't appear to care for precise notation. But there's one exception in Greece—the astronomers—who used the symbol for zero the placeholder that we recognize today: the big oh. The origins of this are hazy, and it's not known whether it was considered as anything more than a punctuation mark. For example, did it exist as an abstract idea? Certainly, zero as a *number* hadn't reached ancient Greece.

Student: I don't get how that can be.

Professor: It does seem strange. I guess if you look at it from a practical perspective, it's easier. Let's say you're a goat farmer. Well, you're likely to know how many animals you own, and use a number for that. If, by some bad luck, you lose all your goats, you probably describe that in words. We still do this in English. We say: "I've got three children," but we don't say: "I've got zero children." We prefer: "I don't have *any* children." Furthermore, getting back to that ancient Greek farmer, there's no point at which he has *negative* animals—that is, *minus* twenty-three goats. Where there's no concept of negative numbers, there's also no concept of zero the number.

Student: So who invented zero the number?

Professor: There are two main contenders. Let's consider Indians first. Some historians of science believe the Indian conception of zero owed something to the Greek astronomers; others make unsupportable claims that zero as an empty placeholder dates back seventeen thousand years. All we can say with certainty is that the first genuine written use—on a stone marker not too far from Delhi—is 876 AD.

Zero the number, however, is a different story. This time, Indians do lead the way. In 628 AD, an Indian mathematician, Brahmagupta, tried to give rules for zero the number and negative numbers. He couldn't figure out how to subtract zero from

other numbers or what happened when trying to divide zero—that came five hundred years later—but basically, he had zero as an idea pretty well under control.

Student: I read that the Mayans in Central America used zero as a number as well.

Professor: That's true. A little later than the Indians, around 665 AD, they had a base-twenty numbering system that included a symbol for zero. Unfortunately, Mayan civilization only lasted until 900 AD, and it didn't influence many other cultures.

Student: What about China? Didn't the Chinese understand zero early on?

Professor: It seems not. Most likely, the spread of Indian ideas influenced them. In a Chinese mathematical treatise written in 1247 AD, the symbol for zero appears for the first time.

But Europeans didn't find out about zero until 1200 AD, and it wasn't *widely* used for another four hundred years.

Understanding zero is still an issue. I'm the only person I know who *didn't* celebrate the millennium on January 1st, 2000. When the ancient Romans devised the calendar we still use, there was no Year Zero, and no one's fixed it since! That's why I was partying on January 1st, 2001.

Narrator: Now answer questions 12 to 17. Circle the letter of the answer.

ANSWERS AND EXPLANATIONS

12. D Zero has a curious history. (Gist-content) Option D is correct because the professor discusses events in the development of zero in chronological order. He also mentions odd things like unproven Indian claims and his own atypical celebration of the millennium in 2001. Option A is incorrect because only zero as an empty placeholder is an ancient idea; zero as a number is relatively modern. Option B is incorrect because although the professor mentions that zero has caused confusion, this is a minor part of his lecture. Option C is incorrect because zero as an empty placeholder is not a difficult concept, but zero as a number is.

13. A By context (Connecting content) Option A is correct because the professor says, "In many cultures with sophisticated mathematical systems, like the ancient Babylonians in the Middle East, zero the empty placeholder didn't exist for a long time." The professor adds, "Context indicated which number was being discussed." Option B is incorrect because the Babylonians dealt with zero as an empty placeholder by adding little hooks, not symbols like stars. Option C is incorrect because zero as a big O was used by the ancient Greeks, not the Babylonians. Option D is not supported by information in the lecture.

14. **B   By astronomers to track the positions of stars (Detail)** Option B is correct because the professor says, "The [ancient Greek] astronomers . . . used . . . zero the placeholder." Option A is incorrect. Ancient Greek architects did not use zero, because they relied on geometry. Option C is not supported by information in the lecture. Option D is incorrect because ancient Greek merchants did not "appear to care for precise notation," so they did not use zero.

15. **C   To demonstrate why zero the number was not needed (Inference)** Option C is correct

because the professor says, "Let's say you're a goat farmer. Well, you're likely to know how many animals you own, and use a number for that. If, by some bad luck, you lose all your animals, you probably describe that in words. Furthermore, . . . there's no point at which [you] have *negative* animals—that is: *minus* twenty-three goats. Where there's no concept of negative numbers, there's also no concept of zero the number." Option A is incorrect because while the anecdote may be amusing, this is not its main function. Option B is incorrect because though the professor suggests that ancient Greeks were mainly practical, this is not the main function of the anecdote. Option D is not supported by information in the lecture.

16. **(Organization/Drag-and-drop)**

ANSWER	EXPLANATION
1. **B** The Babylonians start to use zero as an empty placeholder.	The professor says, "Zero as an empty placeholder came into existence for the Babylonians around 700 BC."
2. **D** An Indian mathematician tries to give rules for zero as a number.	"In 628 AD, an Indian mathematician, Brahmagupta, tried to give rules for zero the number and negative numbers."
3. **A** The Mayans start to use zero as a number.	"Around 665 AD, [the Mayans] had a base-twenty numbering system that included a symbol for zero."
4. **C** The symbol for zero first appears in a Chinese document.	"In a Chinese mathematical treatise written in 1247 AD, the symbol for zero appears for the first time."
5. Around 1600 AD, zero as a number becomes widely used in Europe.	

17. **C   To show that understanding zero as a number remains problematic (Inference)** Option C is correct because the professor says, "Understanding zero is still an issue. I'm the only person I know who didn't celebrate the millennium on January 1, 2000. When the ancient Romans devised the calendar we still use, there was no Year Zero, and no one's fixed it since!" Option A is incorrect because the professor's story is not connected to how deeply he understands the topic, but to his individual actions. Option B is not supported by information in the passage. Option D is contradicted by information in the conversation.

Questions 18–22

TRACK 131 AUDIO SCRIPT

Narrator: Listen to part of a conversation between a student and a university employee.

Employee: Hello. May I help you?

Student: Is this where I register a new student club?

Employee: Yes, it is. Is it a cultural club or a sports club?

Student: Umm—

Employee: Cultural clubs are assigned meeting rooms in the Student Union, and sports clubs get small offices upstairs in the gym. For a sports club, I have to give out information on health and safety to meet the university's insurance requirements. And starting this year, it costs thirty dollars more to register a sports club because the gym is expensive to run.

Student: Uh-huh.

Employee: So, what kind of club is yours?

Student: We're called Reading Reach-Out. Let me explain. Most of us in Reading Reach-Out are education majors, and we've being researching reading habits. We think that getting mothers and fathers to read to their preschoolers is key to children's educational success.

Employee: Don't people on campus already do that?

Student: Yes, they do. We're an outreach group. We're focusing on the community beyond campus where learning to read is an issue.

Employee: So what kind of meeting space do you need?

Student: A small room's fine as long as it's got a large locker. We're planning to give away picture books and easy-to-read books to children in town, so we'll need some storage.

Employee: I'll see what I can do. Once you've filled in the application, a deposit on the meeting room is necessary. If everything's fine with the room at the end of the year, you'll get your twenty dollars back.

Student: No problem.

Employee: By the way, on this form, you can apply for some financial support from the college. Answer the questions and prepare a budget. A student committee will decide if you get the money.

Student: Great. One last thing—can we advertise by writing in chalk on the sidewalks on campus to let other students know about upcoming events? The chalk lasts for a couple of days before the rain washes it away.

Employee: Sure. However, the rules say that you may only advertise in chalk two days before an event. Otherwise the whole place'd be covered in chalk!

Student: I see your point.

Narrator: Now answer questions 18 to 22. Circle the letter of the answer.

TRACK 132 AUDIO SCRIPT

Narrator: Listen again to part of the conversation. Then answer the question.

Student: One last thing—can we advertise by writing in chalk on the sidewalks on campus to let other students know about upcoming events? The chalk lasts for a couple of days before the rain washes it away.

Employee: Sure. However, the rules say that you may only advertise in chalk two days before an event. Otherwise the whole place'd be covered in chalk!

Narrator: What does the employee mean when she says this?

Professor: Otherwise the whole place'd be covered in chalk!

ANSWERS AND EXPLANATIONS

18. **D   Register a cultural club (Gist-purpose)** Option D is correct. The student wants to register a club called Reading Reach-Out. This is a cultural club because it encourages reading. Options A, B, and C are not supported by information in the conversation.

19. **C   Young children in town (Detail)** Option C is correct because the student says, "We're planning to give away picture books and easy-to-read books to children in town." Option A is incorrect. Reading Reach-Out is composed of students majoring in education; it does not want to help education students. Option B is incorrect. Reading Reach-Out will target preschoolers, not adults, in the wider community. Option D is incorrect because high school students are too old to be targeted by Reading Reach-Out.

20. **A   Giving away children's books (Detail)** Option A is correct because the student says, "We're planning to give away picture books and easy-to-read books to children in town." Options B, C, and D are not supported by information in the conversation.

21. **B   Fill out a form and prepare a budget (Detail)** Option B is correct because the employee says, "Answer the questions and prepare a budget. A student committee will decide if you get the money." Options A and C are not supported by information in the conversation. Option D is contradicted by information in the conversation.

22. **A   She wants to show her approval of the rule. (Function/Replay item)** Option A is correct because the employee shows her approval of campus regulations when she says, "The rules say that you may only advertise in chalk two days prior to an event. Otherwise the whole place would be covered in chalk!" The sentence "Otherwise the whole place would be covered in chalk" means that if students advertise more than two days before an event, the sidewalks would be covered with chalk writing. The tone of the employee's voice shows that she thinks this rule is sensible. Option B is incorrect because if the employee were merely showing her awareness of campus regulations, her tone of voice and vocabulary would be different. Options C and D are not supported by the replay.

Questions 23–28

TRACK 133 AUDIO SCRIPT

Narrator: Listen to part of a lecture in an engineering class. The professor is talking about geothermal energy.

Professor: Energy produced by heat from inside Earth is called geothermal energy. Within Earth's core, there is a gradual radioactive decay of iron, nickel, and other elements, which produces huge amounts of heat. This heat permeates the rocky layers and aquifers above. Ultimately, it can be harnessed for electricity.

Male Student: Pardon me, but I read that the amount of heat captured by geothermal systems is minuscule in comparison to what reaches us from the sun.

Professor: Uh-huh.

Male Student: Sure, Earth's core is molten—something like six thousand degrees Kelvin—but we can't get to that core. We can't even drill two hundred kilometers down to the Upper Mantle; our limit's ten kilometers into the crust, where the temperature's around three hundred degrees Celsius.

Professor: Well, three hundred degrees is pretty hot *and* commercially viable. Cost-effective electricity from geothermal plants only requires hot water or steam to reach one hundred twenty degrees Celsius.

Male Student: Still, our poor technology means that most wells are only three to five kilometers deep, which is kind of useless.

Professor: My feeling is that since so much research is being done in this field, we'll get to that magical ten kilometers fairly soon. There's already an eight point five-kilometer well in Germany. But back to your claim about heat from Earth versus the sun.

Male Student: Energy that rises towards Earth's surface is around zero point zero six watts per square meter whereas what reaches us from the sun is around one thousand watts. That makes solar power way more appealing.

Professor: I'm with you on that. However, solar energy provides intermittent supply; oil, gas, and geothermal are constant—there's no variation in output related to time of day or changes in weather.

Female Student: What about sticking with oil and gas, then? Haven't lots of new fields been discovered?

Professor: A few have, but burning fossil fuel produces pollution that damages the ozone layer, and neither oil nor gas will last long. A US government agency has estimated that global geothermal resources are around fifteen thousand times greater than *all known* oil and gas reserves.

Male Student: What about the location of geothermal reserves? Aren't some of them in the middle of the sea? After all, Earth's crust is thinnest below the ocean.

Professor: That's very pertinent. Like solar, geothermal energy is often found far from where it's needed; transporting it to urban and industrial centers adds to its cost. Nevertheless, there are already twenty countries using geothermal, so let's assume the trend is going to continue.

Female Student: How does geothermal work?

Professor: There are two main systems: one, in operation since 1904, uses naturally occurring hot water or steam trapped in or circulating through permeable rock to power turbines. These natural hydrothermal resources are quite rare, existing around the edges of tectonic plates. Also, the heated water contains debris and pollutants, which have to be filtered. New Zealand and Iceland use this system. The UK has recently negotiated a deal with Iceland to supply one-third of its energy via a deep-sea cable, and some of that energy is geothermal.

France and Germany favor a slightly different geothermal system, in use since the 1970s. In this, heat is extracted from hot rock by *artificially* circulating water through the rock.

Male Student: Do you really think geothermal's going to take off?

Professor: I know there are drawbacks. Principally, although fuel is free and maintenance costs low, capital expenditure is enormous. Deep wells are needed to capture high temperatures, and only a few exist. Large amounts of energy are lost in the pumping process; nor is the energy supply endless, as is the case with solar: after thirty years of continuous extraction, the hot rock surface cools, and it takes twenty years of dormancy for heat to regenerate.

All the same, as traditional energy costs spiral, as resources diminish, and as greenhouse gases accumulate, geothermal energy becomes more attractive. It sure gets my approval.

Narrator: Now answer questions 23 to 28. Circle the letter of the answer.

ANSWERS AND EXPLANATIONS

23. **D** **The advantages and disadvantages of geothermal energy (Gist-content)** Option D is

correct because the professor spends significant time talking about the benefits of geothermal energy and its challenges. Options A and C are not supported by the information. The talk contains little historical information, and uses in various countries are discussed in only part of the talk. Option B is contradicted by the lecture; the professor clearly supports using geothermal energy.

24. **B She thinks it is worth developing. (Attitude)** Option B is correct. Overall, the professor thinks geothermal energy is worth developing because she says, "As traditional energy costs spiral, as resources diminish, and as greenhouse gases accumulate, geothermal energy becomes more attractive. It sure gets my approval." Option A is incorrect. A student, not the professor, seems to prefer solar power. Options C and D are contradicted by information in the lecture. Geothermal power is already in use.

25. **A When they produce water or steam at 120 degrees Celsius (Detail)** Option A is correct because the professor says, "Cost-effective electricity from geothermal plants only requires hot water or steam to reach 120 degrees Celsius." Options B, C, and D are not supported by information in the lecture.

26. **D One that uses water artificially circulated through hot rock (Detail)** Option D is correct because the professor says, "France favor[s] a slightly different geothermal system, in use since the 1970s. In this, heat is extracted from hot rock by artificially circulating water through the rock." Option A is not supported by information in the lecture. Option B is incorrect because the professor says that steam is produced by artificially circulating water. Option C is incorrect because Iceland, not France, is supplying the UK with energy via a deep-sea cable.

27. **(Detail/Check box)**

	GEOTHERMAL	SOLAR	OIL AND GAS
Intermittent supply		✔ The professor says, "However, solar energy provides intermittent supply; oil, gas, and geothermal are constant."	
Endless supply		✔ "Large amounts of energy are lost in the pumping process; nor is energy supply endless, as is the case with solar."	
Low maintenance costs	✔ "Maintenance costs [are] low."		
Greenhouse gases produced			✔ "Burning fossil fuel produces pollution that damages the ozone layer."

28. **C Initial investment in a well is high.
    D Technology is not advanced enough to
    drill deep wells. (Detail/Special multiple
    choice)** Option C is correct because the professor
    says, "Principally, although fuel is free and
    maintenance costs low, capital expenditure is
    enormous." Option D is correct because the
    professor says, "Deep wells are needed to capture
    high temperatures, and only a few exist." Option
    A is incorrect; though the professor mentions that
    hot rocks cool down, this happens after 30 years,
    not 10. Option B is not supported by information
    in the lecture.

Questions 29–34

TRACK 134 AUDIO SCRIPT

Narrator: Listen to part of a lecture in a zoology class.
The professor is talking about birds.

Professor: Whether killed for food, kept as pets, or
worshiped as gods, birds have had an intimate
relationship with humans for millennia. English is
rich in language related to our feathered friends.
Consider "She's a wise old bird," or the online
service Twitter—a word for the avian equivalent
of "chat." But many expressions are insulting, like
"bird-brained." Today, I'd like to focus on three
relatively common birds that are rewriting our
perceptions of avian intelligence.

Currently, there are more than ten thousand
avian species alive, but only a very few that make
tools. Two of these are the New Caledonian crow
and the palm cockatoo. The Western scrub-jay
isn't a toolmaker, but its behavior has provided
evidence that jays, like humans and *only* humans,
possess a "theory of mind."

New Caledonian crows, which inhabit two
small islands in the South Pacific, flush out insects
with a hooked tool that they make from dead
plant material found on the forest floor. In one
experiment, two captive birds were given straight
wires instead of wood. One crow repeatedly bent
hers to create a hook. This suggests that crows
adjust their behavior to the demands of a specific
task and do not merely follow a set of learned or
instinctive actions.

The palm cockatoo is even more extraordinary.
Found in rain forests and woodlands of New
Guinea and northeastern Australia, it is large, black,
and distinctive. Like all birds, it changes its feathers
one by one each year, growing brighter feathers
for the breeding season. By the way, feathers are

an amazing innovation. I mean, if a bat's wing is
damaged, no part of it regrows, and if the injury
is bad enough, the poor bat dies. However, birds
repair their wings by regrowing feathers.

Anyway . . . the palm cockatoo also has a unique
beak; the upper and lower mandibles don't entirely
meet, so the tongue can hold a nut against the
upper mandible while the lower one works to open
it. This means palm cockatoos can eat nuts with
hard shells. The cockatoo's nut-cracking is skillful
and intriguing. The male palm cockatoo also uses
his beak to wrench off long seedpods or thick
sticks—2.5 centimeters in diameter—from living
trees. From June to September, he flies around
drumming with his stick against hollow boughs,
perhaps to attract mates or to alert other males to
his territory. The noise is so loud it can be heard
up to 100 meters away. After drumming, the male
may strip the stick into pieces to line the hollow
for a nest. A third theory holds that female palm
cockatoos may assess the size of a hollow by the
resonance of the drumming. A suitable cavity
needs to be large enough to last several years.

Palm cockatoos lay one egg every second year,
having one of the lowest breeding rates of any
parrot. However, they can breed late in life and live
a long time. Recently, one cockatoo reproduced at
the age of fifty; many have survived until ninety.
Aside from their drumming and longevity, palm
cockatoos do not fly in flocks, and produce an array
of complex calls.

The Western scrub-jay poses an interesting
question: do birds project their own experience onto
another bird's in what is known by psychologists as
the "theory of mind"? The answer seems to be "yes."
Just a decade ago, no scientist would've believed
this.

In experiments, scrub-jays who have stolen
another bird's food and have been *observed* hiding
that food are more likely to move their own food
to another site than if they haven't been observed.
The jays are using memories of past experience to
prepare for their future. OK, let's say there's a busy
road, and blackbirds nest nearby. Well, the birds
learn when to fly down onto that road to pick up
food and when to fly away to avoid traffic. But this
response is to one variable only—traffic—and it
doesn't suggest planning or interpreting motive.
The jays that change the location of their stockpiles
have figured out that if they don't do so, another
thieving jay'll come along and take their supply.
They're interpreting the future in a more cunning
way than a bird that's dodging cars.

No one knows how these three different birds acquired their aptitudes—research hasn't been done into the anatomy of their brains—but whatever else, they're certainly not bird-brained.

Narrator: Now answer questions 29 to 34. Circle the letter of the answer.

ANSWERS AND EXPLANATIONS

29. **B   They are changing scientists' views on the intelligence of birds. (Gist-content)** Option B is correct because the professor says, "I'd like to focus on three relatively common birds that are rewriting our perceptions of avian intelligence." Option A is incorrect because while the professor mentions that one of the birds, the palm cockatoo, lives for a long time, this is not the main topic. Option C is incorrect because only two of the three birds make tools from branches and other plant material. Option D is not mentioned in the lecture.

30. **C   They make hooked tools. (Detail)** Option C is correct because the professor says, "New Caledonian crows . . . flush out insects with a hooked tool that they make from dead plant material found on the forest floor." Option A is incorrect because the professor says, "crows adjust their behavior to the demands of a specific task and do not merely follow a set of learned or instinctive actions." Options B and D are incorrect. They are about a bird's unusual beak and living in Australia, but they relate to palm cockatoos, not New Caledonian crows.

31. **D   To make an interesting but irrelevant comment (Function)** Option D is correct because the professor's mention of bats is not useful to his overall argument. The professor is discussing the intelligence of birds, not the success of feathers. Option A is incorrect because it assumes some connection between birds' intelligence and feathers that is not stated by the professor. Option B may be true, but it is not mentioned by the professor. Option C is incorrect because this point is irrelevant to the professor's argument.

32. **A   To attract mates   B   To stake out territory (Detail/Special multiple choice)** Option A is correct because the professor says a male palm cockatoo "flies around drumming with his stick against hollow boughs, perhaps to attract mates." Option B is correct because a male palm cockatoo might drum "to alert other males to his territory." Option C is not supported by information in the lecture. Option D is incorrect because the female palm cockatoo, not the male, may assess the size of a potential nest cavity by drumming.

33. **C   The ability to project one's own experience onto another individual's (Detail)** Option C is correct because the professor says, "The Western scrub-jay poses an interesting question: do birds project their own experience onto another bird's in what is known by psychologists as the 'theory of mind'? The answer seems to be 'yes.'" Option A is too general. Options B and D are not supported by information in the lecture.

34. **A   They use memories of past experiences to plan their future. (Connecting content)** Option A is correct because the professor says, "The jays are using memories of past experience to prepare for their future." Later he says, "They're interpreting the future in a . . . cunning way." Option B is not supported by information in the lecture. Option C is incorrect because producing complex calls relates to the palm cockatoo, not the Western scrub-jay. Option D is incorrect because successfully avoiding dangerous traffic relates to blackbirds, not Western scrub-jays.

Speaking (Page 600)

Item 1

TRACK 135 AUDIO SCRIPT

Narrator: You will now speak about a familiar topic. Prepare your response in fifteen seconds. Then allow forty-five seconds to record your response. Describe a local festival from your hometown that you enjoy. Include specific examples and details in your description.

Item 2

TRACK 136 AUDIO SCRIPT

Narrator: You will now give your opinion about a familiar topic. Prepare your response in fifteen seconds. Then allow forty-five seconds to record your response. Some people take a year off between high school and college or university. Other people prefer to go directly from high school into college or university. Which do you think is better for students? Explain why.

Item 3

TRACK 137 AUDIO SCRIPT

Narrator: You will now read a short passage on a campus-related topic and listen to a conversation on the same subject. Then you will hear a question. Prepare your response in thirty seconds. Then allow sixty seconds to record your response. Northeastern University is introducing a night bus service. You will have 50 seconds to read the announcement from Student Services about the night bus service. Begin reading now.

TRACK 138 AUDIO SCRIPT

Narrator: Now listen to two students discussing the announcement.

Man: At last, a night bus service on campus.

Woman: Yeah, but from the announcement, it looks kind of limited to me.

Man: What do you mean?

Woman: First up, it won't start operating till seven in the evening. In winter, it gets dark here around four-thirty. It's the dark that worries people, especially new students. There'll be plenty of new students in September.

Man: I suppose so.

Woman: Also, the bus won't be leaving campus. It may connect with two major gates where there are other transport services and a parking building, but I think it'd be more useful if it kept on going into town, where lots of students live.

Man: Yes, but can't people change to a city bus at Gate 8?

Woman: Maybe, but they will have to wait there in the cold and dark.

There's another odd thing: there are two dorms near Gate 6, so I think Gate 6 should be one of the bus stops. The way it's currently routed, students who live in those dorms have to walk behind the Student Union and through a parking lot to get home. That parking lot is really dark at night.

Narrator: The woman expresses her opinion of the announcement by Student Services. Briefly summarize the announcement. Then state her opinion about the announcement and give her reasons for holding that opinion.

Item 4

TRACK 139 AUDIO SCRIPT

Narrator: You will now read a short passage on an academic topic and then listen to a talk on the same subject. Then you will hear a question. Prepare your response in thirty seconds. Then allow sixty seconds to record your response. Now read a passage from an art history textbook. You have 50 seconds to read the passage. Begin reading now.

TRACK 140 AUDIO SCRIPT

Narrator: Now listen to part of a lecture on this topic in an art history class.

Professor: The Temple of Bacchus at Baalbek in Lebanon was built around 200 AD. It was probably dedicated to Bacchus, the Roman god of nature, fertility, and wine. The Romans were impressive builders and cunning propagandists. The temple was huge and was constructed in a part of the city that had been sacred for centuries.

The people of the new province understood what to worship—both the emperor in Rome and new Roman gods—but they did so within a familiar architectural context, for most Roman temples combined three styles. They borrowed from earlier Greek temples, and they used Roman and local elements.

Greek features at Baalbek include the stone temple's rectangular shape and columns on all sides. The columns support a horizontal section with carvings.

Roman features include its frontal aspect—the temple can only be entered from the east. There is a single *cella* inside.

Notable local features include its height above ground and its size. Most Roman temples have one flight of steps—Baalbek has three. The temple is sixty-six meters long, thirty-five meters wide, and thirty-one meters high. In addition, there are two towers on each side of the doorway. Its ornate carvings are particularly eastern. Inside, the statue of the god stood on a raised platform. This was not in a recess in the wall as typically but beneath an elaborate marble canopy.

Narrator: The professor describes the Temple of Bacchus at Baalbek. Explain the temple's functions and how its design is typical of Roman temples. Use information from the reading and the talk.

Item 5

TRACK 141 AUDIO SCRIPT

Narrator: You will now listen to part of a conversation about a campus-related situation. Then you will hear a question. Prepare your response in twenty seconds. Then allow sixty seconds to record your answer. Now listen to a conversation between two students on campus.

Man: Hi, Tina. How are you?

Woman: Actually, I'm in a bad mood; I'm so frustrated.

Man: Why's that?

Woman: I've got this biology test coming up, and I can't—I just can't—remember all the new terminology. I mean, have you ever heard of a xylem cell or a cambium cell?

Man: Yes, I have. I took biology last year.

Woman: Oh, great!

Man: I had the exact same problem until I came up with two ways to make things easier. I got pretty good grades.

Woman: Really? What did you do?

Man: First, I used a simple memory device. You probably remember it from junior high. Y'know, you take the initial letter of a word and find another word with the same letter that's easier to remember, and then you put all the words into a crazy phrase. So: My Very Early Marriage Just Suited Uncle Ned stands for the planets: Mercury, Venus—

Woman: Right. What was the other system?

Man: I bought a roll of see-through baking paper and traced my diagrams. I traced each one really neatly in black pen and labeled it really carefully, or half-labeled it. I did ten of every single diagram. It took me a whole weekend. Now, don't laugh, but this did work. I stuck my little traced drawings all over my room. Everywhere. The ones with complete labels, I just enjoyed looking at. The ones with partial labels, I filled in as I began to remember them.

So, memory device or tracing—take your pick.

Narrator: Summarize briefly the problem that the speakers are talking about. Then say which of the two solutions from the conversation you would recommend. Explain your reasons for your recommendation.

Item 6

TRACK 142 AUDIO SCRIPT

Narrator: You will now listen to part of a talk on an academic topic. Then you will hear a question. Prepare your response in twenty seconds. Then allow sixty seconds to record your answer. Listen to part of a lecture in a food and nutrition class.

Professor: Nutritionists have long held that individuals eagerly eat high-calorie food as it provides a pleasurable experience. Recent research has confirmed this belief.

Sophisticated brain scans have shown that language affects a person's perception of taste. Several regions of the brain are associated with taste and pleasure. One such is the orbito-frontal cortex, or OFC. In 2008, one study reported that the OFC was activated after subjects were presented with positive words, such as *family*, *love*, and *home*, while eating different kinds of food. This shows that positive words encourage us to eat.

In 2011, Julie Hudry found that visual cues influence taste. Her subjects were given a neutral taste generated by a tiny electric current to the tongue. The perception of this taste altered after subjects viewed images of food with varying calorific content. Again, OFC activity was marked. Confirming nutritionists' beliefs, subjects described pizza, pastries, and lamb chops as "very pleasant" even though a neutral taste was on their tongue. For watermelons, green beans, and yogurt, the neutral taste seemed little more than neutral.

This is great news for food producers who can confidently erect giant posters of calorie-rich food or bombard us with junk-food ads peppered with positive words like "mother" and "love." Mothers, doctors, and governments, however, may hope future research will find regions of the brain that can limit appetite in a world plagued by obesity.

Narrator: Using points and examples from the talk, explain which factors influence taste and pleasure in food consumption.

EVALUATION

There are many ways to answer these items. If you do not have a recording device, ask a friend to listen and evaluate your responses. If you have a recording device, ask a teacher or an English-speaking friend to listen to your responses and evaluate them. Or wait a day or two and evaluate them yourself. For Items 1 and 2, use a copy of the Independent Speaking Rubric in Appendix D. For Items 3 to 6, use a copy of the Integrated Speaking Rubric in Appendix D.

Compare your responses to the following high-scoring responses:

 Item 1

 Item 2

 Item 3

 Item 4

 Item 5

Item 6

After evaluating your responses, follow the instructions in the TOEFL iBT Personalized Study Planner on pages 76–77 to find ways to improve your performance.

Writing (Page 606)

Item 1

TRACK 143 AUDIO SCRIPT

Narrator: Now listen to part of a lecture on the topic you just read about. You may take notes in the space provided.

Professor: I don't know if you noticed the article in the *University Daily* a couple of days ago. The campus art museum just agreed to return one of its holdings, a very valuable Italian painting, to the church in Italy where it came from. It seems that a collector bought the painting many years ago and didn't know it was stolen, and then donated it to the university. No one really knew the church it had come from until an art historian saw it while visiting campus. He arranged for the painting to be returned to the church it came from, and in return the museum in that town lent us another painting that will hang in the same space.

This is a timely topic because of our reading last night. As you can see, not just iconic works, such as the Elgin Marbles or the Rosetta Stone, can be the subject of ownership disputes. But in this case, an agreeable settlement was reached. Clearly, the museum had no right to keep the painting, but by accepting another painting from the same town as a loan, the museum protected the rights of the real owner of the painting and ensured that students and visitors can have access to authentic works of art. So the university is providing a great example. But still many museums are unwilling to return important works, even when their rights to the works are in question. So what can museums do? When there is a dispute that can be documented, the museum should make every effort to return

the work. A trade or a loan can help the museum ensure that its holdings are legal and can allow visitors to continue to enjoy works of art from other countries. But what about valuable works that are too big or too fragile to move, such as the Elgin Marbles? I would argue that in many cases, the museum can continue to hold such works, but transfer the ownership to the original country. That protects the dignity of the other country while avoiding a costly and dangerous trip for priceless works. Other works, such as the Rosetta Stone, however, should be returned. There is no reason why such a small, easily transported work should not be returned to its country when it was acquired under such doubtful circumstances.

TRACK 144 AUDIO SCRIPT

Narrator: Summarize the points made in the lecture, being sure to explain how they oppose the specific points made in the reading passage.

EXPLANATION

There are many ways to answer this item. Compare your answer to this high-scoring response. Then evaluate your essay. Follow the instructions on page 497. Use a copy of the Simplified Integrated Writing Rubric in Appendix E.

SAMPLE ESSAY RESPONSE

The reading and the lecture are about art that is in museums that the works do not belong to. According to lecture, many museums have art that was taken during war or colonization. Two examples are Elgin Marbles and Rosetta Stone. Both of these works are in a famous British museum, and many people visit them every day. The problem is that Greece and Egypt think that these works of art belong to them.

The musueum got Elgin Marbles because someone bought them from the government of Greece. But the government really did not have the right to sell this art to anybody, and this art really belongs to Greece today. The same for the Rosetta Stone. A foreign soldier found it, and then the British army captured it and took it to England. According to the reading, many problems prevent the museum from returning the art. Musueums say that art is too big or old to travel, for example.

The professor has a different idea. He thinks that the museums should always return art, just as his school returned a stolen painting to Italy. In return, people in Italy were happy, and the school got a different painting from the town to enjoy. Another plan is needed for large or fragile works that cannot travel. The museum gives the object to the other country, but keeps it as a loan. The museum might pay something to the country, or return other objects that are small and easy to move.

In conclusion, there are many problems related to stolen art, and museums may not know about the problems or be responsible for them. The professor gives good suggestions on how to solve this problem.

Item 2

EXPLANATION

There are many ways to answer this item. Compare your answer to this high-scoring response. Then evaluate your essay. Follow the instructions on page 525. Use a copy of the Independent Writing Rubric in Appendix E.

SAMPLE ESSAY RESPONSE

Many people say that students should not get married until after they complete their studies. I am married, and I agree with this statement whenever I have a disagreement with my husband, but mostly I am happy being a student and married at the same time.

First, I was married before I started to study. I married my husband after I graduated from college, and I thought that my studies were finished. But then I lost my job, so decided to go back to school. So being single is not an option for me.

Another reason is that I have the help of my husband while I am in school. He has a good job. That helps pay tuition and expenses. And we did all the housework together even before I returned to school. Now when I am busy preparing for a test, for example, he takes care of housework and cooking.

Last, because I am older than other students and married, I think I am wise. I use my wisdom to help my studies. I have experience from life that single students don't have. I study psychology, and I understand people's psychological problems better because of my experience.

In conclusion, when I was young, I thought that I shouldn't get married until after I finished my studies. But now that I am married and in school, I think it's a good way to go to school.

After you evaluate your responses to Items 1 and 2, use the TOEFL iBT Personalized Study Planner on page 617 to find ways to improve your performance.

CHAPTER 8

TOEFL iBT Final Practice Test 2

Chapter at a Glance

In this chapter, you will learn:

This TOEFL iBT Final Practice Test 2 is designed to help you assess the skills you will need to score your best on the TOEFL iBT.

Completing the entire test takes about 3 hours and 30 minutes, the same amount of time as the actual TOEFL iBT. If possible, complete the test in one sitting to simulate the actual test experience. If you cannot complete the test in a single sitting, use the TOEFL iBT Test At a Glance to help you plan how much time to allow for each part. The table also indicates the materials you will need for each section of the test.

TOEFL iBT Final Practice Test 2

SECTION	TIME	YOU NEED
Reading	60 minutes	Watch or timer on your computer or mobile phone
Listening	60 minutes	Watch or timer, disk, and player
Break	10 minutes	The actual TOEFL iBT includes a break between Listening and Speaking.
Speaking	20 minutes	Watch or timer, disk and player, audio recorder on your mobile phone or computer
Writing	60 minutes	Watch or timer, disk and player, computer to keyboard your response
All sections		Paper and pencil or pen for taking notes during all sections of the TOEFL iBT. (Note-taking is allowed on all sections of the TOEFL iBT.)

After you take this test, use the Answers, Explanations, Audio Scripts, and Sample Responses on pages 708–727 to check your work. Then use the TOEFL iBT Personalized Study Planner on pages 702–707 to analyze your results and find the skills you need to review before you take the actual TOEFL iBT.

Reading

Directions: The Reading section of the TOEFL iBT asseses your ability to understand academic reading passages in English. To simulate actual TOEFL iBT conditions, follow these instructions:

- Use your watch or the timer on your mobile phone or computer to keep track of the time.
- Give yourself 20 minutes to read each passage and respond to the items that are about it.
- Allow 60 minutes to read all the passages and answer all the items.
- As on the actual TOEFL iBT, you may look back at the passage when answering items. You can skip items and return to them.
- If you do not finish all the items when the test ends, mark your place. Then continue working as quickly as you can. When you finish, take note of the total time. This will give you an idea of how quickly you need to work on the actual TOEFL iBT to answer all the items in 60 minutes.

Now begin the Reading section of TOEFL iBT Final Practice Test 2.

Directions: Give yourself 20 minutes to read the passage and answer Items 1–14.

Among major historical figures of all times, one of the best known, but perhaps one of the least understood, is the last queen of France, Marie Antoinette. Both romanticized and vilified, she was executed by guillotine two week before her 38th birthday at the beginning of the Reign of Terror during the French Revolution. For some, she was a symbol of the excesses of the French monarchy, a selfish queen whose lavish spending and irresponsible behavior was a contributing factor to the overthrow of the monarchy. To others, she was the naïve and tragic victim of both the intrigue of the French court and the cruelty of the Reign of Terror. Who was the real Marie Antoinette? And how did she come to be understood so differently by different people?

Confusion about Marie Antoinette begins with her name. An Austrian archduchess, she was born in 1755, the daughter of Empress Maria Theresa, Queen of Austria and Bohemia, and Holy Roman Emperor Francis I. The day after she was born she was named Maria Antonia Josepha Johanna, but she was also called Maria Antonia Josephina Johanna. Her family called her Antonia at home, but at court she was called Madame Antoine. She only received the name Marie Antoinette after her engagement.

The Austrian court lacked the elaborate ritual and ceremony that Marie Antoinette would later encounter at the French court at Versailles. Unlike many countries at that time, the Austrian court was open not only to nobles and high officials but also to commoners "of merit." This facilitated social mobility. The Austrian imperial family tried to live a relatively simple life for a royal family. In times away from court, the family dressed like a middle-class family of the time and the children played with neighborhood children, not with the children of the nobility. She received an education typical of a young woman of her station, but she was at best a mediocre student. The only subject she excelled at was music, and she learned to sing and play four instruments well, including harpsichord and harp. The Austrian court was multilingual, and she spoke Italian well, but her German and French were poor, according to reports from her teachers and observers at court.

The diplomatic balance of power was shifting in Europe at the time, and France and Austria, previously enemies, had created a new alliance. As was the practice at the time, intermarriage among royal families was used to build and maintain alliances. Upon the death of the son of Louis XV, his young grandson, Louis-Auguste, became heir to the French throne. The two countries arranged the marriage of Marie Antoinette, then aged 12, to the future Louis XVI, who was only 14 years old at the time. Such engagements were not unusual at the time, and the marriages generally did not take place until the couples were of sufficient age. Marie Antoinette traveled to France to marry in 1770, but problems soon developed. She was not ready for marriage and felt homesick frequently. She disliked the elaborate protocol of the French court, where nearly every action of the royal couple was a public event. Even getting up in the morning or going to bed at night involved elaborate ceremonies attended by servants and nobles. Despite the gossip and intrigue of the French court, she was popular among the people. However, she and her husband did not have complementary personalities. While her husband was quiet and shy, Marie Antoinette was an extrovert who loved to dance, go to parties and the theater, and visit friends. Ascending to the throne in 1774, the king tended to get up early to attend to affairs of state, but the queen usually got up at about noon after staying up late to attend parties, dinners, and plays. To make matters worse, the minister responsible for the alliance with Austria was dismissed, and the historical tensions between the countries reemerged. Many people doubted her loyalty to France and came to believe that she was a spy or an agent of Austria. As a result, her popularity declined, the king felt unable to trust her, and she lost nearly all her influence on politics.

As queen, Marie Antoinette was expected to be a symbol of France and to wear the best French fashions, jewels, and perfumes. Marie Antoinette enjoyed this role, but her costly jewels and gowns made her unpopular among the people, especially as economic problems grew. As her marital unhappiness increased, her spending increased proportionally. A number of scandals about her spending on gowns and jewels became public knowledge. Even though she was not implicated in any of them, they contributed to her negative image. Many people blamed France's high level of debt on her spending, even though most of it was the result of high wartime spending, and began to call her "Madame Deficit" because of the scandals. People felt she was indifferent to their suffering. Allegedly, when told, "The people have no bread," she replied, "Then let them eat cake." Though this story is a fabrication, it shows the intensity of people's anger toward her.

Shortly after the outbreak of the revolution, the new government moved the royal family to Paris. The king agreed to a new constitution that removed most of his powers. After the royal family attempted to escape abroad, they were taken prisoner. First the king was tried for treason, convicted, and executed by guillotine. Several months later, Marie Antoinette suffered a similar fate. To some a victim, and to others an enemy of the people, it is clear that the negative image of the queen, not entirely deserved, contributed to the outbreak of the revolution and her ultimate demise at the hands of the revolutionaries.

Directions: Now answer the questions.

PARAGRAPH 1

Among major historical figures of all times, one of the best known, but perhaps one of the least understood, is the last queen of France, Marie Antoinette. Both romanticized and vilified, she was executed by guillotine two week before her 38th birthday at the beginning of the Reign of Terror during the French Revolution. For some, she was a symbol of the excesses of the French monarchy, a selfish queen whose lavish spending and irresponsible behavior was a contributing factor to the overthrow of the monarchy. To others, she was the naïve and tragic victim of both the intrigue of the French court and the cruelty of the Reign of Terror. Who was the real Marie Antoinette? And how did she come to be understood so differently by different people?

1. According to the paragraph, which is true of Marie Antoinette?

   Ⓐ She died at the end of the Reign of Terror.

   Ⓑ She caused the French Revolution.

   Ⓒ She was not a real person.

   Ⓓ There is disagreement about her.

Confusion about Marie Antoinette begins with her name. An Austrian archduchess, she was born in 1755, the daughter of Empress Maria Theresa, Queen of Austria and Bohemia, and Holy Roman Emperor Francis I. The day after she was born she was named Maria Antonia Josepha Johanna, but she was also called Maria Antonia Josephina Johanna. Her family called her Antonia at home, but at court she was called Madame Antoine. She only received the name Marie Antoinette after her engagement.

2. In paragraph 2, why does the author mention the various names used to refer to Marie Antoinette?

   Ⓐ To provide an example of confusion about her identity

   Ⓑ To show that she used false names and identities

   Ⓒ To indicate that at this time people changed names frequently

   Ⓓ To show that royal families gave their children complicated names

The Austrian court lacked the elaborate ritual and ceremony that Marie Antoinette would later encounter at the French court at Versailles. Unlike many countries at that time, the Austrian court was open not only to nobles and high officials but also to commoners "of merit." This facilitated social mobility. The Austrian imperial family tried to live a relatively simple life for a royal family. In times away from court, the family dressed like a middle-class family of the time and the children played with neighborhood children, not with the children of the nobility. She received an education typical of a young woman of her station, but she was at best a mediocre student. The only subject she excelled at was music, and she learned to sing and play four instruments well, including harpsichord and harp. The Austrian court was multilingual, and she spoke Italian well, but her German and French were poor, according to reports from her teachers and observers at court.

3. What was the Austrian royal family's attitude toward common people?

   Ⓐ Common people were looked down on.

   Ⓑ Common people were accepted.

   Ⓒ Common people were granted special honors and privileges.

   Ⓓ Common people had no role in the royal court.

4. Which of the following best expresses the essential information in the highlighted sentence? Incorrect choices change the meaning in important ways or leave out essential information.

Ⓐ The Austrian court was multilingual, and according to reports from court observers and her teachers, she spoke Italian well, but her German and French were poor.

Ⓑ The Austrian court was multilingual, according to reports from court observers and her teachers, and she spoke Italian well, but German and French poorly.

Ⓒ According to reports from court observers and her teachers, she spoke Italian well, but her German and French were poor.

Ⓓ According to reports from multilingual court observers and her teachers, she spoke Italian well, but German and French poorly.

5. In which of these ways were the French court and the Austrian court different?

Ⓐ The Austrian court was multilingual and the French court was not.

Ⓑ The French court was open to common people and the Austrian court was not.

Ⓒ The Austrian court was more relaxed than the French court.

Ⓓ The French court was refined and elegant, and the Austrian court was simple and backward.

6. The word "mediocre" in the passage is closest in meaning to

Ⓐ only good at music

Ⓑ typical for the time

Ⓒ only good at Italian

Ⓓ not very good

The diplomatic balance of power was shifting in Europe at the time, and France and Austria, previously enemies, had created a new alliance. As was the practice at the time, intermarriage among royal families was used to build and maintain alliances. Upon the death of the son of Louis XV, his young grandson, Louis-Auguste, became heir to the French throne. The two countries arranged the marriage of Marie Antoinette, then aged 12, to the future Louis XVI, who was only 14 years old at the time. Such engagements were not unusual at the time, and the marriages generally did not take place until the couples were of sufficient age. Marie Antoinette traveled to France to marry in 1770, but problems soon developed. She was not ready for marriage and felt homesick frequently. She disliked the elaborate protocol of the French court, where nearly every action of the royal couple was a public event. Even getting up in the morning or going to bed at night involved elaborate ceremonies attended by servants and nobles. Despite the gossip and intrigue of the French court, she was popular among the people. However, she and her husband did not have complementary personalities. While her husband was quiet and shy, Marie Antoinette was an extrovert who loved to dance, go to parties and the theater, and visit friends. Ascending to the throne in 1774, the king tended to get up early to attend to affairs of state, but the queen usually got up at about noon after staying up late to attend parties, dinners, and plays. To make matters worse, the minister responsible for the alliance with Austria was dismissed, and the historical tensions between the countries reemerged. Many people doubted her loyalty to France and came to believe that she was a spy or an agent of Austria. As a result, her popularity declined, the king felt unable to trust her, and she lost nearly all her influence on politics.

7. Which of the following is NOT a reason for Marie Antoinette's marriage problems?

   (A) She missed her family and country.

   (B) Her husband was jealous of her popularity.

   (C) She and her husband were not compatible.

   (D) She disliked the rituals of the French court.

8. The word "extrovert" in the passage is closest in meaning to

   (A) someone who does not have a complementary personality

   (B) someone who is reserved

   (C) someone who likes to be with other people

   (D) someone who likes to sleep late

P
A
R
A
G
R
A
P
H

5

As queen, Marie Antoinette was expected to be a symbol of France and to wear the best French fashions, jewels, and perfumes. Marie Antoinette enjoyed this role, but her costly jewels and gowns made her unpopular among the people, especially as economic problems grew. As her marital unhappiness increased, her spending increased proportionally. A number of scandals about her spending on gowns and jewels became public knowledge. Even though she was not implicated in any of them, they contributed to her negative image. Many people blamed France's high level of debt on her spending, even though most of it was the result of high wartime spending, and began to call her "Madame Deficit" because of the scandals. People felt she was indifferent to their suffering. Allegedly, when told, "The people have no bread," she replied, "Then let them eat cake." Though this story is a fabrication, it shows the intensity of people's anger toward her.

9. Why does the author mention that people began to call her "Madame Deficit"?

Ⓐ To show how people associated her with the country's growing debt

Ⓑ To show that popular criticism of her spending was unfair

Ⓒ To show how her spending on clothing and jewels drove France into debt

Ⓓ To show that the people continued to respect her because they called her Madame

10. The word "they" in the passage refers to

Ⓐ purchases

Ⓑ people

Ⓒ gowns and jewels

Ⓓ scandals

11. The word "it" in the passage refers to

Ⓐ her spending

Ⓑ the scandal

Ⓒ the debt

Ⓓ wartime spending

PARAGRAPH 6

Shortly after the outbreak of the revolution, the new government moved the royal family to Paris. The king agreed to a new constitution that removed most of his powers. After the royal family attempted to escape abroad, they were taken prisoner. First the king was tried for treason, convicted, and executed by guillotine. Several months later, Marie Antoinette suffered a similar fate. To some a victim, and to others an enemy of the people, it is clear that the negative image of the queen, not entirely deserved, contributed to the outbreak of the revolution and her ultimate demise at the hands of the revolutionaries.

12. Why was the royal family put in prison?

Ⓐ The government moved the royal family from Versailles to Paris.

Ⓑ The royal family tried to escape from France.

Ⓒ The king agreed to a new constitution.

Ⓓ The king was found guilty of treason.

PARAGRAPH 6

Shortly after the outbreak of the revolution, the new government moved the royal family to Paris. **A** The king agreed to a new constitution that removed most of his powers. After the royal family attempted to escape abroad, they were taken prisoner. First the king was tried for treason, convicted, and executed by guillotine. **B** Several months later, Marie Antoinette suffered a similar fate. **C** To some a victim, and to others an enemy of the people, it is clear that the negative image of the queen, not entirely deserved, contributed to the outbreak of the revolution and her ultimate demise at the hands of the revolutionaries. **D**

13. Look at the four squares (■) that indicate where the following sentence could be inserted into the passage.

She had very little time to prepare her defense and was found guilty in a trial lasting only a few days.

Where would the sentence best fit?

14. An introductory sentence for a brief summary of the passage is provided. Complete the summary by selecting the THREE answer choices that express important ideas in the passage. Some sentences do not belong in the summary because they express ideas that are not presented in the passage or are minor details in the passage. *This item is worth 2 points.*

Write the letters of your answer choices in the spaces where they belong.

> **The passage is about the life of Marie Antoinette.**
>
> •
>
> •
>
> •

Answer Choices

A Marie Antoinette's extravagant spending contributed to a negative view of the monarchy.

B Marie Antoinette received a fair trial before her execution.

C Marie Antoinette spoke good Italian, but her French and German skills were poor.

D A number of scandals contributed to negative popular opinion about Marie Antoinette.

E Marie Antoinette was both a symbol of the excesses of the monarchy and a victim of the revolution.

F Marie Antoinette was executed for treason because she was a spy for Austria.

Directions: Give yourself 20 minutes to read the passage and answer Items 15–28.

Plants are the only organisms on Earth that can make their own food. All other organisms have to find their own food by consuming other organisms. Most plants make their own food using photosynthesis, a process that allows plants to use energy from the sun to synthesize food that the plants use as a source of energy. Some plants, such as mushrooms and other kinds of fungi, cannot make their own food because they lack chlorophyll. These plants obtain their food from other plant matter. However, at least a few plants get some nutrients by trapping and digesting animals, usually insects or spiders. These carnivorous plants tend to live in places with soil that cannot supply needed nutrients, such as nitrogen, so they had to obtain them in other ways. It is important to note that, contrary to popular belief, while these plants obtain needed nutrients from the meat they consume, they still derive their energy from food they make themselves through photosynthesis.

To be considered as carnivorous, plants have to meet three criteria: plants need to attract prey, kill prey, and digest prey. There are more than 630 different species of plants that fully meet this definition. All of these are flowering plants, and they fall into five main groups, based on how they attract and kill their prey: pitfall traps, flypaper traps, snap traps, bladder traps, and lobster pot traps. Some of these involve movement, while others do not. Scientists call plants that snap shut or use other movement active traps. Passive traps often use sticky or slippery coatings on leaves to catch their prey.

Pitfall traps generally take the form of rolled-up leaves whose edges are sealed together so that water or digestive fluids can gather at the bottom and not leak out. These plants generally use scent to lure insects inside the rolled-up leaves. Once insects are inside, slippery coatings tire the insects as they try to escape from the plant. Eventually, the insects grow careless, slip on the coating, and fall into the digestive fluids where their nutrients are extracted for use in other parts of the plant. Other pitfall traps have leaves that have small openings that insects use to get inside the rolled-up leaf. The rolled-up leaves have small patches that are white, not green, and look like exits. The trapped insects begin to look for the exits, but they soon become tired and confused by the false exits. Eventually, they slip and fall into the digestive juices. A major problem with these plants is that they live in rain forests with high amounts of rainfall. This causes the rolled-up leaves to become full of water and overflow. To compensate for this, some plants that use pitfall traps have developed folds in their leaves that cover the top opening to prevent water from getting in.

Flypaper traps use mucilage to catch their prey. The leaves of these plants contain special glands that secrete this sticky, gluelike substance. In the most simple flypaper traps, after an insect lands on the plant, the plant secretes enough glue to trap the insect. Some larger insects are strong enough to escape, but most are hopelessly stuck. More sophisticated flypaper traps are active traps. Some of them are able to move their leaves to form indentations where insects land and stick. Digestive fluids then gather in these indentations to digest the insects. Other plants can fold or bend their leaves to surround and digest an insect that is stuck in the mucilage. Some of these plants can bend their leaves 180 degrees in less than a minute to trap an insect.

Much rarer than pitfall traps and flypaper traps are snap traps, which snap shut around their prey. Only two varieties of snap traps are known to exist, the venus flytrap and the waterwheel plant. These two plants are related and may have a common ancestor. In general, the trapping part of the plant has two halves that can open and shut. Along the edges of the trap are some long hairs. When an insect lands on the trap and touches one of the hairs, the two halves close quickly, trapping the insect, which is then digested.

Lobster pot traps work by luring an insect into an enclosed chamber inside the plant. The chamber is lined with small hairs all pointing in the same direction. Once an insect enters the chamber, it can move only in the direction the hairs point. Thus the insect can move only in one direction, which leads to the plant's digestive organ.

The last kind of carnivorous plant is the bladder trap. A bladder is a kind of empty sack or bag made of plant material. These aquatic plants create a kind of partial vacuum inside the bladder. When prey comes near a small door on the bladder, trigger hairs (similar to the ones on snap traps) cause the door to open, and the vacuum sucks in the prey.

Directions: Now answer the questions.

P A R A G R A P H 1

Plants are the only organisms on Earth that can make their own food. All other organisms have to find their own food by consuming other organisms. Most plants make their own food using photosynthesis, a process that allows plants to use energy from the sun to synthesize food that the plants use as a source of energy. Some plants, such as mushrooms and other kinds of fungi, cannot make their own food because they lack chlorophyll. These plants obtain their food from other plant matter. However, at least a few plants get some nutrients by trapping and digesting animals, usually insects or spiders. These carnivorous plants tend to live in places with soil that cannot supply needed nutrients, such as nitrogen, so they had to obtain them in other ways. It is important to note that, contrary to popular belief, while these plants obtain needed nutrients from the meat they consume, they still derive their energy from food they make themselves through photosynthesis.

15. Which of the following is true of carnivorous plants?

Ⓐ They eat insects to get nutrients they cannot get from the soil.

Ⓑ They cannot make their own food, unlike other plants.

Ⓒ They make their own food from insects that they digest.

Ⓓ They get their food from other plant matter.

16. The word "them" in the passage refers to

Ⓐ nutrients

Ⓑ carnivorous plants

Ⓒ places

Ⓓ insects and spiders

17. The word "derive" in the passage is closest in meaning to

Ⓐ release

Ⓑ waste

Ⓒ consume

Ⓓ obtain

P A R A G R A P H 2

To be considered as carnivorous, plants have to meet three criteria: plants need to attract prey, kill prey, and digest prey. There are more than 630 different species of plants that fully meet this definition. All of these are flowering plants, and they fall into five main groups, based on how they attract and kill their prey: pitfall traps, flypaper traps, snap traps, bladder traps, and lobster pot traps. Some of these involve movement, while others do not. Scientists call plants that snap shut or use other movement active traps. Passive traps often use sticky or slippery coatings on leaves to catch their prey.

18. All of the following are true of carnivorous plants EXCEPT:

Ⓐ They kill prey.

Ⓑ They digest prey.

Ⓒ They follow prey.

Ⓓ They attract prey.

19. The word "their" in the passage refers to

Ⓐ coatings'

Ⓑ passive traps'

Ⓒ leaves'

Ⓓ scientists'

20. Why does the author use the phrase "contrary to popular belief" when she mentions that carnivorous plants get their energy from food they make themselves through photosynthesis?

Ⓐ To prove that carnivorous plants are different from most plants

Ⓑ To show how carnivorous plants are similar to fungi

Ⓒ To correct a common misconception about the plants

Ⓓ To demonstrate that carnivorous plants really do not consume meat

Pitfall traps generally take the form of rolled-up leaves whose edges are sealed together so that water or digestive fluids can gather at the bottom and not leak out. These plants generally use scent to lure insects inside the rolled-up leaves. Once insects are inside, slippery coatings tire the insects as they try to escape from the plant. Eventually, the insects grow careless, slip on the coating, and fall into the digestive fluids where their nutrients are extracted for use in other parts of the plant. Other pitfall traps have leaves that have small openings that insects use to get inside the rolled-up leaf. The rolled-up leaves have small patches that are white, not green, and look like exits. The trapped insects begin to look for the exits, but they soon become tired and confused by the false exits. Eventually, they slip and fall into the digestive juices. A major problem with these plants is that they live in rain forests with high amounts of rainfall. This causes the rolled-up leaves to become full of water and overflow. To compensate for this, some plants that use pitfall traps have developed folds in their leaves that cover the top opening to prevent water from getting in.

21. How do pitfall plants lure insects inside?

   (A) Digestive juices extract insects' nutrients.

   (B) A nice smell attracts insects.

   (C) Slippery walls tire insects.

   (D) Insects get careless and fall.

P A R A G R A P H 4

Flypaper traps use mucilage to catch their prey. The leaves of these plants contain special glands that secrete this sticky, gluelike substance. In the most simple flypaper traps, after an insect lands on the plant, the plant secretes enough glue to trap the insect. Some larger insects are strong enough to escape, but most are hopelessly stuck. More sophisticated flypaper traps are active traps. Some of them are able to move their leaves to form indentations where insects land and stick. Digestive fluids then gather in these indentations to digest the insects. Other plants can fold or bend their leaves to surround and digest an insect that is stuck in the mucilage. Some of these plants can bend their leaves 180 degrees in less than a minute to trap an insect.

22. Which of the following can be inferred about flypaper traps?

   (A) These carnivorous plants eat only flies.

   (B) These plants cannot catch small insects.

   (C) Some are active traps and some are passive traps.

   (D) These plants all use motion to catch their prey.

23. The word "mucilage" in the passage is closest in meaning to

   (A) glands

   (B) digestive fluids

   (C) scent

   (D) glue

P A R A G R A P H 5

Much rarer than pitfall traps and flypaper traps are snap traps, which snap shut around their prey. Only two varieties of snap traps are known to exist, the venus flytrap and the waterwheel plant. These two plants are related and may have a common ancestor. In general, the trapping part of the plant has two halves that can open and shut. Along the edges of the trap are some long hairs. When an insect lands on the trap and touches one of the hairs, the two halves close quickly, trapping the insect, which is then digested.

24. Which of the following can be concluded about snap traps?

    (A) There are many varieties of snap traps.

    (B) Snap traps do not digest prey.

    (C) Snap traps are active traps.

    (D) Snap traps catch insects in long hairs.

25. Which of the following best expresses the essential information in the highlighted sentence? Incorrect choices change the meaning in important ways or leave out essential information.

    (A) The two halves of the trap close together quickly when an insect lands on the trap, touches one of the hairs, and is digested.

    (B) The two halves close together very quickly, trapping and digesting the insect when it lands on the trap and touches one of the hairs.

    (C) When an insect lands on the trap, touches one of the hairs, and is digested, the halves of the trap close.

    (D) The two halves close quickly when an insect lands on the trap and touches it.

> P A R A G R A P H 5
>
>   Much rarer than pitfall traps and flypaper traps are snap traps, which snap shut around their prey. Only two varieties of snap traps are known to exist, the venus flytrap and the waterwheel plant. **A** These two plants are related and may have a common ancestor. In general, the trapping part of the plant has two halves that can open and shut. **B** Along the edges of the trap are some long hairs. **C** When an insect lands on the trap and touches one of the hairs, the two halves close quickly, trapping the insect, which is then digested. **D**

26. Look at the four squares (■) that indicate where the following sentence could be inserted into the passage.

Then the two halves reopen and the wait for prey begins again.

Where would the sentence best fit?

PARAGRAPH 7

The last kind of carnivorous plant is the bladder trap. A bladder is a kind of empty sack or bag made of plant material. These aquatic plants create a kind of partial vacuum inside the bladder. When prey comes near a small door on the bladder, trigger hairs (similar to the ones on snap traps) cause the door to open, and the vacuum sucks in the prey.

27. In paragraph 7, why does the author indicate that trigger hairs on bladder traps are similar to hairs on snap traps?

Ⓐ To remind readers how trigger hairs work

Ⓑ To indicate that bladder traps are a kind of snap trap

Ⓒ To prove that bladder traps are active traps

Ⓓ To show that hair on snap traps, bladder traps, and lobster pot traps work the same

28. From the following seven phrases, select the two phrases that correctly characterize active traps and the three phrases that correctly characterize passive traps. Two of the phrases will NOT be used.

Complete the following table to summarize information about the active traps and passive traps. Match the appropriate statements to the group with which they are associated.

ACTIVE TRAPS	PASSIVE TRAPS
Select 2	Select 3
•	•
•	•
	•

Answer Choices

A Some of them use trigger hairs to operate their traps.

B They include all flypaper traps.

C They include snap traps and bladder traps.

D Their slippery leaves help them catch prey.

E They include pitfall traps and lobster pot traps.

F They cannot produce their own food.

G They do not use movement to trap prey.

Directions: Give yourself 20 minutes to read the passage and answer Items 29–42.

The invention of the submarine is, in large part, a reflection of the history of technology. A submarine is a boat that is capable of traveling under the sea using its own power. To build a submarine, at least three technological problems had to be overcome. First, a way had to be devised for the submarine to dive underwater and return to the surface. Second, a power source was needed, and the power source needed to be supplied with fuel and air. Third, a way to supply the crew with oxygen, which would be quickly used up when diving below the surface, had to be invented, or everyone on the boat would suffocate.

Though most people think of the submarine as a relatively modern invention, inventors have been thinking about them for centuries. Many historians of science believe that the first known drawings of a submarine were made by the Italian Renaissance artist Leonardo DaVinci. Though cryptic, the drawings apparently show a way to build a small submarine with one or two crew members. The submarine's purpose, according to the drawing, was to sink enemy ships during a war. DaVinci apparently kept the drawings a secret because he did not want his invention to contribute to making war more terrifying than it already was. The first recorded instance of the successful building of a submarine is from about 1620. A Dutch builder names Cornelis Drebbel working for King James I of England built and tested at least three prototypes between 1620 and 1624 following designs created by a British mathematician, William Bourne. These early models were built primarily with undersea exploration in mind, but the military applications soon became apparent. Writing in 1648, John Wilkins indicated that submarines could be used to blow up enemy ships from below and attack enemy ports secretly. An advantage of submarines over ships, according to Wilkins, was that submarines could remain safe from bad weather by diving undersea during a storm.

Despite the obvious military uses, the first military submarine was the *Turtle*, which was built during the US Revolutionary War. This hand-powered submarine, the first submarine ever that could move independently, failed in its first mission, which was to sink a British ship that was blockading New York harbor during the Revolutionary War. The first large-scale military use of submarines was during the US Civil War. Both the North and the South designed and built submarines, and at least 20 different models of submarines were designed or built during the war, though not all of them saw action during the war. The first navy submarine was the *Alligator*. This was the first submarine to use compressed air as an air supply. The South was interested in using submarines to attack Northern ships that were blocking the entrances to its harbors. In contrast, the North was more interested in using submarines to clear waterways of obstacles, but then began developing attack submarines, too. These early submarines solved two of the biggest technical problems. First, compressed air solved the problem of having a reliable air supply while submerged. Second, the invention of the double hull helped solve the problem of how a submarine could dive and surface. The double hull allowed for air to be trapped between the two hulls. Large tanks in between the two hulls, called ballast tanks, could be filled and emptied of water. For the submarine to dive, water was pumped into the tanks. It was pumped back out for the submarine to return to the surface. However, submarines still were all powered by hand. Both sides had tried to develop submarines powered by electrical motors or combustion engines, but the engines were not strong enough or used too much oxygen to be practical. Submarines began to be designed and produced in many countries, including Ecuador, Peru, France, Germany, and England. Many of these early submarines no longer exist because they were destroyed during war to keep them from falling into enemy hands.

The first self-powered submarine was the *Ictineo II*, designed by Narcis Monturiol, of Barcelona, Spain. Monturiol designed an ingenious chemically powered engine that produced oxygen instead of consuming it. However, the submarine could not stay underwater long because of the large amount of heat generated. The first workable submarine powered by steam was built in 1879 and the first powered by electricity in 1884. This was also the first mass-produced submarine. As technology improved, so did submarines. By the time of World War I, large and sophisticated submarines were in use. These submarines could stay submerged for long periods of time and had extensive arsenals that could be used to sink ships. However, they still had to return to the surface periodically to replenish their air supplies. Not until the development of the nuclear-powered submarine would it be possible for submarines to stay underwater for weeks or even months at a time. German submarines, called U-boats, though small in number, were put to terrifying effect, since they could find and sink enemy ships without ever coming to the surface. The Germans used these submarines to attack enemy trade, though they were never able to stop the trade significantly. The sinking of the passenger ship *Lusitania* by a U-boat was a major factor in the United States' decision to enter World War I. The terror produced by these U-boats, which were capable of sudden, surprise attacks, certainly verified DaVinci's apprehension about the terrifying nature of submarines.

Directions: Now answer the questions.

> P A R A G R A P H 1
>
> The invention of the submarine is, in large part, a reflection of the history of technology. A submarine is a boat that is capable of traveling under the sea using its own power. To build a submarine, at least three technological problems had to be overcome. First, a way had to be devised for the submarine to dive underwater and return to the surface. Second, a power source was needed, and the power source needed to be supplied with fuel and air. Third, a way to supply the crew with oxygen, which would be quickly used up when diving below the surface, had to be invented, or everyone on the boat would suffocate.

29. The author's definition of a submarine mentions which of the following?

   Ⓐ The invention of the submarine was dependent on resolving technical problems.

   Ⓑ A submarine is a boat that can travel underwater.

   Ⓒ The history of technology is a reflection of the invention of the submarine.

   Ⓓ A submarine needs to have access to a supply of fresh air.

30. The word "suffocate" in the passage is closest in meaning to

   Ⓐ die from lack of oxygen

   Ⓑ stop working from lack of oxygen

   Ⓒ lose power from lack of oxygen

   Ⓓ faint from lack of oxygen

P
A
R
A
G
R
A
P
H

2

Though most people think of the submarine as a relatively modern invention, inventors have been thinking about them for centuries. Many historians of science believe that the first known drawings of a submarine were made by the Italian Renaissance artist Leonardo DaVinci. Though cryptic, the drawings apparently show a way to build a small submarine with one or two crew members. The submarine's purpose, according to the drawing, was to sink enemy ships during a war. DaVinci apparently kept the drawings a secret because he did not want his invention to contribute to making war more terrifying than it already was. The first recorded instance of the successful building of a submarine is from about 1620. A Dutch builder names Cornelis Drebbel working for King James I of England built and tested at least three prototypes between 1620 and 1624 following designs created by a British mathematician, William Bourne. These early models were built primarily with undersea exploration in mind, but the military applications soon became apparent. Writing in 1648, John Wilkins indicated that submarines could be used to blow up enemy ships from below and attack enemy ports secretively. An advantage of submarines over ships, according to Wilkins, was that submarines could remain safe from bad weather by diving undersea during a storm.

31. According to paragraph 2, which of the following is true about the invention of the submarine?

Ⓐ Leonardo DaVinci built the first workable submarine.

Ⓑ Cornelis Drebbel invented the submarine.

Ⓒ William Bourne designed the first submarine ever built.

Ⓓ John Wilkins designed the first attack submarine.

32. According to paragraph 2, all of these are advantages of submarines EXCEPT:

Ⓐ They can be used to blow up an enemy ship from underwater.

Ⓑ They can avoid bad weather by diving underwater.

Ⓒ They can be used to attack an enemy port.

Ⓓ They do not need to return to the surface for air.

33. Why does the author cite John Wilkins's ideas about the uses of submarines?

(A) To show that people thought of submarines mostly for underwater exploration

(B) To provide support for the statement that military uses of submarines were quickly discovered

(C) To prove that submarines had several possible uses

(D) To show that Leonardo DaVinci correctly believed that submarines increased people's fear of war

PARAGRAPH 3

Despite the obvious military uses, the first military submarine was the *Turtle*, which was built during the US Revolutionary War. This hand-powered submarine, the first submarine ever that could move independently, failed in its first mission, which was to sink a British ship that was blockading New York harbor during the Revolutionary War. The first large-scale military use of submarines was during the US Civil War. Both the North and the South designed and built submarines, and at least 20 different models of submarines were designed or built during the war, though not all of them saw action during the war. The first navy submarine was the *Alligator*. This was the first submarine to use compressed air as an air supply. The South was interested in using submarines to attack Northern ships that were blocking the entrances to its harbors. In contrast, the North was more interested in using submarines to clear waterways of obstacles, but then began developing attack submarines, too. These early submarines solved two of the biggest technical problems. First, compressed air solved the problem of having a reliable air supply while submerged. Second, the invention of the double hull helped solve the problem of how a submarine could dive and surface. The double hull allowed for air to be trapped between the two hulls. Large tanks in between the two hulls, called ballast tanks, could be filled and emptied of water. For the submarine to dive, water was pumped into the tanks. It was pumped back out for the submarine to return to the surface. However, submarines still were all powered by hand. Both sides had tried to develop submarines powered by electrical motors or combustion engines, but the engines were not strong enough or used too much oxygen to be practical. Submarines began to be designed and produced in many countries, including Ecuador, Peru, France, Germany, and England. Many of these early submarines no longer exist because they were destroyed during war to keep them from falling into enemy hands.

34. The word "that" in the passage refers to

Ⓐ Southern leaders

Ⓑ submarines

Ⓒ Northern ships

Ⓓ entrances

35. The word "submerged" in the passage is closest in meaning to

Ⓐ underwater

Ⓑ in port

Ⓒ at the surface

Ⓓ with a power source

36. The word "it" in the passage refers to

Ⓐ air

Ⓑ water

Ⓒ surface

Ⓓ submarine

PARAGRAPH 3

Despite the obvious military uses, the first military submarine was the *Turtle*, which was built during the US Revolutionary War. This hand-powered submarine, the first submarine ever that could move independently, failed in its first mission, which was to sink a British ship that was blockading New York harbor during the Revolutionary War. ▐A▌ The first large-scale military use of submarines was during the US Civil War. Both the North and the South designed and built submarines, and at least 20 different models of submarines were designed or built during the war, though not all of them saw action during the war. ▐B▌ The first navy submarine was the *Alligator*. This was the first submarine to use compressed air as an air supply. ▐C▌ The South was interested in using submarines to attack Northern ships that were blocking the entrances to its harbors. In contrast, the North was more interested in using submarines to clear waterways of obstacles, but then began developing attack submarines, too. These early submarines solved two of the biggest technical problems. First, compressed air solved the problem of having a reliable air supply while submerged. Second, the invention of the double hull helped solve the problem of how a submarine could dive and surface. The double hull allowed for air to be trapped between the two hulls. Large tanks in between the two hulls, called ballast tanks, could be filled and emptied of water. For the submarine to dive, water was pumped into the tanks. It was pumped back out for the submarine to return to the surface. However, submarines still were all powered by hand. Both sides had tried to develop submarines powered by electrical motors or combustion engines, but the engines were not strong enough or used too much oxygen to be practical. Submarines began to be designed and produced in many countries, including Ecuador, Peru, France, Germany, and England. Many of these early submarines no longer exist because they were destroyed during war to keep them from falling into enemy hands. **D**

PARAGRAPH 3

37. Look at the four squares (■) that indicate where the following sentence could be inserted into the passage.

   Other early submarines suffered mishaps and sank or were destroyed.

   Where would the sentence best fit?

PARAGRAPH 4

   The first self-powered submarine was the *Ictineo II*, designed by Narcis Monturiol, of Barcelona, Spain. Monturiol designed an ingenious chemically powered engine that produced oxygen instead of consuming it. However, the submarine could not stay underwater long because of the large amount of heat generated. The first workable submarine powered by steam was built in 1879 and the first powered by electricity in 1884. This was also the first mass-produced submarine. As technology improved, so did submarines. By the time of World War I, large and sophisticated submarines were in use. These submarines could stay submerged for long periods of time and had extensive arsenals that could be used to sink ships. However, they still had to return to the surface periodically to replenish their air supplies. Not until the development of the nuclear-powered submarine would it be possible for submarines to stay underwater for weeks or even months at a time. German submarines, called U-boats, though small in number, were put to terrifying effect, since they could find and sink enemy ships without ever coming to the surface. The Germans used these submarines to attack enemy trade, though they were never able to stop the trade significantly. The sinking of the passenger ship *Lusitania* by a U-boat was a major factor in the United States' decision to enter World War I. The terror produced by these U-boats, which were capable of sudden, surprise attacks, certainly verified DaVinci's apprehension about the terrifying nature of submarines.

38. Which of the following innovations would let submarines stay underwater for long periods of time?

 Ⓐ The invention of a chemically powered engine

 Ⓑ The invention of a nuclear-powered engine

 Ⓒ The invention of a steam-powered engine

 Ⓓ The invention of an electrically powered engine

39. Which of the following best expresses the essential information in the highlighted sentence? Incorrect choices change the meaning in important ways or leave out essential information.

 Ⓐ It would not be possible for submarines to stay underwater for long periods until the nuclear-powered submarine was invented.

 Ⓑ Staying underwater for long periods would not be possible until nuclear power was invented.

 Ⓒ Not until the nuclear-powered submarine was invented would it be possible for submarines to stay submerged.

 Ⓓ It would not be possible for nuclear power to be invented, until submarines stayed underwater for weeks or months at a time.

40. Which of the following can be inferred about U-boats during World War I?

 Ⓐ Their small numbers showed that military leaders did not believe they would be effective.

 Ⓑ Using U-boats was a mistake because it brought the United States into the war.

 Ⓒ U-boats were an effective way for Germany to stop enemy trade.

 Ⓓ U-boats had a major effect on the war despite their small numbers.

41. Why does the author mention Leonardo DaVinci again in paragraph 4?

 Ⓐ To show that DaVinci was right about the emotional impact of submarine warfare on people

 Ⓑ To prove that DaVinci was the true inventor of the submarine

 Ⓒ To show that solutions to all the technological problems of submarines were found

 Ⓓ To prove that DaVinci correctly realized that submarines should never be built

42. An introductory sentence for a brief summary of the passage is provided. Complete the summary by selecting the THREE answer choices that express important ideas in the passage. Some sentences do not belong in the summary because they express ideas that are not presented in the passage or are minor details in the passage. *This item is worth 2 points.*

Write the letters of your answer choices in the spaces where they belong.

> **The passage is about the development of the submarine.**
>
> •
>
> •
>
> •

Answer Choices

A The design of submarines has improved greatly since their invention.

B Only nuclear submarines can stay underwater for weeks and months at a time.

C Leonardo DaVinci drew the first known design for a submarine.

D Submarines were not used effectively for military purposes until World War I.

E The invention of compressed air allowed submarines to stay submerged for months at a time.

F A submarine is a kind of boat that is capable of traveling underwater using its own power.

Answers and Explanations for the Reading section of TOEFL iBT Final Practice Test 2 begin on page 708.

Listening

Directions: The Listening section of the TOEFL iBT assesses your ability to understand conversations and lectures in English. To simulate actual TOEFL iBT conditions, follow these instructions:

- Listen to each conversation or lecture only once. You may take notes while listening and use your notes as you answer the items.
- After each conversation or lecture, answer the items that follow in the order in which they appear. After you answer an item, do not go back. Continue with each lecture or conversation and its items until you complete the test or time has ended.
- Use your watch or the timer on your mobile phone or computer to keep track of the time. Allow 60 minutes to listen to all the passages and answer the questions.
- If you do not finish all the items when the test ends, mark your place. Then continue working as quickly as you can. When you finish, take note of the total time. This will give you an idea of how quickly you need to work on the actual TOEFL iBT to answer all the items in 60 minutes.

The Audio icon appears each time you need to listen to an audio track. For some items, you need to listen to another audio track besides the conversation or lecture to answer the items.

Now begin the Listening section of TOEFL iBT Final Practice Test 2.

Directions: Listen to a conversation between a student and a professor.

Directions: Now answer the questions. Circle the letter of the answer.

1. What difficulty is the student having?

   Ⓐ Understanding the topic of her term paper

   Ⓑ Defining the topic of her term paper

   Ⓒ Focusing her presentation topic

   Ⓓ Feeling confident enough for her presentation

2. What initial advice does the professor give the student about her presentation?

   Ⓐ Define key terms

   Ⓑ Include relevant examples

   Ⓒ Refer to several sources

   Ⓓ Keep her information simple

3. Why might economists wish to discuss the premodern Chinese salt monopolies?

   Ⓐ To show why China did not develop a free-market economy

   Ⓑ To point out the dangers of capitalism

   Ⓒ To contrast different kinds of monopolies

   Ⓓ To illustrate the profitability of the salt industry

4. 🎧 **152** Listen again to part of the conversation. Then answer the question.

(A) Chinese salt merchants did not make enough profit to invest in other industries.

(B) Chinese salt merchants contributed less to economic development than they might have.

(C) Chinese salt merchants did not know if other industries were profitable.

(D) Under the Qing dynasty, the Chinese economy as a whole was weak.

5. What is one reason the professor gives for the low social status of Chinese merchants under the Qing dynasty?

(A) Scholars looked down upon merchants who wasted their wealth.

(B) Emperors wanted to limit merchants' political power.

(C) Merchants were extremely rich but mostly uneducated.

(D) Merchants contributed less to society than scholars or craftsmen.

Directions: Listen to part of a lecture in a history class. The professor is talking about World War I.

History

Serbia

Chancellor Otto
von Bismarck

Prussia

Austro-Hungarian Empire

Map of Germany in 1866 before the unification of Germany

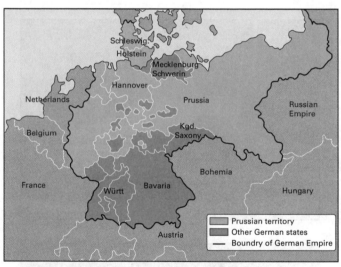

Map of Germany in 1871 after the unification of Germany

Directions: Now answer the questions. Circle the letter of the answer.

6. What is the primary topic of this lecture?

(A) The Treaty of London that brought Britain into World War I

(B) The system of treaties that contributed to the outbreak of World War I

(C) Bismarck's belief that Germany could win a war with Russia and France

(D) Conflict between Germany and Britain over colonies in Asia

7. According to the professor, what was a major problem with the alliance system?

   Ⓐ It was based on mistrust among countries in Europe.

   Ⓑ It reduced the role of diplomacy.

   Ⓒ It cost over one billion dollars to maintain.

   Ⓓ It led to the German domination of Europe.

8. Why does the professor focus mainly on Germany in the prewar period?

   Ⓐ Because she admires Bismarck's leadership

   Ⓑ Because she thinks Germany is unfairly accused of causing World War I

   Ⓒ Because German unification changed the power balance in Europe

   Ⓓ Because the German army was almost invincible

9. According to the professor, what did Bismarck think Germany would gain from alliances?

   Ⓐ New territories in Europe

   Ⓑ Expanded markets around the globe

   Ⓒ Italian military aid in case of a war in Europe

   Ⓓ A period of stability in which Germany could prosper

10. What does the professor think brought Britain back into the alliance system?

   Ⓐ British fears that Germany would attack its coastline

   Ⓑ The potential German threat to Britain's colonies

   Ⓒ Improved relations between Britain and Japan

   Ⓓ Improved relations between Britain and France

11. The professor mentions some important events leading up to World War I. Put the events in order from earliest to latest.

Write your answer choices in the spaces where they belong. You can either write the letter of your answer choice or you can copy the statement. The first one is done for you. *This item is worth 2 points.*

1.	Britain signs the Treaty of London to protect Belgium.
2.	
3.	
4.	
5.	

Answer Choices

A   Germany and Austria-Hungary form the Dual Alliance.

B   France, Russia, and Britain formally become allies.

C   Many separate German-speaking territories make up a united empire.

D   The Germans invade Belgium on their way to attack France.

Directions: Listen to part of a lecture in a design class. The professor is talking about furniture.

Design

Chair by Karen Ryan

Sofa by Frank Willems

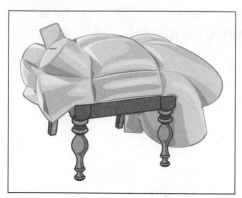

Nina Tolstrup

Marcel Duchamp

Directions: Now answer the questions. Circle the letter of the answer.

12. What is the main point of this lecture?

Ⓐ Designers of repurposed furniture create expensive trash.

Ⓑ Repurposed furniture is only for the rich.

Ⓒ Repurposed furniture has become an art form.

Ⓓ Designers of repurposed furniture make false claims about their work.

13. Why does the professor talk about his student days?

   Ⓐ To introduce the idea of recycling

   Ⓑ To lead into the topic of the lecture

   Ⓒ To sympathize with poor students

   Ⓓ To complain about his difficulties when he was a student

14. According to the professor, why might wealthy people choose recycled or repurposed furniture? *Choose 2 answers.*

   A They are interested in art history.

   B They favor ironic design.

   C They want to save money on decorating.

   D They dislike consumerism.

15. Why does the male student object to the work of Nina Tolstrup?

   Ⓐ He thinks her production process lacks craft.

   Ⓑ He considers it ugly.

   Ⓒ He dislikes recycled furniture.

   Ⓓ He finds the assembly process too complicated.

16. What does the male student think of the work of the Frankfurt designer who repurposes shopping carts as armchairs?

   Ⓐ It is reasonably priced.

   Ⓑ It is very fashionable.

   Ⓒ It is not really what it claims to be.

   Ⓓ It has blatantly copied the work of Duchamp.

17. Why does the professor refer to Marcel Duchamp?

   Ⓐ To remind the students of Duchamp's past importance

   Ⓑ To demonstrate the significance of materials

   Ⓒ To show how furniture design has been influenced by fine art

   Ⓓ To encourage the students to be more playful in their work

Directions: Listen to a conversation between a student and a university employee.

Directions: Now answer the questions. Circle the letter of the answer.

18. What does the student want?

Ⓐ To work as a professional counselor

Ⓑ To become a volunteer mentor

Ⓒ To teach a summer school course

Ⓓ To go on a student exchange program

19. In the opinion of the employee, what is one reason the student is an ideal candidate?

Ⓐ She is studying sociology.

Ⓑ She has lived abroad and speaks Korean.

Ⓒ She knows where to get decent noodles in Springfield.

Ⓓ She is from New Jersey.

20. Listen again to part of the conversation. Then answer the question.

Ⓐ Applicants who have a first aid certificate have a better chance of being accepted.

Ⓑ Applicants must have a first aid certificate before submitting their applications.

Ⓒ Applicants do not need any special qualifications.

Ⓓ Applicants who do not have a first aid certificate must get one after they are accepted.

21. According to the employee, which is particularly difficult for international students?

    (A) Struggling in class

    (B) Having financial problems

    (C) Experiencing feelings of isolation

    (D) Finding food from their countries

22. Why does the student mention her cousin?

    (A) To prove that her cousin would make a good mentor

    (B) To describe her cousin's freshman experience with a mentor

    (C) To show that she has already been an unofficial mentor

    (D) To demonstrate how hard life as an international student can be

Directions: Listen to part of a lecture in psychology class. The professor is talking about left-handedness.

Psychology

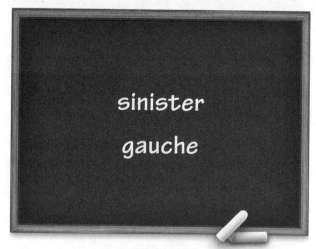

sinister

gauche

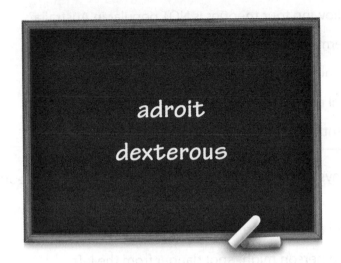

adroit

dexterous

Directions: Now answer the questions. Circle the letter of the answer.

23. What is the main point of this lecture?

Ⓐ There are many theories, but the true cause of left-handedness remains unclear.

Ⓑ Left-handedness is caused by genetic factors.

Ⓒ Left-handedness is not beneficial to individuals or society.

Ⓓ People who are left-handed tend to be creative, intelligent, and wealthy.

24. At the beginning of the lecture, what does the professor note about left-handedness?

Ⓐ There is something correct and appropriate about it.

Ⓑ Psychologists have convincing theories for it.

Ⓒ Neurologists do not believe it exists.

Ⓓ Scientists still cannot explain it.

25. Why does the professor spend so much time on defining certain words?

Ⓐ Because English vocabulary is extremely complex

Ⓑ Because vocabulary reflects social attitudes toward left-handers

Ⓒ To remind students that precise understanding of language is important

Ⓓ To prove that left-handed people are sinister

26. Which of the following four theories is NOT popular in Australia?

    (A) Chance determines left-handedness.

    (B) Genes determine left-handedness.

    (C) High prenatal estrogen levels cause left-handedness.

    (D) Being an identical twin causes left-handedness.

27. What are two ways in which being left-handed may be advantageous? *Choose 2 answers.*

    [A] A left-handed athlete has a special advantage.

    [B] A left-handed person might spot danger from the left.

    [C] A left-handed person will probably earn more money.

    [D] A left-handed person is likely to live longer.

28. Why does the army use the shoe test?

    (A) To demonstrate that true left-handers put on the left shoe first

    (B) To prove that misconceptions about handedness persist in the modern world

    (C) To show that strong beliefs about handedness mean a test is needed to expose lies

    (D) To determine who will be best able to manipulate weapons and equipment

Directions: Listen to part of a lecture in a nutrition class. The professor is talking about humans eating insects and spiders.

Nutrition

entomophagy

chitin

efficiency conversion
index = ECI

Directions: Now answer the questions. Circle the letter of the answer.

29. What is the main point of this lecture?

Ⓐ Insects are destroying the world's food supply.

Ⓑ All humans consume insects as a food source already.

Ⓒ There are not enough kinds of edible insects to become a major food source.

Ⓓ Insects are becoming an increasingly important food source for humans.

30. What does the professor think will probably happen by 2035?

Ⓐ Increased population will dramatically reduce the price of food.

Ⓑ Increased population will make eating insects more common.

Ⓒ Increased population will mean that fewer people eat meat.

Ⓓ Increased population will lead to widespread malnutrition.

31. In regard to insect usage, what is notable about the Dutch?

Ⓐ They consume more insects than anyone else in Europe.

Ⓑ They sell all kinds of snacks and candy that contain insects.

Ⓒ They are trying to reduce the labor costs of insect production.

Ⓓ They are organizing methodically for an expanded insect market.

32. Indicate whether each of the statements is true or false, according to the professor.

Place a check (✔) in the correct box. This item is worth 2 points.

	TRUE	FALSE
Insects are cheap to produce.		
Many insects are healthful to eat.		
Insect chitin has few uses.		
Insects have a high ECI.		

33. What happens when people in developing countries choose a Western meat-based diet?

   Ⓐ They consider themselves less civilized than in the past.

   Ⓑ They experience more weight problems and environmental pollution.

   Ⓒ They spend significantly more money on food.

   Ⓓ They suffer from more insect plagues.

34. How does the professor himself feel about eating insects?

   Ⓐ He is an ardent supporter.

   Ⓑ He is a reluctant opponent.

   Ⓒ He has mixed feelings about it.

   Ⓓ He does not show his feelings.

Answers and Explanations for the Listening section of TOEFL iBT Final Practice Test 2 begin on page 713.

Speaking

Directions: The Speaking section of the TOEFL iBT assesses your ability to speak in English on a variety of academic and general-interest topics. Some of the items assess only your speaking skills, while others assess your ability to integrate information from reading and/or listening passages into your speaking. To simulate actual TOEFL iBT conditions, follow these instructions:

- For items that integrate listening, listen to each conversation or lecture only once.
- For items that integrate reading, use your watch or timer to keep track of the time. After reading time is up, do not refer back to the reading as you answer.
- As you read, listen, and plan your response, you may take notes to use when giving your response.
- Use your computer's or mobile device's *record* function to record and play back your responses. If your device does not have this function, ask a friend with strong English skills to listen to your responses. You or your friend can evaluate your responses using the simplified scoring rubrics in this book.

 The Audio icon appears each time you need to listen to an audio track.

When this icon appears, record your response on your computer or mobile device. If your device does not have a *record* function, ask a friend with strong English skills to listen to your response.

Now begin the Speaking section of TOEFL iBT Final Practice Test 2.

1. You will now speak about a familiar topic. Prepare your response in 15 seconds. Then allow 45 seconds to record your response.

> Describe the first day of your most recent class or your most recent job. What did you like or dislike? Include specific details in your description.
>
> | Preparation Time: 15 seconds |
> |---|
> | Response Time: 45 seconds |

2. 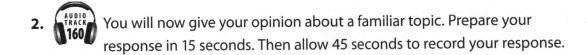 You will now give your opinion about a familiar topic. Prepare your response in 15 seconds. Then allow 45 seconds to record your response.

> Some college students work part-time while they are studying. Other college students prefer to concentrate totally on their studies. Which do you think is better for students? Explain why.
>
> | Preparation Time: 15 seconds |
> |---|
> | Response Time: 45 second |

3. You will now read a short passage on a campus-related topic and listen to a conversation on the same subject. Then you will hear a question. Prepare your response in 30 seconds. Then allow 60 seconds to record your response.

Reading Time: 50 seconds

Announcement from the Head of the Psychology Department

The Psychology Department is seeking volunteer subjects for research studies. In all cases volunteers will be paid a nominal amount, and in some cases they will earn credit toward psychology courses. Volunteers must be over the age of 18 and must undergo a medical examination prior to their participation. This examination will be paid for by the department. For most studies, volunteers must be available for three semesters.

 Now listen to two students discussing the announcement.

The man expresses his opinion of the announcement by the head of the Psychology Department. Briefly summarize the announcement. Then state his opinion and explain the reasons he gives for holding that opinion.

Preparation Time: 30 seconds
Response Time: 60 seconds

4. You will now read a short passage on an academic topic and listen to a talk on the same subject. Then you will hear a question. Prepare your response in 30 seconds. Then allow 60 seconds to record your response.

Reading Time: 50 seconds

Problems with Navigation

Beginning around 1500, European powers began to expand their colonies and trade networks. It became necessary to improve the speed and safety of sea voyages. Accurate maps and sophisticated equipment that showed navigators their exact position were required.

However, the exact position was hard to calculate since Earth is not completely spherical. Navigators could find their position with regard to latitude—an east-west measure of the Earth's surface—but not longitude, a north-south measure. This meant, even as late as 1700, that thousands of sailors and hundreds of ships were lost in wrecks.

Now listen to part of a lecture on this topic in a history class.

Explain how John Harrison's chronometer solved a major navigational problem. Use information from the reading and the talk.

Preparation Time: 30 seconds
Response Time: 60 seconds

5. You will now listen to part of a conversation about a campus-related situation. Then you will hear a question. Prepare your response in 20 seconds. Then allow 60 seconds to record your response.

Summarize briefly the problem that the speakers are talking about. Then say which of the two solutions from the conversation you would recommend. Explain your reasons for your recommendation.

> **Preparation Time: 20 seconds**
> **Response Time: 60 seconds**

6.  You will now listen to part of a lecture on an academic topic. Then you will hear a question. Prepare your response in 20 seconds. Then allow 60 seconds to record your response.

> Using points and examples from the talk, describe three different leadership styles that contribute to contingency theory.
>
> | Preparation Time: 20 seconds |
> | --- |
> | Response Time: 60 seconds |

Explanations and Sample Responses for the Speaking section of TOEFL iBT Final Practice Test 2 begin on page 724.

Writing

Directions: The Writing section of the TOEFL iBT assesses your ability to communicate in writing in academic settings. This section has two items. To simulate actual TOEFL iBT conditions, follow these instructions.

ITEM 1: INTEGRATED WRITING

- Read the passage in 3 minutes. Use your watch or the timer on your phone or computer to keep track of time. You may take notes as you read and listen, and use your notes when you answer the question.
- Start the audio program and listen to the passage one time as you take notes.
- Read the question, plan your response, and write it in 20 minutes. You may use your notes and refer back to the reading passage as you write.

ITEM 2: INDEPENDENT WRITING

- Set your timer for 30 minutes and start working. You may take notes to plan your essay and to use as you write.

 The Audio icon appears when you need to listen to an audio track.

If you do not finish your essays when the time ends, mark your place. Then continue working as quickly as you can. When you finish, take note of the total time. This will give you an idea of how quickly you need to work on the actual TOEFL iBT to write both essays in 60 minutes.

Now begin the Writing section of the TOEFL iBT Final Practice Test 2.

1. Integrated Writing

   A. Read the passage in 3 minutes. Use your watch or the timer on your phone or computer to keep track of the time. You may take notes in the space provided.

   Hybrid vehicles offer many advantages to consumers and society. Hybrid vehicles offer lower operating costs and reduced emissions. Strictly speaking, a hybrid vehicle combines two kinds of power sources, an internal combustion engine (powered by burning gas or another flammable substance) and an electrical motor. However, hybrids can include other power sources as well. When we think about hybrid vehicles, we often think of automobiles, but hybrids are already used on trains, heavy trucks, ships, and aircraft.

   In most hybrid automobiles, the engines are arranged so that both the engine and the motor can power the vehicle at the same time or independently. In parallel hybrid vehicles, the internal combustion engine and the electric motor can power the vehicle independently. When both are powering the vehicle, the engine and the motor are running at the same speed. Thus, when both are powering the vehicle, each is providing 50 percent of the power. A second type of hybrid, a mild parallel vehicle, uses the electrical motor to supplement the power of the engine when extra power is needed for increased speed, for example. Power-split engines have the advantage of being able to power the engine with any proportion of power from either the engine or the electric motor. The electric motor can provide 100 percent of the power, or 0 percent, or any value in between, as can the internal combustion engine.

   A primary advantage of a hybrid vehicle is fuel economy. Hybrid vehicles consume much less gas than cars with only an internal combustion engine. This results in much lower emissions as well. A secondary advantage is that a vehicle can have a smaller engine but have additional power when needed.

B. Now listen to part of a lecture on the topic you just read about. You may take notes in the space provided.

_____

_____

_____

_____

_____

_____

_____

_____

C. Take 20 minutes to plan, write, and revise an essay of about 150 to 225 words. Use a watch or timer to keep track of time. You may refer to the reading and your notes as you plan and write your essay. Pay attention to the quality of your writing and on how well you present the points in the lecture and their relationship to the reading passage.

 Summarize the points made in the lecture you just heard, explaining how they oppose the points made in the reading passage.

Response Time: 20 minutes

2. Independent Writing

Take 30 minutes to plan, write, and revise an essay on the following topic. Use your mobile phone or computer to keep track of the time. As on the actual TOEFL iBT, use notepaper to gather and organize your ideas. Then keyboard your essay on a computer, if possible. An effective essay will be about 300 words.

> **Response Time: 30 minutes**

Do you agree or disagree with the following statement?

The best things in life are free.

Use specific reasons and examples to support your answer.

_____

_____

_____

_____

_____

_____

_____

_____

_____

_____

_____

Explanations and Sample Responses for the Writing section of
TOEFL iBT Final Practice Test 2 begin on page 726.

TOEFL iBT Personalized Study Planner

Reading

Use your answers to the Reading section of TOEFL iBT Final Practice Test 2 and this chart to focus your preparation for the actual TOEFL iBT. Follow these steps.

1. Review all your correct and incorrect answers in the Answers and Explanations, which begin on page 708.
2. In the chart, circle the number of each item you answered incorrectly.
3. Review again the Answers and Explanations for each item you answered incorrectly, this time in the order they are grouped in the chart.
4. For each item type and item format where you want to improve your performance, study the pages listed in the third column.

ITEM NUMBERS	ITEM TYPE	STUDY PAGES
1, 5, 12, 15, 21, 24, 29, 31, 38	Factual information	109–116
7, 18, 32	Negative factual information	116–121
6, 8, 11, 17, 23, 30, 35	Vocabulary	122–131
10, 16, 19, 34, 36	Reference	132–139
4, 25, 39	Sentence simplification	139–148
3, 22, 40	Inference	154–158
2, 9, 20, 27, 33, 41	Rhetorical purpose	159–162
13, 26, 37	Insert text	163–167
14, 42	Prose summary	170–176
28	Fill in a table	176–182

Listening

Use your answers to Listening section of TOEFL iBT Final Practice Test 2 and these charts to focus your preparation for the actual TOEFL iBT. Follow these steps.

1. Review all your correct and incorrect answers in the Answers and Explanations, which begin on page 713.
2. In each chart, circle the number of each item you answered incorrectly.

3. Review again the Answers and Explanations for each item you answered incorrectly, this time in the order they are grouped in these charts.

4. For each item type and item format where you want to improve your performance, study the pages listed in the third column.

ITEM NUMBERS	ITEM TYPE	STUDY PAGES
6, 12, 23, 29	Gist-content	260–269
1, 18	Gist-purpose	270–274
2, 3, 7, 9, 10, 14, 16, 17, 19, 21, 24, 26, 30, 32, 33	Supporting detail	275–281
13, 20, 22, 25, 28	Understanding the function of what is said	284–286
34	Understanding the speaker's attitude	287–291
11	Understanding organization	294–300
8	Connecting content	300–304
4, 5, 15, 27, 31	Making inferences	304–307

ITEM NUMBERS	ITEM FORMAT	STUDY PAGES
14, 27	Special multiple choice	254
4, 20	Replay items	254–256
32	Check box items	256
11	Drag-and-drop items	257–258

Speaking

Use your responses to the Speaking section of TOEFL iBT Final Practice Test 2 and this chart to focus your preparation for the actual TOEFL iBT. Follow these steps.

1. Review your responses by comparing them to the sample responses that begin on page 724.

2. Evaluate your responses with the rubrics. If possible, ask a teacher or an English-speaking friend to help you. Or wait a day or two and evaluate yourself. Use the TOEFL iBT Simplified Independent Speaking Rubric on pages 370–371 to score your responses to Items 1 and 2. Use the TOEFL iBT Simplified Integrated Speaking

Rubric on pages 398–399 to score your responses to Items 3 to 6. Write your scores on the lines.

1. _____   3. _____   5. _____

2. _____   4. _____   6. _____

3. What skills do you do well? Which skills do you want to improve? Review your rubrics for Items 1 and 2 together, and check the boxes of the skills you do well. Then review the pages that are listed for the skills you want to improve.

ITEMS 1 AND 2: INDEPENDENT SPEAKING

SKILL	STUDY PAGES
☐ Answers the question	376–377
☐ Has a main idea	377
☐ Has supporting details	377–378
☐ Follows a logical order	378–379
☐ Uses signaling words and phrases to show relationships among ideas	380–382

4. Now review your completed rubrics for Items 3 to 6 together and check the boxes of the skills you do well. Then review the pages for the skills you want to improve.

ITEMS 3 TO 6: INTEGRATED SPEAKING

SKILL	STUDY PAGES
☐ Answers the question	411, 420–421
☐ Has a main idea and supporting details	404–408, 422–423
☐ Integrates information from reading and/or listening passages	412–416
☐ Follows a logical order	434–435
☐ Uses order and signaling words and phrases to show relationships among ideas	413–416, 424

Writing

Use your responses to the Writing section of TOEFL iBT Final Practice Test 2 and these charts to focus your preparation for the actual TOEFL iBT.

ITEM 1: INTEGRATED WRITING

1. Review your responses by comparing them to the sample responses that begin on page 726. Evaluate your essay using the instructions on page 497.

   Write your score on the line. _____

2. Check the box of your rating in each row of the Integrated Writing Rubric that begins on this page.

3. Review your ratings in each row. Which areas do you want to improve? Study the pages listed for those areas in the column on the right.

SCORE	DESCRIPTION	STUDY PAGES
5	A **Level 5** response: ☐ Selects relevant and important information from the lecture and presents it in relation to similar information in the reading. Includes supporting detail and examples.	483–487
	☐ Is well organized and makes sense. Uses signaling words and phrases to connect information and show the relationships among ideas.	490–494
	☐ Includes occasional errors in vocabulary and grammar that do not result in inaccurate or confusing presentation of information or connections among ideas.	495–497
4	A **Level 4** response: ☐ Generally selects relevant and important information from the lecture and presents it in relation to relevant and important information in the reading, but may have minor inaccuracies, vagueness, or omissions that cause minor confusion to readers.	483–487
	☐ Includes errors in vocabulary and grammar that are more frequent than in a Level 5 response but cause only minor problems with clarity or connection of ideas.	495–497

(continued)

SCORE	DESCRIPTION	STUDY PAGES
3	A **Level 3** response: ☐ Contains some information from the listening and makes some connections to the reading	483–487
	A response at this level has one or more of these problems: ☐ The response addresses the task, but some information may be inaccurate or incomplete. Makes only general, vague, or unclear connections between points in the reading and the lecture.	483–487
	☐ The response omits one major point made in the lecture.	483–487
	☐ Some key points in the lecture or reading, or the connections between them, are unclear, incomplete, inaccurate, or general.	490–494
	☐ Vocabulary and grammar errors may be more frequent than in a Level 4 response and may cause confusion to readers.	495–497
2	A **Level 2** response: ☐ Has some relevant information from the lecture, but has inaccuracies or omissions of important ideas from the lecture.	483–487
	☐ Makes inaccurate or incomplete connections with information from the reading.	483–487
	A response at this level shows one or more of the following: ☐ Omits or inaccurately presents the relationship between the lecture and the reading.	483–487
	☐ Omits or inaccurately presents important points in the lecture.	483–487
	☐ Contains language errors or expressions that obscure meaning.	495–497
1	A **Level 1** response: ☐ Provides little or no meaningful or relevant information from the lecture.	483–487
	☐ Has problems with vocabulary and grammar that make the essay difficult to understand.	495–497
0	A response at this level contains only ideas copied from the reading passage, does not address the topic, is not written in English, or is blank.	

ITEM 2: INDEPENDENT WRITING

1. Evaluate your essay using the instructions on page 525.

    Write your score on the line. _____

2. Check the box of your rating on each row of the Independent Writing Rubric on the next page.

3. Review your ratings in each row. Which areas do you want to improve? Study the pages listed for those areas in the column on the right.

SCORE	DESCRIPTION	PAGES
5	A **Level 5** response largely:	
	☐ Addresses the topic and the task.	515–517
	☐ Is organized and well developed; uses appropriate detail, examples, and explanations.	517–518
	☐ Stays on topic, flows, and makes sense.	519–520
	☐ Uses language well. Has variety in sentence patterns, vocabulary, and idioms, and only minor errors of vocabulary and grammar.	524–525
4	A **Level 4** response largely:	
	☐ Addresses the topic and the task, though some points are not well developed.	515–517
	☐ Is generally well organized and developed; uses appropriate detail, examples, and explanations.	517–518
	☐ Stays on topic, flows, and makes sense, but may have some problems with repetition, staying on topic, or unclear connection of ideas.	519–520
	☐ Uses language fairly well. Has variety in sentence patterns, vocabulary, and idioms, and only minor errors of vocabulary and grammar, but may have some errors in grammar, word form, or natural language that do not cause unclarity.	524–525
3	A **Level 3** response is characterized by one or more of the following:	
	☐ Addresses the topic and the task, but with somewhat developed detail, examples, and explanations.	515–517
	☐ Stays on topic, flows, and makes sense, but connection of ideas might be unclear at times.	517–518
	☐ May show inconsistent ability in grammar and vocabulary that may cause occasional unclarity.	524–525
	☐ Accurate but limited range of sentence structures and vocabulary.	524–525
2	A **Level 2** response will show one or more of the following weaknesses:	
	☐ Limited development of topic and task.	515–517
	☐ Poor organization or connection of ideas.	517–518
	☐ Not enough or inappropriate detail, examples, and explanations.	515–517
	☐ Poor choice of words or word forms.	524–525
	☐ Many errors of sentence structure or vocabulary.	524–525
1	A **Level 1** response is seriously harmed by one or more of these weaknesses:	
	☐ Disorganized or lacks development.	517–518
	☐ Little or no detail, examples, and explanations, or does not respond to the task.	515–517
	☐ Serious errors in sentence structure or vocabulary.	524–525
0	A response at this level contains only ideas copied from the topic, does not address the topic, is not written in English, or is blank.	

Answers, Explanations, Audio Scripts, and Sample Responses

Reading (Page 643)

1. **D There is disagreement about her. (Factual information)** Option D is correct because the passage indicates at least two different interpretations of her. Option A is incorrect because she died at the beginning of the Reign of Terror. Option B is not supported by the information in the passage, which says that she was a "contributing factor" to the revolution. Option C misstates the main idea of the paragraph. She was a real person, but there is controversy about her role in history.

2. **A To provide an example of confusion about her identity (Rhetorical purpose)** Option A is correct because the first sentence of the paragraph says that confusion about her identity extends to her names. The examples support this statement. Options B and C are not supported by the information in the passage. Option D is incorrect because although it may be true that royal families gave their children complicated names, this is not the reason the author mentions Marie Antoinette's names.

3. **B Common people were accepted. (Inference)** Option B is correct because the passage indicates that unlike at many other European courts, at the Austrian court commoners "of merit" were allowed, and the royal parents wanted their children to play with the children of commoners. This indicates that commoners were accepted. For this reason, Options A and D are incorrect. Option C is not supported by information in the passage.

4. **A The Austrian court was multilingual, and according to reports from her teachers and court observers, she spoke Italian well, but her German and French were poor. (Sentence simplification)** Option A is correct because only this option restates the essential ideas of the sentence without omitting information, introducing information that is incorrect or not in the passage, or changing the meaning. Option B is incorrect because it changes the meaning of the sentence: in the original sentence the observers and teachers are commenting on her language skills. In Option B, they are commenting that the court was multilingual. Option C is incorrect because it omits a key detail: the court was multilingual. Option D is incorrect because it changes the meaning of the sentence in a key way. In the original sentence, the court was multilingual. In Option D, the observers and teachers are multilingual.

5. **C The Austrian court was more relaxed than the French court. (Factual information)** Option C is correct because the passage states that Marie Antoinette disliked the elaborate ritual of the French court and that commoners were allowed to attend the Austrian court, which both indicate that the Austrian court was more relaxed than the French court. Option A is not supported by information in the passage. While the passage states that the Austrian court was multilingual, it does not say that the French court was monolingual. Option B is contradicted by information in the passage. Common people were allowed in the Austrian court, not the French one, according to the passage. Option D is not supported by the information in the passage.

6. **D not very good (Vocabulary)** Option D is correct because the passage says that she was "mediocre at best" and "only excelled at a few subjects." The phrase "at best" implies that her performance could have been worse, and the phrase "only excelled at a few subjects" means that her performance was generally not outstanding. Together, these statements imply that she was not a very good student. Options A and C are incorrect because she was good at both Italian and music. Option B is not supported by information in the passage.

7. **B Her husband was jealous of her popularity. (Negative factual information)** Option B is correct because this option is not supported by information in the passage. Options A, C, and D are all mentioned in the passage as sources of Marie Antoinette's marital problems and are therefore incorrect.

8. **C   someone who likes to be with other people (Vocabulary)** Option C is correct because the passage indicates that Marie Antoinette liked to go to parties, dinners, and plays. It also says that her personality was not compatible with that of her husband the king, who was quiet and shy. Option C is the only answer option that captures this meaning. For this reason, Option B is incorrect. Option A is incorrect because it is about differences among people's personalities, not the meaning of *extrovert*. Option D is not supported by information in the passage. There is no connection between being an extrovert and the time people like to get up.

9. **A   To show how people associated her with the country's growing debt (Rhetorical purpose)** Option A is correct because people began to call her this name because of her heavy spending and association with scandal. Option B is incorrect because while it may be true that criticism of her spending was unfair, this is not the reason that the author includes this information in the passage. Option C is contradicted by the passage, which states that most of the debt was the result of wartime spending. Option D is also contradicted by the passage: she lost the people's respect because of her spending.

10. **D   scandals (Reference)** Option D is correct because both *them* and *they* refer to the same antecedent. *Implicate* means "show someone's involvement in an illegal or harmful activity." Of the answer options, only Option D involves these kinds of activities. Therefore, the other options are incorrect.

11. **C   the debt (Vocabulary)** Option C is correct because the sentence is mainly about money problems that were blamed on Marie Antoinette's spending but were actually caused by wartime spending. The only option that makes sense in this context is "the debt." Option A does not make sense because Marie Antoinette's spending was not caused by wartime spending. Option B is not supported by information in the passage. The scandal was related to Marie Antoinette's spending, not wartime spending. Option D does not make sense because wartime spending cannot be both the cause and the effect.

12. **B   The royal family tried to escape from France. (Factual information)** Option B is correct because the passage states that after the family tried to escape abroad, they were put in prison. Options A and C are incorrect because the family was moved to Paris and the king agreed to the new constitution before they were put in

prison. The revolutionaries had agreed to the new constitution, so this would not have been a reason to put the royal family in prison. Option D is incorrect because the king was found guilty after the family was put in prison.

13. **C   (Insert text)** Option C is correct because this detail about Marie Antoinette's trial best comes after the first general sentence about what happened to her—that she suffered the same fate as the king. For this reason, Option B is incorrect because this detail makes no sense before the general statement about her fate. Options A and D are incorrect because these parts of the paragraph are not about Marie Antoinette's trial.

14. **(Prose summary)** If you completed the summary correctly, it should look like this:

The passage is about the life of Marie Antoinette.
- **A** Marie Antoinette's extravagant spending contributed to a negative view of the monarchy.
- **D** A number of scandals contributed to negative popular opinion about Marie Antoinette.
- **E** Marie Antoinette was both a symbol of the excesses of the monarchy and a victim of the revolution.

These answers are correct for these reasons.
- **A   Marie Antoinette's extravagant spending contributed to a negative view of the monarchy.** This response sums up one of the main ideas: the queen's excessive spending contributed to the negative view of the monarchy that led to the French Revolution.
- **D   A number of scandals contributed to negative popular opinion about Marie Antoinette.** This option states one of the main ideas of the passage, so it belongs in the summary.
- **E   Marie Antoinette was both a symbol of the excesses of the monarchy and a victim of the revolution.** This sentence sums up a main idea of the passage, so it belongs in the summary.

Incorrect options do not belong in the completed table for these reasons:
- **B   Marie Antoinette received a fair trial before her execution.** This option is contradicted by information in the passage, so it does not belong in the summary.
- **C   Marie Antoinette spoke good Italian, but her French and German skills were poor.** This option is a minor detail in the passage, so it does not belong in the summary.

· **F Marie Antoinette was executed for treason because she was a spy for Austria.** This option is not supported by information in the passage, so it does not belong in the summary.

15. **A They eat insects to get nutrients they cannot get from the soil. (Factual information)** Option A is stated directly in the passage, so this option is correct. Options B and D are true of fungi, not carnivorous plants, so these options are incorrect. Option C is contradicted by information in the passage. Meat-eating plants use photosynthesis to make their own food, but they get other nutrients from the insects they catch and digest.

16. **A nutrients (Reference)** Option A is correct because this sentence is about how the plants get the nutrients they need, so only this option makes sense in the sentence. Option B is not possible because the antecedent of *they* is *carnivorous plants,* and it does not make sense that the plants find themselves. Option C is incorrect because the plants are looking for nutrients, not places. Option D is incorrect because insects and spiders are the source of nutrients such as nitrogen.

17. **D obtain (Vocabulary)** Option D is correct because the author has already made clear that most plants obtain energy from food they make themselves. Since carnivorous plants also use photosynthesis, it makes sense that they obtain their energy in the same way, and that *derive* means "obtain" in this context. The remaining options do not make sense.

18. **C They follow prey. (Negative factual information)** Option C is correct because while some carnivorous plants use motion, plants are not mobile, so they cannot follow their prey. Options A, B, and D are all mentioned in the passage as being true of carnivorous plants, so they are incorrect.

19. **B passive traps' (Reference)** Option B is correct because *prey* means "the organisms that predators consume." This sentence is about one subset of carnivorous plants, passive traps, so Option B is correct. Options A, C, and D do not make sense.

20. **C To correct a common misconception about the plants (Rhetorical purpose)** Option C is correct because this phrase indicates that despite a belief held by many people, the plants use photosynthesis just like other plants and do not get all of their nutrition from the insects they consume. Option A is incorrect because

the sentence indicates a similarity between the kinds of plants. Option B is incorrect because fungi, unlike other plants, do not have chlorophyll and do not make their own food. Option D is contradicted by information in the passage: the plants clearly catch and digest insects.

21. **B A nice smell attracts insects. (Factual information)** Option B is correct because this answer is stated directly in the passage: "These plants generally use scent to lure insects inside the rolled-up leaves." (*Smell* is another word for *scent*.) Option A is about how the plants get nutrients from their prey, so it is incorrect. Option C is about how the plants get the insects to become tired and careless. Option D is about how the insects fall from inside the plant into the digestive juices.

22. **C Some are active traps and some are passive traps. (Inference)** Option C is correct because the passage first talks about flypaper traps that use only mucilage to catch prey, and then says that more sophisticated flypaper traps use motion to catch prey. This implies that some of them are passive and others are active. Therefore, Option D is incorrect. Option A is not supported by information in the passage. Option B is contradicted by information in the passage.

23. **D glue (Vocabulary)** Option D is correct because this answer is stated directly in the passage: glands in the plant secrete a "sticky, gluelike substance." Option A does not make sense because glands cannot secrete themselves. Option B is incorrect because digestive fluids digest the prey, while the mucilage traps them. Therefore, mucilage cannot be a digestive fluid. Option C is not supported by information in the passage.

24. **C Snap traps are active traps. (Factual information)** Option C is correct because snap traps use motion to catch insects. Option A is contradicted by information in the passage: there are only two known varieties of snap traps. Option B is contradicted by information in the passage. Option D misstates information in the passage. The insects are not caught in the hairs. The hairs act as triggers to close the trap when they are touched.

25. **B The two halves close together very quickly, trapping and digesting the insect when it lands on the trap and touches one of the hairs. (Sentence simplification)** Option B is correct because only this option restates the essential ideas of the sentence without omitting

information, introducing information that is incorrect or not in the passage, or changing the meaning. Options A and C are incorrect because they both introduce the same error. The sentences say that when an insect lands on the trap, touches one of the hairs, and is digested, the trap closes. The insect is digested after the trap closes, not before. Option D is incorrect because it leaves out important information about the trigger hairs and about the insects being digested by the plant.

26. **D** **(Insert text)** Option D is correct because the sentence gives the last stage in the trapping process, so it should come after the other steps in the process. For this reason, the sentence does not make sense in the other positions in the paragraph.

27. **A** **To remind readers how trigger hairs work (Rhetorical purpose)** Option A is correct because the operation of trigger hairs is explained in detail in the paragraph on snap traps. By reminding readers of the previous explanation, the author does not need to repeat it in paragraph 7. Option B is not supported by information in the passage. It is true that bladder traps are active traps because they involve motion, but information about trigger hairs does not prove this, so Option C is incorrect. Option D is incorrect because hair works differently in lobster pot traps than in the other two kinds of traps. In lobster pot traps, the hairs stop the insect from exiting the chamber. The hairs are not triggers, unlike in snap traps and bladder traps.

28. **(Fill in a table)** The correctly completed table should look like this. Answers can be in any order. Answers are correct if only the letter is written.

ACTIVE TRAPS	PASSIVE TRAPS
Select 2	Select 3
• **A** Some of them use trigger hairs to operate their traps.	• **D** Their slippery leaves help them catch prey.
• **C** They include snap traps and bladder traps.	• **E** They include pitfall traps and lobster pot traps.
	• **G** They do not use movement to trap prey.

These answers are correct for these reasons.

Active Traps
• **A** **Some of them use trigger hairs to operate their traps.** This option is correct because it is stated directly in the passage.
• **C** **They include snap traps and bladder traps.** This option is correct because both of these kinds of carnivorous plants use movement to catch prey.

Passive Traps
• **D** **Their slippery leaves help them catch prey.** This option is correct because it is stated directly in the passage.
• **E** **They include pitfall traps and lobster pot traps.** This option is correct because both of these kinds of carnivorous plants do not use movement.
• **G** **They do not use movement to trap prey.** This option is correct because it is stated directly in the passage as the definition of passive traps.

Incorrect options do not belong in the completed table for these reasons:
• **B** **They include all flypaper traps.** This option is incorrect because some of these traps are passive and others are active. Therefore, this statement is incorrect and belongs in neither box.
• **F** **They cannot produce their own food.** This option is incorrect because the passage makes it clear that carnivorous plants, like most green plants, make their own food.

29. **B** **A submarine is a boat that can travel underwater. (Factual information)** Option B is correct because this is part of the definition of a submarine given in the second sentence of the paragraph. While a true statement, Option A is not the answer because this is not a part of the definition of a submarine. Like Option A, Option C is not a part of the definition of a submarine. In addition, Option C misstates the first sentence of

the paragraph, which says that the invention of the submarine was a reflection of the history of technology. While Option D is a true statement, it is incorrect because this sentence describes a feature submarines need to be able to operate, but this feature is not part of the definition of a submarine.

30. **A   die from lack of oxygen (Vocabulary)** Option A is correct because *crew* refers to the people who work on board a ship, submarine, or airplane. If people do not get oxygen, they will die. Options B and C are incorrect because if people do not have oxygen they will die, not lose power or stop working. Combustion engines will stop working or lose power from lack of oxygen, but this sentence is about people, not machines. Option D is incorrect because while people will first faint from lack of oxygen, they will soon die if they do not get access to oxygen very quickly.

31. **C   William Bourne designed the first submarine ever built. (Factual information)** Option C is correct because according to the passage, Drebbel built the submarine according to Bourne's design. For this reason, Option B is incorrect. Option A is incorrect because DaVinci drew plans for a submarine, but that submarine was never built. According to the passage, Wilkins wrote about military applications of submarines, but the passage does not indicate that he ever designed a submarine. Therefore, Option D is incorrect.

32. **D   They do not need to return to the surface for air. (Negative factual information)** Option D is correct because this is the only option that is not mentioned in the paragraph as an advantage of submarines. In addition, it is contradicted by information in the passage. Therefore, Options A, B, and C are incorrect.

33. **B   To provide support for the statement that military uses of submarines were quickly discovered (Rhetorical purpose)** Option B is correct because Wilkins made his statements about military applications of submarines in 1648, only 28 years after Drebbel had built the first prototype. This shows that military applications were found very quickly. For this reason, Option A is incorrect. While it is true that Wilkins identified several uses for submarines (Option C), this is not the reason that the author mentions Wilkins's ideas. Option D is not supported by information in the passage.

34. **C   Northern ships (Reference)** Option C is correct because in a war, one country will block another country's harbors to stop shipping. The

only answer that makes sense is Option C. Option A does not make sense because the Southern leaders would not block their own harbors. Option B is incorrect because submarines were used to stop the ships from blocking the harbors. They were not used to block the harbors. Option D does not make sense because entrances cannot block entrances.

35. **A   underwater (Vocabulary)** Option A is correct because access to oxygen is only a problem when a submarine is underwater. Options B and C are not locations where oxygen would be a problem, so these options are incorrect. Option D does not make sense.

36. **B   water (Reference)** Option B is correct because the previous sentence says that water was pumped into the tanks for the submarine to dive. The only way to get the submarine to surface would be to pump the water back out. Option A is not possible because when the submarine is submerged, water is in the ballast tanks, not air, so air cannot be pumped back out. Options C and D do not make sense.

37. **D   (Insert text)** Option D is correct because it gives an additional idea about why early submarines have disappeared, so it most logically comes in this position, which is after another sentence that gives information about why many early submarines no longer exist. Options A, B, and C all follow information about early submarines, but none of these sentences is about why early submarines have disappeared, so the sentence does not make sense in these positions.

38. **B   The invention of a nuclear-powered engine (Factual information)** Option B is correct because this answer is stated directly in the text. Option A is incorrect because this submarine could only stay underwater for short periods of time because of the amount of heat produced. Options C and D are contradicted by information in the passage.

39. **A   It would not be possible for submarines to stay underwater for long periods until the nuclear-powered submarine was invented. (Sentence simplification)** Option A is correct because only this option restates the essential ideas of the sentence without omitting information, introducing information that is incorrect or not in the passage, or changing the meaning. Option B is incorrect because it leaves out information about submarines. Option C is incorrect because it omits important information about the length of time submarines can stay submerged. Option D is incorrect because it

changes the cause-and-effect relationship. The invention of nuclear power made it possible for submarines to stay underwater for extended periods of time.

40. **D** **U-boats had a major effect on the war despite their small numbers. (Inference)** Option D is correct because despite their small number, they produced great fear and sank many ships. Options A and B cannot be inferred from the information in the passage, so these options are incorrect. Option C is not supported by information in the passage.

41. **A** **To show that DaVinci was right about the emotional impact of submarine warfare on people (Rhetorical purpose)** Option A is correct because at the beginning of the passage, the author discusses DaVinci's concerns about the fear submarine warfare would produce. The fear that U-boats produced in people during World War I confirms DaVinci's belief. Options B and C may be true, but these are not the reason the author mentions DaVinci at the end of the passage. Option D is not supported by information in the passage. It is not reasonable to assume that just because submarines are terrifying they should not be built.

42. **(Prose summary)** If you completed the summary correctly, it should look like this:

The passage is about the development of the submarine.
- **A** The design of submarines has improved greatly since their invention.
- **C** Leonardo DaVinci drew the first known design for a submarine.

- **F** A submarine is a kind of boat that is capable of traveling underwater using its own power.

These answers are correct for these reasons.
- **A** **The design of submarines has improved greatly since their invention.** Most of the passage is about successive improvements to the design of submarines, so this sentence belongs in the summary.
- **C** **Leonardo DaVinci drew the first known design for a submarine.** Since this passage is about the invention of the submarine, the name of the initial inventor is a key detail that belongs in the summary.
- **F** **A submarine is a kind of boat that is capable of traveling underwater using its own power.** This sentence provides a definition of the word *submarine,* the topic of the passage, so it belongs in the summary.

Incorrect options do not belong in the completed table for these reasons:
- **B** **Only nuclear submarines can stay underwater for weeks and months at a time.** This option is a relatively minor detail in the passage, so it does not belong in the summary.
- **D** **Submarines were not used effectively for military purposes until World War I.** This option is not supported by information in the passage, so it does not belong in the summary.
- **E** **The invention of compressed air allowed submarines to stay underwater for weeks at a time.** This option misstates key information in the passage. The invention of nuclear power allowed submarines to stay underwater for weeks at a time.

Listening (Page 670)

Questions 1–5

TRACK 151 AUDIO SCRIPT

Narrator: Listen to a conversation between a student and a professor.

Professor: What can I do for you, Taylor?

Student: My presentation's on Tuesday, and I need some help with my topic. I mean, the particular angle I'm going to take.

Professor: You're working on Chinese salt monopolies and private enterprise under the Qing dynasty, aren't you?

Student: Yes.

Professor: The salt monopolies are fascinating, especially their relationship to the Chinese political and economic system. They lasted for centuries, up until the collapse of the dynasty in 1911. Condensing your research into a twenty-minute talk won't be easy.

Some economists use the history of the monopolies to show why China didn't adopt a free-market economy under the Qing dynasty. Is that your focus?

Student: The truth is I don't know what my focus is!

Professor: Oh, my. What's your starting point?

Student: I've defined "salt monopolies" and "private enterprise." I've used a dictionary definition of private enterprise with some reference to the theories of Weber. There seem to have been two main types of salt monopoly—fiscal and turnover—and I've described both.

Professor: Uh-huh.

Now, while you're an expert on this, your classmates are likely to know very little, so make sure you stick to the basics in your presentation.

Student: If only I could! There are so many concepts involved. There's this caste system thing in China, for one. You know, scholars and officials being at the top socially and economically, craftsmen below them, followed by merchants. Only soldiers and peasants had a lower social status than merchants. This may be one reason why capitalism didn't take off. The moneymakers had very little political power.

Professor: Perhaps.

Student: Plus, when the salt merchants made money—and the thirty families who controlled the industry in 1700 were multimillionaires in today's terms—they, they squandered it, or they spent it trying to worm their way up into the scholar-official elite. Essentially, they were prevented from investing their profits in other industries outside salt, which seems like a no-brainer in terms of developing the whole economy.

Professor: Maybe the state wanted to rein in the salt merchants to stop them from creating their own armies and carving up the kingdom.

Student: Hmm. I hadn't thought of that.

Also, many salt merchants inherited their rights to sell salt. In private enterprise, leadership tends to devolve upon the ablest candidates, not just the sons of the captains of industry.

The salt trade accounted for twenty five percent of the total Chinese economy in 1700, but if it had been run more efficiently, its profits would've been even greater.

Professor: As I said, isn't it in the interests of the emperor and the elite to keep these guys under control? The emperor doesn't want a class of wealthy *and* capable merchants. They might be a threat to the power structure.

Student: Yes, I can see your point.

Narrator: Now answer questions 1 to 5. Circle the letter of the answer.

TRACK 152 AUDIO SCRIPT

Narrator: Listen again to part of the conversation. Then answer the question.

Student: Plus, when the salt merchants made money—and the thirty families who controlled the

industry in 1700 were multimillionaires in today's terms—they, they squandered it, or they spent it trying to worm their way up into the scholar-official elite. Essentially, they were prevented from investing their profits in other industries outside salt, which seems like a no-brainer in terms of developing the whole economy.

Narrator: What does the student mean when she says this?

Student: Essentially, they were prevented from investing their profits in other industries outside salt, which seems like a no-brainer in terms of developing the whole economy.

ANSWERS AND EXPLANATIONS

1. **C** **Focusing her presentation topic (Gist-purpose)** Option C is correct because the student says she needs help with "the particular angle" she's going to take in her presentation. Later, the professor says, "Condensing your research . . . won't be easy." Options A and B are incorrect because the student and professor are not discussing a term paper. Option D is not supported by information in the conversation.

2. **D** **Keep her information simple (Detail)** Option D is correct because the professor says, "Make sure you stick to the basics in your presentation." Options A and B are not supported by information in the conversation. Option C is contradicted by information in the conversation. The professor wants the student to keep her information simple.

3. **A** **To show why China did not develop a free-market economy (Detail)** Option A is correct because the professor says, "Some economists use the history of the monopolies to show why China didn't adopt a free-market economy under the Qing dynasty." Options B, C, and D are not supported by information in the conversation.

4. **B** **Chinese salt merchants contributed less to economic development than they might have. (Inference/Replay)** Option B is correct because if Chinese salt merchants couldn't invest their profits in industries other than salt, they were contributing less to economic development than they might have. Option A is contradicted in the conversation when the student mentions that Chinese salt merchants made huge profits. Options C and D are not supported by information in the conversation.

5. **B** **Emperors wanted to limit merchants' political power. (Inference)** Option B is correct because the professor says, "Maybe the state

wanted to rein in the salt merchants to stop them from creating their own armies and carving up the kingdom." He adds, "Isn't it in the interests of the emperor and the elite to keep [the salt merchants] under control?" Option A is incorrect because although merchants "squandered" or wasted their wealth, the professor does not say whether scholars looked down on merchants for doing this. Options C and D are not supported by information in the conversation.

Questions 6–11

TRACK 153 AUDIO SCRIPT

Narrator: Listen to part of a lecture in a history class. The professor is talking about World War I.

Professor: World War I was a massively destructive conflict involving thirty-two countries. It was the result of many factors. A crisis in Serbia was the immediate cause of the conflict. Leading up to this, however, there was instability and mistrust across Europe.

Today, I'd like to focus on the European alliance system between 1839 and 1914. I've chosen 1839 because that's when the Treaty of London was signed; and 1914, when the war began. This web of alliances was meant to strengthen relationships among signatories, but ultimately, it had the opposite effect.

An ally is a person or country that has some obligation to support or assist another. In international relations, the obligation may be formalized in a treaty or alliance.

The alliance system exacerbated World War I by committing countries to fight that may otherwise have remained neutral. Additionally, countries made and unmade alliances so often in the prewar period that trust seemed in short supply.

Let's look back at Germany in 1866. At that time, Germany was not a country but a patchwork of states, principalities, kingdoms, etc., loosely connected through trade, more closely connected through language and culture. Germany became a unified empire in stages. In 1866, Chancellor Otto von Bismarck was the political leader of Prussia, a kingdom in the north. He wanted Prussia to expand its control over its German-speaking neighbors. The German-speaking Austrians in the Austro-Hungarian Empire opposed Bismarck's plans. The Prussian army defeated the Austrians in several campaigns. Prussia then annexed several north German states allied with Austria, including Hesse

and Frankfurt, as well as the disputed territories of Schleswig and Holstein.

In 1870, the Prussians invaded France. In 1871, while the Prussian armies were besieging Paris, the independent southern German states decided to join Prussia, resulting in the birth of the German Empire. Later that same year, France conceded defeat. The new German Empire annexed the French provinces of Alsace and Lorraine and demanded more than one billion dollars' worth of reparations. Germany was now a richer country than France, and its economy was second only to that of Britain.

Although Bismarck had initially battled Austria-Hungary, he understood that if France tried to fight Germany to regain its lost territory, he would need the assistance of the Austrians. Bismarck hoped alliances would contribute to security so that the newly expanded Germany would have time to coalesce and prosper in peace. In 1879, Bismarck signed an agreement called the Dual Alliance with Austria-Hungary in which the two empires agreed to come to one another's aid militarily if attacked by Russia, and to remain neutral if the other party were attacked by France. This treaty lasted until 1914. It was invoked by Austria-Hungary when the Austrians declared war on Serbia in 1914 at the start of World War I; Austria called for German support since the Serbians were Russian allies.

In 1881, Germany and Austria-Hungary signed an agreement with Italy called the Triple Alliance. It was soon rendered useless when Italy made a secret agreement with France. Nevertheless, the existence of the Triple Alliance led the French and Russians to ally with each other in 1892, in the Franco-Russian Military Convention. In this agreement, if either country were attacked by any signatory of the Triple Alliance, the other country would mobilize.

Bismarck believed that a war on two fronts, with France and Russia, would be disastrous for Germany, but he left office in 1890. His replacement and the German generals were certain they could win a speedy engagement if Britain stayed neutral. They could gain more European territory and more colonies worldwide.

However, Britain, with its own vast overseas colonies, was watching the rise of Germany with alarm. When the Germans began building a large navy, Britain decided to end its neutrality and look for new alliances. For instance, a 1902 military agreement between Britain and Japan was designed to limit Germany's colonial aspirations in the Pacific.

Then in 1904, Britain signed the Entente Cordiale with France. This did little more than offer closer diplomatic ties, but three years later, Britain signed a similar agreement with Russia. Again, no military aid was offered; that came subsequently. In the Anglo-French Naval Convention that Britain and France concluded in 1912, Britain agreed to protect the French coastline from German attack, and France agreed to defend the Suez Canal for Britain.

All these alliances ratcheted up the likelihood of war, yet a treaty with a tiny kingdom—the 1839 Treaty of London pledging Britain to protect Belgium—was what actually brought Britain into World War I. This treaty had been signed because Britain worried that Germany would use Belgium as the route for an invasion of France. And from France, Germany could attack Britain. World War I began on August 4, 1914, when the Germans invaded Belgium on their way to attack France. At that point, Britain honored its treaty with Belgium and came to the aid of France as well. Once this happened, German hopes for a speedy, small-scale conflict were dashed; one of the bloodiest wars in history followed.

Narrator: Now answer questions 6 to 11. Circle the letter of the answer.

ANSWERS AND EXPLANATIONS

6. **B The system of treaties that contributed to the outbreak of World War I (Gist-content)** Option B is correct because the professor says, "I'd like to focus on the European alliance system between 1839 and 1914." She adds, "1914 [was] when the war began." Option A is incorrect because the Treaty of London is only one detail in the lecture. Option C is contradicted by the information in the lecture. Bismarck believed that Germany could not win such a war. Option D is incorrect because this is only one detail mentioned in the lecture.

7. **A It was based on mistrust among countries in Europe. (Detail)** Option A is correct because the professor says, "Countries made and unmade alliances so often in the prewar period that trust

seemed in short supply." Options B and C are not supported by information in the lecture. Option D is incorrect. The professor does mention Germany's powerful position in Europe. She says that in 1871 "its economy was second only to that of Britain." However, this does not mean Germany dominated Europe or that Germany's strength was a result of the alliance system.

8. **C Because German unification changed the balance of power in Europe (Connecting content)** Option C is correct. The professor spends a lot of time talking about Germany in the prewar period because German unification changed the power balance in Europe. Previously, Austria-Hungary and France had been powerful, but Germany defeated them in wars. After 1871, Germany and Britain were powerful. Options A and B are not supported by information in the lecture. Option D is incorrect. The German army was strong, but not "almost invincible."

9. **D A period of stability in which Germany could prosper (Detail)** Option D is correct because the professor says, "Bismarck hoped alliances would contribute to security so the newly expanded Germany would have time to coalesce and prosper in peace." Option A is incorrect because Bismarck gained new territories through fighting Austria-Hungary and France, not through making alliances. Options B and C are not supported by information in the lecture.

10. **B The potential German threat to Britain's colonies (Detail)** Option B is correct because the professor says, "Britain, with its own vast overseas colonies, was watching the rise of Germany with alarm. When the Germans began building a large navy, Britain decided to end its neutrality and look for new alliances. For instance, a 1902 military agreement between Britain and Japan was designed to limit Germany's colonial aspirations in the Pacific." Option A is not supported by information in the lecture. Options C and D are incorrect. While there were improved relations between Britain and Japan and France, it is not clear that these were related to the alliance system.

11. (Organization/Drag-and-drop)

1. Britain signs the Treaty of London to protect Belgium.	This happened in 1839.
2. C Many separate German-speaking territories make up a united empire.	The professor says, "In 1871, while the Prussian armies were besieging Paris, the independent south German states decided to join Prussia, resulting in the birth of the German Empire."
3. A Germany and Austria-Hungary form the Dual Alliance.	"In 1879, Bismarck signed an agreement called the Dual Alliance with Austria-Hungary."
4. B France, Russia, and Britain formally become allies.	"In 1904, Britain signed the Entente Cordiale with France. Three years later, Britain signed a similar agreement with Russia."
5. D The Germans invade Belgium on their way to attack France.	"World War I began on August 4, 1914, when the Germans invaded Belgium on their way to attack France."

Questions 12–17

TRACK 154 AUDIO SCRIPT

Narrator: Listen to part of a discussion in a design class. The professor is talking about furniture.

Professor: Being a student can be tough. It's hard to furnish a new place when you're short of cash or far from home. When I was at college, I made a desk from an old door and a bedside table from a milk crate. I had some pretty strange chairs as well.

These days, another way to find furniture in some places is during designated "throw-away" days when people put unwanted things out on the street. City authorities don't collect these immediately, but leave them for a day or two so that other people can take them in. In Canada and Australia, cities reduce their trash collection and landfill bills by sixty percent with this method. And in the US, thrift stores, yard, and garage sales provide ways to get rid of unwanted items that others buy cheaply.

Even people with plenty of disposable income decorate with salvaged or repurposed chic. Perhaps they don't fully subscribe to a consumerist society, or perhaps they enjoy expensive irony. Their new bedside table may look like a milk crate, but it's been crafted from Douglas fir, "designed" by Jasper Morrison, and it cost three hundred dollars. Whatever the motivation for this trend, it seems that repurposed furniture is on the rise, and I'd like to fit it into an art-historical context.

But first of all, who are some up-and-coming exponents of the style, and what do they produce? Let's start with chairs. Have any of you seen repurposed chairs?

Male Student: Yes, in London last year, I saw the work of the designer Karen Ryan. She makes chairs from stacking or combining parts of broken chairs into hybrid seats. They look weird and uncomfortable, but I sat on one, and they're fine.

Female Student: My favorite is Frank Willems from the Netherlands, who makes sofas from old mattresses. He finds old mattresses, straps them onto four legs, coats the whole thing with a layer of foam, and paints it. The result is more like a sculpture than a sofa.

Professor: Why does he choose mattresses?

Female Student: Because waste-processing machinery has a hard time breaking them down.

Professor: That's right.

Someone else you may not have heard of is Nina Tolstrup. She designed a chair out of a wooden pallet and fifty screws. Avoiding the factory process entirely, she sells instructions for this on her website.

Male Student: Don't you think that's taking things a bit far? It's like telling people to find an old door for a desk and then asking them to pay for the idea.

Professor: I wish I'd done that!

But really, what's your objection? If the chair were assembled and for sale in her store or online, would that be different?

Male Student: I don't know. It seems like there's no craft left in furniture-making.

Professor: That's what people said about the work of many fine artists in the early twentieth century.

Female Student: Personally, I've got a problem with the inflated prices these repurposed items command. I'm from Kuwait. Recently, I saw a show by two Lebanese designers. They buy old furniture in Europe, fix it up, and cover it in fabric embroidered with traditional Middle Eastern designs. They maintain they're encouraging people to value their cultural heritage, but only a millionaire can afford to buy one of their couches. Nice furniture has become the preserve of the super-rich.

Male Student: Or the preserve of a small group of people who determine what is culturally hip.

It's all very well for a designer to say he's made an armchair when he's really selling you a retired shopping cart. There's some guy in Frankfurt who does this. Really, it's a broken-down shopping cart with a cushion, which *he* calls an armchair!

I chose design as a major instead of fine arts because I thought my work'd be sincere. I'm not paying tribute to dead artists, like-like Marcel Duchamp, when I come up with a design. I hope I'm making useful, inexpensive, elegant products.

Professor: I'm glad you've mentioned Duchamp. He shot to fame for appropriating materials from industry and the home to use in works of fine art. He challenged the notions of beauty, craft, and art itself. Whether you like it or not, these ideas are here to stay, and they're now an important part of furniture design.

Narrator: Now answer questions 12 to 17. Circle the letter of the answer.

ANSWERS AND EXPLANATIONS

12. **C   Repurposed furniture has become an art form. (Gist-content)** Option C is correct because the professor says that he wants to discuss repurposed furniture in "an art-historical context." Option A is not supported by information in the lecture. Option B is contradicted by the lecture; inexpensive repurposed furniture is still sold at thrift stores. Option D is an opinion of one of the students, not the professor, and is contradicted by the lecture.

13. **B   To lead into the topic of the lecture (Function)** Option B is correct because the professor talks about his student days before

he begins the actual topic of the lecture. Option A is too broad. While the professor talks about recycling, his topic is recycling and furniture design. Option C is incorrect because although the professor sympathizes with poor students, this is not the function of his introduction. Option D is incorrect. The professor describes his unusual student household, but he does this in order to lead into the topic of furniture design.

14. **B   They favor ironic design. D   They dislike consumerism. (Detail/Special multiple choice)** Options B and D are correct because the professor says, "Even people with plenty of disposable income decorate with salvaged or repurposed chic. Perhaps they do not fully subscribe to a consumerist society, or perhaps they enjoy expensive irony." Options A and C are not supported by information in the lecture.

15. **A   He thinks her production process lacks craft. (Inference)** Option A is correct because the male student says, "Don't you think that's taking things a bit far? It's like telling people to find an old door for a desk and then asking them to pay for the idea." Later he adds, "It seems like there's no craft left in furniture-making." Options B and C are not supported by information in the lecture. Option D is incorrect because the lecture does not include information about the difficulty of assembling Nina Tolstrup's designs.

16. **C   It is not really what it claims to be. (Detail)** Option C is correct because the student says, "Really, it's a broken-down shopping cart with a cushion, which [the designer] calls an armchair!" Options A and B are not supported by information in the lecture. Option D is incorrect because the male student brings up Marcel Duchamp, but he does not claim that the Frankfurt designer copied him.

17. **C   To show how furniture design has been influenced by fine art (Detail)** Option C is correct because the professor says, "Duchamp . . . shot to fame for appropriating materials from industry and the home to use in works of fine art. He challenged the notions of beauty, craft, and art itself. These ideas are . . . now an important part of furniture design." Option A is incorrect because the professor is not reminding students of Duchamp's past importance but of his current importance. Option B is incorrect. While the professor mentions Duchamp's use of unusual materials, this is not the main reason he refers to Duchamp. Option D is not supported by information in the lecture.

Questions 18–22

TRACK 155 AUDIO SCRIPT

Narrator: Listen to a conversation between a student and a university employee.

Employee: Hello. Are you Miss Chen?

Student: Yes, I am.

Employee: You're here about volunteering as a mentor, aren't you?

Student: That's right.

Employee: I see you've filled in the online application. You certainly are the kind of person we're looking for.

Student: Thanks.

Employee: We need more bilingual mentors, and you speak Chinese and some Korean, don't you?

Student: Yes, I do. I was born here, but my parents are from China, and they made me go to Chinese language school when I was a kid.

Employee: How did you learn Korean?

Student: I was an exchange student there.

Employee: That's useful since we've got Koreans and Chinese in our undergrad and summer school programs.

There seem to be two things missing from your application. Do you have a first aid certificate?

Student: I've got to admit, I don't. Is it really necessary?

Employee: It's not essential, but it is desirable. And do you have a driver's license?

Student: Oh, dear, I must've forgotten to check that box.

Employee: OK.

I see you're a sociology major, and you have a counseling diploma from a community college. That's helpful. Still, international students have their own specific set of problems. What do you think mentors mainly deal with?

Student: I suppose academic stuff—y'know, the system's different here from abroad. But probably personal problems, too?

Employee: That's the answer I was looking for. This college generally attracts able scholars; but sometimes they don't reach their potential due to nonacademic issues. Homesickness and loneliness are the big-ticket items. Then there are odd things like where to find decent noodles in Springfield.

Student: I know what you mean. I'm from New Jersey. There's a candy I love that you can't get here. Can you believe I have my brother mail it to me?

Employee: I can.

By the way, have you had any mentoring experience?

Student: My cousin from Hong Kong studies at a college nearby. You could say I informally mentored him when he was a freshman.

Employee: I see.

Narrator: Now answer questions 18 to 22. Circle the letter of the answer.

TRACK 156 AUDIO SCRIPT

Narrator: Listen again to part of the conversation. Then answer the question.

Employee: There seem to be two things missing from your application. Do you have a first aid certificate?

Student: I've got to admit, I don't. Is it really necessary?

Employee: It's not essential, but it is desirable. And do you have a driver's license?

Narrator: What does the employee mean when he says this?

Employee: It's not essential, but it is desirable.

ANSWERS AND EXPLANATIONS

18. **B To become a volunteer mentor (Gist-purpose)** Option B is correct because the employee says, "You're here about volunteering as a mentor, aren't you," and the student agrees. Options A, C, and D are not supported by information in the conversation.

19. **B She has lived abroad and speaks Korean. (Detail)** Option B is correct because the employee says, "We need more bilingual mentors, and you speak Chinese and some Korean." Option A is incorrect because the employee does not suggest that studying sociology is useful to the role of mentor. Option C is mentioned in the lecture, but it is not one of the candidate's strengths. Option D is mentioned in the conversation, but not as a qualification for becoming a mentor.

20. **A Applicants who have a first aid certificate have a better chance of being accepted. (Function/Replay)** Option A is correct. The phrase "It's not essential, but it is desirable" in relation to having a first aid certificate means that if an applicant has a first aid certificate, his or her application will be viewed more favorably and have a better chance of success. An "essential" qualification is 100 percent necessary; a "desirable" one is not 100 percent necessary but is useful. Option B is incorrect because applicants are not required to have a first aid certificate. Options C and D are not supported by the conversation.

21. **C Experiencing feelings of isolation (Detail)** Option C is correct. The employee indicates

that international students experience difficult feelings of isolation when he says, "Homesickness and loneliness are the big-ticket items." Option A is incorrect. The employee suggests that international students at this particular college normally do not have academic problems. Option B is not supported by information in the conversation. Option D is incorrect. The employee mentions finding decent noodles in Springfield, but he says that food issues are not "particularly difficult for international students."

22. **C** **To show that she has already been an unofficial mentor (Function)** Option C is correct because Ms. Chen says, "You could say I informally mentored [my cousin] when he was a freshman." Options A, B, and D are not supported by information in the conversation.

Questions 23–28

TRACK 157 AUDIO SCRIPT

Narrator: Listen to part of a discussion in a psychology class. The professor is talking about left-handedness.

Professor: Before I begin, raise your hand if you're left-handed. One, two, three . . . OK. About five of you.

Now, let's take off our shoes. Don't worry—we'll put them back on soon.

Today's topic is handedness, which remains an area of psychological and neurological mystery.

I've written two words on the board: *sinister* and *gauche*. What do they mean?

Student: *Sinister* is kind of "creepy" or "threatening."

Professor: And *gauche*?

Student: "Shy" or "clumsy."

Professor: Good. "Socially awkward" and "tactless" are also possible.

Originally, *sinister* and *gauche* meant "left." Words associated with *right,* however, like *adroit* or *dexterous,* mean "skillful" or "accomplished."

Student: Are you saying "right" has more positive connotations?

Professor: Yes. Take a look at its synonyms: *correct, appropriate, well,* and *just.* And we all want human rights, not human lefts.

Synonyms for *left* relate to the verb *leave,* describing absence. Therefore, to be left-handed is linguistically loaded. This is the case in many other languages too.

Practically speaking, being left-handed is inconvenient. Scissors, guitars, cameras, and cars are all designed for right-handers. In some countries, children are still forced to write with their right hands, which can cause stuttering and other nervous conditions later in life. Nevertheless, around ten percent of the entire population remains left-handed and has been so over time. Cave paintings of shadow hands show the same proportion of left-handers tens of thousands of years ago.

Student: I read that no gene for left-handedness has been identified. Is that true?

Professor: Not anymore. In 2007, researchers discovered that the LRRTM1 gene is linked to it. Still, with two left-handed parents, the likelihood of a left-handed child is only twenty-six percent, so there are environmental factors that influence handedness as well.

Some neurologists think that there's a spectrum of handedness: that people are not totally right- or left-handed—there are some things they can do well with the other hand.

Student: What else causes left-handedness other than that gene?

Professor: At some time in early childhood, chance or parental guidance influences people. This could explain why left-handers aren't necessarily left-faced or right-brained. A left-hander could have a slight asymmetry on the right side of the face with a higher eye and eyebrow and a dominant right eye; or a left-hander could show a disposition toward left-brained abilities like speech and calculation.

Another theory says handedness is determined in the womb, where fetuses hold one hand close to the mouth. Exposure to high levels of estrogen there is also being considered as a factor.

There's a fourth theory that says that a left-hander was originally part of an identical twin pair in which the right-handed fetus failed to develop. The vanishing twin theory, as it's known, has been strongly refuted in Australia, where there are lots of twins. It just doesn't hold up among twins there.

So, are there any benefits for the population as a whole to left-handedness?

Student: If you're on a sports team—totally. Athletes who play left-handed or left-footed or with both hands or feet are in big demand. Although . . . I've only met a handful.

Professor: You're right—ambidextrousness, total proficiency on both sides, is extremely rare. Curiously, there are people who *tell* others they're ambidextrous, but, when tested, are right- or left-handed with varying ability with the other hand.

There also seems to be some mystique associated with left-handedness: many people believe left-handers are richer, more creative, or more intelligent, but statistics do not bear this out. The only notable thing is that left-handers have a slightly lower life expectancy, possibly due to the stress of constant adaptation.

Yet if left-handers aren't cleverer or more artistic, and if they die young, why do they exist at all?

Student: I guess millions of years ago, predators, like giant cats, would figure out pretty fast if humans were all right-handed or right-eyed. They'd leap onto us from the left every time. Maybe left-handers evolved as lookouts.

Professor: That's possible.

Humans belong to the animal group called bilateria—our body plan is bilaterally symmetrical. However, our brain is not: one hemisphere has become more specialized than the other. The asymmetrical human brain is not well understood, but we do know that other primates are far less asymmetrical, so its advantages must be significant.

Now, let's put our shoes back on.

Did you happen to observe what I, or anyone else, did? Who put the left shoe on first? Were they the same people who declared themselves lefties earlier?

This is how the army tests handedness, because so many recruits lie. Left-handers don't want to be judged as sinister or gauche; right-handers hope to be seen as more creative or just a little different.

Narrator: Now answer questions 23 to 28. Circle the letter of the answer.

ANSWERS AND EXPLANATIONS

23. **A** **There are many theories, but the true cause of left-handedness remains unclear. (Gist-content)** Option A is correct because the professor examines many possible causes of left-handedness and discusses how scientists have rejected or disproved each one. Option B is not supported by the lecture because the professor says that even though a gene for this trait has been identified, only twenty-six percent of people with two copies of this gene become left-handed. Option C is incorrect because several benefits of left-handedness are identified in the lecture. Option D is contradicted by the lecture. The professor says, "Statistics do not bear this out."

24. **D** **Scientists still cannot explain it. (Detail)** Option D is correct because at the start of the lecture, the professor says, "Handedness

. . . remains an area of psychological and neurological mystery." Options A, B, and C are not supported by information in the lecture.

25. **B** **Because vocabulary reflects social attitudes toward left-handers (Function)** Option B is correct because the professor says, "Originally, *sinister* and *gauche* meant 'left.' Words associated with *right*, however, like *adroit* or *dexterous* mean 'skillful' or 'accomplished.'" Options A, C, and D are not supported by information in the lecture.

26. **D** **Being an identical twin causes left-handedness. (Detail)** Option D is correct because the professor says, "The vanishing twin theory, as it's known, has been strongly refuted in Australia, where there are lots of twins. It just doesn't hold up among twins there." Options A, B, and C are incorrect. While all these options are about theories on what causes left-handedness, none of them is connected to Australia.

27. **A** **A left-handed athlete has a special advantage.** **B** **A left-handed person might spot danger from the left. (Inference/Special multiple choice)** Option A is correct because the male student says, "Athletes who play left-handed or left-footed or with both hands or feet are in big demand." Option B is correct because the male student says, "Maybe left-handers evolved as lookouts" to avoid being attacked by giant cats. Option C is not supported by information in the lecture. Option D is contradicted by information in the lecture: a left-hander is likely to have a lower life expectancy than a right-hander.

28. **C** **To show that strong beliefs about handedness mean a test is needed to expose lies (Function)** Option C is correct because the professor says, "[The shoe test] is how the army tests handedness because so many recruits lie. Left-handers don't want to be judged as sinister or gauche; right-handers hope to be seen as more creative or just a little different." Option A is incorrect because while true left-handers will put on their left shoes first, this describes what happens in the shoe test, not why the army uses it. Option B is incorrect because the army is not interested in proving that misconceptions about handedness persist in the modern world. It only wants to find out which recruits are left-handed. Option D is not supported by information in the lecture.

Questions 29–34

Narrator: Listen to part of a lecture in a nutrition class. The professor is talking about humans eating insects and spiders.

Professor: This morning, I was watering the plants on my balcony when I noticed my mint had been badly damaged by caterpillars. As I was removing the offenders, I remembered that in some cultures people eat both the mint and the caterpillars. In fact, by 2035, Earth's population will reach ten billion. The movement towards entomophagy, or eating insects and arachnids, will most likely spread.

Now, as I said, insects are already a minor food source for eighty percent of the world's population, and historically everyone ate them: many ancient texts attest to this. Unintentionally, we *all* eat insects as it is. You can't always wash them off a salad, for example.

Currently, the Food and Agricultural Organization of the United Nations lists around fourteen hundred edible insect or arachnid species. Fourteen hundred—that's quite a few.

Japan and South Korea are two developed countries with moderate insect consumption. In Japan, wasps and grasshoppers are eaten. Silkworm pupae are canned in Korea and, like Thai water bugs, exported to North America. Numerous indigenous communities in Australia and elsewhere enjoy insects. Witchetty grubs, eaten by Aborigines near Sydney, are fed to eager tourists. In 2010, they made their way onto the menus of glamorous city restaurants. This trend has its parallels in Europe. One French insect cookbook is selling so well it's been translated into German and Italian.

In snack aisles, UK supermarket chains stock curried crickets, oven-baked tarantulas, and scorpion candy. Sales of chocolate-covered beetles are rising in California.

Insects have long been grown commercially for bait and pet food. Dutch insect breeders, among the world's most profitable, export forty percent of their stock to pet shops; only one percent goes to supermarkets for human consumption. Recently, however, the breeders founded a trade organization because they're predicting a jump in demand. In 2011, the Dutch government allotted one point four million US dollars to research on insects as human food and to prepare legislation to govern insect farms and the retailing of edible insects. In Canada, industrial methods are being applied to insect farming because the current labor-intensive process means the cost of insects is high. Right now, the majority of farmed insects are more expensive than beef, while locusts are on par with caviar.

Nutritionally speaking, insects are low in cholesterol yet high in beneficial fatty acids and in all kinds of minerals, particularly iron. Four locusts provide as much calcium as one glass of milk; about seventy-five could replace two eggs; and some worms contain more protein than beef.

Less is wasted of insects: three-quarters of a chicken is typically thrown away, but only one-quarter of a locust. Of that quarter, nearly half is the exoskeleton, or shell, made of chitin. Chitin can't be eaten unprocessed; it's the biggest stumbling block in insect farming—it has to be removed, which is a delicate process. However, chitin is a carbohydrate polymer for which there are industrial applications. Shellfish chitin is already added to Japanese cereals as a source of fiber and calcium.

Insects win convincingly on an efficiency conversion index, or ECI. The ECI is the ratio of feed ingested by the animal to the food it produces. Beef cattle have an ECI rating of ten, cockroaches have forty-four, and crickets, fifty-four.

Insects emit a fraction of the greenhouse gas of livestock—estimated to be twenty percent of the global total.

Sadly, while developed nations are contemplating eating more insects, developing nations are eating fewer. People there may believe meat-based Western diets are more civilized. Western junk food has spread throughout the developing world, leading to increased obesity. The dramatic overapplication of chemicals to meat production has polluted soil, air, and water. If more insects were eaten, there'd be far less pesticide use. Indeed, we might all look forward to a plague of locusts.

I've sampled many different kinds of insects and arachnids. Personally, I find most of them too crunchy or too pulpy. I can only cope when they're unrecognizable—concealed by other ingredients. However, experts agree that after 2035, there'll be fewer other food choices, so maybe I'd better get used to the idea of mint-and-caterpillar pie.

Narrator: Now answer questions 29 to 34. Circle the letter of the answer.

ANSWERS AND EXPLANATIONS

29. **D** **Insects are becoming an increasingly important food source for humans. (Gist-content)** Option D is correct because the professor says, "As food security becomes less certain, the movement toward entomophagy, or eating insects and arachnids, will most likely spread." Option A is not supported by information in the lecture. Option B is mentioned in the lecture, but it is only one detail that supports the main idea. Option C is contradicted by information in the passage. The professor says that there are more than fourteen hundred edible insect or arachnid species.

30. **B** **Increased population will make insect eating more common. (Detail)** Option B is correct because the professor says, "By 2035, Earth's population will reach ten billion. As food security becomes less certain, the movement towards entomophagy . . . will most likely spread." Options A, C, and D are not supported by information in the lecture.

31. **D** **They are organizing methodically for an expanded insect market. (Inference)** Option D is correct because the professor says, "Recently [Dutch] breeders founded a trade organization because they're predicting a jump in demand [in edible insects]. In 2011, the Dutch government allotted one point four million US dollars to research on insects as human food and to prepare legislation to govern insect farms and the retailing of edible insects." Founding a trade body and writing new laws show methodical organization. Option A is incorrect. The Dutch produce a lot of insects for export, but the professor does not say how many they consume themselves. Option B is incorrect because the British and Americans, not the Dutch, sell snacks and candy that contain insects. Option C is incorrect because Canadians, not the Dutch, are applying industrial methods to insect farming to reduce labor costs.

32. **(Detail/Check box)** Your completed table should look like this. Reasons to support the answer are in the right-hand column.

	TRUE	FALSE	REASON
Insects are cheap to produce.		✓	The professor says, "The current labor-intensive process means the cost of insects is high."
Many insects are healthful to eat.	✓		"Nutritionally speaking, insects are low in cholesterol yet high in beneficial fatty acids and in all kinds of minerals, particularly iron."
Insect chitin has few uses.		✓	"Chitin is a carbohydrate polymer for which there are industrial applications. Shellfish chitin is already added to Japanese cereals as a source of fiber and calcium."
Insects have a high ECI.	✓		"Insects win convincingly on an efficiency conversion index, or ECI."

33. **B** **They experienced more weight problems and environmental pollution. (Detail)** Option B is correct because the professor says, "Western junk food has spread throughout the developing world, leading to increased obesity. The dramatic overapplication of chemicals to meat production has polluted soil, air, and water." Option A is contradicted in the lecture. The

professor says, "People [in developing countries] may believe meat-based Western diets are more civilized." Options C and D are not supported by information in the lecture.

34. **C** **He has mixed feelings about it. (Attitude)** Option C is correct because the professor says, "I've sampled many different kinds of insects and arachnids. Personally, I find most of them too crunchy or too pulpy. I can only cope when they're unrecognizable—concealed by other ingredients." But he adds, "After 2025, there'll be fewer other food choices, so I'd better get used to the idea of mint-and-caterpillar pie." Option

A is incorrect because an "ardent supporter" totally supports something. Option B is incorrect because a "reluctant opponent" opposes something but not very strongly. Option D is contradicted by information in the lecture.

Speaking (Page 688)

Item 1

TRACK 159 AUDIO SCRIPT

Narrator: You will now speak about a familiar topic. Prepare your response in fifteen seconds. Then allow forty-five seconds to record your response. Describe your first day at your most recent class or your most recent job. What did you like or dislike? Include specific details in your description.

Item 2

TRACK 160 AUDIO SCRIPT

Narrator: You will now give your opinion about a familiar topic. Prepare your response in fifteen seconds. Then allow forty-five seconds to record your response. Some college students work part-time while they are studying. Other college students prefer to concentrate totally on their studies. Which do you think is better for students? Explain why.

Item 3

TRACK 161 AUDIO SCRIPT

Narrator: You will now read a short passage on a campus-related topic and listen to a conversation on the same subject. Then you will hear a question. Prepare your response in thirty seconds. Then allow sixty seconds to record your response. The Psychology Department is looking for volunteers for research studies. You will have 50 seconds to read the announcement from the head of the department. Begin reading now.

TRACK 162 AUDIO SCRIPT

Narrator: Now listen to two students discussing the announcement.
Woman: Too bad I'll be away next semester. Otherwise I would've signed up.
Man: Really? I was part of a psych experiment in March, and it was a big waste of time.

Woman: How so?
Man: Well, we were all kept in the dark—literally and figuratively. We were in this horrible basement computer lab. Then we were given the briefest of outlines about the purpose of the experiment. Sure, instructions for what we did were clear enough, but I didn't see the point of it. Seems we played a few computer games, got a cup of cold coffee, and then played games some more.
Woman: Was that your pay?
Man: Well, we made fifty dollars, but I was stuck in the lab twice for two hours.
Woman: Oh dear. Did you find out the result of the experiment?
Man: We were told it might be published in two or three years.
Woman: Hmm. (*Said neutrally*) Still, how else can researchers test their hypotheses?
Man: Yeah. That's a tough one. To be honest, I don't think college students are the best research subjects.
Woman: I'd've thought you were perfect for anything related to computer games!
Man: We're all so similar—rich kids with the same ideas. I doubt there was much diversity in our responses.
Woman: Maybe. (*Said neutrally*)
Man: Plus there's the commitment. Being available over three semesters is asking a lot.
Narrator: The man expresses his opinion of the announcement by the head of the Psychology Department. Briefly summarize the announcement. Then state his opinion about the announcement and explain the reasons he gives for holding that opinion.

Item 4

TRACK 163 AUDIO SCRIPT

Narrator: You will now read a short passage on an academic topic and then listen to a talk on the same subject. Then you will hear a question. Prepare your response in thirty seconds. Then allow sixty seconds to record your response. Now read a passage from a history textbook. You have fifty seconds to read the passage. Begin reading now.

TRACK 164 AUDIO SCRIPT

Narrator: Now listen to part of a lecture on this topic in a history class.

Professor: In 1707, a shipwreck off the coast of Britain killed more than two thousand sailors and the admiral of the fleet. Parliament decided to take action. It set up a Board of Longitude with a large prize for the inventor of a system or device that could accurately establish longitude.

Navigators could already determine latitude with the aid of solar tables. A leading British astronomer and highly educated man, Nevil Maskelyne, believed that longitude could also be found by using charts called lunars, which essentially showed the moon's position.

In the meantime, John Harrison, an uneducated carpenter, began building very accurate clocks called chronometers. He believed longitude could be calculated if a ship carried two chronometers—one showing London time, the other, the time at the ship's position. Despite long opposition from Maskelyne, parliament awarded Harrison the prize money for solving the longitude problem in 1773.

Initially, Maskelyne's lunars were used at sea, but Harrison's chronometers superseded them, being cheaper, simpler, and more reliable. That is, until the age of telegraphy, radio, and GPS.

Narrator: Explain how John Harrison's chronometer solved a major navigational problem. Use information from the reading and the talk.

Item 5

TRACK 165 AUDIO SCRIPT

Narrator: You will now listen to part of a conversation about a campus-related situation. Then you will hear a question. Prepare your response in twenty seconds. Then allow sixty seconds to record your answer. Now listen to a conversation between two students on campus.

Man: Hi, Sofia.

Woman: Hello, Baxter.

Man: Everything OK?

Woman: Afraid not. One of the reasons I chose this college was the reputation of its creative writing program, but I'm so upset I'm, I'm ready to quit.

Man: Oh dear. Why don't you tell me what's bothering you.

Woman: This probably sounds irrational, but I feel the professor has it in for me. She's never given me more than a B grade, and today she told me in private that some of my classmates had complained about me. I was shocked.

Man: Hmm. What are you supposed to have done?

Woman: She accused me of being domineering. Said I wasn't giving the other students a chance to participate. But they're all so mousy—half of them never utter a word, and when the others do, they seldom say anything original.

Man: I see.

You've got a couple of choices. You could quit, or you could think about what the professor said. Keep attending class, but—well, try to take a backseat.

Woman: I told the professor it was her role to facilitate, to make sure everyone contributes. But she doesn't do that. On top of which—

Man: Look, Sofia, here's my bus. Best of luck with whatever you choose.

Narrator: Summarize briefly the problem that the speakers are talking about. Then say which of the two solutions from the conversation you would recommend. Explain your reasons for your recommendation.

Item 6

TRACK 166 AUDIO SCRIPT

Narrator: You will now listen to part of a lecture on an academic topic. Then you will hear a question. Prepare your response in twenty seconds. Then allow sixty seconds to record your answer. Listen to part of a lecture in a business class.

Professor: For thousands of years, philosophers have debated the qualities that constitute leadership. In 1939, Kurt Lewin and two other authors defined three effective styles. These are authoritarian, democratic, and laissez-faire leadership styles. Let me say that again: authoritarian, democratic, and laissez-faire.

An authoritarian leader takes total control, never allowing subordinates to make suggestions or show initiative. This style is effective when a rapid response or decision is needed, for example, in a time of crisis.

A democratic leader seeks contributions from others and practices social equality. This style is suitable in the day-to-day running of an enterprise, especially where team members are highly motivated and possess similar expertise. It allows for creative ideas from all organizational levels to float to the top.

A laissez-faire leader adopts a hands-off approach—subordinates have a high degree of responsibility or may even be left to fend for themselves. This is appreciated for the freedom it permits.

These days it is believed a leader should not rely on one leadership style. This is called contingency theory. And a leader is judged as successful by his or her ability to flexibly use those different styles.

Narrator: Using information from the lecture, describe three different leadership styles that contribute to contingency theory.

EXPLANATIONS

There are many ways to answer these items. If you do not have a recording device, ask a friend to listen and evaluate your responses. If you have a recording device, ask a teacher or an English-speaking friend to listen to your responses and evaluate them. Or wait a day or two and evaluate them yourself. For Items 1

and 2, use a copy of the Independent Speaking Rubric in Appendix D. For Items 3 to 6, use a copy of the Integrated Speaking Rubric in Appendix D.

Compare your responses to the following high-scoring responses.

 Item 1

 Item 2

 Item 3

 Item 4

 Item 5

 Item 6

Writing (Page 694)

Item 1

TRACK 167 AUDIO SCRIPT

Narrator: Now listen to part of a lecture on the topic you just read about. You may take notes in the space provided.

Professor: Hybrid cars have been rightly touted as a potential way to reduce emissions and reduce the operating cost of vehicles. Hybrid vehicles use significantly less fuel than cars with only internal combustion engines, and as a consequence, produce fewer emissions. However, in many ways, hybrids create additional challenges as well. First, hybrid vehicles need to carry batteries to store electricity produced by the engine while braking and to power the vehicle's electric motor. These batteries are themselves an environmental hazard. Two of the most common types of batteries contain lead or nickel, metals that are known to cause cancer. While lithium batteries are much less hazardous than batteries that contain nickel or lead, these batteries continue to be expensive and impractical for many kinds of hybrid vehicles.

Second, hybrid vehicles, especially power-split vehicles, need elaborate systems to combine power from the motor and the engine in constantly

varying proportions. As we saw a few years ago, these systems are not always uniformly safe and have prompted several product recalls. I have driven all the major hybrid vehicles on the road, and sometimes they are not very responsive when compared to nonhybrid vehicles.

Third, hybrid vehicles do nothing to address a major societal issue, the underfunding and underuse of public transportation. That is, hybrid vehicles offer nothing if the result of the savings and efficiencies is more vehicles on streets and fewer people taking public transportation. The real solution to the economic and environmental cost of internal combustion engines ultimately resides in fewer, not more, vehicles of greater efficiency on the road.

TRACK 168 AUDIO SCRIPT

Narrator: Summarize the points made in the lecture, being sure to explain how they oppose the specific points made in the reading passage.

EXPLANATION

There are many ways to answer this item. Compare your answer to this high-scoring response. Then evaluate your writing. Follow the instructions on page 497. Use a copy of the Simplified Integrated Writing Rubric in Appendix E.

SAMPLE ESSAY RESPONSE

The article and the lecture are about hybrid cars. Hybrid cars are cars that have two sources of power. The power can come from a gas engine. This is called an internal combustion engine. The power also comes from an electric motor. There are different kinds of hybrid cars, depending on the arrangement of the engines. But according to the article, all of them save gas and lower pollution.

The professor agrees that hybrid cars use less gas and make less pollution. But he disagrees with it, too. First, he says that hybrid cars need large batteries. The metals in these batteries can be very dangerous. Nickel is used in a lot of these batteries, and that metal can cause cancer. In order to use these batteries, we need to find safe ways to get rid of the batteries. I also think that maybe these batteries can cause a problem in an accident or fire.

In addition, the professor says that the power systems of these cars are not completely safe. He talks about how some cars had safety problems. Gas engines do not have all of these safety problems.

Finally, he says that pollution and gas use will not go down if we keep adding more cars. If we use the savings from hybrid cars to put more cars on the road, traffic jams will be worse. And we will use the same amount of fuel with more cars on the road. So the only way to really improve is to use more public transportation. I think that the professor wants us to produce more hybrid trucks, trains, and buses, and not more cars. Making more cars will make us lose all of the savings from the hybrids.

In conclusion, hybrid cars are good, but there are some problems to be solved if we will really save money and stop pollution.

Item 2

EXPLANATION

There are many ways to answer this item. Compare your answer to this high-scoring response. Then evaluate your writing. Follow the instructions on page 525. Use a copy of the Independent Writing Rubric in Appendix E.

SAMPLE ESSAY RESPONSE

Many people have heard the old saying, "The best things in life are free." I only agree with this statement partly. I agree because the most important things in life are not possessions, but other precious things like love, friendship, and family. Cars, clothes, and other possessions are less important, but sometimes we focus on them and not on more important things. The best times in life are always with the people we love. For example, I love to spend time with my family. Besides my mother and father, I have four brothers and sisters, eight aunts and uncles, and more than twenty-five cousins. Some of my cousins were my classmates in elementary school, and we had a lot of fun together. I hope that I will get married to a nice person and have children. No one can put a price on the love of your family. I also have a lot of friends—from school, from work, and from my neighborhood. There is no price for having a good friend.

However, I don't agree with this statement in other ways. First, we need money to do things like get married, have a home, or raise children. Without money, we could never have any of these things. I hope that when I marry, I can give my children a good home and send them to good schools. I hope that they can also study outside of our country too, just like I want to do. All of that costs money.

I also disagree with this statement because all of these "free" things take a lot of work. A relationship is a lot of work. For example, my uncle had many problems with his marriage. Finally, he and my aunt solved the problems, but it took a lot of work. And my little brother caused a lot of problems for my mother and father. It took work for them to solve those problems, too. So we cannot say that friends, family, and children are free. They take work.

In conclusion, this saying is valuable because it helps us remember that cars, clothes, and possessions are not so important as other things in life. But friends, family, and children have a cost, too.

After you evaluate your responses to Items 1 and 2, use the TOEFL iBT Personalized Study Planner that begins on page 705 to find ways to improve your performance.

Appendixes

APPENDIX A
Academic Vocabulary

This list contains more than 150 top academic vocabulary words. Each word may have other related words. For example, *achieve* has related words such as *achievement* and *achiever*. By studying a few of these words, and their related words, each day, you can build your academic vocabulary and improve your performance on the TOEFL.

achieve	conclusion	demonstrate	factor
acquisition	conduct	derive	feature
administration	consequence	design	final
affect	considerable	discoverer	financial
alternative	consist	distinction	focus
analysis	constant	distribute	formula
approach	constraint	document	framework
appropriate	construction	dominant	function
area	context		funds
aspect	contribution	economic	
assessment	convention	elements	identify
assistance	coordination	emphasis	impact
assume	core	ensure	implies
	corresponding	environment	indicate
benefit	create	established	initial
	credit	estimate	instance
category	criteria	evaluation	institute
circumstance	culture	evidence	interaction
comment	cycle	exclude	interpret
complex		exist	involve
component	data	experiment	issues
compose	deduction	export	items
concept	definition		

justification

layer
legal
legislation
link
location

maintenance
major
maximum
method
minorities

negative
normal

obtain
occur
outcome

participate
partnership
perceive
percent
period
philosophy
physical
policy
positive
potential
previous
primarily
primary
principle
procedure
process
proportion
publish

range
reaction

region
registered
regulation
relevant
reliance
remove
require
research
resource
response
restrict
role

section
sector
select
sequence
shift
significant
similar
site

source
specific
specify
strategy
structure
sufficient
survey

technical
technique
technology
text
theory
traditional
transfer

validity
variable

APPENDIX B

Academic Subjects and Sample Topics

These lists contain sample topics for academic subject areas tested throughout the TOEFL iBT.

ARTS

Architecture and urban planning

Art and art history (painting, photography, sculpture, etc.)

Folk music and art

Music and music history

Poetry and literature

LIFE SCIENCE

Cell structure

Ecology, conservation, sustainability

Cycles in nature (such as the nitrogen cycle)

Photosynthesis

Public health

Biomes and habitats

Viruses, bacteria, and one-celled organisms

EARTH SCIENCE

The solar system

Earth's structure

Cycles in nature (such as the water cycle)

Natural resources and conservation

Weather

PHYSICAL SCIENCE

Chemistry and physics

Computers and computer science

Matter and properties of matter

Properties of light and sound

Radiation and radioactivity

Wave theory

SOCIAL SCIENCE

Anthropology and sociology

Education

Geography

Human development

Language and linguistics

Mass communication (TV, radio, Internet)

Modern history

APPENDIX C

Campus-Related Topics

These lists contain sample campus-related topics tested throughout the TOEFL iBT.

CLASS-RELATED

Asking questions about a grade

Asking questions about a test or
  assignment

Finding out course requirements

Getting clarification on a class topic

Getting feedback on performance on a test,
  paper, or in-class presentation

SCHOOL SERVICE-RELATED

Asking about parking, local transportation,
  etc.

Using campus services (library, residence
  halls, registrar, cashier, recreational
  sports, student advising, etc.)

SCHOOL-RELATED

Talking over campus news and
  announcements

Talking about extracurricular activities
  and student life (clubs, sports,
  performances, residence life, etc.)

APPENDIX D

Simplified Speaking Rubrics

TOEFL IBT SIMPLIFIED INDEPENDENT SPEAKING SCORING RUBRIC

SCORE	GENERAL DESCRIPTION	DELIVERY	LANGUAGE USE	TOPIC DEVELOPMENT
4	**The response:** • Answers the question • Is complete • Is understandable • Makes sense • Stays on topic • Has few pauses, hesitations, or interruptions • Includes ALL of the items listed in the columns to the right	**The speech:** • Is well paced • Is fluent • Is clear • May include minor problems with pronunciation or intonation • Is understandable overall	**The language:** • Shows effective use of correct grammar and vocabulary • Shows good control of basic and advanced structures • Has minor errors that do not affect understanding	**The content:** • Answers the question • Is sustained (has no pauses or interruptions) • Stays on topic • Has a main idea • Includes supporting details • Has ideas and details in a logical order • Uses signaling words and phrases to show the relationships among ideas
3	**The response:** • Answers the question, but is not fully complete • Is generally understandable • Has fluid expression, but there may be some pauses or gaps in expression • Includes TWO of the items listed in the columns to the right	**The speech:** • Is generally clear • May have minor pronunciation or intonation problems that require the listener to pay attention to understand • Is understandable overall	**The language:** • Shows fairly effective use of correct grammar and vocabulary • May have some improper or limited use of grammar and vocabulary that reduces fluency but not clarity	**The content:** • Generally makes sense most of the time • Mostly sustained • Has limited development of ideas • Lacks detail • At times, the relationship among ideas is not clear

SCORE	GENERAL DESCRIPTION	DELIVERY	LANGUAGE USE	TOPIC DEVELOPMENT
2	**The response:** • Answers the question • Has limited detail and development • Has problems with delivery or completeness and meaning is unclear at times, but is understandable overall • Includes TWO of the items listed in the columns to the right	**The speech:** • Is basically understandable, though listeners need to pay attention to understand • Has pronunciation, intonation, or rhythm problems that make meaning unclear in places	**The language:** • Shows limited range and use of grammar and vocabulary that prevents full expression of ideas • Uses only simple sentence structures correctly • Consists mainly of short sentences with simple or unclear connections among ideas • Lists ideas or joins them with simple linking words and expressions such as *and*	**The content:** • Answers the question, but number of ideas or their development is limited • Uses mostly basic ideas • Has limited development or detail • Is vague or repeats at times • Has unclear connections among ideas • Has poor or limited use of linking words and phrases
1	**The response:** • Is very limited in content, is only minimally connected to the question, or is mainly not understandable • Includes TWO of the items listed in the columns to the right	**The speech:** • Has consistent problems with pronunciation, stress, and intonation that make comprehension difficult • Is choppy or fragmented • Has frequent unnatural pauses and hesitations	**The language:** • Shows limited grammar and vocabulary that prevent expression of ideas • Has limited use of linking words and expressions • May make heavy use of practiced or memorized vocabulary and expressions	**The content:** • Lacks relevant ideas except for the most basic • Does not use the time available or answer the question • May repeat the question to fill time
0	No response, response is off topic, or response is not understandable.			

TOEFL IBT SIMPLIFIED INTEGRATED SPEAKING SCORING RUBRIC

SCORE	GENERAL DESCRIPTION	DELIVERY	LANGUAGE USE	TOPIC DEVELOPMENT
4	**The response:** • Answers the question • Is complete • Is understandable • Makes sense • Stays on topic • Has few pauses, hesitations, or interruptions • Includes ALL of the items in the columns to the right	**The speech:** • Is generally fluent and sustained • May have small problems with pace as speakers try to remember information • Is generally clear • May have minor problems with pronunciation or intonation • Is highly understandable overall	**The language:** • Shows effective use of correct grammar and vocabulary that allows for automatic expression of ideas • Shows good control of basic and advanced structures • Has only minors errors that do not affect understanding or meaning	**The content:** • Includes information necessary to answer the question • Is in a logical order • Uses order and signaling devices to show relationships among ideas • Includes appropriate detail, though there may be small errors or omissions of detail
3	**The response:** • Answers the question, but is not complete • Is generally understandable • Has fluid expression, but there may be some pauses or gaps in expression • Includes TWO of the items in the columns to the right	**The speech:** • Is generally clear and somewhat fluent • May have minor pronunciation, intonation, or pacing problems that require the listener to pay attention to understand • Is understandable overall	**The language:** • Shows fairly effective use of correct grammar and vocabulary • May have some improper or limited use of grammar and vocabulary that reduces fluency but not clarity of the information	**The content:** • Is sustained • Gives relevant information to answer the question • Has some incompleteness or inaccuracy • Lacks some detail, or has unclear or choppy progression of ideas because of improper order or lack of signaling devices

SCORE	GENERAL DESCRIPTION	DELIVERY	LANGUAGE USE	TOPIC DEVELOPMENT
2	**The response:** • Answers the question but lacks some information or is inaccurate • Contains some understandable speech, but problems with understandability or relevance may make meaning unclear at times • Includes TWO of the items in the columns to the right	**The speech:** • Is clear at times, but has problems with pronunciation or intonation that may require significant listener effort • May not be sustained at a consistent level • Has problems with understandability that make meaning unclear at times	**The language:** • Has limited range and control of grammar and vocabulary • Contains errors in complex structures • Lacks automatic use of structures except in memorized phrases • Has limited or vague expression of relevant ideas or inaccurate use of signaling devices	**The content:** • Includes some relevant information, but is incomplete or inaccurate • Omits key ideas or refers to key ideas vaguely • Lacks understanding of key ideas from the stimulus • Presents unrelated or unordered ideas or lacks appropriate signaling devices to show relationships among ideas
1	**The response:** • Has very limited content, is only minimally connected to the question, or is mainly not understandable • Includes TWO of the items in the columns to the right	**The speech:** • Has consistent problems with pronunciation, stress, and intonation that make understanding difficult • Is choppy or fragmented • Has frequent unnatural pauses and hesitations	**The language:** • Shows limited grammar and vocabulary that prevent expression of ideas • Has limited use of signaling devices • May rely on only words or phrases to communicate ideas	**The content:** • Fails to give relevant information • Ideas are often inaccurate, vague, or repetitive (including repeating the question)
0	No response, response is off topic, or response is not understandable.			

APPENDIX E

Simplified Writing Rubrics

TOEFL IBT SIMPLIFIED INTEGRATED WRITING SCORING RUBRIC

SCORE	DESCRIPTION
5	A **Level 5** response: • Selects relevant and important information from the lecture and presents it in relation to similar information in the reading. Includes supporting detail and examples. • Is well organized and makes sense. Uses signaling words and phrases to connect information and show the relationships among ideas. • Includes occasional errors in vocabulary and grammar that do not result in inaccurate or confusing presentation of information or connections among ideas.
4	A **Level 4** response: • Generally selects relevant and important information from the lecture and presents it in relation to relevant and important information in the reading, but may have minor inaccuracies, vagueness, or omissions that cause minor confusion to readers. • Includes errors in vocabulary and grammar that are more frequent than in a Level 5 response, but cause only minor problems with clarity or connection of ideas.
3	A **Level 3** response contains some information from the listening and makes some connections to the reading, but it has one or more of these problems: • The response addresses the task, but some information may be inaccurate or incomplete. Makes only general, vague, or unclear connections between points in the reading and the lecture. • The response omits one major point made in the lecture. • Some key points in the lecture or reading, or the connections between them, are unclear, incomplete, inaccurate, or general. • Vocabulary and grammar errors may be more frequent than in a Level 4 response and may cause confusion to readers.
2	A **Level 2** response has some relevant information from the lecture, but has inaccuracies or omissions of important ideas from the lecture, or makes inaccurate or incomplete connections with information from the reading. A response at this level shows one or more of the following: • Omits or inaccurately presents the relationship between the lecture and the reading. • Omits or inaccurately presents important points in the lecture. • Contains language errors or expressions that obscure meaning.
1	A **Level 1** response: • Provides little or no meaningful or relevant information from the lecture. • Has problems with vocabulary and grammar that make the essay difficult to understand.
0	A response at this level contains only ideas copied from the reading passage, does not address the topic, is not written in English, or is blank.

TOEFL IBT SIMPLIFIED INDEPENDENT WRITING SCORING RUBRIC

SCORE	DESCRIPTION
5	A **Level 5** response largely: • Addresses the topic and the task. • Is organized and well developed; uses appropriate detail, examples, and explanations. • Stays on topic, flows, and makes sense. • Uses language well. Has variety in sentence patterns, vocabulary, and idioms, and only minor errors of vocabulary and grammar.
4	A **Level 4** response largely: • Addresses the topic and the task, though some points are not well developed. • Is generally well organized and developed; uses appropriate detail, examples, and explanations. • Stays on topic, flows, and makes sense, but may have some problems with repetition, staying on topic, or unclear connection of ideas. • Uses language fairly well. Has variety in sentence patterns, vocabulary, and idioms, and only minor errors of vocabulary and grammar, but may have some errors in grammar, word form, or natural language that do not cause unclarity.
3	A **Level 3** response is characterized by one or more of the following: • Addresses the topic and the task, but with somewhat developed detail, examples, and explanations. • Stays on topic, flows, and makes sense, but connection of ideas might be unclear at times. • May show inconsistent ability in grammar and vocabulary that may cause occasional unclarity. • Accurate but limited range of sentence structures and vocabulary.
2	A **Level 2** response will show one or more of the following weaknesses: • Limited development of topic and task. • Poor organization or connection of ideas. • Not enough or inappropriate detail, examples, and explanations. • Poor choice of words or word forms. • Many errors of sentence structure or vocabulary.
1	A **Level 1** response is seriously harmed by one or more of these weaknesses: • Disorganized or lacks development. • Little or no detail, examples, and explanations, or does not respond to the task. • Serious errors in sentence structure or vocabulary.
0	A response at this level contains only ideas copied from the topic, does not address the topic, is not written in English, or is blank.

APPENDIX F

TOEFL iBT Speaking and Writing Personalized Study Planners

Speaking

Use your Speaking responses and this chart to focus your preparation for the actual TOEFL iBT. Follow these steps.

1. Review your responses by comparing them to the sample responses in the Answers, Explanations, and Sample Responses.

2. Evaluate your responses with the rubrics. If possible, ask a teacher or an English-speaking friend to help you. Or wait a day or two and evaluate yourself. Use the TOEFL iBT Simplified Independent Speaking Rubric in Appendix D to score your responses to Items 1 and 2. Use the TOEFL iBT Simplified Integrated Speaking Rubric in Appendix D to score your responses to Items 3 to 6. Write your scores on the lines.

   1. _____   3. _____   5. _____

   2. _____   4. _____   6. _____

3. What skills do you do well? Which skills do you want to improve? Review your rubrics for Items 1 and 2 together. Next, in a copy of the chart, check the boxes of the skills you do well. Then review the pages that are listed for the skills you want to improve.

ITEMS 1 AND 2: INDEPENDENT SPEAKING

SKILL	STUDY PAGES
☐ Answers the question	376–377
☐ Has a main idea	377
☐ Has supporting details	377–378
☐ Follows a logical order	378–379
☐ Uses signaling words and phrases to show relationships among ideas	380–382

4. Now review your completed rubrics for Items 3 to 6 together and check the boxes of the skills you do well. Then review the pages for the skills you want to improve.

ITEMS 3 TO 6: INTEGRATED SPEAKING

SKILL	STUDY PAGES
☐ Answers the question	411, 420–421
☐ Has a main idea and supporting details	404–408, 422–423
☐ Integrates information from reading and/or listening passages	412–416
☐ Follows a logical order	434–435
☐ Uses order and signaling words and phrases to show relationships among ideas	413–416, 424

Writing

Use your Writing responses and these charts to focus your preparation for the actual TOEFL iBT.

ITEM 1: INTEGRATED WRITING

1. Evaluate your essay using the instructions on page 497 and a copy of the Integrated Writing Rubric in Appendix E.

Write your score on the line. _____

2. Check the box of your rating in each row of a copy of the following chart.

3. Review your ratings in each row. Which areas do you want to improve? Study the pages listed for those areas in the column on the right.

SCORE	DESCRIPTION	STUDY PAGES
5	A **Level 5** response: ☐ Selects relevant and important information from the lecture and presents it in relation to similar information in the reading. Includes supporting detail and examples.	483–487
	☐ Is well organized and makes sense. Uses signaling words and phrases to connect information and show the relationships among ideas.	490–494
	☐ Includes occasional errors in vocabulary and grammar that do not result in inaccurate or confusing presentation of information or connections among ideas.	495–497

(continued)

SCORE	DESCRIPTION	STUDY PAGES
4	A **Level 4** response:	
	☐ Generally selects relevant and important information from the lecture and presents it in relation to relevant and important information in the reading, but may have minor inaccuracies, vagueness, or omissions that cause minor confusion to readers.	483–487
	☐ Includes errors in vocabulary and grammar that are more frequent than in a Level 5 response but cause only minor problems with clarity or connection of ideas.	495–497
3	A **Level 3** response:	
	☐ Contains some information from the listening and makes some connections to the reading	483–487
	A response at this level has one or more of these problems:	
	☐ The response addresses the task, but some information may be inaccurate or incomplete. Makes only general, vague, or unclear connections between points in the reading and the lecture.	483–487
	☐ The response omits one major point made in the lecture.	483–487
	☐ Some key points in the lecture or reading, or the connections between them, are unclear, incomplete, inaccurate, or general.	490–494
	☐ Vocabulary and grammar errors may be more frequent than in a Level 4 response and may cause confusion to readers.	495–497
2	A **Level 2** response:	
	☐ Has some relevant information from the lecture, but has inaccuracies or omissions of important ideas from the lecture.	483–487
	☐ Makes inaccurate or incomplete connections with information from the reading.	483–487
	A response at this level shows one or more of the following:	
	☐ Omits or inaccurately presents the relationship between the lecture and the reading.	483–487
	☐ Omits or inaccurately presents important points in the lecture.	483–487
	☐ Contains language errors or expressions that obscure meaning.	495–497
1	A **Level 1** response:	
	☐ Provides little or no meaningful or relevant information from the lecture.	483–487
	☐ Has problems with vocabulary and grammar that make the essay difficult to understand.	495–497
0	A response at this level contains only ideas copied from the reading passage, does not address the topic, is not written in English, or is blank.	

ITEM 2: INDEPENDENT WRITING

1. Evaluate your essay using the instructions on page 525 and a copy of the Independent Writing Rubric in Appendix E.

   Write your score on the line. _____

2. Check the box of your rating on each row of a copy of the chart on this page.

3. Review your ratings in each row. Which areas do you want to improve? Study the pages listed for those areas in the column on the right.

SCORE	DESCRIPTION	PAGES
5	A **Level 5** response largely:	
	☐ Addresses the topic and the task.	515–517
	☐ Is organized and well developed; uses appropriate detail, examples, and explanations.	517–518
	☐ Stays on topic, flows, and makes sense.	519–520
	☐ Uses language well. Has variety in sentence patterns, vocabulary, and idioms, and only minor errors of vocabulary and grammar.	524–525
4	A **Level 4** response largely:	
	☐ Addresses the topic and the task, though some points are not well developed.	515–517
	☐ Is generally well organized and developed; uses appropriate detail, examples, and explanations.	517–518
	☐ Stays on topic, flows, and makes sense, but may have some problems with repetition, staying on topic, or unclear connection of ideas.	519–520
	☐ Uses language fairly well. Has variety in sentence patterns, vocabulary, and idioms, and only minor errors of vocabulary and grammar, but may have some errors in grammar, word form, or natural language that do not cause unclarity.	524–525
3	A **Level 3** response is characterized by one or more of the following:	
	☐ Addresses the topic and the task, but with somewhat developed detail, examples, and explanations.	515–517
	☐ Stays on topic, flows, and makes sense, but connection of ideas might be unclear at times.	517–518
	☐ May show inconsistent ability in grammar and vocabulary that may cause occasional unclarity.	524–525
	☐ Accurate but limited range of sentence structures and vocabulary.	524–525
2	A **Level 2** response will show one or more of the following weaknesses:	
	☐ Limited development of topic and task.	515–517
	☐ Poor organization or connection of ideas.	517–518
	☐ Not enough or inappropriate detail, examples, and explanations.	515–517
	☐ Poor choice of words or word forms.	524–525
	☐ Many errors of sentence structure or vocabulary.	524–525

(continued)

SCORE	DESCRIPTION	PAGES
1	A **Level 1** response is seriously harmed by one or more of these weaknesses:	
	☐ Disorganized or lacks development.	517–518
	☐ Little or no detail, examples, and explanations, or does not respond to the task.	515–517
	☐ Serious errors in sentence structure or vocabulary.	524–525
0	A response at this level contains only ideas copied from the topic, does not address the topic, is not written in English, or is blank.	